Design for Health

One of the most complex global challenges is improving wellbeing and developing strategies for promoting health or preventing 'illbeing' of the population. The role of designers in indirectly supporting the promotion of healthy lifestyles or in their contribution to illbeing has emerged. This means designers now need to consider, both morally and ethically, how they can ensure that they 'do no harm' and that they might deliberately decide to promote healthy lifestyles and therefore prevent ill health.

Design for Health illustrates the history of the development of design for health, the various design disciplines and domains to which design has contributed. Through 26 case studies presented in this book, the authors reveal a plethora of design research methodologies and research methods employed in design for health.

The editors also present, following a thematic analysis of the book chapters, seven challenges and seven areas of opportunity that designers are called upon to address within the context of healthcare. Furthermore, five emergent trends in design in healthcare are presented and discussed. This book will be of interest to students of design as well as designers and those working to improve the quality of healthcare.

Emmanuel Tsekleves is Senior Lecturer in Design Interactions at Imagination@Lancaster, Lancaster University. Emmanuel conducts research on designing creative and technology-inspired health-promoting interventions aimed at improving quality of life. Emmanuel blogs regularly for *The Guardian* and *The Conversation* on design in healthcare.

Rachel Cooper OBE is Distinguished Professor of Design Management and Policy at Lancaster University. Her research interests cover design thinking, design management, design policy, design for wellbeing and socially responsible design. She is the series editor of the Routledge series Design for Social Responsibility.

Design for Social Responsibility
Series Editor: Rachel Cooper

Social responsibility, in various disguises, has been a recurring theme in design for many years. Since the 1960s several more or less commercial approaches have evolved. In the 1970s designers were encouraged to abandon 'design for profit' in favour of a more compassionate approach inspired by Papanek. In the 1980s and 1990s profit and ethical issues were no longer considered mutually exclusive and more market-oriented concepts emerged, such as the 'green consumer' and ethical investment. The purchase of socially responsible, 'ethical' products and services has been stimulated by the dissemination of research into sustainability issues in consumer publications. Accessibility and inclusivity have also attracted a great deal of design interest and recently designers have turned to solving social and crime-related problems. Organisations supporting and funding such projects have recently included the NHS (research into design for patient safety), the Home Office (design against crime) and the Engineering and Physical Sciences Research Council (design decision-making for urban sustainability).

Businesses are encouraged (and increasingly forced by legislation) to set their own socially responsible agendas that depend on design to be realised. Design decisions all have environmental, social and ethical impacts, so there is a pressing need to provide guidelines for designers and design students within an overarching framework that takes a holistic approach to socially responsible design. This edited series of guides is aimed at students of design, product development, architecture and marketing, and design and management professionals working in the sectors covered by each title. Each volume includes: the background and history of the topic, its significance in social and commercial contexts and trends in the field; exemplar design case studies; and guidelines for the designer and advice on tools, techniques and resources available.

Design for Transport
A User-Centred Approach to
Vehicle Design and Travel
Edited by Mike Tovey

Design for Policy
Christian Bason

Design against Crime
Caroline L. Davey and Andrew B. Wootton

Design for Health
*Edited by Emmanuel Tsekleves
and Rachel Cooper*

Design for Personalisation
Edited by Iryna Kuksa and Tom Fisher

Design for Health

Edited by Emmanuel Tsekleves
and Rachel Cooper

LONDON AND NEW YORK

First published 2017
by Routledge

2 Park Square, Milton Park, Abingdon, Oxfordshire OX14 4RN
52 Vanderbilt Avenue, New York, NY 10017

Routledge is an imprint of the Taylor & Francis Group, an informa business

First issued in paperback 2020

British Library Cataloguing in Publication Data
A catalogue record for this book is available from the British Library

Library of Congress Cataloging in Publication Data
Names: Tsekleves, Emmanuel, 1981– editor. | Cooper, Rachel, 1953– editor.
Title: Design for health / edited by Emmanuel Tsekleves and Rachel Cooper.
Description: Abingdon, Oxon ; New York, NY : Routledge, 2017. |
Includes bibliographical references and index.
Identifiers: LCCN 2016048323 | ISBN 9781472457424 (hardback) |
ISBN 9781315576619 (ebook)
Subjects: | MESH: Health Facility Environment | Facility Design and Construction |
Environment Design | Health Promotion | Social Determinants of Health
Classification: LCC RA967 | NLM WX 140.1 | DDC 725/.51–dc23
LC record available at https://lccn.loc.gov/2016048323

ISBN: 978-1-4724-5742-4 (hbk)
ISBN: 978-0-367-66970-6 (pbk)

Typeset in Bembo
by Out of House Publishing

Contents

Figures

Tables

Editors

Rachel Cooper OBE is Distinguished Professor of Design Management and Policy at Lancaster University, where she is Chair of Lancaster Institute for the Contemporary Arts and also Imagination@Lancaster. Her research interests cover design thinking, design management, design policy and, across all sectors of industry, a specific interest in design for wellbeing and socially responsible design. She has published extensively on these topics, including the books *Designing Sustainable Cities* (2009), *Constructing Futures* (2010) and *Handbook of Wellbeing and the Environment* (2014). She is also series editor of the Routledge series Design for Social Responsibility covering topics such as designing for sustainability, inclusivity, service design, sport, health, transport and policy.

She is currently working on Liveable Cities, an Engineering Physical Sciences Research Council-funded six-year research programme working to identify design and engineering solutions that will lead to low-carbon, resource-secure, future cities in which societal wellbeing is prioritised. She is also involved with the Creative Exchange, an Arts and Humanities Research Council (AHRC) Knowledge Exchange hub looking at the growth of the creative industries through exploring the 'digital public space'. She is Co-Investigator of an AHRC project on Design Value in Innovation and Co-Director of HighWire (Digital Economies Innovation Doctoral Training Centre).

Rachel is a non-executive director of the Future Cities Catapult, and a lead expert for the UK Government Foresight Programme on the Future of Cities, and is on the Academy of Medical Sciences working group addressing 'the health of the public 2040'.

She was a member of the 2014 Blackett review on the Internet of Things. She is founding and past president of the European Academy of Design, founding editor of the *Design Journal*, and a trustee of the Research and Development Management Association. She was a member of the EU Design and Innovation Leadership Board and has undertaken several advisory roles to national and international universities, government and non-governmental organisations.

Emmanuel Tsekleves is Senior Lecturer in Design Interactions, Imagination@Lancaster, Lancaster University. Emmanuel designs interactions between people, places and products by forging creative design methods along with digital technology. His design-led research in the areas of health, ageing and wellbeing has generated public interest and attracted media attention. Emmanuel designs technology-inspired health-related innovations and services that are created by end users and that link the physical with the digital world through play and playful interactions. His research also looks at exploring the futures that ordinary people would prefer, by using design fictions. He is currently working with people in the early stages of dementia, people with Parkinson's, with families of children with autism and in the area of public health on the design of playful technology and interactions that promote healthy behaviours. His current research also looks into how participatory design fictions can be used as a tool to provoke and generate debate around policy initiatives and emergent technology amongst diverse groups in the area of ageing and dementia. Emmanuel is a member of Lancaster University's multidisciplinary Centre for Ageing Research, Health and Work Forum and blogs regularly for *The Guardian* and *The Conversation* on the design and use of technology in health.

Contributors

Charles Abraham is a professor and an applied psychologist specialising in design, evaluation and implementation of interventions to change health-behaviour patterns. He is Head of the Psychology Applied to Health group at Exeter University Medical School and holds honorary chairs at Sussex, Nottingham, Maastricht and Curtin Universities. He was the founding chair of the UK British Psychological Society, Division of Health Psychology and is a practising health psychologist (registered by the UK Health and Care Professionals Council). He has acted as a research consultant to the UK Department of Health, was a member of the National Institute for Health and Care Excellence groups that developed guidelines on 'Behaviour Change' in 2007 and extended these in 2013. In 2010–11 he was the scientific advisor to the UK House of Lords Select Committee on Science and Technology, 'Inquiry into Behaviour Change'. He was one of seven psychologists included in the UK Science Council's list of the leading 100 practising scientists in the UK, published by the UK Academy of Science in 2014.

Marco Ajovalasit is Senior Lecturer in Human Factors at Brunel University, London. His research interest is in the field of experience-based co-design, human–product interactions, psychophysics and multisensory perception. Particular emphasis is placed on designing the sensory stimuli of products, systems and services for the purposes of meaning, interaction and emotion. He is Principal Investigator of an FP7 EU Grant-funded project 'Light. Touch.Matters' (2013–16), which brings together a multidisciplinary team of designers and material scientists for a design-driven development of a fully new generation of smart materials that combine touch sensitivity with luminescence, based on latest developments in polymeric piezo materials and flexible OLEDs for wellbeing and care applications.

Richard Bibb graduated from Brunel University with a BSc in Industrial Design in 1995 and moved to the National Centre for Product Design and Development Research (PDR) to undertake rapid prototyping research. In 1998, he established the Medical Applications group at PDR to conduct research into the medical applications of design technologies including additive manufacturing/3D printing. He moved to Loughborough University in 2008 where he is affiliated with the university's multidisciplinary Additive Manufacturing research group and he established the Design School's Design for Digital Fabrication research group in 2014. His research focuses on the application of design techniques and technologies in medicine specifically addressing maxillofacial surgery, prosthetic rehabilitation, orthotics, dental technology and archaeology.

Alison Black is Professor of User-Centred Design and Director of the Centre for Information Design Research in the Department of Typography and Graphic Communication,

University of Reading. A cognitive psychologist by training, her research focus is the explanation of complex information and simplification of complex tasks, using methods and media appropriate to audience and context. Much of her work has focused on health and healthcare, but she also works on communication to support professional and consumer decision-making in areas of complexity and potential risk, such as the communication of extreme weather events and decision-making regarding legal and contractual information.

Christopher T. Boyko is a 50th Anniversary Lecturer in Design at Lancaster University. With Rachel Cooper OBE he is currently examining the relationship between wellbeing and the built environment as part of the UK EPSRC-funded Liveable Cities project. This research builds on previous research about urban density within the planning process and maps sustainable urban design decision-making processes for the EPSRC-funded Urban Futures and VivaCity2020 projects, respectively. Christopher's general research interests include urban design, sustainability, use of digital technology in cities and wellbeing in urban environments.

Josefina Bravo Burnier is a PhD candidate at the University of Reading. She is also a freelance graphic designer with specialisation in the areas of corporate identity, information design and editorial design. She has experience in leading integral design projects and in handling internal and external work teams.

Matthew Brook is a specialist registrar in renal medicine at the Royal Berkshire NHS Foundation Trust.

Clare Carey is an information designer, director at Studiolift and currently a University of Reading student, researching apps in the classroom.

Valerie Carr works for Snook, an award-winning service design agency with offices in Glasgow and London. She is an experienced service designer who focuses mostly on co-designing health and social care services, improving both the experience of the citizen and the efficiency and effectiveness of service delivery. She has a PhD in Healthcare Service Design and is motivated by creatively addressing the challenges associated with engaging patients and citizens in co-producing public services. Recent clients have included NHS24, Department of Health, Department for Education, Capita, NHS Ayrshire and Arran and Lankelly Chase.

Paul Chamberlain is Professor of Design, head of the Art and Design Research Centre and Co-Director of the interdisciplinary research group Lab4Living at Sheffield Hallam University. Paul's interest lies in designing and developing tools and methods to encourage and engender social innovation and he applies this with a focus on healthcare, disability and ageing. His work explores the multisensory aspects of design and the role of artefacts that help define pertinent societal questions as much as present solutions. He has led major interdisciplinary projects and delivered keynote lectures at leading international venues on innovation strategies and sustainable approaches to design and manufacture that have played a significant role in supporting regional industrial reconstruction.

Ricardo Codinhoto is a qualified architect with practical, teaching and research experience. Ricardo holds a senior lecturer position within the University of Bath where he is Director of Studies for the MSc on Modern Building Design. Within the Department of Architecture and Civil Engineering at the University of Bath, Ricardo's research is aligned with the themes studied within the Centre for Advanced Studies in Architecture. Ricardo has developed research funded by EPSRC, MRC, ESRC and NIHR, including a study commissioned by the Government Office for Science. He is active in a number of research initiatives that relate health and wellbeing to the design, construction and maintenance of healthcare facilities design, construction and maintenance, with a particular focus on older people and people with dementia.

Claire Craig is a reader in design and creative practice at Sheffield Hallam University and is Co-Director of Lab4Living with Paul Chamberlain. Claire has a health background and her clinical work and research interests have focused on quality of life for older people and people with dementia. Her research has explored the role of design and the arts in promoting wellbeing and she has published a number of books in this area. Claire is particularly interested in research methods to engage marginalised communities and projects have included photography as a method in care home research and the potential of critical artefacts as a way of building understanding of the experiences of older people in Europe. Claire lectures nationally and internationally and was awarded a national teaching fellowship in 2011. She also holds a fellowship from the College of Occupational Therapists in recognition of her contribution to the field.

Sarah Denford is Research Fellow in the Psychology Applied to Health research group at the University of Exeter Medical School. She has a background in health psychology and public health. Her research interests include self-management of chronic conditions, evaluation of public health interventions, qualitative methodologies and systematic reviewing. Her previous work has attempted to identify processes that are associated with behaviour change in complex interventions. Her current research focuses on the evaluation of public health interventions, sexual health interventions, and environmental factors that influence alcohol consumption.

Alan Dilani is a professor and founder of the International Academy for Design and Health and the journal *World Health Design*. He has been engaged worldwide in several universities in the field of design and health developing 'salutogenic design', in both medical and design institutions. He holds a Masters of Architecture in Environmental Design from the Polytechnic of Turin, Italy and a PhD in Health Facility Design from the Royal Institute of Technology, Stockholm. His research at the Karolinska Institute, Medical University, which developed a multidisciplinary research approach, led to a new definition called 'salutogenic design'. He has designed all types of healthcare facilities and has been consulted as an advisor for several ministries of health around the world. He lectures worldwide and is author of numerous articles and books in the field of design and health. Alan was awarded a Presidential Citation in 2010 from the American Institute of Architects, Academy of Architecture for Health for his promotion of high-quality design research.

K. Downey is a doctoral researcher at the Department of Design, Fashion and Business within the School of Materials at the University of Manchester. Her research is an exploration of computer-aided design and additive manufacturing for the design and fabrication of custom-made spinal braces. Part of the research involves understanding how young people and their families can contribute to co-designed braces through design research.

Sarah Drummond is Co-Founder and Managing Director of Snook, an award-winning design consultancy working at the forefront of civic, public-sector and democratic innovation. Sarah focuses on making social change happen by rethinking public services from a human perspective and regularly lectures and speaks around the globe on service design, innovation and civic engagement. Sarah is a serial idea generator. She has co-founded MyPolice, CycleHack, Dearest Scotland and The Matter. For this work she was awarded a Google Fellowship for her work in technology and democracy.

Michelle Goonasekera is at the Oxford University Hospitals NHS Trust, with expertise in renal medicine.

Marianne Guldbrandsen heads up the Service Innovation and Strategic Partnership team at Macmillan Cancer Support. It is a human-centric service design team focusing on the future of support and healthcare services. By using design and innovation methodologies the team co-design, prototype and scale new service solutions to support cancer patients and their families, delivered with private, public and third-sector partners. The process builds on expressed and latent needs of people affected by cancer, a knowledge of the gaps in existing healthcare services and the challenges of higher demand and reduced resources. In this context, empathy, creativity, multimethods and co-creation is the only way to innovate successfully. In the past Marianne has worked as an innovation consultant with emphasis on design strategy, user insights/ethnography and service design, for clients such as Mars/Wrigley, Nokia, Nissan, Toyota, Volvo, Ford, LEGO, Walt Disney, Orange, Novartis and Novo Nordisk. Prior to this she worked at the Design Council where she provided strategic direction across programmes such as Independence Matters (aging population), Low Water Living and Reducing Violence and Aggression in A&E. Marianne holds qualifications in design-driven innovation, research, psychology and coaching.

Sue Hignett is Professor of Healthcare Ergonomics and Patient Safety at Loughborough University. Over the last 30 years she has experienced the healthcare industry as a clinician, ergonomist, researcher and patient. Her research looks at a wide range of issues including the design of safer systems, building and vehicle (ambulance) design, emergency and CBRNe response, staff wellbeing and an innovative approach to patient falls. Sue is an editor for 'Ergonomics', Chair of the Education and Training panel at the Chartered Institute of Ergonomics and Human Factors; and past chair of the International Ergonomics Association Technical Committee on Healthcare Ergonomics.

Peter Jones is an associate professor in the Faculty of Design, OCAD University, Toronto. Peter is a co-founder of the Systemic Design Research Network and the Relating Systems Thinking to Design symposia. In his practice with the Redesign Network, Peter has led the design and research of leading resources for clinical, educational and scientific practice throughout the internet era. His research adapts applied cognitive and social methodologies for complex systems in healthcare, governance and organisational design domains. He publishes in design and innovation literatures, including his most recent book *Design for Care: Innovating Healthcare Experience* (2013).

Alastair S. Macdonald is Senior Researcher in the School of Design at the Glasgow School of Art. He has a track record of research council-funded research working within multidisciplinary healthcare teams, addressing patient-centred issues in, e.g., physical rehabilitation, spinal injury, dementia, infection control and malnutrition. Using collaborative co-design and mixed-method approaches with substantial stakeholder involvement to address complex healthcare challenges, he and his team have developed a number of innovative healthcare interventions, using iterative narrative and prototyping methods.

Victor Margolin is Professor Emeritus of Design History at the University of Illinois, Chicago. He is Co-Editor of the academic design journal, *Design Issues*, and is the author, editor or co-editor of a number of books including *Design Discourse, Discovering Design, The Idea of Design, The Designed World* and *The Politics of the Artificial*. Margolin has been a visiting professor and lecturer at numerous colleges and universities throughout the world. Margolin was presented with a Lifetime Achievement Award by the organisers of the LearnXDesign conference in Chicago in 2015, for his 'exemplary contributions to design history, research, education and practice' and a Lifetime Achievement Award by the Design Research Society in 2016.

Susan Mawson originally trained as a physiotherapist and worked initially in South Africa. While there she learned to develop novel seating and sleeping equipment out of cardboard boxes for the children living in the Cape flats townships. On returning to the UK, she completed her BSc (Hons) in Physiotherapy and her PhD in Stroke Rehabilitation. Sue is Director of the NIHR CLAHRC YH and Professor of Health Services Research in the School for Health and Related Research at the University of Sheffield, where her role is to develop stronger links between researchers at ScHARR, the NHS, industry and the voluntary sector. She has a specific focus on rehabilitation research into novel interventions and technologies for people with disabilities, older people and people with long-term conditions.

David Meredith is based at the Royal Berkshire Hospital NHS Foundation Trust.

Massimo Micocci is a Design PhD student within the School of Engineering and Design at Brunel University. His research focuses on human-centred design, and in particular on the application of a new generation of smart materials that can sense touch and respond with luminescence in the field of care and wellbeing applications. His research aims to classify key products' features that affect the user with positive experiences by using design techniques such as virtual and tangible prototypes. Massimo's first aim is to make available for designers a toolkit for meaningful experiences iterate over time.

Sarah Morgan–Trimmer is a social scientist working in the Psychology Applied to Health group at the University of Exeter Medical School. Her research experience is in qualitative methods, process evaluations of public health, randomised controlled trials, evaluation research, research on socioeconomic inequality and conducting research with children. Her current work is focused on understanding not just whether health interventions work but how they work, through developing process evaluation methods for complex interventions.

Jeremy Myerson is a professor and leading academic, author and activist in design and innovation. He holds the Helen Hamlyn Chair of Design at the Royal College of Art, London and is Visiting Fellow at the Oxford Institute of Population Ageing, University of Oxford. He is also Director of the Worktech Academy, a new global knowledge network exploring the future of work and workplace. A former journalist and editor on such titles as *Design, Creative Review* and *World Architecture*, he founded *Design Week* magazine in 1986 and later co-founded the Helen Hamlyn Centre for Design in 1999, which he directed for 16 years until autumn 2015. The author of more than 20 books in the field, his most recent titles include *Time and Motion: Redefining Working Life* (2014) and *Life of Work* (2015). He has consulted with governments and businesses around the world, and sits on the advisory boards of design institutes in Korea, Switzerland and Hong Kong.

Lenny Naar is a design strategist at HELIX Centre – short for Healthcare Innovation Exchange – inside St Mary's Hospital, London. The team uncovers root problems and co-designs solutions to improve healthcare at scale. Lenny recently co-founded Prescribe Design, a community aimed at expanding the role of design and designers working in healthcare. As Lead Design Strategist at Aetna's innovation group Healthagen in San Francisco, he worked on creating digital tools to engage patients and clinicians. Formally trained as a communication designer, Lenny worked with Paula Scher at Pentagram Design on large-scale brand projects and has also held positions with Doblin, SYPartners and Smart Design.

Anna Olsson-Brown is a medical doctor and research fellow in Molecular and Clinical Pharmacology at the Institute of Translational Medicine at the University of Liverpool.

Jari Pallari is Vice President of Operations and Innovation at Pofdo and previously has been a research and development manager at Peacocks Medical Group. He has been at the fore-front of the additive manufacturing healthcare frontier, with a decade of experience in the medical applications of the technology, participating in a number of research projects in the area.

Abby Paterson graduated from Loughborough University with a BSc in Industrial Design and Technology in 2008. In 2013, she was awarded a PhD, which focused on novel applications of computer-aided design and additive manufacturing technologies for custom-made orthoses. In 2012, she became Lecturer in Computer Aided Design at the School of Materials, University of Manchester. Abby returned to Loughborough University as Lecturer in Industrial/Product Design in 2014, where she is now a member of the university's Additive Manufacturing research group and recently formed Design for Digital Fabrication research group. Her research interests span the development of 3D scanning protocols and customised computer-aided design/manufacturing methodologies for a range of industrial, product and fashion design applications.

Alison Prendiville is Senior Researcher at the School of Graphic Design at LCC, UAL London. Her research focuses on design for service in local government and healthcare sectors. She has recently completed, as Co-Investigator, the AHRC-funded Mapping and Developing Service Design Research in the UK and the AHRC Design for Service Innovation and Development. Currently she is working as Co-Investigator on the AHRC-funded Public Collaboration Lab with Central St Martins and Camden Council. Her research interests also encompass design and digital anthropology. She has an MA in Design Management and an MSc in Digital Anthropology from University College London.

Gail Ramster is Senior Research Associate at the Helen Hamlyn Centre for Design Work and City Research Lab, exploring how people-centred design and co-design approaches can be applied within different settings including urban planning, community development and employee wellbeing. She joined the centre in 2009 working on projects with both academic and industry partners. Gail began her professional life as a mechanical engineer working in the UK, USA, France and Spain before completing an MA at the Royal College of Art and moving into industrial design, information design and wayfinding. She is one of the creators of the Great British Public Toilet Map; a website and database developed from the TACT3 research project funded through New Dynamics of Ageing that holds the largest database of publicly accessible toilets in the UK.

Debbie Rosenorn-Lanng is an executive coach (holding the Institute of Leadership and Management, ILM Level 7), a visiting professor with Henley Business School and a visiting lecturer with Keele University. She has over 20 years of experience as a doctor, seven years of which were as a hospital consultant. During that time frame she gained over 20 years of experience in medical education. She is an approved Royal College of Physicians educator. Her area of special interest is Human Factors in Healthcare, which is also the title of her book published by Oxford University Press.

Chris Rust is Emeritus Professor of Design at Sheffield Hallam. His principal interests now are in independent creative work rather than an academic or institutional role. His research has been concerned with the role of tacit knowledge in design, arising from experience of research projects in which design plays an instrumental part in investigations into problems in other disciplines. Chris has taken an active role in the development of practice-led research and doctorates in design and the creative disciplines. He has also been developing and running the Nether Edge Bikebus, a practical Design and Social Action project to get more people cycling in his part of Sheffield and a narrative song documentary about the history of war in the 20th century. Chris was the chair of the Design Research Society Council 2006–9 and has been a committee member in several other prestigious committees and conferences. He has been invited to give talks on practice-led research in several universities across Europe.

Aaron Sklar is Managing Director of Experience Strategy and Design at Healthagen and Co-Founder of Prescribe Design. Throughout his career, Aaron has led design teams focused on improving people's quality of life, health and wellness. Prior to joining Healthagen he spent 14 years at IDEO, an award-winning global design firm where he managed projects for more than 50 international organisations. Aaron has been published by the Rockefeller Foundation, *GOOD* magazine and in the HIMSS book *Engage!*

Jane R. Smith joined the University of Exeter Medical School as a post-doctoral Research Fellow in November 2012 to support the work of Professor Charles Abraham, which focuses primarily on the development and evaluation of evidence-based interventions to promote health-related behaviour change. Jane brings to this role her skills in quantitative health services research and broad interests in psychosocial aspects of health and illness. Her research includes systematic reviews, randomised controlled trials of complex interventions and process evaluations alongside interventions, development and testing of outcome measures and other related, mixed-methods research investigating the role of behavioural and other psychological factors in health, illness and healthcare.

Gabriella Spinelli is Reader in Design Innovation in the Department of Design at Brunel University, London. She is interested in research exploring the relationship between identity, behaviour and artefacts. In the last five years her research has focused on how the design of products, services and systems can support the wellbeing of the ageing population. Gabriella's research is people-centred to ensure integrity and inclusion. She has attracted research funds from EPSRC, ESRC, TSB, Innovate UK and commercial schemes. She is a visiting scholar at the Royal College of Art and an associate editor for the *Journal of Design, Business and Society*.

David Swann is a graduate of the Royal College of Art, gaining his PhD in 2011 and MDes in Industrial Design in 1991. David began his academic career in 1992 at the University of Huddersfield and in February 2015 joined the Sheffield Institute of Arts at Sheffield Hallam University as Principal Lecturer. David's design research is grounded in global healthcare design with many of his award-winning medical innovations exhibited worldwide. Notable achievements include 2015 Unicef Wearables for Good Challenge finalist, 2014 London Design Museum's Design of the Year nomination and winner of the 2014 International Council for Societies of Industrial Design World Design Impact Prize.

Samantha Van Beurden is a PhD candidate in Medical Studies as part of the Psychology Applied to Health group at the University of Exeter. Her main research interest is in facilitating behaviour change through impulse management. In 2008 Samantha obtained her BSc in Psychology from the University of Plymouth which was followed by an MSc in Psychological Research Methods in 2009.

Karel van der Waarde gained his PhD from Reading University and has owned a design-research consultancy in Belgium since 1995. The company develops and tests patient information leaflets, medicine packaging, instructions for use, forms, medical protocols and the information architecture for websites. Karel teaches part-time at the Basel School of Design and frequently publishes about visual information design. He is a life fellow of the Communications Research Institute (Melbourne, Australia), a board member of the International Institute for Information Design (Vienna, Austria) and editorial board member of *Information Design Journal, Journal of Communication Design* and *Visible Language*.

Emma Vaux is Consultant Nephrologist, Director of Quality Improvement at the Royal Berkshire NHS Foundation Trust and Associate Medical Director of the Royal Colleges of Physicians Training Board, leading core medical training and national recruitment, the 'Learning to Make a Difference' quality improvement programme and the 'Making Every Moment Count' pilot enabling trainees of all specialties and grades to develop quality improvement skills as part of their usual training.

Sue Walker is Professor of Typography in the Department of Typography and Graphic Communication at the University of Reading and Director of the AHRC-funded Design Star Doctoral Training Centre. Her research interests include the analysis and description of graphic language, in particular the relationship between prescription and practice in everyday documents, typographic design for children and information design in public service. She is an active participant in the Associate All-Party parliamentary group on Design and Innovation, Co-Chair of the Information Design Association and Fellow of the Design Research Society.

Daniel Wolstenholme undertook a first degree in neuroscience before training and working as a nurse. During this time, Dan completed an MMedSci in Nursing and Healthcare Studies and lectured on pre- and post-registration nursing courses within the School of Nursing at the University of Sheffield. Following this Dan worked in research management and governance in Chesterfield and Sheffield Hospitals before taking up his role as project manager and clinical researcher on the user-centred healthcare design project within CLAHRC SY. Dan's own research interests lie in exploring the potential of the theory and practice of design in healthcare.

Andy Young is a design and innovation consultant, an ideas person with a passion for start-ups and entrepreneurship. He works across the private, public and third sector designing for customer experience and has a particular interest in making things happen at the intersection point between service design and technology. Andy's expertise as a service designer, prototyper and his background in product design mean his capabilities extend across the full spectrum of design. He believes in asking difficult questions and challenging why things are the way they are.

Introduction and chapter summary

Rachel Cooper and Emmanuel Tsekleves

Introduction

Ever since the King's Fund Hospital Bed project began in 1962 designers have been undertaking projects for health, and architects have been designing hospitals ever since these institutions were established. These design projects have, however, remained within the different professional domains in design, i.e. product, communication and architecture. It is only relatively recently that we have seen a greater body of work from diverse design work and an increase in design research focusing on health and healthcare issues. Traditionally designers have paid particular attention to acute and chronic care, through new medical products, prostheses and hospital, clinic and care home design, i.e. they have focused on the restoration of health through design and technology. More recently the complex picture of maintaining population wellbeing and of health (illbeing) prevention has begun to emerge, and thus has the role of designers indirectly in supporting the promotion of healthy lifestyle or in their contribution to illbeing (Cooper and Boyko, 2011). This responsibility means designers perhaps now need to consider morally and ethically how they can ensure that they 'Do no harm' and that they might deliberately decide to promote healthy lifestyles and therefore prevent ill health.

Figure 1 illustrates this dichotomy and provides examples of the four disciplines and the attention they can pay to health prevention and care. There are of course many more areas in health prevention and healthcare that designers can focus their skills and attention on; genetic and childhood health and an ageing society and the growth of dementia are just two examples. Indeed designers might benefit from assessing their contribution against the life course from prenatal, childhood, adulthood through to older life and death, looking at the individual and their community in the context of various environments such as cities, various geographies and continents, various socioeconomic situations and various behaviour conditions.

Design has now broadened its skill base and its application. Service design has introduced a new opportunity to address the improved delivery of products and service both within and outside the healthcare system. The 'design in policy' field is introducing new approaches to developing policy and aiding innovation in organisational, local, regional and national governance. Design interactions are a new way of considering how we can improve the relationship between people, products, places and services, and of course technology trends such as the 'Internet of Things' offer great opportunities in providing new ways to connect people with services and products that can contribute to healthier lifestyles and mechanisms to support people with acute and chronic conditions.

Furthermore, the strength in user-centred design has led to participatory design, co-design and co-creation, whereby a much closer relationship is developed between the design professional and the individuals and communities who have a stake in the outcome of any design

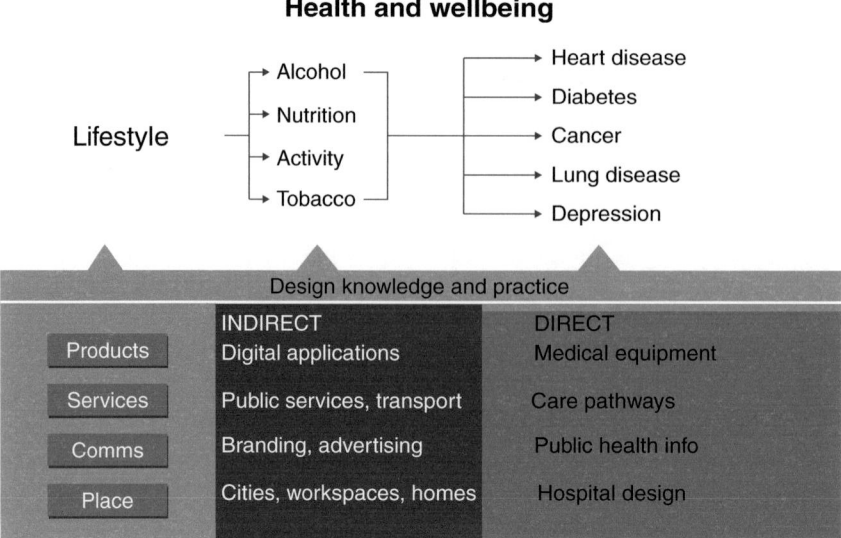

Figure I.1 The relationship between design and non-communicable diseases
Source: Adapted from Cooper and Boyko, 2011

activity. In the same way multi/interdisciplinary teams that embrace not only the user but also the diverse range of skills and expertise related to a specific challenge are a common feature of project teams; the opportunity is for designers to take a lead and facilitate that collaborative approach.

This book illustrates the history of the development of design for health, the various design disciplines and domains to which design has contributed providing a body of work upon which we can build a more comprehensive and joined-up approach to design for health.

Brief summary of chapters

Part I: Setting the scene

Chapter 1

In Chapter 1 Chris Rust presents a very brief overview of the history of medicine from ancient Greece to the modern day. It is interesting to see that although hospitals have been transformed from 'a place to die to temples of technology', hygiene is still compromised in modern hospitals and infection control has become a nightmare due to 'efficient' utilisation of resources resulting in overcrowding. Also we seem to have lost the 'patient as person movement', person-centred healthcare approach of the pre-1940s to a more scientific and technical healthcare that although it focuses on cure often neglects care and personal support.

During this brief journey into history Chris highlights some of the key challenges for healthcare in which designers have a crucial role to play. This includes the design of hospitals that effectively eradicate infections whilst embedding state-of-the-art technology and provide a more humane and person-centred healthcare service. Designers have also a role to play in the design of medical technology and tools for diagnosis, surgery and treatment but also in the design of the built environment to facilitate better public health. He therefore concludes that designers can take responsibility for understanding the problems around healthcare through research and develop ideas and solutions that can make a real difference to the healthcare community.

Chapter 2

In his chapter David Swann sets the scene for the book by discussing the key challenges faced in health today and uses those to draw the reader upon the opportunities for design and designers. Key challenges include an ageing population, the exponential demand of healthcare services and the rising costs associated with it. As we live longer we are more likely to develop at least one chronic and long-term health condition, placing more stress on the already overburdened healthcare system. To cope with this there is a move, especially in the developed world, towards community and the patient's home care. Thus a key challenge that arises is how to maintain high-quality healthcare at an affordable cost.

Design is well placed to provide service improvements and healthcare innovations. Through presentation of the design of the King's Fund hospital bed David illustrates that designers have the tools, methods and competencies to facilitate mass behaviour change that can be the root of several of the many health-related problems. In fact, design for health is now emerging as a discipline of its own.

An ongoing challenge faced in healthcare is the translation of applied research into tangible patient benefits through the widespread adoption and dissemination of design interventions. Co-producing innovations with healthcare professionals and patients as well as evidence-based design provide opportunities for contributing in this field. Lastly, David argues that as currently the majority of design focuses on the development of products and services for the top 10 per cent of the world, there is an unmet challenge and opportunity for tackling global health through design innovation.

Part II: Designing for health

Theme 1: Design for public health

CHAPTER 3

In Chapter 3 Peter Jones discusses the importance of social determinant factors and their impact on our health. Similarly to other chapter authors he highlights the holistic nature of health and how the environment we live in shapes and affects it. He stresses the need for health service design and interventions at a community as well as an individual level. He argues that social determinant factors, such as environment, housing, social lifestyle and food accessibility are so embedded in our community setting that on one hand they are often not perceived as a threat to our health and on the other hand, traditional healthcare providers do not have the resources for intervening or changing these factors that have a such a causal effect on our health. He discusses and presents a systemic design approach adapted from flourishing mental health and flourishing societies. Flourishing addresses multiple societal concerns by creating community cohesion and providing opportunities for improving many aspects of a localised social ecology.

He presents a framework for community-centred approaches to facilitate flourishing through the design of soft services and provides a use case to guide the reader through the framework. His proposal of a soft service design approach focuses on design interventions that primarily engage the 'soft' social and community fields of interaction, with attention to communicative and passive structural design to influence preventive health or health promotion.

In Chapter 4 Denford et al. discuss the value of behaviour-change design interventions by highlighting the importance of health-promoting lifestyles for healthcare professionals and the methodology that designers can follow. The authors recognise that there are many determinants of health-related behaviour patterns including individual, community, legislative, policy and several others, but focus their chapter on interventions targeting changing individual behaviours. They present an intervention mapping model which includes six stages, critical in identifying, planning, implementing and evaluating behaviour-change interventions.

The authors highlight the importance of sustainability and continuity of an intervention following successful implementation but critically indicate that this is often overlooked. Through the presentation of a use case, a weight-management mobile application, they discuss and explain the value of intervention mapping and how to employ it in practice as well as how to evaluate its efficacy based on different outcomes. They conclude that in changing unwanted habits it is important to break such habits by introducing alternative behaviours that individuals can follow when cued from internal (personal) or external (environmental) cues.

CHAPTER 5

In his chapter Alan Dilani presents the principles and benefits of salutogenic design in planning future built environments with the aim of creating a healthier society. He argues that the way we live, where we work and the way we interact with the built environment have a great impact on our emotions and experiences, which are central parts of the health process. As such, the design of health built environments should go beyond hospitals to also include schools, the workplace and public and urban spaces. And since salutogenic design focuses on a preventative care strategy, it offers a more holistic healthcare model that goes beyond the traditional medical model of disease detection and cure.

Alan emphasises that current and next generation of designers, architects and engineers need to learn how to apply ecological and salutogenic design principles in their work and explores how to design for a sustainable healthy future by looking at:

> How we embed health, science and innovation in the creation of healthy built environments.
> How we plan our city, workplace, healthcare facilities, schools and public institutions so they successfully support human health and wellbeing.
> How we implement research-based design to promote health and wellness.

In Chapter 6, Sue Walker discusses the value and importance of visual information design and typography in the communication of health. Through the presentation of public health visual communication examples she provides several practical guidelines on the successful and effective design of health communication visual and textual material. She emphasises that apart from the provision of information, health-related communication should attract the attention of the intended audience.

She draws upon previous research to showcase the importance of working with experts in a particular field and with intended users in the design of health communication material. More precisely, she identifies that successful health communication benefits from the application of best practice from typography and graphic communication but also information design. Putting the user first and including them in the design process and decision-making increases the likelihood of a document's effectiveness.

Theme 2: Design in acute health

CHAPTER 7

In Chapter 7 Ricardo Codinhoto discusses how architecture contributes to health and wellbeing by studying the relation between health, person and place. He argues that design of acute care settings involves much more than simply providing a space for the delivery of care services and highlights the importance of social interaction as part of the healing process that acute healthcare services should take into account.

After placing emphasis on evidence-based and evidence-informed design, the chapter offers practical recommendations on how designers can embed evidence that links the built environment to wellbeing. By presenting a use case of a hospital design in the UK, the author provides the reader with practical examples on how design can enhance acute care settings and the importance of place-making to acute care design. Lastly he draws on the value of co-design in the development of new built environments for healthcare.

CHAPTER 8

Sue Hignett discusses how design can support patient care, treatment, recovery and safety through the application of a human factors and ergonomics framework in the design of products in acute health. She presents two case studies which offer a practical guide on the research process and methods employed for the design of products in two distinct acute healthcare settings. The first case study looks at the design of hospital beds and bedside furniture with the aim of reducing slips, trips and falls risks, whilst the second focuses on the redesign of products used in the delivery of pre-hospital emergency care, such as ambulatory stretchers and portable pods.

The author showcases through the presented use cases how the design of supporting products and technologies has limited changes in pre-hospital urgent and emergency care services. She concludes that designers need to have a comprehensive and rigorous understanding of human behaviour (capabilities and limitations) to ensure that the design of products and equipment provided to acute healthcare are effective, efficient and avoid unwanted side effects.

CHAPTER 9

Black et al. advocate the value of communication design in an acute healthcare setting and promote the role of information designer. Through the presentation of a use case aimed at designing a care bundle for the recognition and treatment of acute kidney injury, they provide an insight to the challenges designers face. The authors also provide a set of general design recommendations for the development of communication tools to support complex clinical processes. The chapter reveals the value of co-production and participatory design in the development of communication documentation and demonstrates that well-designed paper documentation has the potential to contribute to quality improvement to supporting both the implementation and communication of new processes in a healthcare setting.

Theme 3: Design in chronic health

CHAPTER 10

In this chapter Craig and Chamberlain explore the role of design in the context of behaviour change in chronic health. Through the presentation of three case studies across different chronic health conditions, such as motor neurone disease, spinal cord injury and cystic fibrosis, they offer discussion on the benefits but also the complexities of design in health behaviour change. With regards to the latter they highlight the challenges of scaling up any intervention focusing on behaviour change because of the number of variables that are at play and the ethical dilemmas that arise in the area of health self-management.

The authors provide several recommendations on the design of behaviour-change interventions in chronic health, such as working closely with end users, drawing on people's strengths and positioning them as experts in the design process, following a holistic design process and the value of interdisciplinarity in this field. They conclude that supporting through design the individual in adjusting their behaviour and lifestyle to cope with the chronic condition is a topic that merits further exploration.

CHAPTER 11

Following from the previous chapter, Alison Prendiville continues the discussion on the use of technology for chronic health. She discusses the rise of patient health self-management through personal medical devices as a result of people living longer and changing lifestyles. Despite the usefulness of technology, overemphasis on it falls short of delivering systematic changes. The author draws attention on how design can, due to its interdisciplinary nature, provide a much-needed coordinated healthcare strategy for the use of digital products in chronic health.

Through the presentation of a digital glucose-monitoring personal medical device use case, the author raises and discusses the issues of self-hood and compliance within broader social and cultural domains such as commensuration, discipline and surveillance. She concludes that for health professionals, design's contribution lies in its ability to capture the human and social complexities created by the use of healthcare technologies in the home and to offer experimental spaces through creative practice to engage with different stakeholders involved in managing chronic illnesses.

CHAPTER 12

In Chapter 12, Chamberlain et al. revisit from a service design perspective the subject of self-management discussed in the previous chapter, in light of their increased use in healthcare and chronic health. They discuss the value of co-production and participatory design within multidisciplinary health teams to enable the self-management of chronic conditions. Through two use cases, a stroke survivor and service improvement, they provide practical knowledge on the use and value of co-design and experience design methodologies in the development of products and services in chronic health. The use cases illustrate the value of design in offering a paradigm shift in the way it can deliver healthcare following the increase of chronic health conditions on an ageing population.

The authors draw attention to the importance of the interplay between product and service design in healthcare. They conclude that as products are 'touch points' in a healthcare service system, they should not be developed in isolation but as part of the service design process.

CHAPTER 13

Paterson et al. present in their chapter the value and processes of digital design when applied to the development of products for chronic health. They particularly focus on the advent of 3D printing and computer-aided design as tools that seek to enable health practitioners to produce better-quality products, increasing productivity and reducing waiting times. This has a potentially beneficial impact for relieving the strain currently placed on healthcare providers, especially in light of under-resourced staff and an increasingly ageing population.

Through the presentation of four distinct use cases, namely hearing aids, foot/ankle orthoses, wrist splinters and spinal braces, the authors offer a comparison and discussion of how new digital design processes improve or complement traditional processes in the development of healthcare applications for chronic health. In their future direction section they conclude that although overall there are perceived benefits in cost and clinical effectiveness when applying digital design process, there is an urgent need for more research in terms of both cost—benefit analysis and clinical efficiency through more robust clinical trials of new products. The authors also draw attention to the close link between products and service design within healthcare and the regulatory as well as investment and technical challenges that lie ahead.

CHAPTER 14

At the outset of the theme on design in chronic health, Christopher Boyko presents the impact of urban environment design on wellbeing. He focuses the discussion on the urban design issues of deprivation, population density, natural environments and walkable neighbourhoods. After providing definitions of urban design, built, natural environment, wellbeing and illbeing, the author sheds light on the relationship between urban design and people's physical and mental wellbeing.

Through the description of a case study that examines urban environments across four different neighbourhood wards in the city of Birmingham in the UK, the author demonstrates the link between wellbeing, deprivation and urban density. Preliminary results indicate that although the low-density, low-deprivation ward was the best in terms of supporting residents' wellbeing, the high-density, low-deprivation ward had the best environmental quality. Lastly, a number of recommendations are offered in this chapter on how to improve wellbeing through urban design and the role of health professionals and local authorities in enhancing wellbeing in cities.

CHAPTER 15

In this chapter Marianne Guldbrandsen provides interesting insights on how to embed innovation in a charity through design thinking and a design process. She discusses how Macmillan Cancer Support, a UK charity supporting people living with or affected by cancer, developed a design process by adapting the Design Council's double-diamond design model. Furthermore the author draws attention to the importance of co-designing ideas with users and the value of layering research as a means to gaining better insights and sense-making. She also offers discussion on the distinction between prototyping and piloting and the value of both on the testing and scaling up of designed solutions.

Theme 4: Design for ageing well

CHAPTER 16

In this chapter Carr et al. discuss how service design methods and tools have been used in practice to engage older people in reflecting on the barriers to integrated networks of support for an ageing community. Through three case studies, namely building relationships in deprived general practice environments, care information redesign in Scotland and IT-based personalised care service design, the authors demonstrate the value of involving older people in co-designing new services related to health and social care. In their discussion section the authors present the lessons learned from each case study. They highlight that a holistic approach of a 'whole person'–'whole system' model should be followed and similarly to the authors in Chapter 13 draw attention to the importance of designing products as part of healthcare services and not as standalone touch points.

CHAPTER 17

In Chapter 17 Alastair Macdonald offers a discussion on the role of design and the designer within the emerging landscape of experience based co-design (EBCD) within healthcare. He advocates that there is a value in integrating traditional randomised control trials (RCT) with participatory co-design practices. Through a case study focusing on product development for stroke rehabilitation the author demonstrates how a participatory co-design process assisted in the co-development of the intervention before the RCT and helped to improve the understanding of the effects of the intervention during and after the RCT. By presenting a case study aimed at the development of a food-management and nutrition-monitoring system, the author discusses how EBCD-based practitioners could capitalise more on designers' skills in using prototyping and visual methods both as a means to conduct research and make tangible a greater range and type of possible near-future solutions than appear to be currently generated using EBCD.

CHAPTER 18

Karel van der Waarde discusses how communication design can add value to medicine packaging targeting older users. Through a case study of European ibuprofen packaging, he demonstrates how design can uncover and provide solutions to the information and visual design challenges faced by older people. The author highlights the value of prototyping and user involvement in the design of medicine packaging and calls for an 'information strategy' that is patient- and user-centric. He concludes that there is a need for change in the regulatory framework to accommodate for ageing processes and to make sure that medicine can be taken correctly by older patients.

CHAPTER 19

In Chapter 19, Myerson and Ramster explore the relations between health and wellbeing and the workplace in relation to productivity and stress. More precisely they investigate how to improve health and wellbeing in the office workplace. They present a workplace and wellbeing case study use that has employed participatory design to improve levels of mental wellbeing in office workers. Their research findings reveal that participation in the design of the workplace can have some beneficial effect on wellbeing at work. Lastly they present a conceptual model that suggests that better health and wellbeing can be achieved in the office workplace by aligning organisational purpose more closely with both the functional and psychological needs of the individual.

CHAPTER 20

Spinelli et al. review several behavioural strategies displayed by older people in selecting, purchasing and using technology-based products within the context of health. They highlight the impact and importance of the social support group in the adoption of new technology. After drawing attention to the demanding challenges faced by an ageing population and a range of new technologies, the authors focus the discussion on smart materials. Smart materials have the ability to display smart behaviours by sensing a stimulus from their environment and reacting to them in a useful, reliable, reproducible and usually reversible manner. The authors conclude that smart materials can be seen as an interesting and emerging opportunity for the design of more intuitive technology-based healthcare products.

Part III: Research methods, recommendations and foresight

Chapter 21

Victor Margolin, a design historian/theorist who unfortunately became a patient, provides an insider's view into the medical equipment, products and procedures that surround the patient throughout diagnosis, treatment and recovery. Looking through an insider's lens, he illustrates how much more designers and design researchers can do, from process and procedure explanation and understanding, to patients' options and medical decisions, to the design of the technology, not only from the patient's perspective but also from the medical and support team's use-ability perspective.

Chapter 22

Sklar and Naar provide a design-practice perspective on design in healthcare. They start their chapter by offering a discussion on why the healthcare industry at large has been slow to embrace design as a tool for problem-solving. Following this they present 12 distinct areas where design can make a notable difference in healthcare, by providing examples from relevant design research and practice projects.

Chapter 23

In the final chapter of the book, Tsekleves and Cooper provide insights and discussion into the challenges, opportunities and trends in design for health that emerge from analysis of the chapters presented in the book as well as drawing from the literature. Based on the thematic analysis of the contributed chapters, the authors present and discuss the 18 themes which have appeared across the four different healthcare settings and five design disciplines in the book. Based on the 26 case studies presented in the book the authors draw on the research methodologies and methods in design for health and present these in relation to the healthcare settings and design disciplines they have been employed in. Lastly, a number of recommendations are offered based on the analysis of the chapter contributions and relevant work in the literature.

Reference

Cooper, R. and Boyko, C. (2011) Design for health: The relationship between design and non-communicable diseases. *Journal of Health Communication*, 16: 134–57.

Part I
Setting the scene

1 A brief history of Western medicine and healthcare

Chris Rust

Non-Western systems of healthcare, particularly those of China and India, have their own important foundation of scholarship and experience, but for most readers of this book, the Western medical tradition will dominate their work and sets a great part of the agenda for designing.[1] To understand the forces at work in that tradition it is a good idea to know something about its history, which might be considered as a play with four acts, each one shorter and more intense than its predecessor.

Act 1 starts in prehistory, finds its feet with the ancient Greek and Egyptian doctors and philosophers and comes to a climax around AD200 with the work of Galen of Pergamum, doctor to the Emperor Marcus Aurelius. In Act 2, Renaissance scientists start to question the body of accepted wisdom inherited from Galen and his predecessors and develop a new understanding of anatomy. Act 3 begins when 19th-century doctors start to develop a modern professional/academic framework and recognise that they do not have effective 'cures' for most of the serious diseases. They commit themselves to systematic investigation of illness while developing a tradition of care, which emphasises personal support rather than cure. Finally, around 1940, Act 4 starts when the preceding century of research starts to bear fruit and doctors go on the attack with a growing armoury of drugs, therapies and diagnostic tools that transform their role from carer to technologist.

Today's healthcare institutions are products of Act 4 but they still carry the imprint of the previous acts and some of the answers to problems in today's system may well be found in those earlier ideas and practices, as we will see.

The story outlined above does have one serious omission. The art of surgery has strong connections to our four-act play but it has also marched to a different, often military drummer. Surgery is interesting to many designers and it is discussed in more detail later on in this chapter.

Act 1: from prehistory to the Roman Empire

Archaeologists have established that the surgical procedure of trepanning, drilling a hole in the skull to relieve pressure on the brain, was practiced 10,000 years ago when the only tools available were made of sharpened stone. It is fascinating to speculate on the events and ideas that led people to fashion a tool to invade a skull in this way. Whatever the genesis of the practice it is notable that people still undertake it outside mainstream medicine and claim great benefits from a spiritual and wellbeing perspective (Dobson, 2000) as well as an approach to specific illness.

The first well-documented studies of medicine in the Western tradition are found in ancient Greece and include Eristratus' investigations of anatomy and the empiricists' focus on identifying successful therapies by reviewing past experience. At that time Egypt and Greece had a wide range of specialist physicians using a variety of surgical procedures and a review of Indian surgery compiled during that period lists 121 different surgical instruments (Porter, 1996: 203). This act culminates in the work of Galen of Pergamum who emphasised both the study of anatomy and a rigorous approach to observing and diagnosing illness. His writings became the principal source of medical knowledge for succeeding generations. After him, the long drawn-out decline of the Roman and Greek civilisations led to an emphasis on preserving and interpreting Greek philosophy and science that came to be seen as the wisdom of the ancients, rather than a living body of knowledge that might be questioned and advanced.

Act 2: the Renaissance

The Renaissance changed all that. In 1543 Andreas Vesalius published *On the Structure of the Human Body*, a study of anatomy that broke the ancient authorities' hold on medical knowledge, and anatomical investigation became the foundation of modern medical science. This did not come out of the blue. A series of innovations, including the growth of hospital-based care from around AD400, the establishment of a medical school in Salerno in 1080 and the creation of Italian city 'health boards' in the 1400s to develop public health strategies in the face of the Black Death, all point towards new kinds of healthcare and provided an audience for Vesalius' work. Medieval medicine had been based on communal consensus but these new institutions and rules created a divide between people and practitioners that we can recognise in today's institutions.

With the rise of anatomy, the new 'natural philosophy' of the Renaissance promoted the idea that the body was a kind of machine and Descartes formalised this by asserting that the mind or soul has consciousness but all else obeys mechanical laws. Physics and chemistry became the methods to understand our bodies and our health and by the time the Industrial Revolution was underway we had a large and growing body of scientific knowledge together with evidence, from industry, that it had practical uses.

Act 3: taking stock

> Shall we begin by taking it as a general principle – that all disease, at some period or other of its course, is more or less a reparative process... an effort of nature to remedy a process of poisoning or of decay, which has taken place weeks, months, sometimes years beforehand, unnoticed, the termination of the disease being then, while the antecedent process was going on, determined?
>
> (Florence Nightingale, 1860)

Despite the great increases in our understanding of health during the 18th and 19th centuries, little changed in our ability to cure sick people. Infectious diseases were the main cause of illness and death and doctors came to realise that their medicines and therapies could not much affect the course of these infections (Shorter, 1996: 142). This new realism is reflected in the quote above from Florence Nightingale who believed, with good reason, that the outcome of a disease was largely predetermined and all her efforts were aimed at giving the patient the best chance of surviving the process through good nursing care, nutrition and a healthy environment.

The other side of this coin was the growth of the study of illness itself, adding pathology to the established sciences of anatomy and physiology. Increasingly, doctors were expected to apply scientific methods to healthcare and the growth of large public hospitals gave them a laboratory for the study of sick people. As doctors became part of a more unified system of education and licensing they also gained a new idea about their purpose in life. For the leaders of the profession the study of diseases became their priority and patients who came to hospital for care and comfort became statistical examples of their condition, studied in great numbers to gain a better understanding of how each disease worked.

This was not immediately helpful to more humble practitioners who still had to make a living in their communities and whose patients still hoped for a cure. However, it led to a new approach to medical practice from around 1880 to 1940, known as the 'patient as person' movement. Doctors might not have had effective cures, although they still prescribed pills since that was what patients wanted, but they could provide a different kind of therapy. By listening to the patient, examining them and paying attention to their condition a doctor provided very practical help to people struggling through illness. This approach, which we now characterise as 'old-fashioned' doctoring, was greatly appreciated by patients and has been described by a modern psychotherapist as 'Practising psychotherapy without ever studying it' (Shorter, 1996: 143).

The new kind of doctoring was characterised by careful history-taking, physical examination and the use of an increasing range of diagnostic tools including thermometers, microscopes, stethoscopes, x-rays and electro-cardiographs. All of these found their way into the general practitioner's toolkit and designers should reflect on the way that this widespread use of scientific tools gave patients reassurance and a feeling that their illness was important. However, of equal importance was the role of the doctor in administering the tests and giving personal attention to the patient.

During this period there were great improvements in urban people's health and life expectancy, but it is usually argued that this flowed mainly from better nutrition, sanitation and living conditions, supported by public health policies and a general concern for improving the quality of life in towns, rather than from any medical treatments developed by science. However, that picture was to change, and very rapidly.

Act 4: doctors go on the attack

> Whither Medicine?… Why whither else but straight ahead.
>
> (Lord Horder, 1949)[2]

In 1935 the first 'sulpha' drugs were identified and doctors finally had a treatment for a range of infectious diseases. This was followed by the introduction of antibiotics and successful treatments for cancer and heart disease and the whole emphasis of healthcare changed. Doctors had cures in their repertoire and they had increasingly subtle ways to diagnose illness; the old emphasis on personal contact and support faded away as medicine became more specialised and technical.

The new scientific technique of the clinical trial became ever more important in working out which therapies were most effective and safest, hospitals became dominated by technology and the role of nursing was overshadowed by that of the hospital doctor, an often remote figure who prescribes treatment but may have very little contact with the patient. The design of hospitals has been led mainly by the technical requirements of medical specialisms and a hospital's 'mission' can become confused by modern concerns with productivity or the increasingly uneasy relationship between the medical establishment and patients who want the benefits of modern medicine but find its environment to be alien.

The self-confidence of late 20th-century medicine has led to some well-publicised disasters that add to public concern and make individuals increasingly willing to challenge the authority of doctors and hospitals. The loss of the old-style personal care by general practitioners has led people to look for alternative kinds of healthcare provided by complementary therapists who can still give time and personal attention.

The past 60 years has seen an astonishing change in healthcare and none of us would willingly return to earlier times, especially if we suffer from cancer or need a new hip joint, but the picture is not uniformly positive and there are shortcomings in today's system that need our attention. Designers can shoulder some of the blame for difficulties that people experience as patients or professionals in healthcare but we also have an opportunity to make a big difference, by creating the environment for all of us to understand what is happening to us, feel supported and cared for and have the conditions we need for good healing. In tandem we can do a great deal to help health professionals to be both effective and satisfied in their work.

The art of surgery

As mentioned already, the development of surgery has not followed the same timetable as other medical practices and in some respects it has led the way.

Until modern times surgeons had lower status than physicians. They did manual work, getting their hands and clothes dirty with blood and pus, and their work was seen as a craft, likened to the work of butchers and barbers, rather than an intellectual profession suitable for educated men. During the 19th century, this situation was gradually reversed and surgeons came to enjoy the highest status of any medical practitioner, casting off the stigma of the 'barber surgeon'.

It is not true that most surgeons were simply barbers who turned their hand to amputation. Up to the 18th century they might have done some barbering to keep up their income when surgical cases were not plentiful but there were plenty of well-trained, knowledgeable people in the profession. Their work was not as dramatic and bloody as often portrayed. It included dealing with skin complaints, wounds, ruptures, bone setting and the occasional amputation. Most of the surgery we know today was impossible before the mid-19th century although operations had been developed to remove, for example, bladder stones or breast tumours.

That picture was transformed by the twin innovations of anaesthesia and antisepsis (or asepsis as it became once we understood how to sidestep infection rather than just block it with chemicals). With these radical new techniques, operations that would have been excruciatingly painful and accompanied by shock and fatal infections became relatively bearable and safe. A century before the big advances in drug-based therapies allowed physicians to go on the attack against disease, surgeons could embark on a host of inventive new treatments which propelled them to the forefront of medicine.

Before that the main stimulus for surgeons was warfare, which ensured a plentiful supply of interesting wounds and broken bones to test their skills and inventiveness; many leading surgeons learned and advanced their trade in the navy or army. For example, the introduction of firearms led to much more complicated injuries with shattered bones and a greater risk of infection, demanding new surgical techniques. War provided a great number of cases to experiment on and gradually that experience led to better treatments, such as amputation techniques designed for better healing and to ease the fitting of artificial limbs.

When faced with a non-military problem, surgeons used the plentiful supply of poor people for their experiments. In France the huge public hospitals, which had become showcases for the study of pathology, also provided patients for surgeons to practice on. In the southern

United States the abundant supply of slaves also stimulated surgical innovation. We may look back on these times and feel that our modern society has put such abuses behind us but it has been argued (Srinivasan, 1998) that practice has merely moved on to reflect changing conditions, using patients in poor countries for medical experiments as the supply of poor people in the developed countries has declined.

The new climate of modern surgery from the 1850s onwards led to heroic innovations that restored many lives. From removing damaged or diseased parts of the body surgeons moved on to reconstructing tissue, replacing parts of the body with donated or artificial parts and implanting gadgets that ensured the continued functioning of our bodies. These developments were also design challenges calling for inventive partnerships between surgeons, manufacturers and a variety of designers.

The optimistic growth of surgery also led to some questionable practices. Patients underwent fashionable treatments for no good reason, or surgeons mutilated people for reasons that owe more to the prejudices of the day than any medical need. Again we may believe that our advanced society has put all that behind us but we can never be sure that practices believed to be rational today will not be condemned as barbaric or foolish by future generations. For example, in recent years, the growth of cosmetic surgery led to the enthusiastic use of silicone gel breast implants, which were subsequently banned as too risky by health authorities in several countries (Tweed, 2003).

Modern surgery, like all of today's medicine, is enormously complex. It uses a great array of tools and equipment and presents fascinating challenges to designers and manufacturers. It also subjects patients to frightening and uncomfortable experiences and every aspect of their experience can be made better or worse by the information they receive, the environment they are in or their confidence in the system. The effects of the cleverest techniques and therapies can be wiped out by misunderstandings, human error or an unhealthy environment. All of these challenges can be framed as design problems and designers must share responsibility for meeting them.

Hospitals: from places to die to temples of technology

So far this short history has concentrated on what doctors do and what they know, however, the places where healing is expected to take place are equally important.

The first hospitals, which started to appear around AD400, were more like today's hospices, charitable places where sick and dying people could be cared for rather than somewhere to go for a cure. They were small, often run for religious purposes and concerned about sufferers' immortal souls as they approached death. The idea that patients might be cured of their disease was not in the forefront of people's minds, perhaps reasonably given the limitations of medicine at the time.

The background for these hospitals was an urban society that was itself a killer. Until quite recently cities were unable to sustain their populations without a ready supply of immigrants from the countryside since crowding and poor sanitation ensured that disease exacted a steady toll on urban populations. If you consider the technical effort required today to get fresh water into our towns and sewage out, not to mention keeping food fresh, it's easy to see how our predecessors were prey to infection.

Until the Reformation, and much later in Catholic countries, hospitals continued to be run mainly as a religious duty and every monastery had an 'infirmary'. In the 12th century, city hospitals expanded, some gained a medical focus and other kinds of hospitals emerged which were more concerned with isolating people with infectious diseases from the rest of the community. Lepers were the first to be treated like this but later these 'pest hospitals' were used to isolate plague victims.

In the 18th century, with the continuing rise of scientific thinking, large hospitals for the poor became both centres for treatment and places where disease could be studied and the idea of medical specialisms and specialist hospitals became more established. Unfortunately, the concentration of sick people and a poor understanding of infection meant that hospitals were not healthy places. Early maternity hospitals had appalling rates of death through infection and probably their main value was to provide somewhere to learn obstetric skills that would benefit better-off women in the healthier environment of their own homes. Once again we cannot afford to feel too superior about the limitations of our predecessors since hospital-acquired infection is one of the most difficult challenges for healthcare today and one in which designers have a crucial role to play.

In the 19th century, as understanding of infection and pathology improved, hospitals became more recognisably like today's institutions. Nurses became professionalised and an important part of the healthcare system. Medical schools were integrated with hospitals, specialist clinics and specialist doctors became more normal and healthcare practices were based increasingly on scientific knowledge. Hospitals cast off their sense of themselves as charitable institutions and, as treatments came to depend more on technology which could not be taken to the patient's home, they became places for treatment of both rich and poor.

In the 20th century, the hospital became a quintessentially modernist enterprise. Specialist doctors became the high priests of a system that believed deeply in the power of science to cure us. Disease, its symptoms and its treatment have been analysed and measured with amazing precision. Organisational thinking has taken on the same obsession with measurement and hospitals have been built and operated as machines for treatment.

Great benefits have flowed from this movement but many people have come to feel that hospitals have lost something. The community values of the original religious hospitals and the personal therapy approach of pre-1940s practitioners seem to have been swept aside in the modernist adventure. Even the advances in hygiene and public health in the 19th and early 20th centuries seem to be compromised by the 'efficient' throughput and resource utilisation (or crowding) of some modern hospitals, and infection control has become one of their biggest headaches.

This has not gone unnoticed and later in this book we will look at recent developments that marry science and some traditional values in very creative ways. Leading healthcare architects in the USA, for example, have claimed (Ulrich et al., 2004) that we have a once-in-a-lifetime chance, with so many new hospital building programmes going on, to embed a more humane, healing philosophy in the physical fabric of our science-based healthcare system. The problem does not lie with doctors or managers but in the hands of designers. If designers can take responsibility for understanding the problems and explaining their ideas in terms that make sense to the healthcare community, then they can make a difference. If designers expect others to understand them and think like them, they have failed before they start.

Nursing

Whether a sick person is in a hospital or in their own home they need somebody to look after their physical needs and, as medical treatments have become more complicated, somebody to administer the therapies that doctors prescribe.

Until the 19th century nursing was low-status work. It was dirty and demeaning to clean up after sick people and, outside the hospitals, the work was casual with nurses moving from patient to patient. A common caricature of the 18th-century nurse was a drunken unreliable slattern. Ideas about nursing were also confused and few people had much idea of what a patient needed to support healing. Ill-formed folk theories and lack of understanding of the basic needs of hygiene or sources of infection were rife. Most hospitals, rooted in religious rather than healing traditions, were little better.

If this was a problem in civilian life it was even more so for a soldier. Armies paid little attention to their sick and wounded and huge numbers died, nursed by unskilled 'camp followers' in unsanitary conditions. The Crimean War story of Florence Nightingale's work to deal with these problems is well known but it is worth visiting here since Nightingale's career marked the turning point in the nursing profession.

Of course Florence Nightingale did not invent modern nursing on her own, she was drawing on many traditions and had been trained in one of Europe's first modern nursing schools, the Kaiersworth Deaconess Institute founded in 1836 near Düsseldorf in Germany. Nightingale's great strength was her passionate desire to change things and her persuasive abilities, she was also an excellent statistician who used scientific evidence to back up her work. The Crimean War, where she was sent by the British government after newspaper reports of the plight of sick troops, was the laboratory in which she could develop and demonstrate better ways to care for sick people and her results were dramatic, reducing the death rate from 40 per cent to 2 per cent in six months.

Her Crimean achievement also gives us one of the first recorded examples of a famous designer making a difference in healthcare. In October 1855 a new military hospital was opened at Renkioi in Crimea. The engineer Isambard Kingdom Brunel designed it to be prefabricated in the UK and transported to Crimea in five ships. Florence Nightingale described the buildings, which confirmed her beliefs about the value of ventilation, as 'those magnificent huts', and they influenced her work on the design of hospitals when she returned to England. So, although they never met or worked directly together, it might be said that the woman who did more than any other individual to set out the course of modern nursing depended in part on the practical ability of one of the 19th century's greatest designers.

Nightingale's work had three aspects: firstly, following her Crimean enterprise, she set up a national system of nurse training which laid the foundation for the nursing profession that we know today. In that context she also set out many of the principles that governed the design of hospitals and the term 'Nightingale ward' is still used to describe the open-plan ward design used in hospitals until very recent times.

Her second contribution was to write about nursing and healthcare, publishing 200 books and pamphlets, including writing aimed at ordinary people caring for their own families. She gave very clear descriptions of the forces that make for bad health – poor ventilation or ventilation that spreads infection, poor sanitation, lack of calm, inappropriate lighting, poor nutrition – and experienced hospital designers often comment that she understood very well the design principles that we need today, even if her thinking was based on scientific ideas that have been left behind.

The third arena she entered was that of public health, changing the physical nature of our homes and towns to remove the causes of ill health at source. Again she was concerned with both public policy and self-help, offering criticism and policy thinking to public authorities and advice to individuals – especially mothers, who carried the greatest burden of caring for households and their sick members (Seymer, 1954).

Nightingale was not the only significant figure in Victorian healthcare and public health, but her work gives a clear picture of that arena and the very important improvements that were made. Her practicality, insight and activism, underpinned by rigorous scientific work, provide exactly the recipe that designers need to apply today.

Having taken in the history behind modern medicine we now need to understand something of its culture and how that relates to design.

Notes

1 While a number of sources have been helpful in compiling this chapter the main oversight is drawn from the *Cambridge Illustrated History of Medicine*, edited by Roy Porter (1996). Material not attributed to any other source is based on that work, which provides an excellent foundation for designers wishing to gain a fuller understanding of the history of medicine.
2 Lord Horder was the Queen's physician, speaking right at the start of the 'modern' era of Western medicine.

References

Dobson, R. (2000) Doctors warn of the dangers of trepanning. *British Medical Journal*, 320(7235): 602.

Horder, Lord T.J. (1949) Whither medicine? *British Medical Journal*, 1: 557–60. (Originally a talk given to the West London Medico-Chirurgical Society during 1949.)

Nightingale, F. (1860) *Notes on Nursing, What It Is and What It Is Not*. London: Harrison and Sons. Available at: www.gutenberg.org/etext/12439, accessed 16 August 2005.

Porter, R. (1996) Hospitals and surgery, in Porter, R. (ed.), *The Cambridge Illustrated History of Medicine*. Cambridge: Cambridge University Press, 202–45.

Seymer, L.R. (ed.) (1954) *Selected Writings of Florence Nightingale*. New York: Macmillan.

Shorter, E. (1996) Primary care, in Porter, R. (ed.), *The Cambridge Illustrated History of Medicine*. Cambridge: Cambridge University Press, 118–53.

Srinivasan, S. (1998) Clinical trials: Some ethical issues. *Issues in Medical Ethics*, 6(2): 45–6.

Tweed, A. (2003) Health complications from breast implant surgery. *Common Network Magazine*, 6(2/3).

Ulrich, R., Quan, X., Zimring, C., Joseph, A. and Choudhary, R. (2004) The role of the physical environment in the hospital of the 21st century: A once-in-a-lifetime opportunity. Designing the 21st Century Hospital Project, Center for Health Design.

2 Challenges and opportunities for design

David Swann

In his seminal book, *On the Origin of Species*, Charles Darwin (1859) proposes that our survival as a species was not attributed to our intelligence or physical prowess, but to our ability to adapt. Our innate creativity has enabled us to keep pace with a world in acceleration, as we experience, with increasing frequency, many waves of social, technological, economic and environmental change (Toffler, 1970; Bostrom, 2009). The world has changed. Healthcare is transforming. Design is responding.

The United Kingdom's National Health Service (NHS) was conceived in 1948. While its journey to date has not been without its difficulties, the challenges that it now faces are some of the toughest yet encountered. Healthcare systems in France, Germany, Japan and the United States of America are all experiencing the same pressures perpetuated by an ageing population, exponential demand and rising cost of care (Appleby, 2013).

Albert Einstein astutely observed that in the middle of difficulty lies opportunity. Design for health is now emerging from the shadows to be recognised as a distinct design discipline in its own right. A new discipline with patient safety at its heart, an evidence-based practice that necessitates systems thinking and collaboration to tackle complex challenges and a practice governed by a stringent ethical framework. This chapter describes the difficult challenges that unite all healthcare providers and reports on the opportunities arising from healthcare engaging with design and design engaging healthcare – whether it be at a global, national or local level. World-class exemplars, such as Bruce Archer's pioneering King's Fund bed, demonstrate the value of professional convergence. All the exemplars and initiatives identified in this chapter merit further investigation. Finally, I hope to share the knowledge I have gained through my own research practice with those who wish to engage more deeply with the emergent discipline of design for health.

Design in healthcare challenges

The constitution of the World Health Organization (WHO; 1946) articulates that health is a state of complete physical, mental and social wellbeing and not merely the absence of disease or infirmity. Indeed the determinants that influence an individual's state of health are many and varied. Socioeconomic factors, physical environments, a person's characteristics and behaviour all play a part. Dahlgreen and Whitefield's diagram (1993) illustrates the macro forces and relationships of these determinants (Figure 2.1).

It is evident that these health and wellbeing interdependencies have a major influence on an individual's engagement with or withdrawal from social, educational, economic, civic and political participation. Significantly, it illustrates the reach of design in healthcare and, perhaps surprisingly to some, how design permeates into the research territories of education, work

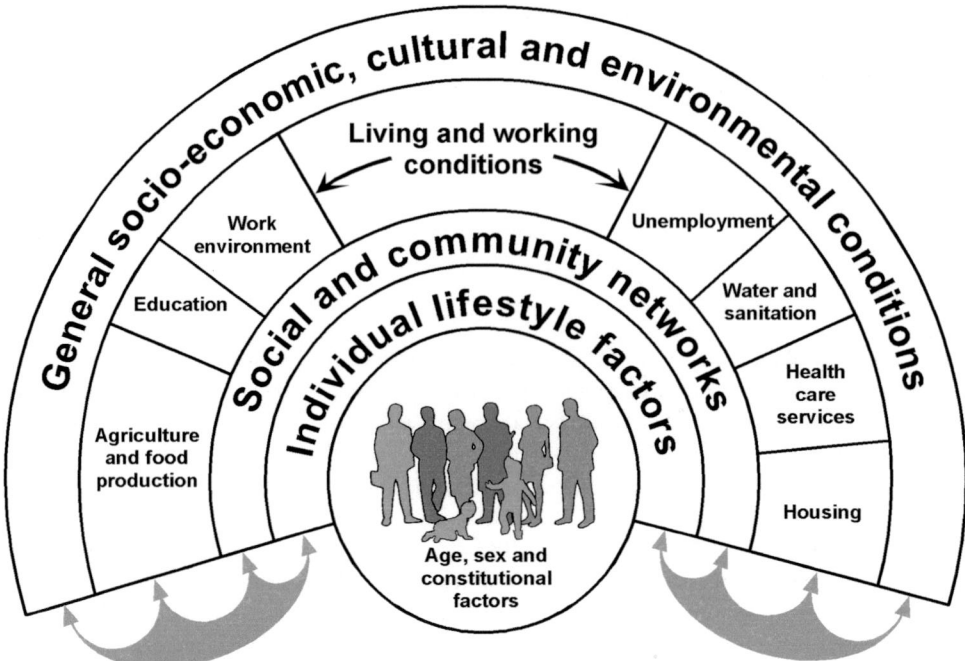

Figure 2.1 Dahlgren and Whitehead's main determinants of health
Source: Dahlgren and Whitefield, 1993

and food production. Healthcare design is an important point of intersection that unites us all: as individuals, as families and as a global community. Therefore it is not surprising that this intricacy offers considerable scope and breadth for both design and clinical communities to impact positively on ordinary people's lives through interventions across the policy, service and product continuum.

In a global context the recognition of health and its wider connectivity is encapsulated by the new Sustainable Development Goals (SDGs) – as outlined in the United Nation's *Transforming Our World: The 2030 Agenda for Sustainable Development*. These SDGs supersede the former Millennium Development Goals. This ambitious agenda seeks to stimulate action and progress across 17 goals and 169 targets that are contained within a thematic framework centred upon the planet, people, prosperity, peace and partnerships. For example, the objective of Goal 3 is the attainment of healthy lives and the promotion of wellbeing for all at any age and is underpinned by nine specific targets that encompass issues such as the ending of preventable deaths of newborns, halving the number of road deaths and injuries due to road traffic accidents and reducing the number of deaths and illnesses associated with hazardous chemicals, pollution and contamination. The scope of healthcare issues described by Goal 3 is wide-ranging and provides a clear call for action for design researchers, clinicians and manufacturers.

The world's population presently stands at 7.3 billion people. Medical advances and better healthcare together with a decline in morbidity and fertility rates have contributed to a population boom worldwide.

Nevertheless, there remains a significant disparity where Design to Improve Life initiatives are actually occurring and who it is actually benefiting. As Polak (2007) states, 'Ninety-five per cent of the world's designers focus all their efforts on developing products and services exclusively for the richest ten per cent of the world's customers. Nothing less than a design revolution is needed to reach the other 90 per cent.'

A recent review funded by the Arts and Humanities Research Council, and led by researchers at Lab4Living based at Sheffield Hallam University, the Helen Hamlyn Centre of Design at the Royal College of Art, London, together with researchers from Coventry and Glasgow Universities sought to establish a greater understanding of the extent of design theory and practice within the context of health (Chamberlain et al., 2015). Their findings seem to support Polak's assertion. A comprehensive search of library databases revealed a landscape dominated by research inquiries around ageing and disabilities, normal life and hospital settings, and artefact outputs driven by health informatics and assistive technologies.

A paucity of design practitioners and researchers engaging with global healthcare issues may be attributed to practical issues. However, the potential reciprocal benefit to providers of healthcare in high-resource settings are presently being overlooked (Howitt et al., 2012). The valiant work of organisations such as INDEX: Design to Improve Life, Unicef's Innovation Unit, the International Council of Societies of Industrial Design, Program for Appropriate Technology in Health and the Bill and Melinda Gates Foundation has created a momentum for engagement with this challenging context. It is also true to say that the visibility of grand challenges has entered our field of vision assisted by the global media coverage of award-winning and socially responsible innovations such as the ingenious Colalife, BetterShelter and U-Report projects (all 2015) by global media organisations. As Polak and Warwick (2013) observed in their recent book, *The Business Solution to Poverty*, there remains an urgent imperative to address this imbalance, from a humanitarian perspective but increasingly from the compelling economic argument.

Today, low- and middle-income countries continue to shoulder a disproportionate amount of the world's disease burden. Simple frugal interventions, if developed locally and adopted at scale, could achieve substantial human impact. Since 2012, global health innovation has become the primary focus of my own design research: ABC syringe (2013), Ebola: bleach dilution gauge (2014) and WAAA! (2015). The ABC project addressed one of the WHO's key research priorities, that of deterring the reuse of injection syringes in a curative context. The project's resultant innovation strategy proposed a transformative colour-changing label which signalled to unsuspecting patients the prior use and subsequent non-sterility of the syringe, therefore empowering them to make better risk decisions (Figure 2.2). After all, once the packaging has been removed how do you tell the difference between a sterile syringe and a used syringe that has been washed?

Engaging with global healthcare challenges through responsible research and innovation requires a different methodical approach to the traditional product-development process. Here, the United Nation's Committee on Economic and Social Council (2000) provides a useful perspective. Article 12 of the 1966 International Covenant on economic, social and cultural rights outlines the right to the highest attainable standard of health. In addition to this, the UN Committee on Economic, Social and Cultural Rights which monitors compliance outlines four essential performance requirements that are used to assess potential projects in relation to the minimum standards of health service delivery: availability, accessibility, acceptability and appropriateness (World Health Organization, 2007). More commonly known as the 4As, these parameters are an extremely useful tool to aid the evaluation of formative design propositions within a new product-development programme and will certainly reveal any incongruity in

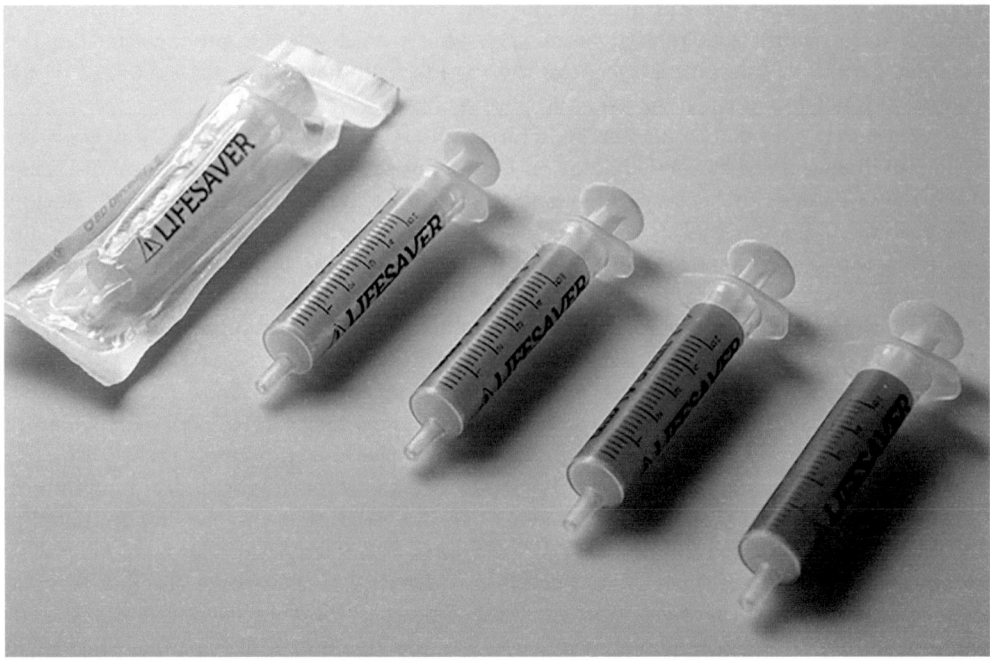

Figure 2.2 A behaviour-changing syringe
Source: Swann, 2013

approach or thinking when designing for a low-resource setting. Inappropriate design think-ing and solutions developed for this challenging context can be characterised by the following attributes: a reliance on mains electricity or costly batteries, a need for consumables, main-tenance requirements, absence of reparability and a product that denies local manufacture. Further to this, a thorough examination of the implementation process is strongly advised, together with detailed knowledge of the organisations, networks and standards/directives. The significance of this must not be underestimated. Past case studies are a useful resource to under-stand this landscape in greater detail and will reveal the invisible barriers, some political, some logistical, that will ultimately determine the success of your project. Identifying these obstacles early on will enable you to make tactical design decisions and so avoid unnecessary cost and the dreaded valley of death. On this subject I have a few further observations. Design and designers can sometimes be blinded by aesthetics, the attainment of design perfection, and often imbue solutions with unnecessary functionality as if to justify and valorise their own creative virtuosity. Design is a broad church, but this mindset is in conflict with the basic principles of designing for a low-resource setting. Operating within this complex field, my experience has led me to believe that no matter how great the healthcare challenge is, or how inextricable the problem may seem to be, this will necessitate a *satisfice* solution as opposed to an optimum solution. When the scale of the problem is perceived to be low, or a first-world problem, the range of the viable solutions and design options is great (concept, design, materials, processes). However, this is inversely true for complex, grand challenges where the scale of challenge and the array of stakeholders involved in realising its mass implementation necessitates the simplest of solutions – a satisfice solution. Figure 2.3 seeks to illustrate this point of view.

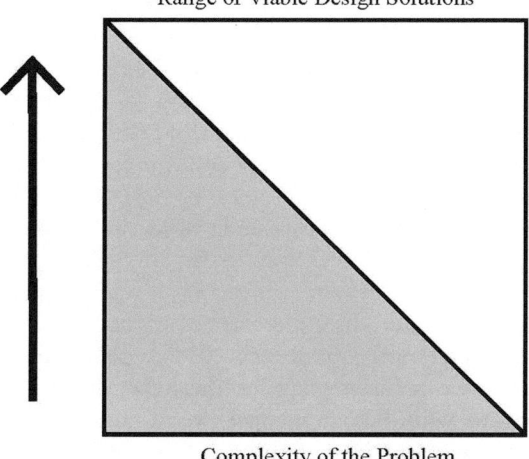

Range of Viable Design Solutions

Complexity of the Problem

Figure 2.3 Complexity of challenge versus complexity of solution
Source: Swann et al., 2015

Satisficing is a blended word derived from the words satisfy and suffice. Conceived by the decision-making theorist Herbert A. Simon (1956), in this context it succinctly describes the creation of a consensus design solution that satisfies the needs of the problem yet is acceptable to all parties even if it may not be the best solution. As Sir Jonathan Ive KBE, Apple's Chief Design Officer, once said at a small design seminar that I attended at the Royal College of Art, 'sometimes the bravest thing you can do as a designer is the most simplest and quietest of things'. It is a philosophy that resonates and underpins global healthcare innovation, and in my opinion demands greater intellectual rigour to achieve the greatest human benefit using limited resources and delivered for the smallest cost possible. Be brave. Be frugal. Be economical.

The NHS is the fifth-largest employer in the world and employs over 1.6 million people (NHS Choices, 2015). Like all healthcare systems, the NHS has been shaped by history, culture and politics. For identification purposes healthcare systems are normally defined by their financing systems: Bismark or Beveridge systems. Regardless of their financing arrangements, all healthcare service providers share a common ideal to provide an inclusive and responsive service to the masses. We are all living longer, assisted by advances in medication and surgical procedures, yet should acknowledge that our final years will be shared with one or more long-term conditions such as chronic heart disease, chronic pulmonary disease or diabetes. Living with a long-term condition also has an impact on our quality of life in our later years with men and women respectively living their last seven to nine years with a disability (Office for National Statistics, 2012). Long-term conditions are not the only physiological conditions requiring prolonged managed care or frequent treatment. The 2015 Later in Life factsheet produced by Age UK highlights many of the physical challenges experienced by older people:

- 6.4 million have some form of hearing loss;
- 3.2 million suffer from urinary incontinence;
- 2 million suffer from sight loss which affects their day-to-day living;
- 30 per cent are unable to cut their own toenails.

Today, 75 per cent of NHS users are aged 65 and over and consume 70 per cent of the acute and primary care spend, 58 per cent of all GP appointments and 77 per cent of inpatient bed days (Department of Health, 2008). Statistical evidence reveals that 80 per cent of an individual's greatest healthcare expenditure during their lifetime occurs in their final years. The average cost of providing NHS hospital care for a patient aged 65–74 is £949, £1,684 for those aged 75–84, rising to £2,639 for those over 85 (Office for National Statistics, 2010). In 2008 the average hospital bed stay for a patient in England was 6.8 days, for patients with dementia it was 68.2 days, circulatory diseases 11.4 days and diabetes 10 days (Office for National Statistics, 2008a). Not surprisingly this is fuelling the migration of services into the community and patient's homes, where new intermediate healthcare teams are bridging the space between hospitals and doctors' surgeries.

The number of people living with a long-term condition is predicted to escalate from 15 million to 18 million by 2025 (House of Commons Health Committee, 2014), with the future cost of providing long-term care presenting a serious challenge to healthcare providers. But, the greatest threat to society and providers rests with the exponential rise of non-communicable diseases such as smoking, physical inactivity, obesity, poor diet and increased alcohol consumption (Wanless, 2002). Evidence indicates that obesity will soon supersede tobacco as the most common cause of premature death and the proliferation of long-term conditions requiring continuous managed care (Ipsos MORI, 2006). In adults, obesity increases the likelihood of Type 2 diabetes by 80 per cent and coronary heart disease by 66 per cent (McKinsey Global Institute, 2014). The WHO (2011) attributes these health risks for 80 per cent of deaths caused by major diseases. The cost to the NHS in providing long-term care for all obesity-related diseases is approximately £7 billion per year and is projected to rise to £12 billion by 2030. The consequence of an increasingly obese society is already being felt in countries such as the USA where public buildings, vehicles and products are being specially adapted or designed to cater for this group's larger anthropometrics. With four out of five children in England never playing outside (Office for National Statistics, 2008b) it appears that we are following a familiar trajectory with 62 per cent of adults classified as overweight or obese (Health and Social Care Information Centre, 2015). Excessive food consumption is not the only adversary that the NHS faces. Alcohol and dementia pose significant threats to spiralling costs as well. Excessive alcohol consumption significantly increases the likelihood of health problems such as high blood pressure, cancer and cirrhosis in later life. The number of alcohol-related deaths continues to grow for both sexes: 18.3 per 100,000 for males and 8.8 per 100,000 for women in all age groups. Perhaps the most shocking figure for alcohol-related deaths is amongst those aged 55 to 74 where there are 44.6 deaths per 100,000 (Office for National Statistics, 2008c). In the UK it is estimated that 3.3 million live with diabetes (Diabetes UK, 2015), with a further 850,000 people living with the effects of dementia that costs the UK economy £24 billion each year (Alzheimer's Research UK, 2014). Parallel to this, it is important to consider the ratio of inactive elderly to the total labour force as this will become an increasingly influential factor in sustaining present levels of healthcare investment to meet future demand. Projected figures for the United Kingdom indicate that the number of people of working age for every person of state pension age (old-age dependency ratio) will rise from 23.8 (2005) to 29.7 (2020) (Office for National Statistics, 2006). With the gap between system capacity and patient need set to widen, this will place a heavier dependency on a diminishing workforce to sustain an NHS in demand as forecasted by Derek Wanless (2002). To illustrate the magnitude of the problem, without any significant changes to the labour-force pattern it is estimated that 20 per cent of all working Europeans will be working in healthcare by 2020 (European Health Telematic Association, 2008). The challenge facing future governments is to maintain present levels of high-quality patient care at an affordable cost.

In rising to the challenges of the 21st century, our innate creative and innovative nature will need to be harnessed if providers of health care are to evolve into sustainable, patient-centred world-class services. If the NHS and other healthcare providers are to achieve their strategic objective of maintaining a safe, first-class patient service within tight fiscal constraints, design innovation is now seen as an indispensable ingredient. In 2001, Borins conducted a comprehensive study of innovation in the public sector and identified that there were five common characteristics of successful projects: the use of a systems approach, the use of new information technology, process improvement, the involvement of the private/voluntary sector and the empowerment of communities and staff. Harris and Albury (2009) further extended these criteria by suggesting that a supportive organisational culture is required to enable innovation to flourish without risk, a need to strengthen the approach and methods used to innovate public service and an ability to view problems through a different lens. Professional diversity can bring the necessary *fresh eyes* to complex or wicked problems by introducing new perspectives and creative thinking to stimulate innovation (Maher et al., 2007). Design is well placed to contribute to service-improvement projects across the strategy, system, service and product continuum. Working alongside health service innovation teams, designers can make an effective contribution to support the transformation of a global industry and shape how future healthcare is delivered, experienced and accepted, because we have the capacity to see things differently and think differently. But more importantly, we have the tools, methods and competencies to affect mass behaviour change that can be the root cause of many health problems.

It is true to say the Royal College of Art (RCA) has led the vanguard of evidence-based healthcare design practice, with activities dating back to the original King Edward's Hospital Fund for London's hospital bed project of 1963. The King's Fund bed as it became known established the British standard for future hospital bed design. A design team lead by RCA research fellow Leonard Bruce Archer developed the parameters for a standardised hospital bed that continues to be used in 85 per cent of NHS hospitals to this day. The King's Fund bed project is an important reference point for all budding and early stage healthcare design practitioners. This ground-breaking project established an evidence-based approach to healthcare design research. Ghislaine Lawrence's authoritative Ph.D. thesis (2001) provides a detailed account of the design processes, development and manufacture of the King's Fund bed project. Lawrence details the methodological processes used within two distinct project phases. A first phase consisted of an information-gathering exercise that involved a comprehensive literature review and the engagement of relevant stakeholders through design workshops. One such meeting held on 3 September 1963 consisted of two matrons, one ward sister and a nursing research officer. The primary aim of these inclusive design workshops was to identify design challenges, opportunities and barriers. This phase included an innovative televised design survey conducted via the BBC's *Panorama* programme. The survey results from participating hospitals provided qualitative feedback to establish the necessary parameters to inform a user specification. A second phase involved a range of simulated trials. At the RCA, user simulations included practising nurses demonstrating the bed-making process with qualitative data informing a design-development programme. A second phase of evaluations involved a clinical trial of 20 design prototypes at Chase Farm Hospital in Enfield. These evaluations lasted for a period of five months and involved a comparative study of the original beds and the proposed design intervention using observational research methods. This trial identified a number of mechanical and user comfort issues which were addressed prior to a second user trial of a revised design at the Royal Berkshire Hospital, Reading. In July 1967, the King Edward's Hospital Fund for London published a comprehensive review (Campbell-Preston et al., 1967) that outlined the final design, user and manufacturing performance and specification requirements: lying/work surfaces, bed perimeter, bed attachments, mobility/stability and manufacturing/construction. The success of the RCA's King's Fund bed lies not only in its design, but also in the pioneering and rigorous processes and methods used during its development. Through this exemplary project, Bruce Archer established the concrete principles for inclusive and evidence-based design research for us all. Today, these emergent design principles and methods continue to influence contemporary design research worldwide and projects at the RCA: Design for Patient Safety, Designing Out Medical Error and Smart Pods.

Design in healthcare opportunities

Both design and designers have a critical role to play in shaping the way healthcare is delivered and experienced in the future. In the last decade the NHS has introduced many initiatives to create the necessary conditions for innovative thinking to emerge and to drive transformative change – both internally and externally. In 2008/9, the Chief Executive of the English NHS, David Nicholson, outlined a range of initiatives in his annual report to increase efficiency and productivity across the NHS. These were to be realised through an innovation-led approach of QIPP: Quality, Innovation, Productivity and Prevention, and as Andrew Lansley, the then Secretary of State for Health, stated in his *Shared Ambition to Improve Outcomes* speech delivered on 2 July 2010:

> All those who work on the frontline should be thinking carefully, and imaginatively, about how we can do things differently. The QIPP process is a home for this in the NHS and the way that we can implement the best and brightest ideas across the service. As the Prime Minister said: 'Don't hold back – be innovative, be radical, challenge the way things are done.

The thematic principles defined by QIPP are still pertinent today, as they remain an influential driver for the improvement of regional and local healthcare services. The QIPP programme offers designers a common narrative to support the co-production of interventions with healthcare professionals and patient groups, to improve the patient experience, patient safety and the efficiency of service delivery.

A second initiative that is actively promoting innovation and professional convergence is the recently introduced Academic Health Science Networks (AHSNs). Formed in May 2013 by the government following Lord Darzi's recommendation, as their name suggests, each AHSN has a remit to build a culture of collaboration and partnership across the NHS, patients, academia and industry to identify, develop and accelerate the adoption of new products and services. Specifically, the 15 AHSNs in England have four core objectives:

- Focus on the needs of patients and local populations: support and work in partnership with commissioners and public health bodies to identify and address unmet medical needs, whilst promoting health equality and best practice
- build a culture of partnership and collaboration: promote inclusivity, partnership and collaboration to consider and address local, regional and national priorities

- speed up adoption of innovation into practice to improve clinical outcomes and patient experience – support the identification and more rapid spread of research and innovation at pace and scale to improve patient care and local population health
- create wealth through co-development, testing, evaluation and early adoption and spread of new products and services.

The changing landscape, culture and environment provide a timely opportunity for students, designers and healthcare communities to connect. However, one of the greatest obstacles experienced by all these communities of practice is translation of applied research into tangible patient benefits through the widespread adoption and diffusion of the design intervention. In an NHS context this is especially problematical and challenging due to its structure. NHS England is comprised of 209 Clinical Commissioning Groups that are responsible for planning and commissioning local health services. As you can imagine, marketing a new innovation and securing a procurement contract across this entire landscape is difficult and time-consuming for any entrepreneur or small business. But there is another way. Innovate UK regularly features open healthcare competitions through its Small Business Research Initiatives (SBRI). SBRIs seek to connect public-sector challenges with innovative ideas from industry while supporting economic growth and providing direct business opportunities for companies. SBRI Healthcare provides a perfect vehicle for engagement for any designer, entrepreneur or small business that has a smart idea or technology that can solve a specific problem. Past calls have spanned a variety of health challenges including the design of a paediatric transport chair, changing people's behaviour to reduce obesity and improving end-of-life experiences. A unique feature of this initiative is a six-month first stage that finances (<£100,000) the development and testing of the idea. Upon completion, projects are further assessed and if successful progress onto a second stage (<£1 million) to prepare the innovation for commercialisation and future adoption by the NHS or other healthcare providers. Most of the projects funded to date have involved different communities of practice where specialist knowledge and expertise has sharpened and refined the quality of the final outcome. SBRIs are a valuable resource for innovators and small enterprises as they provide early-stage funding and a high level of visibility within the NHS, thus providing a potential gateway into supplying the NHS.

Design for health trimtabs

To draw this chapter to a close, it is clear that design-for-health practitioners have a critical role to play in future healthcare. Previously, we have briefly surmised the social and economic challenges that every healthcare service provider is facing. We have also identified emergent global and national opportunities that will undoubtedly influence and spark future design-for-health projects, and along the way cited project exemplars where co-creation and evidence-based design is a vital ingredient that has contributed to their success. These exemplars are extremely well documented and certainly merit closer scrutiny as they will undoubtedly provide valuable insights and can serve as models of best practice; knowledge, innovation tactics and design methods that would undoubtedly shape your own thinking and project strategy. We have also highlighted the new channels such as the AHSNs and SBRIs that are purposefully being created to promote the convergence of health, academia and business communities, which should accelerate innovation to the NHS to deliver a leaner, safer and better health service. However, to achieve the necessary spread, adoption and impact at a national scale, a new partnership model will need to proliferate where designers are placed at the very heart of the clinical setting and service-improvement communities to maximise the effectiveness of design *in* healthcare. Here Buckminster Fuller's analogy of a designer acting as a 'trimtab' and a force for transformative change is an appropriate metaphor (Farrel, 1972):

> Something hit me very hard once, thinking about what one little man could do. Think of the Queen Mary – the whole ship goes by and then comes the rudder. And there's a tiny thing at the edge of the rudder called a trimtab. It's a miniature rudder. Just moving the little trimtab builds a low pressure that pulls the rudder around. Takes almost no effort at all. So I said that the little individual can be a trimtab. Society thinks it's going right by you, that it's left you altogether. But if you're doing dynamic things mentally, the fact is that you can just put your foot out like that and the whole big ship of state is going to go. So I said, call me Trimtab.

References

Age UK (2015) Later in life in the United Kingdom. London: Age UK. Available at: www.ageuk.org.uk/Documents/EN-GB/Factsheets/Later_Life_UK_factsheet.pdf?dtrk=true, accessed 25 November 2015.

Alzheimer's Research UK (2014) Defeat dementia: The evidence and vision for action. Cambridge: Alzheimer's Research UK. Available at: www.alzheimersresearchuk.org/wp-content/uploads/2015/01/Defeat-Dementia-policy-report.pdf, accessed 24 November 2015.

Appleby, J. (2013) Spending on health and social care over the next 50 years. Why think long-term? London: King's Fund. Available at: www.kingsfund.org.uk/sites/files/kf/field/field_publication_file/Spending%20on%20health%20…%2050%20years%20low%20res%20for%20web.pdf, accessed 14 August 2015.

BetterShelter (2015) Millions of people live under tough conditions far away from home. Available at: www.bettershelter.org, accessed 20 August 2015.

Borins, S. (2001) *The Challenge of Innovating in Government*. London: Price Waterhouse Coopers Endowment for the Business of Government.

Bostrom, N. (2009) The future of humanity, in Berg Olsen, J.-K., Selinger, E. and Riis, S. (eds), *New Waves in Philosophy of Technology*. New York: Palgrave Macmillan.

Campbell-Preston, R.M.T., Friend, P.M., Grant, W.R., Heeran, T., Howard, G.P.E., Hunt, J.F., Jolly, C.R., Roberts, I. (1967) *A King's Fund Report: Design of Hospital Bedsteads*. London: King Edward's Hospital Fund.

Chamberlain, P., Wolstenholme, D., Dexter, M. and Seals, E. (2015) *The State of the Art of Design in Health: An Expert-Led Review of the Extant of the Art of Design Theory and Practice in Health and Social Care*. Sheffield: Sheffield Hallam University.

ColaLife (2015) ColaLife building alliances to save children's lives. Available at: www.colalife.org, accessed 20 August 2015.

Dahlgren G. and Whitehead, M. (1993) Tackling inequalities in health: What can we learn from what has been tried? Working paper prepared for the King's Fund International Seminar on Tackling Inequalities in Health, September, Ditchley Park, Oxfordshire. Also printed in: Dahlgren G. and Whitehead, M. (2007) *European Strategies for Tackling Social Inequities in Health: Levelling Up Part 2*. Copenhagen: WHO Regional office for Europe. Available at: www.euro.who.int/__data/assets/pdf_file/0018/103824/E89384.pdf.

Darwin, C. (1859) *On the Origins of Species by Means of Natural Selection*. London: John Murray.

Department of Health (2008) *Raising the Profile of Long-Term Conditions Care: A Compendium of Information*. London: DH Publications.

Diabetes UK (2015) Number of people living with diabetes up 60% in the last decade. Available at: www.diabetes.org.uk/About_us/News/diabetes-up-60-per-cent-in-last-decade, accessed 15 August 2015.

European Health Telematics Association (2008) *Sustainable Telemedicine: Paradigms for Future-Proof Healthcare*. Brussels: Sustainable Telemedicine Task Force.

Farrel, B. (1972) Interview with Buckminster Fuller. *Playboy*, February, 59–70, 194–203.

Harris, M. and Albury, D. (2009) *The Innovation Imperative*. London: NESTA. Available at: www.nesta.org.uk/sites/default/files/the_innovation_imperative.pdf, accessed 14 August 2015.

Health and Social Care Information Centre (2015) Health survey for England: 2013. Available at: www.hscic.gov.uk/catalogue/PUB16076, accessed 14 August 2015.

House of Commons Health Committee (2014) Managing the care of people with long-term conditions: Second report of the session 2014–2015. London: Stationary Office. Available at: www.publications. parliament.uk/pa/cm201415/cmselect/cmhealth/401/401.pdf, accessed 14 August 2015.

Howitt, M.A., Darzi, A., Yang, G., Ashrafian, H., Blakemore, A., Bull, A.M.J., Car, J., Conteh, L., Cooke, G.S., Ford, N., Gregson, S.A.J., Kerr, K., King, D., Kulenran, M., Malkin, R.A., Majeed, A., Matlin, S., Merrifield, R., Penfold, H.A., Reid, S.D., Smith, P.C., Stevens, M.M., Templeton, M.R., Vincent, C. and Wilson, E. (2012) Technologies for global health. *Lancet*, 380(9840): 447–535.

Ipsos MORI (2006) Food for thought: Obesity on the rise. Available at: www.sigmascan.org/Live/Issue/ViewIssue.aspx?IssueId=63&SearchMode=1, accessed 2 February 2011.

Lansley, A. (2010) *A Shared Ambition to Improve Outcomes*. Speech, 2 July. Available at: http://webarchive. nationalarchives.gov.uk/+/www.dh.gov.uk/en/MediaCentre/Speeches/DH_117103, accessed 26 October 2015.

Lawrence, G. (2001) Hospital beds by design: A social–historical account of the King's Fund bed, 1960–1975. PhD, London University.

Maher, L., Pisek, P., Garrett, S. and Bevan, H. (2007) *Thinking Differently*. Coventry: NHS Institute for Innovation and Improvement.

McKinsey Global Institute (2014) Overcoming obesity: An initial economic analysis. New York: McKinsey and Company. Available at: www.mckinsey.com/insights/economic_studies/how_the_world_could_better_fight_obesity, accessed 14 August 2015.

NHS Choices (2015) *The NHS in England*. London: Department of Health. Available at: www.nhs.uk/NHSEngland/thenhs/about/Pages/overview.aspx, accessed 14 August 2015.

Office for National Statistics (2006) Labour force projections 2005–2020. Cambridge: Palgrave Macmillan.

Office for National Statistics (2008a) United Kingdom health statistics no.3 2008. London: Palgrave Macmillan.

Office for National Statistics (2008b) Social trends no.38. Cambridge: Palgrave Macmillan.

Office for National Statistics (2008c) Population trends summer 2008. London: Palgrave Macmillan.

Office for National Statistics (2010) Health expectancy at birth and at age 65 in the United Kingdom, 2005–07, statistical bulletin. London: Office for National Statistics.

Office for National Statistics (2012) Health expectancy at birth and at age 65 in the United Kingdom, 2008–10, statistical bulletin. London: Office for National Statistics.

Polak, P. (2007) Design for the other ninety percent, in Kim, C.R. (ed.), *Design for the Other Ninety Percent*. New York: Cooper-Hewitt, 19–25.

Polak, P. and Warwick, M. (2013) *The Business Solution to Poverty: Designing Products and Services for Three Billion New Customers*. San Francisco: Berrett-Koehler Publishers.

Simon, H.A. (1956) Rational choice and the structure of the environment. *Psychological Review* 63(2): 129–38.

Swann, D. (2013) A behaviour changing syringe: Making invisible risk, visible to deter the reuse of syringes in a curative context. 2nd Global Forum on Medical Devices: Priority Devices for Universal Health Coverage, Centre International de Conférences Genève, Geneva, 22–4 November.

Swann, D., Bartys, S., Martin, H., Keaton, J. and Minhua, M.A. (2015) WAAA! Available at: http://shura.shu.ac.uk/12450/.

Toffler, A. (1970) *Future Shock*. New York: Bantam Books.

United Nations (2000) The right to the highest attainable standard of health. Article 12 of the International Covenant on Economic, Social and Cultural Rights. E/C.12/2000/4, 11 August.

U-Report (2015) U-report, voice matters. Available at: http://ureport.ug, accessed 20 August 2015.

Wanless, D. (2002) *Securing Our Future Health: Taking a Long-Term View*. London: HM Treasury.

World Health Organization (2007) Fact sheet. Geneva: WHO. Available at: www.who.int/mediacentre/factsheets/fs323_en.pdf, accessed 24 November 2015.

World Health Organization (2011) Global status report on non-communicable diseases. Geneva: WHO. Available at: www.who.int/nmh/publications/ncd_report_full_en.pdf, accessed 14 August 2015.

Part II

Designing for health

Introduction

Emmanuel Tsekleves

This book is aimed at both healthcare professionals and designers. In terms of the former the focus is on providing through practical use case studies of the value of design and design thinking as a tool for innovation in healthcare, that goes beyond graphics and application design but into problem-finding and problem-solving. In terms of the latter the focus is on exposing the theory, research methods, tools and spheres of challenges and opportunities in healthcare where design can play an active and much needed transformational role.

Although this is by no means an exhaustive list of design theory, methods and projects in healthcare, it offers a carefully selected and balanced overview of the value, trends, challenges and opportunities for design in healthcare and for healthcare in design. For this reason this section, which forms the main body of the book, has been divided into four healthcare thematic units, namely Design for public health, Design in acute health, Design in chronic health and Design for ageing well. The contribution and potential of design in healthcare is explored in each of these thematic units through the lens of traditional design disciplines, namely architecture design, communication design, product design, service design and behaviour design. Figure PII.1 illustrates how the design disciplines cross the four healthcare themes, with a chapter dedicated to examine each one. An overview of each thematic unit and design disciplines within it is offered below.

Architecture design refers to the process of designing and laying out spaces and buildings as well as non-building structures. It can be considered 'as the definition and integration of physical and conceptual entities and fixing their location in space' (de Vries et al., 2001: 604). Architecture design focuses on planning and designing form as well as interactions between people, spaces and their environment. As such it frames our behaviour, attitudes and often impacts on our lifestyles. Architecture design can be considered from an aesthetic, functional, emotional, social and environmental perspective.

For more information on this topic recommended reading includes *Basics: Architectural Design* by Bielefeld and *Designing Architecture: The Elements of Process* by Pressman.

Product design often blurs the boundaries between specialist areas such as graphics, fashion interaction and industrial design (Rodgers and Milton, 2011) but broadly refers to the process of creating a new product. Morris defines product design as 'the efficient and effective generation and development of ideas through a process that leads to new products' (Morris, 2009: 22). It includes a number of stages and a range of activities that oversee the whole process from product conception to product delivery and marketing, often beginning with the perception of a market opportunity and ending in the production, sale and delivery of a product (Ulrich and Eppinger, 2011).

For more information on product design suggested readings include the books by Rodgers and Milton, *Product Design* and by Ulrich and Eppinger, *Product Design and Development*.

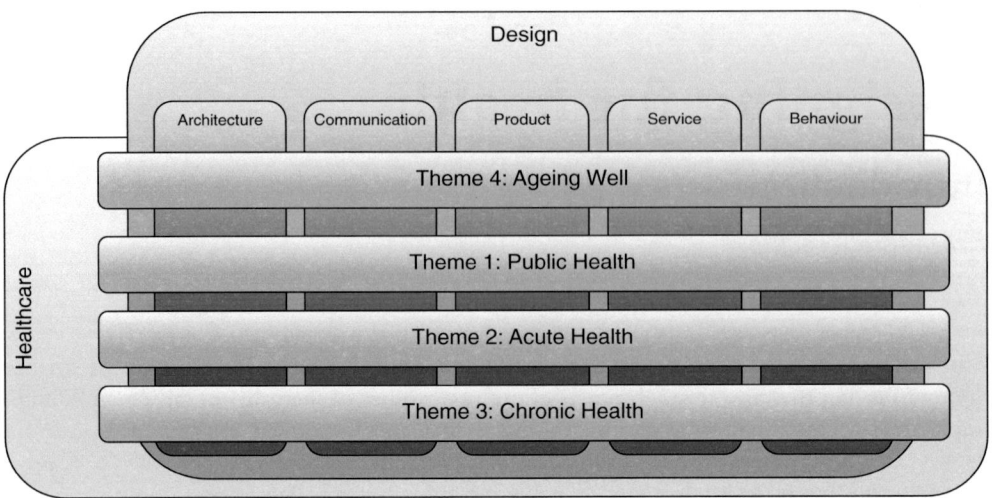

Figure PII.1 How the disciplines of design and healthcare overlap and are presented in this section of the book

Communication design is a discipline that marries graphics design with information design, aimed at the development of material – print, crafted, electronic, online – as well as different media channels specially designed to communicate with people. It is 'the process of conceiving, programming, projecting, and realizing visual communications that are usually produced through industrial means and are aimed at broadcasting specific messages to specific sectors of the public' (Frascara, 2004: 2). The output of communication design is typically focused on increasing the intended target audience's knowledge, perception, attitudes and even behaviour towards a designed direction.

Recommended books in this field include *Communication Design: Principles, Methods, and Practice* by Frascara and *Communication Design: Insights from the Creative Industries* by Yates and Price.

Service design: unlike product design, service design is a form of conceptual design. Although a number of different definitions exist (Nisula, 2012), the most commonly accepted is that it is 'the activity of planning and organizing people, infrastructure, communication and material components of a service in order to improve its quality and the interaction between service provider and customers, (Service Design Network, 2016). It is a multidisciplinary and emerging field and as such employs research methodologies from different disciplines. The role of the end user (service user) is central in the service design process, with the designer often being that of 'an actor able to listen to users and facilitate the discussion about what to do' (Meroni and Sangiorgi, 2011).

For more information on service design readers are encouraged to look at *Service Design: From Insight to Implementation* by Polaine et al. and *Design for Services* by Meroni and Sangiorgi.

Behaviour design focuses on how design can influence and/or shape human behaviour. Behaviour design incorporates theories of behavioural change from psychology and other related disciplines. Behaviour-change interventions – sets of activities designed to change specified behaviour patterns, are often employed and developed (Michie et al., 2011). Such interventions can span across objects, services, spaces and environments, therefore behaviour design seeks to enable consideration for the actions and services associated with any design and its context, and the consequences of these actions (Niedderer et al., 2014).

Recommended books in this field include *Designing for Behavior Change: Applying Psychology and Behavioral Economics* by Wendel and *Motivating Change: Sustainable Design and Behaviour in the Built Environment* by Crocker and Lehmann.

Public health: one of the most common definitions for public health is the one coined by the Institute of Medicine in 1988 as 'what we as a society do collectively to assure the conditions in which people can be healthy' (Institute of Medicine, 1988: 19). In 2003 the definition was updated by the same institute to refer to 'the health of a population as measured by health status indicators and as influenced by social, economic, and physical environments, personal health practices, individual capacity and coping skills, human biology, early childhood development, and health services' (Institute of Medicine, 2003: xii). However, the leading definition, accepted by the WHO, is that defined by Acheson: 'the art and science of preventing disease, prolonging life and promoting health through the organized efforts of society' (Acheson, 1988) and expanded by Wanless 'the science and art of preventing disease, prolonging life and promoting health through the organised efforts of society' (Wanless, 2004: 26).

As such public health is inherently multidisciplinary requiring healthcare professionals to work with other professional groups (i.e. city and government authorities) to monitor the health status of the population, identify health needs, develop programmes to reduce risk and screen for early disease and control communicable diseases. A key distinction of public health from acute, chronic or any other type of healthcare is that it adopts a wider health approach, where the focus is placed beyond the health status of individuals but at health activities aimed at increasing health at the population level. Although public health covers preventive, curative and rehabilitative actions, its main emphasis and effort is placed on prevention, to minimise the risk and impact of illness. In addition, a public health is the subject of policy across different sectors of life and society at a national, regional and international level, with the fostering of public policies aimed at promoting health, evaluating healthcare provision and implementing change. For instance, all European Union (EU) policies are required by the EU treaty to follow a 'Health in all Policies' approach (European Commission, 2016).

Readers wishing to know more about public health can read *The New Public Health* by Baum and/or *New Perspectives in Public Health* by Griffiths and Hunter.

Acute health is defined as 'care aimed at contributing to improved health or to the diagnosis, treatment and rehabilitation of sick people' (Hirshon et al., 2013). The term acute in the context of healthcare refers to illnesses and conditions which have severe symptoms and are usually short term (although may lead to long-term conditions), requiring diagnostic tests, treatment and follow-up care. Acute care responds often to immediately life-threatening health conditions. Therefore, acute care services typically include emergency medicine, ambulatory services, trauma care, acute care surgery and provide secondary care, ranging from relatively small district hospitals to large city teaching hospitals (Hirshon et al., 2013).

Although books around acute healthcare are mostly based on acute medicine of the management of acute patients, they nevertheless provide insights into current practices. Readers wishing to know more about this subject can read *Essential Guide to Acute Care* by Cooper et al. and/or *Initial Management of Acute Medical Patients* by Wood and Garner.

Chronic health refers to the care and management of chronic conditions. Chronic or non-communicable diseases (often referred to as long-term conditions) are health problems that are not passed from person to person but are of long duration (over a period of years or decades) and generally slow progression, requiring ongoing management (World Health Organization, 2002). Although there are several chronic conditions, the WHO has identified four main types. These are cardiovascular diseases (like heart attacks and strokes), cancers, chronic respiratory diseases (such as chronic obstructed pulmonary disease and asthma) and diabetes (World Health Organization, 2014).

Although nowadays chronic diseases are very common, with several people often having more than one chronic condition, many chronic diseases are also preventable. Many are linked to socioeconomic, cultural, political and environmental determinants (globalisation, urbanisation, population ageing) and to lifestyle choices (diet, physical activity, smoking, etc.). Therefore, focus in chronic health is placed on the prevention, diagnosis, care, management and support of people with chronic diseases.

Readers wishing to know more about chronic health conditions can read Weisz's *Chronic Disease in the Twentieth Century: A History* and/or Larsen's *Lubkin's Chronic Illness: Impact and Intervention*.

Ageing well: framed within the context of an ageing population, ageing well refers in this book to actions aimed at improving the quality of life in older age. Although other terms may be found in the literature, such as active ageing or successful ageing, the premise is the same, as identified by Fernández-Ballesteros et al. as 'being defined on the basis of physical, cognitive, emotional-motivational and social domains' (Fernández-Ballesteros et al., 2010: 45). Under this theme topics focus on how to support older people in later life, in living with multiple chronic health conditions, widen social inclusion, strategies for adoption of new technology-based health products and living environments providing independency.

Readers wishing to know more about this theme are encouraged to read Bowling's *Ageing Well* and/or Dangour's *Ageing Well*.

References

Acheson, D. (1988) *Report of the Committee of Inquiry into the Future Development of the Public Health Functions and Community Medicine*. London: Stationery Office.

Baum, F. (2003) *The New Public Health*. Oxford: Oxford University Press.

Bielefeld, B. (2013) *Basics: Architectural Design*. Berlin: Birkhauser Verlag AG.

Bowling, A. (2005) *Ageing Well: Quality of Life in Old Age*. London: McGraw-Hill Education.

Cooper, N., Forrest, K. and Cramp, P. (2008) *Essential Guide to Acute Care*. Chichester: John Wiley and Sons.

Crocker, R. and Lehmann, S. (2013) *Motivating Change: Sustainable Design and Behaviour in the Built Environment*. London: Routledge.

Dangour, A.D., Grundy, E.M. and Fletcher, A.E., eds (2007) *Ageing Well: Nutrition, Health, and Social Interventions*. Abingdon: CRC Press.

European Commission (2016) Health in all policies. Available at: http://ec.europa.eu/health/health_policies/policy/index_en.htm, accessed 12 January 2016.

Fernández-Ballesteros, R., Garcia, L.F., Abarca, D., Blanc, E., Efklides, A., Moraitou, D., Kornfeld, R., Lerma, A.J., Mendoza-Numez, V.M., Mendoza-Ruvalcaba, N.M. and Orosa, T. (2010) The concept of 'ageing well' in ten Latin American and European countries. *Ageing and Society*, 30(1): 41–56.

Frascara, J. (2004) *Communication Design: Principles, Methods, and Practice*. New York: Allworth Press.

Griffiths, S. and Hunter, David J. (2007) *New Perspectives in Public Health*. 2nd edition. Abingdon: Radcliffe Publishing.

Hirshon, J.M., Risko, N., Calvello, E.J., Ramirez, S.S.D., Narayan, M., Theodosis, C. and O'Neill, J. (2013) Health systems and services: The role of acute care. *Bulletin of the World Health Organization*, 91(5): 386–8.

Institute of Medicine (1988) *The Future of Public Health*. Washington, DC: National Academy Press.

Institute of Medicine (2003) *The Future of the Public's Health in the 21st Century*. Washington, DC: National Academy Press.

Larsen, P.D. (2014) *Lubkin's Chronic Illness: Impact and Intervention*. 9th edition. Burlington, MA: Jones and Bartlett Learning.

Meroni, A. and Sangiorgi, D. (2011) *Design for Services*. Farnham: Gower Publishing.

Michie, S., van Stralen, M.M. and West, R. (2011) The behaviour change wheel: A new method for characterising and designing behaviour change interventions. *Implementation Science*, 6(1): 42.

Morris, R. (2009) *The Fundamentals of Product Design*. Worthing: Ava Publishing.

Niedderer, K., Mackrill, J., Clune, S., Lockton, D., Ludden, G., Morris, A., Cain, R., Gardiner, E., Gutteridge, R., Evans, M. and Hekkert, P. (2014) *Creating Sustainable Innovation through Design for Behaviour Change: Summary Report*. Wolverhampton: University of Wolverhampton.

Nisula, J.V. (2012) Searching for definitions for service design: What do we mean with service design? Tagungsband 3rd Service Design and Service Innovation Conference, Espoo, Finland.

Polaine, A., Løvlie, L. and Reason, B. (2013) *Service Design: From Insight to Implementation*. New York: Rosenfield Media.

Pressman, A. (2012) *Designing Architecture: The Elements of Process*. Abingdon: Routledge.

Rodgers, P. and Milton, A. (2011) *Product Design*. London: Laurence King Publishing.

Service Design Network (2016) Service design. Available at: www.service-design-network.org/intro/.

Ulrich, K.T. and Eppinger, S. (2011) *Product Design and Development*. 5th edition. London: Tata McGraw-Hill Education.

Vries, B. de, van Leeuwen, J. and Achten, H. (2001) Computer-aided architectural design futures. Proceedings of the CAAd Futures 9th international conference.

Wanless, D. (2004) *Securing Good Health for the Whole Population*. London: HM Treasury.

Weisz, G. (2014) *Chronic Disease in the Twentieth Century: A History*. Baltimore, MD: Johns University Press.

Wendel, S. (2013) *Designing for Behavior Change: Applying Psychology and Behavioral Economics*. Farnham: O'Reilly Media.

World Health Organization (2002) Innovative care for chronic conditions: Building blocks for actions. Geneva: World Health Organization.

World Health Organization (2014) Global status report on noncommunicable diseases 2014. Geneva: World Health Organization.

Wood, I. and Garner, M., eds (2012) *Initial Management of Acute Medical Patients: A Guide for Nurses and Healthcare Practitioners*. Chichester: John Wiley and Sons.

Yates, D. and Price, J. (2015) *Communication Design: Insights from the Creative Industries*. London: Bloomsbury Publishing.

Theme 1

Design for public health

3 Services

Soft service design outside the envelope of healthcare

Peter Jones

Abstract

Better alternatives to improving population health have been sought by healthcare policymakers and the front-line clinicians who see patients in everyday care settings. While public health experts and primary care clinicians recognise the significant effects on health from social determinant factors they have limited tools for addressing these causal factors in their patients' lives. Systemic improvements to a population's social ecology are considerable challenges from within the envelope of a healthcare system. In mental health and primary care contexts, systemic factors, social determinants of wellness and illness (such as environment, housing, social lifestyle, food accessibility) account for a significant proportion of presented conditions. Social determinants are embedded in a community setting, are multicausal and interrelated, have indeterminate risks and are not typically perceived by individuals as health threats. A community's population and traditional primary providers have few resources for intervening or changing source social causes and contributing factors that diminish individual wellbeing. Without addressing these social sources and determinants through channels other than ensured care delivery, their pervasive influence will persist and will continue to be accommodated as effects in larger healthcare systems.

A systemic design approach developed from the theories of flourishing mental health and flourishing societies has been adapted to identify and guide supports for socialising collective health. Flourishing entails individual and family health, the movement toward 'a good life', and ultimately the sustainment of human and all life. Toward these ends we present a framework for community-centred approaches to facilitate flourishing through the design of soft services. Current cases in university campus mental wellness, and peer health coaching are developed as models for eliciting design principles and approaches that have been effective in interventions in the social systems surrounding practices of care, outside the envelope in which the healthcare system operates.

Constraining envelopes of community-based health services

The truism of 'all things are connected' is readily acknowledged in public health and mental health. When mental illnesses or impairments arise, such second-order effects as emergency accidents, chronic addictions and the neglect of physical health commonly result. Globally, the literature shows a large and increasing proportion of emergency department visits from persons suffering from chronic mental health disorders (Baetz et al., 2015; Ford et al., 2004; Byrne et al., 2003). Ameliorating the sources of these continuing social concerns requires intervention upstream into community and local social settings wherein initial conditions started and trigger events arise. Awareness and responsibility for personal health and prevention also take place within the social context. We can identify these contexts as opportunities for advanced design of community-located services that promote and facilitate better health outside the envelope of healthcare provision by primary care or acute facilities.

Healthcare services are structured to provide care accorded to specialty and function (such as emergency, ambulatory, chronic care, trauma care). However, the front lines of care – primary and community medicine and mental health – are concerned with and consumed by the everyday, immediate and social health concerns across the entire spectrum of health issues. One of the most challenging concerns faced in service system design, particularly in healthcare, is the structural inability of a design programme to direct or evaluate changes to system-level policy. Service design is user-centred and business-oriented, and typically aims for improvements to customer–patient interactions within a repeatable activity system, as an end-to-end horizontal journey. Service design projects generally have no mandate to reform policies defining the functions of the service system. The scope of service design occasionally extends to new activities unsupportable by a payer or policy, such as community outreach or extensive home care for mental health programmes, but until supported by policy these programmes may be unsustainable. A complementary design opportunity arises to identify and evaluate person-centred social interventions in community settings aligned to regional and government health policy.

Whether the boundaries of the health provision system are national (e.g., France or the UK), provincial (Canada), regional-private (India) or a national-private mix (US), the predominant modes of service delivery are dictated by the constraints of the payer system. Primary care and mental health services are typically delivered within the traditional 'provider' model, characterised by coverage of patients within a catchment area or insured pool who present themselves physically for examination, diagnosis and treatment service.

Integration points for social systems of care

Systems of care are organised as social services and are subject to changes in policy and funding. The definition of healthcare as a service delivery model by design excludes community-based health support and complementary modes of care. Providers offer clinical services in response to physically presented symptoms, and for the most part only clinical services are reimbursed according to policy.

Changes to practice must be validated by supporting evidence, at least with knowledge from prior clinical cases and up to the gold standard of randomised trials. We present a service design approach for primary care and mental health that does not change service within the envelope of clinical practice but instead addresses community and social factors. Along with social determinants and environmental factors, these contributing factors might appear to be nearly invisible in the causation of illness. Yet these factors present significant opportunities for elusive population health interventions, and could mitigate the burden of healthcare by treating foreseeable causative factors in the upstream problem system.

Seventy thousand diagnosis codes for presented illnesses and incidents are distinguished in the recently institutionalised International Classification of Diseases Rev. 10 (ICD-10; World Health Organization, 2010) used as standard references for diagnoses, procedures and billing. ICD codes are useful for aggregating descriptive statistics of measured health problems in a community, based on presentation and diagnosis. They include a significant section on psychosocial problems (health hazards related to socioeconomic and psychosocial circumstances) which support epidemiological and public health statistics. The codes also constrain the range of the care envelope, in that while social conditions might be identified by codes, only certain codes and procedures are amenable to billing reimbursement by payers, and social determinants are not among these. In practice, physicians record the codes that define the illness at hand, and even if there might be psychosocial drivers (unemployment or low income, environmental hazards) these are often rendered secondary and not considered options for intervention.

The proposed approach in this chapter addresses these upstream, multiple causative contributing factors. From design studies in mental health and primary care, we propose a model for enhancing the functions of health occurring before and around the envelope of healthcare. As in public health, we consider the central context that of a person's community and their social ecology. This is an immediate and intimate locus of care that is largely inaccessible to traditional health promotion and disease-prevention programmes.

Science and design research are both discovering, through differing modes of investigation, the deeply implicated relationship between social and environmental contexts on health. As we might seek changes to clinical practice as a result of these findings, meaningful evidence will be necessary to convince policymakers and the research community of the right changes and situations. The approach discussed in our account presents a design research intervention, supported by research into behavioural interactions with environments.

A consideration of growing significance in healthcare policy and practice is the recognition of individual illnesses as emergent concerns stemming from unresolved mental health issues. The extent to which underlying mental and physically symptomatic disorders are systemically related will perhaps always be analytically ambiguous. Yet emergency physicians indicate universally that treating presented incidents without attention to mental health issues fails to treat the patient's situation, and the probability of hospital readmission is high. Unfortunately, even treating these patients in the emergency room (ER) may reinforce the behaviours acted out from underlying mental disorders, as the ER continues to provide a local safety net.

Primary care and mental health services continue to be delivered within the traditional mode of patient presentation, as mental disorders are inaccessible to treatment unless persons experiencing their pain declare them as such. Emergency and primary care physicians are well aware of the predominance of mental disorders instigating trauma events and their co-occurrence with chronic diseases and addictions. Innovative approaches to integrating modes of care to address mental disorders contributing to preventable or acute illnesses have been advocated for over a decade (Chisholm et al., 2000).

Design for social determinants of health

The relevance of social determinants of health (Marmot et al., 2008) to mental disorders is well known. The continuing health impacts of structural factors and living conditions present challenges to policy and system change (Carey and Crammond, 2015a, 2015b) and calls for better system design approaches. Better alternatives to improving population health have been sought by healthcare policymakers and the front-line clinicians who see patients in everyday care settings. While public health experts and primary care clinicians recognise the significant effects on health from social determinant factors (such as environment, housing, social lifestyle, food accessibility) they have limited tools for addressing these underlying causal factors in their patients' lives.

Most design approaches to healthcare also treat health problems in a service delivery context. The exceptions to these models are service design for health delivery in developing countries, supplementing their typically less-developed healthcare systems. In mental health and primary care contexts, social determinants of health (SDH) account for a significant (but unquantifiable) proportion of presented conditions. Social determinants are embedded in one's community setting, are multicausal, of indeterminate risk and are not typically perceived by individuals as health threats. A community's population and traditional physicians have few resources for identifying source social causes and contributing factors that diminish individual wellbeing. Without addressing these social sources and determinants through channels other than ensured care delivery, their pervasive influence will persist and will continue to be accommodated.

A systemic design approach developed from the theories of flourishing mental health and flourishing societies has been adapted to guide supports for socialising collective health. Flourishing entails individual and family health, the movement toward 'a good life' and ultimately the sustainment of human and all life. Toward these ends we present a framework for community-centred approaches to facilitate flourishing through the design of soft services. Current cases in community-based senior care, mental wellness and peer health coaching are developed as models for eliciting design interventions in the social systems surrounding practices of care, but not within the healthcare system.

Social determinants of flourishing

Flourishing as sustainability was defined by Ehrenfeld (2000) as 'the possibility that human and all life on earth might flourish on our planet forever'. For individual and social flourishing we take Keyes' (1998, 2002) research defining human flourishing as a composite of qualities that demonstrate a healthy sense of wellbeing and social integration. These formulations of flourishing can be measured by various indicators of qualities, which we might recognise as output effects of individual awareness and social activities, not as the sources of flourishing themselves.

Flourishing provides an idealisation principle for both mental health (as it is for Keyes) and primary care (as relevant to SDH). The integrated definition offers a normative goal of public health and health promotion, yet one not achieved through traditional health science methods and measures. It is a longer-term, cultural innovation within societies that might be accomplished by significant shifts in social norms and community-level communications. Such movements might be best fostered by a multidisciplinary, systemic design approach, not a public health intervention approach.

From social determinants to social ecologies

The social ecosystem model of Bronfenbrenner (1979) is adapted to identify the functions and initial measures of flourishing across a social system. Figure 3.1 represents this model as the inclusion of four system boundaries within which an individual interacts over time, arranged topologically from the microsystem to the macrosystem (in Bronfenbrenner's terms). It shares aspects in common with complex adaptive systems (Plsek, 2001) or living systems approaches, yet there are key differences appropriate to design contexts. Living systems are considered whole, symbiotic systems with interdependent living subsystems (Miller, 1972; Capra, 1996). Here the social ecology presents a series of social systems, each with a boundary and nested within larger social systems. They are developmental, that is the complexity of each social system increases with learning through interaction, rather than symbiotically. The whole

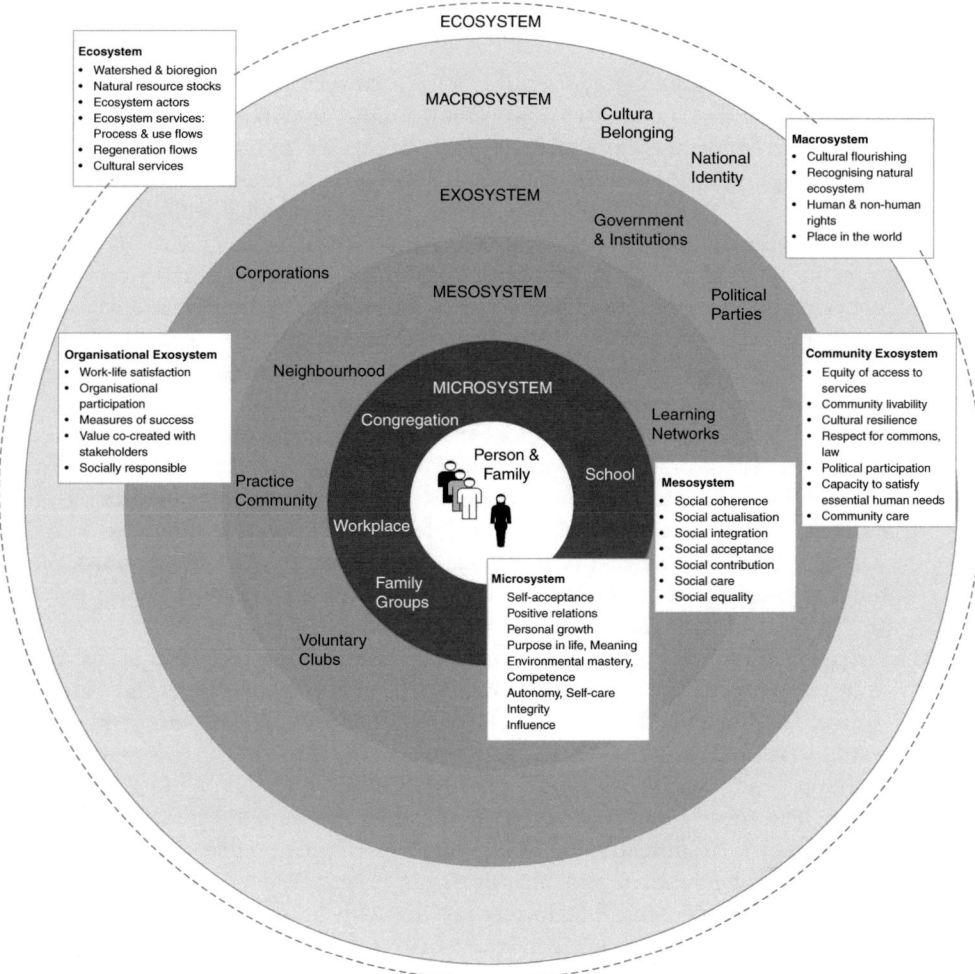

Figure 3.1 Flourishing in the social ecology
Source: Jones, 2015

ecosystem is affected by its parts, but the greater health effects are found in the interaction of parts (individuals) within the social subsystems.

Service design proposals draw from the socioecological system perspective (e.g., the Tavistock tradition of action research), and within the social ecology a social systems perspective (Luhmann, 1997; Christakis and Bausch, 2006) is taken for intervention design. Social systems approaches enable design both materially (e.g., artefacts) and analytically (explaining behaviours at each level of intervention).

Bronfenbrenner's (1979) bioecological theory of human development references these boundaries, within which the research articulations of flourishing are assigned. Rather than individual human development, our interest was to locate individual flourishing (an outcome of development) in a sociocultural context for better understanding flourishing for complex social design.

Five nested social systems are shown in proximal (and temporal) relationship with one another:

Microsystem: The complex set of relations of a person to their immediate containing social context. For an adult citizen in the community context, this might typically entail their family and close relations, their workplace and their immediate friends and social groups. Consistently with Keyes' (2002) notion of flourishing, the measures and values associated with this level would include individual wellbeing and social cohesion and inclusion, as defined previously.

Mesosystem: The meso level is defined as a system of individual microsystems. This is not primarily an aggregate of individuals, it is a number of containing social systems that initiate and reinforce social engagement. The workplace as a system of relations, schools for younger people and community or service organisations may be typical in the meso level of ecosystem.

Exosystem: The exosystem level includes the enduring institutions and major societal references that all individuals within a social boundary would understand as 'part of society'. The exosystem entails workplaces and their larger organisational settings, business networks, neighbourhoods and local government institutions accessible within the experience of the individual. This is the level of the business model function, and would be the level at which social and institutional reform practices are designed for a similar flourishing society model.

Macrosystem: The society and cultures may be described as macrosystems in the societal flourishing model. The macrosystem defines the enduring archetypes and 'blueprints' for societal functions that are repeatable across contexts. The macrosystem includes institutional, infrastructure, media and information structures that are expressed at the inner levels.

Ecosystem: The final system ring necessarily includes the natural ecosystem, which was not defined as an influence or social system in Bronfenbrenner, but establishes an environmental boundary and inclusive final system. While micro–macro systems can change in value and influence over time with human interaction, the natural ecosystem changes both independently of social behaviour and with direct and indirect human activities as a complex adaptive system (Levin, 1998).

Relationship to social determinants of health

The social ecosystem of flourishing portrays relationships between individuals (personal health), social and community contexts and social determinants of health. The tension between microsystem factors of flourishing (self-acceptance, purpose in life, personal growth), macrosystem (cultural influences and fit) and exosystem (community and workplace structures) factors reveals contradictions between personal agency and structures, which may present barriers in navigating health concerns. Individuals living within compromised community circumstances may have limited agency to reorient themselves, and may be unable to locate the types of resources they might prefer or expect in their personal or cultural knowledge. Social determinants have a leveraged effect on persons who are already struggling with a compromise such as limited or insecure income, fragmented family situations or a degraded built environment (Marmot et al., 2008). The socioecological model suggests that the meso (social) and other system levels inhibit flourishing when opportunities for growth and self-determination remain inaccessible due to structural community factors.

Table 3.1 Social determinants of health mapped to the social ecosystem

1.	Income	Exosystem (family, microsystem)
2.	Social status	Mesosystem
3.	Education	Mesosystem
4.	Employment/working conditions	Exosystem
5.	Aboriginal status	Microsystem
6.	Social environments	Meso-exosystems
7.	Physical environments	Micro-mesosystems
8.	Personal health practices and coping skills	Microsystem
9.	Healthy child development	Micro-mesosystems
10.	Gender	Microsystem
11.	Culture	Macrosystem

The following social determinants of health are often recognised (Raphael, 2009), here inclusive of at least one uniquely identified in Canada (aboriginal status) that may have corresponding ethnocultural status in other countries. These can be mapped to the social ecologies in Table 3.1, and from a developmental perspective, we could identify a chronological journey (e.g., a chronosystem) from the initial confrontation of these challenges in the microsystem of family life, progressing through life and coping with social and educational settings, toward the eventual independence and work life.

Societal factors tend to accrue over time and the presence of one may aggravate another or all. An individual born into a poor household (1) may be faced with low social status (2) and barriers to better education (3) in many cases. Aboriginal status (5) and social and physical environments (6, 7) compound these relationships and contribute to mental and physical health problems at earlier ages and in greater proportion than in communities with fewer SDH concerns.

Social factors can erode mental health, even if specific mental illnesses or corresponding diseases are not manifested. Health policy acknowledges SDH factors as contributing to poor health and limiting the effectiveness of prevention programmes. Social determinants function completely outside the envelope of healthcare. Clinical (primary) practices rarely address home and community conditions unless these reveal in critical symptoms. While a service design intervention might not directly bridge the individual's community with healthcare provision, we might realise that such a systemic problem cannot be addressed by episodic or sequential health services.

Soft service design for campus mental health

An account of soft service design is developed from an action research case of designing interventions for campus mental health conducted at OCAD University in Toronto. The case provides a structure for distinguishing design approach and practices relevant to community health design. Emerging models of public health (Coburn et al., 2003; Hepworth, 2015) expand the boundaries of public health to populations of concern, addressing the social ecology from individual wellness to public housing, as in the socioecological model. We adopt this expansive approach for campus mental health.

The soft service approach re-envisions social determinants in community settings as a systemic situation requiring health services normally considered peripheral or complementary. Soft services design interventions engage social and community fields of interaction, with attention to communicative and passive structural design to influence preventive health or health promotion. Soft service design attends to the open and nearly unlimited range of opportunities in human lifeworlds for everyday activities accessible outside of the envelope of health services. It differs from public/community health in that meeting health outcomes or measures would not necessarily be the goal of design, or even a driver. If we are interested in human flourishing, a wide range of socioecological frames (Figure 3.1) can be considered its canvases.

The designation of a soft service indicates a situation where value co-creation can arise in a context outside of the service provision boundary. A significant public investment in medical or mental health deals with 'failure demand', resulting from local socioecological systems that generate illnesses or critical incidents requiring care intervention. Due to healthcare policy, payer structure, medical resource availability and cost, such interventions are provided today as care transactions.

One aim of soft services design is to disclose opportunities for discovery in a population's *health commons*, proposing designable common resources that positively contribute to health in a community setting. Ordinarily service organisations or professional services are made available to health seekers (users) as formal service offerings. Walk-in clinics, emergency rooms and pharmacies are clearly displayed and made accessible, and commonly branded as distinct entities. However, clear boundaries or entry points for a *specific* service, or for certain customer, payer or user needs may not be distinguishable. Campus mental health, though based on a well-defined population of students and a university setting, fits this frame. Student health needs cannot be identified by observation, or even data (given privacy laws protecting health information). Design interventions for engaging and helping students were discovered as 'pre-services', as opportunities for informing rather than direct care. Health interventions within the campus commons include peer communications, education and locating health accessibility features.

In this case where no end user can be identified (as there is no 'user' in the cycle) a beneficiary can be re-envisioned as a person in a population coping with everyday health concerns. We refer to this identity as the health seeker. The health seeker (Jones, 2013) refers to a person as an active agent with conscious and non-aware orientation toward a balance between health (growth orientation) and entropy (potentially life diminishing) in a situation. This allows us to represent persons as uniquely, internally aware of their motivations to improve their health, whether sick or not. The theory of health seeking provides a basis for relating individual motivations and growth behaviours (agency) in the socioecological model. At each system (from micro to macro) one's orientation to flourishing enlarges, from the individual self to the social and to a community exosystem, where individual flourishing might be reflected in one's participation in a community. It offers a qualitative frame for identifying and evaluating changes introduced in soft services design.

Campus mental health research context

Canadian universities and health policymakers have made significant investments in providing for the mental wellness and emotional health of students to facilitate the educational mission, campus climate and safety and successful graduation rates. Campus mental health is a strategic concern, with numerous intervention programmes evaluated across schools (Popovic, 2012). In Kirby and Keon (2006) over 100 recommendations were lodged by a Canadian senate committee to inform institutions addressing people living with mental illness. The central notion that individual *recovery* was deemed as critical to Canada's mental health strategy, defined as 'living a satisfying, hopeful, and productive life even with the limitations caused by mental illness'. This policy definition is consistent with Keyes' (2002) definition of flourishing for mental health. The senate committee established the Mental Health Commission of Canada, whose strategy published six strategic directions for policy and service development:

1. Promote mental health across the lifespan in homes, schools and the workplace and prevent mental illness and suicide wherever possible.
2. Foster recovery and wellbeing for people of all ages living with mental health problems and illnesses and uphold their rights
3. Provide access to the right combination of services, treatments and supports when and where people need them.
4. Reduce disparities in risk factors and access to mental health services, and strengthen the response to the need of diverse communities and Northerners.
5. Work with First Nations, Inuit and Metis to address their mental health needs, acknowledging their distinct circumstances, rights and cultures.
6. Mobilise leadership, improve knowledge and foster collaboration at all levels.

From the socioecological perspective, several of these directions might be met through a soft services model as opposed to direct therapy model. In particular, the vision for reaching broad sectors of society with mental health disorders is being challenged by several trends: the continuing perceived stigma within target population sectors, particularly college-age males (Eisenberg et al., 2009), the lack of knowledge about mental health therapies and their effectiveness, and meaningful access and affordability across the spectrum of mental healthcare.

Canadian universities deliver mental health services within a traditional clinical service, with on-campus clinics providing mental health and basic primary care, typically with a full-time clinical director and part-time physicians and counsellors. Mental health services include individual counselling, encounter groups, mental health promotion, student follow-up and medical psychiatric referral.

A National Collegiate Health Assessment survey (2013) disclosed a higher prevalence of mental health-related issues at OCAD University, in particular depression and suicide, than at other post-secondary schools. Our research identified several factors believed to contribute to this finding:

- sensitivity of personality traits of students choosing art and design education;
- high workload, demanding coursework and associated stress in student environment;
- nature of creative work (to be original, imaginative) places continuing personal stress on students; and
- intensive critique practices in art and design, with real-time critical assessment of work by faculty and peers.

Young adults typically face many significant personal challenges in their transition from a secondary school in their hometown to any residential university. Incoming university students face social pressures and responsibilities associated with first-time independent living, the developmental challenges of establishing new, adult and institutional relationships, and the initial formation of personal economics and households. In our research we found a significant additional stress burden on art and design students imposed by the unique academic and creativity demands.

Design-driven action research

We employed a design-driven participatory action research approach (Swann, 2002; Gloster, 2000) for the campus mental health study, following a process of iterative planning and performing studies, finishing with proposals. A prior account of the study was published in 2014 (Jones et al., 2014).

Over an eight-week period a series of interviews and observations were conducted with students and staff to build an account of experiences with campus services and mental health concerns, of clinician and service provider work activities in context. Figure 3.2 presents the structure and relationship of research activities conducted by the team in support of discovering and proposing new service models for the Health and Wellness Centre (HWC) facility.

The research team conducted structured observations of the HWC facility and flows and exchanges of students/clients and providers and staff in the active work setting. Using the POEMS framework (Kumar and Whitney, 2007) the research team captured references and details for observations of 'people, objects, environments, messages, and services' in the clinic and common campus areas. Observations included the HWC reception and waiting area, the adjoining rooms, the building itself and its entry and egress points, and the use of space and architectural features. Photographs and analysis contributed to contextual description of the contribution of space to the health-seeking experience.

Small-sample interviews with four clinicians and staff and six students/clients were held within the clinic environment, to develop contextual understanding. The interviews were oriented to the students' experience of the HWC and services. Staff interviews asked about mental health service and counselling processes and the unique nature of art and design students.

Two group dialogue methods were employed for student/client and public/expert engagement. With the service design lead, the HWC held a series of private student client dialogues to learn the range of experiences and attitudes from counselling clients. The student group dialogues were held as facilitated, open-ended focus groups and recorded by a team member for later analysis. The public dialogue was an open, community-focused engagement convened by the research team for students, faculty and professionals to explore the experience and struggles of mental health and the enhancement of health services in a public dialogue. The inquiry was focused around several key questions of interest:

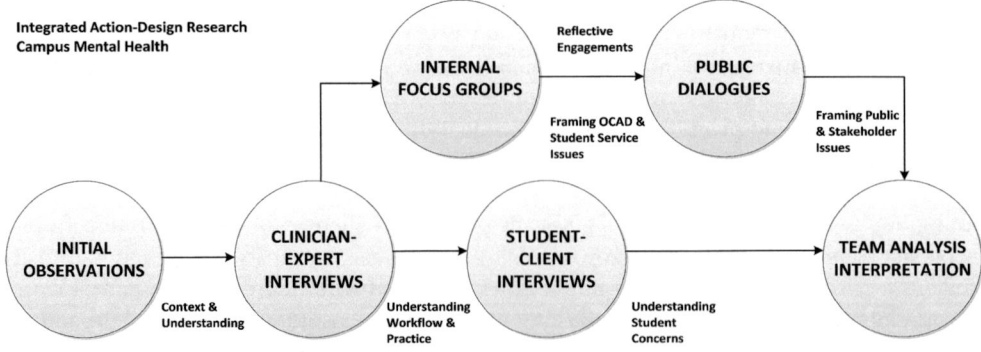

Figure 3.2 Mixed-method approach for design action research
Source: Jones, et al., 2014

- Are there innovations in community and social health that might enhance awareness and improve mental wellbeing?
- How can we move beyond the conventional views of mental health and learn from each other?
- What might we understand together to cultivate empathy and insight about the experience of emotional and mental health journeys?

Rethinking service touchpoints and interaction

A service designer in the research team constructed a service blueprint of the counselling workflow as a baseline process model (a core section of which is referenced in Figure 3.3), contributing to the learning and analysis.

Campus clinical mental health services were primarily for crisis management, and life management through counselling. The study found these services were provided too late in the lifecycle of an individual's developing wellness issue to support the capacity for flourishing, in the Keyes (2002) sense of self-acceptance and personal development. From a systemic perspective we identified the most productive (leveraged) opportunities for enabling and promoting individual and social flourishing.

The study further questioned the normative model of mental health service that has held for at least two generations. The design research team developed early hypotheses (based on observations of media use and communication) that the current generation of students may express a different relationship to health services than in prior years, possibly affecting service design and supporting touchpoints.

Students face many, daily stressors and learn to face expected stressful situations with resilience. The onset of most mental and emotional stress disorder symptoms and feelings are not typically recognised as crises, requiring intervention, as the associated demands of student life are expected. Emotional disorders may develop slowly, and can co-occur with exogenous stressors (such as exams and critiques) that lend social proof to the experience of even significant stress, short of breakdowns, as 'normal' and expected. Gradual mental health languishing (as Keyes refers to the state) does not occur to individuals as an acute, medical situation that requires intervention.

As such concerns emerge in a student's life, they must also cope with the multiple stressors of a new environment, significant workload and school demands, and the attendant social pressures, especially in coping with first-year social integration. Especially with college-age males, the risk of an acute or urgent stress problem increases if supports in the local social

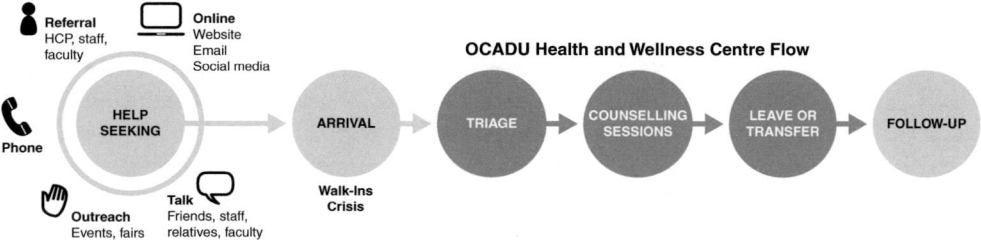

Figure 3.3 Basic workflow from HWC service blueprint
Source: Jones, et al., 2014

ecology of peers, work activities, positive relationships with faculty and school staff and other 'unsought' requirements are not met.

In further analysis, the research team recognised that the service delivery of current mental health offerings would benefit from some service improvements such as a simple client registration form, better online information and some changes in scheduling to benefit identified student demand cycles. A slate of service changes were defined, including the major change of providing walk-in counselling for crises wherever possible and covering the noon lunch hour for student walk-ins and appointments.

Through comprehensive journey mapping of the full lifecycle of student experience, from secondary school through university graduation, the design research team identified and interpreted the significance of salient points of communication and awareness across the lifecycle. Several intervention opportunities were identified for inclusions of salutogenic enhancements (Antonovsky, 1996), such as peer engagement, campus health campaigns and built environment enhancements. The well-defined boundary of the university, its campus and service infrastructure contribute to the design of communications and support services for students in a non-client capacity. While such a context might not be recognised in the same way for people not in a school or campus environment, living in urban or rural communities, we suggest that other community contexts can learn from the design for flourishing in campus settings.

Soft service design can be seen as design for a health commons, providing supportive and complementary resources within a social ecology for the emergence of benefits for potentially all participants in a social system. Providing soft services to promote flourishing outside the envelope of care, or in the case of HWC, 'in advance of arrival', was deemed to have a significant contribution on students' personal awareness of health and reduction of individuated stress. The value to the HWC was seen as possibly significant over time, by reducing the number of crisis visits and the level of stress attending their presentation, and by improving the knowledge and awareness of mental health overall and its contribution to individual flourishing.

Figure 3.4 shows a graphical model of the soft service design for campus mental health developed from the design-action research. Three inferred stages of pre-arrival (peri-diagnostic) encounter can precede the initial presentation at the HWC clinic, represented as Awareness, Understanding and Connection. Each support stage addresses the escalation of concerns discovered in ethnographic inquiry, shown in the shaded bars at the top of the diagram:

- **lack of awareness** (about mental health, concerns, with stigma, lack of knowledge);
- **uncertainty** (of one's health status, of service should one seek help);
- **isolation** (the result of continuing to live with a growing or emerging concern in the face of increased stressors).

The proposed pathway of individual learning and self-management is represented by the arrows, indicating the potential to raise awareness and understanding, while reducing anxiety and concern, through individual and peer interaction with supports and communicative materials. We hypothesised that anxiety can be reduced sufficiently to facilitate student resilience and reduce crisis incidents that would lead to the mental health service encounter.

Further development of design contributions emerged from the research and soft service proposals. Projects were defined to help student health seekers better navigate the campus service system and to enhance the accessibility of mental health services, three touchpoints of which are notably soft services:

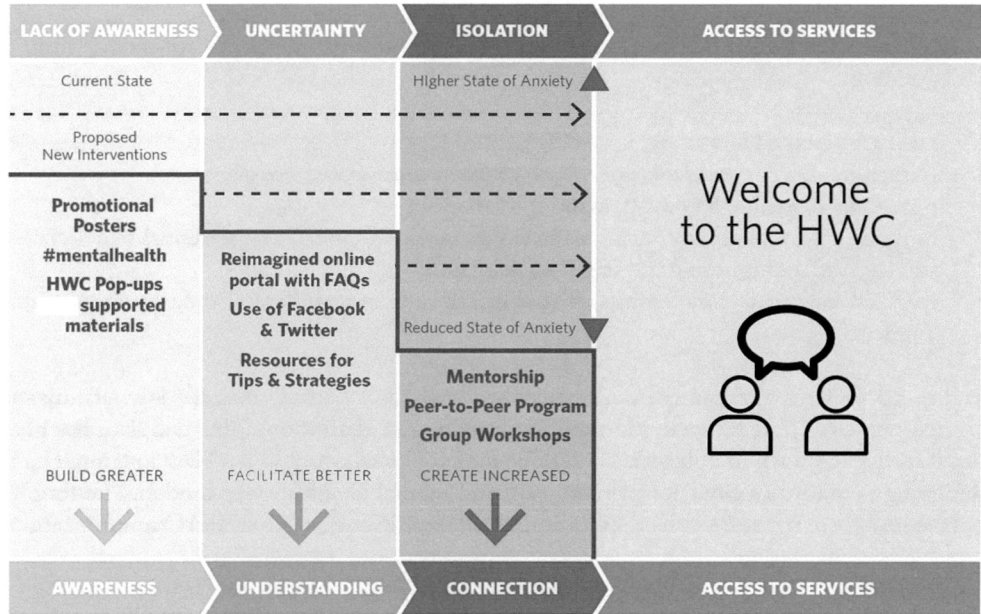

Figure 3.4 Soft service lifecycle in mental health access
Source: Jones, et al., 2014

- Enhance communication processes to promote the resources that are available and better articulate the role of mental health services and the HWC.
- Develop an online resource for the health seeker specific to mental health including FAQs, online tips and strategies and available resources.
- Formalise the broad range of support that is available (self-directed, peer-supported, email counselling, group counselling, individual counselling and crisis support).
- Establish business processes that allow for some self-service (e.g., insurance opt-out process, form requests and scheduling), better allocation of resources (e.g., use of volunteers) and improved flow (e.g., separate administrative roles from triage function).

A soft service design method for social ecologies

Soft services address the continuity of health-seeking experience by people in a community not specifically seeking care. The designation draws from the discovery of significant opportunities for communication, peer engagement and community support within the critical time preceding the need for service. In the campus mental health context, soft services might be designed as ambient information and peer and community support practices made available and accessible in advance of any service encounter, or between major episodes of care.

Soft services not only fall outside the envelope or boundary of professional encounters, they are not even typically activities or activity systems, but background (but not backstage) services accessible to anyone within a social context. Soft services provide layers of undesignated communication, significations and wayfinding for support or further help. Combined with direct care services, soft services provide continuous contexts, a 'commons of care' for continuous availability of basic service, through supports and accessible communication.

A soft services model addresses interventions at pre-service stages of care access within a social ecology:

- raising individual awareness;
- mitigating stigmas and reversing stigmas related to outdated norms;
- providing accessible and on-demand information;
- enabling informal communications between service supports and potential beneficiaries;
- service wayfinding for all the stages of help; and
- feedback related to touchpoints, so that health seekers can identify their location within a process.

Figure 3.5 presents a design method referred to as the 4C journey map for formulating soft service proposals (full lifecycle journeys and touchpoint definition). This template has been developed and evaluated in healthcare service design workshops, and has been instrumental in designing new formulations for primary care and mental health service models. The four 'C' concepts apply in any soft service application: Context, Constraints, Cues and Communications.

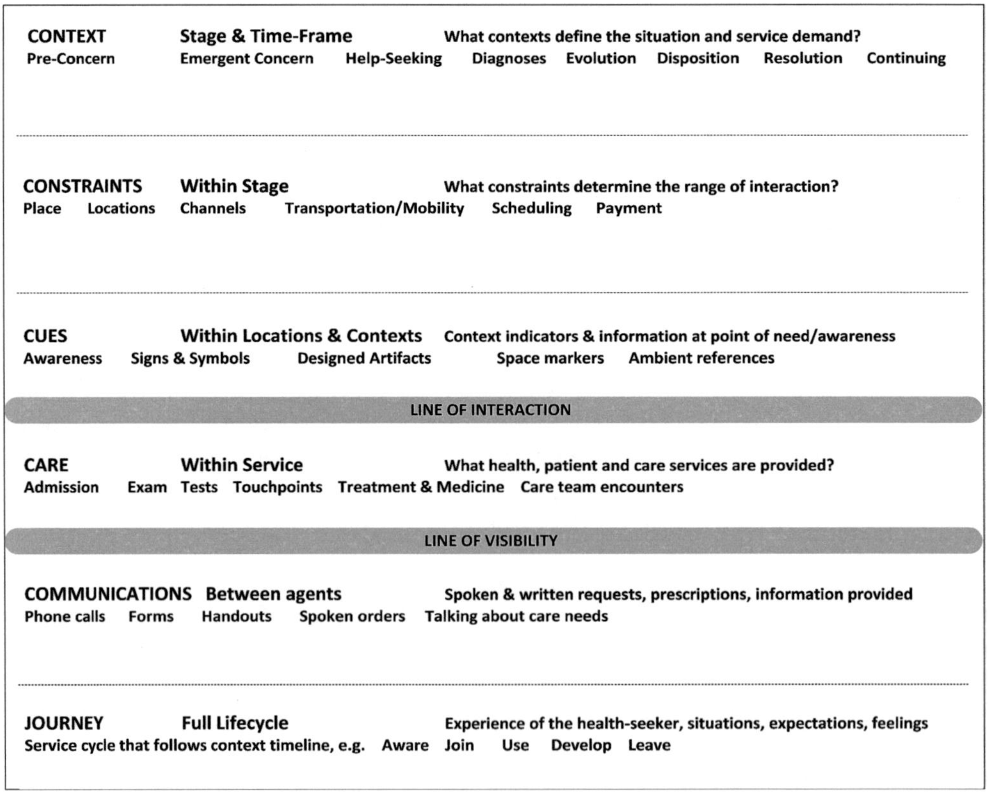

CONTEXT **Stage & Time-Frame** What contexts define the situation and service demand?
Pre-Concern   Emergent Concern   Help-Seeking   Diagnoses   Evolution   Disposition   Resolution   Continuing

CONSTRAINTS **Within Stage** What constraints determine the range of interaction?
Place   Locations   Channels   Transportation/Mobility   Scheduling   Payment

CUES **Within Locations & Contexts** Context indicators & information at point of need/awareness
Awareness   Signs & Symbols   Designed Artifacts   Space markers   Ambient references

LINE OF INTERACTION

CARE **Within Service** What health, patient and care services are provided?
Admission   Exam   Tests   Touchpoints   Treatment & Medicine   Care team encounters

LINE OF VISIBILITY

COMMUNICATIONS **Between agents** Spoken & written requests, prescriptions, information provided
Phone calls   Forms   Handouts   Spoken orders   Talking about care needs

JOURNEY **Full Lifecycle** Experience of the health-seeker, situations, expectations, feelings
Service cycle that follows context timeline, e.g.   Aware   Join   Use   Develop   Leave

Figure 3.5 4C journey – soft service design method template
Source: Jones, 2015

'Care' defines the direct touchpoints and process of healthcare provision and is specific to healthcare. In another service context Care would be replaced by the direct service functions of a different domain of provision.

The overall frame of the soft service design template represents a timeline of defined and opportunistic interactions accessible to participants in a socioecological system. The six guiding constructs across the temporal journey represent the conditions created by an action design team associated with stages or emergent movement over the journey. The novel value identified in the application of the soft services model and template is discerned in discovering the locations for a beneficiary or user to encounter relevant information, peers and other users, and to learn from contexts in the environment, in advance of service.

The layered bands from Context to Journey are not designated in a relevant order or series but are spatial placements, suggestive of the accessibility of designated signs and reference touchpoints associated with the environment (Context) or the health seeker in a Journey (series of steps that make progress toward a goal). The designer using this approach in a canonical way would organise the context and time frame initially, to identify known stages and time markers along a continuum of typical service. The labels in the template suggest the various indications of stages or milestones in an ecological soft service. We start with Context as follows, which might include stages of developmental experience as indicated by:

- pre-concern;
- emergence or incident;
- help-seeking.

Context also includes five formal healthcare service stages, as conventional across many applications:

- diagnoses;
- evolution;
- disposition;
- resolution;
- continuing.

The *Journey* stages, indicated at the bottom of the template, suggest the stages of experience recognised within and outside of the service context. This band of the model represents the experience of the health seeker, the expected and typical situations, their expectations and feelings during the journey.

A service design model is indicated for the stages in the template (Aware, Join, Use, Develop, Leave) based on Polaine et al. (2013). In most soft service applications these journey milestone stages would be contingent, defined for relevance to the health seeker rather than service stages. The other bands are described briefly to suggest their use from applications.

Constraints represents the various sociomaterial process and physical entities that guide or limit the degrees of progress or agency the health seeker may wish to express in the setting. These include:

- channel constraints (i.e., internet, member of an organisation, benefits group);
- wait lists and other operational constraints;
- physical locations and accessibility – the relative ease of access or constraints of location;
- payment and insurance, and other legal and financial constraints affecting access to service.

Cues are context indicators to people in a service system, both providers (backstage) who might be aware of and construct cues, and participants (frontstage) who might attend to cues as ambient information at the point of need or awareness. Cues are represented 'above' the line of Interaction, which represents the 'service stage' itself, where a participant encounters service providers. Yet cues are here considered more indicators of context rather than direct communication of meaning. These include signs and symbols relevant to the service ecology (but perhaps foreign to a participant, such as in medical contexts), visible and provided artefacts and situations, such as the cues for medication or a lab test, various spatial cues and environmental markers, and ambient references such as magazines or print media, various forms and tools of the trade.

Care services directly provided to clients or health seekers can be situated between the line of interaction (as interaction is direct) and the line of visibility (services and artefacts may not be disclosed or visible to the patient). Direct health and care services are indicated within the care as service band. The stages here show the series of touchpoints (care encounters), treatments, examinations, clinical tests and other care team encounters, including physicians, counsellors, pharmacists, etc.

The Communications band indicated defined and designed communications to participants in the ecology, whether in care or pre-care (soft) service environments. We include material forms and physician orders, voiced requests, prescriptions, information provided to patients, caregiver conversations and peer-to-peer communications. As with any communication modes, media can include all forms of spoken, printed, online, image and mixed forms (phone calls, forms, handouts, spoken orders, conversation).

Soft service theory and practice

The developing theory associated with the model describes the behaviours contributing to individual, social and societal flourishing, conceived of as interconnected relationships in a socioecological system.

This foundation model of flourishing in social systems was developed in prior work by Upward and Jones (2016) and was influential in the mental health study. We have extended it to the social ecology of mental wellness in higher education campuses. We believe that the model will have general applicability to public health promotion, preventive care and primary care as these are multipurpose practices that provide resources for health effects identified and presented within their socially embedded environment.

There are distinctive differences in design practice for soft service design. A significant body of service design research has been established from a constructivist approach (Meroni and Sangiorgi, 2011). An interpretive epistemology is advanced, advocating ethnographic methods for understanding service needs and interactions from the perspective of a participant's experience. Yet in practice, most service design projects are performed following client-centred practices derived from user experience methodologies. The tools of service design fall short of motivating clients to expand the boundaries of service to peripheral, possibly uncontrolled, supporting services in the service system.

A systemic design approach to soft services endorses reasonably similar steps and methods in a design application situation to that of service design practice. Within the scope of a given design process model (as critiqued in Jones, 2014) the steps in Table 3.2 are recommended to ensure that field research insights and design options support a soft service approach.

Table 3.2 Endorsed steps toward soft service design

1)	Identify the scope and boundaries of service provision, to be defined as the envelope of formal service (both Context and Care in the template).
2)	Define the (formal service) value proposition and its canonical service flow. Identify current and expected new touchpoints (Care and Journey in the template).
3)	Discover participants and locate them by role in the social ecology. Identify health seekers (and patients), clinicians and staff providers, community stakeholders and other community members.
4)	Map the structures of anticipated needs and satisfactions, expected experiences and service context across a full lifecycle (Care and Journey).
5)	Discover and propose complementary resources as soft services across the range of journey and context not fulfilled by formal service (Context, Cues and Journey on the template).

Conclusion: designing for contexts of flourishing

The reported research in this chapter describes a theory-supported and qualitative evidence-oriented service design methodology in summary. Soft service design is derived from design research and practice knowledge in a particular domain where the complementary service model emerged as a predominant approach for improving accessibility and awareness of conventional mental health services.

Developmental research on the methodology remains to be completed on the methodology and its constituent methods, and design researchers are encouraged to work with the methods and report at conferences or the literature. The reported methods and models (Flourishing model, Soft Service Design, 4C Journey) have been used in various other contexts but only reported in the mental health study, due to research protocols (our licence to report on the study).

Numerous service design methodologies have been developed and offered by global design practices as tools for enabling service providers to develop competitive or high-value service offerings with beneficial economic and social value. Service design perspectives been developed to recognise services across numerous configurations:

- as product service systems (Manzini and Vezzoli, 2003; Tukker and Tischner, 2006);
- sociotechnical systems (e.g., in healthcare, Jones, 2013);
- sociomaterial configurations, as 'designing for service' (Kimbell, 2011);
- transformation and transformative services (Sangiorgi, 2011).

This chapter advocates a contextualised and complementary approach to systemic service design to enable flourishing in community settings. While not arguing against public health models of intervention in social determinants of health, the theoretical approach is based on the social systems model of a social ecology that supports the same outcomes of health services, but by addressing sources in the community setting and not (only) in the care practice setting.

A systemic approach developed as the soft service design model was informed by theories of flourishing in mental health and flourishing societies from the ecological literature. An integrated model oriented to this outcome has been adapted to identify and guide supports for social interventions in collective health settings. We propose that this approach will be found effective in use by other organisations for intervening in the social systems surrounding practices of care, outside the envelope of the healthcare system.

References

American College Health Association (2013) *National College Health Assessment II: Reference Group Executive Summary Fall 2012.* Hanover, MD: American College Health Association.

Antonovsky, A. (1996) The salutogenic model as a theory to guide health promotion. *Health Promotion International*, 11(1): 11–18.

Baetz, M., Meng, X., D'Arcy, C. and Muggli, T. (2015) High frequency users with mental health complaints of emergency departments in a Canadian prairie city. *European Psychiatry*, 30: 355.

Bronfenbrenner, U. (1979) *The Ecology of Human Development: Experiments by Nature and Design.* Cambridge, MA: Harvard University Press.

Byrne, M., Murphy, A.W., Plunkett, P.K., McGee, H.M., Murray, A. and Bury, G. (2003) Frequent attenders to an emergency department: A study of primary health care use, medical profile, and psychosocial characteristics. *Annals of Emergency Medicine*, 41(3): 309–18.

Capra, F. (1996) *The Web of Life: A New Scientific Understanding of Living Systems.* New York: Anchor.

Carey, G. and Crammond, B. (2015a) Action on the social determinants of health: Views from inside the policy process. *Social Science and Medicine*, 128: 134–41.

Carey, G. and Crammond, B. (2015b) Systems change for the social determinants of health. *BMC Public Health*, 15(1): 662.

Chisholm, D., James, S., Sekar, K., Kumar, K.K., Murthy, R.S., Saeed, K. and Mubbashar, M. (2000) Integration of mental health care into primary care. *British Journal of Psychiatry*, 176(6): 581–8.

Christakis, A.N. and Bausch, K.C. (2006) *How People Harness Their Collective Wisdom and Power to Construct the Future in Co-Laboratories of Democracy.* Greenwich, CT: Information Age Publishing.

Coburn, D., Denny, K., Mykhalovskiy, E., McDonough, P., Robertson, A. and Love, R. (2003) Population health in Canada: A brief critique. *American Journal of Public Health*, 93(3): 392–6.

Ehrenfeld, J.R. (2000) Colorless green ideas sleep furiously: Is the emergence of 'sustainable' practices meaningful? *Reflections*, 1(4): 34–47.

Eisenberg, D., Downs, M.F., Golberstein, E. and Zivin, K. (2009) Stigma and help seeking for mental health among college students. *Medical Care Research and Review*, 66(5): 522–41.

Ford, J.D., Trestman, R.L., Steinberg, K., Tennen, H. and Allen, S. (2004) Prospective association of anxiety, depressive, and addictive disorders with high utilization of primary, specialty and emergency medical care. *Social Science and Medicine*, 58(11): 2145–8.

Gloster, M. (2000) Approaching action research from a socioecological perspective. *Systemic Practice and Action Research*, 13(5): 665–82.

Hepworth, J. (2015) Public health psychology: A conceptual and practical framework. *New Directions in Health Psychology*, 4: 229–45.

Jones, P.H. (2013) *Design for Care: Innovating Healthcare Experience.* Brooklyn, NY: Rosenfeld Media.

Jones, P. (2014) Design research methods in systemic design. *Proceedings of RSD3 Relating Systems Thinking to Design Symposium.* Oslo: Oslo School of Architecture and Design.

Jones, P. (2015) Can we design for a flourishing society? Proceedings of Relating Systems Thinking and Design (RSD4) Symposium, Banff, Canada, September 1–3.

Jones, P., Robinson, J., Yip, A., Oikonen, K. and Starkman, A. (2014) Human-centred mental wellness: Discovering touchpoints before a service encounter. *Touchpoint: Journal of Service Design*, 6(2): 58–61.

Keyes, C.L. (1998) Social well-being. *Social Psychology Quarterly*: 121–40.

Keyes, C.L. (2002) The mental health continuum: From languishing to flourishing in life. *Journal of Health and Social Behavior*: 207–22.

Kimbell, L. (2011) Designing for service as one way of designing services. *International Journal of Design*, 5(2): 41–52.

Kirby, M.J. and Keon, W.J. (2006) Out of the shadows at last: Transforming mental health, mental illness and addiction services in Canada. Standing Committee on Social Affairs, Science and Technology, Senate of Canada.

Kumar, V. and Whitney, P. (2007) Daily life, not markets: Customer-centered design. *Journal of Business Strategy*, 28(4): 46–58.

Levin, S.A. (1998) Ecosystems and the biosphere as complex adaptive systems. *Ecosystems*, 1(5): 431–6.

Luhmann, N. (1997) Globalization or world society: How to conceive of modern society? *International Review of Sociology*, 7(1): 67–79.

Manzini, E. and Vezzoli, C. (2003) A strategic design approach to develop sustainable product service systems: Examples taken from the 'environmentally friendly innovation' Italian prize. *Journal of Cleaner Production*, 11(8): 851–7.

Marmot, M., Friel, S., Bell, R., Houweling, T.A., Taylor, S. and Commission on Social Determinants of Health (2008) Closing the gap in a generation: Health equity through action on the social determinants of health. *Lancet*, 372(9650): 1661–9.

Meroni, A. and Sangiorgi, D. (2011) A new discipline. *Design for Services*: 9–33.

Miller, J.G. (1972) Living systems: The organization. *Behavioral Science*, 17(1): 1–182.

Plsek, P. (2001) Appendix B: Redesigning health care with insights from the science of complex adaptive systems, in IOM Committee on Quality of Health Care in America, *Crossing the Quality Chasm: A New Health Care System for the 21st Century*. New York: Institute of Medicine, 322–35.

Polaine, A., Løvlie, L. and Reason, B. (2013) *Service Design: From Implementation to Practice*. Brooklyn, NY: Rosenfeld Media.

Popovic, T. (2012) *Mental Health in Ontario's Post-Secondary Education System*. Toronto: College Student Alliance.

Raphael, D. (2009) *Social Determinants of Health: Canadian Perspectives*. Toronto: Canadian Scholars' Press.

Sangiorgi, D. (2011) Transformative services and transformation design. *International Journal of Design*, 5(2): 29–40.

Swann, C. (2002) Action research and the practice of design. *Design Issues*, 18(1): 49–61.

Tukker, A. and Tischner, U. (2006) Product-services as a research field: Past, present and future. Reflections from a decade of research. *Journal of Cleaner Production*, 14(17): 1552–6.

Upward, A. and Jones, P. (2016) An ontology for strongly sustainable business models: Defining an enterprise framework compatible with natural and social science. *Organization and Environment*, 29(1): 97–123.

World Health Organization (2010) International Classification of Diseases Revision 10 (ICD10). International Statistical Classification of Diseases and Related Health Problems. Geneva: World Health Organization.

4 Behaviours

Behaviour-change interventions for public health

*Sarah Denford, Charles Abraham, Samantha Van Beurden,
Jane R. Smith and Sarah Morgan-Trimmer*

Abstract

In this chapter, we focus on the design of interventions to change health-related behaviours. Such interventions can enhance wellbeing, promote health and prevent disease and facilitate the management of chronic conditions. We discuss design and evaluation principles and practices that optimise intervention effectiveness and evaluation quality.

The importance of behaviour change

Smoking, poor diet, lack of exercise and excessive alcohol consumption are just four behaviour patterns that increase the risk of early mortality (Loef and Walach, 2012; Behrens et al., 2013). Among a group of 20,000 people, Khaw et al. (2008) found that those who smoked, consumed greater quantities of alcohol, were not physically active and did not eat five portions of fruit and vegetables a day were more than four times more likely to have died over an 11-year period than those with healthy lifestyles. Similarly, Kvaavik et al. (2010) followed 4,886 individuals and found that those who smoked, consumed less than three portions of fruit and vegetables daily, did less than two hours physical activity per week, and consumed more than 14 units of alcohol had an all-cause mortality risk equivalent to being 12 years older than those who did not engage in these behaviours.

How we live strongly affects our health and lifespan. Yet many people do not live health-promoting lifestyles. In England 64 per cent of the population are overweight, with 25 per cent classified as obese (Public Health England, 2012), 20 per cent of the population smoke (Office for National Statistics, 2014) and 34 per cent of men and 28 per cent of women drink more than the recommended daily intake of alcohol (Robinson and Bugler, 2008). Changing these behaviour patterns could extend life and enhance its quality. Being overweight or obese, for example, can have detrimental effects on social interaction, sexual functioning and mental wellbeing (Kushner and Foster, 2000; Kolotkin et al., 2001, 2006). By contrast, regular exercise and a Mediterranean diet promotes a higher quality of life (Bize et al., 2007; Sanchez et al., 2012). Preventing the adverse health consequences of health-threatening behaviour patterns, including diabetes, heart disease and various cancers, would also reduce healthcare costs. The cost of treating obesity alone is estimated at £45.5 billion per year in the UK (Vandenbroeck et al., 2007) and, unsurprisingly, a review of the UK National Health Service (Wanless, 2002) concluded that the service would only remain affordable if the population became more engaged in looking after their own health.

Interventions to support people changing health-related behaviour patterns can be effective. Reductions in smoking and unsafe sexual behaviour, increases in physical activity and consumption of healthy diets, improved self-care for chronic conditions and uptake of health screening have all been observed following targeted interventions (Denford et al., 2013; Greaves et al., 2011). The UK's National Institute of Health and Care Excellence commissioned a review that included data from 103 systematic reviews of interventions targeting one of six behaviours (cigarette smoking, alcohol consumption, physical activity, healthy eating, drug use and sexual risk taking). This review found that, although the degree of effectiveness varied between populations and intervention characteristics, overall, interventions were found to be successful in changing behaviour patterns (Jepson et al., 2010; and see also Johnson et al., 2010).

There are many determinants of health and health-related behaviour patterns. Individual behaviour must be understood in relation to cultural, legislative and economic contexts. The socioecological model provides a useful multilayered model of influences on population health from intrapersonal and interpersonal processes to organisational, national and international change (Bartholomew et al., 2011). The physical, social and socioeconomic environments in which people live shape their behaviour and directly affect population health. Consequently, health-promoting interventions may operate at a variety of levels from targeting international legislatures (e.g. to regulate health-damaging products) to promoting organisational change (e.g. to increase physical activity at work) (Whitehead and Dahlgren, 1991). Acknowledging this, in this chapter we will focus on interventions targeting individual change. Within any given social context, there are important principles of intervention design and evaluation that can be abstracted.

Designing and implementing behaviour-change interventions

Designing, planning and evaluating interventions aimed at changing behaviour is complex. Numerous documents provide guidance to researchers and practitioners (Craig et al., 2013; Centers for Disease Control and Prevention, 1999). We use and recommend the Intervention Mapping framework (Bartholomew et al., 2011, www.interventionmapping.com) because it provides a comprehensive and helpful guide to optimal design and evaluation procedures.

Intervention Mapping

Intervention Mapping (IM) involves six design stages. First, a needs assessment is conducted to provide a description of *the health problem* in terms of the impact on quality of life and *causes* of the health problem (behavioural and environmental). Second, when the needs assessment indicates that an intervention is needed (and sometimes it is not) underlying mechanisms of change are identified. These *determinants* are those that (i) are maintaining current (unwanted) behaviour patterns and (ii) could generate behaviour changes. These mechanisms of change are then mapped onto targeted behaviour changes, or *performance objectives*. This allows the *selection of change objectives*, which specify what needs to change and who will need to change what to achieve the relevant health and quality of life objective. Third, using the specified change objectives, relevant *theoretical models* and *evidence-based change techniques* are identified. Techniques, with evidence of effectiveness, are selected to bring about changes in the determinants in order to achieve the change objective and are translated into practical strategies, or delivery formats. Fourth, these practical strategies are then used to create the programme materials. This set of modifiable processes, techniques capable of bringing about change and specified change objectives is often represented in a 'logic model' that maps out the anticipated effects of the intervention (Moore et al., 2014). When the interventions targets more than one group as when a school-based intervention targets both teachers and students' behaviour patterns (e.g. Lloyd et al., 2011; Reinaerts et al., 2008), it is important to map performance objectives and modifiable determinants separately for each target group.

In the fifth stage of IM, implementation planning takes place. This involves anticipating how the intervention will be used or delivered in everyday contexts. For example, how can the intervention be delivered in a manner that is attractive, feasible and sustainable in context? Although many interventions are designed with a focus on successful implementation, the sustainability of an intervention, or continuation after research funding has ended, is often overlooked (Johnson et al., 2004). Consequently, this step involves exploring the capacities, resources and strengths of organisations or communities to sustain interventions. For example, what are the motivations and resources of those who will deliver the intervention? If the intervention is not tailored to these needs, it may not be adopted or sustained past a research study and so may be ineffective (Glasgow et al., 1999). Once developed, interventions should initially be piloted to ensure that the intervention is acceptable to the target population. For example, if the resources necessary for the delivery of the intervention are not available or sustainable then the intervention may have to be redesigned to enable faithful implementation in everyday practice.

The final stage is evaluation: does the intervention change the specified behaviours in the given context? Although listed as a last stage, IM is an iterative process with later stages feeding back into earlier ones. So the nature of the evaluation must be considered when mechanisms of change and performance objectives are defined. These will determine the shape of the evaluation. Feasibility studies can pilot the evaluation and ensure that it will work in practice, testing, for example, whether sufficient participants be recruited and required outcome and process measures can be used as planned.

ImpulsePal: an IM case study

ImpulsePal is a smartphone app designed to support weight management. We use the intervention design process for this intervention to illustrate IM. When the impact of a behaviour pattern on health and quality of life has already been established a complete needs assessment may not be necessary (Green and Kreuter, 2005). So, in this case we already know that people needed help in managing their weight. Our needs assessment highlights the potential utility of an acceptable intervention that could provide 'in the moment' support and help to modify and manage impulsive processes related to eating behaviour. The target audience for this intervention was anyone over 16 years of age with a desire to lose weight and who may struggle when faced with temptations.

For ImpulsePal, the programme outcomes were weight loss and weight maintenance. The key performance objective was that app users would reduce unplanned unhealthy snacking. Given the need for 'in the moment' intervention a mobile phone app was selected as the delivery mode because this allowed users to carry it with them and use it as needed throughout the day.

Once behavioural objectives are set, modifiable change mechanisms are identified. In this case the mechanism underpinning unplanned snacking was identified as an impulsive process that were not heavily consciously monitored. This is what makes much of everyday eating 'mindless' (Wansink, 2007). People do not necessarily intend to snack, rather they do so as well-learnt responses are initiated by environmental cues. Thus ImpulsePal incorporates change techniques designed to alter impulsive processes (Strack and Deutsch, 2004) and enhance self-efficacy (Bandura, 1977).

In the third and fourth steps identified change objectives, underpinned by determinants or regulatory mechanisms, are mapped onto change techniques likely to enhance intervention effectiveness (Abraham and Michie, 2008; Abraham, 2012). Determinants can be changed using multiple techniques which themselves may be delivered in many different ways. For example, one might seek to enhance self-efficacy through reminding individuals of past success, or by observing others as role models. The choice of change techniques and practical strategies (or delivery) is constrained by the context. For example, a behaviour may be demonstrated by watching a teacher in a live demonstration, by watching a video or by looking at a series of labelled diagrams. In each case the technique employed is the same but the delivery format varies. Different change techniques and formats may be more or less effective in particular delivery contexts, thus implementation context must be anticipated when designing interventions. In this case the selection of change techniques was informed by a systematic review of which techniques have been found effective in changing impulsive processes (van Beurden et al., under review).

To promote the adoption and faithful delivery of interventions over time, it is crucial that stakeholders are involved in intervention development. During the development of ImpulsePal, discussions with service users, app developers and behaviour-change experts led to the selection of a combination of different intervention techniques that would not only target the necessary change objectives, but were also able to be translated into programme materials that were deliverable via a smartphone app in a manner that would be readily understood and accessed by users. The challenges of promoting adoption and engagement by users was anticipated in the very early stages of the development of ImpulsePal and 'engagement with the smartphone app' was identified as a separate performance objective throughout.

An exploratory trial has been planned for autumn 2015 in the south west of England to test the acceptability of the materials and delivery methods as well as the feasibility of evaluation following the development of ImpulsePal. Interviews and focus groups with the intervention users alongside will allow for a reflection on, and refinement of the change techniques, delivery formats and measurement methods.

Identifying determinants of behaviour

IM emphasises the use of relevant theories and models in the identification of change mechanisms (Craig et al., 2008; Kok et al., 2004). A variety of theories can direct intervention developers towards mechanisms underpinning particular behaviour patterns. In psychology, for example, a plethora of theories identify mechanisms that may or may not be unique to any theory (Abraham et al., 1998). Single theories may be narrow in their focus, for example, specifying particular cognitive processes, but failing to consider wider influences on behaviour patterns (Crossley, 2001; Spicer and Chamberlain, 1996). Consequently, identifying the behavioural determinants underpinning a selected behaviour and making these explicit in a logic model is arguably more useful in designing an intervention than relying on one specific psychological theory (Kok et al., 2004). Once regulatory mechanisms are identified reviews of empirical research can identify tested techniques that are capable of changing those mechanisms.

Reflective and automatic processes

Frequently, people know what they should do (so they are informed), yet they fail to take action. This may be because they do not want to behave in ways that are good for them (they are not motivated). Or it may be that, despite their best intentions, they simply cannot perform certain behaviours (because they may not have the necessary skills, for example). It may also be that the behaviour patterns in question occur mindlessly, with little or no thought, and in a habitual manner that has been repeated frequently in the past. It is now widely acknowledged that behaviour patterns are influenced by two interacting systems: the reflective system and the impulsive system (Borland, 2014; Strack and Deutsch, 2004; Kahneman, 2011). Choices made reflectively involve consideration of values and conscious reasoning. In contrast, actions regulated by the impulsive system have low levels of conscious monitoring and high levels of automaticity (Bargh, 1994) and are said to be habitual. ImpulsePal, for example, focuses mainly on changing impulsive processes underpinning 'mindless' eating.

Changing reflective processes

The Information, Motivation, Behavioural skills model (Fisher and Fisher, 1992) suggests that behaviour change underpinned by reflective processes requires individuals to be well informed, highly motivated and have the necessary skills to undertake the new behaviours. It is important to establish whether information, motivation or behavioural skills should be targeted. It is often not necessary to target all three. For example, to lose weight an individual must be expending more calories than they are consuming. This requires some basic knowledge of how many calories are in food they eat, and how many calories they use during the day. However, if an individual is already sufficiently informed, providing further information may have no effect.

People may be able to recognise foods that are high in fat and high in calories, and still consume them. This may be because they are not sufficiently motivated to lose weight. Motivation refers to how strongly we intend, or want, to perform a behaviour, and maintain that behaviour over time. Based on an integration of a number of theories of motivation, Fishbein (2001) identify five modifiable determinants of motivation. According to this model, motivation will be greatest when individuals believe that: (i) the advantages of changing their behaviour outweigh the disadvantages, (ii) performing the behaviour will make them feel good (i.e. they anticipate a positive emotional reaction), (iii) others around them are performing the behaviour and want them to change (i.e. they perceive normative pressure), (iv) the behaviour is consistent with their own self-image, and (v) they are capable of changing their behaviour (i.e. they have high self-efficacy).

A wide range of techniques can be used to increase motivation. For example, fear appeals are often used to increase motivation for behaviours such as smoking cessation. Fear appeals increase motivation by making individuals aware of risk and the likely consequences of a specified behaviour (Witte and Allen, 2000). They are most likely to be effective when the target audience lacks motivation but has the necessary skills to perform the behaviour (Ruiter et al., 2001, 2004). If individuals are lacking in behavioural skills, fear is unlikely to be effective. Many smokers, for example, are highly motivated to stop smoking, but lack the behavioural skills to do so. Increasing fear without providing support to enable individuals to enact the behaviour increases anxiety because the individual is faced with a potentially severe threat that they believe they cannot avoid. One way to escape from this uncomfortable psychological state is to deny or undermine the relevance of the threat ('it won't happen to me', 'it's all exaggerated'). Such defensive responses undermine rather than support change motivation (Rogers, 1975; Witte and Allen, 2000). It is important, therefore, to carefully assess the target population before using fear appeals and to ensure that they empower the target audience to avoid the emphasised threat.

People can be highly motivated but do not change their behaviour. Based on ten meta-analyses, Sheeran (2011) found that intentions explained only 28 per cent of the variance in behaviour. Thus a substantial gap remains between what people intend to do and what they actually do. This may be due to a skill deficit. For example, to eat healthy foods individuals may need to learn how to buy, prepare and cook healthy meals. To exercise, individuals may need to learn how to use specific equipment. Individuals may also need to develop social skills to resist peer pressure to engage in social situations that, for example, involve the consumption of calories. Finally, individuals may need to learn self-regulatory skills. These include the skills needed to set goals, monitor progress towards goals and review and revise goals. These techniques are likely to be most effective when motivation and self-regulatory skills are lacking.

Changing automatic processes

In some situations, counterproductive behaviour, such as unhealthy snacking, may be largely controlled by the impulsive system. Such behaviour patterns may be highly rewarding and difficult to change – even when a person is motivated (Kessler, 2009). Although we may intend to eat healthy snacks, the temptation of warm cookies is too much to resist, and we act in accordance with our desires. It is important to recognise behaviours that are regulated by the impulse system because, for such behaviours, targeting consciously controlled regulatory process (including goal setting) may have little impact.

Habits are behavioural patterns that are elicited automatically when in contexts. They require very little conscious monitoring (Verplanken and Aarts, 1999; Gardner et al., 2012). Eating is a behaviour that is highly susceptible to becoming habitual. People are largely unaware of the majority of food-related decisions they make multiple times a day and our food choices are greatly influenced by environmental factors that we are not aware of. For example, people eat more ice cream if given a larger scoop (Wansink, 2005).

If rewarding contexts are consistently encountered, a habit will get stronger over time and will override motivational determinants of behaviour. So, even if an individual is highly motivated to lose weight and give up unhealthy snacks, when this motivation conflicts with a strong habit, the individual will usually act in accordance with the habit (Gardner et al., 2011). In order to change the behaviour, it is necessary to first break the habit (Danner et al., 2008). This requires the individual to consciously recognise the situations that trigger the behaviour and either avoid the trigger or, if this is not possible, rehearse new responses to these triggers, substituting the habitual response for an alternative. This requires the individual to prepare and practise new cognitive, emotional and behavioural responses to contexts that trigger unhealthy behaviours.

One effective technique for breaking habits involves asking people to make 'if then' plans. Such plans make contextual cues (the 'if') salient and can trigger a desired alternative response (the 'then') (Gollwitzer and Sheeran, 2006). For example, if it is morning coffee time, then I will have an apple instead of a cake. Such simple plans can have substantial effects if people are already motivated (Luszczynska et al., 2007). Thus, through a process of identifying triggers, planning and practising new thought patterns and behavioural responses, we can change habits. However, this requires considerable cognitive and emotional effort, and this is not sustainable in the longer term (Baumeister et al., 1998). Replacing one habit with another habit means that new behaviour patterns become prompted automatically by everyday environmental cues, and so require less conscious monitoring. This means new behaviour patterns are more likely to be maintained (Verplanken, 2006; Rothman et al., 2009). So changing impulsively regulated behaviour patterns necessitates both breaking and making habits.

Evaluating interventions

In order to assess whether an intervention has been effective, and its design fit for purpose, interventions need to be evaluated in terms of both outcomes and processes (Moore et al., 2014). Evaluations allow us to identify effective and cost-effective interventions and, through process evaluations, to understand how interventions can be improved.

Outcome evaluation

Outcome evaluation tells us how effective an intervention is. A rigorous outcome evaluation is likely to constitute a trial comparing the intervention to a no-intervention control group or another intervention group (as is the case when an intervention is compared to routine care) – or both. Typically, post-intervention levels of outcome measures are compared, controlling for any pre-intervention levels. Ideally we do not expect differences between intervention and control groups before the intervention but in practice these may occur. Randomisation to intervention and control groups minimises differences between groups and may be done at an individual level or organisational level (e.g. GP practice, school), as is the case in a cluster trial. Where randomisation is impossible, matched groups need to be carefully scrutinised to ensure that differences other than exposure to the intervention are not responsible for observed differences in outcome.

Outcome evaluations usually calculate an effect size (e.g. standardised mean differences or Cohen's *d*) to indicate how effective the intervention was (Cohen, 1992). Anticipating the likely effect size in advance is important to ensure that enough participants are included to detect change. Attrition rates, that is the number of people who drop out of the study, are also important. For example, if an intervention requires persistence and 50 per cent of those in the intervention group drop out then, even if the intervention is very successful amongst the remaining 50 per cent (compared to no-intervention controls) the overall impact of the intervention may be limited.

Validated measures of behaviour are, of course, required to evaluate behaviour-change interventions but as well as key behavioural outcomes (e.g. exercise levels or eating behaviour). Various other outcomes may be measured before and after the intervention, including social and psychological determinants specified in the logic model designed during the IM process. Finally, health outcome measures (such as weight loss or STI rates) are valuable to check the hypothesised link between behaviour change and health. For example, behaviour-change interventions focusing on increasing physical activity or promoting a healthy diet may weigh participants in intervention and control groups before and after the intervention (e.g. Luszczynska et al., 2007).

Cost-effectiveness evaluation may also be conducted to assess the costs and effects of delivering the intervention relative to a comparative course of action. This type of evaluation is especially important to commissioners who must decide between alternative interventions within limited budgets.

Process evaluation

Process evaluations complement outcome studies by examining the process through which an intervention produces its outcomes. The value of process evaluation is to understand not just whether an intervention works, but *how*. Process evaluations are particularly important when evaluating complex interventions which have a number of interacting components, operating at different levels, and which may address complex problems or seek to produce multiple outcomes (Campbell et al., 2007). When nested in pilot or feasibility trials, process evaluations can establish how an intervention and trial might be optimally designed, before conducting a definitive trial. They may also help to understand why interventions do not work: for example, the underlying theory may be sound but the intervention may not have been delivered as intended. They can aid understanding of why the intervention works for some population groups or in some contexts but not for others. These are all important findings which can contribute to better-designed interventions and trials in the future.

Recent Medical Research Council (MRC) process evaluation guidance (Moore et al., 2014) recommends, like IM, using theories and models to identify mechanisms of change. This 'theory of change' articulates how the intervention is expected to operate and generate change its target population. It provides a structure for the process evaluation design, data collection and analysis and corresponds to stage 2 of the IM process. The MRC guidance also recommends producing a logic model to represent the intervention theory of change. This model can represent stages of an intervention and the causal pathways theorised to occur, from the delivery of the intervention through to mechanisms of change in participants and to outcomes (WK Kellog Foundation, 2004). The MRC Guidance provides a framework which describes key elements of an intervention that a process evaluation might investigate: *intervention delivery*, the *mechanisms of change* of an intervention and *contextual factors* (Moore et al., 2014). Process evaluations typically examine elements related to delivery and implementation processes such as fidelity, dose and reach (for example, was it delivered as planned?). The mechanisms of change are concerned with how an intervention has an effect on participants, including their response to the intervention and its influence on determinants of behaviour, to bring about outcomes (for example, did it change the identified regulatory processes?). Context can affect and be affected by an intervention; contextual factors may include an individual's characteristics, family, social network, organisation (such as a school) or local community (for example, did the intervention work better for older or younger people or in particular types of schools?).

Complex interventions can have many interacting components, and logic models representing intervention processes may also become complex. A logic model can be used to structure the evaluation, for example identifying key processes on which to collect data, but in complex interventions, activity may have to be further prioritised in terms of key research questions or causal pathways of interest; gaps in existing knowledge and theory; and pragmatic decisions about resources and methodological feasibility (Weiss 2000). The trade-off between having a simple (and useable) logic model, and having a logic model which reflects the complexity of the empirical world needs to be balanced by the feasibility of conducting the process evaluation.

Process evaluations typically use mixed methods to answer multiple research questions about how an intervention operates. For example, quantitative data may be used in moderation and mediation analyses that test whether key variables alter how the intervention operates (moderating variables – e.g. participant type) and explain how it works (mediating variables – e.g. regulatory process such as self-efficacy). Qualitative methods can be used to explore processes in detail, such as participant perceptions of interventions and how the intervention and its context interact with each other. Furthermore, since trials always produce quantitative outcomes data, and process evaluations normally employ qualitative methods, mixed-methods analysis will commonly be required in process evaluations that seek to use process data to explain outcomes. Iterative approaches to data collection and analysis may also be useful, in order to pursue emerging themes. For example, if unexpected events occur, such as poor implementation or low recruitment levels, interviews with intervention staff or participants could be conducted to investigate the reasons for this. In this way, one type of data (e.g. qualitative data from interviews) can be used to expand on findings from another type of data (e.g. quantitative data on attendance rates). However, this requires flexibility in the research design. A further challenge for process evaluations using mixed methods is to integrate different data at the analysis stage, in order to explain how the causal pathways of the intervention operate and how they are theorised to produce the intervention outcomes. Since process evaluations nested within trials can be methodologically complex studies, the process evaluation team should be carefully selected in terms of their expertise and ability to integrate into the overall evaluation team.

A distinction can be drawn between the function of process evaluations in relation to (i) pilot and feasibility studies and (ii) definitive outcome trials. In the former, findings of the process evaluation can be used as a basis for further intervention development and redesign of research methods, including outcome measures. In the latter, the process evaluation should be conducted in a manner that does not alter the intervention or contaminate the outcome evaluation. Although, of course, the results of a process evaluation may necessitate intervention redevelopment or further outcome studies, for example, when an intervention is found to be ineffective for reasons elucidated by a process evaluation. Close collaboration between process and outcome researchers is needed to optimise intervention development in feasibility studies, while blinding and firewall procedures may be needed in definitive tests of a finalised intervention.

Retrospective process evaluation

It is also possible to evaluate processes that may be linked to the effectiveness of interventions retrospectively. Such 'retrospective process evaluation' involves systematically identifying existing trials of interventions targeting a specific health issue and extracting and synthesising data on intervention characteristics and measures of processes including dimensions of delivery (e.g. whether delivered one to one, or to a group), mechanisms (e.g. determinants targeted, change techniques used) and context (e.g. participant characteristics, settings).

Statistical approaches, such as meta-regression and meta-analysis of sub-groups of interventions may then be used to identify characteristics and processes that are associated with effectiveness. For example, if a sub-group of interventions that employ substantial face-to-face interaction with a professional are found to be significantly more effective than a similar group of interventions that are self-delivered this would suggest that face-to-face interaction with professionals may be needed to optimise the effectiveness of this particular type of intervention. In statistical terms, inclusion of this delivery mode helps explain the heterogeneity of effect sizes across the whole set of interventions. However, each sub-group may differ in terms of the number of trials, sample sizes, etc. so the power to detect a significant effect will vary across such meta-analyses. Weighting of individual trials is applied so that larger trials have more influence than smaller trials (Sutton and Higgins 2008). It is not possible, however, to conclude definitively that the distinguishing variable (e.g. degree of face-to-face interaction with professionals) is responsible for the difference in effectiveness between groups of trials even when such sub-groups differ significantly in effect sizes (Higgins and Green, 2011). The trials may differ in other respects that have not been tested but such analyses can provide guidance to developers suggesting that some features may be 'better bets' than others when designing such interventions.

Some such analyses have successfully identified features likely to increase or decrease the effectiveness of an intervention (Albarracín et al., 2005; Denford et al., 2013; Greaves et al., 2011). For example, in a large meta-analysis of HIV prevention interventions, Albarracín et al. found that the most effective interventions included: (1) information, (2) arguments to promote positive attitudes toward condom use, (3) behavioural skills relevant to condom use, and (4) self-regulatory or skills training. Provision of condoms and HIV counselling and HIV testing also enhanced intervention effectiveness. However, inclusion of threat or fear appeals did not enhance the effectiveness. Albarracín et al. also found some approaches to be effective with one target group but not another. Arguments targeting normative beliefs were found to enhance intervention effectiveness when the target audience was under 21 years of age but to reduce effectiveness amongst older recipients. Thus age moderates the relationship between inclusion of normative arguments and intervention effectiveness.

Despite the potential of retrospective process evaluations, there are some major limitations, and research using this approach must be conducted and interpreted with caution. Such coding of intervention components and content relies on the assumption that published articles describe interventions in sufficient detail to allow the intervention components to be accurately identified, but some findings question this assumption (Abraham and Michie, 2008). Similarly, such research assumes that interventions are delivered as reported, and that there is no variation in the quality of intervention delivery. However, this is often unlikely to be the case, and intervention protocols may not always be available. Differences in control groups may also influence the apparent effectiveness of trials. For example, a high-quality usual care comparison can make an intervention appear less effective than when it is compared to a poor usual care group (de Bruin et al., 2010). However, it is rare that good descriptions of control conditions are provided. Furthermore, this approach usually considers individual components, delivery modes or change techniques in isolation. This precludes considering interactions, such as the effectiveness of different techniques in different contexts.

It should also be noted that associations between the outcome and the variable are associative – not causal. This is because whilst participants are (usually) randomised to intervention or control conditions, there is no randomisation at the level at which these meta-analyses work. For example, participants are not randomised to receive a specific delivery mode or not. A second major concern is that of power. Power refers to an estimation of the likelihood of detecting a significant result. If a study is underpowered, there is a risk that associations are erroneously considered to be non-significant (type II error). It is usually recommended that trials have at least 80 per cent power to detect a clinically meaningful difference at the 5 per cent significant level. Power to detect a significant result increases as the sample size increases. It has been reported that no less than ten trials per variable should be used when performing such meta-regressions (Higgins and Green, 2011). However, the number of trials needed to detect a significant association is likely to depend on many factors, including the sample size of each trial (Simmonds and Higgins 2007). Consequently, it is not clear when meta-analyses of ten evaluations where the intervention includes a particular component versus ten evaluations where the intervention does not contain this component provides sufficient power to detect significant associations. Nonetheless, despite these limitations, where large samples of outcome evaluations are available that systematically differ in relation to intervention design and content, retrospective process evaluation can provide guidance on best-bet intervention components.

In summary:

- Retrospective process evaluation can be used to identify components of interventions that may be associated with effectiveness.
- This approach involves systematically identifying existing trials, and extracting data on key features.
- Statistical approaches can be used to explore which key features explain the most heterogeneity of effect size.

- However, there are limitations with this approach, and research using this approach should be interpreted with caution.
- The description of the intervention may not reflect what is delivered or received.
- Associations between outcome and variable are associative and not causal.
- Despite limitations, they can provide guidance on best-bet intervention components.

Conclusions

Population behaviour change is important to promote health and longevity and to reduce accelerating healthcare costs. Intervention Mapping provides a useful guide to behaviour-change intervention design that can be used in tandem with guidance on outcome and process evaluations. In identifying regulatory mechanisms to be targeted in behaviour-change interventions it is helpful to differentiate between reflective and impulsive processes and to consider whether the potential intervention recipients have sufficient information, motivation and behavioural skills. When attempting to change unwanted habits, it is important to initiate and then consolidate alternative behavioural responses to eliciting cues, so breaking and making habits. Outcome evaluations can tell us how effective an intervention is. Economic evaluations can tell us how expensive an intervention is, given its level of effectiveness. Process evaluations can tell us how, for whom and in what contexts an intervention is effective or optimally effective. The findings of process evaluations may allow an intervention to be better designed or targeted. Retrospective process evaluations involve use of meta-analyses to consider whether the presence of particular intervention features across groups of outcome evaluations is associated with greater or less effectiveness and, despite important methodological limitations, can provide evidence useful to intervention designers.

Acknowledgement

The work was partially funded by the UK National Institute for Health Research (NIHR) Collaboration for Leadership in Applied Health Research and Care of the South West Peninsula but the views expressed in this chapter are those of the authors and not necessarily those of NIHR or the UK Department of Health.

References

Abraham, C. (2012) Designing and evaluating interventions to change health–related behavior patterns, in Boultron, I. and Ravaud, P.M.D. (eds), *Randomized Clinical Trials of Nonpharmacologic Treatments*. London: Chapman and Hall, 357–68.

Abraham, C. and Michie, S. (2008) A taxonomy of behavior change techniques used in interventions. *Health Psychology*, 27(3): 379–87. doi.org/10.1037/0278-6133.27.3.379.

Abraham, C., Sheeran, P., and Johnston, M. (1998) From health beliefs to self-regulation: Theoretical advances in the psychology of action control. *Psychology and Health*, 13: 569–91. doi.org/10.1080/08870449808407420.

Albarracín, D., Gillette, C.J., Earl, A.N., Glasman, L.R., Durantini, M.R. and Ho, M. (2005) A test of major assumptions about behavior change: A comprehensive look at the effects of passive and active HIV prevention interventions since the beginning of the epidemic. *Psychological Bulletin*, 131: 856–97. doi.org/10.1037/0033-2909.131.6.856.

Bandura, A. (1977) Self-efficacy: Toward a unifying theory of behaviour change, in Baumeister, R.F. (ed.), *The Self in Social Psychology: Key Readings in Social Psychology*. Philadelphia, PA: Psychology Press/Taylor and Francis, 285–98.

Bargh, J.A. (1994) The four horsemen of automaticity: Intention, awareness, efficiency, and control as separate issues. *Handbook of Social Cognition*, 1: 1–40.

Bartholomew, L.K., Parcel, G.S., Kok, G., Gottlieb, N.H., and Fernandez, M.E. (2011) *Planning Health Promotion Programs: An Intervention Mapping Approach.* London: Wiley Press.

Baumeister, R.F., Bratslavsky, E., Muraven, M. and Tice, D.M. (1998) Ego depletion: Is the active self a limited resource? *Journal of Personality and Social Psychology*, 74: 1252–65. doi.org/10.1037/0022-3514.74.5.1252.

Behrens, G., Fischer, B., Kohler, S., Park, Y., Hollenbeck, A.R. and Leitzmann, M.F. (2013) Healthy lifestyle behaviors and decreased risk of mortality in a large prospective study of US women and men. *European Journal of Epidemiology*, 28: 361–72. doi.org/10.1007/s10654-013-9796-9.

Bize, R., Johnson, J.A. and Plotnikoff, R.C. (2007) Physical activity level and health-related quality of life in the general adult population: A systematic review. *Preventative Medicine*, 45: 401–15. doi.org/10.1016/j.ypmed.2007.07.017.

Borland, R. (2014) *Understanding Hard to Maintain Behaviour Change: A Dual Process Approach.* Chichester: Wiley Blackwell/Addiction Press.

Campbell, N.C., Murray, E., Darbyshire, J., Emery, J., Farmer, A., Griffiths, F., Guthrie, B., Lester, H., Wilson, P. and Kinmonth, A.L. (2007) Designing and evaluating complex interventions to improve health care. *British Medical Journal*, 334(7591): 455–9.

Center for Disease Control and Prevention (1999) Framework for program evaluation in public health. *Morbidity and Mortality Weekly Report*, 48: RR-11.

Craig, P., Dieppe, P., Macintyre, S., Michie, S., Nazareth, I. and Petticrew, M. (2008) Developing and evaluating complex interventions: The new Medical Research Council guidance. *British Medical Journal*, 337: a1655. doi.org/10.1136/bmj.a1655.

Craig, C., Gwilt, I., Langley, J. and Partridge, R. (2013) Thinking through design and rehabilitation. *Assistive Technology Research Series*, 33: 798–803.

Crossley, M.L. (2001) Rethinking psychological approaches towards health promotion. *Psychology and Health*, 16: 161–77. doi.org/10.1080/08870440108405497.

Cohen, J. (1992) A power primer. *Psychological Bulletin*, 112(1): 155. doi.org/10.1037/0033-2909.112.1.155.

Danner, U.N., Aarts, H. and Vries, N.K. (2008) Habit vs. intention in the prediction of future behavior: The role of frequency, context stability and mental accessibility of past behavior. *British Journal of Social Psychology*, 47: 245–65. doi.org/10.1348/014466607X230876.

de Bruin, M., Viechtbauer, W., Schaalma, H.P., Kok, H., Abraham, C. and Hospers, H.J. (2010) Standard care impact on effects of highly active antiretroviral therapy adherence interventions: A meta-analysis of randomized controlled trials. *Archives of Internal Medicine (JAMA Internal Medicine)*, 170: 240–50. doi.org/10.1001/archinternmed.2009.536.

Denford, S., Taylor, R.S., Campbell, J.L. and Greaves, C.J. (2013) Effective behavior change techniques in asthma self-care interventions: Systematic review and meta-regression. *Health Psychology*. doi.org/10.1037/a0033080.

Fishbein, M., Hennessy, M., Kamb, M., Bolan, G.A., Hoxworth, T., Iatesta, M., Rhodes, F. and Zenilman, J.M. (2001) Using intervention theory to model factors influencing behavioral change: Project RESPECT. *Evaluation and the Health Professionals*, 24: 363–84. doi.org/10.1177/01632780122034966.

Fisher, J.D. and Fisher, W.A. (1992) Changing AIDS-risk behavior. *Psychological Bulletin*, 111: 455–74. doi.org/10.1037/0033-2909.111.3.455.

Gardner, B., Bruijn, G.J. and Lally, P. (2011) A systematic review and meta-analysis of applications of the Self-Report Habit Index to nutrition and physical activity behaviours. *Annals of Behavioural Medicine*, 42: 174–87. doi.org/10.1007/s12160-011-9282-0.

Gardner, B., Abraham, C., Lally, P. and de Bruijn, G.J. (2012) Towards parsimony in habit measurement: Testing the convergent and predictive validity of an automaticity subscale of the Self-Report Habit Index. *International Journal of Behavioral Nutrition and Physical Activity*, 9: 102. doi.org/10.1186/1479-5868-9-102.

Glasgow, R.E., Vogt, T.M. and Boles, S.M. (1999) Evaluating the public health impact of health promotion interventions: The RE-AIM framework. *American Journal of Public Health*, 89: 1322–7. doi.org/10.2105/AJPH.89.9.1322.

Gollwitzer, P.M. and Sheeran, P. (2006) Implementation intentions and goal achievement: A meta-analysis of effects and processes. In Mark, P.Z. (ed.), *Advances in Experimental Social Psychology*. New York: Academic Press, 69–119.

Greaves, C., Sheppard, K., Abraham, C., Hardeman, W., Roden, M., Evans, P., Schwarz, P. and IMAGE Study Group (2011) Systematic review of reviews of intervention components associated with increased effectiveness in dietary and physical activity interventions. *BMC Public Health*, 11(1): 119. Available at: www.biomedcentral.com/1471–2458/11/119.

Green, L.W. and Kreuter, M.W. (2005) *Health Program Planning: An Educational and Ecological Approach*. New York: McGraw-Hill.

Higgins, J.P.T. and Green, S. (2011) *Cochrane Handbook for Systematic Reviews of Interventions Version 5.0*. Cochrane Collaboration. Available at: www.cochrane-handbook.org/, accessed 14 December 2016.

Jepson, R.G., Harris, F.M., Platt, S. and Tannahill, C. (2010) The effectiveness of interventions to change six health behaviors: A review of reviews. *BMC Public Health*, 10. WOS:000282239600005.

Johnson, K., Hays, C., Center, H. and Daley, C. (2004) Building capacity and sustainable prevention innovations: A sustainability planning model. *Evaluation and Program Planning*, 27: 135–49. doi.org/10.1016/j.evalprogplan.2004.01.002.

Johnson, M., Jackson, R., Guillaume, L., Meier, P. and Goyder, E. (2010) Barriers and facilitators to implementing screening and brief intervention for alcohol misuse: A systematic review of qualitative evidence. *Journal of Public Health*, 33(3): 412–21.

Kahneman, D. (2011) *Thinking, Fast and Slow*. London: Macmillan.

Kessler, D.A. (2009) *The End of Overeating: Taking Control of the Insatiable American Appetite*. New York: Rodale Books.

Khaw, K.T., Wareham, N., Bingham, S., Welch, A., Luben, R. and Day, N. (2008) Combined impact of health behaviors and mortality in men and women: The EPIC-Norfolk prospective population study. *PLoS Medicine*, 5: e12. doi.org/10.1371/journal.pmed.0050012.

Kok, G., Schaalma, H., Ruiter, R.A., van, E.P. and Brug, J. (2004) Intervention mapping: Protocol for applying health psychology theory to prevention programmes. *Journal of Health Psychology*, 9: 85–98. doi.org/10.1177/1359105304038379.

Kolotkin, R.L., Meter, K. and Williams, G.R. (2001) Quality of life and obesity. *Obesity Review*, 2: 219–29. doi.org/10.1046/j.1467-789X.2001.00040.x.

Kolotkin, R.L., Binks, M., Crosby, R.D., Ostbye, T., Gress, R.E. and Adams, T.D. (2006) Obesity and sexual quality of life. *Obesity*, 14: 472–9. doi.org/10.1038/oby.2006.62.

Kushner, R.F. and Foster, G.D. (2000) Obesity and quality of life. *Nutrition*, 16: 947–52. doi.org/10.1016/S0899-9007(00)00404-4.

Kvaavik, E., Batty, G.D., Ursin, G., Huxley, R. and Gale, C.R. (2010) Influence of individual and combined health behaviors on total and cause-specific mortality in men and women: The United Kingdom health and lifestyle survey. *Archives of Internal Medicine*, 170: 711–18. doi.org/10.1001/archinternmed.2010.76.

Lloyd, J.J., Logan, S., Greaves, C.J. and Wyatt, K.M. (2011) Evidence, theory and context-using intervention mapping to develop a school-based intervention to prevent obesity in children. *International Journal of Behavioral Nutrition and Physical Activity*, 8: 73. doi.org/10.1186/1479-5868-8-73.

Loef, M. and Walach, H. (2012) The combined effects of healthy lifestyle behaviors on all cause mortality: A systematic review and meta-analysis. *Preventative Medicine*, 55: 163–70. doi.org/10.1016/j.ypmed.2012.06.017.

Luszczynska, A., Sobczyk, A. and Abraham, C. (2007) Planning to lose weight: Randomized controlled trial of an implementation intention prompt to enhance weight reduction among overweight and obese women. *Health Psychology*, 26: 507–12. doi.org/10.1037/0278-6133.26.4.507.

Moore, G., Audrey, S., Barker, M., Bond, L., Bonell, C., Hardeman, W., Moore, L., O'Cathain, A., Tinati, T., Wight, D. and Baird, J. (2014) Process evaluation of complex interventions: Medical Research Council guidance. MRC Population Health Science Research Network, London.

Office for National Statistics (2014) Opinions and lifestyle survey. Available at: www.ons.gov.uk/ons/about-ons/products-and-services/opn/index.html, accessed 9 December 2014.

Public Health England (2012) Adult obesity. Available at: www.noo.org.uk/visualisation/adult_obesity, accessed December 2014.

Reinaerts, E., De Nooijer, J. and De Vries, N.K. (2008) Using intervention mapping for systematic development of two school-based interventions aimed at increasing children's fruit and vegetable intake. *Health Education*, 108(4): 301–20.

Robinson, S. and Bugler, C. (2008) General lifestyle survey: Smoking and drinking among adults. London: ONS.

Rogers, R.W. (1975) A protection motivation theory of fear appeals and attitude change. *Journal of Psychology*, 91: 93–114. doi.org/10.1080/00223980.1975.9915803.

Rothman, A.J., Sheeran, P. and Wood, W. (2009) Reflective and automatic processes in the initiation and maintenance of dietary change. *Annals of Behavioral Medicine*, 38: 4–17. doi.org/10.1007/s12160-009-9118-3.

Ruiter, R.A., Abraham, C. and Kok, G. (2001) Scary warnings and rational precautions: A review of the psychology of fear appeals. *Psychology and Health*, 16(6): 613–30.

Ruiter, R.A., Verplanken, B., De Cremer, D. and Kok, G. (2004) Danger and fear control in response to fear appeals: The role of need for cognition. *Basic and Applied Social Psychology*, 26: 13–24. doi.org/10.1207/s15324834basp2601_2.

Sanchez, P.H., Ruano, C., de Irala, J., Ruiz-Canela, M., Martinez-Gonzalez, M.A. and Sanchez-Villegas, A. (2012) Adherence to the Mediterranean diet and quality of life in the SUN project. *European Journal of Clinical Nutrition*, 66: 360–8.

Sheeran, P. (2011) Intention-behavior relations: A conceptual and empirical review. *European Review of Social Psychology*, 12: 1–36. doi.org/10.1002/0470013478.ch1.

Simmonds, M.C. and Higgins, J.P.T. (2007) Covariate heterogeneity in meta-analysis: Criteria for deciding between meta-regression and individual patient data. *Statistics in Medicine*, 26(15): 2982–99. doi.org/10.1002/sim.2768.

Spicer, J. and Chamberlain, K. (1996) Developing psychosocial theory in health psychology problems and prospects. *Journal of Health Psychology*, 1: 161–71. doi.org/10.1177/135910539600100202.

Strack, F. and Deutsch, R. (2004) Reflective and impulsive determinants of social behavior. *Personality and Social Psychology Review*, 8: 220–47. doi.org/10.1207/s15327957pspr0803_1.

Sutton, A.J. and Higgins, J. (2008) Recent developments in meta-analysis. *Statistics in Medicine*, 27(5): 625–50. doi.org/10.1002/sim.2934.

van Beurden, S.B., Greaves, C.J., Smith, J.R. and Abraham, C. (under review) Techniques for managing impulsive processes associated with unhealthy eating: A systematic review.

Vandenbroeck, P., Goossens, J. and Clemens, M. (2007) Foresight, tackling obesities: Future choices – building the obesity system map. London: Government Office for Science.

Verplanken, B. (2006) Beyond frequency: Habit as mental construct. *British Journal of Social Psychology*, 45: 639–56. doi.org/10.1348/014466605X49122.

Verplanken, B. and Aarts, H. (1999) Habit, attitude, and planned behavior: Is habit an empty construct or an interesting case of goal-directed automaticity? *European Review of Social Psychology*, 10: 101–34. doi.org/10.1080/14792779943000035.

Wanless, D. (2002) Securing our future health: Taking a long-term view. London: HM Treasury, 16.

Wansink, B. (2007) *Mindless Eating: Why We Eat More than We Think*. London: Random House Digital.

Wansink, B. and Kim, J. (2005) Bad popcorn in big buckets: Portion size can influence intake as much as taste. *Journal of Nutrition, Education and Behaviour*, 37: 242–5.

Weiss, C.H. (2000) Which links in which theories shall we evaluate? *New Directions for Evaluation*, 87: 35–45. doi.org/10.1002/ev.1180.

Whitehead, M. and Dahlgren, G. (1991) What can be done about inequalities in health? *Lancet*, 338: 1059–63. doi.org/10.1016/0140-6736(91)91911-D.

Witte, K. and Allen, M. (2000) A meta-analysis of fear appeals: Implications for effective public health campaigns. *Health Education and Behavior*, 27: 591–615. doi.org/10.1177/109019810002700506.

WK Kellog Foundation (2004) *Logic Model Development Guide: Using Logic Models to Bring Together Planning, Evaluation, and Action*. 2nd edition. Battle Creek, MI: Kellog Foundation. Available at: www.wkkf.org/resource-directory/resource/2006/02/wk-kellogg-foundation-logic-model-development-guide.

5 Architecture

The beneficial health outcomes of salutogenic design

Alan Dilani

We shape our buildings; thereafter, they shape us.

(Sir Winston Churchill)

Abstract

There is an urgent and ever-growing awareness worldwide of the need to invest in healthy and sustainable infrastructure. By applying salutogenic design principles that seek to promote greater health, this landmark shift can begin to occur. The resulting and striking healthful outcomes of such existing structures bring these concepts to the forefront of global building opportunities. This approach now comprises the leading edge of change in our society. By embracing these precepts to shape our built environments and infrastructure, we engage in shifting the quality of such environments. Salutogenic architecture is taking its rightful place in the vanguard of preventative care strategies that have the potential to change our lifestyle for the better.

Health has become a commodity that is not equally distributed within society. Certain groups of individuals are more successful than others in having access to proper health-related knowledge and information. This data gathering is very often supported by a healthier lifestyle, in combination with lower exposure to risk factors within the built environment.

The author discusses the principles and ideas for a salutogenic design approach in planning future built environments with one simple goal: to create a healthier society. For design professionals (architects, planners, designers, etc.), the focus on and concern for designing a sustainable healthy future society is the most compelling task to be addressed and implemented in all societal sectors where human beings live, work and play.

Introduction

In 1997, the WHO identified that the health 'arena' should include these frequently used priority spaces: the workplace, schools, hospitals, correctional institutions, commercial offices, public spaces within our towns and cities, and indeed our own homes as the apex of health promotional activities in the 21st century.

During the 66th General Assembly Meeting of the United Nations in September 2011, the socioeconomic challenge of non-communicable diseases was discussed for the first time. The author argues that built environments have a significant impact on human health and states his commitment to bringing this understanding to the design and health professions to help reduce the prevalence of lifestyle diseases that are becoming a major health problem on our planet. Embracing a salutogenic approach when shaping our built environments creates a preventative care strategy that changes the current focus from risk factors and treatment of disease to a more holistic understanding and evolution towards a healthier society.

For this shift to occur, there must be an ever-increasing emphasis on the promotion of a healthful society that is supported by investment in healthy and sustainable public, social, institutional and domestic infrastructure. Research on the salutogenic direction highlights the impact that design factors can have, inspiring both designer and planner to create a healthy society.

For the designer, the compelling question is: 'How do we design for a sustainable healthy future?' First of all, we need to envision how such architecture might look if it is to be sustainable and salutogenic. This query necessitates an expanded understanding by addressing the health consequences of architectural design's functions and processes. This shift includes finding new models for design, seeking new construction and production systems, materials and processes, along with the action we must to take to realise this new vision with comprehensive salutogenic strategies.

On a global level, businesses and industries face similar concerns – seeking to understand the environmental consequences of their workplace, with new business models, new production systems, materials and processes for better health performance.

The salutogenic design approach becomes an opportunity for the architectural profession to not only help the world with its problems, but also to stop creating new issues. Salutogenic design must become the core essence of all architecture, changing the way we design. But how should we shape our future environment so it responds to the pressing demands of our society?

We are living in a post-industrial age amidst the knowledge (Google) society; in this milieu, architecture should provide positive stimuli that promote creativity. Therefore, a new way of looking at the role of the built environment is required within the context of health and well-being: this new perspective *is* salutogenic design.

Salutogenic design highlights the impact of design factors that inspire both the designer and planner to create a healthy society: (1) by developing healthy urban design that stimulates healthy behaviour and thereby (2) supporting the prevention of diseases and the promotion of health.

Increased consideration of a salutogenic design approach leads to social innovation. Salutogenic design requires an interdisciplinary application of psychosocial factors with architecture that actually promote a healthy lifestyle. In order to reduce the global burden of disease in an efficient way, major investments need to be made in the promotion of healthy lifestyles and development of healthy spaces.

Theoretical framework of design and health

Promoting healthy lifestyle and spaces depends upon ecological designs with infrastructure that creates clean air, clean water, clean food and clean land – through water management and retention, natural heating and cooling and renewable energy – which in turn are necessary for human health. These life-giving principles are intertwined with those of salutogenic design, which supports human health in daily behaviour (Yeang, 2012). Improving population health as the foundation for social and economic development will only be achieved through salutogenic and ecological design principles. Salutogenic design can provide social organisation, structure and function in society while ecological design works to continually restore the natural environment.

Ken Yeang, the father of eco architecture, linked the relationship between an ideal building and its environment to a human being with a prosthetic device (2006). He considers that only if the device is in complete harmony with the body will it function optimally. In the same way, nature can be considered as the 'host organism' to man-made infrastructure, with the same level of biointegration required if the whole system is to succeed.

The world requires a new paradigm, and the creation of a healthy global society is a vision we should all embrace. Ecological design deals with infrastructure that creates clean air, clean water, clean food and clean land – and these ideals are focused on achieving an ideal interaction between the built and the natural environment.

Research has shown that well-designed and people-friendly spaces stimulate walking, cycling and the use of public transportation. High levels of greenery also encourage physical activity, which lowers blood pressure, decreases the risk of heart disease, stroke and diabetes, and prevents falls in the elderly. Evidence also shows that attractive and open public spaces reduce mental fatigue and stress.

All these elements contribute to a reduction in the burden of disease, which may eventually reduce the costs of healthcare. 'Global health means making major investments in the promotion of healthy lifestyles throughout the world and the development of healthy spaces to reduce the burden of disease', Julio Frenk, Dean of Public Health at Harvard University told the author in an interview for *World Health Design* in October 2010.

Largely informed by global recognition of the urgent need to reshape our built environment and tackle the 21st-century challenges of chronic and non-communicable diseases, the International Academy for Design and Health has undertaken nearly two decades of dialogue and interdisciplinary, research-based design. While significant progress has been achieved to understand the value of salutogenic and eco design, there are still inadequacies when it comes to implementation.

One of the most pressing subjects is the rehabilitation of our existing cities and built environments into eco-cities that can actually create healthy societies. We need the new generation of designers, architects and engineers to learn how to apply ecological and salutogenic design principles in their work. In the meantime, we also need the support of governments around the world to understand the value of manifesting a healthy and sustainable society.

Science, research and innovation in eco design, as well as development of the built environment, includes hospitals, schools, workplaces, public places and urban spaces and must drive the policies and building practices of national governments. The author continues the search for a common strategy that is based on eco design, alongside salutogenic principles, to effectively create a healthy global society.

The principles of salutogenic design

Despite improvements in the health status and life expectancy of people from developed countries living in the 20th century, global healthcare systems face new challenges. These are characterised by increasing healthcare costs, an ageing population and a rise in the level of lifestyle diseases, most notably diabetes and obesity.

We are living in a post-industrial age, known as the 'knowledge' or 'Google' society, where health policy should be focusing upon providing 'wellness' as well as treating illness. We need to design healthcare infrastructure and city master plans that help prevent disease by creating an active life in which people walk and have exposure to positive stimuli from the beauty of urban design. This formula requires a new way to look at the impact of architecture and design so it truly promotes and supports human health and wellbeing.

We call this 'health promoting' or the salutogenic design approach to architecture and urban planning; it is completely compatible with eco design and sustainability. Greater consideration of the possibilities of salutogenic architecture lead to social innovation and economic growth through an interdisciplinary application of sciences, such as architecture, medicine, public health, psychology, design and engineering in connection with culture, art and music.

Colleagues from government municipal and health departments, universities, health providers and industries are the main figures who are responsible for connecting with designers and architects, planners and engineers to discuss the following: how can science, research and innovation in the field of eco design and salutogenic principles drive the development of healthy built environments and city infrastructures in our society?

Let us explore here the principles of salutogenic design that lend clarity to the following topics:

- How do we embed health, science and innovation in the creation of healthy built environments?
- How do we plan our city, workplace, healthcare facilities, schools and public institutions so they successfully support human health and wellbeing?
- How do we implement research-based design to promote health and wellness?

Definitions of health and salutogenesis

According to Ewles and Simnet (1994), health is difficult to define since it is a subjective experience. It is affected by norms and expectations – and it is also formed by previous experiences. The following are different definitions of health:

- Lawrence has defined health as 'a condition where resources are developed in the relationship between humans and their biological, chemical, physical and social environment' (Lawrence, 2002).
- According to the WHO, 'Health is a state of *complete physical, mental and social well-being* and not merely the absence of disease or infirmity'.
- 'The enjoyment of the highest attainable standard of health is one of the fundamental rights of every human being, without distinction of race, religion, political belief, economic or social condition' (Preamble of World Health Organization Constitution, 1948).

According to Dilani (2001), the model (see Figure 5.1) describes how the physical environment is the foundation upon which the social organisation, structure and function is built in our society – and in the long run, it promotes either health or disease. The model is used within the field of architecture to integrate design elements with health and wellbeing.

Health is considered a process composed of psychosocial factors, lifestyle, emotions and experiences that lead to either disease or health. But there are also the biological and measurable factors between them that determine the status of health or disease. The state of health for each of us is a matter of the balance between the two processes. The 'salutogenic' approach strengthens health processes, whereas the pathogenic approach highlights the process of diseases. For the latter, medical scientists have found 8,000 diagnoses or symptoms of diseases; but medical science has ignored the search for the *causes* of health. They could also identify 8,000 causes of health or wellness factors that could lead to a healthier society.

Emotions and experiences are central parts of the health process and can be strengthened by exposure to positive stimuli from surrounding environments where we live, work and

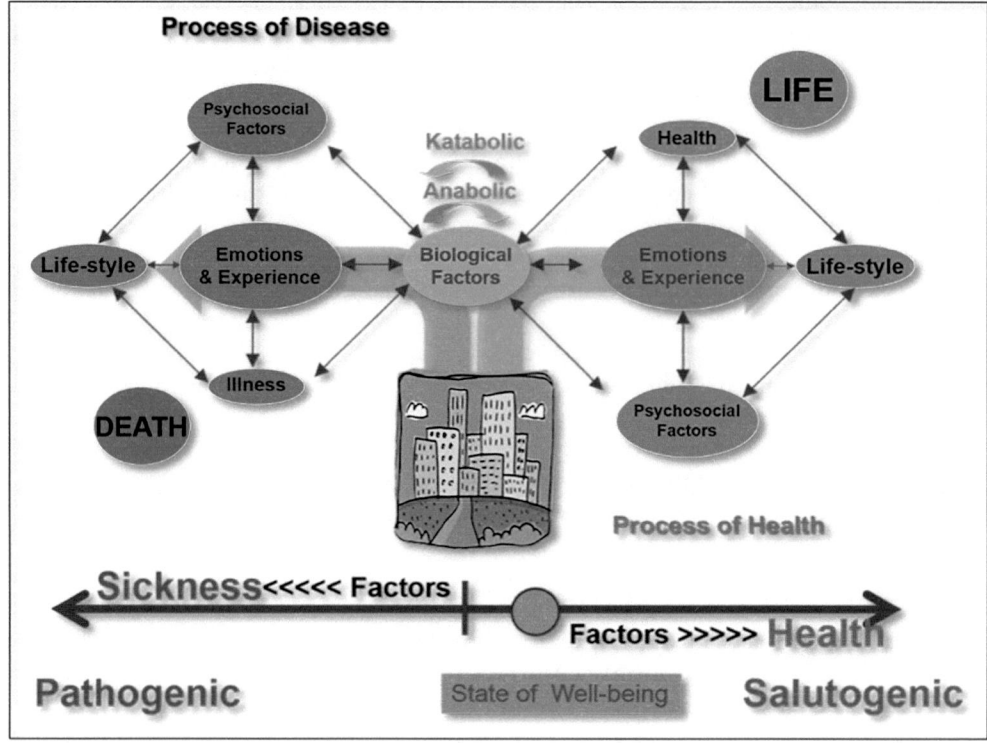

Figure 5.1 The processes of health and disease
Source: Dilani, 2001

play. The place where we live and work and the way we interact with the built environment, along with exposure to the stimuli from the built environment, strongly influences our moods and thereby health processes, emotions and experiences, our state of mind and behaviour.

Health can be divided into two different perspectives: the biomedical and the holistic. From a biomedical viewpoint, health is considered to be a condition without diseases (Andersen et al., 2004). In the Western world, the biomedical perspective has been the leading perspective and has therefore informed the medical and healthcare field (Nordenfelt, 1991).

The holistic viewpoint emphasises multiple dimensions of health, including the physical, psychological, emotional, spiritual and social (Nordenfelt, 1991). From a research perspective, health can be divided into a pathogenic and salutogenic starting point. Pathogenic research focuses on explaining why certain etiological factors cause disease and how they are developed in the physiological organism (Antonovsky, 1979). The primary aim of pathogenic research is often to find medical treatments.

Salutogenic research is based on identifying wellness factors that maintain and promote health, rather than investigating factors that cause disease (Antonovsky, 1991). Together, the salutogenic and the pathogenic approach offer a deeper knowledge and understanding of health and disease. To be able to answer the salutogenic question, we must ask, 'What is causing and maintaining healthy people?'

Antonovsky (1991) developed the concept of a sense of coherence. It maintains that a person with a high sense of coherence chooses the most appropriate coping strategy in a stressful situation. For example, the person may decide to fight, flee or be quiet, depending on what kind of stressor the individual is exposed to. Research has shown that it is possible to measure a person's sense of coherence and thereby predict an individual's health (Suominen et al., 2001).

A strong sense of coherence predicts good health and a low sense of coherence predicts poor health. In his study, Heiman (2004) showed that students with a high sense of coherence did not experience high levels of stress. The research also showed that coping strategies were significantly correlated with the individual's sense of coherence. The concept of sense of coherence has three vital components: (1) comprehensibility, (2) manageability and (3) meaningfulness (Antonovsky, 1991). A person with a strong sense of coherence scores high on all three components.

According to Antonovsky (1991), the term comprehensibility implies that the individual perceives the surrounding environment and that which is happening in the world as coherent. If something unexpected is happening, such as an accident or personal failure, the person who understands why these things are happening has a higher sense of coherence than one who cannot. A person with a low sense of coherence perceives himself as unlucky.

Manageability means that the individual experiences that she has all the required resources necessary to cope with a given challenge or demand. This means that the individual feels that she is influencing that which is happening around her and does not perceive herself as a victim of circumstance. Antonovsky (1991) believes that a person's sense of meaningfulness is connected to his or her perception that there are important and meaningful phenomena in life. Meaningfulness is the component that motivates a person's sense of coherence.

According to the salutogenic theory, a sense of coherence is fostered by people's ability to comprehend the built environment (comprehensibility), to be effective in his behaviour (manageability) and to find meaning from the stimuli and exposure from their built environment (meaningfulness).

Ken Yeang (Antonovsky, 1991) describes the key salutogenic components as the following:

(1) 'environmental comprehensibility' that requires environmental orderliness, predictability and legibility. This includes, for instance, the importance of creating visual order in the built environment with legible, intuitive wayfinding, the elimination of visual chaos, etc. (2) 'Environmental manageability' requires effective family and social support, and (3) 'Environmental meaningfulness' requires the provision of visual and aesthetic meaning, interest, satisfaction and attendant spaces for contemplation in the urban environment.

Impact of built environment on health and wellbeing

There is an interaction between the health of human beings and their built environment. According to Dilani (2006a), the physical environment is not only vital for good health, but can also be a critical stressor for the individual. Physical elements in an organisation can contribute to stress, and therefore are essential design factors that are increasing comfort (Dilani, 2001).

Despite this reality, the majority of humans in the Western world spend most of their time in indoor environments. There is a lack of knowledge about how these environments affect a person's health and wellbeing. There is a general belief that humans are always adapting to the environment (Dilani, 2001). Often called the theory of adaptation, this belief indicates that people become less conscious of the environment the longer they reside or work in that given environment (Carnevale, 1992). A general belief is that if one lets oneself be affected by their physical surroundings, it is a sign of weakness.

In order to create supportive physical environments, it is crucial to understand an individual's fundamental needs (Heerwagen et al., 1995). It is also necessary for different professional disciplines to willingly cooperate in creating the best conditions for humans (Heerwagen et al. 1995; Lawrence, 2002). Before a zoo is built, it is common practice for architects, designers, biologists, landscape architects, animal psychologists and building specialists to collaborate in creating an environment that optimises living conditions for the animals (Heerwagen et al., 1995). Factors such as materials, vegetation and lighting are taken into consideration; animals need enough space to eat, sleep and decide when to be social or seek solitude, and even their need for control and choice have been noticed. The aim is to create an environment that will completely support the animal's physical, psychological and social wellbeing. Ironically, humans do not seem to make the same demands when a workplace for people is going to be designed.

Heerwagen et al. (1995) created a framework and guidelines for a salutogenic design which highlighted the following factors: (1) social cohesion, both formal and informal meeting points; (2) personal control for regulating lighting, daylight, sound, temperature and access to private rooms; (3) restoration and relaxation with quiet rooms, soft lighting, access to nature and a good view.

Stokols (1992) also contributed with design suggestions for health-promoting environments that stem from three different dimensions of health: physical, mental and social. Physical health can be promoted by an ergonomic design with non-toxic environments. Mental health can be promoted by personal control and predictability as well as aesthetic, symbolic and spiritual elements. Social health can be promoted by access to a social support network and participation in the design process.

However, within health research, it is not a new idea to view the physical environment as a health-promoting factor. During the 19th century, Florence Nightingale developed a theory of healthcare which emphasises that physical elements are vital for an individual's health (SHSTF, 1989). For example, noise, lighting and daylight were considered vital factors in affecting a person's mood.

During the 20th century, different researchers developed stress models that illustrate how the physical environment may affect human health and wellbeing (Levi, 1972; Kagan and Levi, 1975; Dilani, 2001, 2006b). Levi founded the stress theory, which was later developed by Kagan and Levi (1975). The model describes how the physical environment is the foundation upon which societal organisation, structure and function is built and in the long run is critical to the promotion of health or disease (Dilani, 2001). The model is based on a system that points to a deeper understanding between the physical environment and different human components (Kalimo, 2005). The model describes that the physical environment is the basis for creating social organisation, structure and function in society.

According to Kalimo (2005) the theory has developed a deeper understanding for the physical environment's effect on humans. Emdad (2005) has developed a model called *Instability of Pyramids of Stress*, where architecture and art are measurable variables. Emdad presents a new framework, which in relation to health in the workplace has taken neuro-ergonomics into consideration. For example, there is a risk that the employee will develop stress-related symptoms and disease if he or she experiences high demands from the surrounding environment, but does not receive any reward. Furthermore, the employee will experience stress if the reward is too low or inadequate. The employee will also experience stress if they do not have any suitable effort strategies in relation to psychosocial factors, home and family factors or neuro-ergonomics. The model integrates all these factors and focuses on health, burnout, cardiovascular disease and short-term memory (Emdad, 2005).

Salutogenic design principles create healthy built environments

Salutogenic design principles serve to create healthy built environments that support users and the local community through the application of a holistic, knowledge-based approach in the delivery of a healthy built environment. This approach is a systematic application of research-based knowledge with a focus on the wellness design factor including exposure of positive stimuli experienced by users as enjoyable when activity promotes health, wellbeing and quality of life.

Salutogenic design environments stimulate and engage people, both mentally and socially, and support an individual's sense of coherence. The basic function of salutogenic design is to start a mental process by attracting human attention, which may reduce anxiety and promote positive psychological emotions. The principles of salutogenic design describes the following.

Space for social support

Social support is an important factor when the aim is to promote an individual's health and wellbeing (Costa et al., 1999; Saito et al., 2005; Jacoby and Kozie-Peak, 1997; Ogińska-Bulik, 2005). The knowledge and consciousness of social support and its relation to health increased in the 1950s (Fleming et al., 1985).

At the same time, researchers established that the ways in which the physical environment influences people's emotions, behaviours and motivation are important to take into consideration when the aim is to promote health and wellbeing. It is therefore essential to identify design factors in the built environment and through a salutogenic approach and create meeting points that can promote spontaneous social interaction and social support (Fleming et al. 1985; Conners, 1983).

Crowding is closely linked to social support and is often defined as the number of persons in a certain area or how much space every individual has received in a certain area (Geas, 1994). Altman (1975) describes crowding as a condition where a person's private sphere is trespassed; for example, when a person or group is exposed to more social interaction than is desirable. If there is too much undesirable contact, an individual may experience a sense of crowding. On the other hand, if an individual experiences too little contact, there is a risk that he or she may feel lonely and isolated. This balance between social interaction and desired loneliness can be regulated and achieved if one can control his or her own levels of social interaction (Maxwell, 2006).

Crowding space

Crowding can be reduced by creating buildings and space, where the individual can control and decide if they would like to be in privacy or participate in social interactions (Altman, 1975). For example, research has shown that a certain length and layout of student dormitories can increase the number of social activities and promote social interaction, creating a higher sense of control and reducing a sense of crowding (Baum and Davis, 1980). Even a high ceiling can contribute to a reduced sense of crowding. Even though the area of the room is the same, people perceive a room with a high ceiling as lighter and more spacious.

Therefore, if architecture and design can create space that minimises crowding, it can reduce the experience of stress and promote social interaction (Baum and Valins, 1977). Crowding can also constrain social interaction and social support (Geas, 1994), which are closely linked to health and wellbeing (Costa et al., 1999; Saito et al., 2005; Jacoby and Kozie-Peak, 1997; Ogińska-Bulik, 2005). This illustrates the importance of identifying factors in the physical environment that promote spontaneous social interaction and social support (Fleming et al., 1985).

Nature and its meaning for health

Most people have some kind of relationship to nature and there are many people who greatly value diverse natural environments. There are also many people who want to get away from everyday life, during weekends and holidays, and regain their strength in relaxing amidst natural recreational areas. What is it that makes people feel at ease in nature? Does the natural environment affect people in different ways? Is it possible to draw any general conclusions about nature's influence on human beings?

Direct and indirect attention

Kaplan and Kaplan (1989) have developed the *Attentional Restorative Theory*, which identifies two attention systems and how they are related. The researchers have chosen to call them direct and indirect attention. Indirect attention does not demand any energy or effort from the person and it is activated when something exciting suddenly happens or when one does not have to focus on anything in particular.

Direct attention is activated as soon as a person needs to concentrate and focus on a task and simultaneously block other disturbing stimuli. After an intense period of direct attention, a person is in need of restoration; otherwise they will easily become mentally exhausted. People who have been using their direct attention without resting often become impatient and irritated; and it has been shown that a mentally exhausted person often commits so called 'human errors'. A person who does not have the capacity to concentrate often becomes careless, less cooperative and less competent (Kaplan and Kaplan 1989; Kaplan 1995; Herzog et al., 2003). Therefore, in order to work efficiently, it is vital to have a well-functioning attention system and find time for restoration.

The restorative environment

In their studies, Kaplan and Kaplan (1989; Kaplan, 1995) have been able to distinguish the following four needs when individuals are in need of restoration and recreation.

(1) The need for being away from everyday life and its surrounding routines, sounds and crowding, etc.
(2) The need for fascinating stimuli which effortlessly stimulate the individual and diminish the risk of boredom.
(3) The need for extent (breathing space) which at the same time can create a feeling of being in a completely different world.
(4) The need for compatibility while performing one's tasks.

The restorative environment should be inviting and well balanced with an aesthetic beauty that allows people to reflect (Herzog et al., 2003). Nature offers various colours, forms and scents, which can encourage humans to forget about their everyday life (Kaplan and Kaplan, 1989; Kaplan, 1995; Herzog et al., 2003). Natural environments often offer an atmosphere in which the individual's needs for harmony and compatibility are met. It is therefore very important that natural environments are accessible at the workplace. The theory has been tested and confirmed by different researchers (Herzog et al., 2003; Tennessen and Cimprich, 1995). One of the studies (Herzog et al., 2003) showed that three of the four components: being away, extent and compatibility, are seen as measurable indicators of how to create a restorative environment.

Several studies have also confirmed that human beings perceive natural environments as more restorative than urban environments (Van den Berg et al., 2007). Therefore, when human beings are tired and mentally exhausted, nature is the appropriate place for restoration. Other studies have shown that viewing nature through a window has positive health outcomes (Moore, 1981–2; Ulrich, 1984; Leather et al., 1998; Frumkin, 2001).

Daylight, sunlight, windows and lighting's effect on health

There is a great deal of research on daylight's positive effects on a human being's psychological wellbeing (Evans, 2003). A lack of daylight can lead to both physiological and psychological difficulties (Janssen and Laike, 2006). Another researcher studied a correctional institution in Michigan and the results proved that inmates who had their windows facing the prison yard were visiting the healthcare facility more often than inmates who had windows facing the forest and farming fields (Moore, 1981–2). Ulrich (1984) showed that hospital patients who were staying in rooms with windows viewing nature were rehabilitated faster than patients who viewed a brick wall. Research has also shown that daylight in a classroom is necessary for pupils to maintain a balanced hormone level (Küller and Lindsten, 1992).

Windows can also have positive health outcomes on patients (Verderber, 1986; Lawson, 2001). For example, the window can contribute to improved health by allowing fresh air and daylight to enter, or by providing a view and a link to the outer world, thus satisfying a patient's or prisoner's need for viewing the seasonal variations (Verderber, 1986; Lawson, 2001). Another study showed that exposure to direct sunlight via windows in a workplace increased the workers' wellbeing and had a positive impact on their attitudes and job satisfaction (Leather et al., 1998).

Rooms without a window can affect human health and wellbeing negatively (Janssen and Laike, 2006; Küller and Lindsten, 1992; Verderber, 1986). One of the studies showed that blue-collar workers who worked in rooms without windows experienced more tension and were more negative towards their physical working conditions than workers who had offices with windows (Heerwagen and Orians, 1986). Patients who are staying in rooms without windows can develop sensory deprivation and depressive reactions and exacerbate perception, cognition and attention (Verderber, 1986).

Since daylight positively influences human physiology, it should be prioritised more than artificial daylight, which claims to have the same effect. According to some research, artificial daylight can positively affect a pupil's cortisol levels and perhaps contribute to fewer sick days (Küller and Lindsten, 1992). Lack and Wright (1993) showed that exposure to lighting at certain times during a 24-hour period can prolong sleep and improve the quality of sleep.

Energy consumption and costs can decrease if the individual has the ability to control the lighting levels (Lack and Wright, 1993), which also has positive effects on environmental resources (Moore et al., 2004). Furthermore, an individual's general satisfaction was higher when they had the ability to control the lighting levels themselves. Küller's (2002) conclusion suggests that lighting will become more important in the future, especially since it is becoming more common to have buildings without windows that have no access to daylight.

The impact of colour on health

Colours can possibly affect the brain's activity and create a sense of wellbeing and originality within architecture (Janssen, 2001). Colours can also have symbolic value and, in that way, contribute to the building's identity and/or cultural meaning. Colours should be of high interest to city planners, mainly because of the aesthetic values, but also because of their symbolic values, which can reflect the organisation's philosophy. The so-called warm colours (red, yellow and orange) are considered to have an activating effect, while the so-called cold colours (blue, purple and green) are considered to have a calming effect (Küller, 1995).

Küller (1995) refers to a well-known colour study from 1958 in which researchers conducted different physiological tests to investigate the brain's activity during exposure to different colours. When the participants were exposed to the colour red, their brain activity increased more than when they were exposed to the colour blue. The results showed differences in blood pressure, breathing and blinking frequencies. Another study showed that restoration was more complete when the participants were exposed to blue light, which confirms that colours do affect brain activity (Ali, 1972).

Goldstein (1942) calls attention to an important viewpoint which asserts that an individual's former experiences can affect their emotions, actions and behaviour, depending on what colour they are exposed to. There are geographical, cultural and historical factors that may affect a person's colour choice and some colours have a religious meaning. Berlyne (1971) and Janssen (2001) highlight that colours should suit the contextual environment and it is important that colour activation should be well balanced to match the environment.

The impact of design as landmark on health and wellbeing

Space both separates people from one another and bonds them together (Lawson, 2001). It is the architecture, with its buildings, rooms, surfaces, dormitories and facilities, that creates the prerequisites for individuals to cooperate, work in privacy, create relationships and fulfil their general social, psychological and physiological needs.

According to Vischer (2005), the organisation's image and identity are viewed and expressed through the architectural facilities. Vischer also maintains that the employee's working identity and role are associated with the working environment and therefore the architectural design partly forms the employee's identity. Furthermore, the physical work environment's design has a pronounced effect on worker performance, and in the long run affects the organisation's productivity. Physical, psychological and functional comfort can have positive outcomes on employee performance and morale.

Other design factors for wellbeing are landmarks in buildings (Dilani, 2004, 2006b). Landmarks are closely related to the perception of space and building related to the level of stress (Dilani, 2004), serving as reference points in the buildings for easy orientation and helping to create cognitive maps of the environment (Dilani, 2006b). These landmarks could be objects such as sculptures, paintings, aquariums or different colours in different areas of the built environment that work as a GPS to navigate us and make wayfinding much easier.

The impact of noise level on health and wellbeing

Noise is one of the most evident problems within public institutions. High noise levels can disturb sleep, increase stress and complicate communication (Janssen and Laike, 2006). Studies have shown that noise can contribute to irritation, which can lead to stress and cause stress-related diseases (van Dijk et al., 1987). Research has also shown that noise can lead to increased levels of cortisol (Brandenberger et al., 1980; Evans et al., 1998). Other researchers proved that noise can increase an individual's blood pressure (Lang et al., 1992; Evans et al., 1998). Noise can also negatively influence the healing process (Fife and Rappaport, 1976) and contribute to mental exhaustion, which in turn may affect the amount of medication that a patient takes (Persinger et al., 1999; Yoshida et al., 1997).

Investigations have also established the connections between noise, irritation and lack of concentration (van Dijk et al., 1987). Finally, other studies indicate that the perception of life quality decreases in a noisy environment (Evans et al., 1998) and high noise levels can also inhibit social interaction (Mathewes and Canon, 1975).

Leather et al. (2003) have shown that noise can have a significant relationship to working demands, where the worker's perception of work stress decreases with lower noise levels. The researchers explain that workers in a less noisy environment need fewer coping strategies for adapting to the physical environment and can therefore focus their energy and coping strategies on other stressful events. In that way, the physical auditory environment can be a vital factor in helping individuals cope with other stressors. It is also important to realise that the experience of sound is highly individual (Staples, 1996). Kryter (1994) describes three variables that affect an individual's sound experience: volume, predictability and possibilities for control.

The impact of music on health

There are sounds that can promote health and Lai et al. (2006) maintain that music is one of these factors, since it may contribute to a decreased activation in the sympathetic nervous system. Music has psychological effects and can unite people, open their senses and help them cope with difficulties and trauma. Music may also lead to lower heart and breathing frequencies and increased body temperature. Lee et al. (2005) conclude that music can be an effective method for decreasing negative physiological effects when people are suffering from anxiety and stress.

Music, either by itself or in combination with therapeutic treatment, can improve a patient's healing process (Nilsson, 2003). For example, McCaffrey and Good (2000) showed that patients who listened to music after surgery experienced less pain, anxiety and fear than those who did not. The patients claimed that, instead of being frustrated over pain and fear, music helped them to focus on healing. In her research, Spychiger (2000) showed that more music lessons in school had positive emotional, social and cognitive effects and that the pupils with more music education cooperated better and had greater motivation for learning than pupils who had fewer lessons.

Paul Robertson (2001) suggests that music is human's richest language that expresses complex, emotional insight and for a long time it has been linked to human wellbeing. Robertson also suggests how different music therapy programmes are used instead of medicine in different treatments, where rhythm and melody distract a patient's perceptions of pain and also reduce a patient's stress hormones. The challenge of salutogenic design is to integrate space for music experiences in the built environment.

The impact of culture on health

Participation in cultural activities has positive effects on human health (Konlaan, 2001). Konlaan's study showed that individuals who did not participate in cultural activities had a

57 per cent higher mortality risk compared to those who participated in cultural activities. The research showed that those who had not been participating in cultural activities, but who changed their behaviour to become active cultural consumers, had almost as good health at the end of the study as those who had been participating in cultural activities from the beginning.

In his study, Konlaan (2001) proved the close connection between being an active cultural consumer and being able to increase one's health status rating. Konlaan also found support for his hypothesis that if a person is changing her behaviour to participate in cultural activities, her health perception becomes more positive.

Another study showed that people who participate in cultural activities have the potential to live a longer life (Bygren et al., 1996). Spychiger (2000) concludes that cultural consumption is very important from a public health perspective.

Music can be a health-promoting activity in a built environment. Silber (2005) studied a choir project for women, where the results indicated that participation in a choir had positive effects on health. For example, the choir became a new social platform where the participants created social bonds with one other. The participants learned to listen to each other, receive criticism and express themselves in a different way. Silber's (2005) research emphasises the value of choirs and explains that the choir can help people to improve their perceptions and relationships to others, including authoritative persons.

In a choir, the members have to follow and trust the conductor, which can be a good training for the person who has difficulty with authoritative figures. In an institution, conflicts can arise regarding power and control between director and employees. With the conductor, the participant has to cooperate and together strive for a common goal, which does not imply power or control (Silber, 2005). Furthermore, the choir generates a dynamic interrelation between its members. Every member has to control his or her own voice and at the same time listen and cooperate.

To achieve this, the members train their self-control, patience, intuition and trust, which can strengthen the participants' self-esteem and give them a more positive self-image. Pratt (1990) considers that music can create a new reality, which can make it possible for participants to find themselves in another context. Music can create a sense of freedom, which can give the participants new inspiration and strength to change their behaviour. It can help the individual to survive, grow and create both a personal and collective identity. Pratt also explains that the space created by music reminds people about their fundamental and psychological need for freedom. Music can make the person forget about worrisome thoughts and emotions, allowing them to temporarily live in the present moment. The research on the choir's positive, social and therapeutic effects in institutional and workplace environments is limited (Silber, 2005).

However, there are several reasons why it is worth investigating how a choir can be a good method for helping people to change their behaviour, such as increasing people's self-esteem, empathy, self-control and decreasing aggression and the need for immediate acknowledgement (Silber, 2005).

Art, healing process and wellbeing

According to art historians, humans today live in a more aesthetic world, where art, fashion and design offer countless aesthetic experiences (Leder et al., 2004). When a person observes and appreciates different visual scenes, such as a piece of art, complex cognitive and emotional processes arise (Keith, 2001). In order to understand the meaning of a painting it is important to understand its different parts before it is possible to understand the whole. During the observation of a painting and in the process of understanding it, a person can, for example, experience joy, participation, discomfort or interest. These emotional and cognitive responses are called *aesthetic experiences* (Keith, 2001) and often lead to positive stimuli, satisfying and rewarding experiences for the viewer (Leder et al., 2004).

According to Kreitler and Kreitler (1972), art psychology is an empirical, scientific discipline that focuses on a person's internal and external behaviour and how they are related to art. There are several psychological theories that try to explain and describe an individual's experience of art. In summary, Kreitler and Kreitler believe that psychological models regarding art perception should be based on the homeostatic behaviour model, which suggests that there is an optimal physical condition in which humans strive to reach the balance between tension and relaxation. This condition of homeostasis can explain some parts of the individual's relationship to art, and that the art experience can help an individual restore the homeostatic balance.

Art therapy (music, dance, painting and drama therapy) has a unique potential to reach patients with psychosomatic diseases who are otherwise difficult to reach with traditional therapeutic methods (Theorell and Konarski, 1998). For example, Argyle (2003) showed how a group of people, identified as being in the risk zone for mental illness, participated in different art projects and improved their social and mental wellbeing. The participants testified that the project had strengthened their self-esteem and given them a sense of belonging to a social group. This health-promoting art project is considered to be cost-effective. Gardner (1994) also maintains that participation in different art processes can give the individual the tools to express feelings and experiences in a way that is non-verbal.

Salutogenic design and productivity

When an organisation's management wants to increase productivity, they often focus on employee competence and personal motivation rather than the physical environment and design (Heerwagen et al., 1995). In his study, Herzberg (1966) observed employee motivation and the relationship between worker behaviour and the physical environment.

When the physical environment is perceived as disturbing it can negatively affect employee motivation and thereby decrease productivity. Herzberg emphasised that it is necessary to have access to a physically supportive environment, which can contribute to employee motivation (1966). Maslow's (1987) theory of motivation is one of the most well-known theories related to human need and motivation. Maslow's theory was developed to analyse and explain the social environment, but it can also be applicable to the physical environment (Heerwagen et al., 1995). For instance, the need for safety can be achieved through designed environments that allow people to have a good visual overview. If humans are not stimulated by their surroundings, they can easily lose interest and this can result in reduced performance (Lawson, 2001). On the other hand, too much stimulation can lead to stress, since a person may not have the capability to deal with the stimulation.

Increased knowledge and consciousness about the relationship between improved health and increased profitability would affect how designers, architects and managers design, build and maintain buildings (Fisk, 2000). For instance, improved indoor climate can improve employee health, decrease the amount of sick days, reduce healthcare needs and increase productivity, which in turn strengthens the human capital and leads to higher company profitability. Ergonomic improvement for employees has also been proven to increase a company's profitability. For example, IBM invested $186,000 in ergonomic education and implemented extended ergonomic changes, whereby they changed the design of the workplace and various working tools (Helander and Burris, 1995).

The improvements contributed to better working positions, improved lighting, lower noise levels and better support with heavy work routines. The project decreased sick days by 19 per cent, which generated an annual profit of $68,000. In addition, the changes contributed to higher productivity and improved quality, which led to an annual profit of $7.4 million. In other words, investments and changes within the physical environment led to profits through an increase in health conditions and productivity (Helander and Burris, 1995).

Discussion and conclusion

As a consequence of our knowledge and idea-driven society, fuelled by the internet, it can be argued that diseases are becoming more psychosocial and psychosomatic in nature. Credible research is also finding that people who frequently experience positive emotions are also more likely to be healthier – they have fewer heart attacks, for example, and fewer colds.

With the link between a positive outlook and good physical health moving from hypothesis to fact, it is time to recognise that the way we live, where we work, the way we interact with the built environment all have a tremendous impact on our emotions and experiences. These emotions and experiences are central parts of the health process that could be strengthened and supported by the stimuli from salutogenic design and psychosocial design factors, among them nature, with the most positive stimuli within the built environment.

The growing prevalence of non-communicable diseases (NCDs), or 'lifestyle' diseases, is highly related to the quality of eco design and built infrastructure and the design of the built environment.

Suggestions about how we can reduce NCDs such as obesity are one of the primary challenges facing the designer and planner. Ageing populations and urban growth are a further two huge challenges to which salutogenic design could be applied to increase life quality and exposure for positive stimuli and active lifestyle behaviour for the elderly. We must focus on the innovative design and planning of ecological, sustainable and salutogenic healthy urban planning around the world. It is the task of the designer and planner to reconsider the value of eco design and health promoting with a knowledge-driven approach to salutogenic design.

The aesthetic value of our surroundings communicates the value of our society; beautiful places are not only stimulating, but they have also been proven to be sources of enjoyment that make us feel less anxious and less stressed. A well-designed built environment can positively shape the social, psychological and behavioural patterns of our society: if we were to bring nature to the built environment through eco design and fill our workplaces with art and culture, then we could optimise brain performance and restore our energies.

The approach of eco design and salutogenic architecture promotes a healthy lifestyle by creating a built environment that focuses on wellness factors that promote health, thereby contributing to the realisation of a healthy society.

An increase in the consideration of the principles of eco design and salutogenic architecture leads to social innovation and economic growth, not least of which is through its interdisciplinary approach, integrating sciences such as architecture, medicine, public health, psychology and engineering with culture, art and music.

Our challenge is to commit to the innovation and innovative ideas that will inspire architects and planners to tackle a demanding economic outlook. The 'eco and salutogenic design' perspective should be considered as a tool for designers to be more competitive: by designing highly salutogenic environments, we can reduce the rising burden of healthcare costs, and save and improve lives on our planet. As more scientific research comes to light on the link between eco and salutogenic design and our health and wellbeing, it becomes even more apparent that we need to develop and apply more research.

The aim of this study was to illustrate how salutogenic design principles are compatible in creating built environments for a healthy global society. The research has shown that the salutogenic perspective forms a theoretical framework for designing our built environment that could stimulate, engage and improve an individual's sense of coherence and thereby strengthen their coping strategies and promote health.

To implement the above-mentioned design principles, it is necessary that the whole organisation, government and/or policy-makers understand the meaning of eco design with a salutogenic perspective. Knowledge of which environment factors contribute to health and wellbeing can thereafter be guidelines in making political decisions. In the process of making decisions it is important to have an interdisciplinary perspective where different individuals with different backgrounds and knowledge work together in this field – people such as psychologists, architects, landscape architects, doctors, behavioural scientists, engineers and health promoters.

Fortunately, it is becoming more common to use an interdisciplinary perspective as a central strategy (Barry, 2007). For example, the IT sector recruits sociologists, anthropologists and psychologists who can study and explain how a product will be used in different cultural contexts. The application of an interdisciplinary approach to work may challenge existing ways of thinking and may make research and innovation more democratic and receptive to public input.

Decision-makers should consider the following factors during the process of building: good lighting; positive interior distractions; and access to daylight and/or nature, art, symbolic and spiritual objects. Other important factors to take into consideration are the individual's need for control over lighting, noise, indoor temperature and the possibility of choosing when to seek social interaction or solitude. It is also important to create attractive and inviting spaces that promote social interaction and social support as well as creating spaces for restoration and private conversations. In order to motivate people to change their lifestyle, it is necessary to offer them activities that strengthen their self-esteem and self-efficacy. This can partly be achieved by participating in different cultural activities.

In summary, this chapter has shed light on salutogenic design principles that can create our cities and our built environment with infrastructure that could promote health, wellbeing and increase productivity and profitability. Secondly, we have shown that there is a need for more empirical studies that verify, investigate and identify more benefits of eco design and salutogenic built environment. Thirdly, we encourage decision-makers to implement eco and salutogenic design that in turn promotes health and wellbeing.

Finally, salutogenic design is still very much in its infancy. The totally salutogenic city does not yet exist – and neither has the complete application of the salutogenic design principle been implemented. We can find some of those principles in the built environment, but not a complete application in any kind of design that the authors have experienced yet. There is still much more theoretical work, technical research and invention, environmental study and design interpretation that needs to be done and tested before we can have a built environment with an entirely salutogenic design.

We all need to continue this great search of our time. It is the most important scientific question of modern civilisation, of the 'Google society'. How do we maintain our health and quality of life far into old age? How do we reduce the burden of lifestyle diseases through shaping our city and built environment and infrastructure that actively promote health in our global society? This study is the basic idea and question to be explored further as a future research agenda that highlights the most important interdisciplinary research programme to be developed and serve humanity in its future. The search for the application of salutogenic design to create a sustainable global healthy society will continue!

Be the change you want to see in the world.

(Mahatma Gandhi)

References

Ali, M.R. (1972) Patterns of EEG recovery under photic stimulations by light of different colours. *Electroencephalography and Clinical Neurophysiology*, 33: 332–5.

Altman, I. (1975) *The Environment and Social Behaviour: Privacy, Personal Space, Territory, Crowding*. Monterey, CA: Brooks/Cole Publishing Company.

Andersen, P., Göransson, A. and Petersson, C. (2004) Hälsa och hälsofrämjande arbete – en studie av vårdpersonalen och landstingspolitikers uppfattningar. [Health and health promoting work – a study of healthcare employees and political decision makers' opinions]. Landstinget Kronoberg.

Antonovsky, A. (1979) *Health, Stress and Coping*. San Francisco: Jossey-Bass.

Antonovsky, A. (1991) *Hälsans mysterium [The Mystery of Health]*. Stockholm: Natur och Kultur.

Argyle, E. (2003) Art for health: The social perspective. *Mental Health Nursing*, 23(3): 4–6.

Barry, A. (2007) The meeting of disciplines: Why interdisciplinary is a central strategy. *Britain Today*, 72.

Baum, A. and Davis, G.E. (1980) Reducing the stress of high-density living: An architectural intervention. *Journal of Personality and Social Psychology*, 38(3): 471–81.

Baum, A. and Valins, S. (1977) *The Social Psychology of Crowding: Studies of the Effects of Residential Group Size*. Hillsdale, NJ: Lawrence Erlbaum Associates.

Berlyne, D.E. (1971) *Aesthetics and Psychobiology*. New York: Appleton-Century-Crofts.

Brandenberger, G., Follenius, M., Wittersheim, G. and Salame P. (1980) Plasma catecholamines and pituitary adrenal hormones related to mental task demand under quiet and noise conditions. *Biological Psychology*, 10: 239–52.

Bygren, L.O., Benson, B. and Johansson, S.E. (1996) Attendance at cultural events, reading books or periodicals and making music or singing in a choir as determinants for survival. *British Medical Journal* 313: 1577–80.

Carnevale, D.G. (1992) Physical settings of work: A theory of the effects of environmental form. *Public Productivity and Management Review*, 15(4): 423–36.

Conners, D.A. (1983) The school environment: A link to understanding stress. *Theory into Practice*, 22(1): 5–20.

Costa, D.D., Clarke, A.E., Dobkin, P.L., Senecal, J-L., Fortin, P.R., Danoff, D.S. and Esdaile, J.M. (1999) The relationship between health status, social support and satisfaction with medical care among patients with systemic lupus erythematosus. *International Journal of Quality in Health Care*, 2(3): 201–7.

Dilani, A. (2001) Psychosocially supportive design: Scandinavian healthcare design, in Dilani, A. (ed.), *Design and Health: The Therapeutic Benefits of Design*. Stockholm: AB Svensk Byggtjänst, 31–8.

Dilani, A. (ed.) (2004) *Design and Health III: Health Promotion through Environmental Design*. Proceedings Book of the 3rd International Conference on Design and Health, Montreal, Canada.

Dilani, A. (2006a) A new paradigm of design and health in hospital planning. *World Hospitals and Health Services*, 41(4): 17–21.

Dilani, A. (2006b) A new paradigm of design and health in hospital planning. *World Hospitals and Health Services*, 41(4): 17–21.

Emdad, R. (2005) Comparison of the 'Instability of Pyramids of Stress (IPS)', occupational health and work environment stressors in dentists and cleaners. *CEJOEM*, 1(1): 33–71.

Evans, G.W. (2003) The built environment and mental health. *Journal of Urban Health: Bulletin of the New York Academy of Medicine*, 80(4): 536–55.

Evans, G.W., Bullinger, M. and Hygge, S. (1998) Chronic noise exposure and physiological response: A prospective study of children living under environmental stress. *Psychological Science*, 9(1): 75–7.

Ewles, L. and Simnett, I. (1994) *Hälsoarbete [Health work]*. Lund: Studentlitteratur.

Fife, D. and Rappaport, E. (1976) Noise and hospital stay. *American Journal of Public Health*, 66(7): 680–1.

Fisk, W.J. (2000) Health and productivity gains from better indoor environments and their implications for the US Department of Energy. *Annual Review of Energy and the Environment*, 25: 537–66.

Fleming, R., Baum, A. and Singer, J.E. (1985) Social support and the physical environment, in Cohen, S. and Syme, S.L. (eds), *Social Support and Health*. Orlando, FL: Academic Press, 327–45.

Frumkin, H. (2001) Beyond toxicity: Human health and the natural environment. *American Journal of Preventive Medicine*, 21(3): 234–40.

Gardner, H. (1994) *The Arts and Human Development*. 2nd edition. New York: Basic Books.

Geas, G.G. (1994) *Prison Crowding Research Re-examined*. Washington, DC: Federal Bureau of Prisons.

Goldstein, K. (1942) Some experimental observations concerning the influence of colors on the function of the organism. *Occupational Therapy and Rehabilitation*, 21: 147–51.

Heerwagen, J.H. and Orians, G. (1986) Adaptations to windowlessness: A study of the use of visual decor in windowed and windowless offices. *Environment and Behavior*, 18(5): 623–39.

Heerwagen, J.H., Haubach, J.G., Montgomery, J. and Weimer, W.C. (1995) Environmental design, work, and well being: Managing occupational stress through changes in workplace environment. *Official Journal of the American Association of Occupational Health Nurses*, 43(9): 458–68.

Heiman, T. (2004) Examination of the salutogenic model, support resources, coping style, and stressors among Israeli University students. *Journal of Psychology*, 138(6): 505–20.

Helander, M. and Burris, G. (1995) Cost effectiveness of ergonomics and quality improvements in electronics manufacturing. *International Journal of Industrial Ergonomics*, 15: 137–51.

Herzberg, F. (1966) *Work and the Nature of Man*. New York: Crowell.

Herzog, T.R., Maguire, C.P. and Nebel, M.B. (2003) Assessing the restorative components of environments. *Journal of Environmental Psychology*, 23: 159–70.

Jacoby, J.E. and Kozie-Peak, B. (1997) The benefits of social support for mentally ill offenders: Prison-to-community transitions. *Behavioral Sciences and the Law*, 15(4): 483–501.

Janssen, J. (2001) Facade colors, not just a matter of personal taste: A psychological account preferences for exterior building colors. *Nordic Journal of Architectural Research*, 14: 17–21.

Janssen, J. and Laike, T. (2006) *Rum för återanpassning- den fysiska miljöns betydelse för ungdomsvården – en miljöpsykologisk översikt [Rooms for readapting – a physical environment's meaning for youth care – an environmental psychological review]*. Statens institutionsstyrelse (SIS). Rapport 2/06, Edita Stockholm.

Kagan, A.R. and Levi, L. (1975) Health and environment: Psychosocial stimuli, a review, in Levi, L. (ed.), *Society, Stress and Disease: Childhood and Adolescence*. 2nd edition. Oxford: Oxford University Press, 241–68.

Kalimo, R. (2005) Reversed causality: A need to revisit systems modeling of work-stress-health relationships. *Scandinavian Journal of Work, Environment and Health*, 31(1): 1–2.

Kaplan, S. (1995) The restorative benefits of nature: Toward an integrative framework. *Journal of Environmental Psychology*, 15: 169–82.

Kaplan, R. and Kaplan, S. (1989) *The Experience of Nature: A Psychological Perspective*. New York: Cambridge University Press.

Keith, M. (2001) Making meaning brings pleasure: The influence of titles on aesthetic experiences. *Emotion* 1(3): 320–9.

Konlaan, B.B. (2001) Cultural experience and health: The coherence of health and leisure time activities. Doktorsavhandling Umeå universitet.

Kreitler, H. and Kreitler, S. (1972) *Psychology of the Arts*. Durham, NC: Duke University Press.

Kryter, K.D. (1994) *The Handbook of Learning and Effects of Noise*. San Diego, CA: Academic Press.

Küller, R. (1995) Färgens inverkan på människan [Colour's effect on humans], in Hård, A., Küller, R., Sivik, L. and Svedmyr, Å. (eds), *Upplevelse av färg och färgsatt miljö [Experience of colour and painted environments]*. Stockholm: Byggnadsforskning, 13–30.

Küller, R. (2002) The influence of light on circa rhythms in humans. *Journal of Physiological Anthropology*, 21(2): 87–91.

Küller, R. and Lindsten, C. (1992) Health and behaviour of children in classrooms with and without windows. *Journal of Environmental Psychology*, 12: 305–17.

Lack, L. and Wright, H. (1993) The effect of evening bright light in delaying the circadian rhythms and lengthening the sleep of early morning awakening insomniacs. *Sleep*, 16: 436–43.

Lai, H-L., Chen, C-J., Peng, T.C., Chang, F-M., Hseih, Huang, M-L. and Cang, S-C. (2006) Randomized controlled trial of music during kangaroo care on maternal state anxiety and preterm infants' response. *International Journal of Nursing Studies*, 43: 139–46.

Lang, T., Fouriaud, C. and Jacquinet-Salord, M.-C. (1992) Length of occupational noise exposure and blood pressure. *International Archives of Occupational and Environmental Health*, 63: 369–72.

Lawrence, R.J. (2002) Healthy residential environments, in Bechtel, T. and Churchman, A. (eds), *Handbook of Environmental Psychology*. New York: Wilyes and Sons, 394–412.

Lawson, B. (2001) *The Language of Space*. Oxford: Architectural Press.

Leather, P., Pyrgas, M., Beale, D. and Lawrence, C. (1998) Windows in the workplace: Sunlight, view, and occupational stress. *Environment and Behavior*, 30: 739–62.

Leather, P. Beale, D. and Sullivan, L. (2003) Noise, psychosocial stress and their interaction in the workplace. *Journal of Environmental Psychology*, 23: 213–22.

Leder, H., Belke, B., Oeberst, A. and Augustin, D. (2004) A model of aesthetic appreciation and aesthetic judgements. *British Journal of Psychology*, 95: 489–508.

Lee, O.K.A., Chung, Y.F.L., Chan, M.F. and Chan, W.M. (2005) Music and its effect on the physiological responses and anxiety levels of patients receiving mechanical ventilation: A pilot study. *Journal of Clinical Nursing*, 14: 609–20.

Levi, L. (1972) *Stress and Distress in Response to Psychosocial Stimuli (Avhandling för doktorsexamen)*. Karolinska institutet.

Maslow, A.H. (1987) *Motivation and Personality*. 3rd edition. Harlow: Longman.

Mathewes, K.E. and Canon, L.K. (1975) Environmental noise level as determinant of helping behavior. *Journal of Personality and Social Psychology*, 32: 571–7.

Maxwell, L.E. (2006) Crowding, class size and school size, in Frumkin, H., Geller, R.J. and Rubin, I.L. (eds), *Safe and Healthy School Environments*. Oxford: Oxford University Press, 13–19.

McCaffrey, R.G. and Good, M. (2000) The lived experience of listening to music while recovering from surgery. *Journal of Holistic Nursing*, 18: 378–90.

Moore, E.O. (1981–2) A prison environment's effect on health care service demands. *Journal of Environmental Systems*, 11: 17–34.

Moore, T., Carter, D.J. and Slater, A. (2004) A study of opinion in offices with and without user controlled lightning. *Lighting Research and Technology*, 36(2): 131–46.

Nilsson, U. (2003) *The Effect of Music and Music in Combination with Therapeutic Suggestions on Postoperative Recovery (Avhandling för doktorsexamen)*. Linköpings universitet.

Nordenfelt, L. (1991) *Hälsa och värde [Health and Value]*. Stockholm: Thales.

Ogińska-Bulik, N. (2005) The role of personal and social resources in preventing adverse health outcomes in employees of uniformed professions. *International Journal of Occupational Medicine and Environmental Health*, 18(3): 233–40.

Persinger, M.A., Tiller, S.G. and Koren, S.A. (1999) Background sound pressure fluctuations (5dB) from overhead ventilation systems increase subjective fatigue on university students during three-hour lectures. *Perceptual and Motor Skills*, 88: 541–56.

Pratt, R. (1990) *Rhythm and Resistance: The Political Uses of Popular Music*. Washington, DC: Smithsonian Institution Press.

Robertson, P. (2001) Music and wellbeing: An introduction to the musical brain. Available at: www.musicmindspirit.org/musicalbrain.html.

Saito, E., Sagawa, Y. and Kanagawa, K. (2005) Social support as a predictor of health status among older adults living alone in Japan. *Nursing and Health Science*, 7(1): 29–36.

SHSTF (1989) *Florence Nightingales anteckningar om sjukvård – ur vårt tidsperspektiv. [Svensk översättning av Florence Nightingales Notes on Nursing – what it is and it is not].* Skellefteå: Artemis Bokförlag.

Silber, L. (2005) Bars behind bars: The impact of a women's prison choir on social harmony. *Music Education Research,* 7: 251–71.

Spychiger, M.B. (2000) Music education is important – why? In Matell, G. and Theorell, T. (eds), *Musikens roll i barns utveckling [The role of music in children's development].* Institutet för psykosocial medicin. Karolinska Institutet, 110–22.

Staples, S.L. (1996) Human response to environmental noise. *American Psychologist,* 51(2): 143–50.

Stokols, D. (1992) Establishing and maintaining healthy environments. *American Psychologist,* 47(1): 6–22.

Suominen, A., Helenius, H., Blomberg, H., Uutela, A. and Koskenvuo, M. (2001) Sense of coherence as a predictor of subjective state of health results of 4 years of follow-up of adults. *Journal of Psychosomatic Research,* 50: 77–86.

Tennessen, C.M. and Cimprich, B (1995) Views to nature: Effects on attention. *Journal of Environmental Psychology,* 15: 77–85.

Theorell, T. and Konarski, K. (1998) *När orden inte räcker.* Stockholm: Natur och Kultur.

Ulrich, R.S. (1984) View through a window may influence recovery from surgery. *Science,* 224: 420–1.

Van den Berg, A.E., Hartig, T. and Staats, H. (2007) Preference for nature in urbanized societies: Stress, restoration, and the pursuit of sustainability. *Journal of Social Issues,* 63(1): 79–96.

van Dijk, F.J.H, Souman, A.M. and De Vires, F.F. (1987) Non-auditory effects of noise in industry. VI. A final field study in industry. *International Archives of Occupational and Environmental Health,* 59: 133–45.

Verderber, S. (1986) Dimensions of person-window transactions in the hospital environment. *Environment and Behaviour,* 18: 450–66.

Vischer, J.C. (2005) *Space Meets Status: Designing Workplace Performance.* New York: Routledge.

Yeang K. (2006) *EcoDesign: A Manual for Ecological Design.* Chichester: John Wiley and Sons.

Yeang, K. (2012) Intersections between ecological design and human health in urban environments. 8th Design and Health World Congress and Exhibition, Kuala Lumpur, Malaysia, 27 June–1 July.

Yoshida, T., Osada, Y., Kawaguchi T., Hosuhiyama, Y., Yoshida, K. and Yamamoto, K. (1997) Effects of road traffic noise on inhabitants of Tokyo. *Journal of Sound and Vibration,* 205: 517–52.

6 Communications

The contribution of typography and information design to health communication

Sue Walker

Abstract

This chapter is about the role that information design and typography and graphic communication play in effective public health communication. It introduces the way that information designers work, particularly in relation to what have been called 'functional texts' – those that enable people to take some kind of action, or to better understand something. Examples of late nineteenth- and early-twentieth-century printed ephemera are used to draw attention to the ways that language and visual presentation work together to enhance the meaning of a particular message. The role of pictures in health communication is discussed with reference to Isotype and the work of Otto and Marie Neurath.

Health communication and information design

Health communication takes many different forms: health promotion and disease prevention, and information to support treatment choices, or to improve the effectiveness of clinical care.[1] Much health-related communication supports decision-making, such as whether to have a child vaccinated, and whether to undergo surgery rather than an alternative route; or is procedural or instructional, such as how to do exercises after an operation or how to use an inhaler. Successful health communication benefits from the application of good practice from typography and graphic communication. An information design perspective puts the reader/user at the centre recognising that visual presentation works with language to successfully communicate with a particular audience.

Public health information can be urgent and complicated, and have several layers of meaning. To be effective, traditional editing or graphic design approaches tend not to be enough and an additional information design perspective can have a transformative effect on the way information is presented. Gui Bonsiepe (1999: 59) puts it well:

> The growth of the information society and the information glut calls for a revision of the traditional view of the graphic designer as primarily a visualizer… The infodesigner structures and arranges information elements and provides orientation aids to enable the user to find a way through the maze of information.

Information designers are particularly concerned to produce materials (whether on paper or digital) that are relevant to a particular audience and intended use. So, if an information designer is working on a project designed to explain the implications for health of a heatwave, it is probable that they would produce different materials for the elderly, for parents with young children and for commuters. They are likely to have worked with the information provider and other stakeholders, including users, to elicit the relevant content and its most effective visual presentation. The material produced is targeted and relevant, which offers a better chance of it being effective.

Effective information design can help people understand, which can be particularly important if a message or set of messages is complicated or confusing. It can mean that people retain information that is relevant to them or their situation, and it can make the difference between taking action or not, or it can change the way people behave. But do we know how many people have taken action as a result of effective information design? Can its effectiveness be measured? There is some evidence to suggest it can. PearsonLloyd's work on a better A&E found that 75 per cent of patients said that improved signage reduced their frustration during waiting times.[2] The work of research-based organisations, such as the Communication Research Institute, led by David Sless, and the Centre for Information Design Research, led by Alison Black, are committed to demonstrating that good information design makes a measurable difference. Their blogs and websites provide examples relevant to healthcare of one kind or another.[3]

Telling the public how they can improve their health and prevent disease and illness is not new. This chapter will use examples of late nineteenth- and early-twentieth-century health communication to draw attention to good and less good practice in health communication that is relevant today. This approach is influenced by the work of Paul Stiff et al. who used 19th-century documents to discuss information design principles (for example, Stiff et al., 2010). It reinforces that much health-related communication is of an everyday nature, produced in line with the conventions of the time, often not by designers but (in the past) by printers and (today) by people working on desktop computers. The illustrations in this chapter are sourced from printed ephemera from late nineteenth- and early- and mid-twentieth centuries, including public health work undertaken by the Isotype Institute.[4]

Successfully communicating information about health is no different to successfully communicating information about anything. This is confirmed to some extent by papers by James Hartley and Patricia Wright in Abraham and Kools' book *Writing Health Communication* (2012). Hartley's chapter, 'Designing easy-to-read text', covers basic principles of typography using as examples text from patient information leaflets found in medication. Wright's 'Using graphics effectively in text' summarises ways of using pictures effectively, drawing on health-related images to make her point. The principles and rules that Hartley and Wright articulate are applicable to clear communication in any context. Such principles have, for example, been used to good effect in particular kinds of health communication, such as patient information leaflets that accompany medication (e.g. van der Waarde, 1999, 2006; Spinillo and van der Waarde, 2013; Spinillo and Amorin, 2014; Dickenson et al., 2001, 2010).

The most effective communication is produced with the needs of the intended audience in mind, which in turn provides the context for making decisions about typography and the use of pictures and text. This way of thinking is embedded in the way that many information designers work, simplified here by David Sless (1992) 9:

- define the problem;
- involve all stakeholders;
- observe and measure the current state of things;
- develop and text prototype solutions;
- iteratively develop and test prototypes until an optimum solution is found;
- implement and monitor the solution in use.

'Informing patients: An assessment of the quality of patient information materials', a project supported by the King's Fund in the UK, reviewed patient information materials about conditions such as back pain, depression, hip replacement and strokes and asked patients' views on the relevance and reliability of the information they received, including their quality and usefulness and the extent to which they contributed to shared decision-making between patients and health professionals (Coulter et al. 1998: xi). A key finding of the project, and one that supports the information design way of working, was that patients (or users) should be involved throughout the process of making the leaflets, and that their questions about a particular topic be considered as a useful starting point for the content of the material. There is also evidence in the emergent field of service design that the approach summarised by Sless is beneficial when applied. Cerne Oven and Predan (2013), for example, brought together service design and information design in several healthcare projects in Slovenia, including healthy eating for people with diabetes, raising awareness of rheumatoid arthritis and stimulating elderly people with dementia. In the UK, the Centre for Information Design's work on a handbook for carers of people with dementia was developed in close collaboration with medics, carers and dementia sufferers, who reviewed and commented on various iterations of the handbook as it was being written and designed (Black and Carey, 2014).

Functional texts

Much health-related communication falls into the category of what Wright (1999) has referred to as 'functional texts'. Such texts might be warnings, reminders, requests or statements of legal responsibilities and rights; many provide information through statements of fact. Functional texts that enable people to take some kind of action, or to better understand something, have interested researchers and practitioners concerned with making documents (on paper and on screen). They are of particular interest to information designers because to work effectively consideration needs to be taken of the linguistic as well as the graphic aspects of the text. Waller (2011), for example, has summarised some of the research that aligns with his definition of a 'good document', and he broke this down into: factors that make it easy for people to understand the words; the visual impact of the document and the way its design influences usability; how far the document establishes a relationship with its users; and how the content is organised to deliver the document's purpose. Gregory (2004), from the technical writing perspective, linked language and visual presentation, and compared guidelines for writing for print with guidelines for writing for the web. She concluded that many of the underlying principles apply to both media arguing that structure and design, writing concisely, scannability, splitting information into coherent chunks and understanding that readers do not read text in the same order were relevant to writing for both print and web. She cited research relevant to these issues in both media and much of this is relevant to clear and accessible writing for functional texts.[5]

The 'Flies and disease' notice shown in Figure 6.1 is not a good functional text. The most noticeable visual characteristic is the large amount of text. It reads as an essay about how flies breed and carry germs rather than a document with easily absorbed key messages. The language combines prescription ('Keep all flies out of your larder'), with platitude ('Prevention is better than cure') and statements of fact ('Flies prefer close and stuffy rooms'). Some sentences are short ('Flies breed in filth'); others are much longer. In addition, although bold type has been used to draw attention to some parts of the text, there is a lack of visual hierarchy to direct the reader. The poster lacks structure; it doesn't help the reader to find the key message. Is it contained in the numbered list at the foot of the page, or is it the sentences picked out in bold type in the body of the text?

NATIONAL HEALTH SOCIETY,

53, BERNERS STREET, OXFORD STREET, LONDON, W.

FLIES AND DISEASE.

The house-fly breeds in rubbish heaps, stable manure, and decaying matter of all sorts. If you are pestered by flies in the house it proves the existence of filth in the neighbourhood. The fly takes about a fortnight to hatch.

Cause, therefore, all rubbish and decaying matter near the house to be burnt or removed every week and you will have no nuisance from flies.

Do not allow rubbish to accumulate. House refuse and stable manure must be regularly and **thoroughly** removed at least once a week from the neighbourhood of dwellings. If, in spite of your keeping your own premises clean, you are still plagued by flies, there must be breeding places on your neighbour's land. Write to the Health Authority stating that you cannot go on living in the house unless the nuisance is remedied.

It is quite useless to attempt to cope with the nuisance by means of fly-papers.

A fly-infested house is one not fit to live in.

Flies which one moment are seen on the manure heap may the next be crawling over your food or dropping in your milk.

If a single fly which has come from a rubbish heap falls into a jug of pure, clean milk, in a short time the milk will be found to be full of germs like those in the manure.

These germs have been carried by the fly and have multiplied in the milk.

It is, of course, possible that some of the germs so carried may be those of disease, and great stress has been laid, more particularly in America, upon the danger of spread of certain diseases, and especially of intestinal diseases, by means of flies.

Some of the biting flies which are met with in foreign countries have been found to spread certain diseases. The two common forms of house-fly usually met with in this country are not, however, biting flies. In any case the attempt should be made to keep all food, and particularly to keep milk, free from fly contamination.

Keep **all** flies out of your larder, therefore, and cover all your food : keep a wire gauze cover over your meat and a piece of gauze over your milk jug.

Your larder must be well ventilated, but cover the ventilation holes with wire gauze to make your larder fly-proof.

Flies prefer close and stuffy rooms to airy and well-ventilated ones.

The points to be especially noted are:—

1. **Flies breed in filth. They are a sign of unhealthy surroundings or of bad management.**

2. **Prevention is better than cure. No dirt—no flies.**

3. **Burn all rubbish in the kitchen Stove or in heaps in the garden. Do not let heaps accumulate.**

4. **Cover with wire gauze all openings to rooms and cupboards in which food is kept.**

Published and Sold by

THE NATIONAL HEALTH SOCIETY, 53, Berners Street, Oxford Street, London, W.

Price ½d. each ; 4½d. per dozen ; 2s. 6d. per 100 ; 10s. 6d. per 1,000.

Figure 6.1 A late 19th-century notice produced by the National Health Society. 252 x 153 mm. This notice aims to tell people that flies harbour disease and explains how to prevent fly infestation

Source: Maurice Rickards Collection, University of Reading

Writing clearly and thinking about the audience

Many would agree that following principles of 'plain English' and using an appropriate tone of voice are essential to successfully communicating a particular message, whether health-related or not. 'Plain English' is a generic descriptor referring to a set of principles for writing clearly.[6] The principles are:

- use short sentences and paragraphs;
- don't use jargon;
- use simple, everyday words rather than complex words;
- be specific rather than general;
- use active verbs;
- think of your audience and use words that are appropriate to them.

Of particular relevance to writing effective health communication is Marieke Kools' work, especially as it is both research-informed and evidence-based in that she promotes testing and iteration as integral to the process. Her 2012 paper, 'Making written materials easy to understand', summarises cognitive processes that take place when people read texts before going on to list features that writing (or rewriting) for effective health communication should contain. These include the generic Plain English principles mentioned above, but she goes into more detail about textual coherence at macro- and micro-levels. Macro-levels, for example, include 'use headings and first and last sentences within a sentence to predict and summarise'; and micro-levels include 'explicitly state the actor in each sentence', explain difficult or unusual words and maintain a 'given-new' order of information within sentences.

An informative title, or an introductory sentence announcing the topic and perhaps specifying an intended audience, are two ways that readers' prior knowledge (of both content and structure) can influence how well they will understand new information (Spyridakis, 2000). The heading in the 'Flies and disease' notice, for example, while describing what the text is about in a short and impactful way, does not engage the user. Perhaps more relevant would be the headings that addressed the reader of the poster as 'you', such as:

How you can stop flies spreading disease; or
How can you prevent disease in your home? Make sure there are no flies.

Keeping text short and to the point is one way of keeping the reader engaged and focused. The 'essence' of the 'Flies and disease' notice, for example, could be as follows:

Flies cause disease
Flies live and breed in rubbish
Keep rubbish away from your house
Keep flies out of your larder
Cover food with gauze to keep flies away from food
An example of how infestation occurs: a fly lands on a manure heap, and then on a jug
   of milk; the milk then becomes full of germs; if you drink the milk you may get ill.

Much research indicates that using the active voice makes content livelier and easier to read and understand. The active voice makes it clear who is doing what. Research has shown that people find text written in the active voice easier to understand than the same text written in

Figure 6.2   Notice to tenant, 1908. Sanitary Department, City of Edinburgh. 125 x 258 mm. An example of a formal tone of voice shown through the use of capital letters, with a more informal tone suggested by use of the active voice in the sentence below the heading

Source: Maurice Rickards Collection, University of Reading

the passive voice (Street and Dabrowska, 2010). Using the active voice can also suggest a link with the reader. The formality and importance expressed through the use of capital letters in the notice in Figure 6.2 is mitigated through the clear and direct use of 'It is your turn'.

This example also demonstrates the relevance of 'tone of voice' (defined as the representation of the brand values of a company, service or other organisation). It works with elements of visual presentation, such as typefaces and use of typographic styles, as well as vocabulary, mode of address and other linguistic considerations. Judy Delin (2005: 11) described tone of voice as being helpful in engaging people with content 'perhaps about products and services they wish to buy but also about benefits and services that they are invited to take part in or claims, such as pensions, tax credits, or advice, health services and screenings, safety information and more'.

Thinking about tone of voice might influence decisions about level of formality (such as use of contractions and colloquial phrases, or whether to address the reader as 'you'). Delin conducted a small survey in a UK government department, and some of her participants thought that information presented in the simplest terms was too friendly for a government agency – and therefore came across as false. They did not want to see contractions such as *you're* and *we'll*; they preferred *please call us* to *give us a ring*; they liked *you are likely to be entitled to a further amount* but thought that *you can get more money* was offensive because it suggested they were childish and greedy. The study participants wanted to write in ways that that were *direct but not too chatty*. They preferred, for example: *complete* to *fill in*; *receive* to *get*. This work suggests that some writers may feel that it is not appropriate to be direct and conversational, even though this might be attractive to a particular user group. However, another study has suggested that some ethnic groups may be offended by the use of direct 'you' (Rose, 1981). Black and Stanbridge (2012) found users can also react negatively to a writing style that overuses motivational features and can interpret this as a patronising or inappropriate style. A balance is needed that takes into account the different levels of understanding and expectations readers bring to a text, and this may be particularly relevant in health communication.

Wright (1999), reinforcing an information design approach, argued that producing effective health information requires special skills, particularly the ability to consider the needs of the users of the text – who may be end users – or the people responsible for the care of those to whom the information is targeted. This, in turn, means that it is important to consider how people *read* functional texts, and Wright provided a summary under the headings of 'access', 'interpretation' and 'application'.[7] She explained that reading functional (healthcare) texts involves a wider range of cognitive activities than reading other kinds of text due to the extent to which people's thinking and feeling affects their engagement with the documents. In producing healthcare texts, then, writers and designers need to anticipate what their readers/ users need and expect.

Shriver (1997: 171–207) presented research looking at health education literature and how teenagers reacted to visual and verbal messages to dissuade them from taking drugs. She annotated five examples of leaflets about the dangers of various kinds of drug misuse with comments from young people about the verbal and visual aspects of them. What this reflected was the importance of and value of getting views from a target audience as well as affirming that even if readers understood the content, hierarchy and structure of a text, there may be other barriers to comprehension. She listed the following observations of what readers may do when reading a text.

- Construct the meanings of the prose and graphic on the basis of their thinking and feeling (cognition and affect).
- Interpret the role they are expected to take, a role established through rhetorical clues set up by the design of the prose and graphics.
- View the messenger of the text (e.g. the persona, organisational voice or corporate identity) and the messenger's attitude about the reader.
- Feel about the way the visual and verbal message constructs them as an intended audience.
- Respond to 'the idea' of the text as a legitimate form of communication.

As an example, the 'Sore throats warning' in Figure 6.3 is a document where the readers may have different views about the 'official warning' being presented by a 'leading expert' giving a lecture. To some this may offer reassurance and validity, to others possibly intimidation or a feeling of 'what has this got to do with me'.

Legibility and hierarchy to guide the reader

Typographers and information designers use a number of techniques to make text visually accessible, including headings and sub-headings, space to group and separate related and non-related items and making sure that the type is legible and, as already noted, James Hartley is one researcher that has provided basic guidance in a health context.[8] The term 'scannable' is used increasingly to describe material organised visually so that key words and important information are clearly distinguished at first glance, especially in relation to information

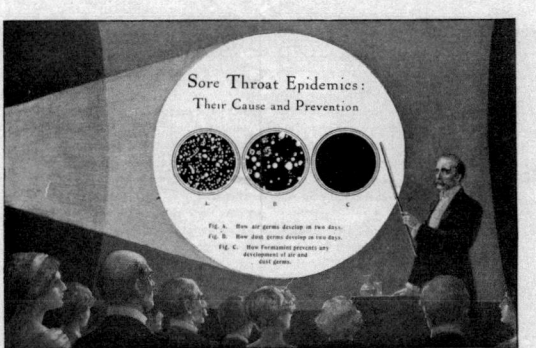

AN

OFFICIAL WARNING.

An Official Warning regarding the dangers of Sore Throat is given in the London County Council's new leaflet entitled "Health Hints to Parents," which states succinctly:

ALL SORE THROATS ARE SUSPICIOUS.

In view of this statement the enclosed leaflet should prove of interest to all householders, its object being to show how infectious diseases may be prevented when their first symptom, namely, sore throat, makes its appearance.

Remarkable Experiments by a Leading Scientist.

No one need suffer from Sore Throat in future, for this painful malady can now be both prevented and cured. Such is the practical significance of the above diagrams, which illustrate a very interesting experiment of Dr. Piorkowski, the famous Berlin scientist.

To understand these diagrams, we must bear in mind that Sore Throat is caught by inhaling germs. These minute organisms multiply rapidly in the mouth cavity, and cause not only Sore Throat, Tonsillitis, Mouth troubles, etc., but also such dread infectious diseases as Diphtheria, Consumption, Scarlet Fever, Measles, etc.

Dr. Piorkowski coated three plates with a substance on which germs thrive.

One (Fig. C) he treated in addition with some saliva in which Formamint had been dissolved. He then exposed all three plates to the air and dust, and afterwards kept them for two days at the temperature of the human body. Plates A and B, not having been treated with Formamint, were covered with germ-growths, but Plate C, treated with Formamint, was absolutely free from them, **proving that Formamint killed all germs which settled there.**

What happened on Plate C is exactly what happens in the mouth and throat of a person who takes Formamint, namely, **the germs which cause Sore Throat and other infectious diseases are all destroyed.**

Figure 6.3 An early 20th-century leaflet telling people about sore throats
Source: Maurice Rickards Collection, University of Reading

presented on the web, but it can apply equally to paper. Morkes and Nielsen (1997), for example, found that 'extremely scannable' text, that is with bulleted lists, bold highlighted key words or short text sections with headings, helped people perform tasks faster with fewer errors and better information recall.

In the 'Food wanted' notice in Figure 6.4 the reader's attention is drawn to particular parts of the text through different degrees of typographic variation as well as the use of vertical space. The use of bold type and capital letters for key words and phrases, in different sizes, gets the message across leaving the reader to decide whether to engage more deeply with the information.

Much day-to-day health communication today is produced by people working with desktop computers and many do not fully understand basic typographic principles. This can result in sub-optimal presentation of information. A typical example is shown in Figure 6.5, a notice

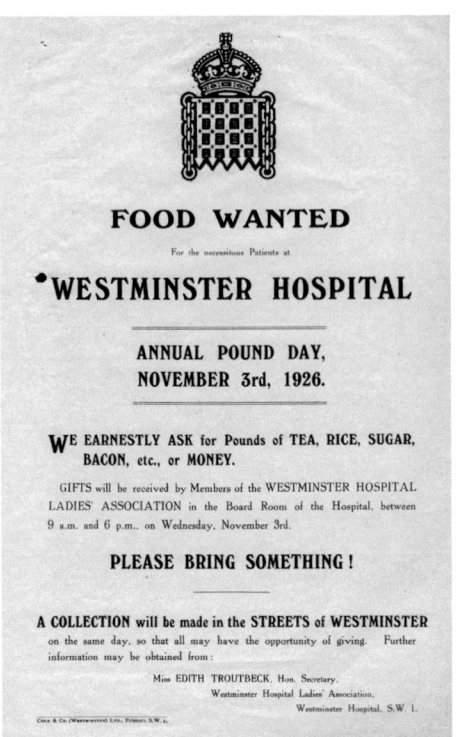

Figure 6.4 A notice produced by Westminster Hospital Ladies' Association, 1926. 325 x 204 mm. An example of a 'scannable' notice with parts of the text picked out in capital letters and bold type

Source: Maurice Rickards Collection, University of Reading

Figure 6.5 Before and after versions of a poster produced to encourage hospital users to wash their hands. 297 x 210 mm.

Source: Author's collection

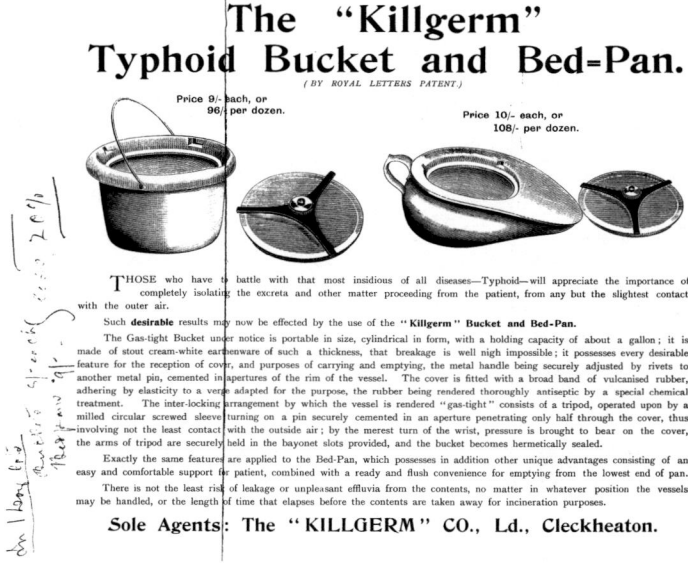

Figure 6.6 Detail from advertisement and description of the working of the 'Killgerm' bedpan, c. 1910. The illustrations, of a technical kind, describe the component parts. 205 x 264 mm.

Source: Maurice Rickards Collection, University of Reading

designed in 2004 to support a 'Clean hands campaign' at a hospital Trust in the UK. The example on the right is the chapter author's reworking to demonstrate to the Trust how typography can help to structure the information and direct the reader. In the reworked example, levels of heading are used to structure the text. The main message of the poster is clear – achieved through type size, colour and use of space. The left-aligned text in two columns follows legibility guidelines, and there are no extraneous features (such as the inexplicable arrows on the original). This approach uses basic principles of typography and graphic communication to facilitate design for reading and for action.

Pictures to help understanding?

Many health information texts use pictures of one kind or another in different ways.[9] In the nineteenth- and early-twentieth centuries many images were reminiscent of illustrations in contemporary scientific textbooks (Figure 6.6). Pictures were typically used to contextualise the information by including images of a target user group, such as the healthy-looking woman in the leaflet explaining the benefits of 'Jolly's "Duchess" pills' (Figure 6.7). Pictures may be used to explain how to take a particular medicine or undertake a medical procedure, such as how to use a condom or an inhaler. Related research considers issues such as the efficacy of the use of arrows and such symbolic devices in aiding understanding and the number of steps that are appropriate to depict in an action (see for example, Spinillo and van der Waarde, 2013; Kools, 2012).

Houts et al.'s (2006) comprehensive review of the role of pictures in health communication taken from the literature from health education, psychology, education and marketing acknowledged that the effective use of pictures is influenced by the context in which they

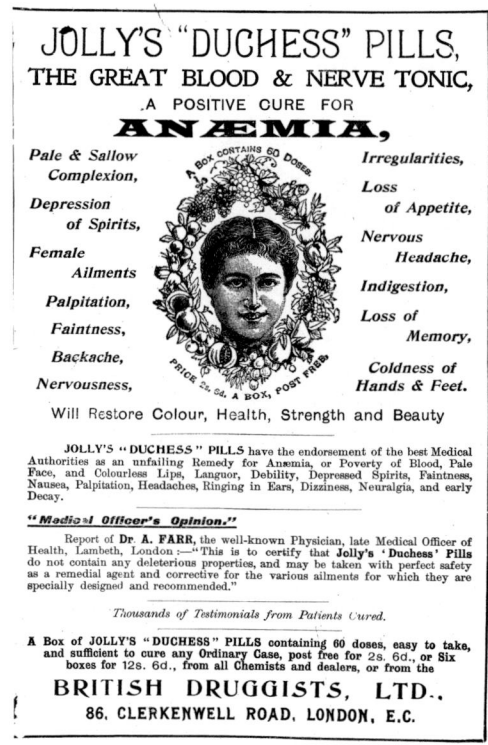

Figure 6.7 Detail from advertisement for Jolly's 'Duchess' pills, produced by British Druggists Ltd, late
19th century. 227 x 142 mm. This illustration associates the product with its likely users
Source: Maurice Rickards Collection, University of Reading

are used, for example, the level of literacy skills, the extent to which they are combined
with written or spoken directions and the graphic form of the picture, whether a line
drawing or a photograph. They presented guidelines for health educators: include pictures;
use simple drawings and photographs; simplify the language used with the pictures; guide
the reader by thinking about the text/picture relationship; be sensitive to the culture of
the intended audience; involve health professionals as well as designers (they use the term
artist!) in the design process; and evaluate their effectiveness with the intended audience.
None of these recommendations would surprise information designers today, and indeed
have already been alluded to in this chapter. Information designers are particularly interested in how pictures can be used to explain things, as were Otto and Marie Neurath in
the 1930s and 1940s.

The distinctive visual presentation of Isotype (if a little outdated) remains relevant today
but it is the Neuraths' approach to designing – including the role of the transformer – that
may be particularly relevant to health communication. 'Transformer' was a term devised by
the Neuraths to mean the person who worked with original and often scientific data and
information to produce explanations (usually in the form of charts) that could be understood by ordinary people.[10] This way of working often involved close collaboration between
the Neuraths and leading scientists or medical professionals, as was the case with their work

for the National Tuberculosis Association in the USA in the 1930s. This work involved the production of a series of large charts that explained how tuberculosis (TB) was contracted and how people with the disease should be cared for.[11] Neurath and his collaborator, the medic H.E. Kleinschmidt, wrote a short booklet explaining their way of working. *Health Education by Isotype*, though published in 1939, advocated principles that remain relevant to health communication today. This part of the chapter draws attention to selected aspects of the Neuraths' work.

Neurath and Kleinschmidt argued that attracting attention was 'a first step in health education' and that this was more easily done through pictures than through words. They believed that explanation using predominantly pictures was more likely to be understood by more people than if it was presented in words only. They suggested that schematic drawings (such as Isotype pictograms[12]) were well-suited to describe structure and mechanism, and as such were better than photographs to explain, for example, how TB germs were spread: 'the schematic drawing omits the non-essentials and emphasizes the structure and phenomena it may be desirable to explain'. They suggested that pictograms were also helpful in explaining a sequence of events 'when it is necessary to show how one situation follows another in evolutionary progress, the symbol language does the task well' (Neurath and Kleinschmidt, 1939: 22). This is demonstrated well in the chart shown in Figure 6.8. The Isotype principles of comparison and contrast are particularly relevant for health communication, this too facilitated by the use of pictograms and consistent use of colour. In the example in Figure 6.9, Neurath explained that comparison was enabled due to identical constants that make it easy to pick out the variables – the main one in this case being advice about what to do when you leave hospital.

Despite the considered and effective use of pictograms, some of the most effective and engaging TB charts are those that use photography, either on its own or in combination with pictograms. Two of the most effective charts are shown in Figure 6.10. In these examples, the headings are clear and succinct and the message is clearly and powerfully conveyed through the use of schematic images rather than text. These charts attract attention through a compelling visual narrative.

Colour, used consistently, was a key component of the Isotype toolkit. On the TB charts produced in the USA, for example, orange was used to represent a healthy person, a healthy part of a lung or a ward in a sanatorium where people are recovering. Neurath and Kleinschmidt (1939: 31) explained:

> For health education purposes, orange is the color adopted for health, the normal or desirable. Black means sick, dead or something undesirable. Red is a good colour to use for protective measures – the doctor, immunizing agents, etc. Blue serves well for water and air, green for outdoors. Yellow is seldom used because it is a weak colour.

The chart in Figure 6.8 shows also how the consistent use of orange (shown in the illustration as mid-grey) and black in the TB charts contributed to making a clear visual explanation.

The Neuraths were acutely aware of the importance of the context within which they worked, and another example related to the use of colour can be found in Marie Neurath's work in the 1950s on a number of health communication projects in the Western Region of Nigeria (Kindel, 2013). One such project was a series of 'poster leaflets': illustrated wall charts that could also be folded and taken home by patients so that they could study them further. A poster leaflet to show causes and symptoms of TB and action to be taken was produced in 1955. Kindel explained how a TB specialist, V.W. Hetreed, in consultation with a Yoruba nurse

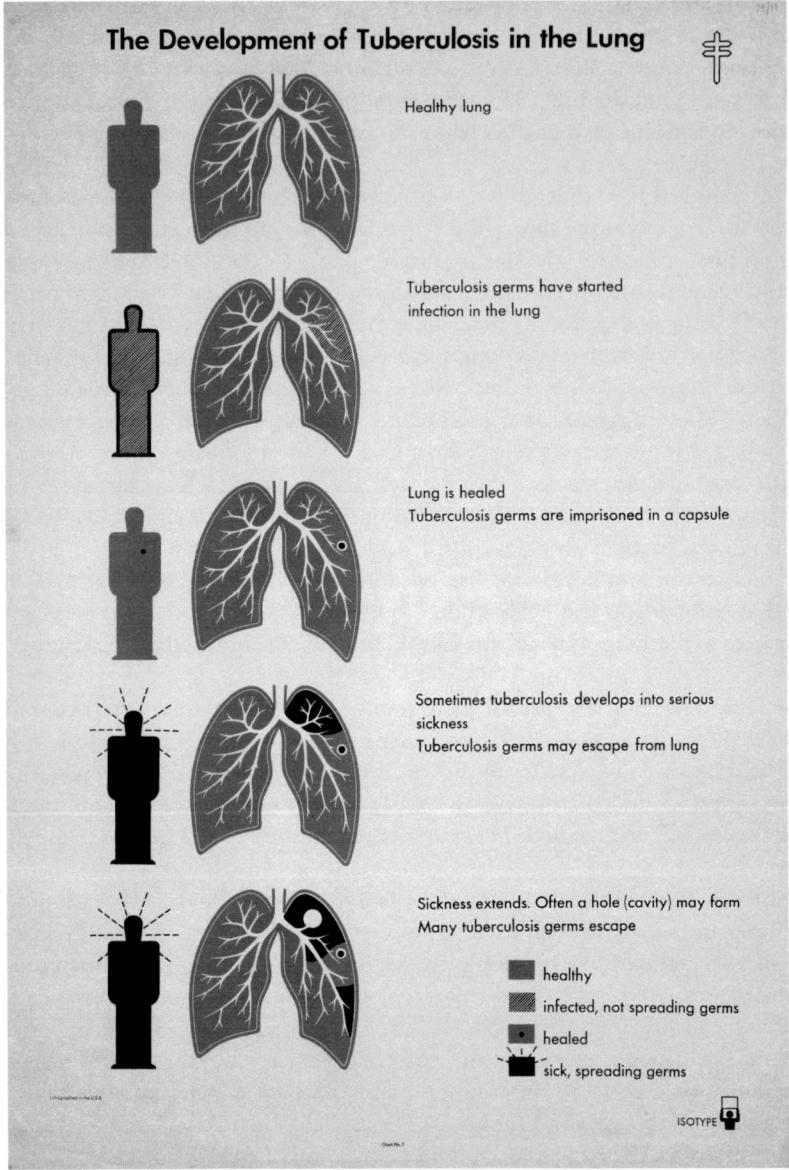

Figure 6.8 'The development of tuberculosis in the lung', 1938. Chart from the 'Fighting tuberculosis' exhibition produced for the National Tuberculosis Association in the USA in 1938. 920 x 610 mm.
Source: Otto and Marie Neurath Isotype Collection, University of Reading

and clerk, advised on the use of colours proposed for the poster leaflet: 'yellow, in his view, had been correctly deployed to designate a healthy person; red, by contrast, should represent tuberculosis because of its Yoruba associations with danger and misfortune; blue, suggesting happiness, was appropriate for depictions of treatment and protection, and for doctors' (Kindel, 2013: 469). This advice resulted in a different range of colours being used in the African TB

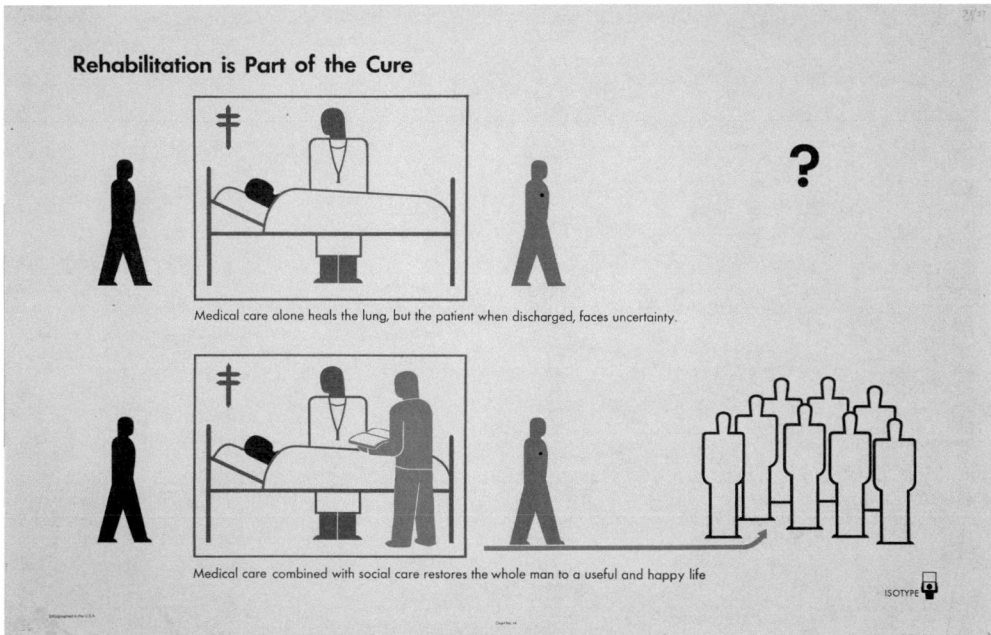

Figure 6.9 'Rehabilitation is part of the cure', 1938. An example showing the powerful effect of comparison between a pair of images. 920 x 610 mm.

Source: Otto and Marie Neurath Isotype Collection, University of Reading

material demonstrating not only the value of consultation, but also of taking account of cultural association and preferences. So, while colours were used consistently to represent different conditions in the African TB materials, the actual colours used were chosen with advice from the people in the relevant community.

Concluding remarks

This chapter has summarised issues that are likely to contribute to effective health communication from the perspective of information design and typography and graphic communication. One thread that runs through the work is the desirability of working with experts in a particular field and with intended users. This does two things: first, it ensures that the content, whether expressed in words or in pictures, is appropriate for a particular purpose, and second, it underlines the importance of feedback and iteration as essential elements in the design process. Asking intended users whether they can read and understand the text, or whether they find a particular graphic representation helpful can provide invaluable guidance to those working towards a final solution. Putting the user first, as has been shown in some of the examples in this chapter, and engaging them in decision making in the design process gives them status as 'part owners' of the documents that are made. This, in turn, increases the likelihood of a document's effectiveness.

Although much health communication material can be improved through the application of basic typographic guidance, there are less easy-to-define qualities that designers, through their training, understand. These include, for example, consideration of the verbal and graphic

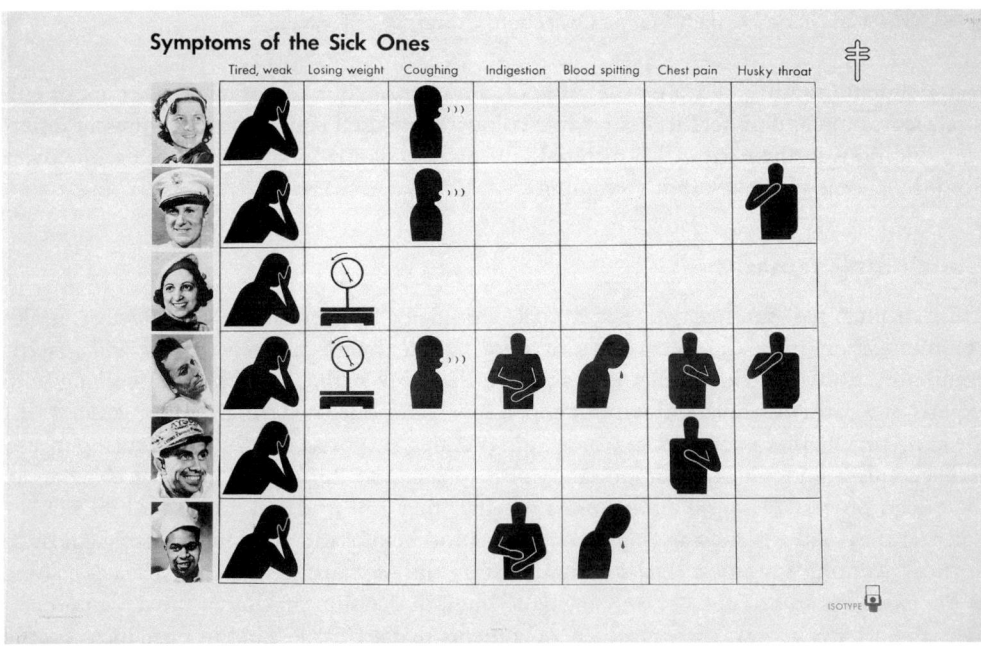

Figure 6.10 'Can you tell who has tuberculosis?' and 'Symptoms of the sick ones', 1938. 920 x 610 mm. A pair of charts using photography as well as pictograms to engage the readers as they try to answer the direct question posed in the heading on the left-hand chart

Source: Otto and Marie Neurath Isotype Collection, University of Reading

conventions that readers might expect to see in a particular document and the impact on readers' rhetorical engagement with a document. As Kostelnick and Hassett (2003: 6–7) note, conventional practice is intrinsically rhetorical:

> Designers must select conventions based on their interpretation of the potential readers and the situational context in which those readers will use them. Often, designers adapt conventions to a situation by re-shaping them, and typically, they integrate them with other conventions in the same communication. This process of selection, adaptation and integration requires rhetorical judgement. Even when a convention demands strict conformity, and the designer acquiesces to that authority, the convention carries the rhetorical weight of the community that sanctions it. In addition, readers bring the same rhetorical elements – interpretation, context, exigence, community – to bear as they 'read' visual language, and they do so in ways perhaps less prescribed even than designers.

Returning to the 'Flies and disease' notice (fig 6.1): looking at this through 21st-century good practice eyes, it has not been organised into 'rhetorical clusters' where the graphic organisation of a text complements and enhances its meaning. It was, however, produced (by a printer) according to the conventions of its time, and as such may have performed perfectly well. Within the context of this chapter it serves to draw attention to the importance of getting conventional attributes right within the context of the genre and circumstances of use. Writers and designers, then, in producing successful functional texts, achieve structure and hierarchy through graphic, as well as linguistic, organisation of the text, and in an effective text integrate this with reader expectation and convention.

The important point to come from the Isotype work is that health-related communication should attract the attention of the intended audience. The Neuraths believed that using pictures, especially Isotype pictograms, was the way to do this. But while the Isotype charts that we have seen in this chapter are visually compelling, more significant are underlying principles of the consistent use of colour, comparison and contrast within the set of clearly defined rules for the way in which the well-known pictograms were organised. And aligning with the way that information designers today work, the innovation that the Neuraths brought to their work, including health communication, was the transformer – someone who ensured that complex information was presented in a way that was accurate and readily understood by the public.

Notes

1 Coulter et al. (1998: 3–12) provide examples of work in each of these categories, including reference to resourcing implications, user involvement, factors that influence decision-making and beneficial outcomes.
2 http://pearsonlloyd.com/2013/11/a-better-aande/.
3 http://communication.org.au and www.reading.ac.uk/cidr.
4 The material used in the discussion is from the Maurice Rickards Collection and the Otto and Marie Neurath Isotype Collection at the University of Reading.
5 Walker et al. (2013) summarised research relevant to writing and organising information visually on the web for www.gov.uk. Much of this is also relevant to what Redish (1989) has referred to as 'reading to do', thus aligning with functional texts.
6 A good description of Plain English, illustrated with examples, is at www.clearest.co.uk/editorsoftware/plain-english/index.html. It also has examples of savings that have been made by governments, councils, multinationals and industry bodies that have adopted Plain English principles.
7 See also Waller (1982): a review of how typography can enhance access and understanding.

8 See Hartley (2012). Dos Santos Lonsdale (2014) provided a thorough review of literature on the legibility of printed text that summarised approaches taken by and findings of researchers and practitioners. Middendorp (2012), writing from a design practice perspective, paid attention to the relationship between content and its visual presentation. Van der Waarde (1999) showed how general principles of typography can be applied to a particular genre of health communication – patient information leaflets in pharmaceutical products.

9 Shriver (1997: 412–30) identifies five ways to describe relationships between text and pictures: redundant, complementary, supplementary, juxtapositional and stage setting, and provides examples of each. Research surveys such as Levie and Lentz (1982) and Goldsmith (1984) present numerous studies about whether pictures or text are better in particular situations, or whether it is more effective to use text and pictures.

10 See Neurath and Kinross (2009: 77–8) and Neurath (1974: 136 for explanations of the transformer's role.

11 The charts are reproduced in Kindel (2013: 342–8).

12 Following Burke, 'pictogram' is used for 'the simplified, modified pictures used by Gerd Arntz and others for Isotype'. Kindel (2013: 17).

References

Abraham, C. and Kools, M. (2012) *Writing Health Communication: An Evidence-Based Guide*. London: Sage.

Black, A. and Carey, C. (2014) How does user research help? Reflections based on a case study of design for dementia care. Paper delivered at the Information Design Conference, London.

Black, A. and Stanbridge, K. (2012) Documents as 'critical incidents' in organization to consumer communication. *Visible Language*, 46(3): 246–81.

Bonsiepe, G. (1999) *Interface: An Approach to Design*. Maastricht: Jan van Eyck Academie.

Coulter, A., Entwistle, V. and Gilbert, D. (1998) *Informing Patients: An Assessment of the Quality of Patient Information Materials*. London: King's Fund.

Cerne Oven, P. and Predan, B. (2013) *Designing an Agenda, or, How to Avoid Solving Problems that Aren't. Focus: Service and Information Design*. Ljubljana: Pekinpah Association.

Delin, J. (2005) Brand tone of voice: A linguistic analysis of brand positions. *Journal of Applied Linguistics*, 2(1): 1–44.

Dickinson D., Raynor, D.K. and Duman, M. (2001) Patient information leaflets for medicines: Using consumer testing to determine the most effective design. *Patient Education and Counseling*, 43: 147–59.

Dickinson D., Gallina, S., Newsom-Davis, E. and Teather, J. (2010) Medicine package leaflets – does good design matter? *Information Design Journal*, 18(3): 225–40.

dos Santos Lonsdale, M. (2014) Typographic features of text: Outcomes from research and practice. *Visible Language*, 48(3): 29–67.

Goldsmith, E. (1984) *Research into Illustration*. Cambridge: Cambridge University Press.

Gregory, J. (2004) Writing for the web versus writing for print: Are they really so different? *Technical Communication*, 51(2): 276–85.

Hartley, J. (2012) Designing easy-to-read text, in Abraham, C. and Kools, M. (eds), *Writing Health Communication: An Evidence-Based Guide*. London: Sage, 7–22.

Houts, P.S., Doak, C.C., Doak, L.G. and Loscalzo, M.J. (2006) The role of pictures in improving health communication: A review of research on attention, comprehension, recall, and adherence. *Patient Education and Counseling*, 61: 173–90.

Kindel, E. (2013) Isotype in Africa, 1952–8, in Burke, C., Kindel, E. and Walker, S. (eds), *Isotype: Design and Contexts 1925–1971*. London: Hyphen Press, 448–97.

Kools, M. (2012) Making written materials easy to understand, in Abraham, C. and Kools, M. (eds), *Writing Health Communication: An Evidence-Based Guide*. London: Sage.

Kostelnick, C. and Hassett, M. (2003) *Shaping Information: The Rhetoric of Visual Conventions*. Carbondale: Southern Illinois University Press.

Levie, W.H. and Lentz, R. (1982) Effects of text illustrations: A review of research. *Educational Communication and Technology Journal*, 26(1): 195–232.

Morkes, J. and Nielsen, J. (1997) Concise, SCANNABLE, and objective: How to write for the web. Available at: www.nngroup.com/articles/concise-scannable-and-objective-how-to-write-for-the-web/.

Middendorp, J. (2012) *Shaping Text*. Amsterdam: BIS.

Neurath, M. (1974) Isotype. *Instructional Science*, 3(2): 127–50.

Neurath, M. and Kinross, R. (2009) *The Transformer: Principles of Making Isotype Charts*. London: Hyphen Press.

Neurath, O. and Kleinschmidt, H.E. (1939) *Health Education by Isotype*. New York: American Public Health Association.

Redish, J.C. (1989) Reading to learn to do. *IEEE Transactions*, 32(4): 289–93.

Rose, A. (1981) Problems in public documents. *Information Design Journal*, 2/3(4): 179–96.

Shriver, K. (1997) *Dynamics in Document Design*. New York: Wiley.

Sless, D. (1992) What is information design? In Penman, R. and Sless, D. (eds), *Designing Information for People*. Canberra: Communication Research Press, 1–16.

Spinillo, C.G. and Amorim, G. (2014) Survey of procedural pictorial sequences in e-PILs, Bulario Eletronico da Anvisa. Unpublished report. Curitiba: Universidade Federal do Parana.

Spinillo, C.G. and van der Waarde, K. (2013) Pictorial instructions in package inserts of Brazil and European Union: Are they for patients? In Fadel, L., Spinillo, C.G., Moura, M. and Triska, R. (eds), *Research and Practice: Selected Readings of the 5th Information Design International Conference*. Florianopolis: Brazilian Society of Information Design, 119–29.

Spyridakis, J.H. (2000) Guidelines for authoring comprehensible web pages and evaluating their success. *Technical Communication*, third quarter: 359–82.

Stiff, P., Esbester, M. and Dobraszczyk, P. (2010) Designing and gathering information: Perspectives on nineteenth-century forms, in Weller, T. (ed.), *Information History in the Modern World: Histories of the Information Age*. Basingstoke: Palgrave Macmillan, 57–88.

Street, J. and Dabrowska, E. (2010) More individual difference in language attainment: How much do adult native speakers know about passives and quantifiers. *Lingua*, 120: 2080–94. Summarised at: www.sciencedaily.com/releases/2010/07/100706082156.htm.

van der Waarde, K. (1999) The graphic presentation of patient package inserts, in Boersema, T., Zwaga, H. and Hoonhout, H. (eds), *Visual Information for Everyday Use*. London: Taylor and Francis, 75–81.

van der Waarde, K. (2006) Visual information about medicines for patients, in *Designing Effective Communications: Creating Contexts for Clarity and Meaning*. New York: Allworth Press, 38–50.

Walker, S., Black, A. and Carey, C. (2013) GOV.UK content principles: Conventions and research background. Commissioned research report. Available at: http://blogs.reading.ac.uk/cidr/2013/06/11/writing-clearly-for-gov-uk/.

Waller, R. (1982) A review of how typography can enhance access and understanding, in Jonassen, D.H. (ed.), *The Technology of Text: Principles for Structuring, Designing, and Displaying Text, Volume 2*. Englewood Cliffs, NJ: Educational Technology, 137–66.

Waller, R. (2011) What makes a good document? The criteria we use. Simplification Centre Technical paper no. 2, University of Reading.

Wright, P. (1999) Writing and information design of healthcare materials, in Candlin, C. and Hyland, K. (eds), *Writing: Texts, Processes and Practices*. London: Longman, 85–98.

Wright, P. (2012) Using graphics effectively in text, in Abraham, C. and Kools, M. (eds), *Writing Health Communication: An Evidence-Based Guide*. London: Sage, 63–82.

Theme 2

Design in acute health

7 Architecture

Healing architecture

Ricardo Codinhoto

Abstract

The purpose of this chapter is to discuss the design of acute care settings with a focus on the evolution of design practice over the last decade. In particular, ideas around healing environments describe how design is contributing to enhanced health and wellbeing and how recent developments are helping to create better designs. The chapter covers aspects of the theoretical hypothesis explaining the relationship between people, the environment and healing with a focus on three elements: how people perceive the environment, social interaction as part of healing and the influence of people's sociocultural background. The chapter looks at evidence-informed design in the context of acute healthcare settings whilst also covering trends, challenges and opportunities in healthcare design, and how this field is developing. A case study demonstrates elements of a real project on a before and after basis. The chapter concludes with the message that design of acute care settings involves much more than simply providing a space for care services to take place.

Introduction

In our lives, we dread the day we have to go to an acute care setting. The experience of going into a hospital is unsettling and, in general, we experience growing levels of anxiety, stress and emotional exhaustion. Constant news headlines announcing a steep rise in hospital admissions, a shortage of funds for the rising costs of care delivery for an ageing population and the pressure for a streamlined and more efficient service delivery just do not help with our confidence. The message is one: to do more with less and, altogether, we wonder whether we are not better off staying in our homes.

However, it is not all bad news. For instance, advancements in technology and treatments support increasingly faster recovery rates. Also, societal changes and a better understanding of patients' and staff demands have led to changes in the way hospitals are designed. Contributing to that is the development of a better understanding of the relationship between the environments surrounding human beings and health, particularly in healthcare settings. These and other positive changes have led to a new briefing for healthcare facilities, in particular acute care settings that are more focused on people's needs.

It is in relation to this last aspect that this section is elaborated. Here, the thematic unit of architecture is introduced to describe how design has been contributing to enhance health and wellbeing. We understand that architecture attempts to bridge the gap between art and practice, between interesting and meaningful design and that both are important. Thus, considering both, perhaps with a bias towards a more technical approach to design, we discuss how recent developments are helping the creation of better designs.

To do that, this section discusses evidence-based design and its development into evidence-informed design in the context of acute healthcare settings. It covers trends in healthcare design as well as the challenges and opportunities, and how it is developing. For this purpose, the chapter is divided into three sections covering theory, practice and an example of acute care design solutions. In this way, the chapter should provide valuable information for planners, designers, healthcare providers and the general public interested in this theme whilst also addressing current debate in this area.

The theoretical principles linking the built environment design and wellbeing

This section on theory discusses the assumption that healing and wellbeing goes far beyond the administration of medication to patients. We discuss here other elements that form part of the healing process and directly or indirectly impact our health and wellbeing, for instance the maintenance of essential human 'functions' such as socialising. The chapter discusses how architecture can support humans engaging in activities, physically and cognitively, individually and/or in groups, introducing the idea of cognitive inclusiveness.

Many theories explain how the design of the built environment affects human life and behaviour. These are important to know as they can influence designers to think differently about their designs. They can give a different sense of purpose for the designs developed. For Sundstrom et al. (1996), amongst the theories that have been guiding research, six appear to be more influential in recent research developments around environment and health: Arousal theory, Environmental load, Stress and adaptation, Privacy regulation, Ecological psychology and behaviour setting theory, and Transactional approach. These theories were generated in the environmental psychology domain and a short extract of their thesis is presented in the following as adapted from Sundstrom et al.'s (1996) work:

> Arousal: Psycho–physiological arousal is... a process that mediates influences of environmental features such as sound and temperature. The arousal hypothesis predicts optimum performance and satisfaction under conditions of moderate arousal, depending on task complexity and other factors (Thayer, 1989; Biner et al., 1989). Extensions of the hypothesis suggest that through arousal, high temperature increases the likelihood of violence, though the nature of the relationship remains in debate (Anderson, 1989; Bell, 1992).
>
> Environmental load: The overload hypothesis assumes that humans have a finite capacity for processing stimuli and information and predicts that we cope with sensory or information overload through (among other responses) selective attention and ignoring low-priority inputs. For instance, selective attention in crossing a road is placed on 'distance to cross', 'oncoming vehicles', 'obstacles in the path', whereas low-priority can be 'background scenery' on the other side of the road. Examples of research in this area include noise and reduced performance in writing (Smith, 1991); masking sound reducing performance deficit due to noise (Loewen and Suedfeld, 1992); and reading comprehension of individuals with internal and external locus of control in quiet and noisy conditions (Veitch, 1990). More recently, this approach has been studied in relation to stress (e.g. Hartig et al., 2003; Hartig, 2007).
>
> Stress and adaptation: This theory associates extremes of temperature, sound and other environmental variables with physiological and psychological stress and with coping and adaptive behaviours that reduce stress or its impact. Environmental stress

research examined prolonged exposures (e.g. Hedge, 1989) and post-traumatic outcomes (Rubonis and Bickman, 1991), including chronic illness and psychological impairment. Such findings reinforce the need for theoretical distinction of acute and chronic environmental stress (e.g. Baum et al., 1990; Hobfoll, 1991; Baum and Fleming 1993).

Privacy regulation: Research on privacy, spatial behaviour, crowding and territoriality together suggests a human tendency to seek optimum social interaction, partly through the use of the physical environment (Altman, 1993). Privacy regulation theory suggests that when a person fails to achieve the subjective, optimum level of social contact for the situation, the resulting stress motivates coping behaviour, which may rely on the physical setting (Brown, 1992). Examples of research include chair arrangement in a work environment and social interaction (Haggard and Werner, 1990); privacy and higher satisfaction in completing complex tasks (Block and Stokes, 1989).

Ecological psychology and behaviour setting theory: This theory analyses environments in terms of behaviour settings: 'small scale social systems composed of people and physical objects configured in such a way as to carry out a routinised program of activities with specifiable time and place boundaries' (Wicker, 1992; Wicker and August, 1995). Research in this area includes the work of McLaren and Hawe (2005) and Sallis et al. (2008).

Transactional approach: An extension of privacy regulation theory, Altman (1993) and colleagues (Brown et al., 1992 and Werner et al., 1992) elaborated their transactional approach, which treats the physical environment as a potential context for social interaction that can support, constrain, symbolise and confer meaning upon various aspects of social relationships. This holistic, systems-oriented analysis incorporates multiple levels and facets, variation over time, and cyclical processes. It describes social relationships and physical settings in terms of dialectics, or tensions between opposing influences. This theory led to the development of the person-environment-occupation theory presented in the work developed by Law et al. (1996) and Rebeiro (2001), amongst others.

In addition to the above theories, *Proxemics* is also a theory that connects humans and their behaviour in the built environment. In other words, it refers to people's use of their perceptual apparatus in different emotional states during different activities, in different relationships, settings and contexts (Hall, 1968). Examples of studies include Cook (1970), Raybeck (1991) and McLaughlin et al. (2008), who investigated privacy and territorial boundaries.

The field of architecture has also made a theoretical contribution, the *Language of the Space* as proposed by Brian Lawson. Lawson (2001, 2010) states that the built environment has signs and specific characteristics that can be 'read' (as interpreted) by its users. Therefore, it is the language of the space and its 'readability' that influences human behaviour. In general, the behaviour is guided by the users' most important needs first and, basically, it varies from conscious to unconscious behaviours, as well as from controlled to uncontrolled ones.

Despite much progress, as argued by Sundstrom et al. (1996) and Gifford (2014), the debate regarding the explanation for how the environment impacts upon a person's health is still wide open and the candidate theories vary considerably. The lack of consensus is not necessarily a bad thing in this context as it gives alternatives for our understanding of this phenomenon and it gives room for necessary trade-offs. Thus the key lesson emerging from the understanding of these theories is that characteristics or different configurations of the built environment can stimulate positive and negative change in psychological, physiological and physical status.

Other important messages can also be highlighted from these theories. The first is that much attention should be given to individual circumstances. In practical terms, designing for a person in need of urgent care will need to be clear and objective and without distracting elements. Conversely, a person in long-term care will need those 'distracting' elements that can be used for supporting social interaction. The built environment is perceived through the use of our senses, which stimulate our cognition in the first place and that can trigger a reaction in the second place. Our physical and/or mental status can be positively and negatively stimulated when the 'natural' environmental balance is disturbed; when there is an unclear message embedded in the design of the built environment; and when the design of the built environment imposes barriers preventing individuals from dealing with their priorities. Secondly, the built environment can support or hinder social interaction. In this respect, in as much as the inclusion of spaces for social interaction is sought, individuals must have, as an alternative, enough space for privacy, reflection and intended seclusion. Finally, the way individuals interpret the environment is also related to their cultural and social background and therefore varies from person to person. As acute care environments are designed to accommodate people with a wide range of backgrounds, finding a design solution that entirely addresses their differences can be impossible.

A changing healthcare sector

Much of the acute care facilities developed in the last 100 years are directly related to care models in vogue at the time the design was conceptualised. Francis (2004) presents five of the more relevant models that link health and design including the 'custodial', 'medical', 'caring', 'holistic' and 'health-promoting' models. Unarguably, these and other care models still directly influence and inform the design of care facilities today.

Another relevant issue that currently impacts on the design of acute care environments is the change in demographics. According to the Office for National Statistics (2014), approximately 15 million people in the UK are aged 60 and above and the number of people aged 100 years or above has reached 15,000 (Office for National Statistics, 2013). As we age, we become more fragile and are prone to develop a range of health-related issues simultaneously. Healing takes longer and our capacity to cope in unfamiliar and stressful environments diminishes. As a result, there has been a shift towards design for older people's needs.

These and other issues to a greater and lesser extent impact the design of acute care environments. In addition to those already mentioned, there is a constant change in organisational care targets as such and the redistribution of care services leading to constant refurbishments and reconfiguration of building layouts. The increase of the population with different cultural backgrounds and the move towards sub-contracting services for the delivery of care in environments created for in-house teams also contributes to changes, as does the increase of c-difficile resistance and the tightening up on infection-control measures. These issues generated a series of themed ideas that address key issues for patients and staff including increased patient control, structured private and social areas and increased building flexibility (Lawson, 2004). These themes are interconnected with unclear boundaries and some of the main ideas are presented in the following.

Patient-centred design

The idea of developing patient-centred facilities is associated with terms such as 'value for money', which seeks to identify the priorities for the development of acute care setting based on patients' needs as identified by the different stakeholder groups (including patients and their families). Initial ideas under this theme were that modern hospitals could not be seen as institutional environments and design became driven by creating an enhanced patient experience, much more related to a hotel-like experience in terms of services and looking homely. Design principles related to this theme aimed at increasing inpatient satisfaction levels and making acute care environments less 'stressful' for those going through difficult times. The use of coordinated colour schemes and neo decade-specific décor in non-clinical communal areas were some of the ideas used to make an environment more patient-centred. Also, programmes mixing single and multiple occupancy and coordinated signage to support wayfinding were part of a patient-centred environment.

Healthcare reconfiguration

At the beginning of the 21st century it became clear that there were threats and challenges in terms of healthcare funding and that the transit of people within hospitals could offer an opportunity to change the configuration of acute care buildings. In an attempt to diminish the running costs of facilities on public pockets, ideas exploring the generation of revenue became more common to the development brief of new healthcare buildings. The new brief would contemplate spaces such as banking, training, cafes and retailing areas that are run by third parties. The incorporation of such ideas was not only incorporated to generate additional revenue but also to give patients and visitors a wider range of things to occupy their time. Clearly, the idea was very well received by the private sector, despite concerns related to the security and safety of patients, visitors and staff.

Service and building design integration

Under the integration theme came the idea that service design impacts on building design and vice versa. As such, co-location and integration of services was sought as a way to positively impact on patients' health, on levels of staff turnover and on care provision. In general, the idea is to understand how healthcare services change through time so as to make the building design more flexible, adaptable and expandable, thus minimising the need for constant refurbishment and reconfiguration whilst also allowing space for decanting activities when unforeseen changes are needed. This idea was of particular relevance at a time when the healthcare system became more centralised and where strategic health authorities would define where and which services would be delivered based on proximity to patients, the need for services and specialisms and the available capacity.

Co-design

Co-design is a process-based idea where the client has a share of direct or indirect responsibility in defining the final product. Within this process, in addition to design expertise, the designer also has the additional role of acting as a facilitator. In general that involves managing stakeholder groups (such as clinical staff, patient groups, heritage, etc.) with regards to their expectations, wishes and needs where the designer works closely with the end users (Bate and Robert, 2006; Sanders and Stappers, 2008). This approach is still widely used in projects where public funding is used for financing the project. Terms that became commonly associated with co-design include 'benefits realisation' and 'fit-for-purpose' facilities.

Information modelling and management

It is not only the design solutions that are changing in the context of healthcare design. The design process as traditionally known has changed considerably in the last decade and more so in the last five years, since the run up for BIM adoption on complex projects (Sebastian, 2011). The possibility of creating a digital model that contains information from the different design, engineering and management disciplines is enhancing our understanding of the interrelationship amongst design solutions. It is fair to say that the engineering disciplines are benefiting more. That is because it is easier to simulate the performance of the physical aspects of the building and its inhabitants than the psychological ones. However, we are not far from a time in which digital models will incorporate intelligent hard and soft information about building occupants.

Therapeutic environments

The idea of therapeutic environments is not new. Ideas around space design and its impact on our healing process can be seen as far back as Hippocrates (400BC). From time to time, these ideas get new insights and, as a result, hospitals gain new configurations. The work of Florence Nightingale (1863), for instance, discussed principles of hospital design and how light and air could improve the healing process. In the 1930s the field of environmental psychology emerged, gaining worldwide momentum in the 1950s and again in the late 1990s and 2000s, giving rise to the dissemination of the evidence-based design (EBD) approach. Amongst the ideas presented, this is the one that still remains strong for many reasons. For Lawson and Phiri (2000), the operational savings resulting from an evidence-based design approach can be in the region of 20 per cent per annum. The design ideas used in therapeutic environments connect the fabric (colour, materials, systems, etc.), the ambient (light, temperature, noise, etc.) and the psychological aspects of spaces (crowd, density, privacy) with healing (Cooper et al., 2008). Several guidance articles, such as CABE (2006), King's Fund (Waller and Finn, 2004; Waller et al., 2013), AEDET, ASPECT and IDEAS (Lawson, 2010; Phiri, 2014), were developed in the UK to support practice. Due to its importance, this theme is discussed in detail in the following sections.

New episteme: shifting to evidence-informed design

Quite convincingly we can think that the idea of therapeutic environments and EBD is the solution for designing acute care settings. We argue here that it can help, but not in the ways most people may think. To explain that, we introduce the general idea of evidence-informed practice, which is used in this section as a derivative of the term evidence-based practice, which in turn is an extension of the idea of evidence-based medicine applied to various fields including management and design. For design, arguably the strength of evidence-based practice is its reliance on the systematic way in which evidence is collected from rigorous scientific reports and incorporated into decision-making in the design process (Malone et al., 2008). Likewise, in medicine this approach has been used to support decisions made between doctors and patients on the best treatment alternative for patients based on individual clinical expertise with the best available external clinical evidence from systematic research (Mulrow, 1994; Sackett et al., 1996). At first sight the idea is so logically rational that it was developed in many other areas such as education (e.g. Reed et al., 2005), economics (e.g. Pignone et al., 2005), management (Tranfield et al., 2003) and design (Malkin, 2008).

For design, EBD is defined as 'a process for the conscientious, explicit, and judicious use of current best evidence from research and practice in making critical decisions, together with an informed client, about the design of each individual and unique project' (Hamilton and Watkins, 2009), 'with the goal of improving outcomes and of continuing to monitor the success or failure for subsequent decision-making' (Malkin, 2008). For Fischl (2006) this approach aims to provide scientific evidence for bridging designers' knowledge gap about humans' social and behavioural attitudes towards the surrounding environment. In this respect, the designer acts as a 'researcher' working as an interpreter in investigating and describing human behaviour needs.

This approach implies a change in the traditional practice of design. Designers are increasingly required to have a considerable amount of expert knowledge that is beyond their own field (Hamilton and Watkins, 2009); for instance, familiarity with multidisciplinary terms. For Hamilton and Watkins, this happens especially because building projects have become more complex as more efficiency and strong links between buildings and services delivered within them are required. Thus, by following this route, it is expected that risks related to design solutions could be reduced up-front once evidence is available to demonstrate the efficiency and effectiveness of tested solutions (CDH, 2008).

In practice, design solutions have to comply with sociotechnical regulations, norms and principles that are put in place after thorough tests have been carried out to set out the standards with which to comply (e.g. norms for health and safety, ergonomics, density, etc.). Such a regulatory system started to be developed in the 1960s by the UK National Health Service (NHS). The NHS developed design guidance for the construction of healthcare environments and, to date, there are approximately 70 health building notes and 240 health technical memoranda that were developed with a basis in evidence and good practice.

Despite the proclaimed importance related to the use of evidence in design, not much can be said about the process steps for its implementation (e.g. Malone et al., 2008; McCullough, 2010; Evans, 2010; Codinhoto et al., 2009). Malone et al. (2008) can be considered the only guidance available, which contains directions for the implementation of EBD through eight process steps: a) the definition of evidence-based goals and objectives; b) the definition of sources providing relevant evidence; c) the critical interpretation of relevant evidence; d) the creation and development of EBD concepts; e) the development of a hypothesis linked to a design proposition; f) the definition and collection of baseline performance measures; g) the monitoring and implementation of the solution within design and construction; and h) the measurement of post-occupancy performance results.

The use of this approach does not come without challenges. As argued in Codinhoto et al. (2009), those unfamiliar with the approach may have difficulties in setting clear aims and objectives. In addition to that, the data source is widespread, fragmented and its compilation and analysis can be confusing due to the different methods used to gather evidence. Also, as highlighted by Lawson (2010), we may want to introduce evidence-based design to our healthcare buildings, but we do not want them to become standardised solutions independent of place, culture and raw creative innovation. However, going through this process is enlightening as it questions the way designers make decisions.

For those willing to use EBD, two activities are very important. First is the systematic compilation, comparison and contrasting of existing evidence through a systematic literature review; second is the development of a method for the collection of empirical evidence after building occupancy. According to Hamilton (2012), EBD currently follows mostly the latter approach and in spite of the added managerial complexity of the design process, it supports the resolution of design trade-offs.

In medicine, the compilation of evidence leads to the development of 'evidence models' that demonstrate multiple cause-effect networks (Mulrow and Cook, 1997). Currently, these

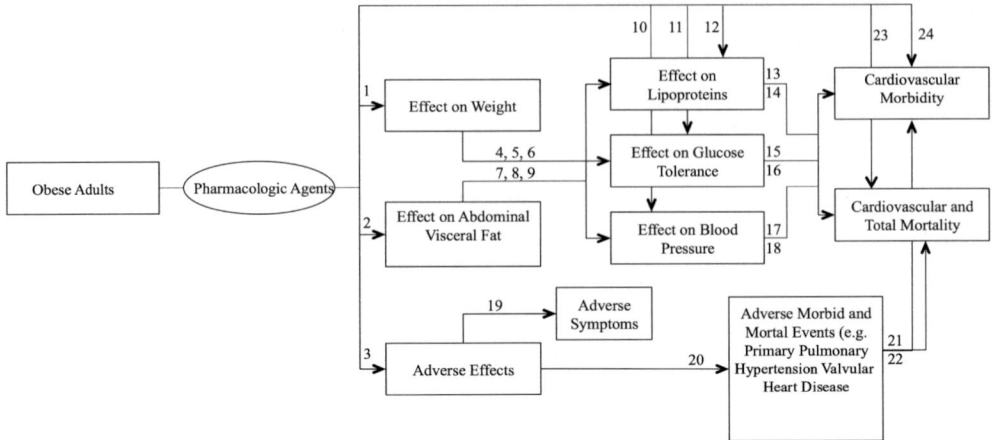

Figure 7.1 An evidence model for the effects of exposure to natural sunlight on older adults

'of the self' models do not exist for design and must be developed by the design team on a case-by-case basis. To illustrate what an evidence model is, Figure 7.1 presents an example developed with a basis on causality and clinically meaningful outcomes relating the built environment and wellbeing. Each arrow represents a possible cause–effect relationship for which research can be conducted (note that the evidence that supports the model is not presented in the links) and only after research is conducted (or found) can the links be confirmed (or disconfirmed) and validated.

In relation to design, the only attempt found that suggests a classification of evidence and a route for incorporating evidence within design is present in the work of Evans (2010). Evans claims that there is a need for proper understanding about how to fill the 'application gap' that links evidence and designing. He suggests revisiting the argument of Hillier et al. (1972) that substitutes the Analysis-Synthesis-Evaluation design process in favour of Popper's Conjecture-Analysis (Bamford, 2002). He then suggests that evidence, to be useful for designers, must be part of 'conjecturing' so as to be used as propositions to support problem finding rather than being used as rules (solutions). However, Evans highlights that the character of evidence generated by science is significantly analytical (too specific) and therefore constitutes a barrier for the implementation of his own suggested approach.

In this respect, Evans' point of view is correct, i.e. design can only be 'informed' rather than 'based' on evidence. Epistemologically, it is impossible to rationally use external evidence from past projects into new ones.[1] The current shift in practice is also aligned with this idea, where studies can generate insights for designers, but the validation of each solution is investigated within its own context, with its own variables and as part of a design composition. In other words, there are difficulties in generalising results as designed environments are the result of compositions created with different material and non-material features that generate space and place. For that reason the term evidence-informed design best represents what can be achieved in practice.

Health, person and place

To provide an in-depth account of all there is that links the built environment and wellbeing in acute care settings would require, perhaps, a whole series of books to discuss the different approaches that there are to investigate this issue. Here, three fundamental aspects are discussed that are relevant: health, place and person.

Health

There are a variety of models, typologies and theories of health and wellbeing out there (e.g. Bergner, 1985; Patrick and Bergner, 1990; Johnson and Wolinsky, 1993). These models tend to consider measures of health and wellbeing based on physical, physiological or psychological outcomes separately. Conversely, Wilson and Cleary (1995) proposed a conceptual model of health-related quality of life, of which the spectrum of outcomes range from biological to psychological aspects. This model has been highly influential in medical research (Ferrans et al., 2005) and as such it is used here as a major reference to the topic. According to Wilson and Cleary (1995), there is a wide spectrum of alternatives for measuring health or the lack of it. They argue that disturbances in health can be perceived at molecular and genetic levels at the one end as well as being broad and subjective measures such as 'feeling well' at the other. According to Wilson and Cleary there are at least five (relevant and practical) different levels of health outcomes: biological and physiological factors; symptoms; functional status; general health perception; and overall quality of life.

Although Wilson and Cleary (1995) argue that molecular and genetic factors are the most fundamental determinants of health status, their model begins with biological and physiological factors because they are more commonly conceptualised, measured and applied in routine clinical practice. Furthermore, in relation to the measurement of health disruption, there are a considerable number of methods and tests for doing so, varying from interviews and the application of questionnaires to patients and their families to highly technological investigations and tests conducted in controlled environments (e.g. blood tests, scans, biopsies, DNA tests, etc.). In addition, Wilson and Cleary argue that there are no clear boundaries between their suggested levels and this is because one level may influence the other. Finally, they argue that health outcomes are influenced by the individuals' characteristics as well as by the characteristics of the surrounding environment.

In this respect, Wilson and Clearly (1995) and Ferrans et al. (2005) consider that the environment has an indirect (rather than direct) impact on patients. For instance, Ferrans et al. consider that characteristics of the environment can be either social or physical. Social characteristics include, for instance, the marital status and interaction between couples. It also includes the social milieu where the patient interacts, such as the specific culture of a haemodialysis clinic, waiting rooms, etc. Physical characteristics, on the other hand, include the distinctive attributes of settings that may influence health outcomes, such as neighbourhood pollution or exercise facilities. According to Wilson and Cleary, 'biological and physiological variables' is the only category that is not affected by the environment and the characteristics of the patient. These authors do not explain why this is. In principle, any health disorder can be captured through Wilson and Cleary's model.

Person

With regards to the person, the number of variables that could possibly characterise patients is considerably large. According to Wilson and Clearly (1995), this is because the characterisation of individuals is also dependent on the health condition of the individual. In this respect, Ferrans et al. (2005) argue that there are four categories of characteristics: (a) demographic; (b) developmental stages; (c) psychological; and (d) biological factors that influence health outcomes, as described below.

We introduce here three other categories to the taxonomy developed by Ferrans et al. (2005) that are related to patients' contextual information: first, the condition of the individual in relation to the intervention to promote health (e.g. pre- and post-operation, during treatment, etc.); second, the type of treatment as related to physical intervention (e.g. surgery), the use of drugs (e.g. chemotherapy, corticoids, etc.) and psychological or psychotherapeutic procedures; and finally, the disease or injury incurred.

In principle, any person can be characterised through this model. However, it is important to highlight that this taxonomy of individuals' characteristics is not exhaustive. For instance, cultural, social and economic characteristics are not included in the model.

Place

The literature about healthcare facilities design (e.g. Kliment, 2000; Miller and Swensson, 2002; Malkin, 2008; Grunden and Hagood, 2012; Purves, 2012; and Clarke, 2012) is, in general, focused on the functional decomposition of the building; for example, by considering main unit areas within hospitals, such as intensive care units (ICUs), maternity, A&E, amongst others. Once each unit is defined as part of the programme, the next step is to define the rooms within each care unit such as wards, waiting areas, examination rooms and so on.

In spite of differences in nomenclature patterns, the presence of one dimension does not necessarily exclude another. In other words, a building type will accommodate many care units that will have within them many settings that are in turn defined by components, furniture and equipment and sub-systems that perform certain functions. At the end of this spectrum there are characteristics that are the minimum elements that ultimately descriptively characterise a space. However, this type of arrangement makes collecting evidence more complex. This is because one characteristic can affect people differently, unless proven otherwise. Thus, collecting evidence for every possible combination of characteristics and settings is almost impossible. Considering this complexity, we propose a classification that includes the specialist type of building (e.g. primary, secondary, tertiary care), care unit (for instance, coronary, A&E, maternity), setting (such as ward, waiting room and operation theatre), component (e.g. wall, celling, door, window), furniture and equipment, sub-systems (for example, air conditioning and ventilation systems) and functions and characteristics (such as colour, texture and light).

We present a health, person and place model that brings together the discussion presented above in Figure 7.2, which summarises the issues that are relevant for the design of acute care facilities when considering an evidence-informed approach. It shows the health outcomes as identified by Wilson and Cleary (1995), the person's characteristics as discussed by Ferrans et al. (2005) and the characterisation of places. In the following section, pieces of evidence are presented to introduce key areas of research linking acute care settings and wellbeing.

What to expect when using evidence to support design

As discussed in the previous section, evidence will appear in all sorts of shapes, sizes and strengths. Anyone attempting to collect evidence will be tempted, soon after starting, to create groups of interconnected findings. The task can be simplified if the designer considers issues related to the scale of observation where the evidence was gathered. The idea of defining a specific setting and finding evidence about design characteristics can help. However, scientific evidence, when presented in the format of systematic reviews such as Devlin and Arneill (2003) and Ulrich et al. (2004, 2008), emphasises specific features such as light, colour,

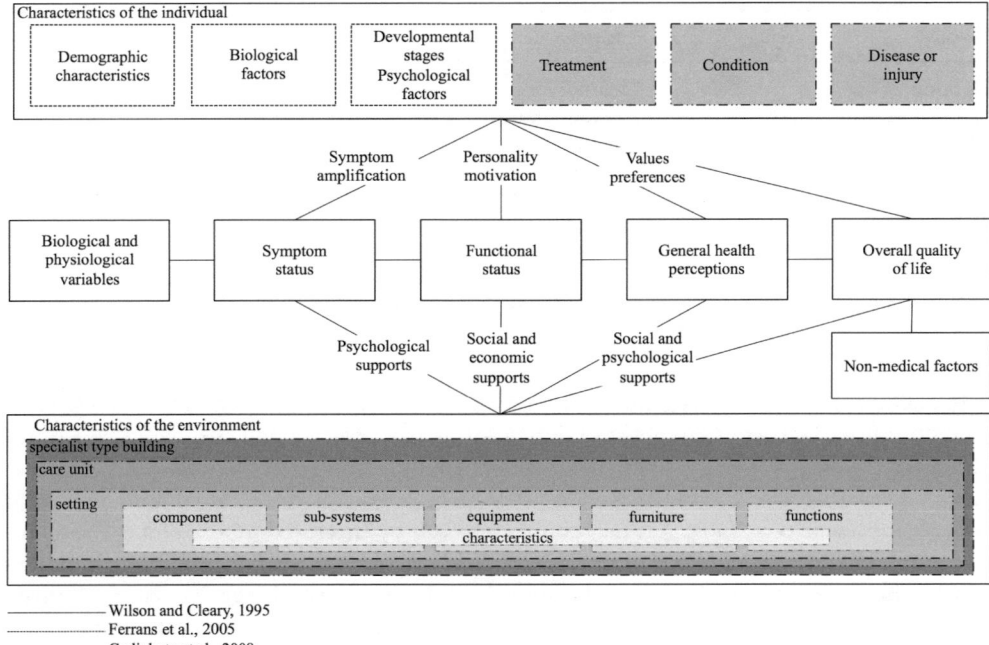

Figure 7.2 Health, person and place model

noise, wayfinding, etc. In this case, the narrative about the functional area investigated is not necessarily always explicit, leading to questions related to generalisation of evidence.

The literature is also rich with regards to the background of the researchers. The subject of built environment and wellbeing has received multidisciplinary attention from designers, architects, artists, engineers, psychologists, environmental psychologists, physicians and nurses, amongst others. Clearly that has led to a large plethora of subjects being explored. In architecture, for instance, considerable attention has been given to design solutions that improve patients' experience (e.g. CABE, 2006; Malkin, 2008). In engineering, research has been focused on the investigation of systems and the improvement of systems' performance (e.g. ventilation, illumination and air conditioning) and how the improvement of these systems affects health and care delivery (e.g. Chow and Yang, 2003).

With regards to impacts on health and wellbeing, the literature brings not just positive, negative and neutral results; some cases also show effects and side effects of the solutions. That is the case when a design solution is analysed in relation to the different outcomes that a single characteristic can produce. This problem was already well described in the seminal Nuffield Provincial Hospitals Trust (NPHT) Report in 1960. According to the NPHT, natural sunlight is a characteristic that may have both a positive and negative impact on wellbeing. On the one hand, it is effective in reducing the levels of *haemolytic streptococci* bacteria, but if the design does not consider the amount of glare generated it may cause discomfort to the patient, therefore leading to falls. Understanding the chain of effects is very important and assembling evidence models assist with a general understanding.

Finally, existing evidence linking the built environment and wellbeing explores different aspects of design. The main dimensions studied include the physical dimension or materiality

Table 7.1 Characteristics and their variants in healthcare facilities

Variables	Variants
Lighting	natural light, artificial light, different types of artificial light
Colour	yellow, orange, red, black, white, blue, green, grey
Pattern	stripes, dots, chequerboard, plain
Textures	smooth, rough, silky
Ventilation	natural ventilation, artificial ventilation
Temperature	cold, hot
Dimension	size, height, width, depth
Material	carpet, copper, steel, aluminium, plastic
Composition	symmetry, balance, rhythm, movement, hierarchy

(e.g. material, colour, texture), the environmental dimension (e.g. temperature, ventilation, dimensions), an aesthetic/composition dimension (e.g. symmetry and balance), a functional dimension of the space (e.g. privacy and maintainability) and a psychological dimension (e.g. crowdedness, secureness, homeliness, etc.). The deployment of these dimensions into their variants is presented in Table 7.1. Each dimension can be measured in different ways, therefore amplifying the possibilities of establishing relationships between the built environment and wellbeing. For Cooper et al. (2008) there are three generic categories that agglutinate these dimensions: the fabric of the environment, the ambience of the environment and the psychological impact of buildings upon humans. The fabric of the environment includes the design and construction of buildings (e.g. floors, walls, doors, ceilings, windows) and the spaces between buildings (e.g. gardens, paving). Consideration should be given to the use of colour (e.g. red, blue, yellow); texture (e.g. rough, smooth, silky); pattern (e.g. checked, stripes, flecks); material (e.g. wood, metal, rubber) and structure (e.g. hard, soft, firm). The ambience of the environment pertains to the surrounding character and atmosphere of the environment. This includes noise (background, white noise, silent, loud, constant); lighting (harsh, stark, mellow, bright, dim); temperature (cold, hot, mild); colour (warm, cool, cheerful, natural, subdued); air quality and ventilation (clear, polluted, dirty, fresh); humidity (damp, dry) and views of nature (natural sunlight). The psychological impacts of the environment are the perceptions of the physical environment and its impact upon individuals such as density (e.g. crowding, desolate); sense of safety or fear; wayfinding (e.g. easy, hard, confusing); accessibility (e.g. difficult, direct, easy, off-putting) and identity (e.g. homely, clinical, institutional, traditional, modern).

Results from systematic reviews (e.g. Ulrich et al., 2004, 2008) show that the range of studies varies considerably from a holistic viewpoint to a reductionist one. Examples of the holistic approach are presented in Qatari and Haran (1999) and Leather et al. (2000). In both studies, specific areas within hospitals were investigated in relation to clients' satisfaction and improved wellbeing. Examples of the reductionist approach can be found in Wilson (1966), Nourse and Welch (1971), Jacobs and Hustmyer, Jr. (1974) and Jacobs and Suess (1975) in relation to the use of colour and its psychological impacts on people within a specific setting and circumstance. Another example can be found in Chow and Yang (2003), who investigated the performance of ventilation systems in relation to temperature control in a non-standard operating room. Chow and Yang concluded that the appropriate ventilation and temperature (in terms of effectiveness in 'washing' bacteria during an operation) might cause discomfort for staff whilst using the space. In addition, it is clear that certain features of the environment are influenced by more than one characteristic. Luminosity within a setting, for instance, can be influenced by the amount of light from natural and/or artificial sources and the colour of the surroundings. In this respect, its perception will also vary: for example, we lose sight capacity with ageing, thus an older person will not perceive the environment in the same way that a younger person does.

Pieces of evidence linking the built environment to wellbeing

A few studies amalgamate a large number of research findings relating the built environment to health and wellbeing. The work of Devlin and Arneill (2003), Ulrich et al. (2004, 2008) and Lawson and Phiri (2005) are amongst those with considerable breadth of work. Here, I do not intend to provide an extensive list of studies, but rather to give examples of research in the area. The list of studies linking the built environment and health outcomes is presented discussing the following individual characteristics within the ambience of the environment: lighting, ventilation, temperature, arts and acoustics. The effects of other environmental variables are also summarised.

In relation to the health outcomes identified, a large proportion is related to psychological disorders as opposed to physical ones. In this respect, the results of the review indicate that outcomes are sought in relation to the presence or reduction of symptoms and improvement of the functional status of the studied groups. In addition, emphasis is placed upon non-medical outputs, such as the overall performance of the care provider in relation to the whole population of patients visiting a particular care institution. In relation to this aspect, results can also be positive or negative. Finally, both positive and negative outcomes (for medical and non-medical categories) can also be measured to different degrees, e.g. relevant or irrelevant to health enhancement or decline.

Lighting

The literature indicates that light (natural or artificial) can be associated directly and indirectly with physical, physiological and psychological health outcomes. In this respect, excessive exposure or lack of exposure to light can have negative impacts on health. Examples of outcomes that are related to light exposure include retinopathy, seasonal affective disorder and melanoma. Conversely, appropriate light exposure is considered to have stimulating properties that affects metabolism and mind. Examples of studies investigating light and its impact on health and wellbeing are presented below:

- Fluorescent light: excessive exposure has been associated with increased risk of developing melanoma in adults (Beral et al., 1982); bright fluorescent light was associated with beneficial effects on seasonal depression. The same effects were not verified on non-seasonal depression (Kripke et al., 1982, 1983; Yerevanian et al., 1986; Kripke, 1998).
- High levels of ambient illumination contribute to the incidence of oxygen-induced retinopathy of premature infants (Glass et al., 1985). Controversially, a study conducted by Ackerman et al. (1989) concluded that there was no difference in the incidence and severity of retinopathy of premature infants. Ackerman et al. (1989) also identified that shielding infants in isolation from incidental lighting has no effect on the development of retinopathy of premature infants.
- Cycled light: exposure was associated with infants' superior rates of weight gain, faster development of the capability of being fed orally and enhanced motor coordination when compared with non-cycled light (Miller et al., 1995).

- Light in intensive care units was associated with variability of patients' sleeping patterns (Richards and Bairnsfather, 1988); low-frequency (red) light waves were associated with less sleep-wake frequency and more sleep thereby contributing to night sleeping. High-frequency (blue) light waves were associated with greater sleep-wake frequency and more waking, thus contributing to day waking or being useful for undesirably sleepy neonates (Girardin, 1992).
- Daylight: exposure to ultra-violet radiation was associated with metabolic stimulation and increased production of Vitamin D (Veitch and McColl, 1993).

Ventilation

Both natural and artificial routes can be used for building ventilation. The literature shows that research related to artificial ventilation and its impact on health outcomes are mainly associated with the dissemination of airborne types of disease. Research about natural ventilation is mainly related to window types and sizes. However, it can be associated with different levels of pressure between adjacent rooms (e.g. bedrooms and corridors). The identified issues are presented below:

- Room pressure: reduction of nosocomial infections through the adoption of negative pressure in settings occupied by infected patients (Anderson et al., 1985); increased risk of airborne bacteria contamination from the surgical team on the patient, and vice versa through the ventilation system (Chow and Yang, 2003).
- Humidifiers: contamination by acremonium kiliense conducted through the humidifier water used in the ventilation system (Fridkin et al., 1996); recommendations for the use of heat and moisture exchangers in patients with acute respiratory failure (Pelosi et al., 1996).
- Combined artificial and natural ventilation system: contamination by staphylococcus aureus (MRSA) (Cotterill et al., 1996); tuberculin conversion among healthcare workers was strongly associated with inadequate ventilation in general patient rooms (Menzies et al., 2000); Charles (2003) presents a compilation of studies looking at comfort generated by the use of localised air distribution systems.

Temperature

The effects of ambient temperature on humans, such as morbidity, stress, cardiovascular and cardiorespiratory episodes are well known. Considering that in hospitals the indoor temperature is expected to be stable, the research in this field is, in general, related to patients' control over ambient temperature rather than the effects of variance in temperature ranges. The literature also demonstrates that there are many parameters that are used to specify the temperature performance of indoor environments that rely on both subjective and objective indicators (Fransson et al., 2007) and these may vary as they are provided by different organisations such as the American Society of Heating, Refrigerating and Air-Conditioning Engineers and the International Standards Organisation. Examples of research related to indoor temperature are presented below.

- Stress: Bell and Green (1982) investigated the impact of temperature on physiological stress; results of the impact of thermal stress is presented in Hickam et al. (2003); Lu and

Zhu (2007) investigated the heat stress and heat tolerance of 148 males. The study proposed physiological limit values at exposure limits.

- Comfort: temperature-related comfort of staff in operation theatres was studied by Chow and Yang (2003) and Hwang et al. (2007).
- Ceiling radiant cooling systems: Nagano and Mochida (2004) investigated the control conditions of ceiling radiant cooling systems and concluded that some measures and parameters that have been used in design should be reviewed.
- The dissemination of waterborne infections due to warm temperature conditions is presented in Joseph (2006).

Acoustics

The investigation of acoustics characteristics is mainly related to noise and its effects on health. In general, noise is associated mainly with sleeplessness and stress. The root causes of noise varies and it is associated with the operation of machines, equipment and tools, staff conversation and transportation of equipment within the facility (Christensen, 2004). It was found that music and music therapy (e.g. Cabrera and Lee, 2000; Devlin and Arneill, 2003; Ikonomidou et al., 2004; CABE and PricewaterhouseCoopers, 2004) have the potential to enhance wellbeing. A review of research within this topic is presented by Konkani and Oakley (2012). Other examples of research include:

- Comfort and recovery: noise disturbance produced by the operation of the facility negatively impacting on patients' comfort and recovery (Bayo et al., 1995); Allaouchiche et al. (2002) found that noise levels above 40 dB does not affect post-anaesthetic patients' comfort.
- Stress: noise produced by the operation of the facility was associated with stress (Topf, 2000; Topf and Thompson, 2001); nurses' increased levels of stress due to noise were found by Morrison et al. (2003). Noise levels were measured in ICU units by Christensen (2007).
- Psycho-physiological effects (e.g. decreased wound healing, sleep deprivation and cardiovascular stimulation): Christensen (2004) investigated excessive noise generated by building occupancy (staff, patients and visitors) and found a correlation between an increased number of people and substantial noise increase. Noise produced by the operation of the facility was associated with sleep disturbance (Richards and Bairnsfather, 1988; Haddock, 1994; Topf et al., 1996; Ersser et al., 2001); noise levels above the international recommendations were found in operating theatres. The measured noise levels exceed the thresholds to produce noise-induced cardiovascular and endocrine effects (Liu and Tan, 2000).
- Patient experience: noise produced by the operation of the facility was associated with patients' bad experience of healthcare service (Douglas and Douglas, 2005).

Art

Art and mental health have been investigated from a myriad of perspectives. These include the use of music with particular attention paid to different types of instruments; the use of live, video or recorded performances; drawings and paintings; and traditional and contemporary art (Staricoff, 2004). The existing literature also distinguishes between art therapy (i.e. the effect of actively getting involved in the development of art work) and the passive exposure to art in specific environments within healthcare settings (Daykin and Byrne, 2006). These authors argue that few controlled and randomised studies of the therapeutic effects of art in mental health have been carried out. Literature reviews specifically looking at art and mental health include ones by Staricoff et al. (2003), Staricoff (2004) and Daykin and Byrne (2006). Other reviews, such as Devlin and Arneill (2003) and Ulrich et al. (2004) also consider the impacts of art on health; however, these reviews are focused on the impact of the physical environment (rather than the built environment) on health. Art and health-related investigations are presented in the following:

- Mental health conditions: a study conducted by Ulrich (1992) revealed that inappropriate visual art styles are related to the disturbance of mental health conditions; according to Philipp et al. (2002), the arts can help mitigate mental health conditions, such as depression, anxiety and low self-esteem. For Philipp et al., art also supports the improvement of social integration and isolation. There is a diverse range of art activities that are incorporated into the study of art and mental healthcare.
- Stress: Mornhinweg (1992) found a significant reduction of stress levels by using patients' pre-selected music in the background; Biley's research (2000) indicates positive (but inconsistent) changes in physiological variables measured; Gerdner (2000) showed that classical music impacts positively in the reduction of levels of agitation of patients with Alzheimer's disease; McGarry and Prince (1998) and Körlin et al. (2000) argue that creative arts programmes induce significant improvements in the communication of psychiatric patients.
- Pain relief: results presented in Onieva-Zafra et al. (2013) show a correlation between pain reduction and music therapy. Gutgsell et al. (2013) observed a similar relationship for patients undergoing palliative care and Vaajoki et al. (2012) for post-surgery patients.
- Research results presented in literature reviews, such as Staricoff (2004) and Daykin and Byrne (2006), suggest that the arts can have a therapeutic effect on people suffering with mental disorders. However, Staricoff (2004) draws attention to the fact that the introduction of creative arts, such as dance, drama, music, visual arts and creative writing in mental health can also bring with them potential risk factors. These are associated with the psychological effects of being engaged in these activities, which could become too demanding for the patient (Staricoff, 2004).

Colour

There are different assumptions about how colour affects humans (Dalke et al., 2006). For instance, there is anecdotal evidence speculating that red, orange and yellow in shiny and polished surfaces stimulate appetite and anxiety (this would explain why these colours are very often used by fast-food chains). Grey, purple and red have been associated with depression and are excluded from the palette of colours of designers designing hospices and psychiatric hospitals. Some other examples of studies about colour and health are presented below:

- Physiological effects (e.g. respiration and heart rate): the study about the effects of red, yellow, green and blue concluded that there is no significant effect of these colours on respiration rates (Jacob and Hustmyer, 1974).
- Anxiety and stress: the study about the effects of red, yellow, green and blue (in non-healthcare environments) concluded that red and yellow can be associated with high levels of anxiety and that blue and green can be associated with low levels of anxiety (Jacobs

and Suess, 1975; Rabin, 1981; Steffes and Thralow, 1985; Edge, 2003; Connellan et al., 2013); the effects of colour on stress and arousal levels in healthcare environments is also discussed by Dijkstra et al. (2006).

- General studies on colour: Etnier and Hardy (1997) studied colour influence on the performance of mentally and physically demanding tasks; Kaya and Crosby (2006) investigated individuals' colour associations with different building types; the effects of colour in hospital design are discussed in Dalke et al. (2006).

Layout

The layout of a setting within acute care facilities is another aspect that affects the way humans behave in general (Zimring et al., 2005), and specifically the way patients and staff react to the environment (e.g. Leather et al., 2003). There are several aspects associated with the layout of the facility or the setting under investigation (Lawson and Phiri, 2005). Privacy seems to be one of the most investigated features, which has been mainly associated with occupancy. There are a variety of studies stating that single-occupancy bedrooms increase privacy and, therefore, it is better for patients and staff because it reduces noise levels and consequently improves sleep rates and reduces stress and the risk of infection. However, anecdotal evidence indicates that single-occupancy rooms are not preferred by patients aged above 45 years of age with a working- and middle-class background. Examples of studies looking at these issues include:

- Occupancy and privacy: Evans and McCoy (1998) and Altimier (2004) associate occupancy and privacy with the development of the social environment, which is relevant to patients' recovery; Grosenick and Hatmaker (2000) associate privacy as one important building characteristic to be considered in the treatment of substance abuse; Chaudhury et al. (2005) present a review of the advantages and disadvantages of adopting single- and multiple-occupancy bedrooms. Improved healthcare experience associated with privacy and occupancy is presented by Douglas and Douglas (2004, 2005).
- Wayfinding: O'Neill (1991) and Passini et al. (2000) explore layout and wayfinding in a nursing home for advanced dementia of the Alzheimer's type; Baskaya et al. (2004); Rooke et al. (2009) and Rooke (2012) discuss this aspect of how the knowledge embedded in objects in healthcare settings support wayfinding.
- Social interaction: whilst providing spaces for privacy is relevant, of great importance is also the provision of spaces for social interaction. This issue is explored in the work of Hair (1998), Fottler et al. (2000), Douglas and Douglas (2004) and Rollins (2009).

Gardens and other green spaces

Finally, positive health outcomes are perceived as related to the exposure of, or having access to, gardens and other green spaces. Some of the outcomes include the reduction of stress and levels of anxiety, increased social interaction and an improved healthcare experience. Researchers looking at this issue include arguably Ulrich (1981, 1984, 1992); Ulrich et al. (2004, 2008); Marcus and Barnes (1999); Marcus (2000); Kaplan (2001); Whitehouse et al. (2001); and Milligan et al. (2004). The incorporation of garden spaces within hospitals has increased in the UK as an alternative to the creation of meaningful activities that keep patients (particularly older patients with dementia) occupied whilst in contact with nature (Söderback et al., 2004). Access to nature is a subject that in 2015 began to gaining momentum again and

Figure 7.3 Royal Sussex County Hospital complex before redevelopment in 2014
Source: 3Ts Hospital and BDP

new evidence related to the impact of accessing nature within hospitals or in our daily lives is expected to emerge.

Practical implementation at Brighton's 3Ts

To conclude this chapter, a case still under development in the UK is presented and by contrasting current versus enhanced design we aim to illustrate the direction for architectural design of acute care settings.

Over the past eight years I have been following the redevelopment of the Brighton and Sussex University Hospitals, for ease referred to from henceforth as 3Ts (for teaching, trauma and tertiary care). The 3Ts hospital is currently an acute teaching hospital working across two sites: the Royal Sussex County Hospital in Brighton and the Princess Royal Hospital in Haywards Heath. The project redevelopment is focused on the Royal Sussex site. Figure 7.3 depicts the current complex with a wide range of buildings, located in central Brighton. The tall buildings in the centre as well as the smaller ones in front of them constitute a rather fragmented hospital complex which imposes difficulties of navigation for patients, staff and visitors and inadequacies of space provision to accommodate patients and current and state-of-the-art equipment.

Current facilities

The redevelopment of the 3Ts hospital is needed for many reasons. The main existing buildings were built nearly 200 years ago (Barry Building was built in 1828 before guidance on hospital design from Florence Nightingale was available). Currently the wards and other clinical and public areas are inadequate and not fit for the delivery of a multitude of care services such as treatment for cancer, infectious diseases and HIV, imaging and cardiac investigations. Changes in technology have also had an impact. Large-size imaging machines simply do not fit in spaces that were not designed for them. More complex is the fact that trauma and neuroscience services are located in different buildings that are considerably far from away each other. This means that currently a person with serious body and head injuries cannot be treated in the 3Ts hospital. In the following, issues demonstrating the need for the redevelopment are presented.

Parking at the 3Ts complex is situated in a central area of Brighton and spaces are less than ideal with regard to allowing easy wayfinding to the main entrances in the case of emergency. As shown in Figures 7.4 and 7.5 there is no control regarding available spaces near the entrances. This type of configuration is commonplace and a cause of distress for patients and families trying to access care services. There is no single entrance to the many buildings and finding a parking space in a moment of emergency is considerably challenging and can consume critical time to care.

Reception areas are the first place patients will look for to gather information regarding their appointment. Figure 7.6 shows an example of a reception desk area that is not fit for purpose, as it does not allow conversations between staff and patients in wheelchairs. Also, the signage hanging from the ceiling is not at sight level for older people and there is no place for confidential conversations.

The main issues with the *examination rooms* are related to clutter from non-integrated equipment. As technology has developed through time, different pieces of kit have been incorporated to clinical spaces in an ad hoc manner (Figures 7.7 and 7.8).

In the past, *wards* used to be open spaces with a series of beds separated, or not, by small barriers such as curtains. Currently, this model does not provide for today's demands of privacy,

Figure 7.4 Current car parking
Source: 3Ts Hospital and BDP

Figure 7.5 Current car parking
Source: 3Ts Hospital and BDP

Figure 7.6 Current reception desk
Source: 3Ts Hospital and BDP

Figure 7.7 Examination room
Source: 3Ts Hospital and BDP

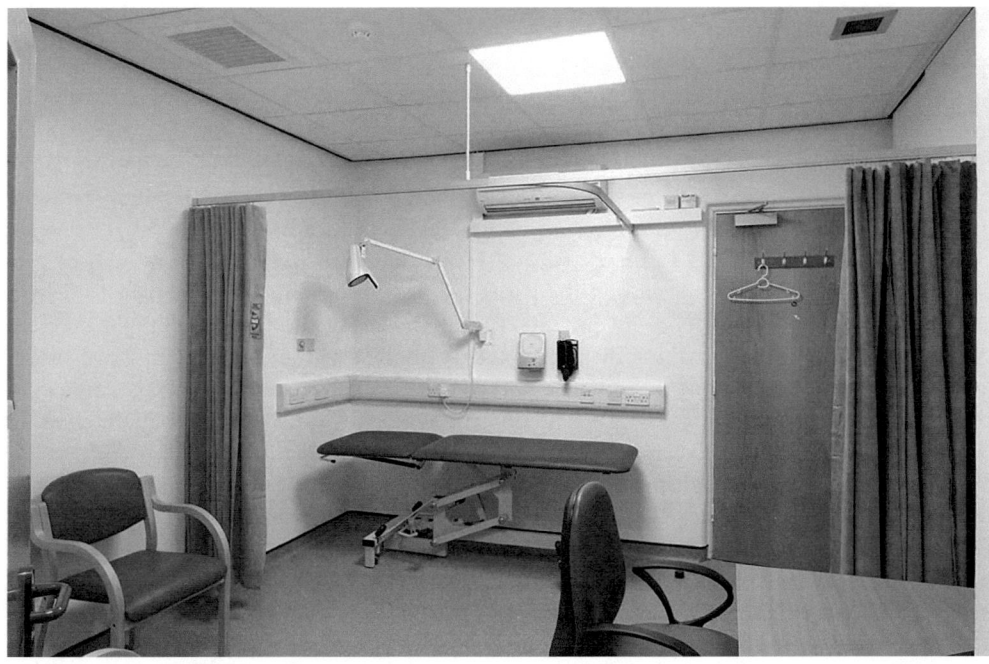

Figure 7.8 Examination area
Source: 3Ts Hospital and BDP

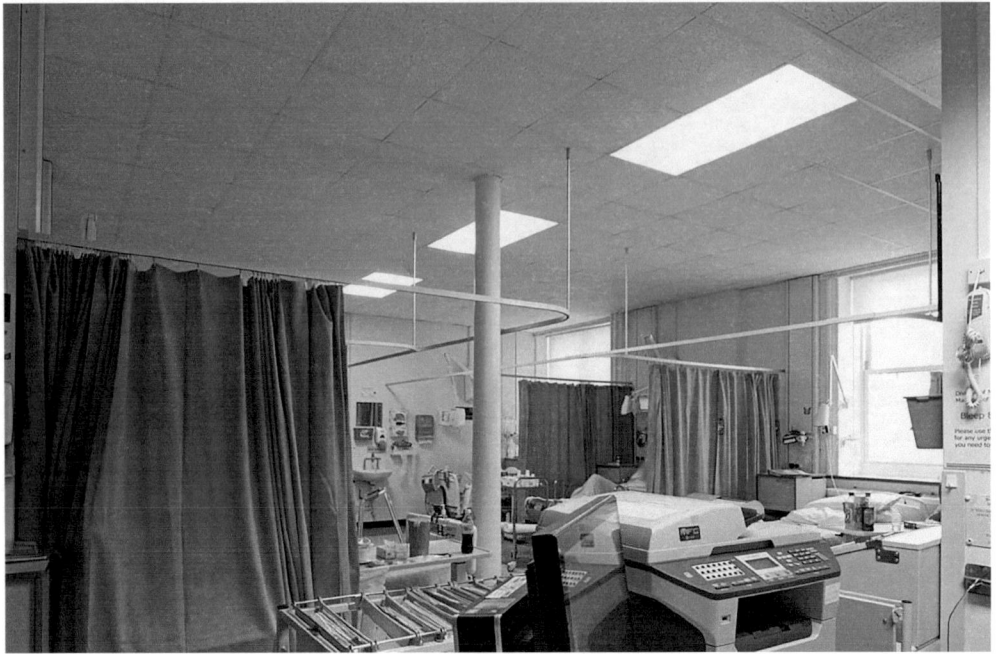

Figure 7.9 Current ward overview
Source: 3Ts Hospital and BDP

dignity and infection control. The small size of wards and the amount of equipment used in modern care makes the space cluttered, thus creating difficulties for maintaining good infection-control practice. Less than 5 per cent of the beds in the Barry Building are in single rooms and the number of toilets per person is below modern standards (Figures 7.9 and 7.10). The space available for staff to perform services (such a bathing patients or simply moving patients within their beds) is below current national standards for manoeuvre.

The same principles apply to *single-occupancy rooms*. New medical kits became part of care delivery and this led to clutter around the patient, thus causing difficulties for staff to deliver care. Patients often feel insecure in moving around and using the toilet facilities. There are very few opportunities for making the room more homelike with personal belongings (assisting those with mental impairment – dementia) and the similarity across all rooms can lead to confusion. Despite some access to natural light, the windows located up near the ceiling do not allow patient control of the environment (Figures 7.11 and 7.12).

Nursing stations are located in areas that do not allow easy observation of patients within different wards. The areas are cluttered with equipment and information (Figures 7.13 and 7.14). The spaces are not the result of carefully thought-out design, but rather the consequence of constant changes happening throughout the years such as the increase of the number of patients and staff.

Corridors are endless and repetitive. Accumulated clutter and information is randomly displayed along patient routes, not considering the appropriate levels of information along the patient route. Natural light is minimal or non-existent in these environments (Figures 7.15 and 7.16).

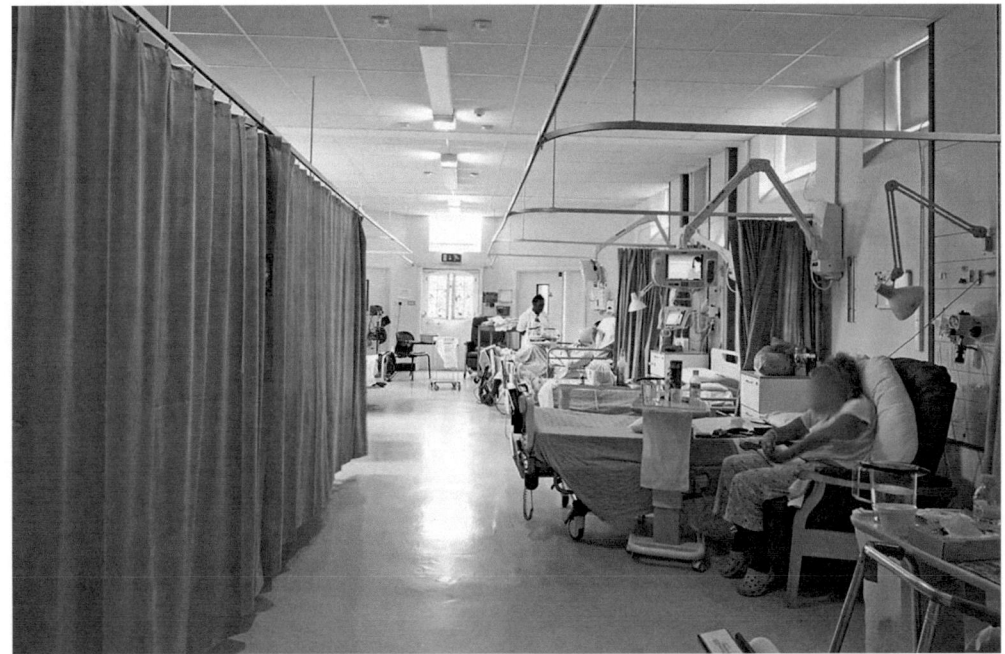

Figure 7.10 Current ward layout
Source: 3Ts Hospital and BDP

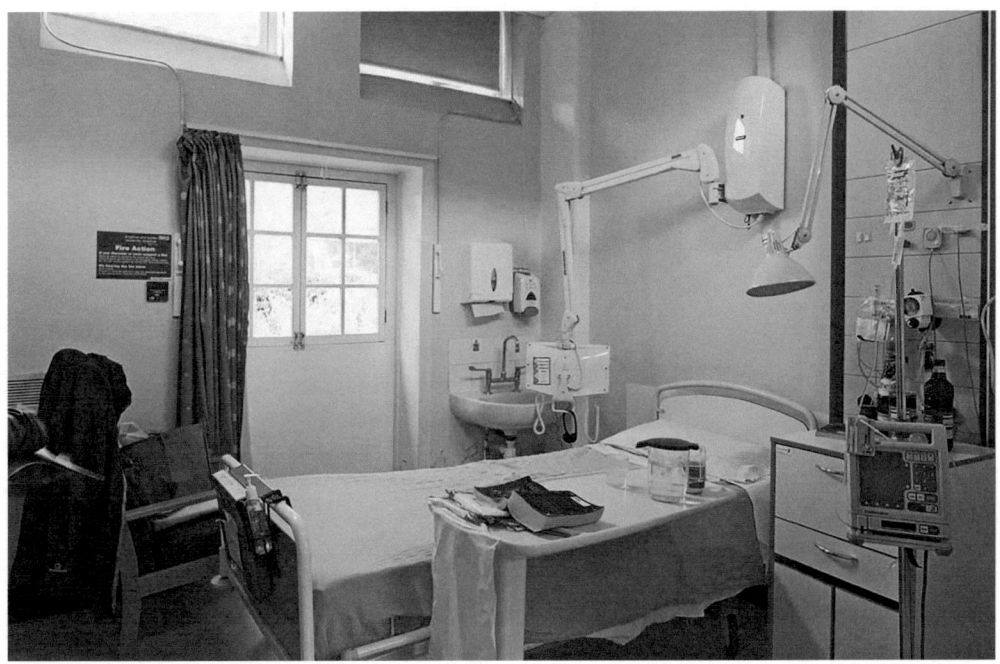

Figure 7.11 Single bedroom
Source: 3Ts Hospital and BDP

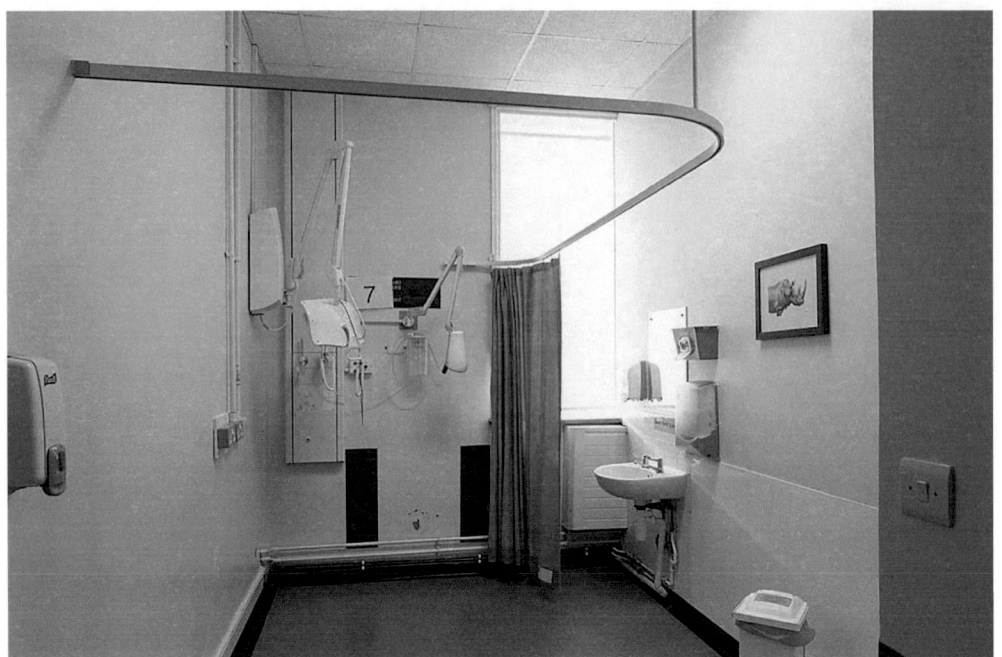

Figure 7.12 En suite shower room
Source: 3Ts Hospital and BDP

Figure 7.13 Nursing station – corridor
Source: 3Ts Hospital and BDP

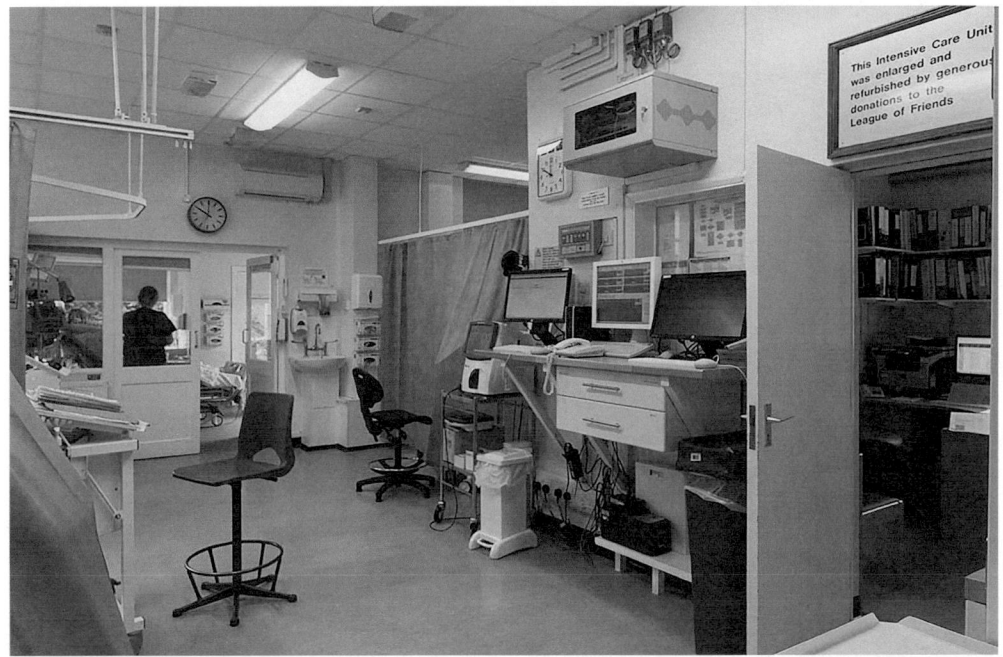

Figure 7.14 Nursing station – ward
Source: 3Ts Hospital and BDP

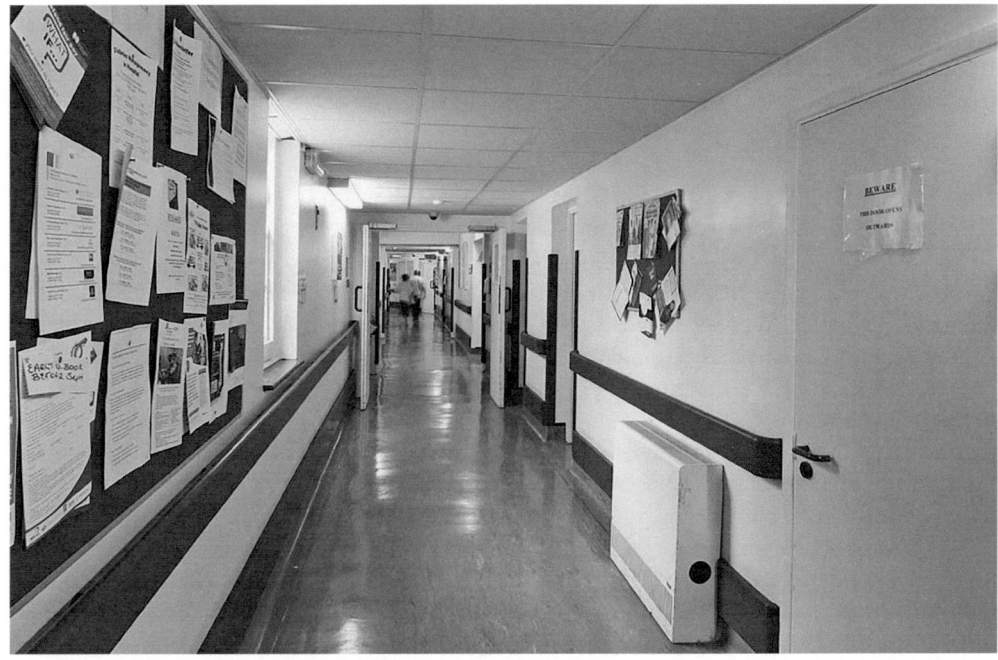

Figure 7.15 Information within corridors
Source: 3Ts Hospital and BDP

Figure 7.16 Clutter within corridors
Source: 3Ts Hospital and BDP

Access points and circulation pathways are not ideal with regards to manoeuvrability and pedestrian zones are located adjacent to traffic areas (Figures 7.17 and 7.18). Attention that should be concentrated on patients during transportation has to be shared with distracting factors such as traffic.

The redevelopment

The redevelopment is much needed for bringing the quality of care delivery up to 21st-century standards (Figure 7.19). The design started with the redefinition of services to be delivered and its location. The new development will have 361 beds of which 75 per cent will be single, en suite rooms and the remaining 25 per cent in single-gender four-bed bays. The Centre for Neurosciences (currently on a split site) will be relocated alongside key emergency services, thus avoiding the transfer of patients to already busy hospitals located in the London area. The capability of services will also be expanded for most services, such as cancer treatment with increased capacity of chemotherapy and radiotherapy services and beds on the oncology ward.

The trauma centre will have a landing pad for emergency cases that together with the neurosciences centre will allow more patients to be treated nearer to home. The redevelopment will provide state-of-the-art teaching, training and research facilities, including a simulation suite for training. All these, and many other changes are necessary and will promote a positive step change in care delivery. The main ward area (the three blocks located on the right side) has been designed to allow more rooms to benefit from outdoor (sea) views and to maximise the use of natural light inside the wards.

Figure 7.17 Access point
Source: 3Ts Hospital and BDP

Figure 7.18 Access point
Source: 3Ts Hospital and BDP

Figure 7.19 New proposed development
Source: 3Ts Hospital and BDP

Parking will be located in a colour-coded multistorey car park with direct access to key areas (Figure 7.20), thus facilitating immediate access to the building. It is not only parking that has been thought through. Patients arriving through other means of transportation (taxi or foot) will be able to easily identify the key access areas to the hospital. External elements of the design were also included to diminish the speed of the wind on the external ground floor and to support easy access to the building. Drop-off areas were designed so people can be collected without impacting on the main flows within the hospital.

Receptions have been redesigned to be inclusive and to allow for privacy when required (Figure 7.21). The space has been designed to accommodate people at peak times and control measures (light and ventilation) were introduced for times when the space in less occupied.

Examination rooms have been designed to incorporate state-of-the-art equipment thus avoiding clutter in the room (Figure 7.22). The space will be fully equipped with washing basins for hand-washing and storage for examination kits.

Ward design is the one that benefited most from the redevelopment. The wards are flooded with natural light and there is adequate space for patients and staff to move around without clutter. The number of bays (four per ward) also helps to reduce noise and whilst it is still a shared space, privacy can be obtained by using the curtain system. The path to the toilet is visible from all beds thereby encouraging patients to use the facilities (Figure 7.23).

Single-occupancy rooms have considered a plenitude of issues such as colour-coded schemes to help patients with wayfinding. Much of the new equipment will be wall-mounted, thus avoiding clutter and the risk of accidents in the room. There will be areas for long-stay patients

Figure 7.20 New designated parking
Source: 3Ts Hospital and BDP

Figure 7.21 New universal reception
Source: 3Ts Hospital and BDP

to bring in personal belongings (Figure 7.24). Enough space is provided for visitors and volunteers to stay with the patient.

Corridors have been reconsidered to maximise the use of natural sunlight and minimum clutter. Support handles will be available in areas where patients may need support for walking. In addition, different colour schemes will be used to facilitate navigation and wayfinding (Figures 7.25 and 7.26).

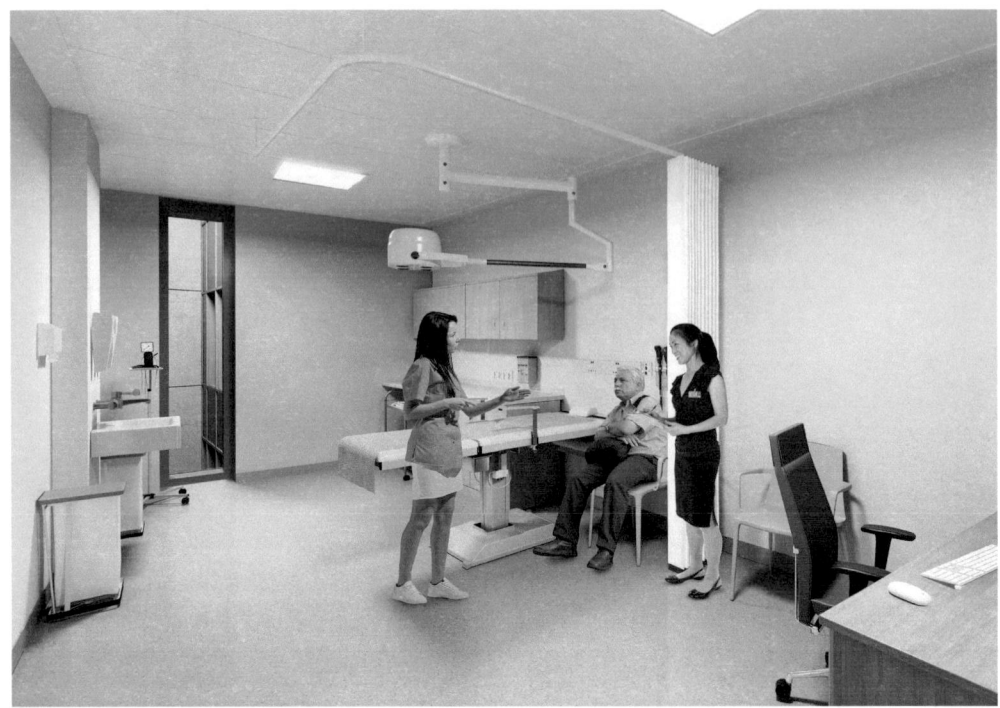

Figure 7.22 Reconfigured exam rooms
Source: 3Ts Hospital and BDP

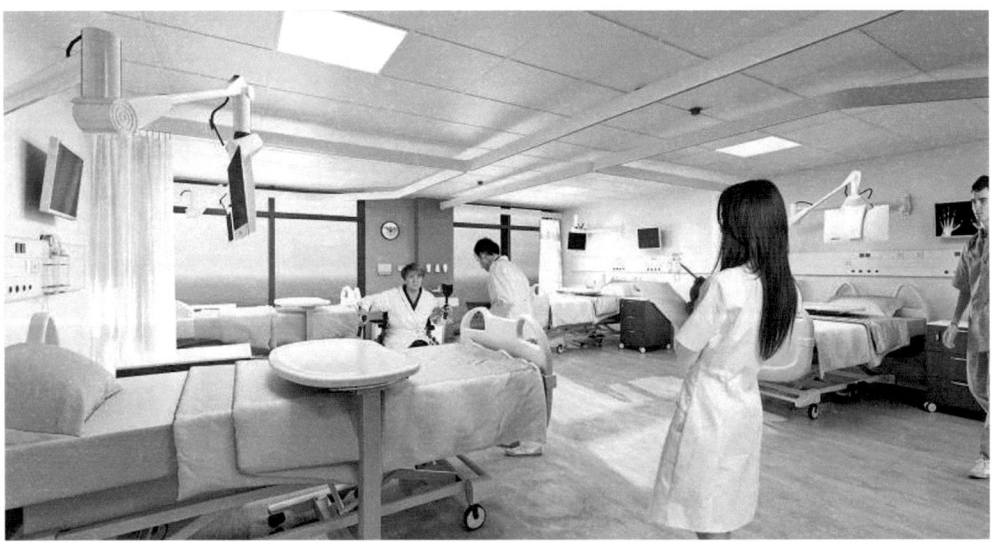

Figure 7.23 Four–bed bay wards with outdoor views
Source: 3Ts Hospital and BDP

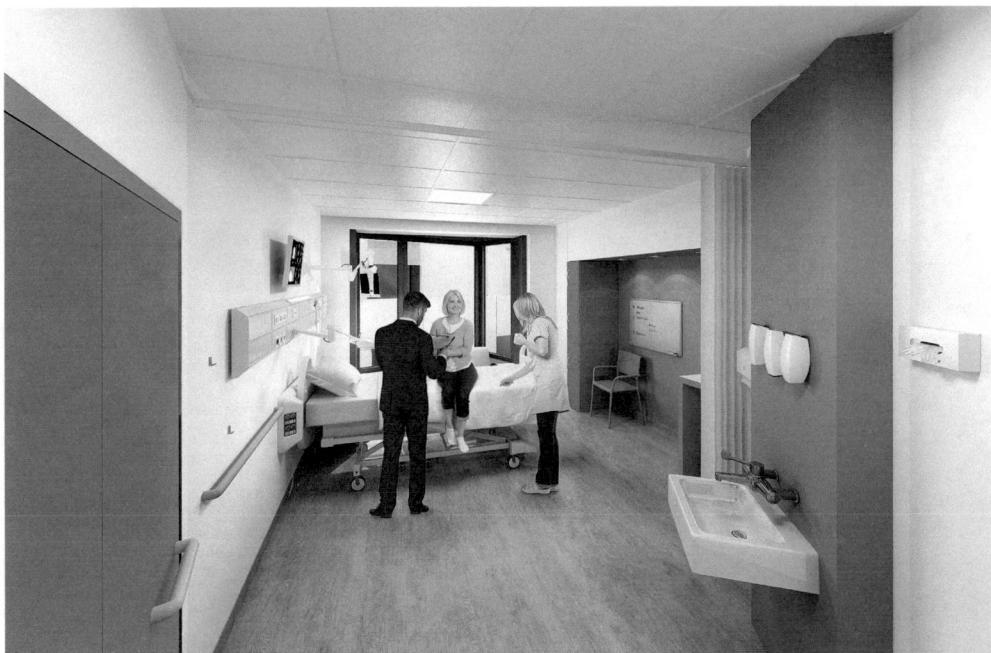

Figure 7.24 Single-occupancy rooms
Source: 3Ts Hospital and BDP

Spaces for social interaction and meaningful activities were included in the design programme. These areas will allow the less vulnerable to socially engage in activities and avoid boredom. These spaces will also be available for staff break-out sessions (Figures 7.27, 7.28 and 7.29).

Spaces for meditation were considered in the project. The space, a multifaith area, should provide privacy for those grieving or looking to meditate and pray (Figure 7.30).

Access to views and nature were created through a roof garden that also benefits from sea views. The garden was designed following principles of design for people with dementia and should support the delivery of care for these patients. The rooftop will be seen from the existing children's hospital, thus also benefiting neighbouring buildings (Figure 7.31).

Patient–public design panel

The design process of the 3Ts hospital had large consultation and participation of the general public. The project director focused on the benefits-realisation process and identified the key changes that were necessary to the trust, both before and throughout the design process. Public engagement was considerably high and wishes and needs accommodated whenever possible. The building is definitely designed for its local public. The idea of evidence-informed design was also implemented and used for issues that caused controversy. An example of such issues is the adoption of open-plan offices to relocate clinical staff. Anecdotal and scientific evidence were sought to show that open-plan offices, when designed with consideration, can lead to increased exchange of multidisciplinary information, a better working environment considering that all rooms will have access to light and rooms for private and confidential

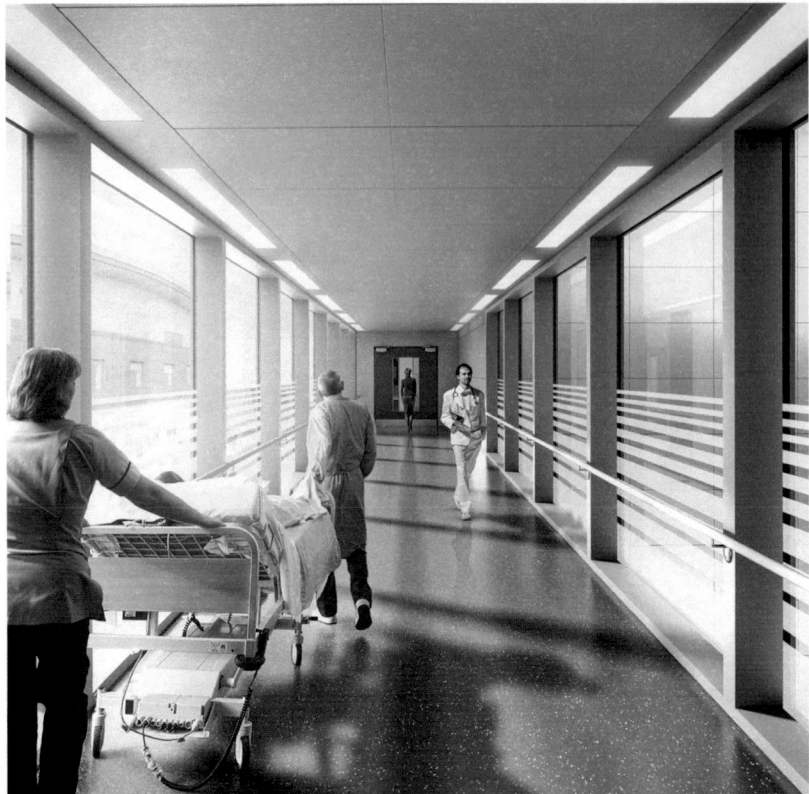

Figure 7.25 Corridor with natural light
Source: 3Ts Hospital and BDP

conversations will be available whenever needed. The building should improve considerably the delivery of care whilst also achieving high standards of sustainability and reduced running costs that were simulated up-front. Issues identified that impacted on service provision and running costs (either service design or building configuration) were dealt with in advance so as to make the scheme a benchmark for care delivery at the same time as being affordable to the trust.

Final remarks

This chapter started with the intention of discussing how architecture contributes to enhanced health and wellbeing. The theoretical arguments developed to date show that when designing, it is essential to consider how people experience the environment in situations of stress related to a lack of health or wellbeing. Within this context, designers must assess ambient characteristics such as noise, light, temperature and information embedded within design that can diminish or exacerbate levels of stress and anxiety. It is also evident that social interaction is part of the healing process and that acute care services and facilities must be configured in such a way as to provide for social interaction without excluding individuality and privacy.

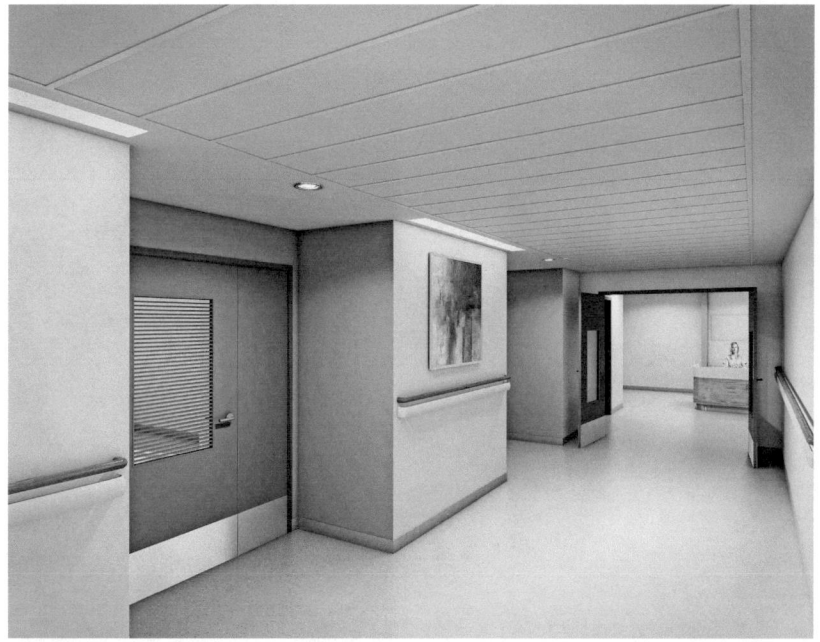

Figure 7.26 Colour-coded corridors
Source: 3Ts Hospital and BDP

Figure 7.27 Multipurpose foyer
Source: 3Ts Hospital and BDP

Figure 7.28 Multipurpose foyer
Source: 3Ts Hospital and BDP

Figure 7.29 Break-out coffee area
Source: 3Ts Hospital and BDP

Figure 7.30 Multifaith area
Source: 3Ts Hospital and BDP

Figure 7.31 Roof garden with sea view
Source: 3Ts Hospital and BDP

Finally, it is clear that there is no solution that fits all in such large and complex buildings, taking into consideration that individual cultural and social backgrounds influence the way people interact with and within their environment.

In practical terms, it is clear that from time to time new approaches to design emerge. This chapter placed emphasis on evidence-informed design and how designers can learn from the evidence that is available. The role of the designer is, to a greater extent, to have a deep understanding of design context and to lessons drawn from evidence that can be merged into new ideas. Finally, perhaps the most important lesson that can be learnt from the 3Ts hospital development is that place-making is central to acute care design. In order for healthcare environments to develop into truthfully healing environments they should be a representation of a popular social expression. The design must focus on people and be designed in collaboration with the people that will benefit from the new environment. There is no space for soulless institutional, factory-like buildings. The lack of health and wellbeing is the primary reason why acute care settings are designed and as such they should be designed to celebrate life through living.

Acknowledgements

The development of this chapter would not have been possible without the support of Professor Duane Passman (3Ts Hospital); Benedict Zucchi and Neil Cadenhead (BDP) and Lindsay McCluskey and Janice McGrory (Salford Royal Foundation Trust), who provided insight and expertise that greatly assisted the research.

Note

1 A thorough justification for this statement is presented in Codinhoto (2013).

References

Ackerman, B., Sherwonit, E. and Williams, J. (1989) Reduced incidental light exposure: Effect on the development of retinopathy of prematurity in low birth weight infants. *Pediatrics*, 83(6): 958–62.
Allaouchiche, B., Duflo, F., Debon, R., Bergeret, A. and Chassard, D. (2002) Noise in the postanaesthesia care unit. *British Journal of Anaesthesia*, 88(3): 369–73.
Altimier, L.B. (2004) Healing environments: For patients and providers. *Newborn and Infant Nursing Reviews*, 4(2): 89–92.
Altman, I. (1993) Dialectics, physical environments, and personal relationships. *Communications Monographs*, 60(1): 26–34.
Anderson, C.A. (1989) Temperature and aggression: Ubiquitous effects of heat on occurrence of human violence. *Psychological Bulletin*, 106(1): 74.
Anderson, J.D., Bonner, M., Scheifele, D.W. and Schneider, B.C. (1985) Lack of nosocomial spread of Varicella in a pediatric hospital with negative pressure ventilated patient rooms. *Infect Control*, 6(3): 120–1.
Bamford, G. (2002) From analysis/synthesis to conjecture/analysis: A review of Karl Popper's influence on design methodology in architecture. *Design Studies*, 23(3): 245–61.
Baskaya, A., Wilson, C. and Özcan, Y.Z. (2004) Wayfinding in an unfamiliar environment different spatial settings of two polyclinics. *Environment and Behavior*, 36(6): 839–67.
Bate, P. and Robert, G. (2006) Experience-based design: From redesigning the system around the patient to co-designing services with the patient. *Quality and Safety in Health Care*, 15(5): 307–10.
Baum, A. and Fleming, I. (1993) Implications of psychological research on stress and technological accidents. *American Psychologist* 48(6): 665–7.

Baum, A., O'Keeffe, M.K. and Davidson, L.M. (1990) Acute stressors and chronic response: The case of traumatic stress. *Journal of Applied Social Psychology*, 20(20): 1643–54.

Bayo, M.V., García, A.M. and García, A. (1995) Noise levels in an urban hospital and workers' subjective responses. *Archives of Environmental Health: An International Journal*, 50(3): 247–51.

Bell, P.A. (1992) In defense of the negative affect escape model of heat and aggression. *Psychological Bulletin* 111, 342–46.

Bell, P.A. and Green, T.C. (1982) Thermal stress: Physiological, comfort, performance, and social effects of hot and cold environments. *Environmental Stress*: 75–104.

Beral, V., Shaw, H., Evans, S. and Milton, G. (1982) Malignant melanoma and exposure to fluorescent lighting at work. *Lancet*, 320(8293): 290–3.

Bergner, M. (1985) Measurement of health status. *Medical Care*, 23(5): 696–704.

Biley, F.C. (2000) The effects on patient well-being of music listening as a nursing intervention: A review of the literature. *Journal of Clinical Nursing*, 9(5): 668–77.

Biner, P.M., Butler, D.L., Fischer, A.R. and Westergren, A.J. (1989) An arousal optimization model of lighting level preferences: An interaction of social situation and task demands. *Environment and Behavior*, 21(1): 3–16.

Block, L.K. and Stokes, G.S. (1989) Performance and satisfaction in private versus nonprivate work settings. *Environment and Behavior*, 21: 277–97.

Brown, B.B. (1992) The ecology of privacy and mood in a shared living group. *Journal of Environmental Psychology*, 12(1): 5–20.

Brown, B.B., Altman, I. and Werner, C.W. (1992) Close relationships in the physical and social world: Dialectic and transactional analyses, in Deetz, S. (ed.), *Communication Yearbook*. Newbury Park, CA: Sage, 509–22.

CABE (2006) Designed with care: Design and neighbourhood healthcare buildings. Available at: http:// webarchive.nationalarchives.gov.uk/20110118095356/ and www.cabe.org.uk/files/designed-with-care.pdf.

CABE and PricewaterhouseCoopers (2004) The role of hospital design in the recruitment, retention and performance of NHS nurses in England.

Cabrera, I.N. and Lee, M.H. (2000) Reducing noise pollution in the hospital setting by establishing a department of sound: A survey of recent research on the effects of noise and music in health care. *Preventive Medicine*, 30(4): 339–45.

Charles, K.E. (2003) A review of occupant responses to localized air distribution systems. *Proceedings: Healthy Buildings*: 304–10.

Chaudhury, H., Mahmood, A. and Valente, M. (2005) Advantages and disadvantages of single versus multiple-occupancy rooms in acute care environments: A review and analysis of the literature. *Environment and Behavior*, 37(6): 760–86.

CHD (2008) Evidence-based design accreditation and certification. Centre for Health Design. Available at: www.healthdesign.org/certification-outreach/edac.

Chow, T.T. and Yang, X.Y. (2003) Performance of ventilation system in a non-standard operating room. *Building and Environment*, 38(12): 1401–11.

Christensen, M. (2004) Noise levels in a general surgical ward: A descriptive study. *Journal of Clinical Nursing*, 14: 156–64.

Christensen, M. (2007) Noise levels in a general intensive care unit: A descriptive study. *Nursing in Critical Care*, 12(4): 188–97.

Clarke, D (2012) Hospitals, in Littlefield, D. (ed.), *Metric Handbook*. New York: Routledge.

Codinhoto, R. (2013) BIM-FM: Manchester town hall complex: Research report. Available at: www.bimtaskgroup.org/wp-content/uploads/2014/03/MCC2_Final-Report_web.pdf.

Codinhoto, R., Tzortzopoulos, P., Kagioglou, M., Aouad, G. and Cooper, R. (2009) The impacts of the built environment on health outcomes. *Facilities*, 27(3–4): 138–51.

Connellan, K., Gaardboe, M., Riggs, D., Due, C., Reinschmidt, A. and Mustillo, L. (2013) Stressed spaces: Mental health and architecture. Doctoral dissertation, Vendome Group.

Cook, M. (1970) Experiments on orientation and proxemics. *Human Relations*, 23(1): 61–76.

Cooper, R., Boyko, C. and Codinhoto, R. (2008) State-of-science review: SR–DR2. The effect of the physical environment on mental wellbeing. Foresight Mental Capital and Wellbeing Project.

Cotterill, S., Evans, R. and Fraise, A.P. (1996) An unusual source for the outbreak of methicillin-resistant staphylococcus aureus on an intensive therapy unit. *Journal of Hospital Infection*, 32(3): 207–16.

Dalke, H., Little, J., Niemann, E., Camgoz, N., Steadman, G., Hill, S., and Stott, L. (2006) Colour and lighting in hospital design. *Optics and Laser Technology*, 38(4): 343–65.

Daykin, N. and Byrne, E. (2006) *The Impact of Visual Arts and Design on the Health and Wellbeing of Patients and Staff in Mental Health Care: A Systematic Review of the Literature*. Bristol: Centre for Public Health Research in the University of the West of England.

Devlin, A.S. and Arneill, A.B. (2003) Health care environments and patient outcomes: A review of the literature. *Environment and Behavior*, 35(5): 665–94.

Dijkstra, K., Pieterse, M.E. and Pruyn, A.Th.H. (2006) Physical environmental stimuli that turn healthcare facilities into healing environments through psychologically mediated effects: Systematic review. *Journal of Advanced Nursing*, 56(2): 166–81.

Douglas, C.H. and Douglas, M.R. (2004) Patient-friendly hospital environments: Exploring the patients' perspective. *Health Expectations*, 7(1): 61–73.

Douglas, C.H. and Douglas, M.R. (2005) Patient-centred improvements in health-care built environments: Perspectives and design indicators. *Health Expectations*, 8(3): 264–76.

Edge, K.J. (2003) Wall color of patient's room: Effects on recovery. Doctoral dissertation, University of Florida.

Ersser, S., Wiles, A., Taylor, H., Wade, S., Walsh, R. and Bentley, T. (2001) The sleep of older people in hospital and nursing homes. *Journal of Clinical Nursing*, 8(4), 360–8.

Etnier, J.L. and Hardy, C.J. (1997) The effects of environment color. *Journal of Sport Behavior*, 20(3): 299–312.

Evans, B. (2010) Evidence-based design, in Lombaerde, P. (ed.), *Bringing the World into Culture: Comparative Methodologies in Architecture, Art, Design and Science*. Valencia, CA: American Scientific Publishers, 227.

Evans, G.W. and McCoy, J.M. (1998) When buildings don't work: The role of architecture in human health. *Journal of Environmental Psychology*, 18(1): 85–94.

Ferrans, C.E., Zerwic, J.J., Wilbur, J.E. and Larson, J.L. (2005) Conceptual model of health-related quality of life. *Journal of Nursing Scholarship*, 37(4): 336–42.

Fischl, G. (2006) Psychosocially supportive design in the indoor environment. Luleå University of Technology.

Fottler, M.D., Ford, R.C., Roberts, V., Ford, E.W. and Spears, Jr., J.D. (2000) Creating a healing environment: The importance of the service setting in the new consumer-oriented healthcare system. *Journal of Healthcare Management*, 45: 91–107.

Francis, S. (2004) Making special places for health care, in Macmillan, S. and Nicholson, R. (eds), *Designing Better Buildings: Quality and Value in the Built Environment*. Abingdon: Routledge, 107–15.

Fransson, N., Vastfjall, D. and Skoog, J. (2007) In search of the comfortable indoor environment: A comparison of the utility of objective and subjective indicators of indoor comfort. *Building and Environment*, 42(5): 1886–90.

Fridkin, S.K., Kremer, F.B., Bland, L.A., Padhye, A., McNeil, M.M. and Jarvis, W.R. (1996) Acremonium kiliense endophthalmitis that occurred after cataract extraction in an ambulatory surgical center and was traced to an environmental reservoir. *Clinical Infectious Diseases*, 22(2): 222–7.

Gerdner, L.A. (2000) Effects of individualized versus classical 'relaxation' music on the frequency of agitation in elderly persons with Alzheimer's disease and related disorders. *International Psychogeriatrics*, 12(1): 49–65.

Gifford, R. (2014) Environmental psychology matters. *Psychology*, 65(1): 541.

Girardin, W.B. (1992) Light wave frequency and sleep-wake frequency in well, full-term neonates. *Holistic Nursing Practice*, 6(4): 57–66.

Glass, P., Avery, G.B., Subramanian, K.N., Keys, M.P., Sostek, A.M. and Friendly, D.M. (1985) Effects of bright light in hospital nursery on the incidence of retinopathy of maturity. *New England Journal of Medicine*, 313(7): 401–4.

Grosenick, J.K. and Hatmaker, C.M. (2000) Perceptions of the importance of physical setting in substance abuse treatment. *Journal of Substance Abuse Treatment*, 18(1): 29–39.

Grunden, N. and Hagood, C. (2012) *Lean-Led Hospital Design: Creating the Efficient Hospital of the Future.* Abingdon: CRC Press.

Gutgsell, K.J., Schluchter, M., Margevicius, S., DeGolia, P.A., McLaughlin, B., Harris, M. and Wiencek, C. (2013) Music therapy reduces pain in palliative care patients: A randomized controlled trial. *Journal of Pain and Symptom Management*, 45(5): 822–31.

Haddock, J. (1994) Clinical sleep: Reducing the effects of noise in hospital. *Nursing Standard*, 8(43): 25–8.

Haggard, L.M. and Werner, C.M. (1990) Situational support, privacy regulation, and stress. *Basic and Applied Social Psychology*, 11(3): 313–37.

Hair, L.P. (1998) Satisfaction by design. *Marketing Health Services*, 6(Fall): 5–8.

Hall, E.T. (1968) Proxemics. *Current Anthropology*, 9(2/3).

Hamilton, D.K. (2012) Creativity, decision making, and evidence-based design. *HERD: Health Environments Research & Design Journal*, 5(2): 111.

Hamilton, D.K. and Watkins, D.H. (2009) *Evidence-Based Design for Multiple Building Types.* Chichester: John Wiley and Sons.

Hartig, T. (2007) Three steps to understanding restorative environments as health resources. *Open Space: People Space*, 163–79.

Hartig, T., Evans, G.W., Jamner, L.D., Davis, D.S. and Gärling, T. (2003) Tracking restoration in natural and urban field settings. *Journal of Environmental Psychology*, 23(2): 109–23.

Hedge, A. (1989) Environmental conditions and health in offices. *International Reviews of Ergonomics*, 3: 87–110.

Hickam, D.H., Severance, S., Feldstein, A., Ray, L., Gorman, P., Schuldheis, S. and Helfand, M. (2003) The effect of health care working conditions on patient safety: Summary. National Center for Biotechnology Information, Bethesda, MD.

Hillier, B., Musgrove, J. and O'Sullivan, P. (1972) Knowledge and design. *Environmental Design: Research and Practice*, 2.

Hippocrates (400BC), in Adams, F. (ed.), *On the Surgery.* Available at: http://classics.mit.edu/Hippocrates/surgery.html (accessed 2 September 2008).

Hobfoll, S.E. (1991) Traumatic stress: A theory based on rapid loss of resources. *Anxiety Research*, 4(3): 187–97.

Hwang, R.L., Lin, T.P., Cheng, M.J. and Chien, J.H. (2007) Patient thermal comfort requirement for hospital environments in Taiwan. *Building and Environment*, 42(8): 2980–7.

Ikonomidou, E., Rehnström, A. and Naesh, O. (2004) Effect of music on vital signs and postoperative pain. *Aorn*, 80(2): 269–78.

Jacobs, K.W. and Hustmyer, Jr., F.E. (1974) Effects of four psychological primary colors on GSR (galvanic skin response) heart rate and respiration rate. *Perceptual and Motor Skills*, 38: 763–6.

Jacobs, K.W. and Suess J.F. (1975) Effects of four psychological primary colors on anxiety state. *Perceptual and Motor Skills*, 41(1): 207–10.

Johnson, R.J. and Wolinsky, F.D. (1993) The structure of health status among older adults: Disease, disability, functional limitation, and perceived health. *Journal of Health and Social Behavior*, 105–21.

Joseph, A. (2006) The impact of the environment on infections in healthcare facilities. Center for Health Design, Concord, CA.

Kaplan, R. (2001) The nature of the view from home psychological benefits. *Environment and Behavior*, 33(4): 507–42.

Kaya, N. and Crosby, M. (2006) Color associations with different building types: An experimental study on American college students. *Color Research and Application*, 31(1): 67–71.

Kliment, S. (2000) *Building Type Basics for Healthcare Facilities.* New York: John Wiley and Sons.

Konkani, A. and Oakley, B. (2012) Noise in hospital intensive care units: A critical review of a critical topic. *Journal of Critical Care*, 27(5): 522-e1.

Körlin, D., Nybäck, H. and Goldberg, F.S. (2000) Creative arts groups in psychiatric care: Development and evaluation of a therapeutic alternative. *Nordic Journal of Psychiatry*, 54(5): 333–40.

Kripke, D.F. (1998) Light treatment for nonseasonal depression: Speed, efficacy, and combined treatment. *Journal of Affective Disorders*, 49(2): 109–17.

Kripke, D.F., Mullaney, D.J., Klauber, M.R., Craig Risch, S. and Christian Gillin, J. (1982) Controlled trial of bright light for nonseasonal major depressive disorders. *Biological Psychiatry*, 31(2): 119–34.

Kripke, D.F., Risch, S.C. and Janowsky, D. (1983) Bright white light alleviates depression. *Psychiatry Research*, 10(2): 105–12.

Law, M., Cooper, B., Strong, S., Stewart, D., Rigby, P. and Letts, L. (1996) The person-environment-occupation model: A transactive approach to occupational performance. *Canadian Journal of Occupational Therapy*, 63(1): 9–23.

Lawson, B. (2001) *Language of Space*. Oxford: Elsevier.

Lawson, B. (2004) Assessing benefits in the health sector, in Macmillan, S. and Nicholson, R. (eds), *Designing Better Buildings: Quality and Value in the Built Environment*. Abingdon: Routledge, 100–6.

Lawson, B. (2010) Healing architecture. *Arts and Health*, 2(2): 95–108.

Lawson, B. and Phiri, M. (2000) Hospital design: Room for improvement. *Health Service Journal*, 110(5688): 24–6.

Lawson, B. and Phiri, M. (2005) Safer environment database. NHS Estates, EFM-Evidence.

Leather, P., Beale, D. and Lee, L. (2000) *A Comparative Study of the Impact of Environmental Design upon Hospital Patients and Staff*. Nottingham: Institute of Work, Health and Organisations.

Leather, P., Beale, D. and Sullivan, L. (2003) Outcomes of environmental appraisal of different hospital waiting areas. *Environment and Behavior*, 35(6): 842–69.

Liu, E.H. and Tan, S.M. (2000) Patients' perception of sound levels in the surgical suite. *Journal of Clinical Anesthesia*, 12(4): 298–302.

Loewen, L.J. and Suedfeld, P. (1992) Cognitive and arousal effects of masking office noise. *Environment and Behavior*, 24(3): 381–95.

Lu, S. and Zhu, N. (2007) Experimental research on physiological index at the heat tolerance limits in China. *Building and Environment*, 42(12): 4016–21.

Malkin, J. (2008) *A Visual Reference for Evidence-Based Design*. Concord, CA: Center for Health Design.

Malone, E., Nanda, U. and Harmsen, C. (2008) *An Introduction to Evidence-Based Design: Exploring Healthcare and Design (EDAC Study Guides, Volume 1)*. Concord, CA: Center for Health Design.

Marcus, C.C. (2000) Gardens and health, in *Design and Health: The Therapeutic Benefits of Design*, 2nd International Congress on Design and Health. Stockholm: Karolinska Institute, 461–71.

Marcus, C.C. and Barnes, M. (eds) (1999) *Healing Gardens: Therapeutic Benefits and Design Recommendations*. Chichester: Wiley.

McCullough, C. (2010) Evidence-based design, in McCullough, C. (ed.), *Evidence-Based Design for Health Facilities*. Indianapolis, IN: R. Wilmeth.

McGarry, T.J. and Prince, M. (1998) Implementation of groups for creative expression on a psychiatric inpatient unit. *Journal of Psychosocial Nursing and Mental Health Services*, 36(3): 19–24.

McLaren, L. and Hawe, P. (2005) Ecological perspectives in health research. *Journal of Epidemiology and Community Health*, 59(1): 6–14.

McLaughlin, C., Olson, R. and White, M.J. (2008) Environmental issues in patient care management: Proxemics, personal space, and territoriality. *Rehabilitation Nursing*, 33(4): 143–7.

Menzies, D., Fanning, A., Yuan, L. and FitzGerald, J.M. (2000) Hospital ventilation and risk for tuberculous infection in Canadian health care workers. Canadian Collaborative Group in Nosocomial Transmission of TB. *Annals of Internal Medicine*, 133(10): 779.

Miller, C.L., White, R., Whitman, T.L., O'Callaghan, M.F. and Maxwell, S.E. (1995) The effects of cycled versus noncycled lighting on growth and development in preterm infants. *Infant Behavior and Development*, 18(1): 87–95.

Miller, R.L. and Swensson, E.S. (2002) *Hospital and Healthcare Facility Design*. New York: W.W. Norton and Company.

Milligan, C., Gatrell, A. and Bingley, A. (2004) 'Cultivating health': Therapeutic landscapes and older people in northern England. *Social Science and Medicine*, 58(9): 1781–93.

Mornhinweg, G.C. (1992). Effects of music preference and selection on stress reduction. *Journal of Holistic Nursing*, 10(2): 101–9.

Morrison, W.E., Haas, E.C., Shaffner, D.H., Garrett, E.S. and Fackler, J.C. (2003) Noise, stress, and annoyance in a pediatric intensive care unit. *Critical Care Medicine*, 31(1): 113–19.

Mulrow, C.D. (1994) Rationale for systematic reviews. *British Medical Journal*, 309(6954): 597.

Mulrow, C.D. and Cook, D.J. (1997) Formulating questions and locating primary studies for inclusion in systematic reviews. *Annals of Internal Medicine, Academia and Clinic, Systematic Review Series*, 127(5): 380–7.

Nagano, K. and Mochida, T. (2004) Experiments on thermal environmental design of ceiling radiant cooling for supine human subjects. *Building and Environment*, 39(3): 267–75.

Nightingale, F. (1863) *Notes on Hospitals*. Cambridge: Cambridge University Press.

Nourse, J.C. and Welch, R.B. (1971) Emotional attributes of color: A comparison of violet and green. *Perceptual and Motor Skills*, 32(2): 403–6.

Nuffield Provincial Hospitals Trust (1960) *Studies in the Functions and Design of Hospitals*. Oxford: Oxford University Press.

Office for National Statistics (2013) Mid-2013 population estimates UK. Available at: www.ons.gov.uk/ons/dcp171778_367167.pdf.

Office for National Statistics (2014) Estimates of the very old, 2002–2012. London: ONS.

O'Neill, M.J. (1991) Effects of signage and floor plan configuration on wayfinding accuracy. *Environment and Behavior*, 23(5): 553–74.

Onieva-Zafra, M.D., Castro-Sánchez, A.M., Matarán-Peñarrocha, G.A. and Moreno-Lorenzo, C. (2013) Effect of music as nursing intervention for people diagnosed with fibromyalgia. *Pain Management Nursing*, 14(2): e39–e46.

Passini, R., Pigot, H., Rainville, C. and Tétreault, M.H. (2000) Wayfinding in a nursing home for advanced dementia of the Alzheimer's type. *Environment and Behavior*, 32(5): 684–710.

Patrick, D.L. and Bergner, M. (1990) Measurement of health status in the 1990s. *Annual Review of Public Health*, 11: 165–83.

Pelosi, P., Solca, M., Ravagnan, I., Tubiolo, D., Ferrario, L. and Gattinoni, L. (1996) Effects of heat and moisture exchangers on minute ventilation, ventilatory drive, and work of breathing during pressure-support ventilation in acute respiratory failure. *Critical Care Medicine*, 24(7): 1184–8.

Philipp, R., Baum, M., Macnaughton, J. and Calman, K. (2002) *Arts, Health and Well-Being*. London: Nuffield Trust.

Phiri, M. (2014) *Design Tools for Evidence-based Healthcare Design*. Abingdon: Routledge.

Pignone, M., Saha, S., Hoerger, T., Lohr, K.N., Teutsch, S. and Mandelblatt, J. (2005) Challenges in systematic reviews of economic analyses. *Annals of Internal Medicine*, 142(12): 1073–9.

Purves, G. (2012) Primary health care, in Littlefield, D. (ed.), *Metric Handbook*. Abingdon: Routledge.

Qatari, G.A. and Haran, D. (1999) Determinants of users' satisfaction with primary health care settings and services in Saudi Arabia. *International Journal for Quality in Health Care*, 11(6): 523–31.

Rabin, M. (1981) Medical-facility colors reduce patient stress. *Contract (New York)*, 23(3): 78–83.

Raybeck, D. (1991) Proxemics and privacy: Managing the problems of life in confined environments. In Harrison, A.A., Clearwater, Y.A. and McKay, C.P. (eds), *From Antarctica to Outer Space: Life in Confined Environments*. New York: Springer-Verlag, 317–30.

Rebeiro, K.L. (2001) Enabling occupation: The importance of an affirming environment. *Canadian Journal of Occupational Therapy*, 68(2): 80–9.

Reed, D., Price, E.G., Windish, D.M., Wright, S.M., Gozu, A., Hsu, E.B. and Bass, E.B. (2005) Challenges in systematic reviews of educational intervention studies. *Annals of Internal Medicine*, 142(12): 1080.

Richards, K.C. and Bairnsfather, L. (1988) Sleep in the ICU: A description of night sleep patterns in the critical care unit. *Heart and Lung*, 17(1): 35–42.

Rollins, J.A. (2009) The influence of 2 hospitals' designs and policies on social interaction and privacy as coping factors for children with cancer and their families. *Journal of Pediatric Oncology Nursing*, 26(6): 340–53.

Rooke, C.N. (2012) Improving wayfinding in old and complex hospital environments. Doctoral dissertation, University of Salford.

Rooke, C.N., Tzortzopoulos, P., Koskela, L.J. and Rooke, J.A. (2009) *Wayfinding: Embedding Knowledge in Hospital Environments.* London: Imperial College Business School.

Rubonis, A.V. and Bickman, L. (1991) Psychological impairment in the wake of disaster. *Psychological Bulletin*, 109: 384–99.

Sackett, D.L., Rosenberg, W., Gray, J.A., Haynes, R.B. and Richardson, W.S. (1996) Evidence based medicine: What it is and what it isn't. *British Medical Journal*, 312(7023): 71–2.

Sallis, J.F., Owen, N. and Fisher, E.B. (2008) Ecological models of health behaviors, in Glanz, K., Rimer, B.K. and Viswanath, K. (eds), *Health Behavior and Health Education: Theory, Research, and Practice.* 4th edition. San Francisco: Jossey-Bass, 465–85.

Sanders, E.B.N. and Stappers, P.J. (2008) Co-creation and the new landscapes of design. *Co-design*, 4(1): 5–18.

Sebastian, R. (2011) Changing roles of the clients, architects and contractors through BIM. *Engineering, Construction and Architectural Management*, 18(2): 176–87.

Smith, A.P. (1991) Noise and aspects of attention. *British Journal of Psychology*, 82: 313–24.

Söderback, I., Söderström, M., and Schälander, E. (2004) Horticultural therapy: The 'healing garden' and gardening in rehabilitation measures at Danderyd Hospital Rehabilitation Clinic. *Developmental Neurorehabilitation*, 7(4): 245–60.

Staricoff, R.L. (2004) *Arts in Health: A Review of the Medical Literature.* London: Arts Council England.

Staricoff, R., Loppert, S., Kirklin, D. and Richardson, R. (2003) Integrating the arts into health care: Can we affect clinical outcomes? *Healing Environment: Without and Within.* London: RCP, 63–79.

Steffes, R. and Thralow, J. (1985) Do uniform colors keep patients awake? *Journal of Gerontological Nursing*, 11(7): 6–9.

Sundstrom, E., Bell, P.A., Busby, P.L. and Asmus, C. (1996) Environmental psychology 1989–1994. *Annual Review of Psychology*, 47(1): 485–512.

Thayer, R.E. (1989) *The Biopsychology of Mood and Arousal.* New York: Oxford University Press.

Topf, M. (2000) Hospital noise pollution: An environmental stress model to guide research and clinical interventions. *Journal of Advanced Nursing*, 31(3): 520–8.

Topf, M. and Thompson, S. (2001) Interactive relationships between hospital patients' noise-induced stress and other stress with sleep. *Heart and Lung: Journal of Acute and Critical Care*, 30(4): 237–43.

Topf, M., Bookman, M. and Arand, D. (1996) Effects of critical care unit noise on the subjective quality of sleep. *Journal of Advanced Nursing*, 24: 545–51.

Tranfield, D., Denyer, D. and Smart, P. (2003) Towards a methodology for developing evidence-informed management knowledge by means of systematic review. *British Journal of Management*, 14(3): 207–22.

Ulrich, R.S. (1981) Natural versus urban scenes: Some psychophysiological effects. *Environment and Behavior*, 13: 523–56.

Ulrich, R.S. (1984) View through a window may influence recovery from surgery. *Science*, 224: 420–1.

Ulrich, R.S. (1992) Effects of interior design on wellness: Theory and recent scientific research. *Journal of Healthcare Design*, 3: 97–109.

Ulrich, R.S., Quan, X., Zimring, C., Joseph, A. and Choudhary, R. (2004) The role of the physical environment in the hospital of the 21st century: A once-in-a-lifetime opportunity. Designing the 21st Century Hospital Project, Center for Health Design.

Ulrich, R.S., Zimring, C., Zhu, X., DuBose, J., Seo, H., Choi, Y., Quan, X. and Joseph, A. (2008) A review of the research literature on evidence-based healthcare design. *Health Environments Research and Design Journal*, 1(3): 61–125.

Vaajoki, A., Pietilä, A.M., Kankkunen, P. and Vehviläinen-Julkunen, K. (2012) Effects of listening to music on pain intensity and pain distress after surgery: An intervention. *Journal of Clinical Nursing*, 21(5–6): 708–17.

Veitch, J.A. (1990) Office noise and illumination effects on reading comprehension. *Journal of Environmental Psychology*, 10: 209–17.

Veitch, J.A. and McColl, S.L. (1993) *Full Spectrum Fluorescent Lighting Effects on People: A Critical Review.* Ottawa: Institute for Research in Construction.

Waller, S. and Finn, H. (2004) *Enhancing the Healing Environment: A Guide for NHS Trusts.* London: King's Fund.

Waller, S., Masterson, A. and Finn, H. (2013) *Improving the Patient Experience: Developing Supportive Design for People with Dementia: The King's Fund's Enhancing the Healing Environment Programme 2009–2012.* London: King's Fund.

Werner, C.M., Altman, I. and Brown, B.B. (1992) A transactional approach to interpersonal relations: Physical environment, social context and temporal qualities. *Journal of Social and Personal Relationships,* 9(2): 297–323.

Whitehouse, S., Varni, J.W., Seid, M., Marcus, C.C., Ensberg, M.J., Jacob, J.R. and Mehlenbeck, R.S. (2001) Evaluating a children's hospital garden environment: Utilization and consumer satisfaction. *Journal of Environmental Psychology,* 21: 301–14.

Wicker, A.W. (1992) Making sense of environments, in Walsh, W.B., Craik, K.H. and Price, R.H. (eds), *Person-Environment Psychology: Models and Perspectives.* Hillsdale, NJ: Hillsdale, 157–92.

Wicker, A.W. and August, R.A. (1995) How far should we generalize? The case of a workload model. *Psychological Science* 6, 39–44.

Wilson, G.D. (1966) Arousal properties of red versus green. *Perceptual and Motor Skills,* 23: 942–9.

Wilson, I.B. and Cleary, P.D. (1995) Linking clinical variables with health-related quality of life: A conceptual model of patient outcomes. *Journal of American Medical Association,* 273: 59–65.

Yerevanian, B.I., Anderson, J.L., Grota, L.J. and Bray, M. (1986) Effects of bright incandescent light on seasonal and nonseasonal major depressive disorder. *Psychiatry Research,* 18(4): 355–64.

Zimring, C., Joseph, A., Nicoll, G.L. and Tsepas, S. (2005) Influences of building design and site design on physical activity: Research and intervention opportunities. *American Journal of Preventive Medicine,* 28(2S2): 186–93.

8 Products

Product design in acute health

Sue Hignett

Abstract

This chapter uses a Human Factors and Ergonomics (HFE) framework to discuss how design has been used to support patient care, treatment, recovery, rehabilitation, experience and safety. Case studies are provided for two new areas for design in acute healthcare: slips, trips and falls (STF) and pre-hospital urgent and emergency care. Human interactions for inpatient STF are described using two new HFE models to illustrate the complexity of human capabilities and limitations. In particular, the importance of understanding the behaviours of all the humans in the sociotechnical system is discussed; in this case study the activities and actions of patients need to be supported with design for safer mobility. The second case study explores the complexity of design in unpredictable treatment environments with innovations such as a portable clinical (clean) work surface for assessment and treatment.

Introduction

This chapter will discuss how HFE design can be used to support patient care, treatment, recovery, rehabilitation, experience and safety by focusing on human interaction with products in the acute sector from pre-hospital/ambulance care to discharge. An HFE approach looks at design within a system (micro-meso-macro) to include all humans, including patients, caregivers (staff and informal) and others who are involved in receiving, delivering and supporting the service delivery.

Products, equipment, medical devices (Hignett et al., 2013a), furniture and consumables are used across a wide range of acute services from domestic environments (ambulance response) through to vehicles and buildings for emergency and planned (elective) care (Hignett et al., 2013b). The potential of HFE design allows for the consideration of physical and cognitive abilities and capabilities (e.g. ageing populations) to recognise limitations and expectations for both caregivers (staff) and care recipients (Hignett, 2013). This includes changes in the culture of care with, for example, encouragement and support for early mobilisation to reduce functional decline, which transforms care from a warehousing (static) culture to a horticultural (dynamic, growing) model (Miller and Gwynne, 1972).

In the UK, design has been seen as an important component in patient safety since the 2000s and there have been design projects on electronic infusion devices, medication labelling, computer interfaces and ambulances (NHS, 2015). This continued in 2015 with initiatives to embed HFE in healthcare across both product and systems led by Health Education England:

to ensure that the practices and principles of human factors are integrated into all train-ing and education… to develop the future healthcare workforce by ensuring it contains individuals with the right skills, attitudes, behaviours and training, to enable the delivery of excellent healthcare and drive improvements for the quality of care provided and the safety of our patients.

(Health Education England, 2015)

Human factors and ergonomics

The need for HFE in healthcare has been recognised since the inception of the profession and discipline but development and growth have been slow (Carayon, 2010). 'Ergonomics (or Human Factors) is the scientific discipline concerned with the understanding of interactions among humans and other elements of a system, and the profession that applies theory, principles, data and methods to design in order to optimise human well-being and overall system performance' (Dul et al., 2012). HFE explores a problem by looking at the people within a system, their interactions with each other and the system, and then redesigning the tasks, interfaces and system. A systems analysis approach is used where people are defined as stakeholders within the system and interventions are developed to give two key outcomes of human wellbeing and performance (Hignett et al., 2015a).

HFE can be described using a dynamic model (Figure 8.1) showing the human as a link point, with interactions at micro, meso and macro levels. To represent the interactions the conical rings move through a vertical axis to link the internal and external factors. So, a

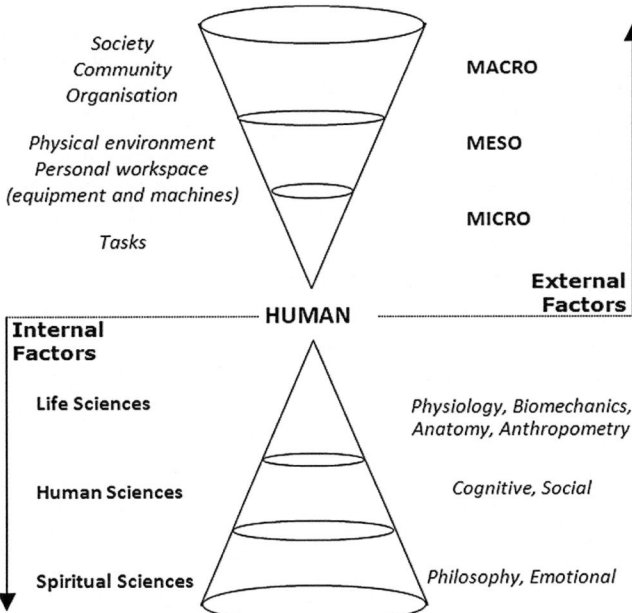

Figure 8.1 Human interactions model
Source: Hignett et al., 2015b

macro-level ring (incorporating issues of society, community and organisation) links with the spiritual sciences (personal philosophy or world view, emotional behaviours) for HFE design issues relating to religious and cultural practices with respect to employment conditions, personal protective clothing and/or working hours.

Two case studies will be used to consider firstly the design (and human interactions) of hospital beds and bedside furniture with respect to slip, trip and falls risks, and secondly how products and equipment are used in emergency situations (ambulance response) away from a care facility.

Case study 1: reducing slips, trips and falls through HFE design

STF by patients in hospital have been described as a 'seemingly intractable cause of harm' (Donaldson et al., 2014). They are the second most frequent cause of death after failure to recognise or act on deterioration, and have been described as one of the 'Geriatric Giants' (Healey et al., 2004). STF account for the greatest number (33 per cent) of adverse event reports to the National Reporting and Learning System in the UK, with 94 per cent occurring in acute inpatient facilities (Healey et al., 2008). The incident rate is approximately three times higher in hospitals and nursing homes than in community-dwelling older people (American Geriatrics Society, 2001). Many clinical interventions have tried to reduce the number of incidents and severity of injuries experienced by inpatients, but there is very little evidence of sustained success over the last 60 years (American Geriatrics Society, 2001; Healey et al., 2008; Coussement et al., 2008; Gillespie, 2004; Chang et al., 2004; Kannus et al., 2005; Oliver et al., 2007).

How can design help? As over 70 per cent of STF are unwitnessed, an HFE design approach seeks to understand the problem through the eyes of the people experiencing the STF – namely the patients.

From the patient's perspective, an STF only occurs when there is movement – an unconscious or paralysed person has a negligible risk level. Movement usually implies a goal and this is likely to be associated with physiological motivators (Morse et al., 1987). Maslow's theoretical model for basic human needs was used to describe a mental model for movement motivation (Figure 8.2; Hignett and Masud, 2006) to look at the problem from the viewpoint of the person in bed ('worm's eye view'; Hignett, 2006). If the level 1 need for self-care (feeding, grooming, bathing, dressing, bowel and bladder care and toilet use) is not supported by caregivers, then the patient may be highly motivated to achieve them independently, resulting in movement from the bed and introducing a risk of falling. Maslow's hierarchy has also been used and modified by Zeisel (2000) to explore altered mental models (related to dementia) as a risk factor for STF. Zeisel combined levels 1 and 2 of the hierarchy to show how interactions between physiological and safety needs may introduce safety risks. The behavioural and functional needs are combined and illustrate not only social activities but also a need for predictability and orderliness.

The first barrier for HFE design of products is the bed, specifically the bed height and bed rails. Bed rails were first introduced in the 19th century for agitated psychiatric patients as a precautionary measure against falls (Levine, 1994). The first bed rails were full length and this design of rail is still the most commonly available and used in the UK (Figure 8.3), whereas in the USA split side rails were introduced in the 1950s and have continued to be used (Hignett et al., 2013b).

Bed rails serve a number of purposes (HBSW, 2003), including security in transit, facilitating turning and repositioning within the bed or transferring in or out of a bed, providing a feeling of comfort and security, facilitating access to bed controls and providing a physical barrier as

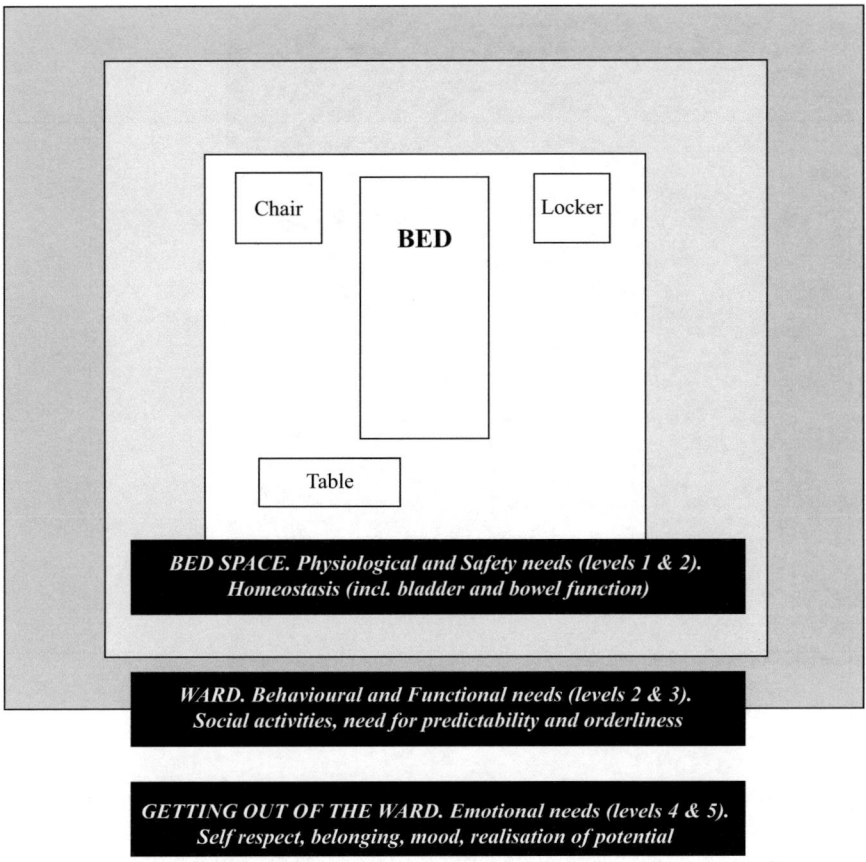

Chair

BED

Locker

Table

***BED SPACE. Physiological and Safety needs (levels 1 & 2).
Homeostasis (incl. bladder and bowel function)***

***WARD. Behavioural and Functional needs (levels 2 & 3).
Social activities, need for predictability and orderliness***

***GETTING OUT OF THE WARD. Emotional needs (levels 4 & 5).
Self respect, belonging, mood, realisation of potential***

Figure 8.2 Maslow's hierarchy for STF for confused patients
Source: Modified from Hignett and Masud, 2006 and Zeisel, 2000

a reminder of the bed perimeters. Bed rails can both support and restrict patient mobility as 'the same device may have the effect of restraining one individual, but not another, depending on the individual resident's condition and circumstances. For example, partial rails may assist one resident to enter and exit the bed independently while acting as a restraint for another' (HBSW, 2003), so if they are not designed to be used by patients then they can become a restraint (Frengley, 1999). They can also obstruct vision, separate the care receiver from the caregiver, create noise and cause trauma if the patient's body strikes or becomes entangled in the side rail (Donius and Rader, 1994).

To provide a framework for HFE design, a new theoretical model (DIAL-F; Figure 8.4) has been proposed to include both staff (caregivers) and patients (care recipients) in an open, dynamic system (Hignett et al., 2013c). A rotary telephone DIAL shape (used for telephone design from 1920s to 1980s; F is for falls) represents the active elements (both within and between layers) with the most transience (dynamic change and motion) in the outer rings and the most stability in the inner rings. The DIAL-F model changes the patient role from predominantly passive to active where the patient is both transient (for both short-term care and

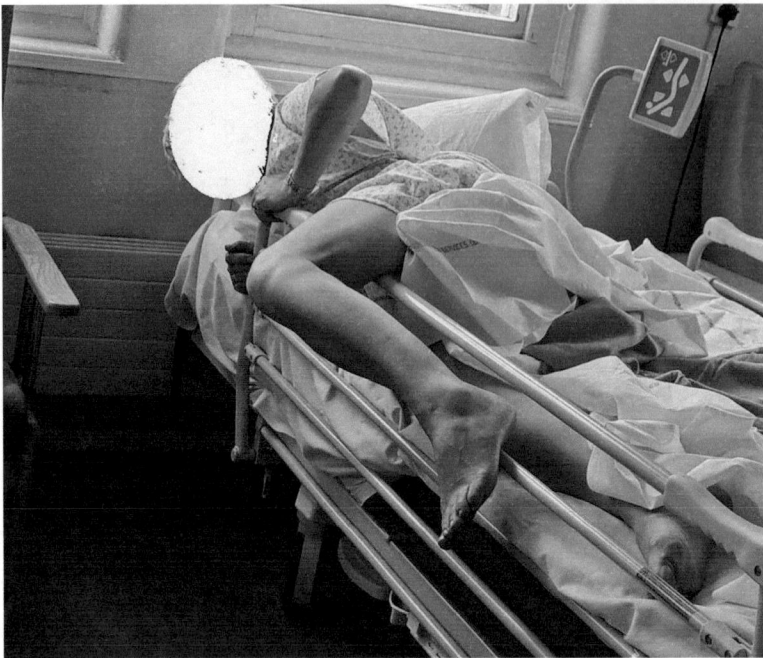

Figure 8.3 Bed rails as a barrier; climbing over bed rail

longer-term care with repeated visits) in the system and independent to choose when (and if) they engage with the system (as a voluntary member of the system rather than an employee). DIAL-F attempts to show a 'horticultural model of care' (active, risk-taking) rather than a passive, minimum risk environment or 'warehousing model of care' (Miller and Gwynne, 1972).

It has been suggested that only about 50 per cent of the patients may participate with STF-prevention initiatives (Nyman and Victor, 2011). This has been explored in two projects using clinical audit (Hignett et al., 2014) and patient interviews (Wolf and Hignett, 2015). The audit found that most of the items on the bedside table (e.g. drink, spectacles) were within reach (>80 per cent) but that the nurse call bell (on a cord from the wall) might have fallen out of reach (with less than 60 per cent within reach). The mobility challenges (and STF risks) faced by the patients (n=156) were increased as only 21 per cent of their walking aids (frames, crutches and sticks) were within reach and over 75 per cent had the bedside table obstructing the area by the bed and introducing a trip hazard. The interview study explored patients' perception of STF risks; it found that almost all interviewed patients (n=30) strongly disagreed that they were at risk of an STF during their hospital stay. Some of the reasons for a low perceived risk of STF included the desire for independence. For example, a high STF-risk patient often forgot to use her call bell when she got out of bed, when the nurse told her they were going to have to put an alarm on her bed she started crying and said she felt she was losing her independence (Wolf and Hignett, 2015). Other reasons included awareness of surroundings, using caution when walking around, denying a need for help, feeling strong and stable while standing and walking and feeling protected and safe in the hospital. These projects suggest that patients have a desire to retain control over their activities and will continue to mobilise independently.

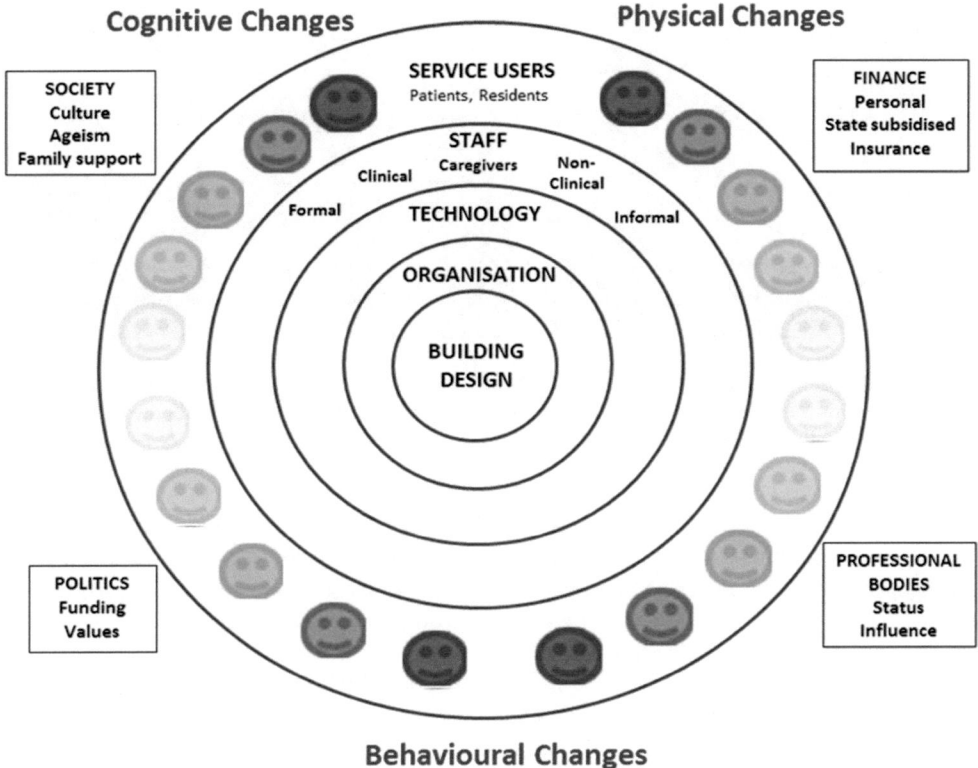

Figure 8.4 DIAL–F; model of STF risk–management system
Source: Hignett et al., 2013c

The HFE design approach looks for a solution to support patient interactions with the products and equipment in the bedside area. Examples for product design interventions could include split bed rails to enable independence (rather than acting as a barrier) and a different combination of locker/table with embedded (design) walking support to encourage mobility (and reduce functional decline). The products in Figure 8.5 are commercially available but have not yet been combined in either the same country or in the same care sector; for example, the walker/table is not used on hospital wards as furniture, it is a product used in home care.

Case study 2: HFE design for pre-hospital acute care (ambulance)

The second case study describes an HFE approach to redesign products used in the delivery of pre-hospital emergency care. Before 2005 the NHS ambulance service (UK) had over 40 different designs of emergency ambulances (Jones and Hignett, 2005). This presented an increased risk to patient safety due to the variation in the location of equipment and consumables in each vehicle, which impacted on safe systems of work and the efficiency of clinical care.

In 2005 the UK Department of Health set out a vision for the provision of future ambulance services by 2010 to increase the range of quality mobile healthcare services for patients

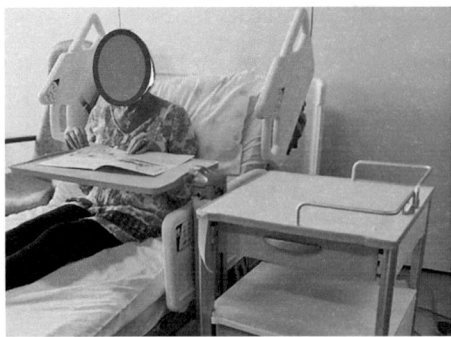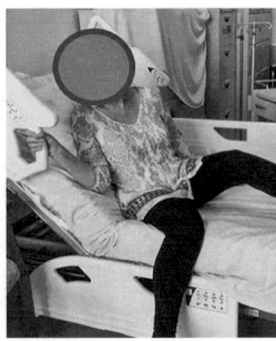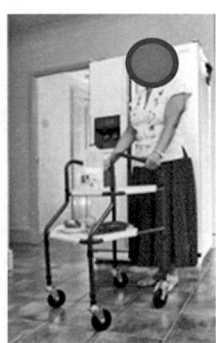

Figure 8.5 HFE design to reduce STF risks (and functional decline) and support independent mobility. From left to right: locker/table to reduce clutter (Germany), assisted bed exit using split bedrail (USA), walker/table (community)

with urgent and emergency care needs. It was identified that the demand for ambulance pre-hospital care was rising by about 7 per cent per annum (approximately 250,000 extra calls) and that the role of the ambulance service was changing, with only 10 per cent of calls relating to life-threatening emergencies with many of the residual 90 per cent having primary care or social needs (Department of Health, 2005).

A programme of HFE research commenced in 2003 with the aim of standardising the design of emergency ambulances. The first scoping project explored activities in emergency ambulances (Ferreira and Hignett, 2005) using link analysis, postural analysis and anthropometry. Paramedics were observed over 16 shifts carrying out a range of clinical tasks. The most frequently occurring clinical tasks were checking blood oxygen saturation, oxygen administration, monitoring the heart and checking blood pressure. Access to the equipment and consumables to support these tasks had been designed for the attendant seat (head end of the stretcher), but the layout of the vehicle interior (including patient position) resulted in paramedics being unable to reach some equipment and storage across the stretcher (Figure 8.6).

To look more closely at the products used in the pre-hospital care setting, the next project focused on stretcher design and use. As well as being used as a treatment platform in the ambulance, the stretcher is also a transportation product. In 2003, there were three stretcher loading systems widely in use in the UK; 42 per cent of services used easi-loader stretchers, 29 per cent used tail lifts and 29 per cent used ramp/winch systems (Jones and Hignett, 2007). The specification and selection of the stretcher system was found to be based on professional experience rather than a rigorous process of product evaluation. To provide an evidence base for purchasing, the HFE project compared the three systems using a range of methods including hierarchical task analysis, critical incident technique, link analysis and postural analysis. Over 660 postures (Figure 8.7) were analysed and the easi-loader stretcher was found to cause the highest postural risks (for musculoskeletal injuries).

A national questionnaire was distributed to explore perceptions of ambulance design features with patient and operator safety ranked as the most important issue, followed by reliability, time to operate, carry chair access, vehicle layout, task complication, weather/environment, clearance, effect of camber, security, infection control, equipment misuse and sensors. These design concepts (challenges) were taken forward in a national specification of emergency ambulances in collaboration with NHS staff (management and operational), patient

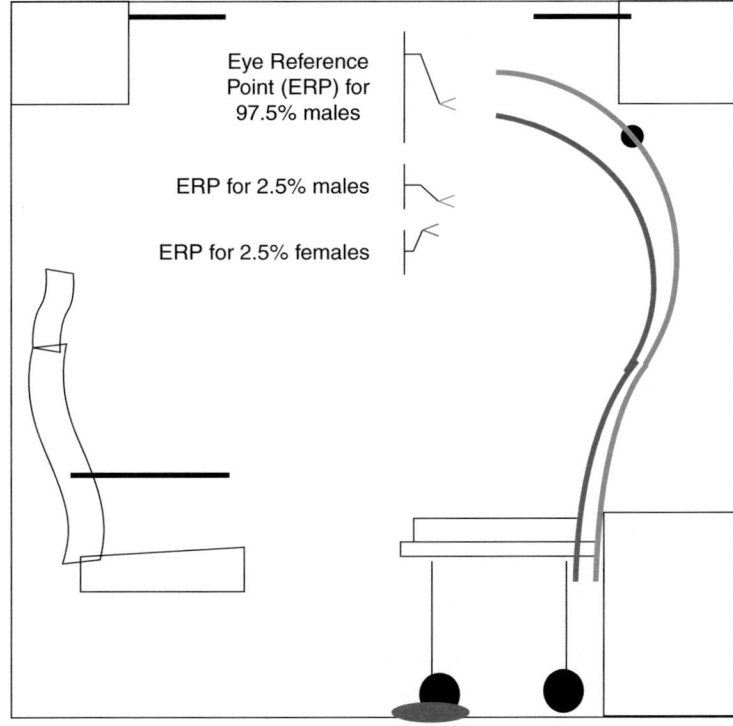

Eye Reference
Point (ERP) for
97.5% males

ERP for 2.5% males

ERP for 2.5% females

Foot Reference Point

Figure 8.6 Anthropometric analysis of ambulance reach distances
Source: Ferreira, 2002

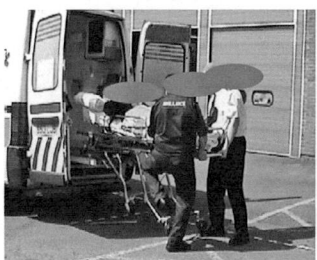 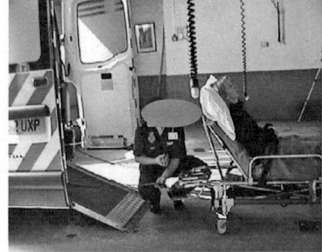 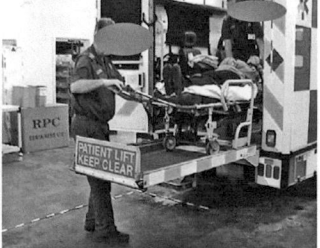

Figure 8.7 Three stretcher loading systems. From left to right: easi-loader stretcher, ramp and winch, tail lift

representatives and vehicle and equipment manufacturers (Hignett et al., 2009). The standardised ambulance vehicle design has been implemented in England, with savings calculated at over £2.5 million from efficiencies in procurement and manufacturing.

However, the emergency ambulance is only involved in a small percentage of treatments, with most of the pre-hospital care being delivered wherever the patient is located (home, street, countryside, shopping centre, etc.). To explore the equipment and consumables used for

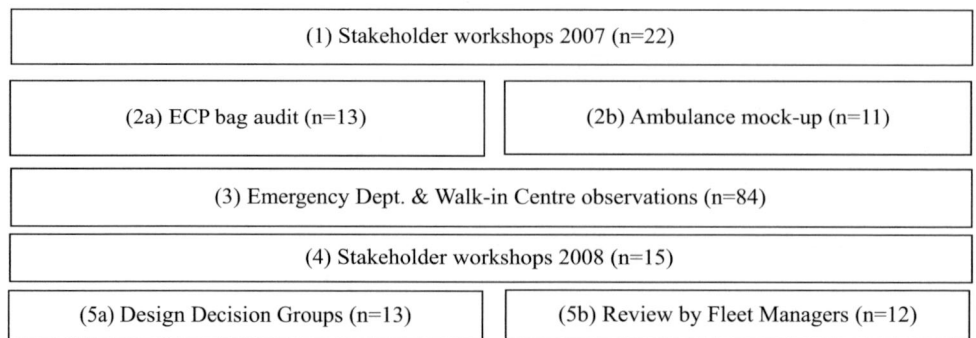

Figure 8.8 Project methodology with five phases of data collection

kerbside care the Smart Pods project investigated activities in acute care centres (emergency department and minor injuries unit) which, it was suggested, could be transferred to pre-hospital or community care. Data were collected with 125 staff and 88 patients over 18 months using stakeholder workshops (2007, 2008), portable technology audits, treatment observations in emergency departments and walk-in centres, and design decision groups (Figure 8.8).

The first phase of the Smart Pods project (stakeholder workshops, 2007) defined the clinical scope as a set of treatment groups with six presenting complaints: breathing difficulties, chest pain, lacerations, falls, neck pain and head injury (Hignett et al., 2011). The second phase explored the current use of equipment and consumables using checklist and interview techniques as an audit; these data were grouped by clinical complaint for comparison with the treatment groups from workshops. A wide range of products were being used from individual personally purchased equipment to adapted bags and systems to reduce the quantity of equipment taken to the care location (Figure 8.9).

In phase 3 observational data were collected about clinical treatment practices for urgent complaints at 85 patient assessments in two emergency departments (acute) and one minor injuries walk-in centre (primary care). Some patients presented with a combination of complaints, e.g. fall and laceration, and one observational session was discontinued due to changes in the patient's condition. The data were recorded and analysed with Link Analysis (Figure 8.10) and Hierarchical Task Analysis for the equipment and consumables used, staff movements and clinical procedures (Jones et al., 2009). Data were collected until theoretical saturation was achieved and no additional information was being generated from the observations. Staff were observed leaving the cubicle for a number of reasons, including to fetch equipment and consumables, ask for second opinions, attend to other patients, check x-rays, print documents, fetch drugs and arrange referrals. For pre-hospital care a paramedic needs to have access to all equipment and consumables, communications, etc. within the vehicle as they do not have immediately available support or storage.

The fourth phase of data collection used a second workshop (2008) with fleet (n=4), clinical (n=5), service (n=4) and health and safety managers (n=2) from five ambulance trusts to explore how medical equipment and products might be (1) better organised, laid out and accessed in vehicles and (2) rationalised to reduce excessive or unnecessary stock. These data supported modularisation by:

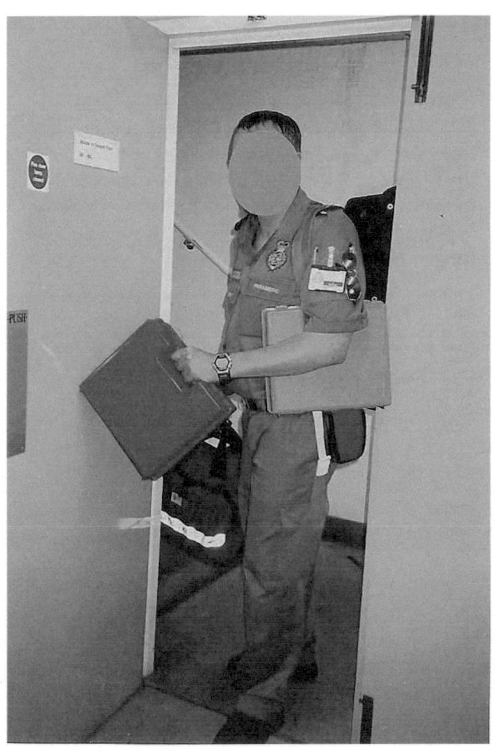

Figure 8.9 Carrying multiple bags for pre-hospital care

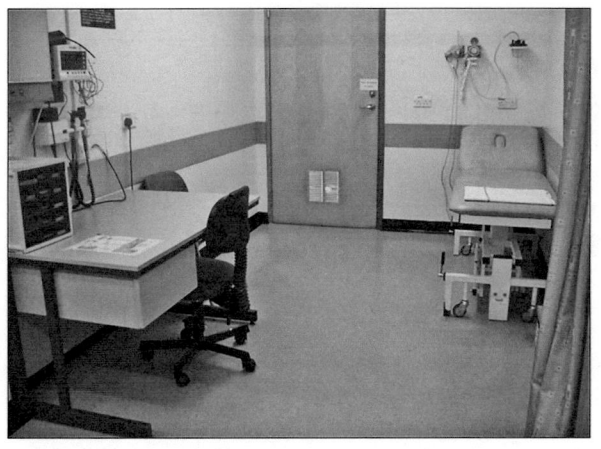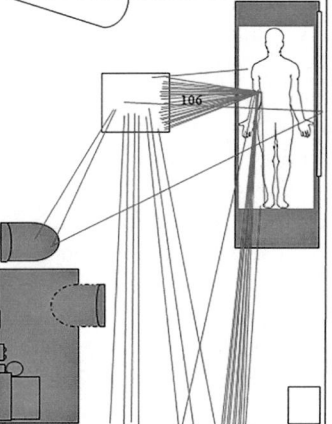

Figure 8.10 Link analysis of minor injuries unit assessment room

Table 8.1 Presenting clinical scenarios for pre-hospital care

Scenario 1 (emergency)	Scenario 2 (urgent)
22-year-old male complaining of severe neck pain after rear end shunt RTC at unrestrained front seat passenger. Car was travelling at 45mph (in 30mph zone). Has pins and needles radiating down both arms (bulls-eye on windscreen). Normally fit and well. No visible haemorrhage; no further injuries reported. Driver is uninjured and currently talking to police. Patient found still in passenger seat.	74-year-old female patient phones in with small (2–3cm) laceration to scalp, feeling generally unwell. Hit head on shelf whilst standing up. Fully conscious and alert. Other medical history: Type 2 diabetes. No known history of hypotension. Social: husband alive, well and able to care for her.

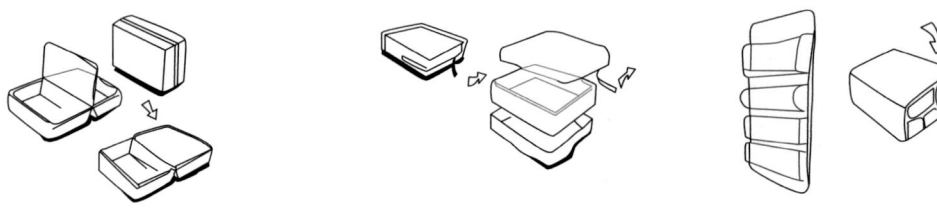

Figure 8.11 Examples of 2D prototypes for portable pod

- standardising contents and layout into clinical presentations, e.g. cardiac, breathing difficulties;
- miniaturising diagnostic equipment by, for example, reconnecting to a base station in vehicle and using wireless technology; and
- using smaller (disposable) portable bags for individual patients, including safe, sterile, disposable containers.

Finally, two design decision groups (Wilson et al., 2005) were held to review current practice and explore opportunities for design through round robins, word maps, mock-ups and prototypes. Two presenting scenarios were used (Table 8.1) to represent different clinical scenarios for emergency and urgent pre-hospital care.

This progressed design ideas from 2D paper-based prototypes (Figure 8.11) in a drawing exercise to create portable pods with improved functionality and usability to 3D prototypes created for session 2 which were used as the focus for the discussion and modification of the design specification.

The five datasets were analysed iteratively using NVivo, a qualitative data-management program that supports coding, searching and theorising (Bazeley and Richards, 2000). Primary (equipment/consumables and procedural issues), secondary and tertiary codes were applied to each dataset and then reviewed by clinical complaint and location. Finally, all data were reviewed and recoded to account for the emerging codes and triangulated to identify functional design requirements. The design outputs were a three-level technology system for personal kit, assessment packages (Table 8.2) and storage for other clinical treatment packages.

The outputs from the Smart Pods project were then taken forward in a knowledge-transfer project (Community Urgent Response Environment) and the products and equipment were designed using iterative prototyping (Figure 8.12) in collaboration with two manufacturers

Table 8.2 Personal kit and assessment/treatment packages for urgent care

Personal kit	Assessment pack	Other packs
Gloves, pen torch, phone, stethoscope, scissors, drugs guide (e.g. British National Formulary), coat, helmet, stab vest, fleece, radio, tourniquet	BP cuff, thermometer, BM kit, urinalysis, peak flow meter, opthalomo/oto-scope, tongue depressor, tendon hammer, KY jelly, apron, patient record form, clinical disposal bag, sharps box	Suture, dressings (including pressure sores), catheter care, maternity, IV access, diabetic, cardiac/respiratory care and treatment

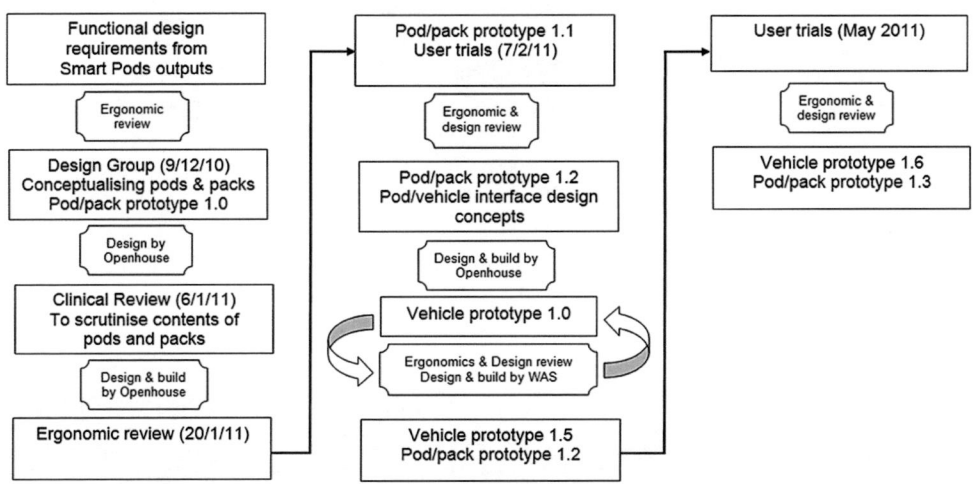

Figure 8.12 Iterative prototyping to design portable pods
Source: Hignett et al., 2012

(Hignett et al., 2012). A full-size mock-up of the ambulance interior was supplied by one manufacturer (WAS) and three portable pod prototypes were provided for user trials by the second manufacturer (Openhouse). These were used in simulation exercises with patient actors in four clinical scenarios: head injury, paediatric febrile convulsion, chest pain/respiratory and collapse from an unknown cause.

The first pod prototype was used to collect 24 data sets with clinical information delivered as a simple radio communication template (pre-arrival at scene) and as a set of test results as appropriate during the user trial (Table 8.1, scenario 2). The observational data sets comprised 72 video datasets (three camera positions) which were amalgamated with the 24 post-scenario debriefing interviews and verbatim transcriptions from the 12 post-trial interviews. This was repeated with the second pod prototype in trial 2. The qualitative analysis involved iterative steps to ensure that all data were accounted for and included in the final results (Figure 8.13).

The final pod prototype included visible fronts (easy content identification) using colour and luminous materials (Figure 8.14). The exteriors were provided with reinforced corners, water resistance and a unique design for a supported work surface (sterile zone) was created. The paramedics gave useful feedback: 'I like the way when you open the wound treatment

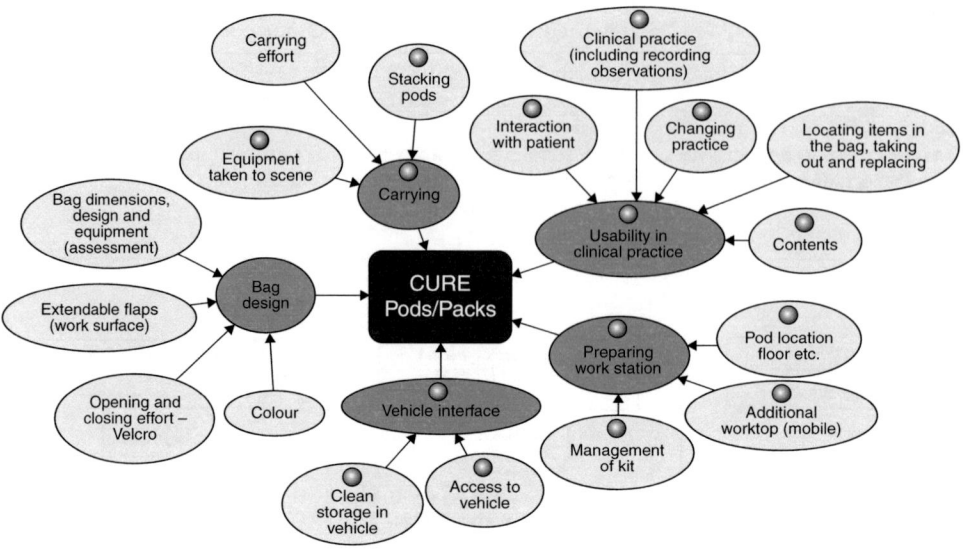

Figure 8.13 Thematic analysis using NVivo9
Source: Hignett et al., 2012

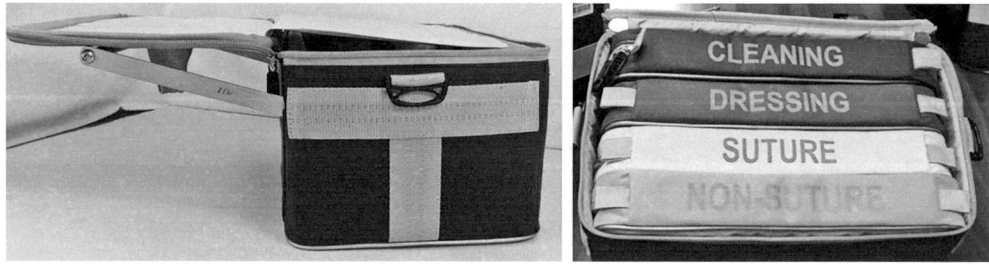

Figure 8.14 Portable pod with sterile work zone

bag they're different colours, that's really good because you can see them straight away' (ECP 5, trial 1, collapse).

The major design innovations were the incorporation of a work surface into the assessment and wound care pods, the small footprint for the portable systems and improved access to equipment and consumables.

Discussion

This chapter has looked at two new areas for design in acute healthcare. The first (slips, trips and falls) focuses on design for patients with a need to understand the very wide range of requirements and behaviours. The human interactions have been represented in two new HFE models (Figures 8.1 and 8.4) to illustrate the complexity of human capabilities and limitations that need to be understood to design solutions based on internal and external factors. The second case study described how changes in pre-hospital urgent and emergency care services have been limited by the design of supporting products and technologies.

The lessons learned from the two case studies include a deeper understanding of design challenges as complex behaviours and human–human interactions (case study 1; CS1) and designing for unpredictable environments in case study 2 (CS2). Using the HFE approach allowed detailed and robust iterative analyses of tasks and human interactions at individual (CS1) and systems (CS2) levels. These are needed for design to understand and define the challenge (specification) and then test/evaluate proposed solutions as paper, 2D/3D and simulated prototypes before real-world implementation and user trials.

Implementing change is a key part of realising the benefits from design improvements. It has been suggested that 80 per cent of the effort when working in healthcare is needed to progress the project due to the complexity of the industry with only 20 per cent on understanding/solving the problem. So using HFE task-analysis methods to gain insight into the role of the product in the systems (human interactions with all stakeholders) and contexts of use will have a major impact on its eventual success or otherwise. For example, improved design may not be incorporated in healthcare products, devices and information technologies because manufacturers have not adopted HFE design principles and purchasers (clinicians) have not demanded them (Hignett et al., 2013b). One of the outcomes from the Health Education England 'Learning to Be Safer' initiative is likely to be raised expectations and demands from staff and patients for better-designed products to support safer care and treatment. In 2004, Clarkson et al. stated that 'to be successful, any design-led initiative must be underpinned by a thorough understanding of the complex systems of interactions'. Designers need to have a comprehensive and rigorous understanding of human behaviour (capabilities and limitations) to ensure that the design of products and equipment provided to support care, recovery and rehabilitation are effective, efficient and avoid unwanted side effects.

Summary

This chapter has described the use of a HFE approach to design for health products. The reconceptualisation of healthcare systems, to include the transient role of patients (DIAL-F), illustrates how poor design can permeate and result in a system that is trying to fit the human to the environment (relying on behaviour changes and training) rather than starting design with people and fitting the environment (physical, organisational and social systems) to the human. HFE can contribute to systems and design initiatives for both patients and clinicians to improve everyday performance and safety, and help to reduce and control spiralling healthcare costs.

References

American Geriatrics Society (2001) Guidelines for the prevention of falls in older persons. *Journal of the American Geriatrics Society*, 49(5): 664–72.

Bazeley, P. and Richards, L. (2000) *The NVivo® Qualitative Project Book*. London: Sage Publications.

Carayon, P. (2010) Human factors in patient safety as an innovation. *Applied Ergonomics*, 41(5): 657–65.

Chang, J.T., Morton, S.C., Rubenstein, L.Z., Mojica, W.A., Maglione, M., Suttorp, M.J., Roth, E.A. et al. (2004) Interventions for the prevention of falls in older adults: Systematic review and meta-analysis of randomized clinical trials. *British Medical Journal*, 328: 680–6.

Clarkson, P.J., Buckle, P., Coleman, R., Stubbs, D., Ward, J., Jarrett, J., Lane, R. and Bound, J. (2004) Design for patient safety: A review of the effectiveness of design in the UK health service. *Journal of Engineering Design*, 15: 123–40.

Coussement, J., De Paepe, L., Schwendimann, R., Denhaerynck, K., Dejaeger, E. and Milisen, K. (2008) Interventions for preventing falls in acute- and chronic-care hospitals: A systematic review and meta-analysis. *Journal of the American Geriatrics Society*, 56: 29–36.

Department of Health (2005) Taking healthcare to the patient: Transforming NHS ambulance services. Available at: www.dh.gov.uk/assetRoot/04/11/42/70/04114270.pdf, accessed 13 January 2012.

Donaldson, L.J., Panesar, S.S. and Darzi, A. (2014) Patient-safety-related hospital deaths in England: Thematic analysis of incidents reported to a national database, 2010–2012. *PLOS Med*, 11(6): e1001667.

Donius, M. and Rader, J. (1994) Use of side rails: Rethinking a standard of practice. *Journal of Gerontology Nursing*, 20: 23–7.

Dul, J., Bruder, R., Buckle, P., Carayon, P., Falzon, P., Marras, W.S., Wilson, J.R. and van der Doelen, B. (2012) A strategy for human factors/ergonomics: Developing the discipline and profession. *Ergonomics*, 55(4): 377–95.

Ferreira, J. (2002) Ergonomic investigation of ambulance design: Paramedics working in the patient compartment. Unpublished MSc dissertation, Loughborough University.

Ferreira, J. and Hignett, S. (2005) Reviewing ambulance design for clinical efficiency and paramedic safety. *Applied Ergonomics*, 36: 97–105.

Frengley, J.D. (1999) Bedrails: Do they have a benefit? *Journal of the American Geriatrics Society*, 47(5), 627–8.

Gillespie, L. (2004) Preventing falls in elderly people. *British Medical Journal*, 328: 653–4.

HBSW (2003) Hospital Bed Safety Workgroup. Clinical guidance for the assessment and implementation of bed rails in hospitals, long term care facilities and home care settings. Available at: www.fda.gov/cdrh/beds/index.html, accessed 28 March 2003.

Healey, F., Monro, A., Cockram, A., Adams, V. and Heseltine, D. (2004) Using targeted risk factor reduction to prevent falls in older in-patients: A randomised controlled trial. *Age and Ageing*, 33: 1–5.

Healey, F., Scobie, S., Oliver, D., Pryce, A., Thomson, R. and Glampson, B. (2008) Falls in English and Welsh hospitals: A national observational study based on retrospective analysis of 12 months of patient safety incident reports. *Quality and Safety in Health Care*, 17: 424–30.

Health Education England (2015) Learning to be safer. Available at: https://hee.nhs.uk/work-programmes/human-factors-and-patient-safety/, accessed 17 April 2015.

Hignett, S. (2006) Someone to watch over me: A worm's eye view on safer design in health care. *SaferHealthCare*, 27 July.

Hignett, S. (2013) *Why Design Starts with People*. London: Health Foundation: Patient Safety Resource Centre. Available at: http://patientsafety.health.org.uk/sites/default/files/resources/why_design_starts_with_people.pdf, accessed 10 June 2013.

Hignett, S. and Masud, T. (2006) A review of environmental hazards associated with in-patient falls. *Ergonomics*, 49(5–6): 605–16.

Hignett, S., Crumpton, E. and Coleman, R. (2009) Designing emergency ambulances for the 21st century. *Emergency Medicine Journal*, 26: 135–40.

Hignett, S., Jones, A. and Benger, J. (2011) Portable treatment technologies for urgent care. *Emergency Medicine Journal*, 28: 192–6.

Hignett, S., Fray, M., Benger, J., Jones, A., Coates, D., Rumsey, J. and Mansfield, N. (2012) CURE (Community Urgent Response Environment) portable work stations. *Journal of Paramedic Practice*, 4(6): 352–8.

Hignett, S., Sands, G., Fray, M., Xanthopoulou, D., Healey, F. and Griffiths, P. (2013a) Which bed designs and patient characteristics increase bed rail use? *Age and Ageing*, 42: 531–5.

Hignett, S., Carayon, P., Buckle, P. and Catchpole, K. (2013b) State of science: Human factors and ergonomics in health care. *Ergonomics*, 56(10): 1491–503.

Hignett, S., Griffiths, P., Sands, G., Wolf, L. and Costantinou, E. (2013c) Patient falls: Focusing on human factors rather than clinical conditions. Proceedings of the HFES 2013 International Symposium on Human Factors and Ergonomics in Health Care, Baltimore, MD, 11–13 March.

Hignett, S., Youde, J. and Reid, J. (2014) Using the DIAL-F systems model as the conceptual framework for an audit of in-patient falls risk management. Proceedings of the HFES 2014 International Symposium on Human Factors and Ergonomics in Health Care, Chicago, 9–11 March.

Hignett, S., Miller, D., Wolf, L., Jones, E., Buckle, P. and Catchpole, K. (2015a) What is the relationship between human factors and ergonomics and quality improvement in healthcare? In Sharples, S., Shorrock, S. and Waterson, P. (eds), *Contemporary Ergonomics 2015: Proceedings of the Annual Conference of the Chartered Institute of Ergonomics & Human Factors*. London: Taylor and Francis, 213–19.

Hignett, S., Jones, E., Miller, D., Wolf, L., Modi, C., Shahzad, M.W., Banerjee, J., Buckle, P. and Catchpole, K. (2015b) Human factors and ergonomics and quality improvement science: Integrating approaches for safety in healthcare, *British Medical Journal Quality and Safety*, 24(4): 250–4.

Jones, A. and Hignett, S. (2005) A comparative analysis of stretcher loading systems. In Bust, P.D. and McCabe, P.T. (eds), *Contemporary Ergonomics*. London: Taylor and Francis, 261–5.

Jones, A. and Hignett, S. (2007) Safe access/egress systems for emergency ambulances. *Emergency Medicine Journal*, 24: 200–5.

Jones, A., Hignett, S. and Benger, J. (2009) Mobile pods: Technology to support the delivery of community-based urgent care. Proceedings of the 17th Triennial Congress of the International Ergonomics Association, Beijing, 9–14 August.

Kannus, P., Sievänen, H., Palvanen, M., Järvinen, T. and Parkkari, J. (2005) Prevention of falls and consequent injuries in elderly people. *Lancet*, 366: 1885–93.

Levine, J.M. (1994) A historical perspective on specialty beds and other apparatus for treatment of invalids. *Advanced Wound Care*, 7: 51–4.

Miller, E.J. and Gwynne, G.V. (1972) *A Life Apart: A Pilot Study of Residential Institutions of Physically Handicapped and the Young Chronic Sick*. London: Tavistock.

Morse, J.M., Tylko, S.J. and Dixon, H.A. (1987) Characteristics of the fall-prone patient. *Gerontologist*, 27(4): 516–22.

NHS (2015) Design for patient safety. Available at: www.nrls.npsa.nhs.uk/resources/collections/design-for-patient-safety/, accessed 17 April 2015.

Nyman, S.R. and Victor, C.R. (2011) Older people's recruitment, sustained participation, and adherence to falls prevention interventions in institutional settings: A supplement to the Cochrane systematic review. *Age and Ageing*, 40(4): 430–6.

Oliver, D., Connelley, J.B., Victor, C.R., Shaw, F.E., Whitehead, A., Genc, Y. et al. (2007) Strategies to prevent falls and fractures in hospitals and care homes and effect of cognitive impairment: Systematic review and meta-analyses. *British Medical Journal*, 334: 82–7.

Wilson, J.W., Haines, H. and Morris, W. (2005) Participatory ergonomics. In Wilson, J.W. and Corlett, E.N. (eds), *Evaluation of Human Work*. 3rd edition. London: Taylor and Francis, 933–62.

Wolf, L. and Hignett, S. (2015) Are patients at risk of falling? Not if you ask them! Proceedings of the 19th Triennial Conference of the International Ergonomics Association, Melbourne, Australia, 11–15 August.

Zeisel, J. (2000) Nonpharmacological treatment for Alzheimer's disease: A mind-brain approach. *American Journal of Alzheimer's Disease and Other Dementias*, 15(6): 331–40.

9 Communications

Designing care bundle documentation to support the recognition and treatment of acute kidney injury: a route to quality improvement

*Alison Black, Josefina Bravo Burnier, Matthew Brook,
Clare Carey, Michelle Goonasekera, David Meredith,
Anna Olsson-Brown, Debbie Rosenorn-Lanng
and Emma Vaux*

Abstract

The chapter describes the development of care bundle documentation, through an iterative, user-centred design process, to support the recognition and treatment of acute kidney injury (AKI). The chapter details stages of user and stakeholder consultation, employed to develop a design response that was sensitive to user experience and need, culminating in simulation testing of a near final prototype. The development of supplementary awareness-raising materials relating to the main care bundle tool is also discussed. This information design response to a complex clinical decision-making process is contrasted with other approaches to promoting AKI care. The need for different but related approaches to the working tool itself and the tool's communication are discussed. More general recommendations are made for the development of communication tools to support complex clinical processes.

Introduction

Hospitals are busy environments in which staff teams work under time pressure to make complex decisions about their patients, in changing conditions (Nemeth et al., 2008: 3), often with many interruptions (Parker and Coiera, 2000). In this context, healthcare processes and systems need to be designed to support staff to deliver best practice and defend against possible errors (Reason, 2000). Clinical communication tools support healthcare processes by enabling the sharing of information across teams and compensating for the disruptive impact of interruptions on information processing and memory (Coiera, 2004). They also facilitate decision-making, by supporting exploration and synthesis of patient data (Mamykina et al., 2012). It is essential that communication tools are designed to fit the process staff are engaged in and, in so doing, minimise any additional cognitive demands on them (Wyatt and Wright, 1998). Lack of fit between communication tools and care process may lead to limited use or abandonment of the tools, with consequences for patient care and safety.

Despite the move to electronic communication in hospitals, paper documentation remains a potent support tool for clinical processes. While the design of interfaces for electronic, clinical documentation has been a focus of applied research (Powsner et al., 1998), the detailed design of traditional, paper documentation has received less attention. A salutary exception is the Royal College of Physicians' (2012) research and recommendations for the use of consistently designed data sheets across all UK hospitals, to record 'early warning' data to improve assessment of and response to changes in the condition of acutely ill patients.

This chapter describes collaboration between information designers and clinicians[1] at an NHS hospital trust to develop effective paper documentation for a care bundle to support the recognition and treatment of AKI.[2] The UK National Institute for Clinical Excellence (NICE) introduced care guidelines for AKI (NICE, 2013), following evidence of deficiencies in care and resulting mortality (NCEPOD, 2009). AKI is seen in 13–18 per cent of hospital admissions, with particular prevalence in the elderly. Costs of treatment are high, estimated as exceeding the combined costs of breast, lung and skin cancer (NICE, 2013: 4).

AKI is sometimes called the 'silent killer' (HSJ, 2011a) because there are no easily observable symptoms in its early stages and patient data may be interpreted as a range of conditions. Furthermore, although almost any acute patient is susceptible, AKI may not be a diagnosis that immediately comes to mind for clinicians who are not renal specialists. Hence, hospitals have used care bundles (focused treatment guidelines for implementation by front-line staff) to support AKI detection and initiation of treatment.

Before starting this project the specialist renal team at the trust had already implemented a documented care bundle. However, they knew that the bundle was rarely used, which they attributed, in part, to its poor fit to staff needs. They were concerned about failure to treat AKI early in its development, and low referral rates to renal specialists when needed. The aim of this project was, therefore, to develop documentation that would support non-specialist staff in recognising AKI in its early stages, initiating treatment and making appropriate referrals to renal specialists.

Context for the project

Care bundles and their adoption

A care bundle is defined as 'a collection of processes needed to effectively and safely care for patients undergoing particular treatments with inherent risks' (IHI, 2006). It comprises scientifically grounded components that have been demonstrated to improve patient care outcomes. First introduced in the United States in 2001 (Resar et al., 2012), care bundles are now used worldwide in the care of many critical conditions.

Diffusion and adoption of new standards in hospital care can be slow, although specific factors seem to support adoption, including the use of printed and online materials that are 'forthright and explain the advantages and potential benefits of changing current clinical practice' and, particularly, ensuring that relevant senior clinicians buy into the standard (Khodyakov et al., 2014). A UK study showed variable uptake of care bundles across hospitals, with consequent effects on mortality in the specific conditions targeted (Robb et al., 2010).

Precedents for information-based approaches to AKI management

Two case studies of the use of training materials to raise awareness of AKI were available. Forde et al. (2012) implemented a training programme based around the mnemonic ABCDE (address drugs, boost blood pressure, calculate fluid balance, dip urine, exclude obstruction), which, over the trial period, improved the detection and management of AKI. Similarly, Bhagwanani et al. (2014) used a mnemonic DONUT (dehydration, obstruction, nephrotoxins, urine, think sepsis) which again improved AKI detection and management to some extent.

The mnemonics used by Forde and Bhagwanani et al. indicate the range of factors that need to be taken into account in managing AKI. There is some, but not complete, overlap in the two approaches, although neither specifies a full AKI management process – one might argue, however, that that is not what mnemonics are intended to do. Both mnemonics 'squeeze' the management process to fit the overall framework. ABCDE builds on the familiarity of a more widely used alphabetic mnemonic for the assessment of patients who are becoming rapidly unwell.[3] The mnemonic cues actions to be taken, although the ordering imposed by the alphabet does not follow a desirable clinical process. It also adds in additional wording ('address, boost, calculate', etc.) in order to fit the listed actions to the alphabet. The DONUT mnemonic mixes potential causes of AKI (dehydration, obstruction of the bladder, nephrotoxic drugs, sepsis) with a symptom (low urine output). Neither mentions a primary indicator of AKI: high or increasing creatinine levels (creatinine is waste metabolic product which builds up in the blood if the kidneys are malfunctioning). Creatinine levels are tested routinely on hospital admission and as part of regular patient monitoring. Together with measurement of urine output, they are key to AKI detection. In the papers describing these two precedents, only Bhagwanani appears to have made a distinction between developing training materials and documentation to support clinical processes, but the tools developed in the study (forms and alert stickers to go in patient notes) were not thought to have been particularly successful.

Outside research publications, the London AKI Network developed comprehensive education and documentation materials, pre-dating the publication of the NICE guidelines. These also included a mnemonic for risk assessment, STOP (sepsis, toxicity, obstruction, parenchymal kidney disease). Note, however, the NICE recommendation that all hospitalised patients be considered at risk of AKI, rather than just those with the conditions in the STOP mnemonic. The ambition of the London AKI Network materials (24 dense pages of guidance and forms) and the design approach used perhaps militated against their use.

Others implementing awareness-raising trials have commented on the fragility of improvements in awareness beyond a trial period (Trotter et al., 2014; Xu et al., 2014) and all the trial reports emphasise the need for all members of multidisciplinary teams (from senior clinicians to junior nurses) to be involved in the implementation of the trial approach, if it is to be successful. In our case we were in the strong position of working on a project led by a senior renal consultant, who had the additional brief of quality improvement lead for the hospital trust.

Significance of multidisciplinary team working

Many care decisions, AKI included, depend on the response of multidisciplinary teams to a developing situation. In the case of AKI this team, initially, may include nurses and doctors who are unlikely to be renal specialists although renal specialists may be called in. Team members are likely to have differing levels of experience and seniority. One of the key indicators of AKI, creatinine level, is reviewed by doctors as part of regular patient monitoring, whereas the other key indicator, low or reducing urine output, is monitored by nursing staff. As discussed above, AKI can be identified and treated by non-specialists; however, if it does not respond to treatment, the intervention of specialists is essential. Hence strong cross-disciplinary awareness and communication are required.

Many studies point to deficiencies in cross-disciplinary communication in healthcare (Donchin et al., 1995; Reader et al., 2007), with the contribution of nursing care often under-acknowledged (Lindeke and Sieckert, 2005). Strategies such as the WHO checklist have promoted sharing of knowledge and responsibility in surgical settings (Haynes et al., 2009). However, checklists have only recently been applied in diagnostic, rather than surgical settings

(Ely et al., 2011) and their impact on interdisciplinary teams in medical care has not been documented.

Existing documentation

The existing documentation, designed by the hospital's renal team, is shown in Figure 9.1. The documentation was designed as a 'peel-off' form to be attached onto patient notes. The section surrounding the form and left on the backing sheet was to be kept for audit. A circular sticker, peeled off this backing sheet, was to go over the front edge of the notes folder (a practice used throughout the hospital to indicate a care bundle was in progress). It transpired, however, that use of the bundle was no longer audited, so the surround area (which reduced space available on the form) was redundant. Additionally the renal team had already concluded that some information in the documentation was not relevant and that other information that was important had been omitted. For example, the form specified measurement of EGFr (estimated glomerular filtration rate – a measure of kidney performance) whereas this is only used in the diagnosis of chronic kidney injury; the form suggested a review of medication but did not indicate that the review should consider whether nephrotoxic drugs had been prescribed.

The design of the documentation broadly followed a style adopted across care bundles used within the hospital, following a centrally available template (see samples of other documentation in Figure 9.2). None of these documents is simple to follow and, of necessity, they include densely packed information. However, other care bundles had a broadly linear (top to bottom) arrangement, while the existing AKI bundle was two-column, with additional information in fields extending across the two-column format.

The development process

The role of the information designer

Given the complex medical and social setting for the care bundle, it might be asked what benefit an information designer might bring, other than, perhaps, to improve the typographic organisation of a reformulated document. That was certainly part of the brief. But there was the potential to work with the renal team to ensure the best possible fit between proposed documentation content and the needs of the staff who would use it. This role, often poorly understood outside (and sometimes within) design, follows in the tradition of the Isotype 'transformer' or 'visual editor' (Twyman 1975), working with subject experts on the information they provide, to formulate it in a way appropriate to its audience (MacDonald-Ross and Waller 2000).

In this project iterative engagement with experts and end users served this process of transformation:

- Meetings with nurses and non-specialist doctors to elicit their awareness of AKI, their experience of diagnosing and treating it and of collaboration with the renal team (due to their technical and potentially sensitive nature, these meetings were led by the renal team, with the designers attending).
- Parallel meetings with the renal team to elicit their expectations for AKI care, to reach consensus about care bundle content, given the outcomes of meetings with non-specialist staff.

Acute kidney Injury care bundle

Ward / Department: .... Date and Time: .... Care Bundle commenced by: .... (BLOCK LETTERS) Role & Grade:	Patient label

Aim of care bundle: To effectively recognise and treat acute kidney injury (AKI)

If eGFR <60 THINK AKI CARE BUNDLE

Doctor completing care bundle: Print name and sign...

Date/Time of admission...   **All *sections must be completed and initialled***

		Yes	No
1. eGFR unchanged from baseline	Monitor U+Es during admission (minimum 72 hrly) Care with prescribing and fluid balance		
2. eGFR changed* from baseline	1. Review patient's medication and doses	Yes	No
AKI stage 1 Creatinine increased 1.5-2 x above baseline And/or urine output <0.5ml/kg/hr (6 hrs)	2. Review fluid balance	Yes	No
	3. Urine dipstick	Yes	No
AKI stage 2 Creatinine increased 2-3 x above baseline And/or urine output <0.5ml/kg/hr (6 hrs)	4. USS renal tract within 24 hrs if suspect retention and/or AKI stage 3	Yes	No
	Be aware of potential complications – potassium, acidosis, pulmonary oedema		
AKI stage 3 Creatinine increased 3x above baseline and/or Cr >350 µmol/l And/or Urine output < 0.3ml/Kg/hour	AVOID urinary catheter **Only** insert a urinary catheter for AKI if for 1. Relief of acute or chronic retention *Use Urinary catheter insertion care bundle*		

Consider early input from Renal team if…	
• AKI stage 3 • Difficult to manage AKI - not responding to initial measures within 24 hours • Complications setting in • Any clinical concern	

* Refer to AKI ward acquired guidelines found on trust intranet (search term AKI) for more detailed information
Please note there is a renal consultant on 24 hours a day; contact via switchboard

V2 mar 2011

Instructions
1. Attach patient details.
2. Detach square sticker place in medical notes, and fill in.
3. Detach round sticker place on inside cover of medical notes.
4. File this backing sheet (with patient label) in designated audit tray.

Figure 9.1 Existing hospital AKI bundle documentation, which had been developed by the hospital's renal specialist team, using an A4 template for care bundles for different conditions

Note: The document is colour-coded, using mauve as a second colour.

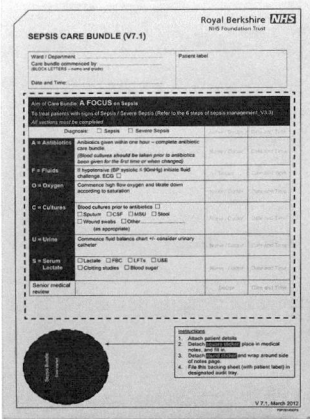 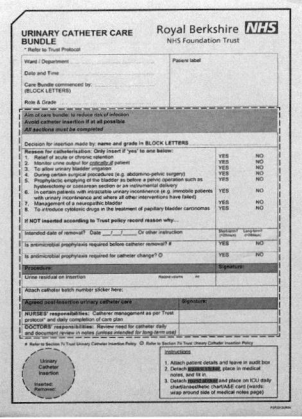 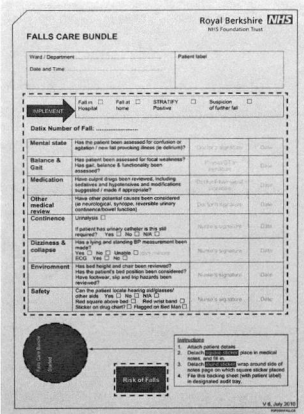

Figure 9.2 Samples of documentation used for care bundles other than AKI, demonstrating the basic A4 format and variations for (from left to right) sepsis, urinary catheter insertion, falls

Note: Note that the bundle documents are colour coded for easy recognition (from left to right, with violet, pink and maroon as second colours).

- Iterative cycles of design and feedback with the renal team to develop a prototype that could be tested against the existing bundle documentation; some further refinement was also carried out after testing.
- Testing use of the bundle in simulated care scenarios with multidisciplinary teams (again, due to their technical nature, testing was led by the hospital's specialist in medical simulation, together with renal specialists, with the designers attending).

The list suggests a more linear process than the actual engagement. Because of the potential complexity of the content and because it was important for project informants and the renal team to see what was possible and usable within the constraints of a standard bundle format, design proposals were presented during the later elicitation meetings. Giving form to ideas helped focus discussion and sparked feedback that shaped development of the documentation.

It is worth noting the constraints on designer involvement in the elicitation and testing stages, partly due to the technical nature of the bundle content, but also to the sensitive nature of research in a service where care quality is subject to scrutiny. These kinds of constraints are not unusual in healthcare research (Black et al. 2013; Katz et al. 2006). However, even with constraints, the engagement was essential to understanding the context for design and invaluable for the development of the design solution.

Understanding user experience

Knowledge gaps

Interviews with doctors and nurses from the hospital's accident and emergency and acute medicine units revealed:

- low awareness of both the NICE guidelines and, as the renal team had thought, the hospital's care bundle;
- awareness of the key indicators, raised creatinine and reduced urine output, but not of the levels that would trigger a response;

- different interpretation across individuals of the reference in existing documentation to 'baseline creatinine levels';
- concern that the weight-based units of measurement for urine output (mls/kg/hr) were unlikely to be used because of the difficulty of weighing acutely unwell patients and because the units appeared unfamiliar and technical to non-specialist nursing staff.

Embedding the bundle in practice

Points were made about the processes and systems linked to use of the care bundle:

- the difficulty of alerting other staff that a care bundle has been initiated, particularly in patients where multiple care bundles were in use, hence the need for dates to be prominent in the notes and on care bundle folder stickers;
- the need to start the care bundle record with a clear statement of why the care bundle had been started, for other staff to pick up on;
- the warning on the care bundle to avoid catheterisation, whereas this might be needed to accurately track patients' urine output;
- the need to trigger investigation of possible AKI on charts used across the hospital to record patients' fluid balance;
- experience of inconsistency in hospital electronic data systems' flagging of potential AKI cases, based on creatinine levels. Hence raised creatinine which was not flagged was sometimes misinterpreted as chronic kidney injury rather than AKI;
- failure of the intranet link given on the existing form.

Interdisciplinary team working

Much discussion stemmed from the different roles of nurses and doctors and, particularly, the scope of nurses to initiate response to AKI:

- Nurses saw the bundle, and particularly its notes sticker, as a tool for alerting doctors to the need for their involvement.
- They commented that while care bundles are, typically, started by nurses, they required a doctor's signature. Finding a doctor to sign documentation wasted valuable time, with little perceived benefit ('[They] have to be signed by doctors who have no investment in the patient. Does it add any value… why can't nurses sign? If the culture is "I'm just signing this box for formality" it's not very useful').
- Some nurses were concerned that doctors would find simplified documentation too basic and would not engage with it.

Input to bundle design

Stemming from this discussion of multidisciplinary working, nurses proposed either that documentation be divided into distinct sections: nurse-facing (dealing with urine output) and doctor-facing (dealing with further investigations). Alternatively, if the bundle was only likely to be used by nurses, the amount of information could be reduced.

More generally, discussion highlighted that the current documentation conflated education (discussion of patients at risk) with instruction about the steps of investigation and treatment: 'This is a care bundle, not a text book', 'It should say "first do this, then do this"'.

Knowledge elicitation with the renal team

The renal team's focus was threefold: raising awareness of AKI, ensuring immediate investigation and treatment and direct involvement of the renal team where needed. They were sensitive to the issues regarding linked systems and processes, raised in user interviews, and had already taken steps to improve the notification of possible AKI on electronic data systems and to include a trigger to 'Think AKI' on fluid balance charts.

Developing bundle content

User experience research (above) confirmed the complexity of decision-making regarding AKI, the potential density of content in bundle documentation and, hence, the limitations of mnemonic approaches used in some of the precedents, discussed above.

A series of project team meetings mapped out the content that needed to be included in the bundle and considered organising frameworks to group the content and support information navigation (Figure 9.3 shows workshop notes using different organising frameworks). A framework was proposed based on a sequence that moved from awareness to action, using the headings 'Risk, recognise, respond, refer'. This was similar to an article, 'Three Rs for reduction', which listed 'reducing risk, early recognition, right response' (HSJ, 2011b). The inclusion of referral as a fourth stage reflected the renal team's focus on specialist involvement. After some debate, and given the requirement to focus on instruction rather than education in the bundle, the first 'R' was removed to give a working framework: 'Recognise, respond, refer'.

Interdisciplinary team working

The project team also considered implementation of the bundle in interdisciplinary teams. The issue of sign-off was discussed but not resolved. It was understood that it imposed a burden on nursing staff and also reduced their sense of agency. An alternative proposal was to break down sign-off so that each part of the bundle was signed by the individual implementing it (nurse or doctor).

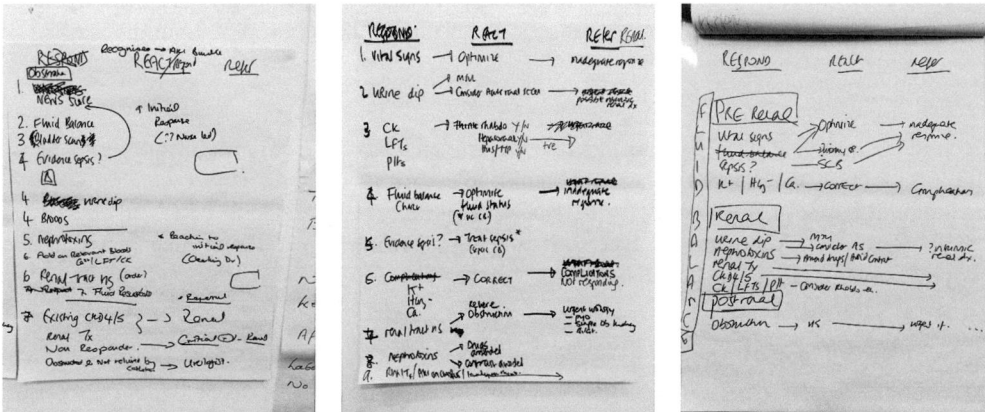

Figure 9.3 Examples of notes taken in meetings to develop care bundle content showing development of the initial three Rs framework: 'Recognise, Respond, Refer'

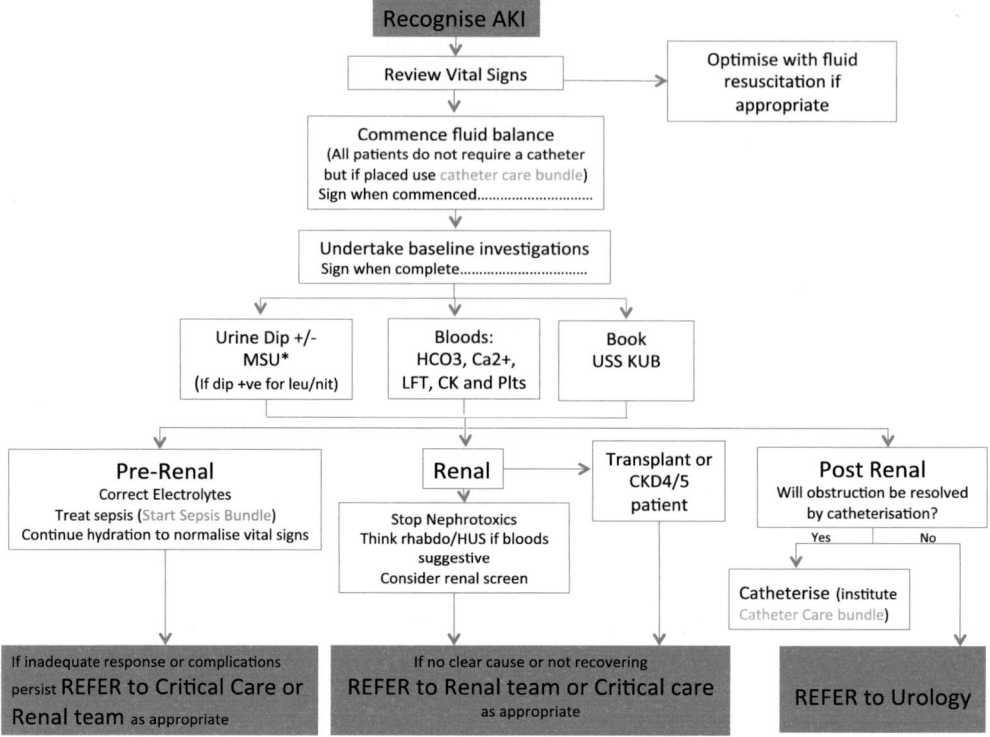

Figure 9.4 Flow diagram representing AKI management process, proposed by a junior doctor participating in knowledge elicitation meetings

Input to bundle design

The use of flow diagrams in the NICE guidelines themselves and in other available documents led to consideration of a similar approach in the care bundle documentation, with one renal team member drafting a flow diagram (Figure 9.4). This approach was abandoned as it appeared to complicate rather than aid content navigation and because a flow diagram's cascading shape was likely to waste rather than maximise space available on the constrained bundle forms.

Raising awareness

Beyond the bundle itself, a separate exercise was initiated to create communications to support the introduction and continuing use of the bundle. Various umbrella terms were considered, including RReact or RResist AKI (the two Rs suggesting Respond and Refer), an alternative 'AKI Aware' and, following a successful campaign, 'Think sepsis', to reduce sepsis in the hospital, an equivalent 'Think AKI'.

Design and feedback

As mentioned above, design was initiated early in the elicitation process to help focus discussion and gather feedback. An initial set of proposals (Figure 9.5) aimed to reflect:

• the communication approaches that had been considered, including variation in the use of two-R (Respond Refer) or three-R (Recognise Respond Refer) approach (compare Figure 9.5a and 9.5b with 9.5c and 9.5d);

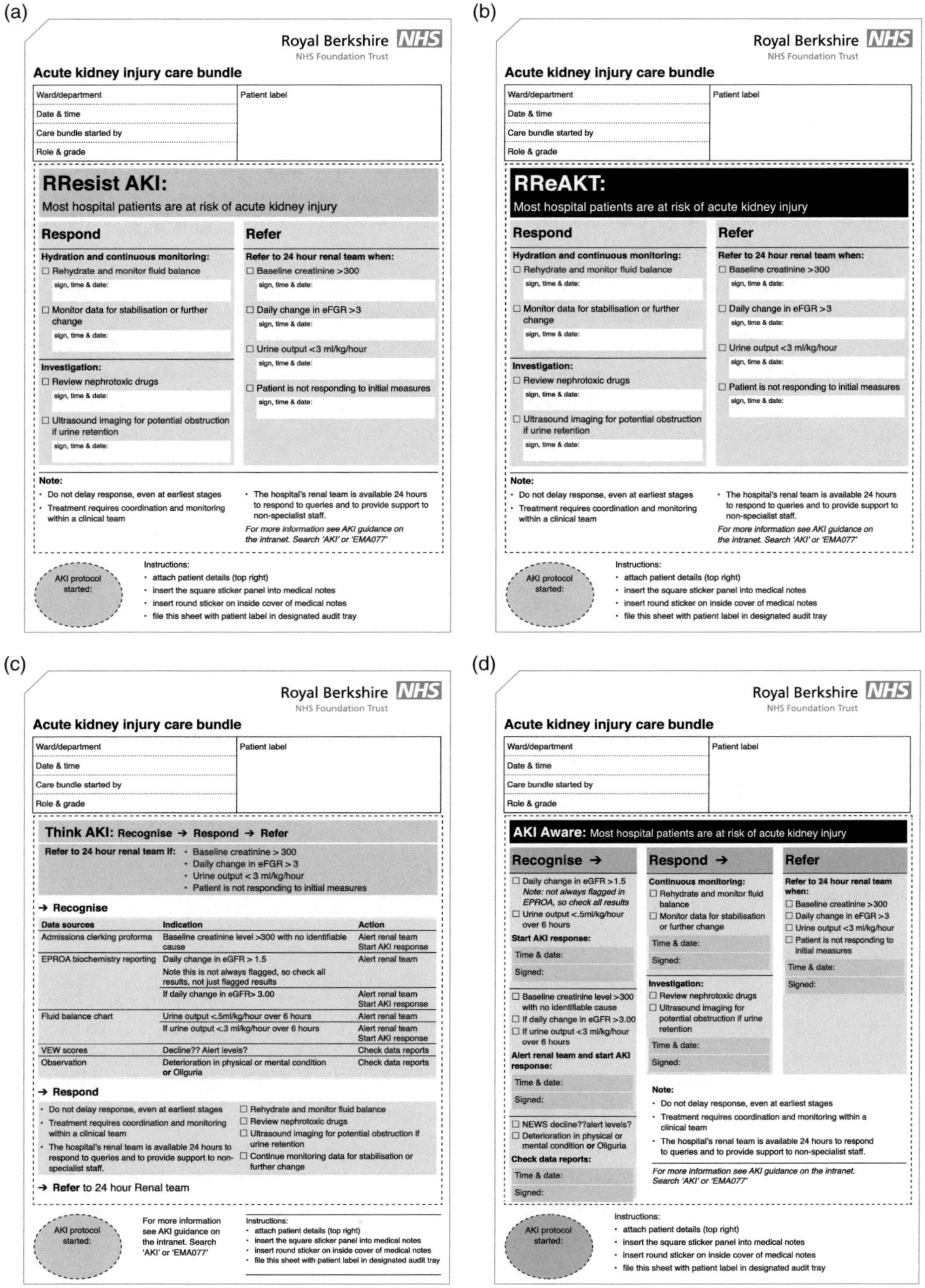

Figure 9.5a–d First set of design proposals showing different approaches to the amount of information included in the care bundle document: (a) Acute kidney injury care bundle; (b) Acute kidney injury care bundle; (c) Acute kidney injury care bundle; and (d) Acute kidney injury care bundle

Note: Documents are A4, black on white with mauve as a second colour to signal the AKI care bundle.

- a 'read down' versus 'read across' arrangement of information (compare Figure 9.5c to 9.5a, 9.5b and 9.5d);
- the inclusion or exclusion of signature boxes (Figure 9.5c signed only by the bundle initiator, 9.5a, 9.5b and 9.5d including signature boxes for each stage of management).

The two-R approach, while creating a less dense document, was rejected because it was felt not to carry adequate information to support bundle implementation. The 'read across' approach was preferred and, in particular, the emphatic statement of 'Recognise Respond Refer' shown in Figure 9.5d.

Further detailed iterations were made to address users' concerns that the reason for starting the bundle should be specified. By implication, including the reason for starting the bundle meant that AKI had been recognised; hence the first of the three Rs was changed from 'Recognise' to 'Review', reflecting more accurately the process being carried out. Document content was aligned to support reading across from 'Review' to 'Respond' with the 'Refer' column treated distinctively, as referral did not follow directly from the steps of the review and response process.

The multiple signature boxes were removed, partly due to the potential barrier to implementation of signature seeking and also, pragmatically, to allow space for content which, with each iteration, was both updated and augmented.

Throughout the process of refinement the design team were concerned to maximise the legibility of increasingly dense information on a necessarily single-sided A4 form. At the same time they contributed to the expansion of content by recommending that some abbreviations were spelled out in full to ensure they would be understood by non-specialist staff.

The established separation of a peel-off form to go into patient notes and an audit sheet was maintained, exerting additional pressure on the limited space until a late decision to override this convention released some space in the (near) final version of the bundle documentation (see Figure 9.6).

Simulation testing

Simulation design

User testing is a key part of the information design process but can be hard to achieve in hospitals and other medical settings. In order to test the new care bundle in as close to real conditions as possible the hospital's simulation suite was used to set up and test simulated scenarios. Nurses and trainee doctors, working in pairs, were presented with patients with typical AKI symptoms and asked to respond to the patients' changing condition.

Two scenarios were used to compare the redesigned documentation with the original, in a balanced study design (each participant pair working on one scenario and with one version of the bundle documentation). Eight nurse/trainee doctor pairs participated (16 participants in all).

Both the simulation scenarios involved a patient in their 70s with multiple health conditions. Study participants were given details of the patients' presenting symptoms and asked to proceed with managing the patient. Appropriate documentation (and also equipment) was provided at the beginning or when requested by participants during the simulation session. Documentation included a drugs chart, urine dip results, blood results and a fluid balance chart (see Figure 9.7). The AKI bundle documentation was available if participants requested it

Acute kidney injury care bundle

Most hospital patients are at risk of acute kidney injury
Do not delay response, even at the earliest stages

AKI care bundle started by: Name: Time: Date:

Due to: ☐ AKI on blood results ☐ Fluid balance: urine output <250ml/6 hours ☐ Critically unwell patient

Review →	Respond →	Refer

Patient assessment
☐ ABCDE
☐ Check early warning score + check for signs of sepsis
	☐ Call for help to resuscitate if patient critical
	☐ Start sepsis care bundle if signs of sepsis
		Immediate referral
		• *Renal*
		  ☐ Existing CKD 4/5
		  ☐ Kidney transplant
		  ☐ Likely intrinsic kidney disease
		  ☐ Complications: K^+ >6.5; anuric; pericarditis; confusion; pulmonary oedema; severe acidosis pH <7.2, HCO_3^- <15

☐ Venous gas (K^+, HCO_3^-, lactate) + send lab bloods	☐ Correct high K^+	
☐ Fluid assessment including fluid balance chart	☐ Fluid resuscitate	
☐ Check previous bloods	☐ Correct abnormalities – add relevant bloods (Ca, LFTs, CK) ☐ Consider glucose levels	• *Urology* ☐ If obstruction and likely pyosepsis, or single kidney, or not relieved by catheter
☐ Urine dip	☐ Consider culture ☐ Consider acute renal screen: ANCA, ANA, anti-GBM, complement, immunoglobulins, BJP	**Within 6 hours of starting bundle** • *Renal* ☐ Cr >300 and non-responder
☐ Bladder scan	☐ If UC used, start UC care bundle. *Avoid urinary catheter unless critically unwell or acute/chronic retention.*	**Within 24 hours of starting bundle** • *Renal* ☐ Inadequate response irrespective of creatinine
☐ Review medication	☐ Stop nephrotoxins: NSAIDs, ACEIs, angiotensin receptor blockers, contrast, diuretics, gentamicin, PPI	• *Urology* ☐ Obstruction on ultrasound scan
☐ Renal tract ultrasound	☐ Contact urology if obstruction	

Note: The renal team is available 24 hours
Renal registrar Monday – Friday 8.30–17.00, bleep number 176 or
contact a consultant through switchboard anytime

For more information see AKI guidance on the intranet. Search 'AKI'

AKI protocol started:

Instructions:
• insert the square sticker panel into medical notes
• insert oval sticker on inside cover of medical notes
• dispose of this sheet

V26 January 2015
Reference number

Figure 9.6 The near final version of the bundle documentation used for simulation testing

Note: Further detailed changes to documentation content were made after testing, and before trial implementation. Printed A4, black on white with mauve as a second colour to signal the AKI care bundle.

(a)
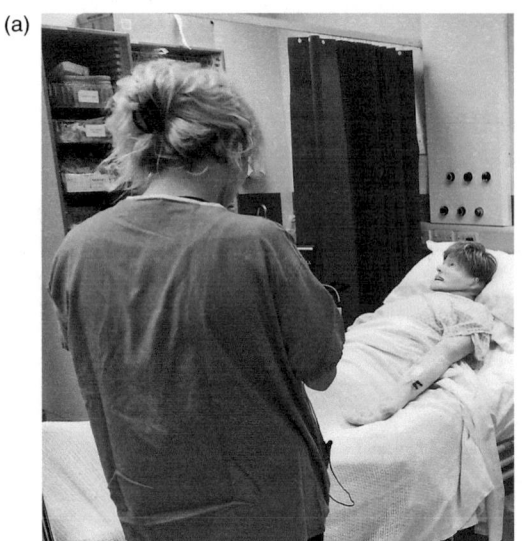

(b)
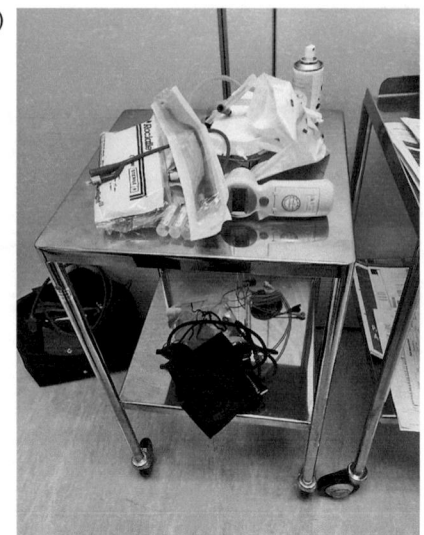

(c)
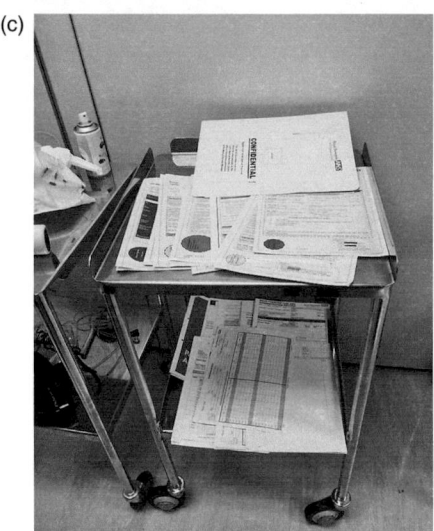

Figure 9.7a–c Detail from simulation testing showing (a) mechanised mannequin (b) equipment and (c) documentation set available at the scenario start

or, if not requested, was handed to participants at a point where the simulation team felt they needed it in order to proceed.

In a structured debriefing session after the simulation the participants were shown the version of the documentation that they had not used (existing or revised) and asked to comment on the two alternatives. They also were asked more generally about the process of embedding use of the bundle in ward practice, particularly how best to communicate it to their colleagues.

Simulation outcomes

In simulation sessions, there was often a delay in identifying the presence of AKI. When prompted with the bundle documentation, those receiving the revised bundle were able to follow it more effectively (including making a referral to the renal team) than those with the original documentation.

In post-simulation debriefing, where participants were given both documents to compare, they commented favourably on the revision, particularly on its step-by-step guidance to AKI management:

> 'Yes, this one [the revision], I would bother to get this out as it is really useful. It's not just paperwork.'
> 'This [current documentation] is written from a doctors' point of view.'
> 'I only remembered to check drugs after looking at the bundle.'
> 'You can just look down the right hand column and see who you should refer to.'

However, some comments questioned the utility of care bundles and aspects of the bundle document design:

> 'I'm quite suspicious of care bundles, I like to think for myself.'
> '... you'd need a little training run through beforehand.'

Comments also highlighted the importance of triggers to start the care bundle:

> '[We need] better triggers on the notes that creatinine levels are high. Alerts will be a massive thing'
> 'We need better fluid balance recording throughout the trust.'
> 'A lot of AKI comes in from the community and the data could be months old.'

Other comments related to past difficulties experienced by trainee doctors in bringing in specialist renal support.

Discussion of possible routes to communicating the bundle highlighted existing communication routes (e.g. weekly briefing meetings for nurses), the need for a high-profile launch and the perceived effectiveness of branded pens (always in use) with a campaign strapline. Participants cited the hospital's successful 'Think sepsis' campaign as a good precedent.

Renal team's conclusions

The team concluded that the bundle document could deliver an improvement in AKI management. Participants' failure to recognise AKI without prompting, however, reinforced the need for improving the triggers to AKI management and for wider communication of the bundle. There was a two fold need to raise awareness among hospital staff, generally, and to overcome perceived barriers to liaison with the renal specialists. In addition, the renal team were already aware of the need to raise awareness among general practitioners treating patients in the community, which was mentioned in comments during debriefing.

Supporting care bundle communication

The design team developed communication materials for a within-trust campaign to raise awareness of the bundle. The strapline for the campaign, 'AKI Aware', was used to develop an illustrated campaign leaflet (Figure 9.8), explaining the three-stage 'Review, respond, refer' process. Since hospital staff must cope with large amounts of paperwork in their professional lives, including abundant information leaflets, the amount of text in the leaflet was limited. Sketch illustrations were included, to attract readers' attention and also to depict the demands on doctors and nurses empathically. The illustrations were made available to the renal team, for use as needed in presentation and training materials.

An additional, awareness-raising version of the AKI bundle was prepared for GPs. Its function differed from the hospital documentation as it was to be accessed via a weblink provided with online reports of blood tests for patients in the community. Where creatinine levels suggested the possibility of AKI, this was flagged, and the link to the bundle document provided. Since awareness of AKI was thought to be lower among GPs than hospital staff, the three Rs were changed from 'Review, respond, refer' to 'Recognise, review, respond', with corresponding instructions to GPs developed by the renal team and a GP specialist (Figure 9.9).

Figure 9.8 Leaflet to support campaign launch
Note: Printed A4 in black and mauve on white.

Royal Berkshire **NHS**

NHS Foundation Trust

Guidance notes for Primary Care

Acute kidney Injury: recognise, review and respond

You have been sent an abnormal alert for AKI.
Consider high risk of AKI or deterioration in heart
failure, CKD, diabetics and transplant patients.

Recognise →	Review →	Respond
AKI Stage 1 • Cr > 1.5-2 × baseline • +/− poor urine output	1. Review/recall patient 2. Medicines: Consider reducing/ stopping diuretics, ACEI/ARBs, NSAIDs, metformin, PPI	**Level 1** Repeat U+E in 1 week *In cases of raised K+, anuria or any clinical concern, contact the Renal Team on-call*
AKI Stage 2 • Cr > 2-3 × baseline • +/− poor urine output	3. See patient to assess • Blood Pressure • Urine output and urine dipstick *If there is infection, do not prescribe trimethoprim or nitrofurantoin* • Blood+/protein (consider intrinsic renal problem)	**Level 2** • Repeat U+E in 48-72hrs *In cases of raised K+, anuria or any clinical concern, contact the Renal Team on-call* • Organise an outpatient USS
AKI Stage 3 • Cr > 3 × baseline • +/− Cr > 350 • +/− no urine output	4. Exclude a palpable bladder. *In obstruction discuss with urology.*	**Level 3** Discuss with the Renal Team

For more information, see NICE guidelines: *https://www.nice.org.uk/guidance/cg169*

The renal team is available 24 hours
Renal registrar Monday – Friday 8.30–17.00, bleep number 176
or contact a consultant through switchboard anytime

Figure 9.9 Adaptation of care bundle documentation for use by general practitioners caring for patients
in the community, for on-screen viewing or on-demand printing by GP

Lessons learned from the project

The impact of information design on the use of technical information and the negative consequences of poor document design have long been understood by information designers (see, for example, Wright 1981; Redish 2000). Given the substantial investment health services make in acquiring and applying medical technologies it is perhaps not surprising that the everyday, ephemeral nature of paper documentation removes it from focus in medical settings. However, as this study has shown, well-designed paper documentation has the potential to contribute to quality improvement. Berwick (2003) has pointed out that for innovations in healthcare to be adopted they must both be easy to use and perceived as useful. Documentation can support both the implementation and communication of new processes, i.e. contribute to both ease of use and perception of usefulness.

This chapter has discussed the role of information designers in the technically and socially complex setting of healthcare innovation. It is prudent to be modest here. The documentation development relied heavily on the renal specialists' nuanced understanding of AKI manage-ment, and their patience in working with non-specialist designers. However, the complementary contribution of designers' treatment of complex information in a constrained graphic context should also be mentioned. Similar descriptions of this complementary development are given by Zender et al., 2017). Furthermore, the design process of iterative prototyping, with input from a wide range of users and stakeholders, shaped the project positively. The availability of early prototypes provided an immediate basis for focused discussion; see Norman (2010) on the contribution of early prototyping to user consultation. While the desire to publish design studies in academic contexts may lead to an aspiration towards methods that pass scrutiny with scientific researchers, pragmatic approaches may be required to achieve results. In this study we were able to combine the two, through a relatively informal, though systematic, approach to user consultation and a more formally structured simulation.

The NHS uses Langley's *Plan Do Study Act* process for improvement (Langley et al. 2009). This study served the Do and Study phases, providing the basis for implementation in the Act phase, which will be proof of the effectiveness of the intervention. The Act phase will comprise not just implementation of the care bundle documentation but the building and sustaining of awareness and practice through training, the example of senior staff, the wider support of the hospital trust and the positive impact of achieving evidence of a reduction in AKI. In this wider context, the detail of the information design supporting the implemented bundle is likely to be lost. Nevertheless, through publication of the designer-clinician collaboration in this project, we hope to build awareness of the potential for quality improvement through design in future, similar initiatives.

Recommendations

Extrapolating general recommendations for the design of communication tools to support quality improvement from the specifics of a single project is not without risk. Nevertheless, we venture the following perspectives.

- Avoid conflating promotion of the process with process documentation itself. Our critique of precursors in AKI care interventions highlights the limitations of leading with promotion rather than the technical information that needs to be communicated. Coming full circle, in the later stages of the project, we were able to develop promotional materials, directing clinical staff to the care bundle itself.

- Design complex information for clarity rather than designing out complexity inappropriately. Participant response in simulation tests indicated that, far from finding the detailed information in the care bundle off-putting, participants responded positively to detail, organised in a navigable structure.
- At the same time, focus the content and design of the documentation on the needs of the people who will use it. Where it is possible to do so, edit out extraneous information – for example, in this case, the technically correct, but rarely used, measurement of glomerular flow rate and the inclusion of a legacy audit form.
- Where possible, link documentation with connecting processes and systems. Triggering initiation of the care bundle through alerts on patient data systems and prompts on fluid balance charts is likely to increase the impact of the care bundle itself once implemented.

Finally, although not specific to information design for clinical settings, we cannot overemphasise the contribution of user and stakeholder consultation throughout the design process. The combination of consultation, prototyping, gathering feedback and iterating design strengthened confidence in the final design solution.

Acknowledgements

The development of the AKI care bundle documentation was supported by funding from the Thames Valley Strategic Clinical Network Innovation and Diffusion fund. We are grateful to Sue Anderson and Jade Twist for their assistance with the simulation study and to the nurses and trainee doctors who gave their time to participate in it.

Notes

1 The clinicians were renal specialists and a specialist in medical simulation.
2 'Acute kidney injury' is sometimes described using the lay term 'kidney failure' outside medical circles.
3 In acute care assessment ABCDE stands for airways, breathing, circulation, disability, exposure. It was used in this sense in the final care bundle documentation (see Figure 9.8).

References

Berwick, D.M. (2003) Disseminating innovations in health care. *Journal of the American Medical Association*, 289(15): 1969–75.

Bhagwanani, A., Carpenter, R. and Yusuf, A. (2014) Improving the management of acute kidney injury in a district general hospital: Introduction of the DONUT bundle. *British Medical Journal Quality Improvement Reports*, 2(2). doi: 10.1136/bmjquality.u202650.w1235.

Black, A., Gibb, A., Carey, C., Barker, S., Leake, C. and Solomons, L. (2013) Designing a questionnaire to gather carer input to pain assessment for hospitalised people with dementia. *Visible Language*, 47(2): 37–60.

Coiera, E. (2004) Four rules for the reinvention of health care. *British Medical Journal*, 328(7449): 1197–9. doi: 10.1136/bmj.328.7449.1197.

Donchin, Y., Gopher, D., Olin, M., Badihi, Y., Biesky, M., Sprung, C.L., Pizov, R. and Cotev, S. (1995) A look into the nature and causes of human errors in the intensive care unit. *Critical Care Medicine*, 23(2): 294–300.

Ely, J.W., Graber, M.L. and Croskerry, P. (2011) Checklists to reduce diagnostic errors. *Academic Medicine*, 86(33): 307–13. doi: 10.1097/ACM.0b013e31820824cd.

Forde, C., McCaughan, J. and Leonard, N. (2012) Acute kidney injury: It's as easy as ABCDE. *British Medical Journal Quality Improvement Reports*, 1(1). doi: 10.1136/bmjquality.u200370.w326.

Haynes, A.B., Weiser, T.G., Berry, W.R., Lipsitz, S.R., Breizat, A.-H.S., Dellinger, E.P., Herbosa, T., Joseph, S., Kibatala, P.L., Lapitan, M.C.M., Merry, A.F., Moorthy, K., Reznick, R.K., Taylor, B. and Gawande, A.A. (2009) A surgical safety checklist to reduce morbidity and mortality in a global population. *New England Journal of Medicine*, 360(5): 491–9. doi: 10.1056/NEJMsa0810119.

HSJ (2011a) Prevent this silent killer: Care of the acutely unwell. *Health Service Journal/NHS Kidney Care Special Supplement*. Available at: www.hsj.co.uk/Journals/2/Files/2011/6/23/HSJ_Supplement_acutekidneyinjur_23june.pdf, accessed 16 February 2015.

HSJ (2011b) Three Rs for reduction. *Health Service Journal/NHS Kidney Care Special Supplement*. Available at: www.hsj.co.uk/Journals/2/Files/2011/6/23/HSJ_Supplement_acutekidneyinjur_23june.pdf, accessed 16 February 2015.

IHI (2006) Raising the bar with bundles: Treating patients with an all or nothing standard. *Joint Commission Perspectives on Patient Safety*, 6(4). Available at www.IHI.org, accessed 16 February 2015.

Katz, M.G., Kripalani, S. and Weiss, B.D. (2006) Use of pictorial aids in medication instructions: A review of the literature. *American Journal of Health-System Pharmacy*, 63(23): 2391–8.

Khodyakov D., Ridgely, M.S., Huang, C., DeBartolo, K.O., Sorbero, M.E. and Schneider, E.C. (2014) Project JOINTS: What factors affect bundle adoption in a voluntary quality improvement campaign? *British Medical Journal Quality and Safety* Online First. doi: 10.1136/bmjqs-2014–003169, accessed 16 February 2015.

Langley G.L., Nolan, K.M., Nolan, T.W., Norman, C.L. and Provost, L.P. (2009) *The Improvement Guide: A Practical Approach to Enhancing Organizational Performance*. 2nd edition. San Francisco: Jossey Bass.

Lindeke, L. and Sieckert, A. (2005) Nurse-physician workplace collaboration. *Online Journal of Issues in Nursing*, 10(1).

Macdonald-Ross, M. and Waller, R. (2000) The transformer revisited. *Information Design Journal*, 9(2–3): 177–93.

Mamykina, L., Vawdrey, D.K., Stetson, P.D., Zheng, K. and Hripcsak, G. (2012) Clinical documentation: Composition or synthesis? *Journal of the American Medical Informatics Association*, 19(6): 1025–31. doi: 10.1136/amiajnl-2012-000901.

NCEPOD (2009) Acute kidney injury: Adding insult to injury. Available at: www.ncepod.org.uk/2009report1/Downloads/AKI_report.pdf, accessed 16 February 2015.

Nemeth, C., Wears, R., Woods, D., Hollnagel, E. and Cook, R. (2008) Minding the gaps: Creating resilience in health care, in *Advances in Patient Safety: New Directions and Alternative Approaches*, Volume 3. Rockville, MD: Agency for Healthcare Research and Quality.

NICE (2013) Acute kidney injury: Prevention, detection and management of acute kidney injury up to the point of renal replacement therapy. Clinical guideline 169. Available at: http://guidance.nice.org.uk/CG169.

Norman, D.A. (2010) Technology first, needs last: The research–product gulf. *Interactions*, 17(2): 38–42. doi: 10.1145/1699775.1699784.

Parker, J. and Coiera, E. (2000) Improving clinical communication: A view from psychology. *Journal of American Medical Informatics*, 7: 453–61.

Powsner, S.M., Wyatt, J.C. and Wright, P. (1998) Opportunities for and challenges of computerisation. *Lancet*, 352(9140): 1617–22.

Reader, T.W., Flin, R. and Cuthbertson, B.H. (2007) Communication skills and error in the intensive care unit. *Current Opinion in Critical Care*, 13(6): 732–6.

Reason, J. (2000) Human errors: Models and management. *British Medical Journal*, 320(7237): 768–70.

Redish, J.C. (2000) What is information design? *Technical Communication*, 47(2): 163–6.

Resar, R., Griffin, F.A., Haraden, C. and Nolan, T.W. (2012) Using care bundles to improve health care quality. Cambridge, MA: Institute for Healthcare Improvement. Available at: www.ihi.org.

Robb, E., Jarman, B., Suntharalingam, G., Higgens, C., Tennant, R. and Elcock, K. (2010) Using care bundles to reduce in-hospital mortality: quantitative survey. *British Medical Journal*. Available at: http://dx.doi.org/10.1136/bmj.c1234.

Royal College of Physicians (2012) National early warning score (NEWS): Standardising the assessment of acute-illness severity in the NHS. Available at: www.rcplondon.ac.uk/resources/national-early-warning-score-news.

Trotter, N., Doherty, C., Tully, V., Davey, P. and Bell, S. (2014) Improving the recognition of post-operative acute kidney injury. *British Medical Journal Quality Improvement Reports*, 3(1). doi: 10.1136/bmjquality.u205219.w2164.

Twyman, M. (1975) The significance of isotype, in Edwards, J.A. and Twyman, M. (eds), *Graphic Communication through Isotype*. Reading: University of Reading, 7–17.

Wright, P. (1981) The instructions clearly state… Can't people read? *Applied Ergonomics*, 12(3): 131–42.

Wyatt, J.C. and Wright, P. (1998) Design should help use of patients' data. *Lancet*, 352(9137): 1375–8. doi: 10.1016/s0140-6736(97)08306-2.

Xu, G., Baines, R., Westacott, R., Selby, N. and Carr, S. (2014) An educational approach to improve outcomes in acute kidney injury (AKI): Report of a quality improvement project. *British Medical Journal Open*, 4(3). doi: 10.1136/bmjopen-2013–004388.

Zender, P.M., Brinkman, W.B. and Widdice, L.E. (2017) Design + medical collaboration illustrated by three cases designing decision support aids, in Black, A., Luna, P., Lund, O. and Walker, S.F. (eds) *Information design: research and practice*. London: Routledge, 655–668.

Theme 3
Design in chronic health

10 Behaviours

Design and behaviour change in health

Claire Craig and Paul Chamberlain

Abstract

This chapter explores the role of design in the context of behaviour change for people living with long-term conditions. A series of short case studies illustrates how design can facilitate the development of products and interventions that better support the needs of individuals and how these can lead to positive coping behaviours. The chapter concludes with a broader discussion of the complexities and ethical issues that design in the context of behaviour change promotes.

Introduction

Design and human behaviour are integrally linked. The design of objects, the wider environment, the way services are configured all elicit particular ways of responding and behaving (Fry, 2008; Niedderer et al., 2013). Interest in this relationship between design and behaviour change has been growing particularly in the context of the broader healthcare environment. This interest stems from an increasing recognition that when certain behaviours are adopted improvements in health outcomes and quality of life ensue (Alcorn and Broome, 2014; Brady et al., 2013; Rabe et al., 2007).

This chapter considers the role that design can play in promoting and facilitating these changes with a particular focus on individuals living with long-term conditions and begins by describing something of the wider context. It explores why an approach that focuses on behavioural change may be particularly relevant and of value to this population group. We then share three examples of research programmes undertaken in Lab4Living at Sheffield Hallam University. These are a product innovation focusing on the development of a neck collar for people living with motor neurone disease; a research programme focusing on design thinking in enabling individuals living with spinal cord injury to better manage their condition and an open-design research project which engaged young people with cystic fibrosis in the design of products to manage their medication. We share some of the findings of the research and suggest some of the principles that enabled positive behaviour change to occur. The chapter then turns to a critical discussion of the complexities of design in health behaviour change, ending with recommendations for future avenues for research and development.

The relationship between design and behaviour change has been recognised for some time. Niedderer and colleagues (2014) suggest that its origins can be traced to design psychology or behavioural design (Norman, 1988) which set out to understand the intuitive use of objects and our responses to them. Over time a shift in emphasis occurred and approaches developed with the express purpose of harnessing the potential of design to explicitly shape behaviour as can be seen in the Loughborough model (Lilley, 2009), the work of Lockton et al. (2010) in the development of design with intent and the emergence of persuasive technology (Fogg, 2003).

Recently there has been increasing interest as to how these approaches might be applied to the emerging field of design for health, particularly in relation to supporting individuals living with long-term conditions.

Defining long-term conditions

The Department of Health defines a long-term condition as a 'health problem that cannot be cured but can be controlled by medication or other therapies' (Department of Health, 2012: 3). Long-term conditions can have a number of causes. Some are genetic in origin. For instance, cystic fibrosis is a chronic, genetic condition that affects individuals from birth. Other long-term conditions may occur at a later point in the life course and arise through a combination of biological vulnerability and environmental factors. For instance, the Stress Vulnerability model initially proposed by Zubin and Spring (1977) has been used to account for a number of chronic mental health conditions including bipolar disorder, manic depression and schizophrenia. Some long-term conditions occur completely as the result of environmental factors including trauma and infection. Brain injury and spinal cord injury would be examples of this. Others such as heart disease, high blood pressure and Type 2 diabetes have strong links to or may be exacerbated by unhealthy lifestyle choices.

At present it is estimated that long-term conditions affect over 15 million people in the United Kingdom (Department of Health, 2012). The complexity of individuals' needs means that at present, people living with chronic conditions occupy 70 per cent of all inpatient bed days, 50 per cent of all GP appointments and 64 per cent of all outpatient appointments. This amounts to approximately 70 per cent of the total health and social care budget (King's Fund, 2015). Future projections regarding this population are at present unclear. Recent reports by the Department of Health suggest that these figures will remain relatively stable until 2018 whilst other reports highlight the correlation between some long-term conditions and ageing and suggest that as the population ages a further £5 billion will be required to provide for care over the next ten years. There is some consensus that the number of people with three or more long-term conditions will rise to 2.9 million by 2018 (an increase in 1 million from 2008).

Current policy directives therefore place emphasis on the prevention and management of multiple morbidities rather than single diseases. Given the role that lifestyle plays in contributing to these morbidities (Mokdad et al., 2004; Scarborough et al., 2011) the aim of health interventions currently revolves around enabling individuals to manage their condition in order to prevent the deterioration of the original condition and the development of secondary problems. This is primarily achieved through a combination of education and practical support in terms of how to adjust behaviour and routines in order to live with the condition (Welsh Assembly Government, 2007).

This adjustment will occur throughout the life course. Living with any long-term condition will require the individual to make changes in behaviour at every level (Alcorn and Broome, 2014). This may be in relation to their day-to-day routines and the decisions they make. It may involve following a treatment regime, making changes in relation to how tasks and activities are undertaken, developing new habits and routines as well as avoiding certain behaviours known to exacerbate a condition (World Health Organization, 2007, 2010). There will be an ongoing process of both physical and psychological adjustment. The process can be complex and will be affected by a host of factors including the individual's personality, coping mechanisms, physical and mental health, resilience, support networks and the nature of the condition (Schutzer and Graves, 2004). For example, a person living with rheumatoid arthritis may have relatively long periods when this is stable interspaced by flare-ups where joint stability is particularly vulnerable and they will struggle to undertake activities of daily living. For a person living with a condition such as cystic fibrosis, treatment and care may be more intensive and ongoing. Each person's response will be unique. However, it can be said that any long-term condition has the potential to impact on every aspect of a person's life including physical functioning, mental wellbeing, social relationships, self-perception and employment (Harris et al., 2003).

Supporting the individual in adjusting their behaviour and lifestyle to cope with the long-term condition is therefore an important area for consideration. At a recent Design for Health event held at the Helen Hamlyn Centre it was highlighted that 'the first six months following diagnosis is a critically important time for chronic care patients to regain control of their lives. Yet almost 30% of post-surgical patients are back in hospital within 30 days because they have trouble adapting to new behaviors after they get home' (Helen Hamlyn Centre, 2013).

What follows is a description of three research programmes undertaken by researchers in Lab4Living. Lab4Living is an interdisciplinary research cluster at Sheffield Hallam University drawing together a cohort of expertise in design, healthcare, creative practice and engineering. The case studies have been chosen to reflect the diversity of approaches relating to a number of long-term conditions.

Three case studies

Case study 1: Head Up

Head Up is a research project led by Joseph Langley and Heath Reed. People with motor neurone disease (MND) often develop weak neck muscles, leading to pain, restricted movement and problems with swallowing, breathing and communication. Ideally, a neck collar would help alleviate these. However, neck collars currently available are of limited use for people with MND and are often rejected by patients. The same is true for patients with neck weakness due to other conditions.

The Head Up research programme was a two-year study funded by the National Institute for Health Research's Invention for Innovation, the principal aim of which was to develop a novel neck orthosis for neck weakness that offered the necessary support whilst allowing freedom to move without negatively impacting on quality of life.

The research represented a close collaboration between clinicians, engineers, creative designers, patients and carers. Individuals participated in a series of workshops where the emphasis was on developing solutions through a co-design methodology. Through this process end users were able to highlight the strengths and limitations of existing products and offer ongoing feedback on the different iterations as the design of the neck orthosis evolved.

A series of comfort assessments offered the designers a first-hand experience of how it felt to wear existing neck collars. In addition, the research included an engineering simulation of the neck and upper torso, which enabled the designers to understand the nature of the contact between body and collar, and the pressure of that contact. Data of this experience was collected using the McGill pain questionnaire and emotional responses to the impact of wearing the collars was documented.

The result of this process is the Sheffield Support Snood that consists of a lightweight snood that fits the back of the neck of the user allowing it to be worn under clothing (Figures 10.1

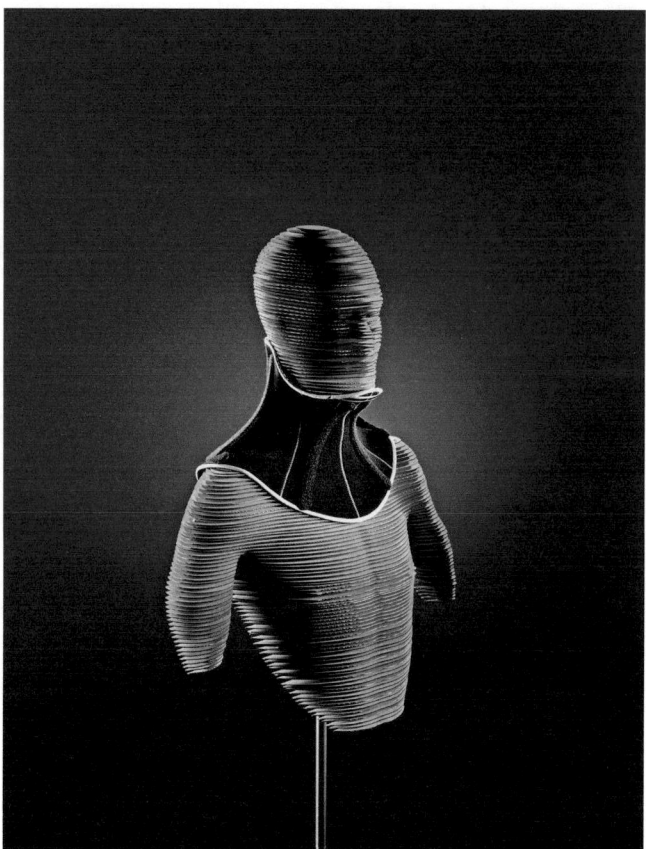

Figure 10.1 The Sheffield Snood

and 10.2). The snood functions as a scaffold for additional lightweight polymer support structures that can be added or removed according to the degree of support required by individual users. Key strengths of the design relate to its aesthetic qualities as well as to improved comfort, as the following quotes by participants reflect:

> 'I love the way you can adjust it in lots of different ways.'
> 'It looks like an item of clothing and you can wear a scarf over it.'

Moreover, findings of a preliminary study to examine the efficacy of the design has shown that the product has increased the amount of time users wear the support by up to 80 per cent – a significant change in behavioural practices (Langley et al., 2014).

Case study 2: design thinking and spinal cord injury

This case study describes an enquiry focusing on individuals living with a degenerative long-term condition. The study explored the potential of design in behaviour change for individuals

Figure 10.2 Testing the Sheffield Snood

living with a sudden onset of a long-term condition acquired as a consequence of trauma or illness.

It is estimated that 40,000 people are currently living with spinal cord injury in the United Kingdom. The degree to which an individual's function and behaviour is affected will very much depend on the nature of the injury. Broadly, spinal cord injuries are frequently categorised into complete or incomplete, depending on the level of damage to the spinal nerves. In complete injury the person will experience paralysis below the level of the injury. For people living with incomplete spinal cord injury there will be some movement and sensation below the injury. Nonetheless, whether complete or incomplete a person experiencing this type of long-term condition will require a significant degree of physical, psychological and behavioural adjustment to cope with the impact of this on their everyday life.

The research programme was part of the Royal Society of Arts (RSA) Design and Rehabilitation Initiative and was a collaboration between designers and researchers in Lab4Living at Sheffield Hallam University, Princess Royal Spinal Injuries Centre and the RSA. The aim of the research, led by Professor Paul Chamberlain, was to evolve a co-productive process of discovery, enabling people with spinal cord injury to gain insight into and develop alternative ways of thinking about and taking control of their interactions with the environment. Underpinning the research was the question as to whether design thinking could facilitate change through building self-efficacy for individuals learning to cope with the injury.

Initial results of the study were very promising and a number of the participants who took part in the research described how the experience had led them to think very differently about their condition which, in turn, had shaped how they approached a number of aspects of their lives. These findings very much reflected Campbell's suggestion that 'if people and not just designers have tools available to be more resourceful then changes may be seen in their self-management ability' (in Craig et al., 2013: 798).

Building on this work, Wolstenholme et al. (2014) developed a series of workshops focusing on design thinking that were shared with 20 people with spinal cord injury on the unit in Sheffield. The results of this study were again very promising. Participants described how they had used the skills learned to change the way they approached aspects of their life, enabling individuals to make changes in their routines and how they adjusted to living with the injury. As one of the participants in the study described, 'I used it when thinking around setting a routine at home, the activities give a framework' (Wolstenholme et al., 2014). Further research is clearly required. However, from these two studies it is possible to see how such an approach may promote changes in social adjustment to the injury.

This chapter has thus far described a potential role of design in supporting change and adjustment to living with a degenerative neurological long-term condition, a long-term condition arising more unexpectedly as a consequence of illness or trauma. How then might design support individuals who are living with a long-term condition that is genetic in origin and present from birth? This is the focus of our final case study.

Case study 3

Cystic fibrosis is a genetic condition affecting the lungs and digestive system, which become clogged with a thick and sticky mucus. The condition has a significant impact on a person's quality of life since management of the condition requires adherence to a strict daily regimen and periodic stays in hospital.

Matthew Dexter's research explored the potential of the open design process as a way of engaging with people living with cystic fibrosis to give individuals a chance to play an active role in the design of products to manage their condition through the process (Dexter et al., 2013). If individuals living with long-term conditions are required to use particular medical products and devices it seems important to involve them in the design of the products to ensure an optimum fit between the design of the product and their requirements.

Given that cystic fibrosis is a condition where compromised immunity can make it difficult for individuals living with the condition to engage in face-to-face collaborative design processes, this research utilised open design to facilitate a design process with people living with the condition. Open design was facilitated by the internet and distributed digital manufacturing (e.g. 3D printing) and as such the participants did not need to travel – instead using bespoke online tools for collaboration in their own home.

This research project recruited individuals living with cystic fibrosis in the UK and the USA to a bespoke online social network, where they designed products from their own lived experience. These were prototyped and made using a MakerBot 3D printer at Sheffield Hallam University's workshop facilities (mimicking a Fab Lab). The participants that did not have access to a Fab Lab or 3D printer themselves had prototypes posted to them by the project leader (Figure 10.3).

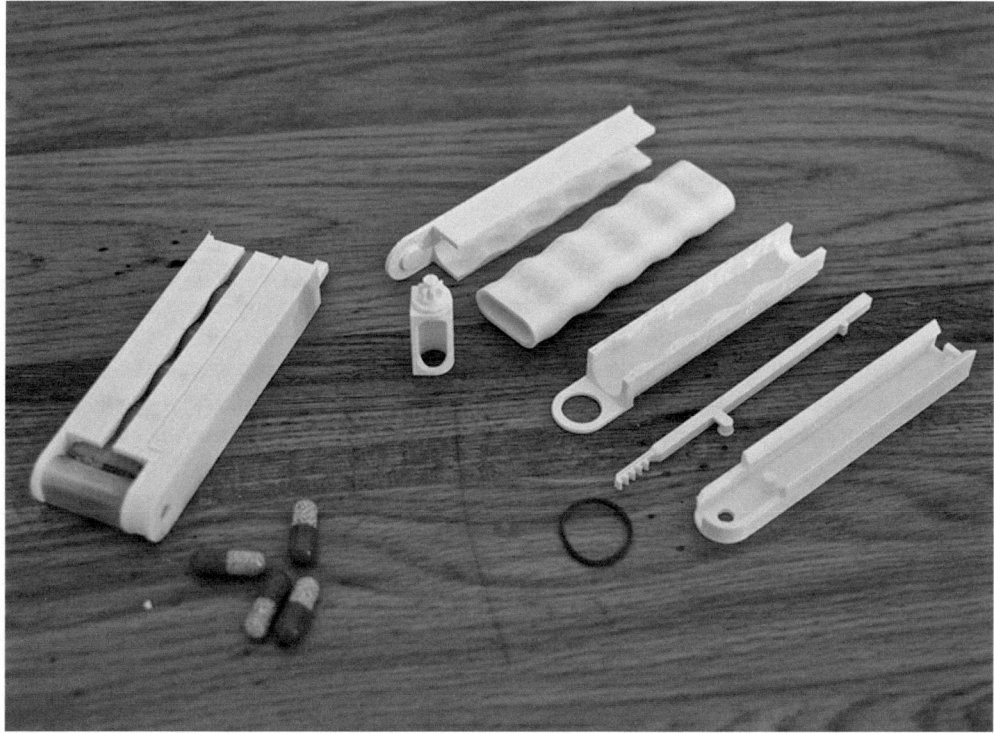

Figure 10.3 One of the designs generated through the open design process

Further research in this area is required in order to determine whether this involvement was sufficient to trigger increased use of and compliance with treatment regimens. However, it marked an important first step in demonstrating that the participants were able to conceive, design and develop complex devices that fitted needs based on their own lived experience.

The use of open design was fundamental for this process, as it allowed for the rapid development of the ideas, with less chance of duplicated work as everyone had access to the project files (Dexter et al., 2013).

Reflections

Whilst the above case studies describe work with very different groups of individuals managing quite distinct challenges we believe that they offer a number of useful insights in relation to design in context and behaviour change.

First and foremost they highlight the dangers of making assumptions as to why a person is behaving in a certain way. It would have been easy to assume, for instance, that the primary reason why people living with motor neurone disease chose not to wear a neck brace was due to discomfort. However, it soon became apparent that the aesthetic of the orthosis and how it related to the person's self-image was as important as the resolution of the current constricting nature of existing neck braces to the individuals we worked with.

The second insight was the importance of not just offering information but of also providing structures and frameworks to scaffold change or to focus and direct energies. The spinal cord project particularly illustrated the value, providing a tangible illustration of how design thinking could provide an important set of tools to enable individuals to conceptualise their spinal injury in a different way and to adopt strategies to adapt to living and behaving with this.

There was great merit in bringing people together, both to share challenges but also to offer potential solutions and alternatives. This was true of all the projects cited and the final case study suggests that creating virtual meeting places is also a viable way forward.

The success of the projects we describe were underpinned by a number of key principles.

First and foremost each of the studies highlight the importance of working with people. We have already acknowledged that how a person experiences and manages their long-term condition is unique to the individual and the importance of spending time to understand these challenges is paramount. The level of participation and partnership was achieved through involving end users at each stage of the research, rather than just consulting at the beginning and the end of the process. Involvement was not confined to simply talking and commenting on issues but on photographing, drawing and responding to objects through active engagement, leading to the development of new and shared insights.

The second key principle we believe these case studies embody is that they draw on people's strengths, positioning individuals as experts because they are experts in living with their condition. At no point did the design process disempower the participants. Rather it took as its starting point the strengths and the abilities of the person. We sought to challenge potential imbalances of power between the researcher and the researched and to work in partnership with individuals. Where new behaviours developed they did so as a consequence of people utilising their strengths and using these as a way of moving forward in a different way. This seems to be particularly important when designing for people with long-term conditions where so much of their self-efficacy and choice has been eroded. An approach that offers new possibilities, showing people what they are able to do feels to be of value.

The case studies also reiterate the value of interdisciplinarity. The research did not only rely on the extensive skills of designers but of engineers, healthcare practitioners, of experts in manufacturing. This way expertise could be pooled in order to develop both potential and real solutions to meet the requirements of individuals participating in the studies.

The final principle to which we wish to allude is the importance of holism, of the need to understand the physical and psychological aspects of living with the condition, of recognising the dimensions of work, home and community and of recognising the importance of the aesthetic in challenging stigma and offering aspects of normalisation.

Interestingly our findings closely reflect the guidance suggested as best practice by the Department of Health, Social Services and Public Safety (2012: 13), which are as follows:

> Working in partnership: The person, and the interests of the person, should be at the centre of all relationships. People, and where appropriate their carers, must be recognised as partners in the planning of services, which should be integrated and based on collaborative working across all sectors.
>
> Supporting self-management: Self-management should provide people with long-term conditions with the knowledge and skills they need to manage their own condition more confidently and to make daily decisions which can maintain or enhance their health and wellbeing as well as their clinical, emotional and social outcomes.
>
> Managing medicines: Individualised support should be available for people with long-term conditions to achieve the best possible outcome from their medicines.

Niedderer et al. (2014: 36) state,

> if in design for behavior change we understand design as a social process we can see that at its heart are people. Therefore at the most elementary level design for behavior change attempts to understand people, why they behave in the way they do and to use design to encourage them to 'do' or 'not do' something.

In the examples we provide this understanding has led to better design of products, the application of design thinking as a way of claiming back and gaining control or the manifestation of products through a shared process of making in open design. This certainly sits well with the original conceptualisation of behavioural design as expounded by Don Norman (1988) with respect to product design.

However, the examples we have included all refer to positive changes, the adoption of new behaviours and ways of thinking. What about the role of design in inhibiting or changing unhelpful behaviour? Poor lifestyle habits can play a significant contributing factor to many long-term conditions (Alcorn and Broome 2014). Poor diet, lack of exercise, smoking and the overconsumption of alcohol can significantly increase the risk of chronic disease including diabetes, cancer and heart disease (Hu et al., 2001; Colaguiuri et al., 2009; Rabe et al., 2007). It can also exacerbate existing problems. For instance, according to Arthritis Research UK, for every pound a person is overweight three extra pounds of stress is placed on the knee joint and six pounds of excess stress is placed on the hip joint. For a person living with chronic arthritis this can significantly exacerbate the condition, leading to further joint instability and pain.

Dizzying arrays of approaches to behaviour change exist including the Theory of Planned Behaviour Model (Ajzen, 1991), the Health Belief Model (Rosenstock, 1988; Sharma and Romas, 2012) and the Stages of Change, also known as the Trans-Theoretical Model (Prochaska and Di Clemente, 1983; Prochaska et al., 1992). Designers have drawn on a number of models from psychology and the behavioural sciences. Lee et al. (2011) for instance have utilised behavioural economics in their design of interventions to reduce the consumption of unhealthy snacks in the workplace, 'presenting choices in a way that leverages people's decision processes and induces them to make self-beneficial choices' (Niedderer et al., 2014: 28).

Closely related to this is nudge: a concept in behavioural science that has been applied by designers (Sunstein and Reisch, 2013). In a similar way to models based on behavioural economics the focus here is on shaping the decisions a person makes by making the healthy choice the default position. However, the key component is that at each point a person has the freedom to opt out if they choose. For instance, in order to encourage its employees to drink more water the company Google placed bottled water on eye-level shelves behind clear glass. Less healthy beverages were placed on the bottom shelves of refrigerators and behind frosted glass. Whilst at no point was the right of the employee not to drink sugary sodas removed, by making the drinking of water the easier position to take, the company increased water consumption by 47 per cent and reduced the drinking of sugar-laden sodas by 7 per cent (Chang and Marsh 2013). Such is the potential of this approach in relation to behaviour change that the 'Nudge Unit' (Behavioral Insights Team) in the British Cabinet Office has been formed bringing together designers and behavioural scientists with the express purpose of finding ways to improve society's behaviour. These approaches are frequently categorised or described as 'libertarian paternalism', the idea being that rather than actively changing a person's behaviour it is possible to simply 'design out' the problem.

These approaches, however, have been criticised on a number of accounts. First and foremost they raise a number of ethical concerns. Whilst acknowledging that at no point are people's choices taken away from them, the covert manipulation of behaviours, particularly when these occur at societal level, raises questions as to the extent to which this impinges on human rights. The second main criticism is the failure of such approaches to result in any long-term behaviour.

Other methods utilised by designers have been more direct, focusing on triggers and prompts to encourage or discourage particular behaviours. For instance, much of e-health is based on the potential of persuasive technology (Fogg, 2003, 2014) to offer a medium, a conduit for change. This may be through raising awareness of the amount of exercise taken or the number of calories consumed, the delivery of motivating feedback messages, or more specific information such as heart rates, body posture, respiration or glucose levels. The utilisation of such technologies has been a key component of enabling people to self-manage their long-term condition and the design of telehealth and telecare interventions has been based on a combination of enabling individuals to monitor their condition and to make small adjustments and changes to their behaviour. Initial findings from the Whole Systems Demonstrator Programme, a government-funded study that looked at the role of telehealth and telecare in enabling people to manage their long-term condition, was extremely promising. Initial figures indicated that this approach led to a reduction in mortality rates of 45 per cent and cut hospital admissions by 25 per cent. However, more recent research has called into question these results, concluding that 'telehealth does not seem to be a cost effective addition to standard support and treatment' (Henderson et al., 2013: 2).

Further research is being undertaken to understand some of the mechanisms involved here. An earlier European study undertaken by Domingo et al. (2012) offers us perhaps a hint of an explanation. This study evaluated a telemedicine intervention for heart failure patients. The study found that those who completed the study experienced a high degree of satisfaction leading to positive behavioural changes. However, over half of those engaged in the research withdrew. The authors of this study concluded that more work was required in relation to understanding the factors that enable or prevent a person from accepting or rejecting the technology. This study underlines the challenges of scaling up any intervention focusing on behaviour change because of the number of variables that are at play. This means that even when one can control some of these there are no guarantees that a specific response will occur. For instance, being able to see a reading of blood pressure does not automatically lead to a reduction in the amount of salt a person consumes. A person's ability to change will depend on their understanding of the consequences of consuming the salt, on their value and belief systems, peer pressure from those around them and on their readiness to change. Equally there is an element of the unpredictability of how people will respond to or utilise a product and the unanticipated and unplanned consequences of some designs.

Perhaps then it is necessary to look to other approaches and methodologies designers can take within this arena. One such approach is mindful design, a promising method expounded by Niedderer (2007, 2013, 2014). Drawing on the work of Langer (1989, 2010) mindful design works on the principle of achieving change through using design to 'disrupt the user's consciousness to raise their awareness'. Examples of mindful design in the literature are limited at present although Neidderer et al. (2014) cite an example from their own work whereby healthcare practitioners were taught how to apply mindful design practices in their interactions with patients so that they began by asking questions regarding positive steps they had taken to manage their own health. The interesting aspect of this example is that amidst all the approaches that are currently expounded perhaps the task of the designer needs to extend to the potential of design on raising awareness, challenging stigma, changing attitudes to healthcare and, rather than focusing solely on the person living with the long-term condition, to direct energies towards enabling the health professionals who work alongside them.

A number of examples regarding this approach exist in the literature. For instance SHIFT MS is an organisation that seeks to support individuals living with the degenerative long-term neurological condition of multiple sclerosis (MS). In a recent piece of work people living with MS were invited to convey their experiences using visual media as a way of building understanding and challenging the stigma that is associated with this condition.

Similar research examples include Debra Padfield's work (2011), which has explored the meaning of pain, again through visual media. Her face2face project focused on the development of a visual communication tool for clinical use, developed out of photographs of the representation of pain, co-created with people experiencing pain. Findings from the research have been extremely positive with increased understanding of the consequences of pain and its impact on behaviour.

Conclusion

In many ways, design for behaviour change in the context of the healthcare of people with long-term conditions is in its infancy and as we have shown, discussion around the role of design here raises more questions than it answers. For instance there are questions relating to how and when to offer interventions, potential ethical dilemmas, whether the focus should be on societal solutions or on approaches that place the onus on the individual. These issues still require further debate and discussion. However, what is clear is that this area offers many possibilities. We have provided examples in this chapter where the design process has offered new insights, leading to the design of better products and hinted at other avenues for exploration where the focus of the designer turns to the health practitioners who work with individuals. Whatever the focus design for behaviour change for individuals living with long-term conditions is, it is a topic that requires further exploration.

References

Ajzen, I. (1991) The theory of planned behaviour. *Organizational Behaviour and Human Decision Processes*, 50: 179–211.

Alcorn, K. and Broome, K. (2014) Occupational performance coaching for chronic conditions: A review of the literature. New *Zealand Journal of Occupational Therapy*, 61(2): 49–56.

Brady, T.J., Murphy, L., O'Colmain, B.J., Beauchesne, D., Daniels, B., Greenberg, M., et al. (2013) A meta-analysis of health status, health behaviours, and health care utilization outcomes of the chronic disease self-management programs. *Preventing Chronic Disease: Public Health Research, Practice and Policy*, 10. Available at: www.cdc.gov/pcd/ issues/2013/12_0112.htm.

Chang, J. and Marsh, M. (2013) The Google diet: Search giant overhauls eating options to 'nudge' healthy choices. Available at: http://abcnews.go.com/Health/google-diet-search-giant-overhauled-eating-options-nudge/story?id=18241908.

Colagiuri, R., Girgis , S., Eigenmann, C., Gomez, M. and Griffiths, R. (2009) *National Evidence Based Guideline for Patient Education in Type 2 Diabetes*. Canberra: Diabetes Australia and the NHMRC.

Craig, C., Gwilt, I., Langley, J. and Partridge, R. (2013) Thinking through design and rehabilitation, in Encarnacao, P. et al. (eds), *Assistive Technology: From Research to Practice*. Amsterdam: IOS Press.

Department of Health (2012) *Long Term Conditions Compendium of Information: Third Edition*. London: HMSO.

Department of Health, Social Services and Public Safety (2012) *Living with Long Term Conditions: A Policy Framework. Northern Ireland*. London: Department of Health, Social Services and Public Safety.

Dexter, M., Atkinson P. and Dearden, A. (2013) Open design and medical products: Irreconcilable differences or natural bedfellows? In *Proceedings of 10th European Academy of Design Conference, Gothenburg*. Gothenburg: University of Gothenburg/European Academy of Design.

Domingo, M., Lupon, J., Gonzalez, B., Crespo, E., Lopez, R., Ramos, A., Urrutia, A., Pera, G., Verdu, J.M. and Bayes-Genis, A. (2012) Noninvasive remote telemonitoring for ambulatory patients with heart failure. *European Journal of Cardiovascular Nursing*, 11(4): 410–18.

Fogg, B.J. (2003) *Persuasive Technology: Using Computers to Change What We Think and Do*. San Francisco: Morgan Kaufman.

Fogg, B.J. (2014) *BJ Fogg's Behavior Model*. Stanford: Stanford University Press. Available at: www.behaviormodel.org/index.html, accessed 1 April 2014.

Fry, T. (2008) *Design Futuring: Sustainability, Ethics and New Practice*. Oxford: Berg Publishing.

Harris J., Piper, S., Morgan H., McClimens A., Shah, S., Reynolds, H., Baldwin, S., Arksey H. and Qureshi, H. (2003) Carers experiences of providing care for people with long term conditions. Social Policy Research Unit, University of York.

Helen Hamlyn Centre (2013) Can we design a better patient event? Helen Hamlyn Centre, 29 January. Available at: http://archive.constantcontact.com/fs179/1102241208570/archive/1112144354478.html.

Henderson, C., Knapp, M., Fernandez, J.L., Beecham, J., Cartwright, M., Rixon, L., Benyon, M., Rogers, A., Bower, P., Doll, H., Fitzpatrick, R., Stevento, A., Bardsley, M., Hendy, J., Newman, S.P. (2013) Cost effectiveness of telehealth for patients with long-term conditions (Whole Systems Demonstrator telehealth questionnaire study): Nested economic evaluation in a pragmatic cluster randomised controlled trial. *British Medical Journal*, 346: 1035.

Hu, F.B., Manson, J.E., Stampfer, M.J., Colditz, G., Liu, S., Solomon, C.G. et al. (2001) Diet, lifestyle, and the risk of Type 2 diabetes mellitus in women. *New England Journal of Medicine*, 345: 790–7.

King's Fund (2015) *Long-Term Conditions and Multi-Morbidity*. London. King's Fund.

Langer, E.J. (1989). *Mindfulness*. New York: Addison Wesley.

Langer, E.J. (2010) *Counterclockwise*. London: Hodder and Stoughton.

Langley J., Reed, H., Stanton, A., Heron, N., Clarke, Z., Judge, S., Shaw, P.J., Quinn, A. and McDermott, C.J. (2014) Conference proceedings: Theme 5 multidisciplinary care and quality of life. Amyotrophic Lateral Sclerosis and Frontotemporal Degeneration, 15: supplement.

Lee, M.K., Kiesler, S. and Forlizzi, J. (2011) Mining behavioral economics to design persuasive technology for healthy choices. *CHI*: 325–34.

Lilley, D. (2009). Design for sustainable behaviour: Strategies and perceptions. *Design Studies*, 30: 704–20.

Lockton, D., Harrison, D. and Stanton, N.A. (2010) The design with intent method: A design tool for influencing user behaviour. *Applied Ergonomics*, 41(3): 382–92.

Mokdad, A.H., Marks, J.S. and Stroup, D.F. (2004) Actual causes of death in the United States, 2000. *Journal of the American Medical Association*, 291(10): 1238–45.

Neidderer, K. (2007) Mapping the meaning of knowledge in design research. *Design Research Quarterly*, 2.

Neidderer, K. (2013) Mindful design as a driver for social behaviour change. Proceedings of the IASDR Conference 2013, August.

Neidderer, K., Cain R., Clune, S., Lockton, D., Ludden, G., Mackrill, J. and Morris, A. (2014) *Design for Behaviour Change*. London: Arts and Humanities Research Council.

Norman, D.A. (1988) *The Psychology of Everyday Things*. Cambridge, MA: MIT Press.

Padfield, D. (2011) Representing the pain of others. *Health*, 15(3): 241–57.

Prochaska, J. and Di Clemente, C. (1983) Stages and processes of self-change of smoking: Toward an integrative model of change. *Journal of Consulting and Clinical Psychology*, 51: 390–5.

Prochaska J.O., Di Clemente, C.C. and Norcross, J.C. (1992) In search of how people change: Applications to addictive behaviours. *American Psychologist*, 47: 1102–14.

Rabe, K.F., Hurd, S., Anzueto, A., Barnes, P.J., Buist, S.A., Calverley, P. et al. (2007) Global strategy for the diagnosis, management, and prevention of chronic obstructive pulmonary disease. *American Journal of Respiratory and Critical Care Medicine*, 176: 532–55.

Rosenstock, L.M., Strecher, V.J. and Becker, M.H. (1988) Social learning theory and the Health Belief Model. *Health Education Quarterly*, 15(2): 175–83.

Scarborough, P., Bhatnagar, P., Wickramasinghe, K.K., Allender, S., Foster, C. and Rayner, M. (2011) The economic burden of ill health due to diet, physical inactivity, smoking, alcohol and obesity in the UK: An update to 2006–7 NHS costs. *Journal of Public Health*, 33(4): 527–35.

Schutzer, K.A. and Graves, B.S. (2004) Barriers and motivations to exercise in older adults. *Preventative Medicine*, 39(5): 1056–61.

Sharma, M. and Romas, J. (2012) *Theoretical Foundations of Health Education and Health Promotion*. Sudbury, MA: Jones and Bartlett Learning.

Sunstein, C. and Reisch, L. (2013) Green by default. *Kyklos*, 66(3): 398–402.

Welsh Assembly Government (2007) Designed to improve health and the management of chronic conditions in Wales. Strategy Unit, Welsh Assembly Government.

Wolstenhome, D., Downes, T., Leaver, J., Partridge, R. and Langley, J. (2014) Improving self-efficacy in spinal cord injury patients through 'design thinking' rehabilitation workshops. *British Medical Journal Quality Improvement Report*, 3.

World Health Organization (2007) Prevention of cardiovascular disease: Pocket guidelines for assessment and management of cardiovascular risk. Available at: www.who.int/cardiovascular_diseases/guidelines/PocketGL.ENGLISH.AFR-D-E.rev1.pdf.

World Health Organization (2010) Burden: Mortality, morbidity and risk factors, in *Global Status Report on Noncommunicable Diseases 2010*. Geneva: World Health Organization. Available at: www.who.int/nmh/publications/ncd_report_chapter1.pdf.

Zubin, J. and Spring, B. (1977) Vulnerability: A new view on schizophrenia. *Journal of Abnormal Psychology*, 86: 103–26.

11 Communications

Communication design in chronic health

Alison Prendiville

Abstract

In developed countries in the 21st century, chronic health is placing a huge burden on healthcare systems. As the number of people with such conditions increases, through living longer and with changing lifestyles, there is the expectation that patients with the support of technology, and in particular personal medical devices (PMDs) may be empowered to monitor and manage their own health status. Yet the emphasis on technology to address this challenge falls short of delivering systematic strategies. To overcome these limitations, design has the interdisciplinary potential to illuminate the complex technological, social and professional relationships that are needed to support patients as part of a coordinated care strategy.

Introduction

This chapter explores design in chronic health from an interdisciplinary perspective of design research, digital anthropology and science and technology studies. The chapter presents how design in chronic health in developed countries falls within Rittel and Webber's (1973) definition of 'wicked problems' and also fits within the conceptual apparatus of Buchanan (2001), Krippendorf (2006) and Jones' (2013) design development trajectories. The work examines the specific nature of chronic health, its demands and uncertainties and how the conditions of chronic health extend beyond the hospital and health clinic into relationships with family and friends and daily practices. Concomitant with this rise in chronic health is an increase and variety of interactive medical devices adopted for healthcare and wellbeing management (Li and Thimbleby, 2013: 1), including the domestication of healthcare technologies. In particular, this chapter draws on anthropology fieldwork within an NHS hospital and a community health centre to explore daily practices and how the digital glucose monitor, as a PMD for the self-monitoring of diabetes, plays out issues of self-hood and compliance within broader social and cultural domains such as commensuration, discipline and surveillance. The chapter concludes by presenting 'wicked problems' from the perspective of design's involvement in complex social problems and also on a human scale through the granularity of living with diabetes and the daily challenges that this presents.

Design and chronic health

Chronic health fits within Rittel and Webber's (1973: 160) definition of 'wicked problems', that is, problems that are socially embedded, difficult and/or impossible to solve, and where the information is ill-formulated and confusing (Churchman, 1967: B141). Equally for Buchanan (1992), design problems are indeterminate as 'design is potentially universal in scope and may be applied to any human experience' (Buchanan, 1992: 15). He emphasises in the 'application of the process, the designer must discover or invent *a particular* subject out of the problems and issues of specific circumstances'. Thus design in chronic health offers the opportunity for the designer to work on many levels – depending on the nature of the context – from standalone devices, to interface and interactions and complex assemblage, 'a configuration of relationships among diverse sites, time and space, people and things' (Marcus and Saka, 2006: 102).

Buchanan's 'Four Orders of Design' (2001) offer a way 'of rethinking and reconceiving the nature of design, not as categories that are rigidly fixed and separated from each other but as representations of how design is increasingly dealing with the rapid rise of complex challenges in the 21st century. This 'rethinking' of design corresponds with design's role in chronic health and also provides a historical overview of its involvement in this area. In the first and second orders, Buchanan sees the establishment of the professions of graphic and industrial design in the 20th century through symbols and the shaping of things. Graphic design grew from visual symbols and the communication of information in words and images originally associated with print material but now encompassing all visual media used for communication. In developed countries within healthcare, since the 1960s and 1970s communication design has primarily been focused on campaigns for non-communicable diseases and the promotion of healthy lifestyles, although these have been acknowledged for their simplicity and limited effectiveness (Nutbeam, 2000: 260). Lupton (2012: 230) presents health promotion as traditionally a low-tech area of public health when compared to the 'vast array of medical technologies used in clinical settings'. Bivins (2012: 18) notes how as the 20th century progressed the domestic management of health, through such household items as bathroom scales, was increasingly technologised and how such items produced accessible tools for self-surveillance and quantitative indicators of health and weight. This growth in domestic medical devices fits within Buchanan's second order of design, when industrial design emerged at the beginning of the 20th century with 'the production of mass-produced consumer goods and explicitly concerned with tangible, physical artifacts – for material things' (Buchanan, 2001: 230).

In the third order Buchanan (2001: 11) focuses on interaction design and how 'humans relate to each other through the mediating influence of products, emphasizing that the products are more than physical objects'. For him they are 'experiences or activities or services all integrated into a new understanding of what a product is or could be' (2001: 12). He then moves towards immaterial systems, 'human systems, the integration of information, physical artifacts, and interactions in the environments of living, working and playing'. Here from my perspective these two orders blur and are not easily distinguishable when considering, in the last five years, the arrival and rapid adoption of mobile medical health devices (mHealth technologies) such as Web 2.0 applications, social media tools and digital devices connected to the web, such as smartphones, tablet computers, iPods and wearable patches (Lupton, 2012: 213). These recent technologies now offer 'the opportunity to directly tailor and target health messages on an individual level to intensify the pervasiveness of these messages and to monitor and record aspects of embodiment of users of mobile devices' (Lupton, 2012: 231). Thus the four orders when applied to chronic health reflect design's evolution from simple health campaigns through to standalone domestic health products to the emergence of assemblages of spatially diverse, complex and interconnected things (Marcus and Saka, 2006), responsible for supporting the challenges of a chronic illness in daily practice and the clinical environment.

Krippendorff's *The Semantic Turn: A New Foundation for Design* (2006) also offers a trajectory to link design to chronic health through a six-tier 'trajectory of artificiality', to represent the changing nature of design practice that starts with products and moves towards more immaterial and abstract manifestations of design. He notes how today's world is more complex and more immaterial when compared to early industrial design practices. In Krippendorff's third trajectory (2006: 8), and similar to Buchanan's third order on interaction design, the focus is on interfaces that 'mediate between complex technological devices and their users: human machine interfaces'. For Krippendorff the design of interfaces shifts the 'designer's attention from a concern for the internal make up and appearance of technology to what mediates between users and technology, the betweeness in which interfaces evolve'. To deal with the complexities of the 21st century, Krippendorff proposes that:

> design needs to move from the appearances of mechanical products that industry is equipped to manufacture to conceptualizing artifacts, material or social, that have a chance of meaning something to the users, that aid larger communities and support a society that is in the process of reconstructing itself in unprecedented ways and at record speeds.
>
> (Krippendorff, 2006: xv)

Jones' (2013: 24) adaptation of Jones and VanPatter's (2009) design geographies illustrates the different level of design's involvement specifically in healthcare. This representation may be conceptually applied to design in chronic health with each level reflecting a higher, less tangible, more complex and assembled involvement in the healthcare context. Design 1.0 is presented as traditional design (patient literature, promotion and advertising); design 2.0 as product/service design (user experience, service design, informatics and decision support); design 3.0 as embracing organisational transformation design (including focus on change making, organisational processes, cross-function action teams); design 4.0 as social transformation design (covering areas such as health policy, healthcare affiliations and social innovation). Each of the theoretical models presented by Buchanan, Krippendorff and Jones foresees design's evolution to different levels of complexity that mirrors design's involvement in chronic health, with each level taking on greater challenges and contributing to broader social–cultural transformative processes. In the following section the specific nature and challenges of chronic health are presented and with this the rapid rise of rise of PMDs to manage this growing area of healthcare.

Definitions and management of chronic disease

The WHO defines chronic health as an:

> ongoing condition that requires management over a period of years or decades, needing a complex response for an extended period of time that involves coordinated inputs from a range of health professionals, access to essential medicines and monitoring systems all of which need to be optimally embedded within a system that promotes patient empowerment.
>
> (Unwin et al., 2006)

Similarly, O'Halloran et al., (2004: 383) defines chronic diseases as 'non-communicable illnesses that are prolonged in duration, do not resolve spontaneously and are rarely cured completely'. These characteristics may be tied to more specific criteria that sees chronic health as 'characteristically a duration that has lasted, or is expected to last, at least six months; has a pattern of recurrence or deterioration; has a poor prognosis; and produces conditions that may lead to other related health issues that may be physical or mental and related to the initial chronic condition' (O'Halloran et al., 2004: 384). Examples that fall within the National Centre for Disease Control and Prevention's (2009) definition include heart disease, cancer, stroke, diabetes, oral conditions, obesity, respiratory conditions, arthritis and asthma.

Accordingly, for Pomerleau et al. (2008: 15) chronic disease is one of the major challenges facing Europe and indeed the world. For the authors such conditions are important as they not only contribute to premature mortality but they also may cause disability and impact on quality-of-life issues and the expectancy of life lived in good health. Populations across the globe are growing older with the shift starting off in industrialised countries well over a century ago, but with developing countries now also having large numbers of older citizens and with the numbers also rapidly increasing (Kinsella and Phillips, 2005: 6). This changing age structure means that the likelihood of contracting a chronic disease is on the increase. To exacerbate this problem further, 'societal and cultural issues, through changes in lifestyle, including diet, greater inactivity and smoking are also contributing to the increase in chronic health issues across the globe' (Nolte and McKee, 2008: xix). The difficulties of living with a chronic condition implicate not only the ill people themselves but also affect their families and friends, communities and society as a whole (Kane et al., 2005: 27). Equally the long-lasting nature of these illnesses means that 'people with such conditions have to learn to cope and participate in everyday life whilst also dealing with periods that may need interventions from the medical profession for the diagnosed condition' (Radley, 1994: 136).

With the rise of chronic health and increasing knowledge of the contributing factors to such illnesses, the growth of mobile technologies with their increasing ubiquity and power has led to the development of PMDs that can be carried or worn by individuals to generate biomedical data and carry out medical interventions (Farrington, 2014). Such devices include the glucose monitor, finger pulse oximeters (blood oxygen and heart rate) and pedometers plus a wide range of mobile phone applications that enable the recording of distances run to food eaten (Weiner et al., 2014: 2). Design's role in such devices now extends to applications that take design into the field of design for service where the focus is not just on physical artefacts but an 'action platform', described as 'a system that makes a multiplicity of interactions possible' (Meroni and Sangiorgi, 2011: 3). Here we see design moving beyond the product to configure relationships through a community; PMDs are now situated within a network of service provision, entangled with multiple actors with the design focusing on the interaction, relationship, data and experience of its users.

For Kane et al. (2005: 137) 'technologies ranging from drug regimens through to PMDs have changed the face of chronic health by not only extending the life expectancy of people with previously fatal illnesses but also supporting them to function more effectively and over long periods of time'. The authors note the revolutionary advances in computers, the internet and more recently mobile technologies that are beginning to change the way people experience chronic health by 'enabling them to remain in their homes, delaying the need for hands on care or decreasing the quantity of direct care needed' (137).

In the following section the glucose monitor is presented as an accepted and established PMD that dramatically changed the management of diabetes at the end of the 20th century. As an example of a PMD the glucose monitor fits within different design levels presented by Buchanan, Krippendorff and Jones, revealing that such devices are not necessarily fixed within one category. On one level a glucose monitor sits within established frames of product design and service design and on another it acts as a human machine interface. However, when observing the quotidian management of diabetes in an NHS hospital clinic and community healthcare centre, through the patients' interactions with the clinical staff, the glucose monitor also demonstrates broader transformational, social–political and cultural issues.

The glucose monitor case study

This section presents data from ethnographic fieldwork the author undertook at an NHS hospital diabetes clinic and a community health centre undertaken during research into anthropological frames into the use of digital artefacts. The material is drawn from audio recordings from consenting patients and informant interviews. This methodological approach offers the researcher the opportunity to listen to and observe the local practices that present the glucose monitor not as standalone technology but a PMD which is transformational and complex.

In the mid-1980s the arrival of the first blood glucose meters for the self-monitoring of blood glucose (SMBG) levels was a significant technology development that led to the 'extensive growth of point-of-care testing' for people with diabetes (Clarke and Foster, 2012: 83). Prior to this the authors present urine tests as the dominant form of glucose monitoring. Today SMBG is viewed as potentially playing a key role in the management of diabetes and in the reduction of risk in secondary clinical complications; SMBG is recommended in all patients taking insulin and advised in others on an individual basis (Clarke and Foster, 2012: 89). For the authors diabetes presents a significant healthcare challenge, 'estimating that in the UK in 2010 diabetes affected 4.3 per cent (2.8 million) of the population representing a dramatic two fold increase, compared to data in 1996. The authors do not attribute this to a rise in Type 1 diabetes, which accounts for 10 per cent of diabetes cases with most commonly early onset (<40 years), but the 90 per cent for Type 2 diabetes, which occurs typically in later life or increasingly in young people with what is called 'lifestyle obesity' (91). Consequently, glucose is one of the most frequently measured analytes in clinical units, primary care and by patients for monitoring at home.

Since the discovery of insulin in 1921, the medical profession has adopted the use of the glucose monitor for people with non-insulin dependent diabetes mellitus and diabetes in general, expecting people with such conditions to learn how to become 'physicians unto themselves' (Ferzacca, 2000: 29). Before the self-monitoring of blood glucose, testing was undertaken in doctors' offices (Clarke and Foster, 2012). Now the glucose monitor, similar to many digital devices in chronic health, delegates biomedical work giving autonomy to the user and creating and distributing new competencies extended through time and space (Prout, 1996: 206). A participant interview with a woman with Type 1 diabetes captures how the autonomy provided in the self-monitoring of the glucose also means she takes on biomedical decision-making and competencies: "If my blood sugar is 14 so therefore it's too high so I have to drop it down the one unit of insulin will decrease my blood sugar level by 3mmol/l. So my rations vary for breakfast it's 1:1 so for 10g of carb I have one unit of insulin."

In these circumstances compliance and non-compliance are recognised by Ferzacca (2000: 44) as never far apart. Observing the consultation between a nurse and woman with Type 2 diabetes, and the examination of glucose readings from a monitor, the nurse describes portion sizes, especially rice, to assist the woman in lowering her blood glucose levels. The patient laughs explaining how much rice she eats. When the nurse leaves the room to see the dietician, the woman turns to the author and says 'how she tries to help herself but she doesn't keep her promise'.

In another clinical encounter between the doctor and a woman with Type 2 diabetes, the patient diligently tests her glucose levels, recording each time that the sugars are very low. When asked how she feels with the onset of low blood sugar the woman replies "I test my blood glucose regularly as it makes me feel safe". Here as with other studies (Horensius et al., 2012) the act of taking a blood glucose reading creates a feeling of safety and confidence, although it does not necessarily lead to actions to raise or lower the blood sugar level, as the doctor in the community centre commented when a woman with Type 2 diabetes left the consultation: "People are deliberately hurting themselves (pricking their fingers to take blood glucose readings) for no benefit whatsoever. Subconsciously thinking by testing their blood glucose they are treating their diabetes rather than going on a diet."

In the case of the self-management of diabetes, it is perhaps easy to view patients in terms of bodily signs, body weight, blood pressure, HbA^{1}c and glucose readings. Haraway (1991) notes the intensification of machine and body relations within the clinic and hospital and sees personal experiences of the body mediated by new technologies, including 'struggles over meaning and means of health environments pervaded by high technology products and process' (1991: 171).

Mol and Law (2004: 4) discuss the role of the glucose monitor in 'not only revealing the body we have, but also the body we are, as this requires knowledge from the inside'. For them 'self-awareness is at least as important as measuring'. To feel sensitive to one's own physical state, to be in tune with the onset of a 'hypo' (dizziness and potential loss of consciousness brought about by a blood sugar level that falls below 4mm/mol) allows one to do something to increase one's blood sugar level (6). The authors acknowledge that this is not straightforward and this too was evidenced in the fieldwork and in the informant interviews. Frequently patients described their need to achieve higher blood sugar levels as embodied in the glucose monitor to overcome their feelings of a hypo. During one of the author's observations in the hospital the consultant asks a woman with Type 2 diabetes what reading she aims for at night, the woman replies, "I think 16 is good." The doctor repeats slightly shocked, "16 at bedtime!" The woman adds, "Even 9 is not going to get me through." The consultant suggests "10 or 12 maybe?" Here the doctor explained that over time too high blood sugar levels makes the body accustomed to the highs, so that when the blood sugar levels drop to a normal range between 4 to 8 mmol/l the body is tricked into feeling the onset of a hypo.

Mol (2009: 1757) observes how the disadvantages of glucose monitoring may outweigh for the patient the onset of complications in the future. She further notes how the daily complexities and messiness of using self-monitoring technologies to exercise control over the diabetic body are likely to fail as the body is open to many fluctuations, as the following quote taken from an informant interview with a woman with Type 1 diabetes from my own research shows:

> Something which is your body and you are looking at data and it's transferred into a mathematical graph and that's really quite weird and it's so easy when you are sat with the nurse and she's pointing at the graph and saying that you can see the pattern every day… and you go away and you look at the data yourself and you are trying to ask yourself those questions to interpret what's happening.

This woman recorded her blood glucose levels using her monitor seven to ten times a day, opening a window into her life that she cannot always interpret through the data.

Many tensions exist with the tight regulation of diabetes with some aspects being good for some parts of the body and bad for others (Mol and Law, 2004: 6). Equally, tight regulation can sometimes just fail and this emerged in my interviews and in the hospital clinic as diabetes is enmeshed in every aspect of a person's life. For Mole and Law (2004) modern medicine is seen as predominantly epidemiological in character, often ignoring the uncertainties that come with the human body. As observed in the hospital the body is complex and has many inputs, therefore, the notion that it can be measured for total control is flawed. In the hospital consultations patients often expressed with resignation that monitoring blood glucose levels was far less controllable, even when they felt they were adhering to strict dietary regulations, "What

I discovered is that it is not an exact science at all it's not any easy thing. Sometimes I think it doesn't matter what I do" (NHS observation).

For Mol and Law (2004: 17) the tight rope of balances needed to manage diabetes requires an approach that will capture 'jagged story-lines' and from my own observations in the hospital clinic the glucose monitoring acted as a catalyst for stories, affording a process of commensuration between the biomedical and the everyday challenge of living particularly with Type 2 diabetes. High readings were explained in relation to eating fish and chips, a weekend break, a stressful week and the death of relative. The glucose monitor facilitated a dialogue, revealing personal snap-shots and the challenges of monitoring blood sugar levels. In particular the hospital observations revealed the role of the monitor and its readings as affording a process of commensuration between the biomedical and the quotidian living of a person with Type 1 and Type 2 diabetes. Espeland and Stevens (1998: 314) define commensuration as the transformation of different qualities into a common metric. Whether it is being used to allay guilt or symbolise disparate forms of value it may take the form of 'rankings, ratios or elusive prices'. The benefit of commensuration is its ability to simplify diverse information into numbers that can easily be compared. Most importantly the authors argue that 'commensuration is no mere technical process but a fundamental feature of social life'.

In the case of diabetes the act of appreciating food is the balancing of ratios and trade-offs concerning food intake, types of insulin, drug dosages and exercise. As Mol and Law (2004: 13) so poignantly acknowledge, 'the body is entangled in ever so many ways with the diabetes it lives with'. In contrast, the glucose monitor in a hospital consultation provides the doctor with a window for the commensuration of measurements of food intake, insulin and exercise whilst for the patient it narrates the early morning coffee before a prayer, a late office dinner or an outing with a friend (social moments described by patients with Types 2 diabetes in the hospital clinic when discussing their blood sugar levels with the doctor).

Davidson (1984: 101, in Povinelli, 2001: 322) notes that 'Torn between the need to make sense of a speaker's words and the need to make sense of his patterns of belief, the best we can do is choose a theory of translation that maximizes agreement'. Here within the hospital the shift from the numerical to the personal is achieved through the glucose monitor. Throughout the fieldwork, and in particular people with Type 2 diabetes, the glucose monitor frequently allowed cultural differences to be negotiated and enacted, and for agreement to be reached between the doctor and patient, as demonstrated in an observation made between the doctor and a woman with Type 2 diabetes. The doctor suggests she gets her readings down to 8 before bed (currently they are 16) but the patient is adamant that, "8 would be too low, I could possibly manage 10."

Espeland and Stevens (1998: 317) see commensuration as fundamentally relative, 'creating relations between attributes or dimensions where value is revealed in the comparison'. In the consultation where the glucose monitor was only produced two thirds of the way through the appointment, the conversation between a man with Type 1 diabetes and the doctor suddenly shifted to one which was more relational. In this instance the doctor starts reviewing the young man's glucose readings from his monitor, whilst examining the readings very carefully, he asks, "Are you sure that you got your basal insulin right?" The patient replies, "Yes, well I think I have." For the authors 'commensuration can be understood as a system for discarding information and organizing what remains into new forms' (317). Here the monitor is essential for selecting the good readings, evaluating the low ones and their impact, to explain the need to get the sugars up. In a consultation between the consultant and a man with Type 1 diabetes, prior to the glucose meter appearing, the opportunity for discussion on the management of the diabetes was very limited and incommensurable. This improved once the meter readings were being examined by the doctor. For example, when the monitor is produced, the patient becomes more cooperative and agreeable as he loo ks at the monitor with the doctor and says, "There, there that will do, I would be happy at 6." The doctor replies, "Yes I would be happy if you were at 6, I wouldn't be happy if you were 3, most of the time, 4 is okay?"

In the nurse/patient consultation the author observed a form of 'public reason' (Habermas, 1989) in which communication was used by the nurse to talk through different aspects of diabetes management (blood glucose levels, eating, exercise) with the emphasis on arriving at a consensus. For Povinelli (2001: 326) 'the procedures of reason and judgment are seen as determining sociological epistemologies and moral obligations, of bending moral sensibilities and making them pliable; and, in doing so, making a shared cultural and moral community'.

> I know if you want to bring that one down to 7.5 we need to get these blood sugars between 4 and less than 8, that's nearly a replication of your target but I want it slightly better. But we can work with this and here anything between 5 and less than 10, to achieve the better percentage – okay so we will look together and see how many numbers are higher than this target.
>
> (Nurse/patient consultation, NHS clinic)

From this example, it is clear that the nurse moves from using 'I' and 'you' whilst addressing the patient's blood glucose levels to using 'we', which implies a collective and consensual effort to address the problems. This technique of using the readings to negotiate a collective effort for reducing blood glucose levels was common in all the nurse–patient consultations; using the glucose readings and the HbA1c score as the tools, the nurse would circle targets, look for highs and lows and open up terms for agreement. According to Habermas with Povinelli (2001: 326) through public reason, 'moral obligations and its conditioning of freedom allows a broader moral horizon, the I-you dyad to a we-horizon' comes into play. Through this approach the author sees the social shifting from the 'bonds of particular persons and groups to recalibrating the scope of the current consensus'.

Povinelli (2001: 326) asks us to think about types of communication used in the foreclosure of socially inconceivable and incommensurate worlds. Her work draws on and asks us to con-sider the 'interactional signals to indicate to persons how they should calculate and calibrate the stakes, pleasures and risks of being a certain type of form in a certain type of formed space'. In the following quote we see the 'institutionalized conventions of risk and pleasure commen-surate social worlds' Povinelli (2001: 325) at the end of the consultation between a nurse and a woman with Type 2 diabetes:

> Don't do it for me do it for yourself – and if you do it for yourself you will start to feel better. First thing is to focus on getting the blood sugar and you will start to feel better but long term you don't want to be having kidney problems or heart problems. (Nurse/ patient consultation, NHS clinic)

According to Lupton (2013a: 261) digital health technologies have disciplinary power as well as surveillance capabilities. Instead of the direct medical gaze confined to the clinical set-ting as outlined in Foucauldian writing, these technologies now create a spatial distance that in turn makes the medical gaze virtual, requiring the patient to turn the gaze onto themselves and become self-governing and report what they observe back to the medical profession.

In the hospital clinic and domestic settings, the glucose monitor played a role in a network of monitoring and surveillance. People with Type 1 diabetes or insulin-dependent Type 2 are required to inform the DVLA (Driving Vehicle Licensing Agency) of their condition and be signed off by a doctor. The DVLA paperwork requires the diabetic person's doctor or in some instances a consultant to undertake a face-to-face question and answer session based on three months of glucose readings. In the hospital ethnography a man is questioned about how he feels when his blood sugars are low and how he counteracts such sensations with the doctor guiding him through the paperwork. After 35 minutes of extensive questions the doctor signs of the documents and says to the man: 'Do you feel thoroughly monitored?'

For Lupton (2013a: 266) the digitally engaged patient may be perceived as part of a wider neoliberal political drive to patient care and preventive health. In Great Britain and other advanced liberal nations, Ong (2007: 4) identifies neoliberalism as a mode of 'governing through freedom' that entails people to be 'free and self-managing in different spheres of everyday life – health, education, bureaucracy and professions'. Additionally, she emphasises the expectation of responsibility at the community level, and new requirements of self-responsibility by individual subjects. As Lupton (2013b: 398) argues, individuals that readily adopt self-tracking in preventative medicine 'have readily adopted the subject of the responsibility, entrepreneurial citizen as it is privileged in neoliberal governmentality, in seeking to take action to achieve healthy and fit embodiment and engaging in self-governance' (in Lupton, 1995b; Petersen and Lupton, 1996). However, health self-monitoring discourses frequently ignore the barriers to digital health empowerment caused by a lack of access to digital technologies because of socioeconomic status, geographical location, disability, lack of skills or reluctance to learn about new digital technologies (Blanchard et al., 2008; Frederico et al., 2012, in Lupton, 2013b: 398).

The ethnographic fieldwork reveals the complex and entangled nature of the glucose monitor in the management of diabetes. As well as providing a window into the internal workings of the body, where it is made visible through a numerical value, the glucose monitor makes a bridge to family and work, states of loneliness and unemployment. The monitor becomes a catalyst for storytelling, an activity which transforms and expands the numeric readings into discussions that allow diabetic, consultant and nurse to make sense of the current challenges and messiness of living with diabetes and, together, to negotiate a future.

Concluding comments and the implications for design

In this chapter the author has looked at Buchanan (2001), Krippendorff (2006) and Jones' (2013) conceptual frames to situate design in chronic health and to demonstrate that artefacts such as PMDs, and in particular the glucose monitor, are not fixed at one specific level of the different design developments. In addition, from the evidence provided in this chapter, it is important to consider design in chronic health from two particular perspectives. In the first, chronic health is a 'wicked problem' fitting Rittel and Webber's (1973) definition of a systemic social problem, whereby the design of PMDs may be seen as part of an assemblage, dispersed over time and space to transform relationships, support political agendas and undertake surveillance activities. However, this higher level of design activity, dealing with intractable social problems as envisioned by Buchanan, Krippendorff and Jones, raises questions concerning the need for designers to consider the ethical and moral issues that are caught up within broader social and cultural debates and to place the individual at the centre of these discussions. If we are looking at design's role in complex assemblages for higher levels of transformative design, questions arise over what is being transformed, for whom and to what ends. Design's ability to work on the human scale with individuals through creative practices offers a space for this exploration, to formulate new agendas and resolve human problems.

Secondly, through the fieldwork conducted in an anthropological framework on the use of the glucose monitor, the author has also shown that when living with a chronic condition, design in the form of PMDs extends beyond the monitoring of blood sugar levels into more social, messier and less bounded areas where narrative forms a crucial part of shared disease management. In this instance, when living with a chronic condition such as diabetes, the granularity of the daily practices reveals 'wicked problems' on a human level that are difficult to locate without the methodological practices of anthropology. Here, the interdisciplinary nature of design could learn from these alternative methodological and theoretical and interpretative standpoints, taking the quotidian of a chronic health condition and to collaboratively create new human centred interventions. For health professionals, design's contribution lies in its ability to capture these complex encounters and to make visible what are often taken-for-granted actions and to offer experimental spaces through creative practice to engage with different stakeholders involved in managing chronic illnesses. For non-designers this approach broadens the understanding of design and in particular PMDs, not as standalone technologies for the self-monitoring of a chronic condition but as one element in a complex social assemblage.

Note

1. HBA1c: Over ten weeks glucose sticks to the haemoglobin to make a glycosylated haemoglobin molecule referred to as A1C or HbA1c. The more glucose in the blood the more haemoglobin A1C or HbA1c will be present in the blood. Red cells live for eight to ten weeks before they are replaced. By measuring the HbA1c it can tell you the average blood sugar levels for the previous weeks. A normal HbA1c is 3.5–5.5 per cent. In diabetes management 6.5 per cent is considered good. Available at: http://medweb.bham.ac.uk/easdec/, accessed 25 May 2013.

References

Bivins, R. (2012) Histories of medicine in the household. Anglo Dutch German Workshop, University of Warwick, 5–7 July. Centre for the History of Medicine, Wellcome Trust, University of Warwick.

Blanchard, M., Metcalf, A., Degney, J., Herman, H. and Burns, J. (2008) Rethinking the digital divide: Findings from a study of marginalised young people's information communication technology use. *Youth Studies Australia*, 27(4): 35.

Buchanan, R. (1992) Wicked problems in design thinking. *Design Issues*, 8(2): 5–21.

Buchanan, R. (2001) Design research and the new learning. *Design Issues*, 17(4): 3–23.

Clarke, S.F. and Foster, J.R. (2012) A history of blood glucose meters and their role in self-monitoring of diabetes mellitus. *British Journal of Biomedical Science*, 69(2).

Churchman, C.H. (1967) Wicked problems. *Management Science*, 14(4): B141–2.

Davidson, D. (1984) Belief and the basis of meaning. In *Inquiries into Truth and Interpretation*. Oxford: Clarendon, 125–39.

Espeland W. and Stevens, M.L. (1998) Commensuration as a social process. *Annual Review of Sociology*, 24: 313–43.

Farrington C. (2014) Understanding personal medical devices: The sensemaking heuristic. Theorising Personal Medical Devices: New Perspectives. University of Cambridge and the Wellcome Trust, 18–19 September.

Ferzacca, S. (2000) 'Actually I don't feel that bad': Managing diabetes and the clinical encounter. *Medical Anthropology Quarterly*, 14(1): 28–50.

Habermas, J. (1989) *The Theory of Communicative Action*. 2 vols. Translated by T. McCarthy. Boston, MA: Beacon.

Haraway, D. (1991) A cyborg manifesto: Science, technology, and socialist-feminism in the late twentieth century, in *Simians, Cyborg and Women: The Reinvention of Nature*. London: Routledge, 149–81.

Horensius, J., Kars, M., Wierenga, W., Kleefstra, N., Bilo, H. and van der Bijl, J. (2012) Perspectives of patients with Type 1 or insulin-treated 2 diabetes on self-monitoring of blood glucose: A qualitative study. *BMC Public Health*. Available at: www.biomedcentral.com/1471–2458/12/167/, accessed 5 January 2015.

Jones P.H. (2013) *Design for Care, Innovating Healthcare Experience*. New York: Rosenfeld.

Jones P.H. and VanPatter G.K. (2009) *Design 1.0.2.0.3.0.4.0: The Rise of Visual Sensemaking*. New York: NextDesign Leadership Institute.

Kane R.L., Priester R. and Totten, A. (2005) *Meeting the Challenge of Chronic Illness*. Baltimore, MD: Johns Hopkins University Press.

Kinsella, K. and Phillips, D. (2005) *Global Aging: The Challenge of Success*. Washington, DC: Population Reference Bureau.

Krippendorff, K. (2006) *The Semantic Turn: A New Foundation for Design*. New York: Taylor and Francis.

Li, Y. and Thimbleby, H. (2013) Design personal medical devices to manage human errors for effective chronic disease management. Chi+med Making medical devices safer. EPSRC Programme. Talk presented at Chinese CHI, Paris, May.

Lupton, D. (1995) *The Imperative of Health: Public Health and the Regulated Body*. London: Sage.

Lupton, D. (2012) M-health and health promotion: The digital cyborg and surveillance society. *Social Theory and Health*, 10(3): 229–44.

Lupton, D. (2013a) The digitally engaged patient: Self-monitoring and self-care in the digital health era. *Social Theory and Health*, 11(3): 256–70.

Lupton, D. (2013b) Quantifying the body: Monitoring and measuring health in the age of m-health technologies. *Critical Public Health*, 23(4): 393–403.

Marcus, E.G. and Saka, E. (2006) Assemblage. *Theory, Culture and Society*, 23(2–3): 101–9.

Meroni, A. and Sangiorgi, D. (2011) *Design for Services: Design for Social Responsibility Series*. Farnham: Gower.

Mol, A. (2009) Living with diabetes: Care beyond choice and control. *Lancet*, 373(9677): 1756–7.

Mol, A. and Law, J. (2004) Embodied action, enacted bodies: The example of hypoglycaemia. *Body and Society*, 10(43).

National Center for Chronic Disease Prevention and Health Promotion (2009) *The Power of Prevention: Chronic Disease: The Public Health Challenge of the 21st Century*. Atlanta, GA: CDC. www.cdc.gov/chronicdisease/pdf/2009-power-of-prevention.pdf, accessed January 2016.

Nolte E. and McKee M. (2008) Caring for people with chronic conditions: A health system perspective. European Observatory on Health Systems and Policies Series, Open University Press.

Nutbeam D. (2000) Health literacy as a public health goal: A challenge for contemporary health education and communication strategies in the 21st century. *Health Promotion International*, 15(3).

O'Halloran, J., Miller Graeme, C. and Britt, H. (2004) Defining chronic conditions for primary care with ICPC-2. *Family Practice*, 21(4).

Ong, A. (2007) Neoliberalism as a mobile technology. *Journal Compilation Royal Geographical Society*, 32(1): 3–8.

Pearlman, D., Kaw, D., O'Connell, S., Jiang, Y. and Goldman, D. (2014) The economic burden of preventable chronic diseases. *Rhode Island Medical Journal*: 36–9.

Petersen A. and Lupton D. (1996) *The New Public Health: Discourses, Knowledges, Strategies*. London: Sage.

Pomerleau, J., Knai, C. and Nolte, E. (2008). *The burden of chronic disease in Europe*. Ed. Nolte E and McKee. Caring for people with chronic conditions, a health systems perspective. Europen Observatory on Health Systems and Policies Series. Open University Press, McGraw-Hill Education.

Povinelli, E.A. (2001) Radical worlds: The anthropology of incommensurability and inconceivability. *Annual Review of Anthropology*. 2001. 30:319–34.

Prout, A. (1996) Actor-network theory, technology and medical sociology: An illustrative analysis of the metered dose inhaler. *Sociology of Health and Illness*, 18(2): 198–219.

Radley, A. (1994) *Making Sense of Illness, the Social Psychology of Health and Disease*. London: Sage.

Rittel, H. and Webber, M. (1973) Dilemmas in a general theory of planning. *Policy Sciences*, 4: 155–69.

Unwin, N., Epping, J. and Bonita, R. (2006) Rethinking the terms non-communicable disease and chronic disease. *Journal of Epidemiology Community Health*, 58: 801–3.

Weiner, K., Will, C. and Henwood, F. (2014) Fleshing out the self in self-monitoring: From discourse to practice. Draft paper prepared for Theorising Personal Medical Devices: New Perspectives. University of Cambridge and the Wellcome Trust, 18–19 September.

12 Services

Service design in chronic health

Paul Chamberlain, Susan Mawson and Daniel Wolstenholme

Abstract

In this chapter, we will explore the specific challenges presented by chronic health or long-term conditions and the role design might have in responding to these challenges. We will do this by describing the fundamental challenge to the traditional ways of delivering healthcare posed by long-term conditions and the paradigm shift required by health practitioners, commissioners, providers and patients to one of self-care.

We will illustrate this through two case studies, which reflect the work of multidisciplinary research teams from Sheffield Hallam University, Lab4Living and two research teams from the National Institute for Health Research Collaborations for Leadership in Applied Health Research and Care Yorkshire and Humber, User-centred Healthcare Design and Telehealth and Care Technologies.

The Intelligent Shoe project is a technology project that used participatory methods in a larger social science health services research approach to develop a platform to support people to successfully undertake rehabilitation following a stroke. Methods from participatory design sat alongside qualitative and quantitative methods to deliver an intervention that has demonstrated clinical impact.

The Better Outpatients Services for Older People project worked using a recognised model of design-led service improvement, experience-based design, to understand the experience of staff and patients of the medical outpatient department of a large teaching hospital. It used narrative to identify emotional highs and lows of the patient journey and mapped this to the 'touchpoints' of that journey. The team then facilitated co-design groups to address shared priorities for improvement and to implement and test them.

Throughout these diverse projects there is the thread of participatory design theory and practice. We will close the chapter by reflecting on design's unique contribution to delivering innovative solutions to address the changing needs of today's and tomorrow's populations.

Introduction

Every day we interact with services. From checking our mobile phone to taking the bus to work, from ordering shopping online to taking money out of the ATM. Most, if not all of these services will have been designed, and we have a sense of which of these services are good or bad, and we can change providers based on this experience.

Now consider health. The majority of the UK's health provision is delivered as a service; in fact, the clue is in the title. The National Health Service (NHS) is the biggest provider of healthcare in the world. In 2014, the NHS employed 150,273 doctors, 377,191 qualified nursing staff, 155,960 qualified scientific, therapeutic and technical staff and 37,078 managers. It comprises 156 acute trusts, its planned expenditure for 2014/15 is £113.035 billion and the NHS deals with over 1 million patients every 36 hours (NHS Confederation, 2015).

Service design is an emergent discipline of design and to date has had limited impact on the development of services in health. This chapter reflects on the challenges changing societal needs will have on the way that healthcare is provided, and how by applying the theory, methods and practice of participatory service design, health services are able to respond and deliver services that 'work' for both patients, carers and health service providers.

The chapter will set out the key challenges to healthcare provision and make the case that in order to address these challenges we need to meaningfully engage with those individuals living with chronic conditions, reflecting on the particular strengths service design brings to involving a diverse range of stakeholders to co-design solutions that work for all.

Self-management programmes are being used worldwide to redesign health systems to be more responsive to the challenges, and associated economic concerns, imposed by an ageing population and the associated increased prevalence of chronic disease. The WHO developed the Innovative Care for Chronic Conditions framework based on the original Chronic Care Model (2002). The framework is focused on a triad partnership between the individual, the healthcare team and the community. The evolving notion of patients' engagement in managing their chronic illness is stressed in this framework. Strategies for engagement include health literacy, shared decision-making and self-management. Providing the scale and adequacy of services to support self-management of long-term conditions requires radical new thinking about how public health services are organised and delivered, including how technologies can be integrated into healthcare systems to promote and support self-management.

A starting point for such thinking is the concept of co-production of health outcomes. To enable self-management, the person with the chronic illness, physician and health professional need to work together within a participatory network of relatives, friends and service organisations. Design has certain key characteristics that allow this goal to be realised.

The designer's role has traditionally been shaped through commissions from industry to respond to a brief formulated by the client to improve or create new products to maximise their market share and profit margin. Designers utilise and apply their aesthetic and technological skills to optimise manufacture and performance of the product and to enhance economic viability and consumer appeal. This has been a familiar model in the design of medical devices and health-related products. These products when launched into the market-place are very often part of a service and become the 'touchpoints' where service providers and recipients interact. The service encounters become a critical part of the customer experience and consequently consideration to the role of the service interaction through the product is an important factor for the designer and manufacturer. Unfortunately, too often service encounters are not the experience we would wish for and this is largely due to the fact that products, the 'touchpoints', are designed and developed in isolation of the service. Conversely services are designed without full consideration of the users' interaction with these services through the 'touchpoints'. 'As Manzini similarly argues, talking of designing for services rather than designing services recognizes that what is being designed is not an end result, but rather a platform for action with which diverse actors will engage over time' (Kimbell, 2011).

So service design can be seen as a process of planning and organising all the elements of a service, including the interfaces, to optimise the customer experience, with co-design between designers, manufacturers, service providers and end service users playing a central role. The benefits of co-design are argued to occur:

- through improving the creative process and organisation of the service project;
- for the service's customers by a better match between offer and needs;
- in the supplier through creativity, awareness of customers and internal cooperation on innovation (Steen et al., 2011).

The traditional role of design and the designer has evolved. Sanders (2001) discussed how we were witnessing a shift in focus from individual to 'collective creativity' that provided a new role for designers as creators of scaffolds or infrastructures upon which non-designers could express their creativity. Chamberlain and Yoxall (2012) have described how designed objects, what we might describe as critical artefacts, do not necessarily present solutions but considered questions and prompts for conversation to develop understanding. Rather than conceptualising design as a problem-solving activity used at the end of the development process to embellish a product, they have frequently employed design through the creation of objects to promote discussion and to aid communication amongst stakeholders (Figure 12.1). Critical artefacts and prototypes can become key in understanding and defining user needs, accessing their tacit knowledge through 'doing' rather than relying on verbal protocols. This can help break down barriers of language, culture, age and gender. Design skills can be employed to make tangible dreams, test future scenarios and can facilitate the engagement of people as active partners in research and design activity rather than as passive respondents.

With an increasing shift to self-managed health programmes as part of health services, it seems creators of services have a moral obligation to engage users of these programmes and services at the heart of their development. From a pragmatic perspective, it could also be suggested that by engaging users throughout the design process, the outcome will be fit for purpose and potentially more valued by those using the service.

This chapter will illustrate the described challenge and explore it through two projects; namely, a stroke survivor case study reflecting how design has engaged and involved users in developing their own self-managed care and a service-improvement case study where users were involved in developing the very services they required.

Intelligent shoes for stroke survivors

The UK National Clinical Guidelines for Stroke (Intercollegiate Stroke Working Party, 2012) provide evidence and recommendations for the commissioning and delivery of services for individual stroke survivors and their families. The guidelines cover the acute phase of management, secondary prevention, the recovery phase and rehabilitation followed by long-term management after the stroke. Whilst there is significant evidence to support rehabilitation post-discharge, delivered by early supported discharge teams and community rehabilitation teams, due to increasing demand on services and financial constraints within health and social care, service needs cannot be met. A recent national audit of stroke services (Intercollegiate Stroke Working Party, 2015) reported evidence of widespread variations in the nationally commissioned portfolio of post-stroke services with 'too many areas failing to commission comprehensive care'.

With this increasing demand on services, financial constraints and an overwhelming amount of evidence for change, this project responded by proposing a radical innovation with the adoption of a self-management paradigm as a way of delivering home-based rehabilitation, thereby repositioning the patient and carer as central to both the design and delivery of their own care.

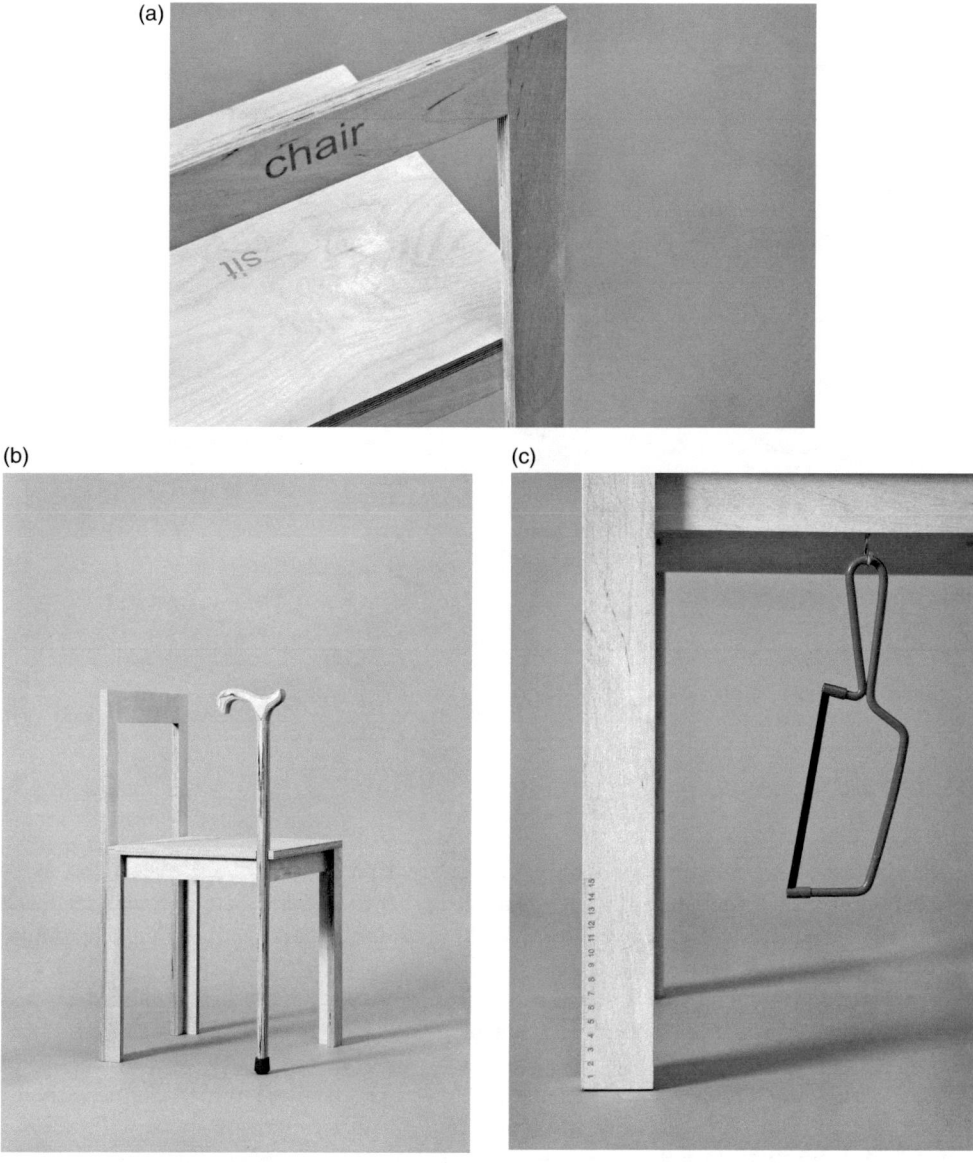

Figure 12.1 A selection from Chamberlain's Stigmas series: (a) 'This is a chair to sit on', (b) 'Rest of your life', (c) 'Adjustable chair'

The research team aimed to deepen understanding of the potential for digital technology to support the self-management of stroke rehabilitation through an iterative health, social care and user-centred design methodology (Wright and McCarthy, 2010). The team designed a personalised self-management rehabilitation system, a prototype integrated with sensor technology, developed to enable stroke survivors to self-manage their rehabilitation with motivational feedback enabling them to achieve identified individualised life goals. The

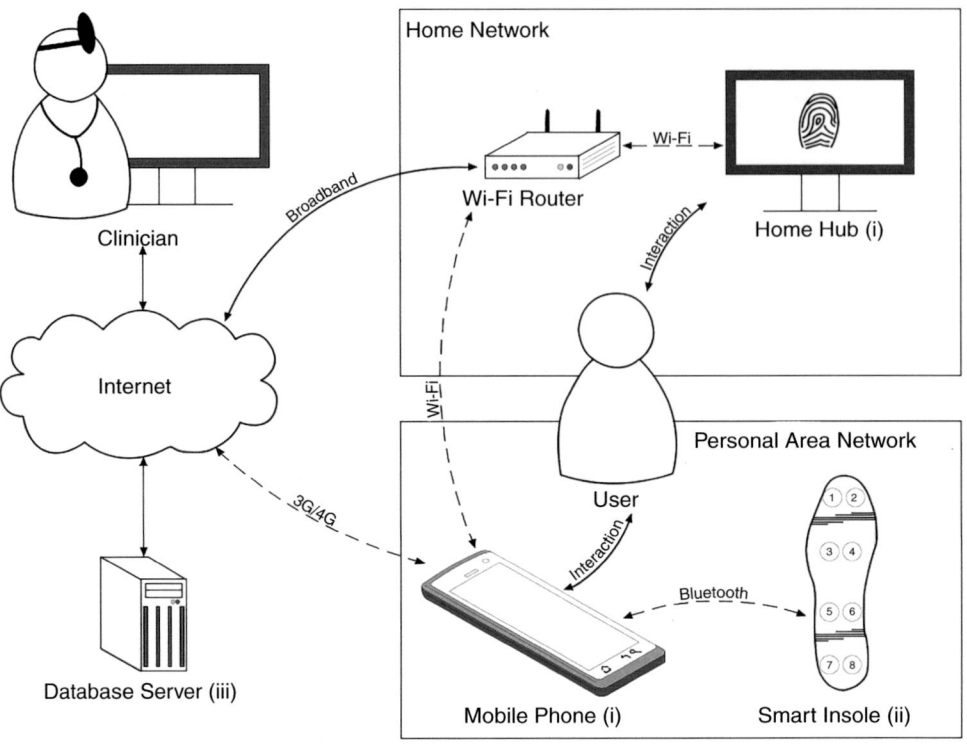

Figure 12.2 Self-management system

self-management system consists of a 'home hub', a smartphone or PC, a server and an intelligent sensored shoe insole, the initial concept being that the system could provide feedback to the stroke survivor, their carers and the clinical multidisciplinary team within community rehabilitation centres (Figure 12.2).

As described, the current care pathway for stroke involves acute care followed by discharge to an early supported discharged team or community rehabilitation team who provide rehabilitation either in the home environment or daycare centres for a maximum of 12 weeks. Following discharge from the service, the stroke survivor has no input from therapists, relying on their prior learning and practice of exercise or private therapy if available. It was envisioned that the self-management system, when designed and developed, would fill the gap in stroke provision, enabling the survivor to self-manage the rehabilitation with feedback on their walking ability from the intelligent shoe after discharge from the health service.

A key component of rehabilitation is relearning how to balance and walk, keeping weight evenly distributed between both feet and placing the heel first when the foot strikes the ground in stepping. The multisensored insole (see Figure 12.3) worn daily provided feedback on both gait parameters through the 'home hub' feedback screens enabling the stroke survivor to visualise their recovery and link that to their exercise programme, also included within the 'home hub' (Figure 12.4).

Figure 12.3 Multisensored insole

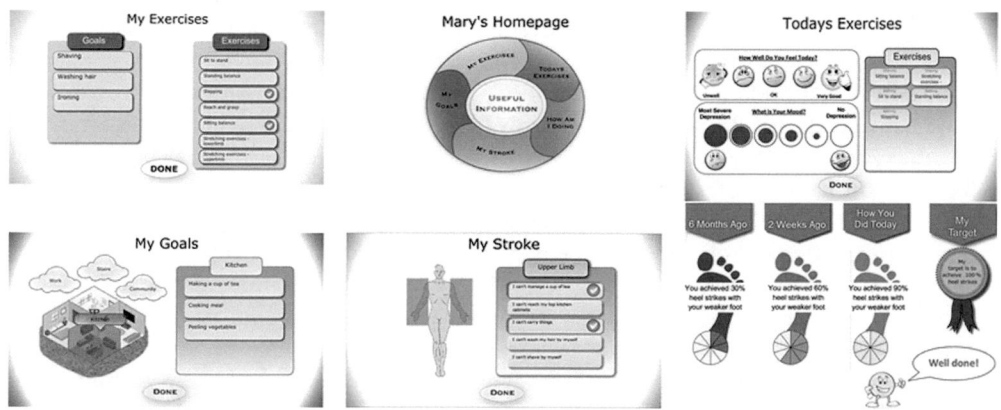

Figure 12.4 Home hub screens

The design and development of the self-management system involved a complex user-centred, participatory process which aimed to:

1. Translate current models of stroke rehabilitation into a technology-based system.
2. Design a system that integrated 'life' goals that reflected the needs of the individual stroke survivor.
3. Explore whether a technology solution that recorded walking ability could be integrated into a personalised system to provide motivational feedback on the attainment of key walking characteristics.
4. Design motivational feedback screens that could translate complex biomechanical data into simple conceptual images.

We undertook a series of home visits, focus groups, in-depth interviews, cultural probes (Gaver et al., 1999) and technology biographies (Blythe et al., 2002) together with cooperative evaluations during the iterative design process. This user-centred approach to design was utilised as a holistic approach in order to understand firstly the users' experience of technology and secondly to ensure that we had a meaningful engagement with the users in co-designing the technology.

Our first focus group was conducted with seven stroke professionals and the second focus group was conducted with seven people with stroke and their carers. Participants' feelings and attitudes towards assistive and information communication technologies were explored by using 'post-it' activities and envisioning cards.

During the home visits, eight participants were given three activities: cultural probes, technology biographies and in-depth interviews. The cultural probes provided valuable information that enriched the data derived from interviews with the participants. The non-verbal data were particularly useful in participants who provided less detailed descriptions of their experiences with stroke and technology. Researchers used a probe kit (package) containing a newspaper, a TV magazine and a diary to enable the observation of participants' interests and concerns over a period of time within their personal and social context or life setting. The team were particularly interested in finding out about relationships and shared experiences and, hence, themes such as 'my family and friends', 'description of an imaginary therapeutic exercise', 'description of four gifts', 'description of an ideal dream-day', 'use of a media diary' and 'a few words about me' were included in the kit which subsequently helped us identify user requirements for developing the system. Stroke survivor and carer dyads were used to create technology biographies in which participants' views, feelings, thoughts and hopes towards technology were explored. The outcome of the technology biographies were merged with the data obtained from the in-depth interviews and cultural probes to examine participants' experiences as a whole.

The technology biography interviews were also undertaken to examine the use of technology in the participants' homes, to explore the personal history of technologies, cultural meaning and the changes that the participants witnessed during their lifetime, and to investigate future technological developments and participants' feelings related to these technological advancements (Mawson et al., 2013).

Researchers also conducted narrative interviews with the aim of inducing narrative responses (Wengraf, 2001) as they took the participants back to their experience of stroke and how and what things had happened since the incident of stroke. The narratives allowed users to express their experiences of stroke and their views on acceptable technologies and desirable design solutions, allowing users as partners in co-design to give a voice to often personal, social and professional aspects of their lives.

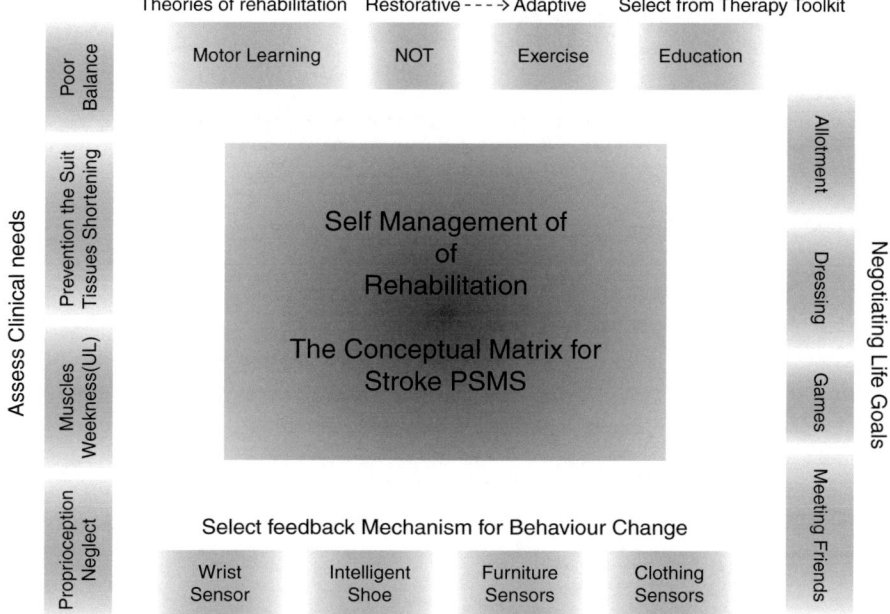

Figure 12.5 The conceptual matrix for a stroke self-managed rehabilitation system

The participants were encouraged to use their imagination to express their ideas about technological solutions for the rehabilitation of stroke by completing the envisioning cards. They supported the idea of a technology to monitor patients between therapy sessions and the idea of integrating patient information in a shareable system. They believed that technology has the potential to augment therapy carry over and to maintain therapy outcomes but had their reservations about the idea of hands-on therapy being replaced by rehabilitation technology. They stressed the significance of meaningful, context-dependent and personalised technology that could be used to redesign and improve rehabilitation services (Parker et al., 2013; Mawson et al., 2013).

In order to understand how to build a system that mirrored, in a virtual sense, the care pathway and model of rehabilitation current in the UK, qualitative data from clinicians and literature reviews were used to design a conceptual matrix of the self-management systems (Nasr et al., 2009).

The matrix, Figure 12.5, was linked to a series of personalised scenarios, Figure 12.6, which were also developed from the focus groups, in-depth interviews and cultural probes. Together they provided a communication tool within the interdisciplinary research team. This gave the team a concrete and tangible representation of the rehabilitation process, the individualised needs of the stroke survivor and the theories of recovery and behaviour change in order to facilitate the co-design of the self-management stroke technology.

The conceptual matrix was translated into a number of modules within the system, each having an interactive screen accessed by touch from the 'home hub'. The screens were designed and tested with stroke survivors, carers and the multidisciplinary team as it was envisioned that the system would be integrated into the stroke care pathway during the final weeks of community rehabilitation. This would allow the customisation and personalisation of the system

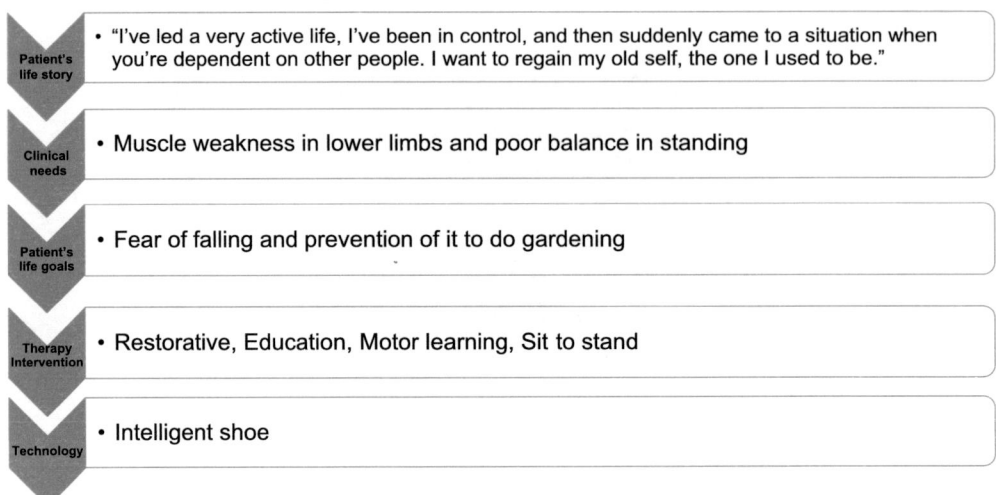

Scenario 1: Michael

Patient's life story
- "I've led a very active life, I've been in control, and then suddenly came to a situation when you're dependent on other people. I want to regain my old self, the one I used to be."

Clinical needs
- Muscle weakness in lower limbs and poor balance in standing

Patient's life goals
- Fear of falling and prevention of it to do gardening

Therapy Intervention
- Restorative, Education, Motor learning, Sit to stand

Technology
- Intelligent shoe

Figure 12.6 Example of a stroke survivor's 'scenario'

for each stroke patient. The following modules with interactive screens were designed to mirror the rehabilitation model reflected in the conceptual matrix: 'My stroke', My goals', 'My exercises', 'Todays exercises', 'How am I doing'.

A number of prototype screen shots were designed, the most complex of the screens being the feedback screens that provided the stroke survivor with information (knowledge) about their walking symmetry and heel strikes. The reason why these two parameters of gait were chosen was the evidence-based link between poor symmetry of gait and the risk of falling, and the cosmetic improvements in gait when a stroke survivor walks more normally, striking the heel in a forward step. As the intelligent insole (shoe) had been chosen from a technology review as the most appropriate measure of walking characteristics, a screen was required that translated the complex sensor data from the insole to the stroke user in both a meaningful way and a way that would promote self-efficacy and motor behaviour change.

Research suggests that in order to achieve rehabilitation outcomes through the use of digital technology, key elements of feedback, such as it being accurate, measurable, rewarding, adaptable, and the user's knowledge of results feedback are required to trigger the mechanisms underpinning self-management and behaviour change (Parker et al., 2010). Therefore, these elements were incorporated into the feedback screens, each of which were paper prototyped. These were evaluated with stroke survivors and their carers using the participatory method of cooperative evaluation and cognitive walkthroughs. Figure 12.7 illustrates the preferred feedback screen shot alongside the traditional, more technical feedback screen.

Following the initial evaluation, the prototypes were evaluated further with nine stroke survivors and their carers in their own homes. Using a cooperative evaluation (Monk et al., 1993), users were encouraged to think aloud while using the self-management system. Users' interactions with the system were audio/video recorded. The aim was to examine how easy or

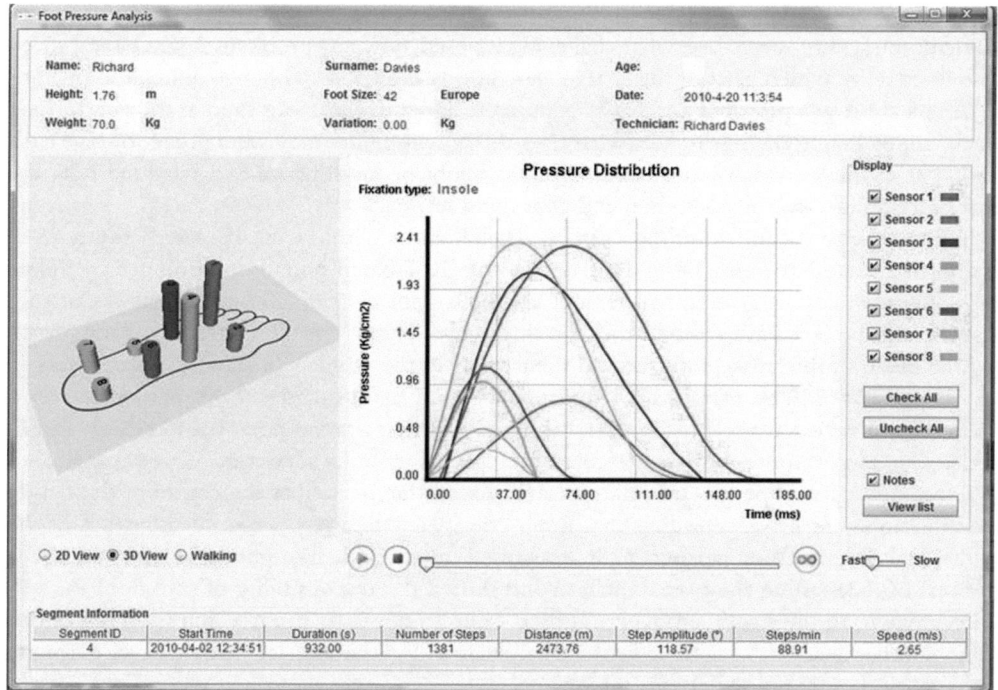

Figure 12.7a Traditional feedback screen

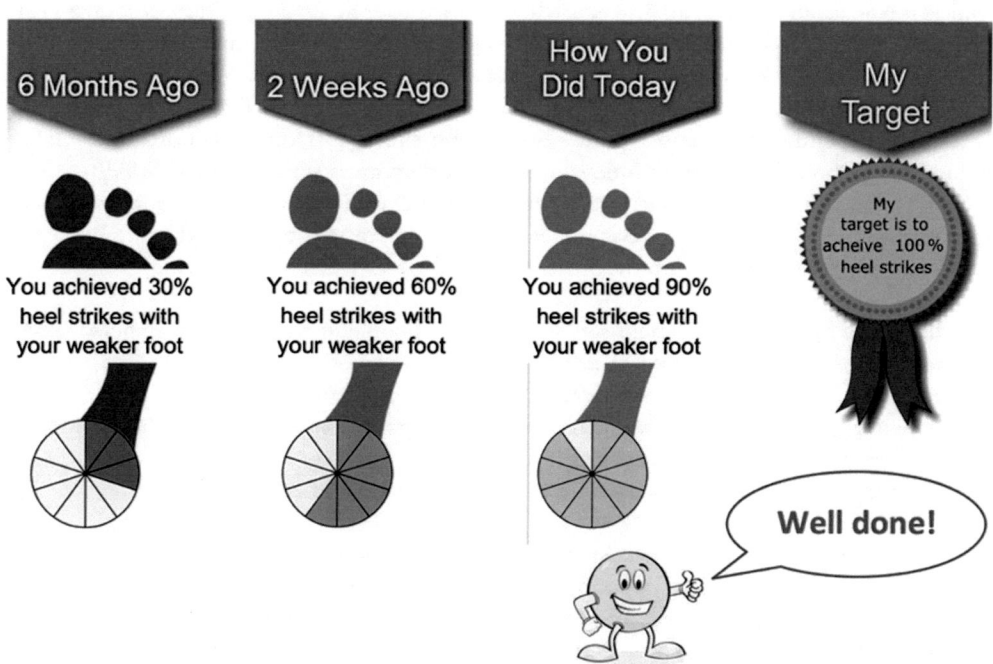

Figure 12.7b Feedback screen designed with users

difficult the system was to use, what challenges it posed, how any problems might be improved and to establish which parts of the system were poorly designed and hence difficult to operate.

A task sheet was prepared and participants were asked to think out loud as they performed each task by telling the researchers what they thought and how they were going to solve each task. For example, which button they thought might be appropriate and why and how the system responded to their activities and gave them feedback.

Different ways of providing post-stroke rehabilitation within a stroke care pathway were explored and how they might be translated into an ICT-based system underpinned by theories of motor relearning, self-management and behaviour change. The design methodologies used in this project have ensured that the interactive technology developed has been driven by the needs of the stroke survivor and their carers in the context of their journey to recovery or adaptation. The participatory and user-centred nature of this work has resulted in a personalised system for self-managed rehabilitation which has the potential to change motor behaviour and promote the achievement of life goals for stroke survivors.

From a pragmatic perspective, the research placed the 'person' at the centre of the design and development process, leading to a more effective system responsive to the needs of the individual; from a moral perspective it recognised the individual's right to be involved in the process of redesigning their rehabilitation and shifted the responsibility of care from the service provider to the stroke survivor and their carer. In doing so, the research team responded to the unmet need for long-term stroke rehabilitation and the societal challenges we currently face within health and social care.

Better outpatient services for older people

Most people's first interaction with hospital services is through the outpatient department. Unless it is an accident or an emergency, when you see your general practitioner/primary care physician, if you need any specialist care you will be referred to the outpatient service.

From the data we know that in the time period 2008–9, nearly 20 million people over the age of 60 attended an outpatient clinic within the NHS in England (Health and Social Care Information Centre, 2009) and yet the research also shows that outpatient areas have fallen behind the technical and service innovations of inpatient areas (Enderby et al., 1999).

The primary aim of the project was to improve the experience of older people with complex needs who use outpatient services. The project team anticipated the following outcomes subject to the priorities and improvements identified by service users and staff:

1.   Improved quality of outpatient services for older people in terms of a more personalised, responsive and dignified experience.
2.   Better access and support for older people using outpatient services.
3.   A better understanding of what matters to older people which can be used to improve and measure the quality of services.
4.   Training material in outpatient skills based upon patients as experts.

The team anticipated that this would result in two main benefits: firstly, older people would receive the particular care and support they need through the outpatient system; and secondly, older people would gain greater health and wellbeing benefits from a service that is more responsive to their needs. The project would therefore directly address a number of criteria in maintaining patient dignity, namely to:

- treat each person as an individual by offering a personalised service;
- enable people to maintain the maximum possible level of independence, choice and control;
- listen and support people to express their needs and wants; and
- assist people to maintain confidence and a positive self-esteem.

In order to measure the impact of the project against these criteria we used a triangulated method of three outcomes:

- the improved experience of older people with complex needs through interviews;
- the implementation of changes in outpatient services through audit with standards set by the design groups; and
- the reduction in rates of Did Not Attends, cancellations and complaints from routine data collection.

The basic approach of the project was to use service design in the context of healthcare to achieve service improvements. The project focused on the points at which people come into contact and interact with medical outpatient services at a large teaching hospital. These 'touchpoints' shape the experience users have of the service and influence the way they access and use the services. The researchers therefore followed the methods of *experience-based design* (EBD) developed by the NHS Institute for Innovation and Improvement. The methods of EBD are well referenced (Wolstenholme et al., 2010; Bate and Robert, 2006; Bowen et al., 2013), but in summary the methods involve a participatory approach where staff, patients and carers are brought together to capture and understand the experience of using the current service; they then co-design aspects of new services and evaluate the changes.

A key aspect of this method is the capturing of experience in the form of emotion maps, which are a powerful way of representing this process. Figure 12.8 is an excerpt from the patient experience map which shows significant interactions on their journey and associated emotions.

The methods used in the project depend upon the involvement of patients and their carers as expert users of outpatients. However, because the focus of this project was older people and their complex needs, there was a need to go beyond conventional approaches to patient involvement to secure the insights from 'less heard' groups and so a local voluntary organisation was engaged to involve patients through a community-outreach model.

Working with this organisation gave access to individuals with mobility and access issues. Interviewing the people in their homes enabled researchers to gather a wider range of the experiences and represent these in the group work. A further benefit of this approach was that these service users had an existing relationship with the voluntary organisation and so felt comfortable and supported to contribute meaningfully to the project.

EBD recognises that it is not just patients who experience a service. Staff inclusion is crucial in terms of their experience and understanding of the clinical and service requirements. The team therefore worked to gather all the key stakeholders' experiences including clerical, nursing and medical staff and the local ambulance service. This core group then expanded as the complexity of the project became apparent to include the local city council, universities and senior managers from across the trust (Figure 12.9).

Staff engagement not only allowed the grounding of any proposed changes in the reality of the workplace, but also allowed a deeper understanding from both staff and patients of each *other's* experience.

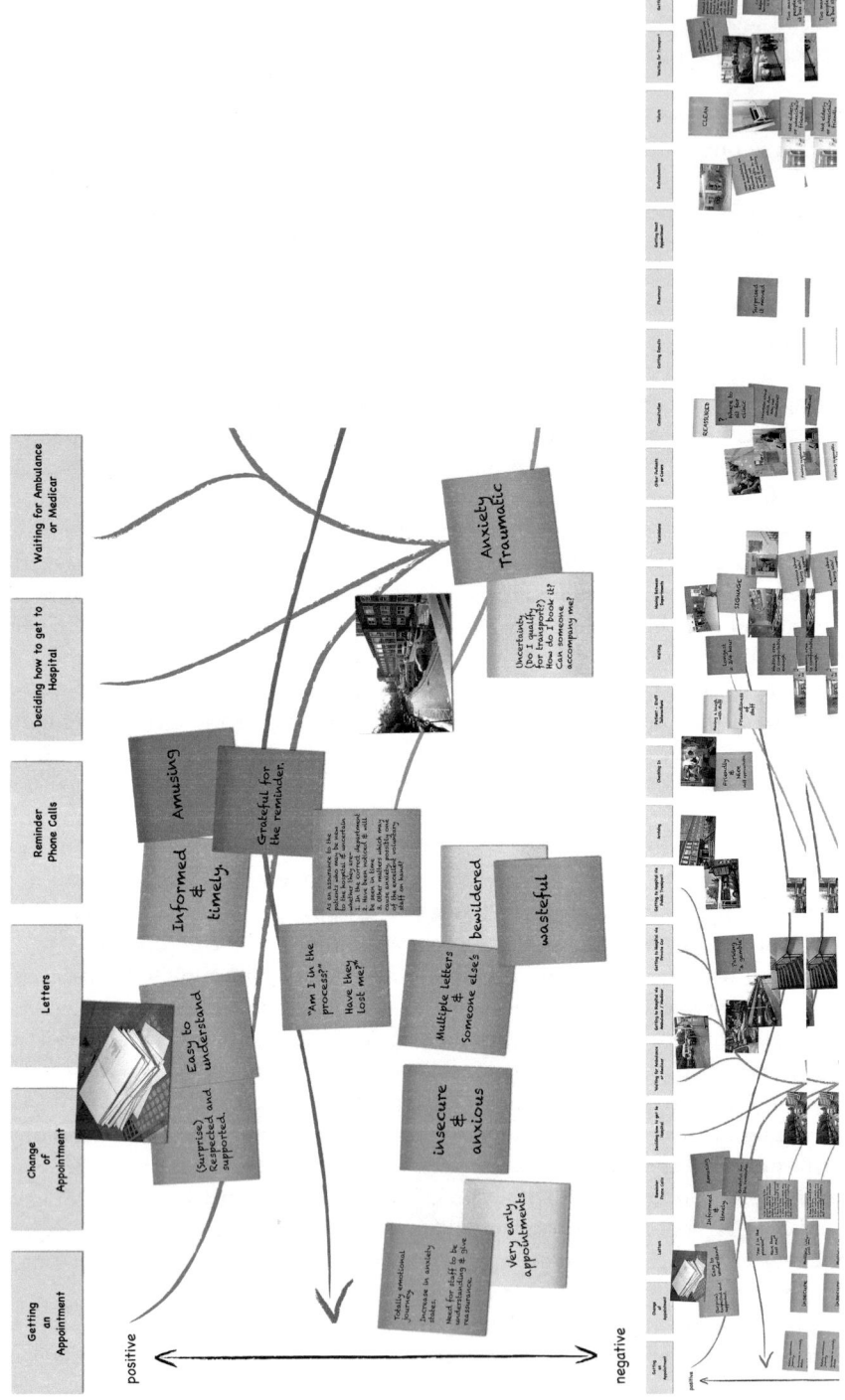

Figure 12.8 Excerpt (a) from the patient experience map (b)

Figure 12.9 Participants at an experience-gathering event

A focus on experience

The project team provided training to the voluntary organisation's staff to enable them to gather evidence from service users. This was achieved by asking patients to tell the story of their last visit to outpatients. These stories allowed people to move past the 'mustn't grumble' and 'don't want to complain' and describe the interactions of the patient journey with a degree of objectivity. For example, the story provided by one of the older patient representatives highlights many issues:

> When you're going to hospital the anxiety starts a long time before. When you get your appointment you begin to get anxious: what's going to happen, what are they going to do to me? Dealing with patients is a very difficult, time-consuming, and emotional responsibility. All the relationships between staff and patients are caught up in this anxiety. Particularly for older people who aren't as able as they used to be to cope with difficult situations: where am I, what am I doing here, have they forgotten me, am I in the right place, am I going to get to my appointment in time? This project is beginning to unpick what I call the leviathan of the hospital which is so vast, and so big.

This illustrates the power of stories here in that:

> Stories need not only be about experiences we have had. They might be about experiences we would like to have, or we plan to have. Imagined stories of possible futures or alternative presents are the basis of our imaginative engagement with the world. Imagining alternative presents or possible futures is of course central to design thinking and is thus of great importance to us here

> (Wright and McCarthy, 2010)

The project was able to create new experiences for staff and patients to provide other insights into the service and utilised 'secret shoppers'. A patient and voluntary organisation staff member made the journey from the centre of town to the outpatients department by public transport, attended a 'virtual' appointment and went on to x-ray, ECG and the pharmacy. They told the story of this, which provided powerful evidence to stimulate design thinking.

Staff were interviewed to understand the reality of working in medical outpatients, and at every opportunity sought to return to the staff and their experience, knowledge and expertise to validate the work we were undertaking. Excellent support was provided from individuals who championed the project in and out of the immediate environment.

Co-design

The second key component of the approach is co-design. Groups of patients, carers, staff and the wider project team were established around themes (Getting to the hospital, arriving at the department), derived from the experience-capture sessions. Techniques of service design and design research (blue sky thinking, modelling, critical artefacts) were used to allow the groups to come up with ideas, develop prototypes and propose ways to test. The groups could request external 'experts' where technical or specialist advice was required to move their ideas forward, but some of the most powerful solutions were developed within the groups over a period of weeks. A range of the proposals are outlined below.

Many patients praised the staff of medical outpatients for their professionalism and understanding, but within the co-design phase of the project, discussion took place around good examples of customer care from different services. To stimulate thinking, the idea of a luxury hotel was the focus of discussion where there is a warm welcome. This experience was recognised as being positive within the group, however, the patients emphasised the significant differences between attending a clinic and staying at a hotel so went on to describe a much more emotionally responsive and caring response required. Consequently, whilst the existing trust customer care e-learning package was a good start, it was not adequate to enable staff to understand and respond more fully to the situation being experienced by many patients. In keeping with the participatory nature of the project, researchers felt that applied theatre would offer a different and memorable insight into the roles of staff and patients in this complex process.

The creative director of the theatre company worked with the design team and the staff and patient experience to develop a script that foregrounded the aspects of interpersonal interaction identified in the experience-capture aspect of the project. This was performed to an audience of staff, patients and carers and allowed a connection with the data and experience that other methods would not have allowed.

The experience mapping highlighted that anxiety for patients often starts with the receipt of the appointment letter. The original appointment letter (Figure 12.10) was described as impersonal and potentially confusing. Staff and patients went away and wrote the letter, from their perspective, that they would like to receive, and then brought their work back to the group to produce the second letter.

The changes made concerned the introduction of a picture of the correct door to use for the clinic, the key information being in bold and the personalisation of the letter so it was addressed from the appointment clerk responsible for the clinic.

This was co-design in action resulting in a letter that reflected the best of patient and staff experience (Figure 12.11). This letter was piloted in outpatients and was being sent out to all new patients over the age of 65. It was the research team's recommendation that the letter should be adopted by the trust for use on appropriate clinics.

Sheffield Teaching Hospitals **NHS**

NHS Foundation Trust

Royal Hallamshire Hospital
Glossop Road
Sheffield S10 2JF

MR P. ATIENT
24 SOME ROAD
WALKLEY
SHEFFIELD
S YORKSHIRE
S6 #AB

Tel 0114 271 1900 Fax 0114 271 1901

22 DECEMBER 2009

Ref: AB####

NHS No: ### ### ####

Dear P. ATIENT

Consultant : DR. A.B. FOOT
On   : Thursday 04 March 2010 at 3.30 pm
Clinic   : GENERAL MED-E   (Ref: ABC#D)

An appointment has been made for you to be seen in the
above clinic which is held in the Medical Out Patient
Department, situated on A floor at the Royal
Hallamshire Hospital.

If you are unable to keep this appointment, please
contact the clinic on Sheffield (0114) 2712953 so that
this appointment may be offered to another patient and
an alternative date arranged for you.

N.B. Please bring your medication or prescription list
to every appointment.

Please bring your appointment card with you when you
attend.

Yours sincerely

Appointments Clerk

Figure 12.10 Original appointment letter

Sheffield Teaching Hospitals NHS
NHS Foundation Trust

Medical Outpatients
Glossop Road
Sheffield
S10 2JF

0114 271 2953

Mr P Atient
101 Nice road
Sheffield
S12 357

Dear Mr Atient   Patient Number DW1452

Welcome to Medical Outpatients, we have arranged the following appointment for you.

Consultant:	**Dr A Anderson**
Date:	**Wednesday 13 November**
Time:	**4.30pm**
Where:	**Medical Outpatients (A Road)**
	Royal Hallamshire Hospital
Transport:	**An ambulance will arrive for you and your**
	escort between 12 noon and 2.00pm

As this is your first visit to clinic you will need to bring:

- A sample of urine in a small labelled pot
- A list of medications and their doses (your prescription list)

Please allow a full morning or afternoon for your visit. After meeting with the doctor you **may** need to have an ECG, Blood tests or an X-Ray. The doctor will tell you if this is necessary during your appointment.

Please contact us as soon as possible if you are unable to attend your appointment as this will allow us to offer the appointment to someone else. We can be contacted on the number at the top of this letter between 8.00am and 5.00pm Monday to Friday. You can also use this number to contact us if you have queries regarding your transport arrangements.

We look forward to seeing you at your appointment

Yours sincerely

Darren Woodward,
Appointments Clerk

Please bring this letter with you to your appointment

Chairman: David Stone OBE • Chief Executive: Andrew Cash OBE

Figure 12.11 New appointment letter

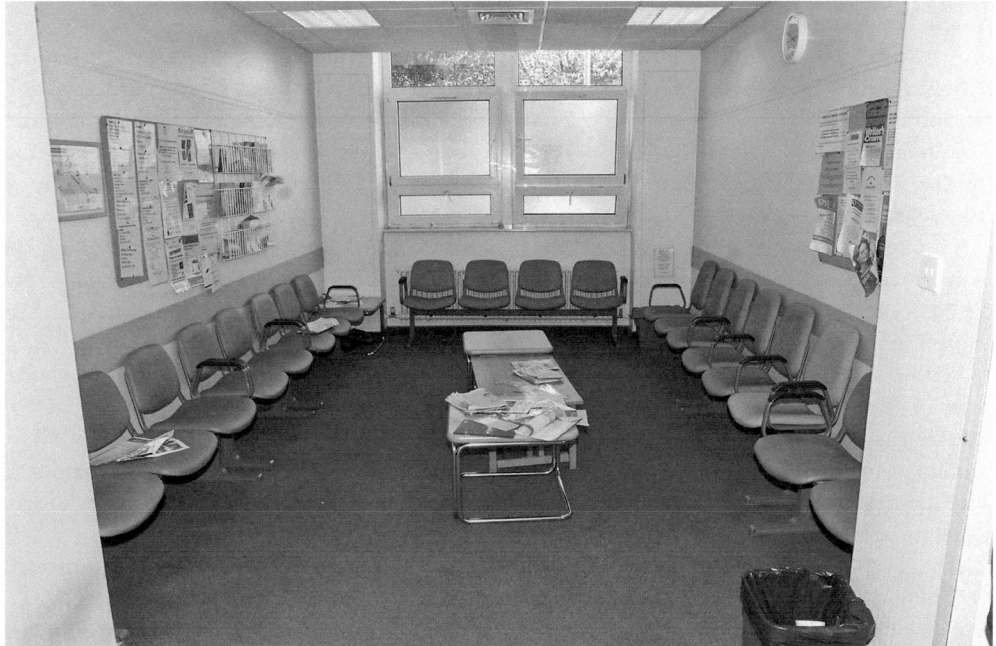

Figure 12.12 Waiting area in medical outpatients

'Am I in the system?' was a concern echoed throughout many of the project groups. In some ways this was an expression of the general anxiety of attending outpatients for a potentially life-changing diagnosis to be delivered, but there was a more specific anxiety about the process of waiting for the consultation. To better explore the former point, the project team commissioned a health psychologist from the local university to undertake a review of the psychological implications and environmental factors that might influence these. 'The overarching aim should be to minimise any additional stress associated with visits to outpatients. If outpatient visits are experienced as distressing, then it will increase the likelihood of missed appointments particularly with individuals who are having difficulty coping' (psychology report).

Patients described not knowing if they were in the right place, if they had been missed and overlooked. Consequently this affected behaviour in the waiting areas. Figure 12.12 is the main waiting area on the outpatients corridor. Anecdotally, this was rarely used outside of the occasions when there was nowhere else to sit. When you sit in this area, you have no connection to the corridor and the feeling is that you are out of the way and almost unseen. A practical solution was to install convex mirrors on the corridor wall opposite to allow patients to see the staff on the corridor and vice versa.

The waiting area is complex with several different clinics running simultaneously. 'Rules' exist regarding who takes priority in clinic lists, and the full effect is disorientating for the casual observer, never mind an anxious patient. A proposal that was explored as a follow-on project is the use of a 'ticketing/waiting' system, which would address some of these concerns. The hypothesis was that by giving patients a tangible token, which differentiates between different clinics and gives people a sense of knowing they are in the system, will improve the patient experience.

A major issue resulting from mapping the patient experience was the difficulty for the patients visiting outpatients to navigate to different departments required during their visit. For instance, visits to ECG were highlighted as being particularly problematic, since the route is complicated, their destination is another building entirely and the signs throughout the journey do not explicitly refer to the ECG department until the patient arrives in Cardiology (the department in which the ECG is performed).

Through the co-design process staff and patients explored potential solutions, drawing on experience from other sectors and their own experience of different hospitals. Simple principles from the retail sector were explored with 'store guides' being cited as a useful model to address some of the complexities of signage.

With this in mind, and as part of the larger topic of wayfinding (wayfinding refers to the ways in which people navigate through an environment from one place to another and the systems that facilitate this including signs, maps, landmarks and building layouts) in BOSOP, prototype signage was commissioned from two university Master's in Graphic Design students. The revised signage was piloted with patient representatives in the medical outpatient department and designed to complement the prototype 'hand-out' maps by utilising the same visual cues and colour palette. Figure 12.13 shows one of the prototype signs held in a proposed location during the field test, by one of the designers.

Also proposed were floor guides which list in alphabetical order the different departments on each floor, with the floor that the patient is currently on highlighted in a bold colour (this colour then corresponds to the rest of the signage on that floor).

Another outcome of the wayfinding work were prototype maps that helped visitors (particularly the elderly) to find other locations within the outpatient department, or a specific location that has been identified as difficult to find (from the experience-gathering sessions with staff and patients), for example, ECG, the pharmacy and phlebotomy (blood testing). Shown in Figure 12.14 is an example of the prototype map to ECG from the outpatient department.

Alongside these maps showing a specific destination, maps showing the entire outpatient department were produced, showing the main destinations that patients visiting ask for; this being the main reception desks, individual departments, toilets and stair/lift access. The maps were taken from original architectural drawings for the building and simplified to show only main entrances and thoroughfares. Figure 12.15 is an example of the architectural plans for the west wing of the outpatients department, A floor. The plans are very detailed, but overcomplicated for the proposed maps to hand out to visitors. Hence, the design was simplified. An example of the first side of a double-sided document showing all three floors of the outpatient department can be seen in Figure 12.16.

There were many more aspects of the service that were addressed through this project, but there were some key attributes of the ideas that gained most traction. Involving designers resulted in very tangible outputs that served to carry the knowledge gained from the project beyond the immediate project team.

The appointment letter became a meme for the project, representing co-production and high production values in something that was very ubiquitous within the organisation. It was a useful object to explain the principle of 'touchpoints' to non-designers, as it set up the expectations and interactions with patients and carers before they even stepped foot in the hospital. The inclusion of an image was very easy to do but also powerfully represented the use of different forms of information for different people. The images of the correct entrances to

Figure 12.13 Prototype signage for medical outpatients

the hospital has subsequently influenced the design of the signage across both hospital sites (Figure 12.17).

The very meaningful way (with tangible outputs) that patients and carers were involved in the project became a positive way for describing patient and public involvement in service improvement. It described some practical steps that staff could take to engage and work with patients and carers to deliver change that worked for all parties.

It also raised the profile of the use of design methods and designers so much so that graphic design students now routinely have briefs set by clinical and service delivery teams as part of their undergraduate programme.

Service improvement happens in hospitals all the time (or at least it should). What is demonstrated through this project was the 'added value' that a service design approach might bring to working with older people. Whilst age is not specifically a chronic condition, it shares many of the attributes one might associate with such conditions. It is hoped that the outputs of this approach would provide confidence for using these methods with others who might have diabetes or, as in the previous case study, have had a stroke.

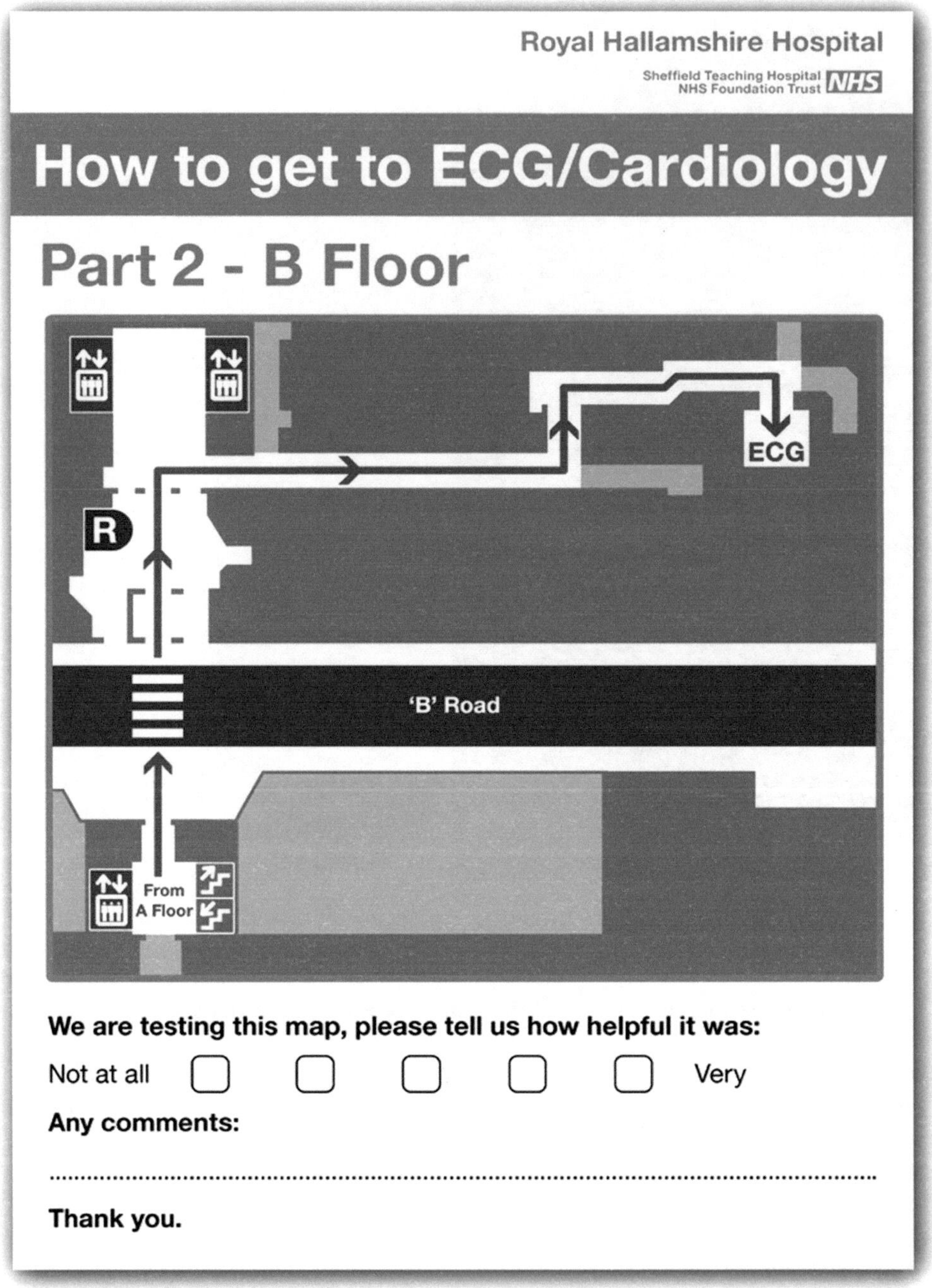

Figure 12.14 Hand-out map to ECG

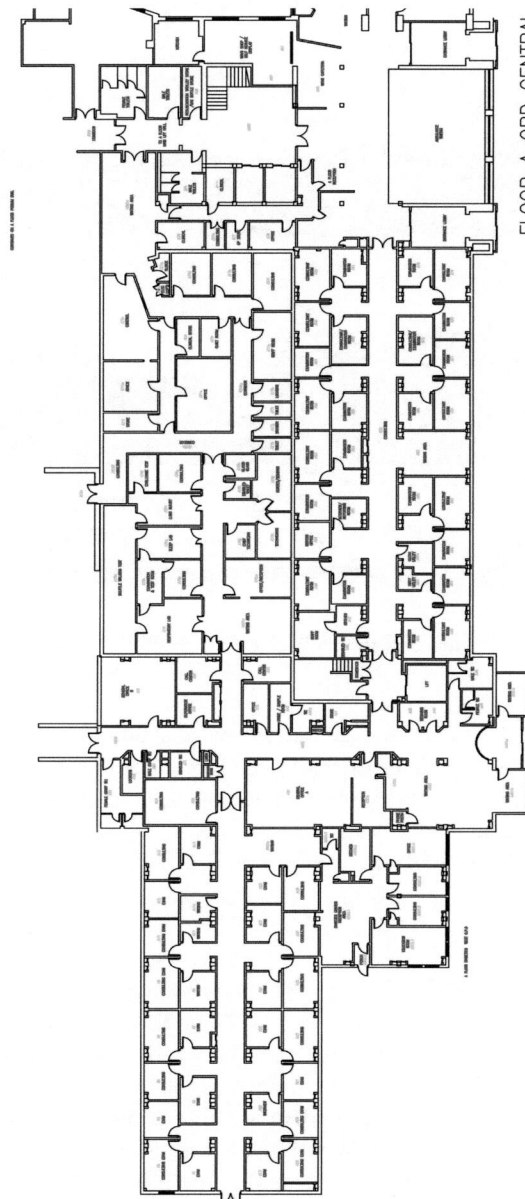

FLOOR A OPD CENTRAL

FLOOR A MEDICAL O P D WEST

Figure 12.15 Architectural plans for Floor A, outpatients department

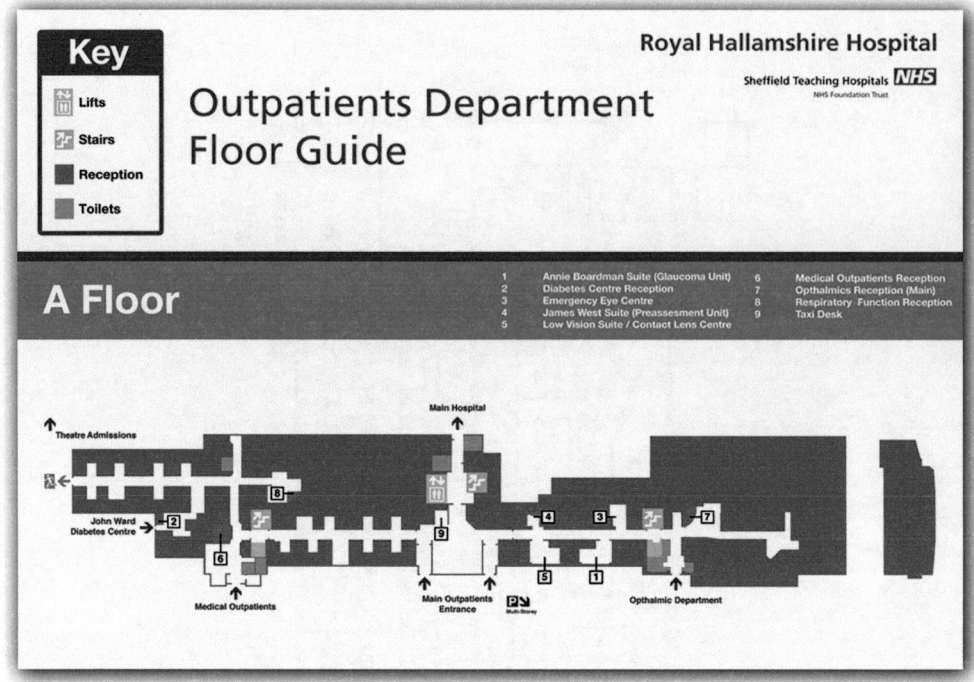

Figure 12.16 Department guide to the outpatients department (prototype)

Many of the techniques of service design are recognisable from other forms of service improvement (Lean, 6-sigma, Microsystems); what service design brings is an explicit attention to experience and the skills of designers allow this experience to be made tangible, which in turn allows a deeper engagement with those people with whom the responsibility of self-care lies as they move forward with their own lives.

Reflections

The challenges facing individuals living with chronic conditions are complex and ever-changing. Within an institution as large as the NHS finding ways to create seamless services that predict, respond to and meet the needs and aspirations of individuals coping with long-term health conditions can be difficult. This is made all the more problematic as health services also seek to address a constantly changing demographic at the same time as reducing overall costs, requiring a reconfiguration of where and how services are delivered. This chapter has illustrated, through case studies, how it is here that the role of design within the healthcare context comes to the fore. We have shown how designers working within multidisciplinary health teams can use design methodologies in order to build understanding of the needs of people living with long-term conditions and to engage and involve people in the redesign of services. We have challenged some of the traditional notions of where designers might be involved, highlighting the importance of engaging designers throughout the process rather than simply at the end. We have also given examples of how design might shape services,

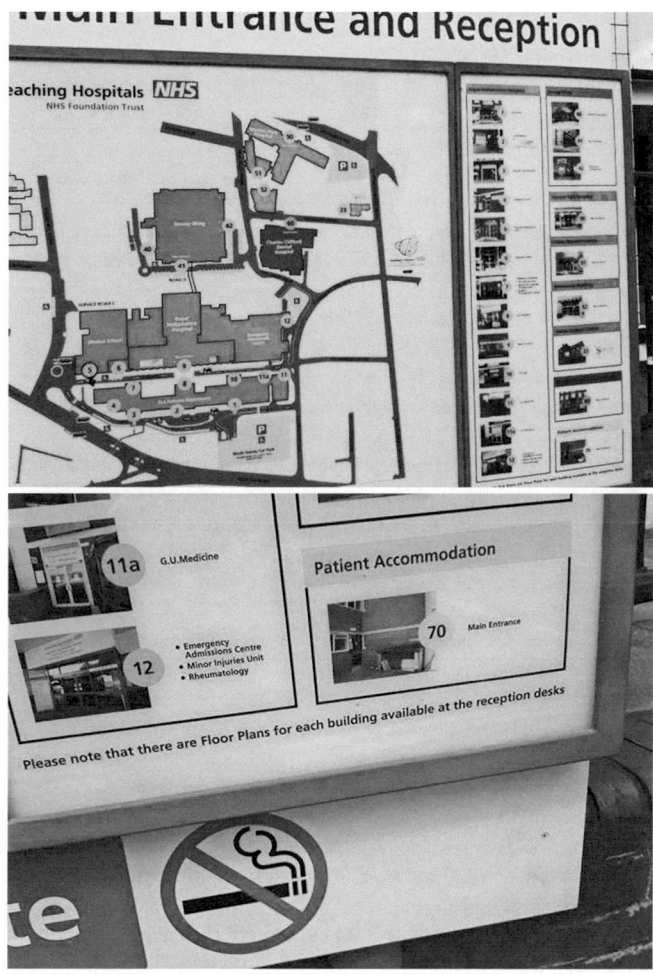

Figure 12.17 Hospital signage implemented as a result of the project

including the role of product design as a starting point in disrupting traditional interventions to reshape how services are then conceptualised. Finally, we have shown the importance of designing the detail and how the interventions that often make the greatest difference can be something as simple as clearer signage or signposting. Above all, we hope that we have shown that at the heart of good service design is the authentic engagement of individuals living with long-term conditions and the staff who work with them. It is only through designing with people that the ultimate aims and aspirations of service design will be achieved.

References

Bate, S.P. and Robert, G. (2006) Experience-based design: From redesigning the system around the patient to co-designing services with the patient. *Quality and Safety in Health Care*, 15: 307–10.

Blythe, M., Monk, A. and Park, J. (2002) Technology biographies: Field study techniques for home use product development. *Extended Abstracts on Human Factors in Computing Systems (CHI'02)*: 658–9.

Bowen, S., McSeveny, K., Lockley, E., Wolstenholme, D., Cobb, M. and Dearden, A. (2013) How was it for you? Experiences of participatory design in the UK health service. *CoDesign*, 9(4): 230–46. Available at: www.tandfonline.com/doi/abs/10.1080/15710882.2013.846384, accessed 25 June 2015.

Chamberlain, P. and Yoxall, A. (2012) 'Of mice and men': The role of interactive exhibitions as research tools for inclusive design. *Design Journal*, 15(1): 57–78.

Enderby, P. et al. (1999) *A Study of Hospital Outpatient Services*. London: King's Fund.

Gaver, B., Dunne, T. and Pacenti, E. (1999) Design: Cultural probes. *Interactions*, 6(1): 21–9.

Health and Social Care Information Centre (2009) Hospital outpatient activity – 2008–09 [NS]. Available at: www.hscic.gov.uk/searchcatalogue?productid=2460&topics=1%2fHospital+care%2fAdmissions+and+attendances&covdate=APR%2c2008%2cMAR%2c2009&sort=Relevance&size=100&page=1#top, accessed 15 December 2015.

Intercollegiate Stroke Working Party (2012) National clinical guideline for stroke. London. Available at: www.rcplondon.ac.uk/sites/default/files/national-clinical-guidelines-for-stroke-fourth-edition.pdf.

Intercollegiate Stroke Working Party (2015) Intercollegiate Stroke Working Party, Sentinel Stroke National Audit Programme, Post Acute Organisational Audit, public report. London. Available at: www.strokeaudit.org/Documents/Results/National/2015/2015-PAOrgPublicReportPhase2.aspx.

Kimbell, L. (2011) Designing for service as one way of designing services. *International Journal of Design*, 5(2): 41–52.

Mawson, S., Nasr, N., Parker, J., Davies, R. and Mountain, G. (2013) Developing a personalised self-management system for post stroke rehabilitation: Utilising a user-centred design methodology. *Disability and Rehabilitation. Assistive Technology*, 9(6): 521–528. Available at: www.ncbi.nlm.nih.gov/pubmed/24131371.

Monk, A.F. et al. (1993) *Improving Your Human-Computer Interface: A Practical Technique*. New York: Prentice Hall.

Nasr, N., Torsi, S., Mawson, S., Wright, P. and Mountain, G. (2009) Self-management of stroke supported by assistive technology. Virtual Rehabilitation International Conference, 2009, p. 193. Available at: 10.1109/ICVR.2009.5174231.

NHS Confederation (2015) Key statistics on the NHS. Available at: www.nhsconfed.org/resources/key-statistics-on-the-nhs, accessed 15 December 2015.

Parker, J., Mountain, G.A. and Hammerton, J. (2010) An investigation into stroke patients' utilisation of feedback from computer-based technology, in Robinson, P., Clarkson, J. and Langdon, P. (eds), *Designing Inclusive Interactions*. New York: Springer, 167–76.

Parker, J., Mawson, S., Mountain, G., Nasr, N., Davies, R. and Zheng, H. (2013) The provision of feedback through computer-based technology to promote self-managed post-stroke rehabilitation in the home. *Disability and Rehabilitation. Assistive Technology*, 9(6): 529–38. Available at: www.ncbi.nlm.nih.gov/pubmed/24131369.

Sanders, L. (2001) Collective creativity. *LOOP: AIGA Journal of Interaction Design Education*, 6(3): 1–6. Available at: www.maketools.com/articles-papers/CollectiveCreativity_Sanders_01.pdf\nhttp://scholar.google.com/scholar?hl=en&btnG=Search&q=intitle:Collective+Creativity#6.

Steen, M., Manschot, M. and de Koning, N. (2011) Benefits of co-design in service design projects. *International Journal of Design*, 5(2): 53–60.

Wengraf, T. (2001) Qualitative research interviewing: Biographic narrative and semi-structured methods. Available at: http://books.google.com/books?id=c2b6jQ8g3sAC&pgis=1.

Wolstenholme, D., Cobb, M., Bowen, S., Wright, P. and Dearden, A. (2010) Design-led service improvement for older people. *Australasian Medical Journal*, 3(8): 465–70. Available at: www.amj.net.au/index.php?journal=AMJ&page=article&op=viewFile&path[]=377&path[]=632, accessed 20 February 2016.

World Health Organization (2002) Innovative care for chronic conditions: building blocks for action: global report. Geneva: WHO. Available at: www.who.int/chp/knowledge/publications/icccglobalreport.pdf.

Wright, P. and McCarthy, J. (2010) Experience-centered design: Designers, users, and communities in dialogue. *Synthesis Lectures on Human-Centered Informatics*, 3(1): 1–123. Available at: www.morganclaypool.com/doi/abs/10.2200/S00229ED1V01Y201003HCI009.

13 Products

Designing products for chronic health

Abby Paterson, Richard Bibb, Kathryn Downey and Jari Pallari

Abstract

This chapter describes four different applications where the design and fabrication of custom-made assistive devices have been affected by disruptive technologies such as Additive Manufacturing (more commonly known as *3D Printing*); applications include hearing aids, ankle-foot orthoses, wrist splints and spinal orthoses. Each application describes prior 'traditional' processes of design and fabrication and explains the potential benefits of the new 'digital design and manufacture' approach along with the impact on the design process and limitations (where appropriate). The order in which the cases appear in the chapter represents their current state of implementation in the healthcare sector, with hearing aids being the most established in the market. The aspects of the different approaches are then discussed, with limitations and challenges for future adoption into the healthcare sector; specifically within the UK.

Introduction

Many chronic (long-term) conditions are incurable and resistant to drug therapies and give rise to a wide variety of physical symptoms that can be relieved or aided by physical products. Conditions such as congenital abnormality, degenerative disease, amputation and stroke lead to permanent or long-term physical or sensory disabilities that can be treated through the application of physical products.

Typically these devices have to fit onto (or into) human anatomy and fall into two categories; generic 'off the shelf' products designed for any user, and custom-fitting (bespoke) products designed and made to fit a specific individual. Both routes create significant challenges for design. In the case of generic devices it is a challenge to provide a wide enough range of sizes or sufficient adjustability to fit any given individual whilst still providing the intended physical function. This typically leads to products that are compromised in their effectiveness and/or appearance. However, they are mass-produced with a consequently lower cost. Custom-made devices are potentially more comfortable and arguably more clinically effective. However, they require bespoke design and fabrication for each individual. As each product needs to be made individually, design is often compromised by the need to use hand crafting, low-cost materials and highly skilled but labour-intensive fabrication processes, leading to higher costs and longer production times. Custom-fitting devices are also highly dependent on the skills and knowledge of individual practitioners, and if appropriate, how well this information is conveyed to fabricators who may be off-site; this also leads to variability and inconsistency of the product. Both routes lead to products that may be unsatisfactory. Discomfort, poor fit, inconvenience and poor aesthetics frequently have a negative effect on patient compliance, which in turn compromises the effectiveness of the treatment.

Recent developments in technology are, however, leading to a convergence between the two previous routes. Increased flexibility of manufacturing processes such as Additive Manufacturing (AM) is enabling more variety and possibly even customisation for mass produced items. Advances in data capture, Computer-Aided Design (CAD) and manufacture have provided opportunities to increase the effectiveness and speed for the production of custom-fitting devices. Other potential benefits for moving away from conventional methods and towards digital interventions include:

- reduced inventory of spare/replacement parts;
- digital storage and instant retrieval of patient and/or customer data, including patient-specific meta-data through to anatomical scan data;
- reduced lead times, from design to fabrication;
- potential for bespoke form and function;
- monitored process control and quantifiable quality control;
- improved physical properties, ranging from aesthetics, fit and function;
- increased patient/customer satisfaction;
- potential for increased productivity of healthcare professionals who prescribe custom devices; and
- financial gain.

Many of these elements are interlinked; for example, there is scope to make significant cost savings in the way in which duplicate devices are made and distributed to patients/customers. By digitising and storing patient-specific scan data, custom devices can be designed to suit and produced on an AM system. Provided that this data is stored, this information can be retrieved at a later date; this is particularly beneficial for patients who would like duplicate devices (e.g. to suit different aspects of their everyday activities). This in turn has scope to reduce waiting times, as the clinician would no longer need to allocate a scheduled session with an individual patient to make a duplicate product for them.

Ultimately, the elimination of labour has potential cost savings. However, reduction in labour must not be confused with the eradication or redundancy of valued healthcare practitioners. Instead, many processes seek to empower healthcare practitioners by allowing them to produce better-quality products, whilst increasing productivity, thereby reducing waiting times further and relieving strain on healthcare providers. With an ageing population and budgets restraints, this reduction is becoming increasingly important, as well as providing new ways to help assist individuals to live independent lives for as long as possible.

These aspects mean that the design process and ultimate success of a new approach to the design and manufacture of custom-fitting products is dependent on the healthcare system it will be implemented into. So for example, a product design optimised for an insurance reimbursement system may not be suitable for a free-at-the-point-of-delivery NHS in the United Kingdom. An important consideration is how the transition is made from a manual to a digital design and manufacture process, how this is achieved in terms of resources and who is actually conducting the design and manufacture. With current 'traditional' methods, the design and manufacture are typically undertaken simultaneously by an individual practitioner (such as an occupational therapist), or may be segregated and completed in consultation with additional trained personnel within laboratories (and more recently, factories) in order to access specialised skillsets and facilities. When moving to a new, digital process the question of who takes over these tasks is raised. Does the clinical specialist become merely a prescriber or do they perform the design? How is the tacit and experiential knowledge of therapists captured and translated into a digital design process?

This chapter explores these questions and the practical considerations encountered in the transition from conventional 'traditional' methods of design and fabrication to new digital processes.

Chapter structure

This chapter consists of four different healthcare applications of digital design and manufacture: hearing aids (Application 1), foot/ankle foot orthoses (Application 2), wrist splints (Application 3) and spinal braces (Application 4). The order relates to their technology-readiness level; Application 1 (hearing aids) for example has already been implemented, whilst Application 4 (spinal braces) is a relatively recent development in need of further research, development and investment. Most of these have been due to the technology readiness of a range of contributing factors, from physical build sizes of AM machines, materials available and the cost-effectiveness of the collective elements. Each application section describes the traditional design and fabrication process, along with newly established or developing production streams in the wake of AM and supporting technologies. Strengths and limitations of their adoption are also defined.

Applications

Application 1: design of custom-made hearing aids

The hearing aid industry has undergone a significant change in recent years due to disruptive technologies, including AM.

'Traditional' design and fabrication can be time-consuming, expensive and laborious; the patient is assessed by an audiologist, who determines the optimum solution for them. The fabrication then involves several key phases (Cortez et al., 2005). An initial impression of the patient's ear canal is taken using a silicone impression material. Once set, the impression is removed from the ear, then sent to a laboratory along with a prescription with specific requirements to the hearing aid manufacturer; this may be on-site or off-site. The impression is submerged in clear silicone to form a negative mould or an 'investment' cast, which can be used as a back-up in the event of a mistake in the fabrication process later on. The impression is then removed; excess material is trimmed off and the impression is then submerged in wax to provide the aid's wall thickness. Once hardened, the wax-covered impression is submerged in a hydrocolloid to make a refined negative mould. Once the hydrocolloid is set, the impression is removed from the mould and the void is filled with acrylic resin, which is set within a UV light container (Masters et al., 2006). Alternatively, a room-temperature cured acrylic resin may be used. Once hardened, the acrylic cast forms the hearing aid shell and offers a near perfect fit for the patient's ear canal; the exterior is hardened whilst the internal remains liquid as the acrylic hardens from the outside inwards due to the containment and curing process. Next, the cast is trimmed and a channel or 'vent' is added to enable air to pass through the device when placing in the ear canal; this avoids extreme changes of air pressure on insertion and removal of the device which could otherwise damage the ear. Electronic components and additional parts are assembled within the device by hand and the device is polished and/or lacquered to give a high-quality finish.

Using a digitised design and manufacturing process, an impression is still taken using a biocompatible fast-curing resin. The impression is then sent to a hearing aid manufacturer. However, rather than generating silicone moulds, the impression is digitised (e.g. using structured light scanners) and a high-resolution 3D point cloud is generated depicting the 3D form (Figure 13.1).

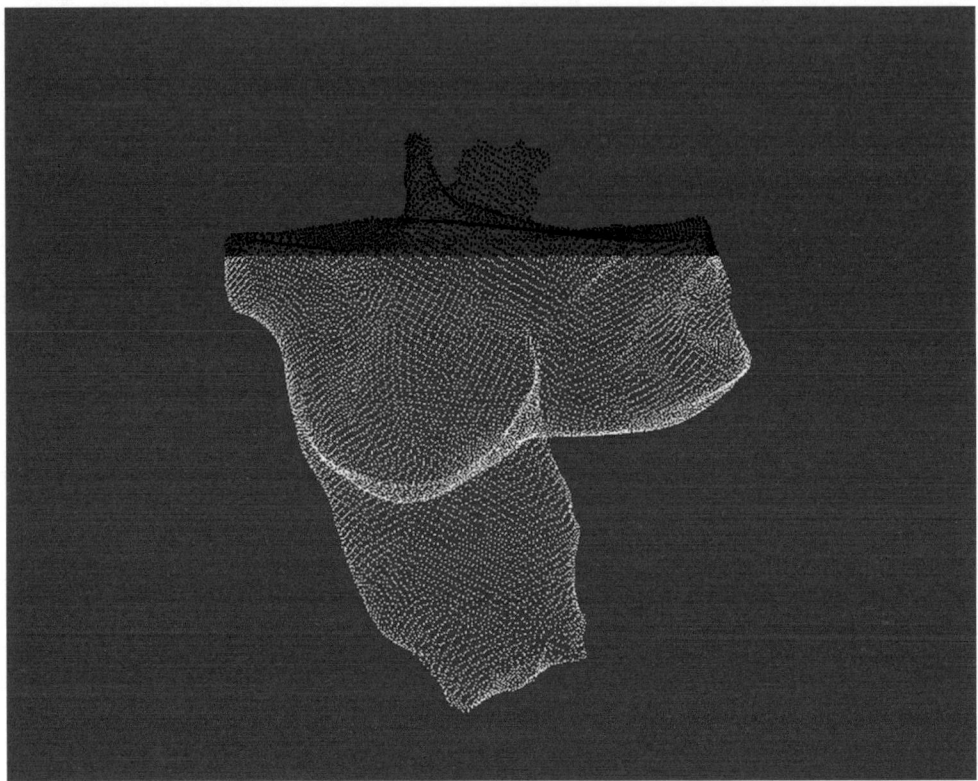

Figure 13.1 Point cloud of scanned ear canal impression
Source: Image courtesy of Phonak

The point cloud is then manipulated by a design engineer using specialised CAD software to give the canal topology a volume by solidifying the scan data. A virtual library of all required custom hearing instruments are then brought into the CAD session in order for the operator to manually position the required component within the solid geometry of the individualised shell.

A tubular channel is also integrated throughout the length of the hearing aid to enable air movement through the device. Once the design has been finalised in CAD, the model is exported to an AM system; liquid-based photopolymer resin systems like stereolithography are typically used due to their high resolution, accuracy and surface quality. A number of follow-on stages are involved, including the physical assembly of parts and components and the laser etching of the unique customer reference number on the device. Each device is then passed through a number of quality control checks, including physical fit, appearance and the overall sound quality. The finished hearing aid is then sent to the audiologist so they can review the physical fit, provide fine tuning and supply wear instructions for the customer.

Siemens,[1] Phonak[2] and Widex[3] provide custom-fitting hearing aid solutions using AM systems, such as powder-based fusion (e.g. laser sintering) and vat photopolymerisation (Rosen, 2014). The digitised fabrication process is equivalent to traditional hearing aids in terms of retention, comfort and ease of insertion/removal, but offers significant benefits, such as the ability to easily replace lost or damaged aids (Fabry, 2002). It is also possible to provide hearing aids in a range of colours to suit the patient's preference.

In response to these successes, Materialise[4] collaborated with Phonak and Siemens to develop dedicated software, called E-Shell, to semi-automate the design of custom-made hearing aids. After capturing a scan of the patient's ear canal impression, the customised software, termed *Rapid Shell Modelling*, is the second phase of the three-stage digital fabrication process prior to AM. The benefits of custom software is a refined workflow, which can help support the entire product lifecycle management of the hearing aid industry for Phonak, including custom tools to simplify the design process in a virtual CAD environment. Within this environment, parameters such as the wall thickness can be defined and internal components can be positioned to fit within the confines of the hearing aid shell; positioning must also comply with certain restrictions regarding proximity of various components within the shell. Given the small size of each shell, it is possible to fill a build platform of a typical AM machine and subsequently many orders can be fulfilled in a relatively short space of time.

Application 2: design of foot and ankle-foot orthoses

Healthy musculature is crucial in the distal lower limb, as the collective strength and movement can enable propulsion, initiate and facilitate swing of the leg in transit and enable/maintain upright posture of an individual (Kepple et al., 1997; Neptune et al., 2001). Foot orthoses (FO) are typically prescribed to improve the gait and posture of an individual and improve mobility; they are also used to protect and correct deformity in addition to preventing the progression of an existing deformity (Kott, 2002; Knutson and Clark, 1991; Meyer, 1974). Users may not necessarily present any form of medical condition; runners for example may be prescribed FOs with high arches to prevent pronation in order to maintain or correct imbalance at the knee and hip joints. FO and ankle-foot orthoses (AFO) can also be prescribed for patients with conditions such as cerebral palsy (Knutson and Clark, 1991) and rheumatoid arthritis. The latter results in increased instability of ligaments and degeneration of joints, resulting in continual degradation of the anatomy (Riskowski et al., 2011), which can be incredibly debilitating for sufferers. This can affect mobility and consequently affects the individual's quality of life through reduced independence.

Similar to Application 1, the 'traditional' process of designing and fabricating FOs and AFOs can be time-consuming and laborious. Whilst processes may vary slightly, the process typically starts with taking an initial cast of the patient's affected ankle and/or foot using fibreglass, plaster of Paris or similar impression-making materials. The negative cast is filled with another material to form a positive mould/buck impression of the ankle and/or foot. This positive buck is then used as a mould, where materials such as carbon fibre (Bartonek et al., 2007) or Low-Temperature Thermoplastic (LTT) are formed around the buck. In the context of LTT, sheets are heated in an oven or water bath and moulded/laminated to the buck to generate a custom device (Lusardi and Neilsen, 2000); this may be done by hand, but can also be achieved using vacuum-forming processes. Cutting of excess material and finishing of edges is also required before a final fit to the patient.

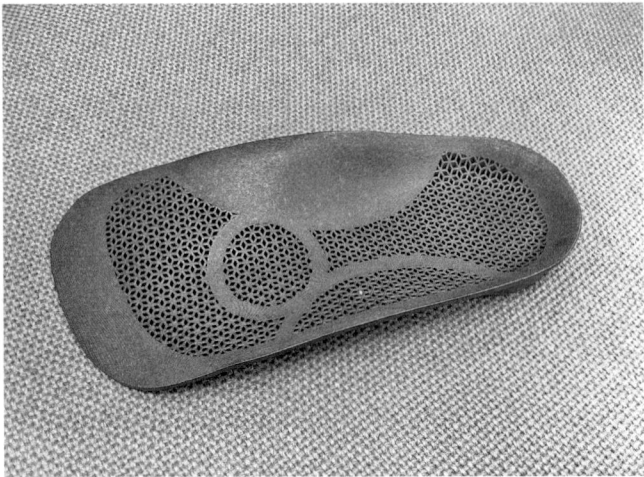

Figure 13.2 Custom-made foot orthosis
Source: Image courtesy of Peacocks Medical Group Ltd

CNC milling has also been routinely used to make bucks in the past; however, the use of direct digital capture (e.g. laser scanning) prior to CAD/CAM is increasing. This enables the acquisition of the patient's limb topography directly, or indirectly by scanning a negative cast of a patient's limb. The buck can then be used for forming the orthosis. Alternatively, the FO can be manufactured directly from scan data (modified in CAD software) without the need for a buck (e.g. using CNC milling).

Further advancements in software have also enabled additional import/export options to support the use of AM and this is beginning to change the landscape. This has a profound effect on the structure and composition of the FO/AFO; lattice structures can be implemented into orthoses to reduce weight and improve ventilation, for example. Evidence suggests that custom-made AM FOs are equivalent to FOs made with traditional methods in terms of fit, function and performance (Pallari et al., 2010). Furthermore, advances relating to Finite Element Analysis and biomechanics including gait analysis can help inform on the shape of the orthosis to suit the biomechanics of the individual. However, many of these areas are still undergoing research.

Podfo is a service provider for custom-made foot orthoses (Figure 13.2) (Podfo, 2015). Owned by Peacocks Medical Group Ltd[5] and an output of the A-Footprint European project, Podfo works with NHS trusts as well as private practitioners within the UK. The patient/customer attends an appointment with an orthotist/podiatrist; a cast, impression or scan of their foot is taken to capture a 3D representation of the anatomy. The design is finalised based on certain parameters which are driven by the orthotist. Once the design is finalised, an order is placed. The virtual geometry is then validated for manufacture and sent to one of many AM machines to be built layer by layer. Once the build is complete, the insole is removed, post-processed and distributed to the orthotist/podiatrist to fit to the patient at a follow-up appointment.

RS Print is another commercial outlet for custom-made foot orthoses, and is a joint venture between RSScan[6] and Materialise (RS Print, 2015). Their design and fabrication process is shown in Figure 13.3; the process is similar to Podfo, except scan data is in the form of a 2D

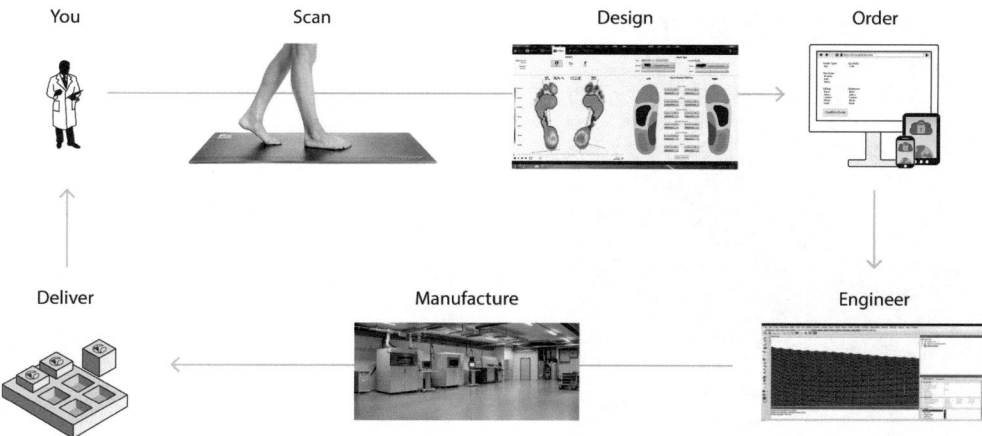

Figure 13.3 RS Print workflow
Source: Courtesy of RS Print

pressure distribution map as opposed to 3D scan data. Pressure distribution of the consumer is captured with a pressure plate by RSScan; combined with their RSScan Footscan V9® software, the equipment is designed to capture the dynamic load distribution of the individual whilst they are in motion. The data is then analysed and parametric design rules are sent off-site where a CAD engineer translates the design rules into a CAD model based on the 2D pressure map. This information is gathered by the RS print centre and the prescribed design is modified to include a number of additional features, including a lattice structure to reduce weight and increase ventilation. The finished orthosis CAD models are then fabricated and distributed back to the customer.

In addition to FOs, the European A-Footprint project also explored AFOs (Figure 13.4). Studies are ongoing to optimise the design and fabrication process of AFOs with given parameters; Creylman et al. (2013) found that AM AFO braces (specifically with laser sintering) displayed performance characteristics that equated and even improved upon AFOs made with the traditional process, including stride length. Aspects such as CAD and design for AM rules are under development to facilitate a more streamlined process (Schrank and Stanhope, 2011).

Application 3: design of upper extremity wrist splints

Conditions such as Carpal Tunnel Syndrome and various forms of arthritis can affect the performance of our wrists and hands, often leading to a multitude of symptoms including reduced range of motion, pain, discomfort and deformity. There are various methods used for treating these ailments, from cryotherapy through to surgical interventions. Every treatment poses different strengths and weaknesses, yet one of the most commonly prescribed products are wrist splints. Taylor et al. (2003), Jacobs (2003) and Callinan and Mathiowetz (1996) state that splints are often prescribed to:

- reduce pain and discomfort;
- stabilise the affected joints;

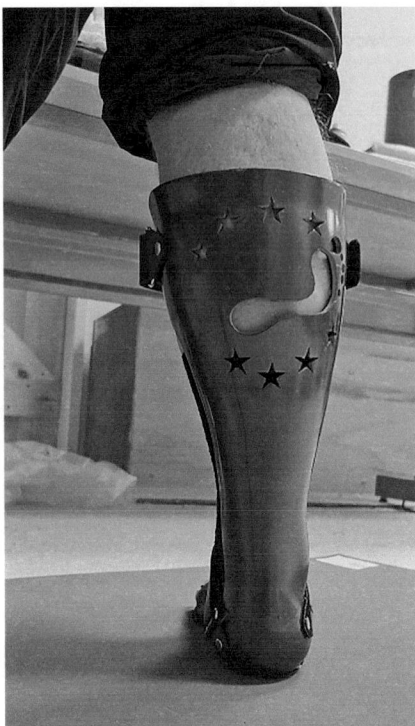

Figure 13.4 A–Footprint ankle-foot orthosis
Source: Image courtesy of Peacocks Medical Group Ltd

- immobilise specific joints;
- promote movement in stiff joints through immobilisation of more prominent, mobile joints; and
- prevent deformity.

Custom-made splints are made by a trained practitioner (e.g. occupational therapist, physiotherapist) and are typically designed and fabricated for each individual patient, on-site, by one clinician. A patient is referred to a trained splinting practitioner and must undergo an assessment. Once a suitable treatment method and regime have been established, the choice of splint is decided. There are many types of wrist splint available depending on the condition and all pose different fabrication processes, so in this instance only a wrist immobilisation splint will be described (Figure 13.5).

Custom-made splints are typically made with LTT. The shape of the splint is planned in 2D profile and is scored or drawn onto the LTT sheet. The LTT is then heated in a water bath until pliable and formed onto the patient. The LTT is then held or wrapped in place on the patient until it has cooled and hardened. To optimise the fit this process is often repeated. Fine adjustments are also made, such as the rolling of the splint edges. Localised adjustments can be made with heat guns, such as cavities over prominent areas or areas prone to swelling, in order to relieve pressure. Fasteners such as Velcro are then attached.

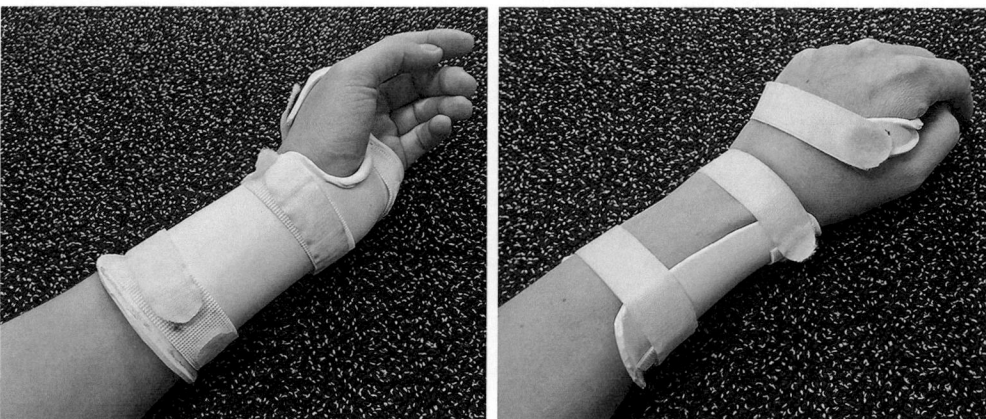

Figure 13.5 Custom-made wrist immobilisation splint made with traditional methods

The design and fabrication time can take approximately 20–40 minutes, depending on the skills and experience of the clinician. Whilst clinicians make many efforts to make their splints safe, tidy and appealing for patients to wear, there are several drawbacks to current splinting methods and practices which can affect patient compliance. Fasteners such as Velcro can collect debris (Veehof et al., 2008), the LTT can induce perspiration (Veehof et al., 2008; Melvin, 1982) and internal padding such as neoprene can collect the perspiration and ultimately can become odorous and unhygienic (Sandford et al., 2008; Coppard and Lynn, 2001). Splints are also difficult to keep clean and patients are often provided with instructions to avoid certain situations and activities such as washing up, as padding can take a long time to dry (Veehof et al., 2008). Patients can also feel stigmatised and embarrassed by their splints, resorting to concealing or even abandoning their splints, particularly in social environments (Louise-Bender Pape et al., 2002).

There are solutions to these issues relating to poor compliance, using digital interventions. Much like Application 1 and Application 2, there are three key phases involved in the digitised splinting process: (i) data acquisition; (ii) modification of scan data using CAD to generate a virtual design of the device (in this case, a wrist splint) and (iii) manufacture using a chosen AM system. As a result, there are many opportunities to improve the aesthetics, form and function. The prospect of using AM for wrist splints has been proposed by many, including Fraunhofer IPA[7] and Oxman (2010); the latter proposed the use of the Stratasys/Objet[8] Connex multimaterial PolyJet AM system to integrate both hard and soft materials in locations across the 'carpal skin' splint to promote or restrict movement (Figure 13.6).

There have also been examples in the press regarding the use of AM for trauma casts (fracture reduction) (Evill, 2013; Karasahin, 2014). However, one of the key areas which were not addressed was the lack of exploration of bespoke software capabilities to enable practitioners to design casts for their patients.

The software element is a crucial stage to enable individuals to capture their design intent. There are two main streams to enable this; either practitioners could relay their prescribed designs to a CAD engineer to translate their design intent using mainstream software such as Solidworks, Rhino, etc., or the practitioner could design the splint themselves. The issue

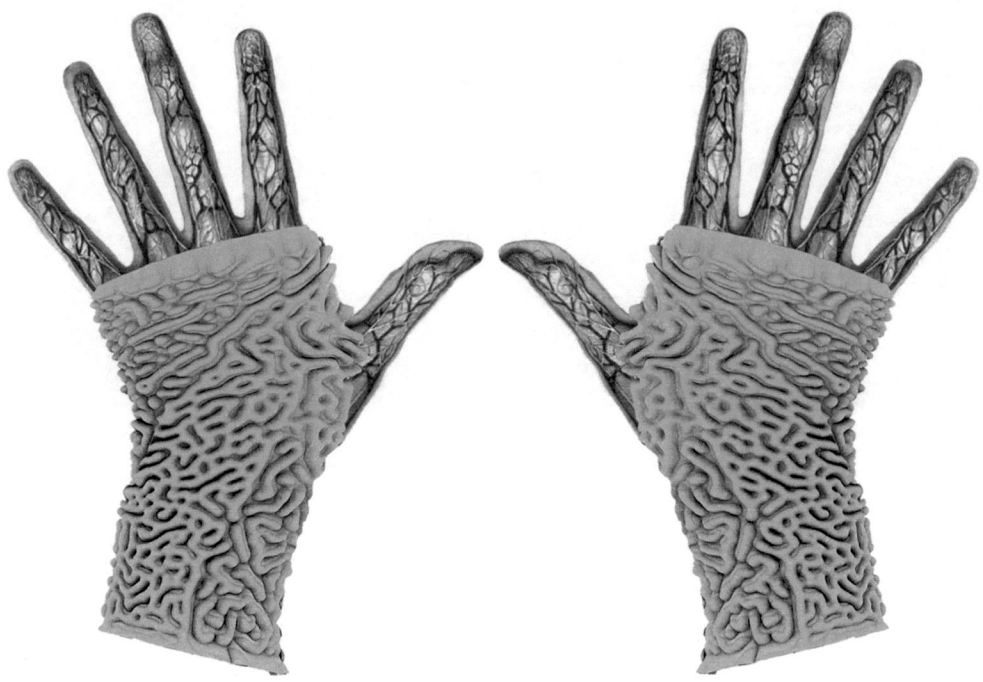

Figure 13.6 'Carpal skin'
Source: Oxman, 2010

with the first stream is the likelihood of miscommunication and resulting human error which in turn could lead to splints being designed and fabricated incorrectly, as the design and fabrication process of splints currently involves tacit skillsets. The second stream would involve training practitioners to use mainstream software, which would be time-consuming and expensive. A solution to the latter was to create specialised software for practitioners to enable them to design splints themselves with minimal training. Paterson et al. (2014b) developed a custom-made software prototype (Figure 13.7) which sought to enable practitioners to design wrist immobilisation splints with additional functionality which was not previously possible; this included steps to design multimaterial splints for added functionality and comfort.

It is also possible to integrate multicolour, multimaterial properties to the splint using AM systems such as the Statasys/Objet Connex3 (Figure 13.8), in addition to textile hinges for easier donning and doffing (Paterson et al., 2014a). It is hoped that with the creation of specialised software, practitioners have a greater range of toolsets available to improve the treatment options for their patients; not just in terms of aesthetics, but also fit and function.

Application 4: spinal braces

This application focuses on spinal braces used to support and stabilise the spine for those with adolescent idiopathic scoliosis (AIS). AIS is the most common spinal deformity seen

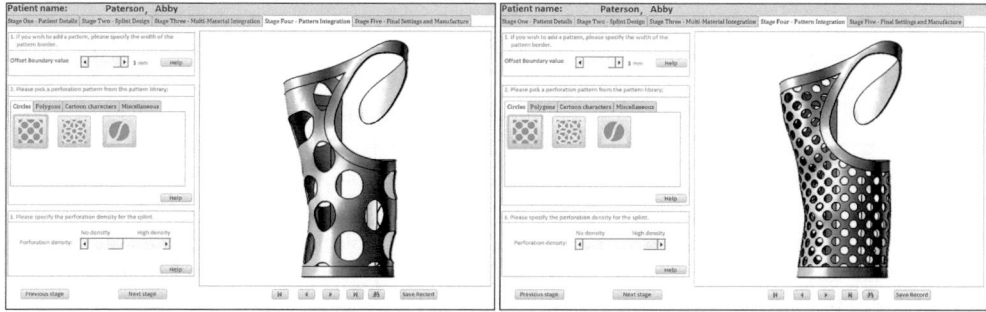

Figure 13.7 Specialised splinting software prototype

Figure 13.8 Multicolour, multimaterial wrist immobilisation splint
Source: Design work by Paterson; photography by Bibb

in children and adolescents, affecting up to 3–4 per cent of the population aged 10–16 years (Weinstein et al., 2008; Shah, 2015). This three-dimensional deformity of the spine and trunk is defined as a deviation in the curve of the spine that measures at least 10° progressing during periods of rapid growth (Nnadi and Fairbank, 2010; Weiss and Moramarco, 2013). AIS has no known cause (Lowe et al., 2000) and is more commonly seen in girls (Lonstein, 1994). If left untreated, the spine may continue to curve, potentially leading to further deformity and other health conditions such as arthritis. In more severe cases, curvature can even cause impaired heart and lung function or kyphosis, when the upper spine starts to twist (Weinstein et al., 2003).

Treatment takes into consideration both long- and short-term outcomes as well as complications of the treatment method. The three main evidence-based treatment pathways are observation, use of a brace, and surgical stabilisation. Where bracing is used, the goal is to limit further progression and stabilise the scoliotic spine rather than correct a curve back to normal (Courvoisier et al., 2013). Brace stabilisation is intended to support the spine, trunk and rib cage during growth whilst applying counteracting forces to correct abnormal curvature, leading to a change in the load being exerted on the growth plates to promote normal growth (Mac-Thiong et al., 2003; Castro, Jr., 2003; Maruyama et al., 2011).

There are several variations of braces available, the most common being the Boston Brace: a prefabricated module consisting of a polypropylene shell lined with polyethylene foam. The edges of the shell are manually trimmed and pressure pads placed at the apex of a curve. This type of brace may need to be worn up to 20 hours a day. Weinstein et al. (2013) concluded the benefit of bracing increased with longer hours of brace wear, whilst Rahman et al. (2005) found a direct correlation between compliance and efficacy. Katz and Durrani (2001) also showed that increased brace wear correlated with not only lack of curve progression but also avoidance of surgical treatment.

Adolescence is recognised as a particularly sensitive developmental stage (Eliason and Richman, 1984; Fällström et al., 1986; Drench, 1994; Sapountzi-Krepia et al., 2001). AIS patients may suffer negative experiences owing to the cosmetic appearance of the brace, functional discomfort resulting from pressure points, and encounter issues with humidity and restriction of movement; all of which can lead to poor compliance (Schiller et al., 2010; Fayssoux et al., 2010; Nicholson et al., 2003; Wong et al., 2008). Diagnosis and treatment of scoliosis adds further distress requiring special adjustment for a chronic disease (Reichel and Schanz, 2003).

The conventional approach to brace construction is to produce a buck of the patient's torso (Figure 13.9a), created by either a negative plaster cast or more recently a 3D scan of the torso area for CNC milling a buck. Sometimes rectifications may be added to the plaster cast prior to forming the brace (Wong et al., 2005). Sheets of LTT are heated until pliable and moulded around the negative torso buck (Figure 13.9b). The spinal brace is created noting anatomical landmarks. If a mistake is made through the thermoforming process the fabrication process may need to be scrapped, and the whole process repeated from the beginning. If errors are made during this process, including exceeding the optimum moulding temperature of the plastic, the integrity of the device can be compromised.

The edges of the brace are trimmed and smoothed for increased comfort (Figure 13.9c). Once moulded, patients attend a follow-up fitting session, where straps and pads are positioned; all aspects are informed by the experience of the orthotist (Visser et al., 2012). Patients require modifications in the coming months and have follow-up appointments to check the brace management. The only design input available for a young person with regards to their brace is adding a pattern to the exterior of the brace during thermoforming (Figure 13.9b). However, the pattern and colour can be distorted during thermoforming.

The use of AM for spinal braces has been previously proposed by 3D Systems (2014)[9] and Andiamo[10] (Figure 13.10); the latter focusing on custom-made medical devices for children. Much like the digitised splinting process proposed by Paterson et al. (2014b), the process involves scanning the anatomy, modifying the captured data in 3D CAD and then manufacturing using a suitable AM system. However, its commercial and clinical uptake has been slow in the past due to limitations of materials, AM processes and supporting infrastructure.

One of the biggest restrictions in adopting this process is the build volume required to fabricate spinal braces. The bounding volume for a child's spinal brace can be very large depending on the size of the child; due to the size of construction of a spinal brace, AM build capabilities are restricted. However, it is entirely plausible to use panelling to construct the brace in multiple pieces to enable 'nesting' on the AM system platform. Panelling will also

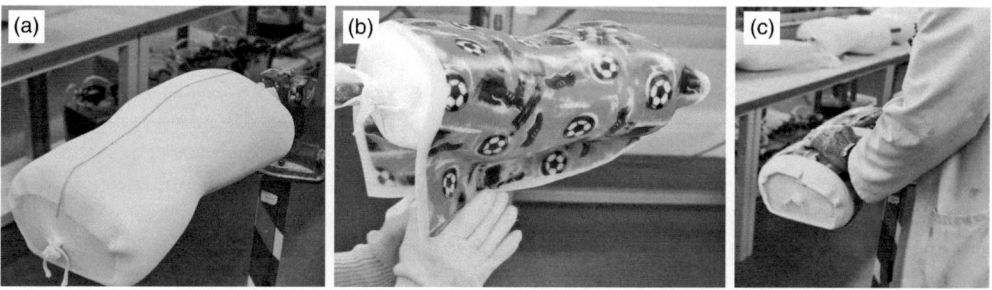

Figure 13.9 Traditional brace fabrication: (a) initial buck of child's torso; (b) LTT being wrapped around the buck; (c) finishing touches to orthosis, including fasteners

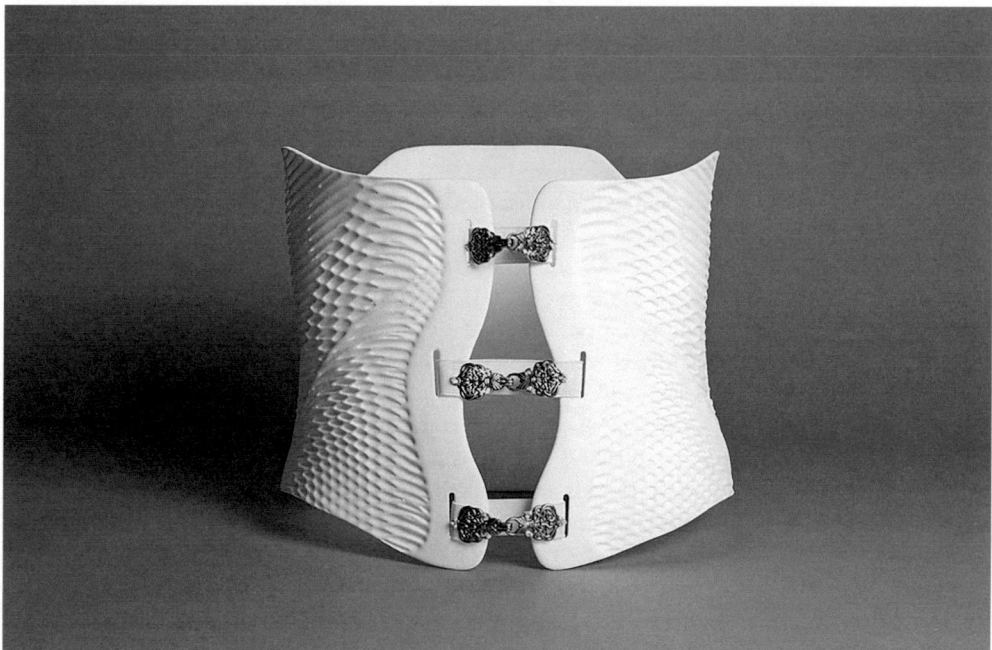

Figure 13.10 Adolescent back brace
Source: Image courtesy of Andiamo and Claire Gaul Photography

facilitate the user getting in and out of the brace with greater ease and the panels could be replaced in a modular fashion as the treatment progresses.

Future directions

Whilst the use of CAD and AM may be well established in the hearing aid industry, there is plenty of scope for optimisation and improvement for other custom-made assistive devices. In addition to the applications described here, custom face masks for example could also be explored further for individuals with severe burns to aid in scar management, and the development of specialised software could further enable the production of such devices (Cazon et al., 2014). AM for bespoke prosthetics and fairings is also an expanding market area, as evidenced by Bespoke Innovations;[11] affiliated with 3D Systems. It is entirely plausible that many of the design features proposed by Paterson et al. (2014a) and Oxman (2011) could also be transferred to other custom devices, including textile hinges for easier donning/doffing, multimaterial regions for added comfort and performance and custom lattice designs; all of which could be co-designed by the patient and therapist together. In turn, patient involvement could lead to improved acceptance and compliance. Whilst design for AM provides a convincing argument through improved quality of life and 'simplified supply chains to increase efficiency and responsiveness in demand fulfilment' (Huang et al., 2013), the full societal and economic impact requires a more comprehensive review for each new application.

Combined with a supporting infrastructure, there is scope for better treatment management; the Internet of Things poses interesting opportunities for monitoring using integrated sensors, particularly with regards to compliance of device wear. Temperature sensors and activity monitoring are now being explored further in the realms of foot orthoses (Telfer et al., 2014) and it is entirely plausible for this to be adapted to the monitoring of other devices such as wrist splints and spinal braces. The inclusion of additional performance-enhancing devices such as bearings, gas springs and adjustable fasteners are also being explored (Telfer et al., 2014), as well as ultrasound functionality to increase the rate of recovery (Karasahin, 2014; Roper et al., 2015). However, these advancements require supporting infrastructure, including data processing, cloud-based connection, software development, knowledge transfer and education to communicate the changes of the traditional processes to digital production streams. The willingness of likely stakeholders and direct end users to adopt digitised approaches is also potentially a limiting factor (Telfer et al., 2012), as practitioners may be unconvinced or uncertain of the impact it will have upon them, their profession and their patients.

The key advantage that a digital design and manufacture approach offers compared to traditional handcraft approaches is the capture and storage of digital data. Under traditional processes, any subsequent products that might be needed, such as spares or replacements, require the whole process to be repeated as there is no economy of scale and may require significant inventory space to store moulds and casts. With a digital approach, the process is split into three main stages: (i) data acquisition (e.g. 3D scanning); (ii) CAD; and (iii) manufacture. Whilst each of these stages may pose several sub-tasks, the separation of these stages could lead to optimised production chains. Whether in-house production is used or not, the continued use of AM could one day enable the majority of clinics to possess their own AM systems to produce a variety of custom-made devices. This could enable the design and fabrication of devices on-site, without outsourcing, which in turn could reduce the complexity and delay of the supply chain. Alternatively, a similar approach to Podfo could be used for different applications; patients could be scanned at their local clinic, whilst the CAD and AM aspects could take place at regional or national centres of expertise. The opportunities to reduce or eliminate travel, manage workflow and distribute manufacture could lead to whole-process savings that far outweigh possible increases in material and/or manufacturing costs. Consequently, the design of these devices needs to be completely reconsidered as a service-product combination.

Ideally, more integrated product lifestyle management software tools could be adopted, with special interfaces for managing each stage involved in the process. Ultimately, there is a need to develop specialised software to enable practitioners to exploit these technologies themselves (Telfer et al., 2012).

Adopting Applications 2–4 will require a significant amount of investment and policy changes to enable service provision in healthcare organisations. This is a significant undertaking and not one to be taken lightly. To change the current service provision model to utilising the latest 2D/3D scanning, AM and supporting software will pose many challenges. There is an urgent need for more thorough cost—benefit analysis and supporting business models relative to different healthcare sectors across the world, with an explicit benefit in cost *and* clinical effectiveness. The provision of clinical services is increasingly evidence-based and robust clinical trials are required to demonstrate that the new devices are at least equivalent to existing devices in a range of characteristics and properties, including material strength or impact that devices have on the individuals directly. These are costly and time-consuming, but a necessity if the approaches are to be implemented.

The uptake also depends on the materials available. Materials should ideally be tested to recognised standards such as ISO 10993 or USP 23 Class VI, with suitable mechanical properties for their application but further research and development of polymers is required, particularly for multimaterial capabilities. For example, Objet digital materials such as FLX-9740-DM currently have very low tear resistance, which limits their current application. Long-term physical properties and environmental degradation is also poor for many AM materials. Cleaning is an issue and the resistance to long-term skin contact, detergents and disinfectants needs to be improved. Build time and clean-up of AM parts is currently very time-consuming, taking approximately 7–15 hours to make a wrist splint, for example. Until AM systems can offer faster build times, the adoption will remain limited, particularly within the context of wrist splinting.

Regulatory issues are a challenge; where each product is customised, there is a need to ensure that design processes and procedures are well proven, safe and traceable. Specific robust design rules for each application are also necessary, to ensure products are safe for individuals with a range of ailments. This would ideally involve an assessment of each individual, with automated adjustment of design parameters to suit their individual condition and circumstance. This may include a range of virtual prototyping tools including Finite Element and Biomechanical Analysis. The application in wrist splinting (Palousek et al., 2013), back braces (Nie et al., 2009) and foot orthoses (Riskowski et al., 2011) is still very limited and in need of further research and investment in clinical testing to establish baseline data if future interventions are to be developed. Whilst some companies have developed internal standards to assess suitability of their devices, it may be necessary in the future to update existing national and international standards, or devise new ones, to ensure the safe provision of these medical devices in light of technological advancements.

Acknowledgements

The authors wish to thank the following individuals, institutions, organisations and businesses for their valuable contribution to this chapter: Naveed and Samiya Parvez at Andiamo, Neri Oxman at the Massachusetts Institute of Technology, Loughborough University, Peacocks Medical Group Ltd., Phonak, Tom Peeters at RSPrint, the University of Manchester and Mike Gilligan of M.G. Gilligan Ltd Orthotic Consultants at the University of Salford.

Notes

1 Siemens Aktiengesellschaft, 80333 Munich, Germany. Corporate website: www.siemens.com.
2 Sonova AG Headquarters, Laubisrütistrasse 28, 8712 Staefa, Switzerland. Corporate website: www. phonak.com.

3 Widex, Nymøllevej 6, 3540 Lynge, Denmark. Corporate website: www.widex.com.
4 Technologielaan 15, 3001, Leuven, Belgium. Corporate website: www.materialise.com.
5 Peacocks Medical Group Ltd., Benfield Business Park, Newcastle upon Tyne, NE6 4NQ. Corporate website: www.peacocks.net.
6 RSscan International NV, De Weven 7, 3483 Paal, Belgium. Corporate website: www.rsscan.com/.
7 Fraunhofer IPA, Nobelstraße 12, 70569 Stuttgart. Website: www.ipa.fraunhofer.de/.
8 Objet, 2 Holtzman St, Science Park, Rehovolt, Israel.
9 3D Systems, Rock Hill, South Carolina. Corporate website: www.3dsystems.com/.
10 145–57 St John Street, London, EC1V 4PW. Website: http://andiamo.io/.
11 Company is no longer – it was acquired by 3D Systems with no further outputs.

Additional reading and resources

Phonak (2013) Phonak Aurora Operations and Distribution Center (AODC). Available at: www.youtube.com/watch?v=1Yp2hbDIm-E, accessed 2 May 2015.
Phonak (2014) Phonak Digital Manufacturing of Custom Products (Custom ITE). Available at: www.youtube.com/watch?v=pa0VraRjnP8, accessed 2 May 2015.
Rosen, D.W. (2014) Research supporting principles for design for additive manufacturing. *Virtual and Physical Prototyping*, 9(4): 225–32. doi: 10.1080/17452759.2014.951530.

References

3D Systems (2014) Media image gallery: Personalized 3D printed scoliosis brace – bespoke braces. Available at: www.3dsystems.com/resources/press-room/image-gallery?field_printers_tid_selective= All&field_industries_tid_selective=438&page=1, accessed 10 May 2015.
Bartonek, Å, Eriksson, M. and Gutierrez-Farewik, E.M. (2007) A new carbon fibre spring orthosis for children with plantarflexor weakness. *Gait and Posture*, 25(4): 652–6.
Callinan, N.J. and Mathiowetz, V. (1996) Soft versus hard resting hand splints in rheumatoid arthritis: Pain relief, preference and compliance. *American Journal of Occupational Therapy*, 50(5): 347–53.
Castro, Jr., F.P. (2003) Adolescent idiopathic scoliosis, bracing, and the Hueter-Volkmann principle. *Spine Journal*, 3(3): 180–5.
Cazon, A., Aizpurua, J., Paterson, A., Bibb, R. and Campbell, R.I. (2014) Customised design and manufacture of protective face masks combining a practitioner-friendly modelling approach and low-cost devices for digitising and additive manufacturing. *Virtual and Physical Prototyping*, 9(4): 251–61.
Coppard, B.M. and Lynn, P. (2001) Introduction to splinting, in Coppard, B.M. and Lohman, H. (eds), *Introduction to Splinting: A Clinical Reasoning and Problem-Solving Approach*. 2nd edition. St Louis, MO: Mosby, 1–33.
Cortez, R., Dinulescu, N., Skafte, K., Olson, B., Keenan, D. and Kuk, F. (2004) Changing with the times: Applying digital technology to hearing aid shell manufacturing. Available at: http://www.hearingreview.com/2004/03/changing-with-the-times-applying-digital-technology-to-hearing-aid-shell-manufacturing/. Accessed 03 March 2017.
Courvoisier, A., Drevelle, X., Vialle, R., Dubousset, J. and Skalli, W. (2013) 3D analysis of brace treatment in idiopathic scoliosis. *European Spine Journal*, 22(11): 2449–55.
Creylman, V., Muraru, L., Pallari, J., Vertommen, H. and Peeraer, L. (2013) Gait assessment during the initial fitting of customizes selective laser sintering ankle foot orthoses in subjects with drop foot. *Prosthetics and Orthotics International*, 37(2): 132–8.
Drench, M.E. (1994) Changes in body image secondary to disease and injury. *Rehabilitation Nursing*, 19(1): 31–6.
Eliason, M.J. and Richman, L.C. (1984) Psychological effects of idiopathic adolescent scoliosis. *Journal of Developmental and Behavioral Pediatrics*, 5(4): 169–72.

Evill, J. (2013) Cortex. Available at: http://www.evilldesign.com/cortex, accessed 3 March, 2017.

Fabry, D. (2002) Hearing aid physical fit: The next revolution? *Hearing Journal*, 55(8): 46–50.

Fällström, K., Cochran, T. and Nachemson, A. (1986) Long-term effects on personality development in patients with adolescent idiopathic scoliosis: Influence of type of treatment. *Spine*, 11(7): 756–8.

Fayssoux, R.S., Cho, R.H. and Herman, M.J. (2010) A history of bracing for idiopathic scoliosis in North America. *Clinical Orthopaedics and Related Research*, 468(3): 654–64.

Huang, S., Liu, P., Mokasdar, A. and Hou, L. (2013) Additive manufacturing and its societal impact: A literature review. *International Journal of Advanced Manufacturing Technology*, 67(5–8): 1191–203.

Jacobs, M. (2003) Splint classification, in Jacobs, M. and Austin, N. (eds), *Splinting the Hand and Upper Extremity: Principles and Process*. Baltimore, MD: Lippincott Williams and Wilkins, 2–18.

Karasahin, D. (2014) Osteoid medical cast, attachable bone stimulator by Deniz Karasahin. Available at: https://competition.adesignaward.com/design.php?ID=34151, accessed 25 March 2014.

Katz, D.E. and Durrani, A. (2001) Factors that influence outcome in bracing large curves in patients with adolescent idiopathic scoliosis. *Spine*, 26(21): 2354–61.

Kepple, T.M., Siegel, K.L. and Stanhope, S.J. (1997) Relative contributions of the lower extremity joint moments to forward progression and support during gait. *Gait and Posture*, 6(1): 1–8.

Knutson, L. and Clark, D. (1991) Orthotic devices for ambulation in children with cerebral palsy and myelomeningocele. *Physical Therapy*, 71(12): 947–60.

Kott, K. (2002) Orthoses for patients with neurologic disorders: Clinical decision making, in Seymour, R. (ed.), *Prosthetics and Orthotics: Lower Limb and Spinal*. Baltimore, MD: Lippincott Williams and Wilkins, 367–426.

Lonstein, J. (1994) Adolescent idiopathic scoliosis. *Lancet*, 344(8934): 1407–12.

Louise-Bender Pape, T., Kim, J. and Weiner, B. (2002) The shaping of individual meanings assigned to assistive technology: A review of personal factors. *Disability and Rehabilitation*, 24(1–3): 5–20.

Lowe, T.G., Edgar, M., Margulies, J.Y., Miller, N.H., Raso, V.J., Reinker, K.A. and Rivard, C. (2000) Etiology of idiopathic scoliosis: Current trends in research. *Journal of Bone and Joint Surgery*, 82(8): 1157.

Lusardi, M. and Neilsen, C. (2000) *Orthotics and Prosthetics in Rehabilitation*. Lutterworth: Butterworth-Heinmann.

Mac-Thiong, J.M., Labelle, H., Charlebois, M., Huot, M.P. and De Guise, J.A. (2003) Sagittal plane analysis of the spine and pelvis in adolescent idiopathic scoliosis according to the coronal curve type. *Spine*, 28(13): 1404–9.

Maruyama, T., Grivas, T.B. and Kaspiris, A. (2011) Effectiveness and outcomes of brace treatment: A systematic review. *Physiotherapy Theory and Practice*, 27(1): 26–42.

Masters, M., Velde, T. and McBagonluri, F. (2006) Rapid manufacturing in the hearing industry, in Hopkinson, N., Hague, R.J.M. and Dickens, P.M. (eds), *Rapid Manufacturing: An Industrial Revolution for the Digital Age*. Chichester: John Wiley and Sons, 195–210.

Melvin, J.L. (1982) *Rheumatic Disease: Occupational Therapy and Rehabilitation*. 2nd edition. Philadelphia: F.A. Davis Company.

Meyer, P. (1974) Lower limb orthotics. *Clinical Orthopaedics and Related Research®*, 102: 58–71.

Neptune, R.R., Kautz, S.A. and Zajac, F.E. (2001) Contributions of the individual ankle plantar flexors to support, forward progression and swing initiation during walking. *Journal of Biomechanics*, 34(11): 1387–98.

Nicholson, G.P., Ferguson-Pell, M.W., Smith, K., Edgar, M. and Morley, T. (2003) The objective measurement of spinal orthosis use for the treatment of adolescent idiopathic scoliosis. *Spine*, 28(19): 2243–50; discussion 2250–1.

Nie, W., Ye, M., Liu, Z. and Wang, C. (2009) The patient-specific brace design and biomechanical analysis of adolescent idiopathic scoliosis. *ASME Journal of Biomechanical Engineering*, 131(4): 041007.1–7.

Nnadi, C. and Fairbank, J. (2010) Scoliosis: A review. *Paediatrics and Child Health*, 20(5): 215–20.

Oxman, N. (2010) Material-based design computation. PhD thesis, Massachusetts Institute of Technology.

Oxman, N. (2011) Variable property rapid prototyping. *Virtual and Physical Prototyping*, 6(1): 3–31.

Pallari, J.H.P., Dalgarno, K.W. and Woodburn, J. (2010) Mass customisation of foot orthoses for rheumatoid arthritis using selective laser sintering. *IEEE Transactions on Biomedical Engineering*, 57(7): 1750–6.

Palousek, D., Rosicky, J., Koutny, D., Stoklasek, P. and Navrat, T. (2013) Pilot study of the wrist orthosis design process. *Rapid Prototyping Journal*, 20(1): 27–32.

Paterson, A.M., Bibb, R.J., Campbell, R.I. and Bingham, G.A. (2014a) Comparison of additive manufacturing systems for the design and fabrication of customised wrist splints. *Rapid Prototyping Journal*, 21(3): 230–43.

Paterson, A.M., Donnison, E., Bibb, R.J. and Campbell, R.I. (2014b) Computer aided design to support fabrication of wrist splints using 3D printing: A feasibility study. *Hand Therapy*, 19(4): 102–13.

Podfo (2015) Podfo: High Performance Orthotics, built for life. Available at: www.podfo.com/#&panel1-1, accessed 3 March, 2017.

Rahman, T., Bowen, J.R., Takemitsu, M. and Scott, C. (2005) The association between brace compliance and outcome for patients with idiopathic scoliosis. *Journal of Pediatric Orthopaedics*, 25(4): 420–2.

Reichel, D. and Schanz, J. (2003) Developmental psychological aspects of scoliosis treatment. *Developmental Neurorehabilitation*, 6(3–4): 221–5.

Riskowski, J., Dufour, A.B. and Hannan, M.T. (2011) Arthritis, foot pain and shoe wear: Current musculoskeletal research on feet. *Current Opinion in Rheumatology*, 23(2): 148–55.

Roper, J.A., Williamson, R.C., Bally, B., Cowell, C.A.M., Brooks, R., Stephens, P., Harrison, A.J. and Bass, M.D. (2015) Ultrasonic stimulation of mouse skin reverses the healing delays in diabetes and aging by activation of Rac1. *Journal of Investigative Dermatology*, 135(11): 2842–51.

Rosen, D.W. (2014) Research supporting principles for design for additive manufacturing. *Virtual and Physical Prototyping*, 9(4): 225–32.

RS Print (2015) RS Print: Supporting your every move. Available at: www.rsprint.be/#, accessed 5 May 2015.

Sandford, F., Barlow, N. and Lewis, J. (2008) A study to examine patient adherence to wearing 24-hour forearm thermoplastic splints after tendon repairs. *Journal of Hand Therapy*, 21(1): 44–52.

Sapountzi-Krepia, D.S., Valavanis, J., Panteleakis, G.P., Zangana, D.T., Vlachojiannis, P.C. and Sapkas, G.S. (2001) Perceptions of body image, happiness and satisfaction in adolescents wearing a Boston brace for scoliosis treatment. *Journal of Advanced Nursing*, 35(5): 683–90.

Schiller, J.R., Thakur, N.A. and Eberson, C.P. (2010) Brace management in adolescent idiopathic scoliosis. *Clinical Orthopaedics and Related Research*, 468(3): 670–8.

Schrank, A.S. and Stanhope, S.J. (2011) Dimensional accuracy of ankle-foot orthoses constructed by rapid customization and manufacturing framework. *Journal of Rehabilitation Research and Development*, 48(1): 31–42.

Shah, S.A. (2015) Nonoperative treatment for adolescent idiopathic scoliosis. *Seminars in Spine Surgery*: 27–32.

Taylor, E., Hanna, J. and Belcher, H.J.C.R. (2003) Splinting of the hand and wrist. *Current Orthopaedics*, 17(6): 465–74.

Telfer, S., Pallari, J., Munguia, J., Dalgarno, K., McGeough, M. and Woodburn, J. (2012) Embracing additive manufacture: Implications for foot and ankle orthosis design. *BMC Musculoskeletal Disorders*, 13(84).

Telfer, S., Munguia, J., Pallari, J., Dalgarno, K., Steultjens, M. and Woodburn, J. (2014) Personalized foot orthoses with embedded temperature sensing: Proof of concept and relationship with activity. *Medical Engineering and Physics*, 36(1): 9–15.

Veehof, M.M., Taal, E., Willems, M.J. and Van de Laar, M.A.F.J. (2008) Determinants of the use of wrist working splints in rheumatoid arthritis. *Arthritis Care and Research*, 59(4): 531–6.

Visser, D., Xue, D., Ronsky, J.L., Harder, J. and Zernicke, R.F. (2012) Computer-aided optimal design of custom scoliosis braces considering clinical and patient evaluations. *Computer Methods and Programs in Biomedicine*, 107(3): 478–89.

Weinstein S.L., Dolan L.A., Spratt K.F., Peterson K.K., Spoonamore M.J., Ponseti I.V. Health and Function of Patients With Untreated Idiopathic Scoliosis A 50-Year Natural History Study. *JAMA*. 2003;289(5): 559–567

Weinstein, S.L., Dolan, L.A., Cheng, J.C., Danielsson, A. and Morcuende, J.A. (2008) Adolescent idiopathic scoliosis. *Lancet*, 371(9623): 1527–37.

Weinstein, S.L., Dolan, L.A., Wright, J.G. and Dobbs, M.B. (2013) Effects of bracing in adolescents with idiopathic scoliosis. *New England Journal of Medicine*, 369(16): 1512–21.

Weiss, H. and Moramarco, M. (2013) Scoliosis: Treatment indications according to current evidence. *OA Musculoskeletal Med*, 1(1): 1.

Wong, M.S., Cheng, J.C. and Lo, K.H. (2005) A comparison of treatment effectiveness between the CAD/CAM method and the manual method for managing adolescent idiopathic scoliosis. *Prosthetics and Orthotics International*, 29(1): 105–11.

Wong, M.S., Cheng, J.C., Lam, T.P., Ng, B.K., Sin, S.W., Lee-Shum, S.L., Chow, D.H. and Tam, S.Y. (2008) The effect of rigid versus flexible spinal orthosis on the clinical efficacy and acceptance of the patients with adolescent idiopathic scoliosis. *Spine*, 33(12): 1360–5.

14 Architecture

Urban design and wellbeing

Christopher T. Boyko

Abstract

The design of the urban environment plays a key role in the health and wellbeing of residents. Often though, cities and their neighbourhoods are not planned and designed with wellbeing in mind. What may result are: (1) pockets of deprivation; (2) high population densities that suffer from inadequate services; and (3) a lack of high-quality, accessible natural environments situated within (4) walkable neighbourhoods. This chapter explores some of the leading, empirical research concerning these four urban design issues and presents a case study that analyses the relationship between the urban design of four neighbourhoods in Birmingham (UK) and the wellbeing of their inhabitants. Recommendations for how to improve wellbeing through urban design are discussed as well as the role of healthcare professionals in delivering healthcare to enhance wellbeing in cities.

Introduction

The UK Department of Health (DoH) (2015) has a simple strapline: 'Help people to live better for longer'. To assist in achieving their aim, the DoH believes it should be responsible for putting health and care at the heart of government, and leading across health and care through the development of national policies and legislation. Implicit in the DoH's remit and responsibilities is that good healthcare and a good healthcare system should mean that its users and the wider population enhance their *wellbeing*, mainly through treatment, prevention and education (Tzortzopoulos et al., 2009). What is less apparent – yet acknowledged by others (e.g. Design Council, 2014; Moore, 2011) – is that the design of the built and natural environment plays a significant role in wellbeing such that, if done correctly, the burden (financial, bureaucratic, etc.) of providing healthcare to the populace may be reduced. Often in cities, though, decision-makers get urban design wrong for a whole host of reasons (some of which will be discussed later in the chapter), resulting in reduced wellbeing, increased illbeing (e.g. depression, anxiety) and burgeoning costs for healthcare service provision. Guided by academic research, some key decision-makers, such as developers, engineers, architects, town planners and urban designers, are beginning to understand the valuable relationship between wellbeing and the design of the urban environment, and what can be done to ensure that citizens get the most out of healthcare in their cities.

This chapter begins by defining key terms: urban design, built environment, natural environment, wellbeing and illbeing. The next section examines some of the key relationships between urban design and wellbeing, highlighting the importance of deprivation, urban density, natural environments and walkable environments to people's health. The third section presents a case study for how the author and his colleagues assessed the relationship between urban design and wellbeing. The chapter ends with speculation on what the literature and the case study mean for relevant stakeholders involved in delivering healthcare.

Definitions

The following terms are important for understanding the relationship between urban design and wellbeing, and therefore require defining.

Urban design: the art and process of designing, creating, making and managing spaces and places for people (Boyko et al., 2005). Key to this definition is that urban design is recognised as an art (Biddulph, 2012; CABE and DETR, 2001; Cowan, 2000; Floyd, 1978; Lynch, 1981; Moughtin et al., 2003; Norberg-Schulz, 1979), connected with notions of creativity and innovation (Leach et al., 2015). Urban design also is a process (Barnett, 1982; CABE and DETR, 2001; DETR and CABE, 2000; Frey, 1999; Gosling, 1984; Madanipour, 1997; Toon, 1988; Webber, 1988; see also Brown, 1971, 1990) through which frameworks, rules and guidelines are followed by decision-makers and stakeholders to orchestrate the physical parts of cities (Frey, 1999: 16).

Built environment: subjective and objective features of the physical context in which people live, work and recreate, including characteristics of urban design, land use and transportation. The built environment influences, and is influenced by, patterns of human activity (adapted from Davison and Lawson, 2006; Handy et al., 2002).

Natural environment: a space that is relatively unchanged or undisturbed by human culture (Johnson et al., 1997). It incorporates biodiversity (including habitats and ecosystems); water quality, supply and demand; the marine environment; the soil environment; landscapes; air quality; and recreation and access (eftec, 2006).

Wellbeing: a positive physical, social and mental state that occurs when several basic needs are met (e.g. education or shelter) and one perceives a sense of purpose, including being able to achieve important personal goals and take part in society (DEFRA, 2010).

Illbeing: negative affect, physiological complaints and a state of worry that develops from a perceived sense of low personal competence, a lack of control and planning over life, socioeconomic deprivation and a poor family situation (Heady et al., 1984, 1985). Depression, low self-esteem, pessimism and self-dissatisfaction are common states when experiencing illbeing (Scheff, 1999).

Relationships between urban design and wellbeing

Increasing evidence suggests that urban environments within the UK – as well as other countries – are connected with poor mental health (McKenzie et al., 2013). In particular, the role of specific urban design features have been found to influence people's wellbeing and illbeing. The following section highlights some of these empirical relationships relating to deprivation, urban density, natural environments and walkable neighbourhoods, all of which have significant consequences for health and healthcare.

Deprivation

Although urban designers, town planners and architects do not intentionally design neighbourhoods and cities to look run-down or to be deprived, the lack of management, maintenance and place keeping (Dempsey and Burton, 2012, Dempsey et al., 2014) – which are part of the process of urban design and planning (Boyko and Cooper, 2009) – may contribute to a perception of neglect. Generally, neighbourhoods that are more run-down enhance residents' illbeing and decrease wellbeing, signalling that a place may be 'out of control' (Grabosky, 1995). Scholars have found that disused and derelict buildings as well as the presence of graffiti, vandalism and litter in neighbourhoods are associated with depression (Burdette et al., 2011; Ellaway and McIntyre, 2009; Galea and Vlahov, 2005; Weich et al., 2002). Indeed, these more street-level incivilities, rather than infrastructural problems, may have a greater effect on residents' depression (Ellaway and McIntyre, 2009). Furthermore, Hill et al. (2005) indicate that neighbourhood disorder, in the form of abandoned houses and other antisocial behaviour (e.g. open drug dealing on the streets), is positively and significantly related to worse general health, which is mediated by psychophysiological distress. Neighbourhood physical neglect also may contribute to decrements in social capital, especially an inability to receive adequate social support (Hill et al., 2013) or form social ties (Ross and Jang, 2000), and trigger a lack of sense of community (Wood and Giles-Corti, 2008).

When an area is improved, however, mental health also may improve. Both Dalgard and Tambs (1997) and Halpern (1995) discovered that in neighbourhoods where urban regeneration has occurred and the built environment is perceived to be better, anxiety and depression levels decreased. Moreover, parents and male children who moved from high-poverty public-housing neighbourhoods to low-poverty, private housing neighbourhoods experienced reductions in distress and depressive symptoms and depressive/anxiety and dependency problems, respectively (Leventhal and Brooks-Gunn, 2003).

Urban density

With more people living in cities than ever before and the consequent need for more housing, the density of cities has become a significant issue for urban designers, town planners and architects to consider and manage. Particularly because of the complexity around the multiple drivers and consequences of urban density, finding design solutions that are sustainable is not easy (Boyko and Cooper, 2011). The academic literature also is undecided in terms of the advantages and disadvantages of urban density: some research indicates that density – and especially crowding – fosters illbeing whereas other research, predominantly work about compact cities, believes that increasing densities in cities may enhance wellbeing.

Regarding the problems of high-density living, the empirical evidence is strong: children (Booth, 1976; Bradley et al., 1994; Essen et al., 1978; Evans et al., 1998; Evans and Saegert, 2000; Gottfried and Gottfried, 1984; Hassan, 1977; Saegert, 1982) and adults (Gabe and Williams, 1993; Ineichen, 1993; Kellett, 1984; Mitchell, 1971) residing in housing and neighbourhoods that are high in density and/or are perceived to be crowded suffer from poor health and illbeing. Such impacts include:

- lower quality of life (i.e. a greater quantity of negative life events) (Cramer et al., 2004);
- psychological stress (Gómez-Jacinto and Hombrados-Mendieta, 2002);
- chronic mental fatigue (Kuo, 1992);
- psychiatric illness (Duvall and Booth, 1978; Paulus et al., 1978);
- psychoses among older people (Gruenberg, 1954);
- less social interaction (Dempsey et al., 2012).

In terms of compact cities (see Jenks et al., 1996; Williams et al., 2000), scholars consider that living in high-density areas means that the greater mix of uses within walking distance, not having to rely only on private vehicles for travel, using less carbon and so on, positively impact physical health. The opposite also is true: residents living in lower-density neighbourhoods suffer from poorer health. For example, Ewing et al. (2004) found that individuals living in areas with less sprawl had lower BMI scores than residents living in more sprawling areas. Related to this research, Troped et al. (2010) discovered that residents living in high-density neighbourhoods (operationalised as population density and housing unit density within a 1km buffer of residents' homes) were more likely to engage in moderate-to-vigorous physical activity than those living in lower-density neighbourhoods. Furthermore, Lopez (2004) established that urban sprawl was positively and significantly related to residents' risk of being overweight or obese.

Although relatively scant, there is research stating that increasing urban densities improves mental wellbeing, with lower densities affecting illbeing (see Kirmeyer, 1978 for additional empirical studies about higher densities and wellbeing). As a result of higher densities, children suffer from less behavioural and emotional problems (Silburn et al., 2006) and increased social contacts (Bernard, 1939; Moore, 1986); older people living in sheltered, social or retirement housing experience enhanced wellbeing (Lawton and Nahemow, 1979; Lawton et al., 1980); and neighbourhood residents across the lifespan have greater social ties, cooperate more with one another (Halpern, 1995) and socially interact more (Talen, 1999; Young and Willmott, 1957).

Walkable neighbourhoods

A walkable neighbourhood is one that, through physical characteristics of the built environment, facilitates or inhibits residents and others to be able to walk or cycle in an area, either for leisure or commuting (Sarkar et al., 2014). Urban design can promote or obstruct walkability in various ways (e.g. adding pavements to both sides of the road; allowing cars to park on the pavement), which may lead to improvements *or* decrements in physical as well as mental health. Two related urban design features, intersection density and street connectivity,[1] highlight the complexity. Li et al. (2005, 2008) and Troped et al. (2010) both found a positive correlation between walking activity and intersection density; Berrigan et al. (2010) and Wells and Yang (2008) produced similar results for street connectivity. However, Forsyth et al. (2008) reported a negative relationship between leisure walking, walking for commuting and intersection density, and Gómez et al. (2010) established that residents living in neighbourhoods with low street connectivity would likely walk less than those living in high street connectivity areas. Finally, other scholars have found no associations: for example, Rutt and Coleman (2005) state that walking activity was not associated with intersection density in a low-income community.

Additional research into urban design features and walkable environments suggests that pavements are important. The absence of pavements and/or the perception of no pavements contribute to a lack of recreational walking (Duncan and Mummery, 2005) and may lead to being overweight and obese (Giles-Corti et al., 2003). Likewise, poor-quality pavements may contribute to a lack of walking among residents (Gilbert and Galea, 2014). However, research has shown that the presence of pavements and/or perceptions of pavements are associated with a higher propensity to walk (Ewing et al., 2004), both for leisure and for commuting (Foster et al., 2011; Kaczynski and Glover, 2012; Saelens et al., 2003); actual minutes walked (Nagel et al., 2008); and decreased chances of obesity (Boehmer et al., 2007).

Finally, the presence or perception of a walkable neighbourhood, comprised of many urban design features, may improve mental health (Leslie and Cerin, 2008). In particular, older men who lived in neighbourhoods considered highly walkable had less depressive symptoms than older men living in poorly walkable neighbourhoods (Berke et al., 2007).

Natural environments

The academic literature has identified the importance of natural environments in cities, particularly greenspaces, to wellbeing and health. Having greenspaces may help to reduce stress as well as increase social support and social cohesion (Sugiyama et al., 2008; van den Berg et al., 2010; Thompson et al., 2012). For children in particular, the ability to spend time in, and interact with, natural environments may help them better manage stress (Wells and Evans, 2003), reduce attention deficit hyperactivity disorder (Kuo and Taylor, 2004; Taylor et al., 2002), facilitate restoration (Korpela et al., 2002) and improve general mental health (Küller and Lindsten, 1992; Milligan and Bingley, 2007). In addition, for people who move to greener urban areas, mental health is found to be better, longitudinally, than those who move to less green areas (Alcock et al., 2014).

One avenue of natural environment research states that the *quantity* of greenspaces is significant, with a positive relationship existing between greater amounts of greenspaces within neighbourhoods and general health (Maas et al., 2006, 2009; Mitchell and Popham, 2007), decreased stress (Beyer et al., 2014; Roe et al., 2013; Thompson et al., 2012), anxiety and depression (Beyer et al., 2014), higher levels of perceived efficacy among users (Cohen et al., 2008), less loneliness and less shortage of social support (Maas et al., 2009) and greater levels of physical activity among children (de Vries et al., 2007). Another avenue indicates that *access* to greenspace is an important factor, although the relationship is less clear; for example, empirical evidence shows that people's overall physical activity is less with greater access to urban greenspace (Hillsdon et al., 2006) whereas specific physical activities have been positively associated with access to certain types of greenspace (see Wendel-Vos et al., 2004) (see also Tamosiunas et al., 2014 for lack of association between access to greenspace and prevalence of non-communicable diseases and cardiovascular risk factors). A third avenue suggests combinations of the above: for example, *quantity* of, and *access* to, greenspaces promotes physical and mental health as well as walking behaviour (Sugiyama et al., 2008); *quality* of and *access* to greenspaces may help to reduce psychological distress (Pope et al., 2015); and *quantity* and *quality* of greenspaces may decrease anxiety and mood disorders (Nutsford et al., 2013) and encourage less stress and greater social cohesion (Groenewegen et al., 2012). Key to all three notions of quantity, accessibility and quality involves having greenspaces that are *close* (Hartig, 2008; Hartig et al., 1996) and *available* (HM Government, 2011a, 2011b) for people to use. In neighbourhoods that are designed with proximity and availability of good-quality greenspaces in mind, a number of benefits may occur, including improved air quality and mental health (Knopf, 2001; DfT and DCLG, 2007).

Liveable cities case study: empirically examining the relationship between urban design and wellbeing

The relationships in the previous section as well as the author's prior research indicate that two particular features within the built and natural environment appear to strongly influence wellbeing and illbeing: deprivation and urban density (e.g. Boyko and Cooper, 2011, 2012, 2013; Cooper et al., 2008, 2009). With colleagues, the author wanted to see if both features together had an impact on individuals' wellbeing at the urban neighbourhood scale.[2] To do so, they undertook a case study in Birmingham (UK) as part of the *Liveable Cities* project.[3]

The authors used two different methods within the case study. The first method was a wellbeing questionnaire, consisting of 25 questions that assessed subjective wellbeing, the local

Figure 14.1 Map of Birmingham with the four wards highlighted with asterisks

Source: Birmingham ward map by © OpenStreetMap (contains Ordnance Survey data © Crown copyright and database right 2010–12), used under CC BY-SA 2.0; asterisks added

environment, perceptions of safety, daily life, water and electricity use and public transport (see Boyko et al., 2015, for more information about the development of the questions for the questionnaire). Hard copies of the questionnaires were given to residents living in four different wards within Birmingham, with each ward varying on urban density (low, high) and deprivation (low, high). The four neighbourhoods (see Figure 14.1) comprised: Ward 1 (low density, low deprivation), Ward 2 (high density, low deprivation), Ward 3 (low density, high deprivation) and Ward 4 (high density, high deprivation) (see Figures 14.2–14.5). Participants were contacted through community support officers within each of the four wards, ensuring consistency of recruitment approach. In total, there were 65 respondents from the wards: 14 in Ward 1, 18 in Ward 2, 17 in Ward 3 and 16 in Ward 4.

Based on participants giving their postcodes, the author and colleagues then could apply the second research method: built environment audits (Lewis, 2011). This method was used to evaluate the objective quality of the local environment in which participants lived within the four wards and took the form of an app that could be used on a tablet. Approximately 300 questions comprised the State of Place app, which was developed from the Irvine-Minnesota Inventory (Boarnet et al., 2006; Day et al., 2006) and asked about the quality of pavements on a road, the type of buildings and mix of building uses, the presence or absence of streetlights and so on. Within each ward, the authors audited approximately 2.5km of roads and 20 roads

Figure 14.2 Image of road in Ward 1 (low density, low deprivation)
Source: Photograph by Christopher T. Boyko, 2014

per ward on average, chosen from within 300m buffer zones around each participants' post-code. Such buffer zones are commonly used in the field of biodiversity to better understand the relevant spatial scales of various species (see, e.g., Hale et al., 2012); therefore, it was an appropriate approach to use with our participants.

Preliminary analysis of the data from the questionnaire and the audits suggest slightly different stories: the low-density, low-deprivation ward is best in terms of supporting the wellbeing of residents whereas the high-density, low-deprivation ward had the best environmental quality. In both instances, deprivation appears to play a larger role than does density, with lower deprivation providing both enhanced wellbeing and better-quality environmental features. Further analysis of the data likely will yield additional nuances between the wards that could help healthcare professionals when designing services for patients accessing healthcare (see below).

Nonetheless, based on these preliminary conclusions, changes could be made to different wards to improve both their urban design and the wellbeing of residents. In the UK, the Health and Social Care Act 2012 states that public health is to be part of the remit of local

Figure 14.3 Image of road in Ward 2 (low density, low deprivation)
Source: Photograph by Christopher T. Boyko, 2014

authorities. Doing so means that health, town planning and urban design now sit within a similar governance structure and help to achieve a similar vision. Small budgets could be created for ward-scale teams that involve public health, town planning and urban design departments. Together, and using empirical research, they could find simple yet effective ways to incorporate wellbeing into urban design. For example, outdoor fitness equipment could be installed in public parks where both ward density and deprivation are high. The equipment allows people, especially older people, to get physical exercise as well as enhance psychological health and socially connect with others. Attention would need to be paid to the maintenance of the equipment and the perceived safety of equipment users (Chow, 2013; Cranney et al., 2016).

A second way that wellbeing could be improved by more effective urban design, particularly in high-deprivation areas with low densities, is through a re-examination of current land use classes in cities. A UK government report by the Social Exclusion Unit (2001) acknowledged that deprived neighbourhoods often lacked basic public and private services, including access to shops with healthy and affordable food options. These 'food deserts' have negative impacts on residents' diet and health (Larsen and Gilliland, 2008; Wrigley, 2002). As with the previous example, public health could work with town planning – as well as local businesses and residents – to map existing wards' provision of available, healthy food. Provision may include mapping of shops, farmers' markets, allotments and the areas around them. They then can examine their city's spatial strategies and explore the possibility of changing or adding new land-use classes to allow for 'healthy shops' to be part of every ward, integrated with public transport, green space and social hubs.

Figure 14.4 Image of road in Ward 3 (low density, high deprivation)
Source: Photograph by Christopher T. Boyko, 2014

Conclusions

This chapter has explored the relationship between urban design and health and wellbeing, citing empirical evidence from the academic literature as well as presenting a case study from a live research project, *Liveable Cities*. The findings from both sets of sources are useful in that they help to elucidate how four built and natural environment features within cities – run-down areas, urban density, walkable neighbourhoods and greenspaces – impact people's physical and mental health. Regarding run-down areas, the evidence is clear that people living in such neighbourhoods are at greater risk of having poor health and illbeing. For the other features, however, the results from the research are inconclusive, at times confusing and somewhat contradictory to expected outcomes. For urban density, many studies point to increases in stress, anxiety and ill health for people living in high-density housing and neighbourhoods whereas other studies state that living closer together may result in more social contact and support when needed. With respect to walkable neighbourhoods, there is consensus that using urban design to create places so that people can be more physically active is favourable; however, the built environment features that some research sees as health promoting, such as increased street connectivity, have been shown to promote fear for safety in the public in other research. Finally, while greenspace is generally regarded as beneficial to health and wellbeing in terms of the potential for physical activity and restoration, scholars are unclear as to whether it is the quantity or quality of greenspace, or the proximity or access to greenspace, that is

Figure 14.5 Image of road in Ward 4 (high density, high deprivation)
Source: Photograph by Christopher T. Boyko, 2014

most advantageous. For urban designers, town planners and architects, these findings provide challenges to the design, planning, management and maintenance of spaces and places in cities in an effort to boost health and wellbeing.

And what of healthcare professionals? What is their role in the above? As mentioned in the previous section, with public health now sitting within local authorities, visions for cities have a better chance of being realised; public health, town planning and urban design departments may be more likely to work together on issues that overlap their respective areas of expertise (e.g. the provision of greenspace for housing amenity versus the provision of greenspace to encourage physical activity). One way that this could have been achieved is through local health and wellbeing boards, which act as a forum for health and care leaders to work together to improve health and wellbeing (Health and Social Care Act 2012). Unfortunately, these boards do not currently require town planners or urban designers to be board members (unless deemed appropriate), although this would be an important change for the future of healthcare in cities.

Another possible route for healthcare professionals to be involved in urban design and its impact on patient health and wellbeing is by extending the notion of 'care pathways'. According to Vanhaecht et al. (2007: 8), the European Pathway Association defines care pathways as, 'a complex intervention for the mutual decision-making and organisation of care processes for a well-defined group of patients during a well-defined period'. This definition currently covers patients' experiences while in healthcare, but does not sufficiently extend to patients' experiences of and with the built environment of healthcare facilities (Codinhoto et al., 2008, 2009; Davies and Gray, 2014; Shibeika and Gray, 2009). Even further, the definition does not cover patients' journeys and experiences to and from healthcare facilities and the urban design barriers that prevent sufficient healthcare from being delivered. This is a potentially new area of research that could expand healthcare service design and policy to the larger scale of neighbourhoods and cities, making health and wellbeing a priority for more people.

Acknowledgements

This work was supported by the UK Engineering and Physical Sciences Research Council under grant EP/J017698/1. The *Liveable Cities* case study was undertaken with Dr. Claire Coulton, Lancaster University, and Dr. James Hale, University of Birmingham.

Notes

1 Intersection density refers to the total number of intersections (know as junctions in the UK) within a defined area divided by the total area (Troped et al., 2010). Street connectivity refers to the directness and availability of different routes from one point to another within a street network (Handy et al., 2002). Although both terms may be defined differently by various scholars, the use of these terms in this chapter is illustrative of the general concepts.
2 The neighbourhood within the city is an appropriate scale for this research as this is where people live and coordinate their private lives (Power and Bergin, 1999).
3 *Liveable Cities* is a five-year, UK Engineering and Physical Sciences-funded programme grant that seeks to transform the design of cities through radical engineering to deliver low-carbon living, resource security and enhanced global and societal wellbeing. More information about the project may be found here: www.liveablecities.org.uk.

References

Alcock, I., White, M.P., Wheeler, B.W., Fleming, L.E. and Depledge, M.H. (2014) Longitudinal effects on mental health of moving to greener and less green urban areas. *Environmental Science and Technology*, 48(2): 1247–55.
Barnett, J. (1982) *An Introduction to Urban Design*. New York: Harper and Row.
Berke, E.M., Gottleib, L.M., Moudon, A.V. and Larson, E.B. (2007) Protective association between neighborhood walkability and depression in older men. *Journal of the American Geriatrics Society*, 55(4): 526–33.
Bernard, J. (1939) The neighborhood behavior of school children in relation to age and socioeconomic status. *American Sociological Review*, 4(5): 652–62.
Berrigan, D., Pickle, L.W. and Dill, J. (2010) Associations between street connectivity and active transportation. *International Journal of Health Geographics*, 9(20). doi: 10.1186/1476-072X-9-20.
Beyer, K.M.M., Kaltenbach, A., Szabo, A., Bogar, S., Nieto, F.J. and Malecki, K.M. (2014) Exposure to neighborhood green space and mental health: Evidence from the survey of the health of Wisconsin. *International Journal of Environmental Research and Public Health*, 11(3): 3452–72.
Biddulph, M. (2012) The problem with thinking about or for urban design. *Journal of Urban Design*, 17(1): 1–20.
Boarnet, M.G., Day, K., Alfonzo, M., Forsyth, A. and Oakes, M. (2006) The Irvine-Minnesota Inventory to measure built environment: Reliability tests. *American Journal of Preventive Medicine*, 30(2): 153–9.
Boehmer, T.K., Hoehner, C.M., Desphande, A.D., Brennan Ramirez, L.K. and Brownson, R.C. (2007) Perceived and observed neighborhood indicators of obesity among urban adults. *International Journal of Obesity*, 31(6): 968–77.

Booth, A. (1976) *Urban Crowding and Its Consequences*. New York: Praeger.

Boyko, C.T. and Cooper, R. (2009) The urban design decision-making process: A new approach, in Cooper, R., Evans, G. and Boyko, C. (eds), *Designing Sustainable Cities*. Oxford: Wiley, 42–51.

Boyko, C.T. and Cooper, R. (2011) Clarifying and re-conceptualising density. *Progress in Planning*, 76(1): 1–61.

Boyko, C.T. and Cooper, R. (2012) High dwelling density as sustainability solution in Lancaster. *Engineering Sustainability*, 165(1): 81–8.

Boyko, C.T. and Cooper, R. (2013) Density and decision-making: Findings from an online survey. *Sustainability*, 5(10): 4502–22.

Boyko, C.T., Cooper, R. and Davey, C. (2005) Sustainability and the urban design process. *Engineering Sustainability*, 158(3): 119–25.

Boyko, C.T., Cooper, R. and Cooper, C. (2015) Measures to assess well-being in low-carbon-dioxide cities. *Urban Design and Planning*, 168(4): 185–95.

Bradley, R.H., Whiteside, L., Mundfrom, D.J., Casey, P.H., Kelleher, K. and Pope, S.K. (1994) Early indications of resilience and their relation to experiences in the home environments of low birthweight, premature children living in poverty. *Child Development*, 65(2): 346–60.

Brown, D.S. (1971) Learning from pop. *Casabella*, 359–60: 15–46.

Brown, D.S. (1990) *Urban Concepts*. New York: St Martin's Press.

Burdette, A.M., Hill, T.D. and Hale, L. (2011) Household disrepair and the mental health of low-income urban women. *Journal of Urban Health*, 88(1): 142–53.

CABE (Commission for Architecture and the Built Environment) and DETR (Department of the Environment, Transport and the Regions) (2001) *The Value of Urban Design*. London: Thomas Telford.

Chow, H.W. (2013) Outdoor fitness equipment in parks: A qualitative study from older adults' perceptions. *BMC Public Health*, 13(1): 1.

Codinhoto, R., Tzortzopoulos, P., Kagioglou, M., Aouad, G. and Cooper, R. (2008) The impacts of the built environment on health outcomes. *Facilities*, 27(3/4): 138–51.

Codinhoto, R., Aouad, G., Kagioglou, M., Tzortzopoulos, P. and Cooper, R. (2009) Evidence-based design of health care facilities. *Journal of Health Services Research and Policy*, 14(4): 194–5.

Cohen, D.A., Inagami, S. and Finch, B. (2008) Non-residential neighborhood exposures suppresses neighborhood effects on self-rated health. *Social Science and Medicine*, 65(8): 1779–91.

Cooper, R., Boyko, C. and Codinhoto, R. (2008) DR-2: The effect of the physical environment on mental wellbeing. *Foresight Project on Mental Capital and Wellbeing: Making the Most of Ourselves in the 21st Century*. London: Government Office for Science.

Cooper, R., Evans, G. and Boyko, C., eds (2009) *Designing Sustainable Cities*. London: Wiley-Blackwell.

Cowan, R. (2000) *Placecheck: A User's Guide*. London: Urban Design Alliance.

Cramer, V., Torgersen, S. and Kringlen, E. (2004) Quality of life in a city: The effect of population density. *Social Indicators Research*, 69(1): 103–16.

Cranney, L., Phongsavan, P., Kariuki, M., Stride, V., Scott, A., Hua, M. and Bauman, A. (2016) Impact of an outdoor gym on park users' physical activity: A natural experiment. *Health and Place*, 37: 26–34.

Dalgard, O.S. and Tambs, K. (1997) Urban environment and mental health: A longitudinal study. *British Journal of Psychiatry*, 171(6): 530–6.

Davies, R. and Gray, C. (2014) Care pathways and designing the healthcare built environment: An explanatory framework. *International Journal of Care Coordination*, 13(1): 7–16.

Davison, K.K. and Lawson, C.T. (2006) Do attributes in the physical environment influence children's physical activity? A review of the literature. *International Journal of Behavioral Nutrition and Physical Activity*, 3: 1–17.

Day, K., Boarnet, M., Alfonzo, M. and Forsyth, A. (2006) The Irvine-Minnesota Inventory to measure built environments. *American Journal of Preventive Medicine*, 30(2): 144–52.

de Vries, S.I., Bakker, I., van Mechelen, W. and Hopman-Rock, M. (2007) Determinants of activity-friendly neighborhoods for children: Results from the SPACE study. *American Journal of Health Promotion*, 21(4s): 312–16.

DEFRA (2010) *Measuring Progress: Sustainable Development Indicators 2010.* London: DEFRA.

Dempsey, N. and Burton, M. (2012) Defining place-keeping: The long-term management of public spaces. *Urban Forestry and Urban Greening*, 11(1): 11–21.

Dempsey, N., Brown, C. and Bramley, G. (2012) The key to sustainable urban development in UK cities? The influence of density on social sustainability. *Progress in Planning*, 77(3): 89–141.

Dempsey, N., Smith, H. and Burton, M. (eds) (2014) *Place-Keeping: Open Space Management in Practice.* London: Routledge.

Department of Health (2015) About us. Available at: www.gov.uk/government/organisations/department-of-health/about, accessed 28 August 2015.

Design Council (2014) *Design for Care: Transforming Care for the 21st Century.* London: Design Council.

DETR and CABE (2000) *By Design: Urban Design in the Planning System: Towards Better Practice.* Norwich: Her Majesty's Stationery Office.

DfT and DCLG (2007) *Manual for Streets.* London: HM Government.

Duncan, M. and Mummery, K. (2005) Psychosocial and environmental factors associated with physical activity among city dwellers in regional Queensland. *Preventive Medicine*, 40(4): 363–72.

Duvall, D. and Booth, A. (1978) The housing environment and women's health. *Journal of Health and Social Behavior*, 19(4): 410–17.

eftec (2006) Valuing our natural environment. Final report NR0103. London: eftec.

Ellaway, A. and MacIntyre, S. (2009) Are perceived neighbourhood problems associated with the likelihood of smoking? *Journal of Epidemiology and Community Health*, 63(1): 78–80.

Essen, J., Fogelman, K. and Head, J. (1978) Children's housing and their health and physical development. *Child: Care, Health and Development*, 4(6): 357–69.

Evans, G.W. and Saegert, S. (2000) Residential crowding in the context of inner city poverty, in Wapner, S., Demick, J., Yamamoto, T. and Minami, H. (eds), *Theoretical Perspectives in Environment-Behavior Research.* New York: Plenum Press, 247–67.

Evans, G.W., Lepore, S., Shejwal, B.R. and Palsane, M.N. (1998) Chronic residential crowding and children's well being: An ecological perspective. *Child Development*, 69(6): 1514–23.

Ewing, R., Schroeer, W. and Greene, W. (2004) School location and student travel: Analysis of factors affecting mode choice. *Transportation Research Record: Journal of the Transportation Research Board*, 1895: 55–63.

Floyd, J. (1978) Urban design… a new profession? *Built Environment Quarterly*, 4(7): 73–7.

Forsyth, A., Hearst, M., Oakes, J.M. and Schmitz, K.H. (2008) Design and destinations: Factors influencing walking and total physical activity. *Urban Studies*, 45(9): 1973–96.

Foster, S., Giles-Corti, B. and Knuiman, M. (2011) Creating safe walkable streetscapes: Does house design and upkeep discourage incivilities in suburban neighbourhoods. *Journal of Environmental Psychology*, 31(1): 79–88.

Frey, H. (1999) *Designing the City: Towards a More Sustainable Urban Form.* New York: E. & F.N. Spon.

Gabe, J. and Williams, P. (1993) Women, crowding and mental health, in Burridge, R. and Ormandy, D. (eds), *Unhealthy Housing: Research, Remedies and Reform.* London: E. & F.N. Spon 137–49.

Galea, S. and Vlahov, D. (2005) Urban health: Evidence, challenges, and directions. *Annual Review of Public Health*, 26: 341–65.

Gilbert, E. and Galea, S. (2014) Urban neighbourhoods and mental health across the life course. In Cooper, R., Burton, E. and Cooper, C.L. (eds), *Wellbeing and the Environment: Wellbeing: A Complete Reference Guide*, Volume 2. Oxford: John Wiley and Sons, 23–50.

Giles-Corti, B., Macintyre, S., Clarkson, J.P., Pikora, T. and Donovan, R.J. (2003) Environmental and lifestyle factors associated with overweight and obesity in Perth, Australia. *American Journal of Health Promotion*, 18(1): 93–102.

Gómez, L.F., Parra, D.C., Buchner, D., Brownson, R.C., Sarmiento, O.L., Pinzón, J.D., Ardila, M., Moreno, J., Serrato, M. and Lobelo, F. (2010) Built environment attributes and walking patterns among the elderly population in Bogotà. *American Journal of Preventive Medicine*, 38(6): 592–9.

Gómez-Jacinto, L. and Hombrados-Mendieta, I. (2002) Multiple effects of community and household crowding. *Journal of Environmental Psychology*, 22(3): 233–46.

Gosling, D. (1984) Definitions of urban design. *Architectural Design*, 54(1–2): 31–7.

Gottfried, A.W. and Gottfried, A.E. (1984) Home environment and cognitive development in young children of middle-socioeconomic-status families, in Gottfried, A.W. (ed.), *Home Environment and Cognitive Development*. New York: Academic Press, 57–115.

Grabosky, P.N. (1995) Fear of crime, and fear reduction strategies. *Current Issues in Criminal Justice*, 7(1): 417–24.

Groenewegen, P.P., van den Berg, A.E., Maas, J., Verheij, R.A. and de Vries, S. (2012) Is a green residential environment better for health? If so, why? *Annals of the Association of American Geographers*, 102(5): 996–1003.

Gruenberg, E.M. (1954) Community conditions and psychoses of the elderly. *American Journal of Psychiatry*, 110(12): 888–96.

Hale, J.D., Fairbrass, A.J., Matthews, T.J. and Sadler, J.P. (2012) Habitat composition and connectivity predicts bat presence and activity at foraging sites in a large UK conurbation. *PLoS ONE*, 7(3): e33300.

Halpern, D. (1995) *Mental Health and the Environment: More Bricks than Mortar?* Oxford: Taylor and Francis.

Handy, S.L., Boarnet, M.G., Ewing, R. and Killingsworth, R.E. (2002) How the built environment affects physical activity: Views from urban planning. *American Journal of Preventive Medicine*, 23(2S): 64–73.

Hartig, T. (2008) Green space, psychological restoration, and health inequality. *Lancet*, 372(9650): 1614–15.

Hartig, T., Book, A., Garvill, J., Olsson, T. and Garling, T. (1996) Environmental influences on psychological restoration. *Scandinavian Journal of Psychology*, 37(4): 378–93.

Hassan, R. (1977) Social and psychological implications of high population density. *Civilisations*, 27(3/4): 228–44.

Heady, B., Holmstrom, E. and Waring, A. (1984) Well-being and ill-being: Difference dimensions? *Social Indicators Research*, 14(3): 115–39.

Heady, B., Holmstrom, E. and Waring, A. (1985) Models of well-being and ill-being. *Social Indicators Research*, 17(3): 211–34.

Health and Social Care Act (2012) Chapter 7. Available at: www.legislation.gov.uk/ukpga/2012/7/contents/enacted, accessed 30 September 2015.

Hill, T.D., Ross, C.E. and Angel, R.A. (2005) Neighborhood disorder, psychophysiological distress, and health. *Journal of Health and Social Behavior*, 46(June): 170–86.

Hill, T.D., Burdette, A.M., Jokinen-Gordon, H.M. and Brailsford, J.M. (2013) Neighborhood disorder, social support, and self-esteem: Evidence from a sample of low-income women living in three cities. *Cities and Community*, 12(4): 380–95.

Hillsdon, M., Panter, J., Foster, C. and Jones, A. (2006) The relationship between access and quality of urban green space with population physical activity. *Journal of the Royal Institute of Public Health*, 120(12): 1127–32.

HM Government (2011a) *Healthy Lives, Healthy People: Update and Way Forward*. London: Department of Health.

HM Government (2011b) *Laying the Foundations: A Housing Strategy for England*. London: DCLG.

Ineichen, B. (1993) *Homes and Health: How Housing and Health Interact*. London: E. & F.N. Spon.

Jenks, M., Burton, E. and Williams, K. (eds) (1996) *The Compact City: A Sustainable Urban Form?* London: E. & F.N. Spon.

Johnson, D.L., Ambrose, S.H., Bassett, T.J., Bowen, M.L., Crummey, D.E., Isaacson, J.S., Johnson, D.N., Lamb, P., Saul, M. and Winter-Nelson, A.E. (1997) Meanings of environmental terms. *Journal of Environmental Quality*, 26(3): 581–9.

Kaczynski, A. and Glover, T. (2012) Talking the talk, walking the walk: Examining the effect of neighbourhood walkability and social connectedness on physical activity. *Journal of Public Health*, 34(3): 382–9.

Kellett, J.M. (1984) Crowding and territoriality: A psychiatric view, in Freeman, H. (ed.), *Mental Health and the Environment*. Edinburgh: Churchill Livingstone, 71–96.

Kirmeyer, S.L. (1978) Urban density and pathology. *Environment and Behavior*, 10(2): 247–69.

Knopf, K. (2001) *Stratford-on-Avon District Design Guide. Issue 1, April*. Stratford-on-Avon: Stratford-on-Avon District Council.

Korpela, K., Kyttä, M. and Hartig, T. (2002) Restorative experience, self-regulation, and children's place preferences. *Journal of Environmental Psychology*, 22(4): 387–98.

Küller, R. and Lindsten, C. (1992) Health and behavior of children in classrooms with and without windows. *Journal of Environmental Psychology*, 12(4): 305–17.

Kuo, F.E. (1992) Inner cities and chronic mental fatigue, in Arias, E. and Gross, M. (eds), *EDRA 23/1992: Equitable and Sustainable Habitats: Proceedings of the Environmental Design Research Association Annual Conference*. Boulder, CO.

Kuo, F.E. and Faber Taylor, A. (2004) A potential natural treatment for attention-deficit/hyperactivity disorder: Evidence from a national study. *American Journal of Public Health*, 94(9): 1580–6.

Larsen, K. and Gilliland, J. (2008) Mapping the evolution of 'food deserts' in a Canadian city: Supermarket accessibility in London, Ontario, 1961–2005. *International Journal of Health Geographics*, 7(16).

Lawton, M.P. and Nahemow, L. (1979) Social areas and the wellbeing of tenants in housing for the elderly. *Multivariate Behavioral Research*, 14(4): 463–84.

Lawton, M.P., Nahemow, L. and Yeh, T.-M. (1980) Neighborhood environment and the wellbeing of older tenants in planned housing. *International Journal of Aging and Human Development*, 11(3): 221–7.

Leach, J.M., Boyko C.T., Cooper, R., Woodeson, A., Eyre, J. and Rogers, C.D.F. (2015) Do sustainability measures constrain urban design creativity? *Urban Design and Planning*, 168(1): 30–41.

Leslie, E. and Cerin, E. (2008) Are perceptions of the local environment related to neighbourhood satisfaction and mental health in adults? *Preventive Medicine*, 47(3): 273–8.

Leventhal, T. and Brooks-Gunn, J. (2003) Moving to opportunity: An experimental study of neighborhood effects on mental health. *American Journal of Public Health*, 93(9): 1576–82.

Lewis, F. (2011) Towards a general model of built environment audits. *Planning Theory*, 11(1): 44–65.

Li, F., Fisher, K.J., Brownson, R. and Bosworth, M. (2005) Multilevel modelling of built environment characteristics related to neighbourhood walking activity in older adults. *Journal of Epidemiology and Public Health*, 59(7): 558–64.

Li, F., Harmer, P., Cardinal, B.J., Bosworth, M., Acock, A., Johnson-Shelton, D. and Moore, J.M. (2008) Built environment, adiposity, and physical activity in adults aged 70–75. *American Journal of Preventive Medicine*, 35(1): 38–46.

Lopez, R. (2004) Urban sprawl and risk for being overweight or obese. *American Journal of Public Health*, 94(9): 1574–9.

Lynch, K. (1981) *Good City Form*. Cambridge, MA: MIT Press.

Maas, J., Verheij, R.A., Groenewegen, P.P., de Vries, S. and Spreeuwenberg, P. (2006) Green space, urbanity, and health: How strong is the relation? *Journal of Epidemiology and Community Health*, 60(7): 587–92.

Maas, J., Van Dillen, S., Verheij, R. and Groenewegen, P. (2009) Social contacts as a possible mechanism behind the relation between green space and health. *Health & Place*, 15: 586–95.

Madanipour, A. (1997) Ambiguities of urban design. *Town Planning Review*, 68(3): 363–83.

McKenzie, K., Murray, A. and Booth, T. (2013) Do urban environments increase the risk of anxiety, depression and psychosis? An epidemiological study. *Journal of Affective Disorders*, 150(3): 1019–24.

Milligan, C. and Bingley, B. (2007) Restorative places or scary spaces? The impact of woodland on the mental wellbeing of young adults. *Health Place*, 13: 799–811.

Mitchell, B.R. (1971) *Abstract of British Historical Statistics*. Cambridge: Cambridge University Press.

Mitchell, R. and Popham, F. (2007) Greenspace, urbanity and health: Relationships in England. *Journal of Epidemiology and Public Health*, 61(8): 681–3.

Moore, P (2011) A model to embed health outcomes into land-use planning. *Community Development*, 42(4): 525–40.

Moore, R.C. (1986) *Childhood's Domain: Play and Place in Child Development*. London: Croon Helm.

Moughtin, C., Cuesta, R., Sarris, C. and Signoretta, P. (2003) *Urban Design: Methods and Techniques*. 2nd edition. Oxford: Architectural Press.

Nagel, C.L., Carlson, N.E., Bosworth, M. and Michael, Y.L. (2008) The relation between neighborhood built environment and walking activity among older adults. *American Journal of Epidemiology*, 168(4): 461–8.

Norberg-Schulz, C. (1979) *Genius Loci: Towards a Phenomenology of Architecture*. New York: Rizzoli.

Nutsford, D., Pearson, A.L. and Kingham, S. (2013) An ecological study investigating the association between access to urban green space and mental health. *Public Health*, 127(11): 1005–11.

Paulus, P.B., McCain, G. and Cox, V.C. (1978) Death rates, psychiatric commitments, blood pressure and perceived crowding as a function of institutional crowding. *Environmental Psychology and Nonverbal Behavior*, 3(2): 107–16.

Pope, D., Tisdall, R., Middleton, J., Verma, A., van Ameijden, E., Birt, C. and Bruce, N.G. (2015) Quality of and access to green space in relation to psychological distress: Results from a population-based cross-sectional study as part of the EURO-URHIS 2 project. European Journal of Public Health. doi: 10.1093/eurpub/ckv094.

Power, A. and Bergin E (1999) *Neighbourhood Management*. London: Centre for Analysis of Social Exclusion, London School of Economics.

Roe, J.J., Thompson, C.W., Aspinall, P.A., Brewer, M.J., Duff, E.I., Miller, D., Mitchell, R. and Clow, A. (2013) Green space and stress: Evidence from cortisol measures in deprived urban communities. *International Journal of Environmental Research and Public Health*, 10(9): 4086–103.

Ross, C. and Jang, S. (2000) Neighborhood disorder, fear, and mistrust: The buffering role of social ties with neighbors. *American Journal of Community Psychology*, 20(4): 401–20.

Rutt, C.D. and Coleman, K.J. (2005) Examining the relationships among built environment, physical activity, and body mass index in El Paso, TX. *Preventive Medicine*, 40(6): 831–41.

Saegert, S. (1982) Environment and children's mental health: Residential density and low-income children, in Baum, A. and Singer, J.E. (eds), *Handbook of Psychology and Health*. Hillsdale, NJ: Erlbaum, 247–71.

Saelens, B.E., Sallis, J.F., Black, J.B. and Chen, D. (2003) Neighbourhood-based differences in physical activity: An environment scale evaluation. *American Journal of Public Health*, 93(9): 1552–8.

Sarkar, C., Webster, C and Gallacher, J. (2014) *Healthy Cities: Public Health through Urban Planning*. Cheltenham: Edward Elgar.

Scheff, T.J. (1999) *Being Mentally Ill*. 3rd edition. New York: Aldine de Gruyter.

Shibeika, A. and Gray, C. (2009) A proposed approach for modelling care pathways for infrastructure design briefing, in Lee, L.H., Kuhl, M.E., Fowler, J.W. and Robinson, S. (eds), *Proceedings of the 2009 INFORMS Simulation Society Research Workshop*. Warwick: INFORMS Simulation Society Research Workshop, 85–9.

Silburn, S.R., Zubrick, S.R., De Maio, J.A., Shepherd, C., Griffin, J.A., Mitrou, F.G., Dalby, R.B., Hayward, C. and Pearson, G. (2006) *The Western Australian Aboriginal Child Health Survey: Strengthening the Capacity of Aboriginal Children, Families and Communities*. Perth: Curtin University of Technology and Telethon Institute for Child Health Research.

Sugiyama, T., Leslie, E., Giles-Corti, B. and Owen, N. (2008) Associations of neighbourhood greenness with physical and mental health: Do walking, social coherence and local social interaction explain the relationships? *Journal of Epidemiology and Community Health*, 62(5). doi: 10.1136/jech.2007.064287.

Talen, E. (1999) Sense of community and neighborhood form: An assessment of the social doctrine of New Urbanism. *Urban Studies*, 36(8): 1361–79.

Tamosiunas, A., Grazuleviciene, R., Luksiene, D., Dedele, A., Reklaitiene, R., Baceviciene, M., Vencloviene, J., Bernotiene, G., Radisauskas, R., Malinauskiene, V., Milinaviciene, E., Bobak, M., Peasey, A. and Nieuwenhuijsen, M.J. (2014) Accessibility and use of urban green spaces, and cardiovascular health: Findings from a Kaunas cohort study. *Environmental Health*, 13(20). doi: 10.1186/1476-069X-13–20.

Taylor, A.F., Kuo, F.E. and Sullivan, W.C. (2002) Views of nature and self-discipline: Evidence from inner city children. *Journal of Environmental Psychology*, 22(1): 49–63.

Thompson, C.W., Roe, J., Aspinall, P., Mitchell, R., Clow, A. and Miller, D. (2012) More green space is linked to less stress in deprived communities: Evidence from salivary cortisol patterns. *Landscape and Urban Planning*, 105(3): 221–9.

Toon, J. (1988) Urban planning and urban design. *Ekistics*, 55(328–30): 95–100.

Troped, P.J., Wilson, J.S., Matthews, C.E., Cromley, E.K. and Melly, S.J. (2010) The built environment and location-based physical activity. *American Journal of Preventive Medicine*, 38(4): 429–38.

Tzortzopoulos, P., Codinhoto, R., Kagioglou, M., Rooke, J. and Koskela, L. (2009) The gaps between healthcare service and building design: A state of the art review. *Ambiente Construido*, 9(2): 47–55.

UK Government Social Exclusion Unit (2001) *Preventing Social Exclusion*. London: Cabinet Office.

van den Berg, A.E., Maas, J., Verheij, R.A. and Groenewegen, P.P. (2010) Green space as a buffer between stressful life events and health. *Social Science and Medicine*, 70(8): 1203–10.

Vanhaecht, K., de Witte, K. and Sermeus, W. (2007) The impact of clinical pathways on the organisation of care processes. PhD thesis, Katholieke Universiteit Leuven.

Webber, P.G. (ed.) (1988) *The Design of Sydney: Three Decades of Change in the City Centre*. Sydney: Law Book Company.

Weich, S., Blanchard, M., Prince, M., Burton, E., Erens, B. and Sproston, K. (2002) Mental health and the built environment: Cross-sectional survey of individual and contextual risk factors for depression. *British Journal of Psychiatry*, 180: 428–33.

Wells, N.M. and Evans, G.W. (2003) Nearby nature a buffer of life stress among rural children. *Environment and Behavior*, 35(3): 311–30.

Wells, N.M. and Yang, Y. (2008) Neighborhood design and walking: A quasi-experimental longitudinal study. *American Journal of Preventive Medicine*, 34(4): 313–19.

Wendel-Vos, G.C., Schuit, A.J., de Niet, R., Boshuizen, H.C., Saris, W.H. and Kromhout, D. (2004) Factors of the physical environment associated with walking and bicycling. *Medicine and Science in Sports and Exercise*, 36(4): 725–30.

Williams, K., Burton, E. and Jenks, M. (eds) (2000) *Achieving Sustainable Urban Form*. London: E. & F.N. Spon.

Wrigley, N. (2002). 'Food deserts' in British cities: Policy context and research priorities. *Urban Studies*, 39(11): 2029–40.

Wood, L. and Giles-Corti, B. (2008) Is there a place for social capital in the psychology of health and place? *Journal of Environmental Psychology*, 28(2): 154–63.

Young, M. and Willmott, P. (1957) *Family and Kinship in East London*. London: Routledge and Kegan Paul.

15 Design innovation

Embedding design process in a charity organisation: evolving the Double Diamond at Macmillan Cancer Support

Marianne Guldbrandsen

Abstract

Structured design and innovation processes have long existed in the private sector and help manage risk and ensure successful outcomes for end customer and business. They are newer to the public and third-sector organisations, such as charities. This article describes the context and need for a structured innovation process for Macmillan Cancer Support, the inspirations that drove how the new process was developed and the different stages in the model. The stages lean on a general design process, although that must have been tailored to the charity's need. A clear distinction between problem definition (design brief) and idea generation has been helpful in the evolution and early stages of implementation across the organisation. Similarly the awareness around divergent versus convergent stages has helped colleagues get a better understanding of the process.

Introduction

When designing a new consumer product or service it is common to follow an outlined process. We have seen this approach in manufacturing and construction for decades in the design of cars, mobile phones, furniture, buildings, etc. (Roozenberg and Eekels, 1995; Roy and Group, 1993; Gemser and Leenders, 2001; Parthasarthy and Hammond, 2002; Reason et al., 2015). Here a process refers to the step-by-step progression that will lead to the creation of an object that serves a specific or several needs. In the last decade this process has been variously described as a design process, an innovation process or a new product-development process. This process methodology used to create physical objects has in the last decade become more widespread, and is now becoming increasingly used in the design of services.

This article will describe such a process, and how it has been evolved and adapted to fit Macmillan Cancer Support, a charity in the UK supporting people living with or affected by cancer. It will describe the context and challenges that lead to the introduction of design expertise into the organisation; the development of a new innovation process and different stages; as well as some of the lessons learned.

The context and challenge

Macmillan Cancer Support is a charity operating in the UK, supporting people living with or affected by cancer. Macmillan's aim is to reach and improve the lives of everyone living with cancer and to inspire millions of others to do the same. The following statements, called the

Nine Outcomes, influence all of Macmillan's work. They are the cancer patients' statements we are working towards achieving.

1.   I was diagnosed early.
2.   I understand, so I make good decisions.
3.   I get the treatment and care which are best for my cancer, and my life.
4.   Those around me are well supported.
5.   I am treated with dignity and respect.
6.   I know what I can do to help myself and who else can help me.
7.   I can enjoy life.
8.   I feel part of a community and I am inspired to give something back.
9.   I want to die well.

'Living with cancer' is a term used to describe people that are at any of four points in their cancer journey: diagnosis; treatment; in recovery or survivorship; or at the end of their life. Equally the charity supports 'people affected by cancer', e.g. people supporting others that are going through cancer, such as family, friends and carers. It also includes people that are concerned about their own risk and potential diagnosis. In this article people affected by cancer will be shortened to PABC, to mean both people living with and those affected by cancer. In helping these groups Macmillan Cancer Support provides emotional, medical, financial and practical advice and support to these people through a broad range of services.

The charity has existed for more than a hundred years and currently employs 1,500 people, 900 based in the head office in London and another 600 in locations across England, Wales, Scotland and Northern Ireland. Macmillan's activities are entirely financed through private and corporate donations. In 2014 Macmillan's total donations came to £220 million. This funding is used in a number of different ways; to finance staff working in the nine geographical areas to provide support across the UK both in terms of designing and delivering localised services; this is done in partnership with local providers such as the NHS or corporations such as financial institutions. Working in this way Macmillan has gained a reputation for coming up with innovative solutions. For example, in the late 1970s the introduction of Macmillan specialist nurses into the NHS was made possible through pump priming, i.e. Macmillan paid for the first three years of a new nurse post, with the agreement that the NHS would continue the post thereafter. As a result of this innovation Macmillan now funds over 7,000 healthcare professionals in the NHS.

In addition to partnership working Macmillan also delivers a number of services directly to people living with or affected by cancer. These 'direct services' include the Macmillan Support Lines, a helpline offering a range of support services, a grant-giving service, information booklets and a website accessed by over 4 million people a year.

The need for cancer support is growing. The latest figures show there are now 2.5 million people in the UK living with cancer and this number is forecast to increase to 4 million by 2030. By 2020 nearly half of the UK population is forecast to be diagnosed with cancer in their lifetime. This potential increase is in part because of improved diagnostics and screening, as well as the fact that people are living longer (cancer is partly a function of old age with three-fifths of cancer sufferers over the age of 65). In the future those living with cancer will also increasingly suffer from other long-term conditions such as diabetes, heart disease or respiratory disease which further increase the complexity of their needs. The impact of these developments means that cancer services will need to change radically to support more people and more holistically, given the increasing complexity of their need and condition. In response to this Macmillan is leading the way in seeking to transform cancer care through the creation and testing of new services, and redesigning or further developing existing services.

Senior sponsorship

The creation of a new design-led innovation team was a strategic decision made by senior directors and the CEO. It resulted from a shared understanding that there was a need to raise the organisation's expertise in innovation management, processes and tools in order to meet the future challenges of cancer care. At the core of this decision was a desire to remain person-centric; hence the focus was on a design-driven approach with a strong anchor in user ethnography and rapid prototyping. This led to the development of the Macmillan innovation process. Crucial to the development of this innovation process was the continued senior sponsorship and buy-in from the rest of the organisation. The development and implementation of a process quickly became an important stream of work in the organisation-wide change-management programme, to create a more effective organisation better equipped to meet the challenges of the future.

Understanding the organisation

Like all good design-driven work, the development started with insight. The need to deeply understand the organisation and its values was a key first step. Careful observation and listening to colleagues and undertaking (informal) in-house user ethnography helped inform the design and evolution of the innovation process. One particular finding was the use of language. The word 'innovation' was used to variously describe any project or activity that appeared to include a new idea. There was no distinction between development, incremental or disruptive innovation. Moreover, innovation described more the idea or vision, rather than the implementation. Having the insights of this nature helped the understanding of what was most important to both define and to communicate in the development of a Macmillan-specific innovation process.

Structure and governance

During the initial in-house user ethnography, it was evident that there was already a high level of skills in the organisation, e.g. research was used widely, the drive for new ideas was omnipresent and many people were engaged in projects across the organisation developing new services and improving existing services. The development of an organisation-wide Macmillan innovation process would seek to support the development of a more coherent structure and organisation for innovation. It further supported better governance and decision-making through for example the introduction of clear gateways and phasing of project development.

Design expertise

The initial buy-in to set up a new design-led innovation team was not directly driven by an understanding of design, but more a need to ensure consistency and good use of resources. The

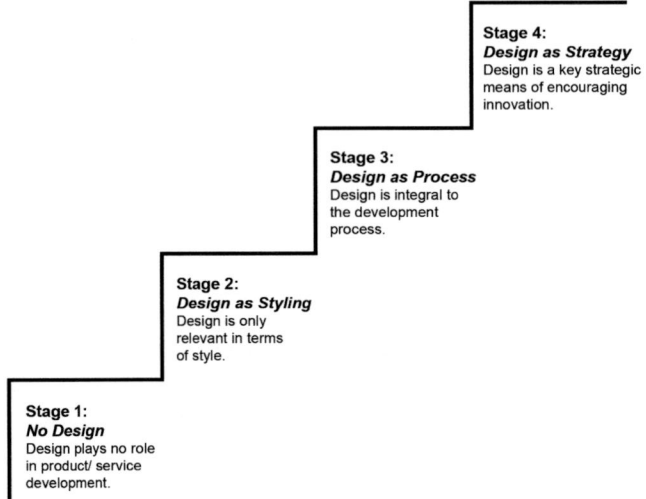

Figure 15.1 The Design Ladder
Source: Danish Design Centre, 2015

concept of design as a discipline was not distinguished from innovation amongst senior leaders, however there was an awareness of two areas where design contributes to innovation: the deep understanding of users, what motivates them and their behaviours, and rapid prototyping. Danish Design Centre developed the Design Ladder (see Figure 15.1) tool to measure the level of design activity in businesses (SEE, 2011). The higher a company was ranked on the Design Ladder, the greater strategic importance was attributed to design.

With the development of a new service innovation team, called Innovation and Strategic Partnerships, Macmillan made the decision to step between stage 2 and stage 3 of the Design Ladder, moving towards seeing design as a process:

> Design is not a result but an approach that is integrated at an early stage in the development process. The solution is driven by the problem and the users and requires the involvement of a wide variety of skills and capacities, for example process technicians, materials technicians, marketing experts and administrative staff.
>
> (Danish Design Centre, 2015)

The work of the Innovation and Strategic Partnerships team over the last three years means that Macmillan's innovation process is now broadly acknowledged in the organisation and it is seen as a strategic and practical way to drive future business areas. In a relatively short space of time the organisation is therefore moving from level 2 to level 4 as defined here:

> Design as Strategy: The designer works with the company's owners/management to rethink the business concept completely or in part. Here, the key focus is on the design process in relation to the company's business visions and its desired business areas and future role in the value chain.
>
> (Danish Design Centre, 2015)

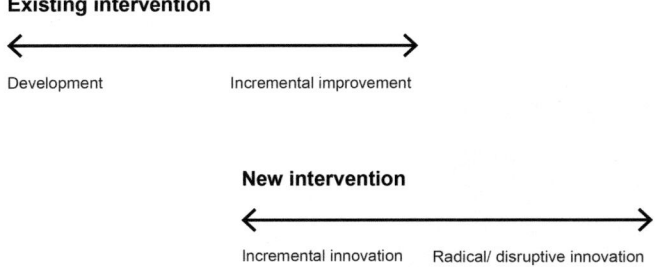

Figure 15.2 Incremental versus disruptive innovation

On innovation

Innovation refers to 'the process of translating an idea (or intervention) into a good or a service that creates value for which the customer will pay. To be called an innovation, an idea must be replicable at an economic cost and must satisfy a specific need' (Business Dictionary, 2015).

In Macmillan customers do not pay for services, instead we are looking at the socioeconomic value for our beneficiaries, which in return will appeal to others to donate money.

Maranville (1992), argues 'Innovation can be viewed as the application of better solutions that meet new requirements, inarticulate needs, or existing market needs'. What seems to distinguish innovation from development is novelty, a new approach to a known problem or a solution to an unarticulated problem. Tan and McAloone (2006) add to this by emphasising that something isn't innovative until it has proven successful: 'Innovation is synonymous with successful development and implementation, and therefore peculiar to innovation is that we do not know if something is innovative until it has been applied and adopted'.

Innovation can be divided into two main categories (see Figure 15.2):

- Incremental innovation is a continuous or evolutionary process brought about by many iterative advantages in features, technology or processes.
- Disruptive innovation is disruptive, radical and discontinuous. It is often based on rethinking current or unmet needs in completely new ways.

Innovation is synonymous with risk taking (see Figure 15.3). Organisations that create disruptive products or services and/or are involved in larger system change, e.g. healthcare, are exposed to greater risk because of the significant shifts in potential new markets, standards and expectations. Macmillan operates in all areas of development, from incremental to more disruptive innovation, as well as in domains ranging from products (such as cancer information booklets or holistic needs assessment tools made available to the NHS by providing the software on iPads) to services and systems (such as the telephone helpline or pathway redesign).

Developing Macmillan's innovation process

The first step in embedding an innovation process into Macmillan was to get a sense of what people understood by 'innovation' and what they would like from a 'process'. In discussions with staff across the organisation, including directors and those involved in delivery and directors about what they saw as good examples of innovation in their current projects and

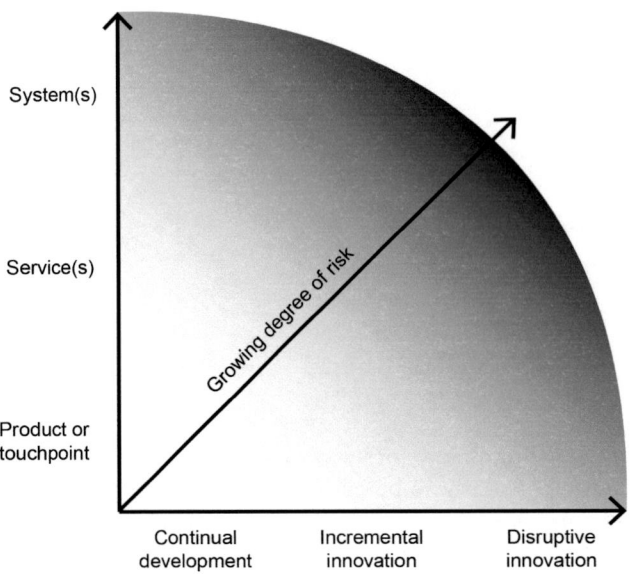

System(s)

Service(s)

Product or
touchpoint

Growing degree of risk

Continual
development

Incremental
innovation

Disruptive
innovation

Figure 15.3 Degrees of risk in innovation

programmes, it became clear that the organisation understood innovation as 'a good idea that will help people affected by cancer'.

It was also clear in discussions that there was an appetite for a more systematic approach, that would ensure new service interventions could be developed in a way where the right questions were asked and answered in the right order, to ensure greater success in their implementation. In looking to which design process to use as a foundation, a number of influencing factors came into play as most processes seem to follow common stages of research/analysis, specification, design and implementation. However, it was felt it was more important to articulate the process in more than just words. There was a need to develop a more visual description and language around innovation.

Equally, the ethos of Macmillan is to serve people affected by cancer with a core value of person-centricity. Consequently, the beginning of any new service solution or influencing work (policy, campaign and partnership) should be started with the end goal in mind; to support people affected by cancer.

From the initial stages of the organisational ethnography it was clear that there was a need to help people involved in innovating to better understand where they were in the process, as ideas were often a starting point and would relatively quickly lead to piloting. There was a general understanding that you need a good idea or a vision to be innovative, but there wasn't much talk about different methods or processes to get good ideas implemented.

One key thing would be to help Macmillan staff who were responsible for coming up with new service solutions to understand where they were in the design-led innovation process. A helpful distinction is to define if colleagues are in a stage of divergence, e.g. opening up, thinking up, coming up with different perspectives or options. Or if they were in a stage of convergence, e.g. the narrowing down of options, refining thinking and making decisions.

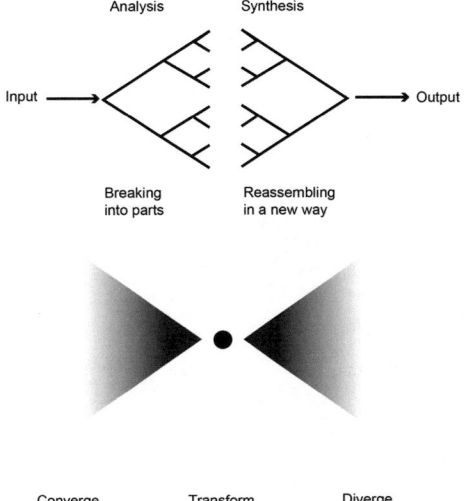

Figure 15.4 The divergent-convergent nature of design
Source: Dubberly, 2005: 22

Alexander (1964) has described these stages as Analysis and Synthesis (see Figure 15.4): the process of breaking problems down into pieces, e.g. decomposing, followed by reordering the pieces based on dependencies or similarities, and then finally knitting all the pieces back together, recombining the pieces. This process of decomposition-recombination echoes the divergent convergent nature of design described by Dubberly (2005).

Banathy, a professor of system theory, has further illustrated the iterative nature of the design process, where the process of divergence (analysis) and convergence (synthesis) is repeated (see Figure 15.5). Banathy (1996) describes how the process starts out diverging as we consider a number of inquiry boundaries, and that this type of divergence-convergence operates in the design solution space, e.g. we create a number of alternatives, and then converse as we evaluate the alternatives and select the most desirable alternative.

More recently the Design Council (2011; a government-funded institution championing and demonstrating the value of design to the advancement of British society as a whole, and public and private businesses in particular), created the Double Diamond based on similar principles (see Figure 15.6).

The Double Diamond again demonstrates the divergent-convergent nature of the design process and breaks this into four stages: 'Discover' insight into the problem, 'Define' the area to focus upon, 'Develop' potential solutions and 'Deliver' solutions that work. Other models were assessed, e.g. Stanford D-school's design process (2015; see Figure 15.7). In general most design processes go through a stage of researching the problem, gaining insights about users, defining the problem and then come up with ideas to solve it and finally prototype and test (Schilling and Charles, 1998; Urban and Hauser, 1993).

On the basis of initial research a repeated diamond illustration was chosen for a number of reasons. It is a model that visually communicates the divergent/convergent nature of design activities. It is easy to remember and has an equal emphasis on the need for understanding

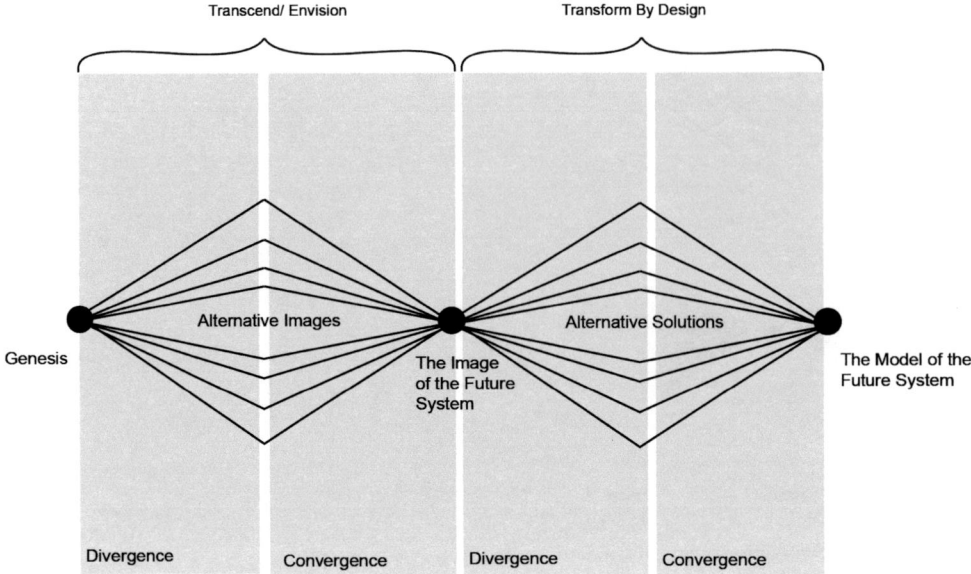

Figure 15.5 The iterative nature of the design process
Source: Banathy, 1996, in Dubberly, 2005

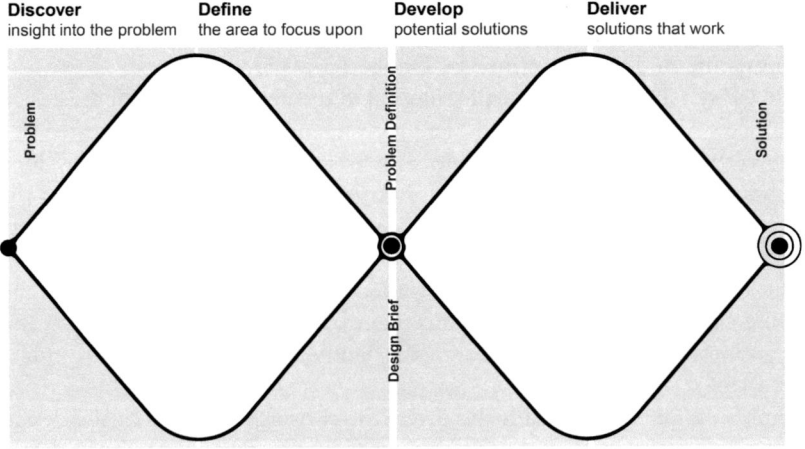

Figure 15.6 The Double Diamond design process
Source: Design Council, 2009

the problem before coming up with solutions, e.g. half of the model is about understanding the problem. This is an important key to success as well as having a good problem definition. This was especially pertinent, as the initial interviews with internal teams had identified a common behaviour of jumping to the ideas stage and then very quickly building and testing one solution.

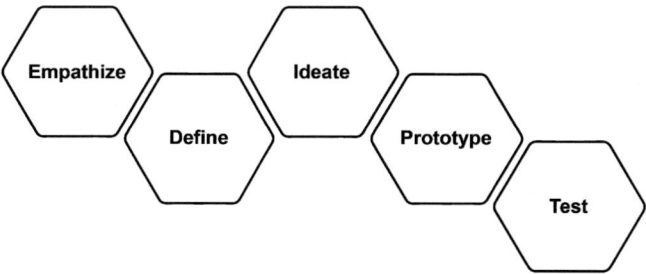

Figure 15.7 Stanford D-schools design process
Source: Stanford, 2015

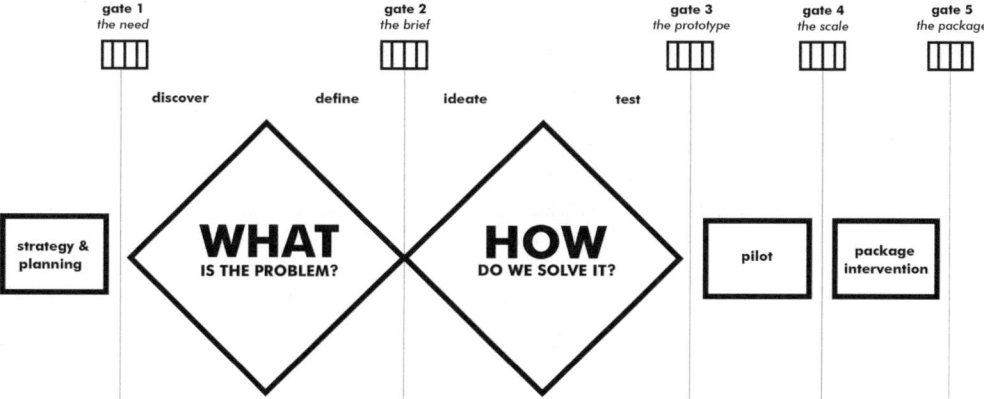

Figure 15.8 Macmillan's innovation process, based on a double-diamond shape

The model has been evolved and prototyped with staff across Macmillan (see Figure 15.8). The generic design process has been broken down to elements that work primarily for new service interventions. The inclusion of decision gates was key to evolve the model into something that would have a governance structure around it and would include unlocking funds.

The first diamond

The *first diamond* is about understanding what the issue is that a solution is sought for. It is about discovering and defining the problem/challenge/unmet need affecting the targeted PABC group. It breaks down to the following stages of activity.

Understanding the problem in context

The start of the process is the period of discovery, it is divergent in nature, focused on identifying user needs in more depth and understanding the context in which these are experienced. It is also a stage where inspiration is gathered. It is here desk research is done, looking for relevant reports, academic articles, blogs, products, services, social media, etc. The objective is to understand different facets of the problem. If for example a certain community demographic in a council area is not diagnosed as early as others in their cancer journey, it is easy to assume that the cause might be down to lack of awareness or lack of information. By unpacking the problem it might come to light, for example, that the target population are shift workers and cannot easily gain access to GP services out of hours. It is about asking the question behind the question, e.g. unpacking why it is a problem or unmet need by placing it in context, i.e. societal, economic, cultural, geographic etc. Data gathered and insights produced will span qualitative and quantitative research methodologies.

One methodology that is gaining more ground in various design and innovation processes is user ethnography. Macmillan has always sought to be close to the people they support and gather insight from them about what needs, wishes and desires they have. But it was new to have a person-centric design team that placed deep ethnographic insights at the heart of the process.

Design ethnography ancestry arises out of anthropological methods, but does not always lean on anthropological theory. In anthropology ethnographic methods have been used to gain understanding of human values, behaviours and life, by a researcher spending months immersed in a sub-culture or context. More recently designers have started to use a similar method but in a more applied way, e.g. a design researcher is likely to spend 1–3 days with the user to gain insights into their lives, experiences and values with a focus on how that might be applied to designing a new product, service or system. It is important to emphasise that the process is not just about talking to people, it is not a longer semi-structured interview, but a much more open format although with a topic guide. The reason for that is that it is not just about understanding the unmet need, but also about getting pointers around general activities, interests and the issues of getting about in daily life, as herein lies valuable knowledge and inspiration about what might lead to a successful solution.

Layering research

Conducting and gathering research does not in itself provide good and useable insights into problems or areas of unmet needs of people living with or affected by cancer; or any other user group for that matter. The value lies in layering these different types of data. Layering research is an activity that allows both quantitative and qualitative data to add to our understanding; it is accumulative, but recognises that there might be gaps in knowledge. Each layer represents a lens, with which the problem is investigated. Examples of what type of research will be relevant to include in research layering are: statistical insights from national healthcare systems, insights from professionals, interviews with experts in the field (not just representing the problem, but also potential inspirational insights that could influence the problem definition or ideation), various types of user insights, such as interviews, focus groups, surveys or user ethnography or online forums, market research identifying existing successful or learnings from not so successful existing interventions. There may also be relevant existing solutions that are worth getting a better understanding of, so as to help identify barriers or enablers: this might influence the problem definition too.

This stage of the process is where there is a tipping point between analysis and synthesis. It is an organic and iterative process, of zooming in and taking things apart through analysis and also zooming out and seeing the 'bigger picture'. Eventually the layering of insights will lead to a new level of sense making, understanding the users' need in context, influencing factors and potential pointers towards what a successful solution or problem solving should build on.

Problem definition and prioritisation

The final stage of the first diamond is about turning the layered insights into problem statements, also called design briefs. It is important to allow the richness of insights to come through by having a number of design briefs rather than one, that is trying to describe all the complex needs of people affected by cancer.

An example from a current project will bring this a bit more to life. At the beginning of a double-diamond process a particular strategic area of unmet need is identified. In this instance the research has shown that emotional wellbeing amongst people in their 20s, 30s and 40s has more of a dip compared to older people (50+) when experiencing cancer and after treatment. This problem was then investigated further through desk research (looking for more quantitative evidence); speaking to experts in mental health; speaking to professionals; and a market analysis of current offers in the space of emotional wellbeing, both within Macmillan, other charities and private organisations. Ethnographic research with 25 people within the target audience also added a deeper understanding and helped define the issue not only from the user perspective, but also in their language. A number of briefs were developed and all framed as opportunities: 'How can I reconnect better with the world', meaning how can I establish my sense of self and my confidence after cancer. The user ethnography added valuable insights by unpacking the 'notion of emotional wellbeing' down to areas such as loss of identity, belonging and purpose.

Layering insights leads to a well-developed design brief which in essence is a clear definition of the fundamental challenge or problem to be addressed through a product or service. The design brief forms the core reference point for all stakeholders, as it informs formal sign-off by project sponsors and sets the boundaries for the development in the second diamond.

The second diamond

The *second diamond* of the innovation process is about coming up with lots of ideas, co-designing and selecting ideas to prototype and finally having a proof of concept for that solution. The second diamond is broken down into the following stages of activity.

Idea generation and development

This stage takes the initial design brief from problem definition into problem solution. The second diamond is essentially about 'how do we solve the problem or unmet need?' There are many different ways of coming up with ideas but a common one used is brainstorming, often done with a broader group of people through a series of workshops. This idea generation is an iterative process of developing ideas, testing and refining them. One example from Macmillan included 40 people from across the organisation in a series of brainstorming workshops. The brief was always the starting point, allowing people both to come up with totally fresh ideas and to build on others' ideas. The core team would then go away and cluster the ideas, write them up in more detail and start a selection process. Ideas on hundreds of Post-It notes were narrowed down to 20–30 key concepts. These were then evolved and sketched up. Drawings of user journeys helped to bring the idea to life and identify where there may be weaknesses or areas of development of the original idea. This process helps further idea generation and maturing. End users and other stakeholders are valuable in this process to help co-design ideas and/or provide early testing of ideas.

Prototyping

Prototyping is testing solutions in a way in which risks are minimised. As stated by Hartmann et al. (2006), prototyping is a pivotal activity that helps structure innovation, collaboration and creativity. Low-level prototyping is achieved through testing with a small number of users, low initial investment and iterative development of selected ideas. It is at first low fidelity, prototyping a few ideas, gaining user and stakeholder feedback and using this iteratively to develop the solution. At this stage that could actually lead to radical shift, e.g. if the prototyped idea is not fulfilling the need specified in the problem definition/design brief, then it is easy to stop the ideas as investment (time and money) has been low. Prototyping continues through a series of prototypes that become more and more defined, moving from low fidelity to high fidelity. At the end of the second diamond process the new ideas will have got to proof of concept, which is the final output. Proof of concept means that the solution has been prototyped to a level where it is known that the solution, the concept, has been proven to work in one context (one location). As part of proof of concept an evaluation is made to demonstrate what impact the solution has had on people affected by cancer and that it is worth investing in.

Prototyping versus piloting

Piloting is deliberately placed outside the second diamond to emphasise the need of getting to proof of concept first. This is because prototyping is new to Macmillan and it was important to develop the proof of concept first before resources are expended on piloting the solution.

Piloting ends with a proof of scalability of the solution. This is a solution built to the highest level of fidelity, based on knowing that it is the right idea for investment. Piloting still allows for iterative learning and tweaking the solution, but piloting means that you are tying down substantial resources and you are not rethinking it at a conceptual level, e.g. if you are building a service delivered via a digital platform, a prototype will still end up with a digital platform but you might tweak the design of it. While in the prototyping stage you will have tested if a digital platform is the right concept to fulfil the need in the first place. The advantage of breaking down the differences between prototyping and piloting means that you are keeping the creative solutions space open for longer, while it is less costly to do so.

Governance via stage gates

Macmillan's innovation process has also been evolved to include gateways. It is a concept first introduced by the stage-gate model, which came out of the field of new product development (Cooper, 1990). Cooper (2008) describes how the stage gate was based on the premise that some projects and project teams understood what it took to succeed, yet still failed to perform. Stage gates was originally developed from research that modelled what successful projects do. Cooper describes how further research revealed that many projects were plagued by missing steps and activities, poor organisational design and leadership, inadequate quality of execution, unreliable data and missed timelines.

A stage-gate process consists of a series of stages, followed by gates, representing where go/no go decisions are made to continue to invest in the project.

Cooper (2008) has described how each gate is similar and consists of 1) deliverables, 2) criteria against which progress should be judged and 3) an output, e.g. a decision to go/stop/hold/recycle.

For Macmillan's innovation process the gates have systematised when in the process it is time to evaluate and reflect on the process, its outputs and resources spent. The series of gates is accumulative, meaning that they build the foundation on which a service solution is validated. There is a gate that kick-starts the double diamond, which is shaped around corporate strategy and priorities. The gate at the end of the first diamond ensures that enough insight has been gathered and that this has provided evidence for the design briefs, and that one has been selected to go into the second diamond. The governance structure 'hangs off' the gates and ensures that sign-off is given before more resources can be given to the project. For each gate a list of 'gate questions' forms the criteria by which a decision is made.

Challenge group and co-design

The development of Macmillan's innovation process was led by people with expertise in design-driven innovation, and co-designed with colleagues across the organisation that would use the process. It was important to ensure that it was designed with a range of people across the organisation. The application of the process is currently being tested and training material developed. It has been important to have input from the challenge group as well as co-designing with colleagues as they provided quick feedback on the stages in the process, the language used and identified where skills were already present. To date the process has been very well received across the organisation. The Innovation and Strategic Partnerships team are working as in-house service design consultants to continue to facilitate roll-out of Macmillan's innovation process, which is spearheading cultural change around how the organisation is developing new service solutions.

Conclusion

With the creation of the Innovation and Strategic Partnership team, Macmillan Cancer Support has embedded design-led innovation expertise in-house. The team's work is both strategic and practical in nature. With the development of Macmillan's innovation process and the work the team is doing to support development of innovative service interventions, there has been a shift from seeing design as styling to seeing it as a key strategic means to encourage innovation. With the evolution of the process there is recognition that structure is needed, but one that does not impede innovation. People affected by cancer's context demands a process that is extremely user-centric, and this process has been developed with that in mind.

The Macmillan-specific innovation process was evolved based on a number of divergent-convergent design processes as well as stage-gate principles. The model is supporting the creation of a shared design language across the organisation, which is needed because many (hundreds) of Macmillan employees innovate.

Macmillan's innovation process helps for a number of reasons – the image or visual nature of the model (not a Word document) has helped people that are not trained in design or innovation understand where and when different activities take place. The model introduces prototyping to the organisation, which allows for better risk management, effective use of resources and a 'test faster at lower fidelity' mindset.

References

Alexander, C. (1964) *Notes on the Synthesis of Form*. Cambridge, MA: MIT Press.
Banathy, B.A. (1996) Information-based design of social systems. *Behavioral Science*, 41(2): 104–23.

Business Dictionary (2015) www.businessdictionrary.org, accessed November 2015.

Cooper, R.G. (1990) Stage-gate systems: A new tool for managing new products. *Business Horizons*, 33(3): 44–54.

Cooper, R.G. (2008) The stage-gate idea-to-launch process–update, what's new and NexGen systems. *Journal of Product Innovation Management*, 25(3): 213–32.

Danish Design Centre (2015) Design ladder. Available at: http://ddc.dk/wp-content/uploads/2015/05/Design-Ladder_en.pdf, accessed March 2016.

Design Council (2011) Design methods for developing services. Keeping Connected Business Challenge competition material. London. Available at: www.designcouncil.org.uk/sites/default/files/asset/document/Design%20methods%20for%20developing%20services.pdf, accessed 14 November 2015.

Dubbley, H. (2005) How do you design? Available at: www.dubberly.com/articles/how-do-you-design.html.

Gemser, G. and Leenders, M.A. (2001) How integrating industrial design in the product development process impacts on company performance. *Journal of Product Innovation Management*, 18(1): 28–38.

Hartmann, B., Klemmer, S.R., Bernstein, M., Abdulla, L., Burr, B., Robinson-Mosher, A. and Gee, J. (2006) Reflective physical prototyping through integrated design, test, and analysis. *Proceedings of the 19th Annual ACM Symposium on User Interface Software and Technology*. ACM, 299–308.

Maranville, S. (1992) Entrepreneurship in the business curriculum. *Journal of Education for Business*, 68(1): 27–31.

Parthasarthy, R. and Hammond, J. (2002) Product innovation input and outcome: Moderating effects of the innovation process. *Journal of Engineering and Technology Management*, 19(1): 75–91.

Reason, B., Lavrans, L. and Flu, M.B. (2015) *Service Design for Business: A Practical Guide to Optimizing the Customer Experience*. Chichester: John Wiley and Sons.

Roozenburg, N.F. and Eekels, J. (1995) *Product Design: Fundamentals and Methods*, Volume 2. Chichester: Wiley.

Roy, R. and Group, D.I. (1993) Case studies of creativity in innovative product development. *Design Studies*, 14(4): 423–43.

Schilling, M.A. and Hill, C.W. (1998) Managing the new product development process: Strategic imperatives. *Academy of Management Executive*, 12(3): 67–81.

SEE (2011) Case study: Design ladder. Available at: www.seeplatform.eu/casestudies/Design%20Ladder, accessed March 2016.

Stanford (2015) An introduction to design thinking: Process guide. Available at: https://dschool.stanford.edu/, accessed 12 November 2015.

Tan, A. and McAloone, T.C. (2006) Understanding and developing innovative products an services: The essential elements. International Design Conference, Design 2006, Dubrovnik, Croatia, 15–18 May.

Urban, G.L. and Hauser, J.R. (1993) *Design and Marketing of New Products*, Volume 2. Englewood Cliffs, NJ: Prentice Hall.

Theme 4

Design for ageing well

16 Services

Exploring how a service design approach can facilitate co-design of supportive communities and service frameworks for older people

Valerie Carr, Sarah Drummond and Andy Young

Abstract

Systems, services, networks, products and places together make up the environment in which we age. This chapter will explore the interconnectedness and transactional nature of the relationship between these elements from a service design perspective. Drawing on case studies from Snook's portfolio of work with older people, we will focus specifically on three projects, outlining the context and methods used to engage with older people and reflecting on the learning from each project.

Background

According to the Organisation for Economic Co-operation and Development (OECD, 2013) the proportion of those aged 80 years and over in OECD countries is expected to increase from 4 per cent in 2010 to nearly 10 per cent in 2050. In the UK it is projected that those aged 65 and over will account for 23 per cent of the total population by 2035, with those over 85 increasing to 5 per cent or 3.5 million people (ONS, 2012).

COSLA et al. (2011) state that 'we need to push back our concept of older age, with less of a focus on "over 65" years and more on "over 75"' and the European Commission (2015) has agreed that there should be a focus on *Healthy Life Years* (or 'disability-free life expectancy') rather than simple life expectancy.

Triggle (2012) suggests that the primary challenge created by our ageing population is the increased number of older people suffering from multiple and complex health conditions. An Office for National Statistics (ONS) study of the 2011 census stated that just over half (52 per cent or 4.6 million) of individuals aged over 65 in England reported health and/or mobility problems which are long term and limited their daily activities, rising to 84 per cent when looking at individuals living in communal housing (ONS, 2013). Various conditions including respiratory illnesses, diabetes and cardiovascular disease are heavily correlated with preventable risk factors such as nutrition, exercise and substance abuse.

Alderwick et al. (2014) concur that most long-term conditions are certainly caused by lifestyle factors, 'yet seven out of ten adults in England fail to adhere to two or more government guidelines in four areas of behaviour that affect health (smoking, alcohol, diet and physical activity)'. They propose a continued move in the NHS towards prevention and lifestyle support.

Loneliness and social isolation are also identified as priority risks to emotional wellbeing and clinical health (Tomaka et al., 2006; Holwerda et al., 2012).

Cartwright (2007) found that the fundamental healthcare needs expressed by older people were: reduction in pain, improved mobility and a sense of control over their health.

Themessl-Huber and colleagues (2007) likewise identified limitations of the current health-care structure related to the homogeneity of services offered: 'Frail older people are high users of services but claim that services are not responsive to their main concerns: meeting individual needs, maximizing independence and helping to live fulfilled lives. Services not catering for these needs are often cancelled or left in abeyance.'

Health inequalities

The Marmot review of 2010, *Fair Society, Healthy Lives*, stated that: 'Health inequalities result from social inequalities. Action on health inequalities requires action across all the social determinants of health.'The report linked improvement in health inequalities with community engagement and suggested that, to really reduce health inequalities, a strong emphasis must be given to individual and community empowerment, creating the conditions for people to take control over their lives. Local services should increase the opportunities for people to participate in the definition of community solutions, enabling a real shift of power: 'Without citizen participation and community engagement fostered by public service organisations, it will be difficult to improve penetration of interventions and to impact on health inequalities' (Marmot, 2010).

Financial sustainability of existing models

Various reports have suggested that, with increases in demand and restrictions on budgets, the NHS will face a funding gap of between £20–30 million by 2017 (Appleby et al., 2009) and certainly around £30 billion by 2020 (Ramesh, 2013). Consequently, priority is given to the healthcare services that focus on prevention and improving population health.

Wanless, in 2004, produced three scenarios of 'fully engaged', 'solid progress' and 'slow uptake', each related to how individuals might take responsibility for maintaining their own health, reducing the cost burden to the NHS of being a

> national sickness service... Our health services must evolve from dealing with acute problems through more effective control of chronic conditions to promoting the maintenance of good health... Many of the benefits of engaging people in living healthier lives occur in the long term but there are also immediate and short-term benefits when demand for health services can be reduced, especially in those areas such as acute services where capacity is seriously constrained.
>
> (Wanless, 2004)

In a follow-on reflection on progress of self-management programmes in 2007, Wanless et al. (2007) found limited progress, or relatively slow uptake, suggesting a continuing increase in demand on the health services.

Cottam and Leadbeater (2004) proposed a new 'open welfare' model to address capacity issues in public services, relying on mass participation of citizens in both the design and delivery of innovative service models.

Positive contribution of older people

The Local Government Association (LGA) Task and Finish Group on Ageing has recognised the important contribution that older people make to civic society:

Older people are part of the solution to the challenges that face us… Older people can contribute to and participate in society in many different ways, whether through employment, volunteering, spending patterns, or the taking on of citizenship roles in various community organisations. Supporting the economic and civic participation of older people as producers, consumers and investors is a key dimension of trying to address ageing strategically, particularly in the context of unprecedented austerity.

(LGA, 2015)

COSLA et al. (2011), in their consultation for the vision document for the Reshaping Care for Older People programme in Scotland, found that:

People wanted to see a whole systems shift towards a greater degree of personalisation. Older people need to be much more involved in planning their own care and therefore needed to be better informed about their options and choices. Anticipatory care planning could not work unless older people were far more involved in decisions about their own care.

The Joint Improvement Team in Scotland, in their report 'Somewhere to go and something to do: Active and healthy ageing: An action plan for Scotland 2014–2016' identified four key themes that older people indicated were important to them.

- 'I want to have fun and enjoy myself.'
- 'I wish to remain connected to my friends.'
- 'I wish to be able to contribute to society for as long as I want.'
- 'Don't talk about me without me, and respect my beliefs and values.'

(JIT and NHS Health Scotland, 2014)

The ONS report of 2013 found that:

The proportion of those aged 65–74 who were economically active in 2011 (16 per cent) was almost double that in 2001 (8.7 per cent), a rise in those economically active of 413,000 people over the decade. The increased proportion of those aged 65–74 economically active reflects the larger number of older people who had continued to work beyond age 65.

(ONS, 2013)

Recognising the different attitudes and expectations of the Baby Boomer generation, Huber and Skidmore explain that,

At every stage of their lives, the baby boomers have been at the forefront of radical social, economic and political change: within the family, within the education system, within the labour market, and beyond. The way that members of this age group, the most influential generation in recent social history, choose to adapt to their changing circumstances will have a similarly dramatic impact in their later life.

(Huber and Skidmore, 2003)

Elg et al. (2012) suggest a model for co-creation and learning in healthcare service development through three learning methods. First, the model may be used as a means for generating and collecting patient ideas; second, a single patient's story can be illustrated and can serve as an incentive for healthcare service development and the creation of patient–centred care; finally, a large number of diaries can be analysed and combined with patient surveys to provide a deeper understanding of how the patient experiences healthcare services.

Service redesign with older people

Given the extensive skills and capacity of older people, and their desire to have more say in shaping services they may currently use, or use in the future, they provide an ideal group for involvement in the co-design of services.

At Snook we have worked with individuals and groups of older people in many of our public-sector projects over the past five years. They are often the demographic most likely to volunteer and to attend community meetings – indeed many third-sector organisations rely heavily on older volunteers to keep them running (Matthews et al., 2014).

The three projects that will be highlighted in the following text were all Snook projects conducted between 2012 and 2015 and involved older people in co-designing new services related to health and social care. They each illustrate in different ways the connections and interdependencies between services, systems, products and places and the capacity of older people to reflect on the challenges of ageing, and co-design alternative service models that allow them to continue to thrive in their homes and communities.

BRIDGE project

The BRIDGE project (building relationships in deprived general practice environments; see Figure 16.1) was funded by the Scottish Collaboration for Public Health Research and Policy as a research and development project to enable health and wellbeing in later life. Snook was commissioned by the Institute of Health and Wellbeing at the University of Glasgow to create a framework enabling older people and other professional and third-sector stakeholders to co-design the pilot services in each locality. The name BRIDGE was chosen as the project focused on trying to connect people who were disconnected and provide them with a link into services.

The project used participatory methods with staff in general practices, community organisations and older people to understand, co-design and 'road test' a system in which general practices in deprived areas identified older people in need and helped them access resources and/or participate in activities known to help prevent or delay disablement and enhance wellbeing (Figure 16.2).

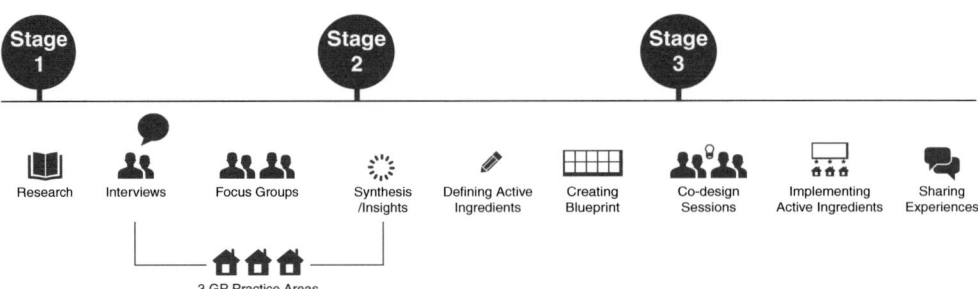

Figure 16.1 BRIDGE project outline

Figure 16.2 Co-production in the BRIDGE project

This project built on the work of the Deep End practices (GPs at the Deep End, 2013). General practitioners at the Deep End work in 100 general practices serving the most socio-economically deprived populations in Scotland. Their report identified some core principles to reduce health inequalities in the most deprived areas, including:

- The principles of co-production, including mutuality and respect, should be applied to serial encounters in general practice and primary care, enabling patients to become more knowledgeable and confident in living with their conditions and in making good use of available resources.
- The principles of co-production should also be applied to the joint work of general practices and area-based services, including attached workers (from social work, mental health, addictions and child health services), on a named basis.
- The lay link worker role should be developed to link practices and patients with community-based services and resources (GPs at the Deep End, 2013).

The project's ambition was to support older people to be less socially isolated and avoid all the implications and complications associated with isolation.

The guiding principles for the project were:

- starting from the knowledge, contact and relationships which general practices already have of older patients;
- basing the project in general practices serving very deprived populations; and
- engaging practices, local organisations and the target population in co-design of the system.

Methodology

Snook was responsible for the development of tools and methods to engage with, and elicit contributions from, all stakeholders, specifically facilitating the involvement of older people in co-designing (Sanders and Stappers, 2008; Hampson et al., 2013) the new service model. Over 100 older people were engaged through groups in community hubs and interviews in the homes of those with mobility or social problems. Initial interviews with older people identified some key factors that caused people to become socially isolated, such as: death of spouse, death of a pet, family moving away, relationship break-ups, moving area (being forced to move house either as a result of physical/mobility problems or reorganisation by the housing association).

In addition we engaged with some key stakeholder groups in the local community, such as community hub managers and those who came into contact with older people on a daily basis, such as local shopkeepers and hairdressers as well as staff from the three key GP practices who would be responsible for the implementation of the pilot project.

The first round of engagement involved quite informal chats and some shadowing of different people to understand their daily, lived experience. Following this we analysed and synthesised the findings from the wide range of material produced and identified some key insights that we then took back to the interviewees to check and comment on. In the second phase we used some bespoke tools to enable participants to reflect on their service experiences and to consider what the framework for a new service might look like, and how it might work. A series of personas and scenario-based story boards were the outputs from these first two phases and these were used with staff from the GP practices to enable them to understand and gain insight into the challenges of the lives of the older people they met every day. The presentation of this material was to enable staff to see beyond the physical and mental symptoms patients presented with and understand the wider social determinants of health.

The final phase of the engagement comprised two large co-design sessions where all three groups (older people, local organisations and GP practice staff) came together. For these workshops Snook had developed some prototypes or potential service touchpoints that could be used by service providers to engage with older people and these were tested out in role play between the different stakeholders. One example was a set of 'trigger' cards that could be used in GP practices to initiate deeper conversations with patients about social isolation, including questions about the seven triggers of isolation identified through the engagement sessions, such as death of a spouse, etc.

Following the co-design sessions Snook created service blueprints (Bitner et al., 2007; Stickdorn, 2012) outlining how the new service model would work in practice; identifying front-stage interactions and the tasks and processes that needed to be put in place back stage to provide the best service experience for older people and the greatest impact for the project. This also involved identifying key roles and the activities related to these roles, such as practice receptionist.

Lessons learned

Engagement with the older people was key to ensuring that there were very bespoke packages that met specific needs, and service staff were not just trying to plug older people into networks and services that already existed, regardless of whether they met their needs. This person-centred approach aimed to ensure that older people felt that the services that were being offered were relevant to them. The service was very much designed to be community-based and accessible, emphasising the importance of a sense of belonging and place to older people's wellbeing.

Taking a service design approach allowed us to develop tools that obtained the most value from the engagements with the different stakeholders, and that were perceived as much more interesting and personal than a questionnaire. Considering the whole system of community services as an interrelated whole, and taking a 'whole-person' approach to understanding the participants' needs, allowed us to produce detailed maps of community networks and assets that could be drawn on as part of the new personalised service model. This project was an attempt to connect the somewhat fragmented services in the three communities and highlighted the interdependencies between different statutory and voluntary-sector services and some of the systems issues that prevented greater cooperation.

Piloting of the new service model in the three general practices provided the following insights:

1. Linking older people with community resources for physical and social activity via general practices is a complex process, involving many different relationships, each of which takes time to develop.
2. The availability, accessibility and acceptability of community resources in some deprived areas were less than expected.
3. Initiation of the process is best carried out by practice staff, who are known to patients.
4. A key step is matching knowledge of individual circumstances and preferences with knowledge of suitable community resources.
5. There is no substitute for local trial and error in developing this approach.
6. Practices could be helped with additional information about local resources.
7. Each link takes time to develop, however, limiting the number of such links that a practice can focus on in the short term.

The final report on the project, summarising the key findings, suggested that:

> There is considerable enthusiasm for the BRIDGE approach. Our close working relationship with the Scottish Government's Joint Improvement Team, the ALISS project and the Deep End Group means that learning will be fed into subsequent approaches to enabling health and wellbeing in later life. The lessons from this project will enable policy makers, practitioners and community groups to consider the key facets of an implementable and sustainable system, easily accessed by older people.
>
> (BRIDGE, 2013)

Care Information Scotland service redesign

Care Information Scotland, an online and telephone-based service, was launched by NHS 24 in 2010, establishing an information service providing access to quality-assured community-care information for older people. This followed publication of Caring Together: The Carers Strategy for Scotland by the Scottish government in 2010, which made reference to the development of a 'Carer's (information) zone' on NHS Inform.

Snook were commissioned by NHS 24 and the Scottish government to review the existing service model for Care Information Scotland, engage users and potential users of the service to gauge opinion on the current remit and extent of the service and to propose recommendations for a future model (Figure 16.3). The goal of redesigning the service was to ensure that

Figure 16.3 Older people participating in the Care Information Scotland service redesign project

the service was more relevant for a wider group of carers, rather than just older people, and to ensure the service was accessible in a format that met the needs of different carer groups. By increasing the relevancy of the information, it was anticipated that access to the service would be increased. One of the guiding principles behind this project was: 'Recognising that effective services must be designed with and for people and communities – not delivered "top down" for administrative convenience' (Christie Commission Report).

Methodology

Snook worked very closely with the client project management team from NHS 24 and the Scottish government Reshaping Care for Older People team, and also with a wider steering group that included carers' group representatives. We used a facilitated co-design approach to guide all stakeholder engagement throughout both phases of the project (Figure 16.4).

We used the standard Snook methodology based on the Design Council double-diamond (Design Council, 2007) approach, appending our kick-off establish phase and a final reflection phase. We have explained in detail the methods and tools used on each of these phases below.

Establish

First phase:

a)   Create an initial service blueprint, mapping the existing service in terms of the client-facing aspects and the back-stage services that deliver the client experiences.

Figure 16.4 Workshop activities in the Care Information Scotland service redesign project

b)   Establish some project outcomes with steering group (including older people's representatives) and key performance indicators for the project.
c)   Define aspirations for the service, identifying some brand principles.

Discover

In the first citizen-engagement phase we used a Design Ethnography approach, meeting
participants for contextual interviews in their homes, spending time with them, talking
through their experience of accessing care and support, allowing them to tell their stories and
express their concerns. We then conducted workshops with groups of older people in various
locations across Scotland, ranging from large urban cities to rural villages.

We devised a set of tools specifically for this project that were designed to elicit the widest
range of insights whilst also providing in depth details of daily experiences. We used similar
tools in both the one-to-one and group sessions. These consisted of:

a)   Experience game – set of hexagonal cards, red, amber, green, allowing participants
to indicate who they would contact for help in urgent, pressing and non-urgent
situations.
b)   Social network map – looking at things from a wider perspective, where do you generally
go for information and support, who do you turn to and what channels do you prefer
to use?

We sent some of the tools out as part of a cultural probe pack to carers' organisations but this was less successful than conducting face-to-face workshops for various reasons, mostly because of the extra work this created for the carers' organisations, but also because face to face worked better when we were able to talk them through the tools.

Define

In this phase we worked with the client steering group to synthesise outputs and findings from the Discover phase and create some guiding principles to take forward. We did this through defining the following:

a)   Personas – a set of eight people stories or 'personas' representing the different types of people who might access the Care Information Scotland service.

b)   Each of the personas were then linked to specific elements drawn from the business model canvas, identifying what they needed from the service and how the service might meet their needs and add value to their experience.

c)   Key insights.

The information and insights identified through these activities served as a checklist for both content and function of the new service.

Develop

In the Develop phase we returned to some of the individuals and groups who were involved in the Discover phase and conducted co-design workshops where we:

•   presented the initial design proposal and mock-ups and supported participants to work through these and comment on usability and desirability of the different functions.

•   asked participants to design an ideal user journey focused on: What do you want to find out? and How do you want to find it?

•   mapped five easy steps to achieving desired outcomes.

We used a magnetic web page with matching magnetic components to allow participants to easily move and map features and functions that they would like to see on the web page. This allowed some of the older people who were not familiar with standard web icons and interfaces to create a web page format that was more intuitive for them. We also supported them to plot key interactions and touchpoints on visual user journey maps.

Deliver

To complete the project in the first phase we presented a detailed final report that included the following elements:

a)   A service blueprint with links through to mock-ups of specific touchpoints (human-centred interactions).

b)   A detailed brand proposal outlining design principles for the service.

c)   A wider system diagram – outlining key partnerships in the Scottish statutory and third-sector context.

d)   An insights map – outlining where the insights came from.

Implementation

Following presentation of the proposals to the client we were invited back to work with the client on the implementation of our recommendations between January and July 2014. The revised ambition for the service was to provide a central, comprehensive, national information resource accessible across a variety of digital channels to the public and professionals, fully encompassing the wide range of information on care and caring, providing a clear structure for information seekers.

The new project initiation document outlined four main streams of work:

1. Content: This work stream identified key sources of content by working with the client to establish relevant content providers and content leads and with user groups to develop protocols and scripts for the helpline. It also considered long-term maintenance of content, and how appropriate documentation might guide content governance.
2. Stakeholder engagement: This work stream focused on engaging with and identifying key stakeholders and establishing what level of input and impact they might have on and within the project and service. It also identified new content they might require and/or provide.
3. Technical: Snook worked closely with the technical architecture team from NHS 24 to identify technical specifications for the functional requirements of the website and the most appropriate design of the interface to accommodate the different abilities and preferences of various groups.
4. Self-assisted support: As phase 1 of the project had identified that people were interested in receiving and providing support as well as information, this work stream focused on identifying existing support services and 'how to' guides which were already available, and also where Care Information Scotland should and could fill any potential gaps in existing services or find new solutions to these.

In phase 2 of the project we were also specifically asked to develop the personas further to include a wider range of protected characteristics, such as lesbian, gay, bisexual and transgender (LGBT) groups, a wider ethnic diversity and those with learning difficulties. To enable us to create realistic and representative personas we held workshops with a Chinese minority ethnic older carers group (supported by a translator); the LGBT Healthy Ageing group in Scotland; and a learning disabilities group, which was then followed by a one-to-one interview with one older man with his support person. We developed outline personas, then had a second round of engagement with the groups to confirm the accuracy of the fictional stories we had created, and explore the specific ways in which a Care Information Scotland service might engage with these service users and meet their needs.

We also set up a website presenting the findings from the first phase of the project, along with the personas from both phases. We used this to engage with a wider range of people throughout Scotland and elicit feedback from them on the veracity of the personas and how we had interpreted their requirements for care information and support. This provided some useful feedback that informed development of the use cases for the final report to the client.

The final outputs from this phase of the project were:

*   A detailed set of design principles to guide future service development.
*   A comprehensive outline of required and desired service functionalities.

- Creation of a set of specific use cases – including detailed mapping of different client requirements and desired channels of interaction with the service. These were very action-focused and linked through to the technical, content and stakeholder workstream specifications.

Lessons learned

It is always rewarding to work with an engaged client who is genuinely looking to implement project findings and work with us as service designers to develop the best service experience for their clients. The Reshaping Care for Older People team in the Scottish government, who initiated the project with NHS 24, are particularly interested in service design methods and tools, and equally focused on user engagement and co-design. This provides very fertile ground in which to work.

Many of the older people we spoke with in carers' groups did not consider that they had care needs or functioned as 'carers' in any way. This was an obstacle to them recognising the usefulness of the Care Information Scotland service. We realised that the name a service is given, and the language used in marketing that service, may actually prohibit engagement with a wider range of people who might benefit from it. The older people involved in the computer users' groups in particular did not want to be identified as 'needy' or a burden, but as the local government authority suggested, be appreciated for what they could give and for the experiences and skills they possessed.

The importance of place was also evident in this project, as many participants in more rural and isolated communities demonstrated greater reliance on online information and support networks. The co-design work with the older people demonstrated that having a set of products, or a variety of 'ways in' to the Care Information Scotland service was clearly an important factor in ensuring universal coverage of the service. Integrating the various service offerings from different parts of the 'system' through one portal is an ambition that has not yet been realised by the new CIS service but the NHS 24 team are continuing to work on stakeholder engagement and building quality approved links with third-sector support networks.

RITA

The RITA (responsive interactive advocate) project developed out of Innovate UK's Long-Term Care Revolution (LTCR) (https://connect.innovateuk.org/web/the-long-term-care-revolution/about-us). This funded programme focuses on radically rethinking current institutional models of long-term care. Innovate UK states that: 'The goal is to create diverse, vibrant and cutting-edge non-institutionalised services and systems addressing the lifestyle needs and wishes of dependent individuals, their carers, and families, delivering long term care options that are fit for purpose and fit for the 21st century.' The initial idea for the RITA project came out of the original LTCR sandpit where the different team members came together to develop the original proposal that was successful in obtaining first-round funding from Innovate UK. RITA is a responsive interactive advocate service that is harnessing emerging technologies from the entertainment industry to innovate future models of personalised care.

The concept of RITA was borne out of the team's experiences with ageing parents and relatives, and their own desires to have more choice and control as they age themselves. Although the humanised avatar, providing a digital champion and friendly interface to the service, is what people remember most, RITA was conceived as an integrated service model. An effective state system that is capable of understanding and responding to the psychological needs and emotional welfare of the user underpins the communication interface of RITA, enabling empathetic communication. This, in turn, is informed by an 'essence' repository, designed to capture the essence of the individual through storage and organisation of all personal and memory-related information, where access is determined by the user.[1]

Methodology

Although the initial concept of RITA was developed by the team for the funding proposal, the actual development of the project involved input from a wide range of older people. Snook was responsible for the user engagement and we deliberately targeted a range of potential service users, from the age of 54 to over 80, as the key focus of the LTCR was to project forward to the year 2040, when today's 55 year olds will be approaching 80. Thirteen individuals aged 54–81, some in couples, some single, were part of our reference group for the project. Some were very fit and active, still working or volunteering. Others were part of a couple where one partner had a significant care need, such as Parkinson's or Alzheimer's. We also engaged with eight voluntary groups comprised of older people, including the LGBT Health and Ageing group. Professional groups such as local authority telecare groups, academic dementia centres and central government older people's committees were also consulted and contributed their opinions related to the functionality and integration of RITA as a prospective supportive service.

Finally, three private care companies were involved in mapping the needs of their clients and staff and identifying where RITA could supplement existing services and add value for clients.

Discover

Initially we asked participants about their understanding and experience of care. For some of the younger group members this related to the care their parents had received (or were receiving) and their perceptions of the good and bad points there. We then asked very general, open questions, such as: How do we want to age? What supportive systems and services can/ should we put in place to help us age well?

Define

In this phase we synthesised the feedback from the initial interviews to identify key insights that would inform the framework for the RITA service. Some of the specific aspects that people felt RITA should help with were:

- memory prompts: reminders, prompts and reassurance for those concerned about their cognitive functioning;
- reminiscing: storing images, sounds and even smells connected with cherished memories;
- connecting with others: helping people with limited mobility to retain their connections to their local communities and also their wider social networks. This may be through digital channels such as Skype, but also through enabling new connections between

people who have similar interests in the local area. This would help overcome the loneliness that has such an impact on older people's quality of life;

- coordinating care and support: helping people understand and negotiate the complex care systems and creating networks of informal care and support where required or desired;
- helping individuals with activities they are finding difficult; helping individuals maintain interests, activities and a link with the wider world as they perhaps lose mobility and cognitive function diminishes. Again this may be through immersive virtual experiences.

Develop

The RITA avatar (Figure 16.5) was developed through an iterative cycle of feedback from the older people regarding the development of the face of RITA, the voice, and the most important aspects and core functionality of the RITA support system. This helped us produce a justification and outline a business case for our initial proof of concept.

The University of Portsmouth team produced some initial facial rigs for the avatar, drawn from their extensive academic research about preferred facial characteristics. We then sourced an actress with similar features and conducted motion capture of her face while talking through some agreed phrases. We worked with our reference group and the wider circle of stakeholders to develop these phrases and also the scripts for two demonstration videos for the project.

Deliver

At the end of the nine-month funded project the RITA team had produced a limited function demonstrator, specifically related to facial and emotional recognition, and two proof of concept videos. We have received very positive feedback from a range of organisations and potential future partners who may provide a route to market. One of the key outcomes has been the

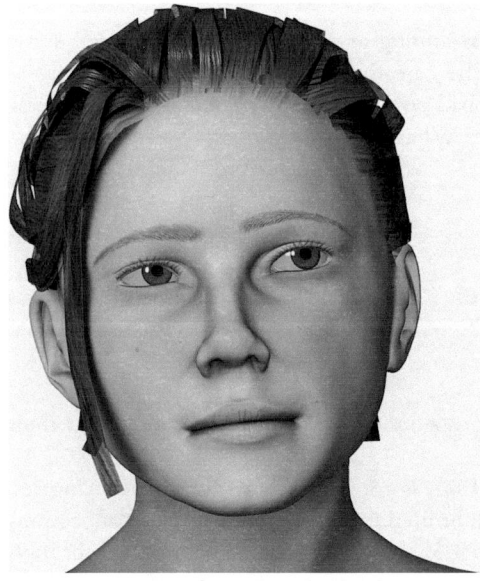

Figure 16.5 The RITA avatar

discussions and enquiries we have received about how RITA may be integrated into other existing services and platforms. The team are currently developing partnerships and a further proposal for funding to take the RITA service concept to the next level.

Lessons learned

Older people are passionate and have strong opinions about retaining control of their own lives and not being perceived as a burden. They want to continue to contribute to society and feel they are valued. When we asked the group to help us develop the scripts for the proof of concept videos, they commented, 'Don't have the people in the scripts too old and frumpy — show older people who have spirit and aren't too passive'.

The older people in the reference group (and in some stakeholder groups that we engaged with, such as the University of the Third Age) were adamant that they did not want computers replacing people in care services, as they valued the human-to-human interaction highly and were afraid to lose this. As Patrick Mankins has stated, 'This means that crafting the relationship between people and the technology we use becomes as critical as building faster processors' (Mankins, 2015). The fragmentation of services (Pearson, 2015) is a major obstacle in attempting to provide a 'whole-person' approach to care and support in later life. There was a recognition by older people in the reference group that 'the system is broken', and a real desire to see RITA as a service that constructed a coordinated interface connecting disparate products, players and networks: creating a person-centred community of support that transcends geographical and systems barriers.

Conclusion

Reflection on learning from the three projects

BRIDGE was an attempt at a community-based solution to social isolation in older people. Involving older people in the co-design of service solutions was important but some systems issues around the availability of appropriate resources and services in the local communities and funding for the 'link' person proved to be barriers to effective implementation of the proposals. With fragmented commissioning previously separating health and social care budgets, the authority paying for preventative services would not necessarily see the savings in their own budgets, even in the long term. This may improve with the new integrated health and social care boards in Scotland and the integration of commissioning with a real focus on improving outcomes.

The Care Information Scotland service redesign has been successfully implemented with a focus on providing information in appropriate modes for different audiences, including increasing video content and the availability of audio descriptions on the website. There were some major obstacles to be overcome in terms of the risk aversion in the statutory sector related to the provenance and quality assurance of information and therefore some of the self-assisted support aspects of the recommendations have not yet been implemented. The service redesign has, however, certainly involved better partnership working with the third sector.

RITA is still in the very early stages of development as an alternative service model improving health and wellbeing in later life. However, the project has attempted to involve a wide range of older people in co-developing a radical concept of how technology might be used to create a network of support around people who face diminishing physical and cognitive capacity. It has attempted to address some of the systems issues related to person-centred services by giving choice and control of information back to the individual. However, the next phase of development will prove whether the existing statutory, private and third-sector providers are ready for such a shift, and particularly whether the very different proprietary IT systems can actually be integrated and interoperable.

Why service design offers some approaches and tools that support healthy ageing

Older people have lived a long time – they have lots of experience and they certainly recognise the difference between good and bad service. However, many older people often have an ingrained respect for professionals, such as GPs and hospital consultants, which means they don't argue or question what they have been told, and can be passively accepting of decisions that are made for them.

In addition to this, older people want access to their own, named doctor and personal care by individuals that they are familiar with, and who also know them. There is little recognition that the model of personal care is changing, and that there will not actually be enough people to provide named personal carers for all those who are ageing (Simmons et al., 2013).

From the RITA project reference group comments, it became clear that many older people are particularly concerned about data privacy in relation to computer-based caring services. This may be because they don't necessarily understand how cloud-based storage or online services work, and they worry about their bank or personal details being stolen or misused.

These elements and attitudes are changing as the Baby Boomers (those born 1946–64) start to encounter health and care services that do not provide the choice and control they have come to expect (Department of Health, 2008; LGA, 2015). This cohort is also more familiar with the concept of co-designing services and using online services.

The key elements of effective services for the ageing population will be their ability to integrate a whole-person with a whole-systems approach. Fragmented services delivered in isolation cannot solve the intractable problems of sustainability in both human and economic terms.

As Charlie Leadbeater has stated, 'The future will belong to companies that assemble whole systems – content, services, software, finance – around their products and as a result help to bring about mass change in behaviour' (Leadbeater, 2013).

Additionally, NESTA suggests that we need to reframe our attitudes and see 'People as assets: so that the skills, experience and strengths of older people are recognised and older people are not defined solely by their "needs"; and People as architects: so that older people can be active players and co–creators in developing solutions' (NESTA, 2013). This chapter has presented a snapshot of how service design methods and tools have been used in practice to engage older people in reflecting on the barriers to integrated networks of support for older people, attempting in some measure to use co-design methods to overcome these. Each of the projects has addressed issues related to systems, services, networks, products and places to varying degrees and highlighted the value of engaging the people who access services in developing new service models, fit for the future.

Although the projects described have not been entirely successful in achieving the aims set out by NESTA above, we believe that the learnings garnered from even small-scale service design projects enable us to continue to evolve a set of effective methods and approaches that enable us to develop services that work at both personal and system levels. We see each project as a 'breaching experiment', breaking through institutional and attitudinal barriers to demonstrate how a whole-person and whole-systems approach can embrace the evolving, transactional nature of the relationship between the two elements (Garfinkel, 1963).

We believe that a service systems and service design approach provides the methods and tools to respond to the complexity of multilayered services, and enables and supports people to co-design new, dynamic and personalised service models that help create a network of supportive communities that will enable us all to age well.

Note

1 The team behind RITA are Valerie Carr from Snook, Wendy Powell from Centre for Creative Industries at University of Portsmouth, Blair Dickson from Affective State, and the project lead, Jane Reeves of the Centre for Child Protection at University of Kent.

References

Alderwick, H., Ham, C. and Buck, D. (2014) *Population Health Systems: Going beyond Integrated Care*. London: King's Fund.

Appleby, R., Crawford, R. and Emmerson, C. (2009) How cold will it be? Prospects for NHS funding: 2011–2017. London: King's Fund.

Bitner, M.J., Ostrom, A.L. and Morgan, F.N. (2007) Service blueprinting: A practical technique for service innovation. Center for Services Leadership, Arizona State University working paper.

BRIDGE (2013) Enabling health and wellbeing among older people: Capitalising on resources in deprived areas through general practice. University of Glasgow, Institute of Health and Wellbeing.

Cartwright, T. (2007) 'Getting on with life': The experiences of older people using complementary health care. *Social Science and Medicine*, 64(8):1692–703.

COSLA, Scottish Government and NHS Scotland (2011) Reshaping care for older people: A programme for change 2011–2021.

Cottam, H. and Leadbeater, C. (2004) *Open Welfare: Designs on the Public Good*. London: Design Council.

Department of Health (2008) High quality care for all: NHS next stage review final report. London: DoH.

Design Council (2007) Eleven lessons: Managing design in eleven global brands. A study of the design process. Available at: www.designcouncil.org.uk/sites/default/files/asset/document/ElevenLessons_Design_Council%20%282%29.pdf.

Elg, M., Engström, J., Witell, L. and Poksinska, B. (2012) Co-creation and learning in health-care service development. *Journal of Service Management*, 23(3): 328–43.

European Commission (2015) Innovation for active and healthy ageing. European Summit on Innovation for Active and Healthy Ageing, Brussels, 9–10 March, final report. Available at: http://ec.europa.eu/research/innovation-union/pdf/active-healthy-ageing/ageing_summit_report.pdf#view=fit&pagemode=none.

Garfinkel, H. (1963) A conception of and experiments with 'trust' as a condition of concerted stable actions, in O'Brien, J. (ed.), *The Production of Reality: Essays and Readings on Social Interaction*. New York: Pine Forge Press.

GPs at the Deep End (2013) What can NHS Scotland do to prevent and reduce health inequalities? Proposals from General Practitioners at the Deep End. Available at: www.glasgow.ac.uk/deepend.

Hampson, M., Baeck, P. and Langford, K. (2013) *By Us, for Us: The Power of Co-design and Co-delivery*. London: NESTA Innovation Unit.

Holwerda, T.J., Beekman, A.T.F., Deeg, D.J.H., Stek, M.L., Van Tilburg, T.G., Visser, P.J. and Schoevers, R.A. (2012) Increased risk of mortality associated with social isolation in older men: Only when feeling lonely? Results from the Amsterdam Study of the Elderly (AMSTEL). *Psychological Medicine*, 42(4): 843–53.

Huber, J. and Skidmore, P. (2003) *The New Old: Why Baby Boomers Won't Be Pensioned Off*. London: Demos.

JIT and NHS Health Scotland (2014) Somewhere to go and something to do: Active and healthy ageing: An action plan for Scotland 2014–2016. Joint Improvement Team, Scottish Government.

Leadbeater, C. (2013) The systems innovator. In Mulgan, G. and Leadbeater, C. (eds), *Systems Innovation*. London: NESTA, 25–56.

LGA (2015) Ageing: The silver lining: The opportunities and challenges of an ageing society for local government. Local Government Association Task and Finish Group on Ageing.

Mankins, P. (2015) Can we design trust between humans and artificial intelligence? Available at: www.fastcodesign.com/3047500/can-we-design-trust-between-humans-and-artificial-intelligence, accessed 27 July 2015.

Marmot, M. (2010) *The Marmot Review: Fair society, Healthy Lives*. Strategic Review of Health Inequalities in England Post-2010. London: Marmot Review.

Matthews, K., Demakakos, P., Nazroo, J. and Shankar, A. (2014) The evolution of lifestyles in older age in England. In Banks, J., Nazroo, J. and Steptoe, A. (eds), *The Dynamics of Ageing: Evidence from the English Longitudinal Study of Ageing 2002–2012* (Wave 6). London: Institute of Fiscal Studies, 40–63.

NESTA (2013) Five hours a day: Systemic innovation for an ageing population. London: NESTA. Available at: www.nesta.org.uk/publications/five-hours-day.

OECD (2013) A good life in old age? Monitoring and improving quality in long-term care. OECD Health Policy Studies, European Commission. Available at: ec.europa.eu/social/BlobServlet?docId=10292&langId=en.

ONS (2012) *Population Ageing in the United Kingdom, Its Constituent Countries and the European Union*. London: Office of National Statistics.

ONS (2013) *What Does the 2011 Census Tell Us about Older People?* London: Office of National Statistics. Available at: www.ons.gov.uk/ons/dcp171776_325486.pdf.

Pearson, M. (2015) We all know about dementia but the lives of the most vulnerable make for sobering reading. *Conversation Online*. Available at: https://theconversation.com/we-all-know-about-dementia-but-the-lives-of-the-most-vulnerable-make-for-sobering-reading-44605, accessed 28 August 2015.

Ramesh, R. (2013) Interview with Chris Hopson: The NHS could keel over in 2016. *Guardian*, 7 August. Available at: www.theguardian.com/society/2013/aug/07/chris-hopson-nhs-keel-over-2016.

Sanders, E.B.-N. and Stappers, P.J. (2008) Co-creation and the new landscapes of design. *CoDesign*, 4(1): 5–18.

Simmons, S.F., Durkin, D.W., Rahman, A.N., Choi, L., Beuscher, L. and Schnelle, J.F. (2013) Resident characteristics related to the lack of morning care provision in long-term care. *Gerontologist*, 53(1): 151–61.

Stickdorn, M. (2012) *This Is Service Design Thinking*. Amsterdam: BIS Publishers.

Themessl-Huber, M., Hubbard, G. and Munro, P. (2007) Frail older people's experiences and use of health and social care services. *Journal of Nursing Management*, 15(2): 222–9.

Tomaka, J., Thompson, S. and Palacios, R. (2006) The relation of social isolation, loneliness, and social support to disease outcomes among the elderly. *Journal of Aging and Health*, 18(3): 359–84.

Triggle, N. (2012) The changing NHS. Available at: www.bbc.co.uk/news/health-19721977, accessed 20 October 2014.

Wanless, D. (2004). *Securing Good Health for the Whole Population*. London: HMSO.

Wanless, D., Appleby, J., Harrison, A. and Patel, D. (2007) *Our Future Health Secured? A Review of NHS Funding and Performance*. London: King's Fund.

17 Products

Negotiating design within sceptical territory: lessons from healthcare

Alastair S. Macdonald

Abstract

Recent co-design initiatives demonstrate successful healthcare innovation and improvement without the need for designers, potentially problematising design's legitimacy in and contribution to this sector. In arguing the case for design, the author explores design's value in the healthcare research domain, where the randomised controlled trial is regarded as the gold standard for scientific evidence. Two case studies are presented, one of the development of a visual tool for stroke rehabilitation, the other of a food-management and nutrition-monitoring system, describing design's contributions within larger multidisciplinary healthcare research teams. These illustrate the value of designers' methods in generating visual narratives and physical prototypes and their role in simultaneously eliciting and embodying particular forms of evidence while making progress in providing a tangible and interactive glimpse of the future.

Introduction

Designing in healthcare settings

Designers working in the healthcare setting could adopt a number of positions. Contrasting three, they could: i) act as sole designers, consulting as required; ii) involve and empower other, non-designers, to design alongside themselves, thereby extending the design team; iii) relinquish their own involvement, provide the tools and processes they use and let others, i.e. non-designers, get on with the designing.

Donetto et al. (2014) summarise the achievements of a decade's work in improving patient experiences in healthcare settings, first planned for and piloted in a head and neck cancer service at Luton and Dunstable NHS hospital in England (Bate and Robert, 2007) in a model that has come to be known as experience-based co-design (EBCD). What is significant about EBCD is the scale of uptake in the healthcare community over the decade since that first pilot, across several countries, the accessibility, usability and adaptability of the tools and processes to local requirements and resources by non-specialists, the value of that critical mass in developing and reporting case studies to share experiences and outcomes, the continuous improvements to tools and the finely calculated economic benefits. More recently this work has led to the development of a more cost-effective 'accelerated' form of EBCD (Locock et al., 2014).

What is interesting about EBCD is that we can witness an approach and process almost exclusively conducted without the involvement of professionally trained designers. We can witness the logical conclusion of the desire for the democratisation of design reflected in recent discussions which develop the understanding of design from one of a practice comprising activities which were once regarded solely as those of the 'professional' (e.g. industrial) designer providing a 'solution' to a problem to the point where design is seen as a 'distributed social accomplishment' (Kimbell, n.d.) where 'stakeholders are co-designers and designers are another kind of stakeholder' (Kimbell, 2009). EBCD pushes this further: designers are not stakeholders in this form of co-design. This appears to be 'designing without designers', arguably a truly democratised form of designing which doesn't require designers *per se* any longer. Should designers rejoice?

This EBCD phenomenon seems to have made significant progress in a manner that may make many designers feel uncomfortable. However, are external, professional designers the best people to be designing within healthcare? Or, are those whom Sanders (2001) defines as the 'real virtuosos', with their deep insights and expertise derived from delivering and experiencing its services, best placed to identify and address issues from within? The evidence from EBCD's *grand projet* appears to suggest that the healthcare professionals and patients involved can do a pretty good job without designers. It is not only from healthcare that we face this attitude. Siodmok (2014) reinforces this point with respect to the use of design-led approaches in government policymaking, stating that: 'Design is too important to be left to designers', citing three reasons why: '90% of design decisions are not made by designers… designers are not the only source of creativity, ingenuity and innovation… ideas are not the only problem… ideas are everywhere… the difficulty is in making them happen' (Siodmok, 2014). This leaves us facing such questions as, is this 'mission accomplished' for design? Is EBCD a form of democratised design legacy? Is there any longer a role for designers and, if so, what might their contribution be?

One easy win in this discussion would be to cite the more traditional product design engineering model with its highly practised range of expertise in healthcare equipment or device design, concerned with the combination of expertise in usability, ergonomics, aesthetics, interaction design, materials specification, component packaging and manufacturability, etc., but we might also have to concede that often the initial ideas for innovations can come from the clinicians and practitioners themselves. But maintaining our focus on co-design, which is defined by Donetto et al. (2014: 45), as 'a complex social intervention whose impacts and outcomes are difficult to evaluate and cannot be reduced solely to the design solutions it generates', can we see different kinds of effects and outcomes if designers are involved in co-design within healthcare?

Despite the substantial growth of interest in – and practice of – design involvement in the healthcare sector, one commentator claims that design: 'does not yet fit into the conventional clinical organisation, and institutional practices have not established meaningful positions for design' (Jones, 2013: xv). 'Healthcare as a domain is strongly influenced by scientific tradition and evidence-based practices. Designers will be expected to understand and adapt to the domain rather than the language of design and user experience' (2013: 17). But already EBCD, working from within the healthcare system, seems to refute this as its practice uses narrative-based techniques to elicit experience as a platform for co-design activity, rather than more 'scientific' types of evidence. The EBCD project provides many examples where experience has been used as the basis for co-designing successful and cost-effective improvements to services and patient and staff experiences ranging from those which are small-scale to those which are more process design-oriented (Locock et al., 2014). However, having raised the spectre of the potential redundancy of designers' involvement in the healthcare setting it is now incumbent on this author to argue the contrary case.

Jones' (2013) statement above raises the interesting issue of the scientific tradition and what is regarded as evidence in its practices. This takes us into the realm of the randomised controlled trial (RCT), regarded as the 'gold-standard' for evidence. Macdonald and Robert (2014) have stated that 'the findings of RCTs or the mandating of quality improvements often do not sit comfortably with the complexities of daily life within a healthcare organisation'. Therefore, can we reconcile some of the tensions of the scientific tradition and the complexities of daily life by exploring ways of integrating, e.g., 'gold-standard' evidence-based approaches fundamental to scientific legitimacy and judgement-making in the biomedical sciences tradition with the more socially oriented concerns and narrative-driven evidence of the user experience, by identifying and exploiting a legitimate contribution from designers?

The issues and questions raised above are now explored in two case studies of collaborative research and development conducted by the author and colleagues, where design approaches and methods were introduced and integrated into the overarching research methodologies of multidisciplinary teams concerned with developing innovative healthcare interventions.

Case study 1: physical rehabilitation following stroke

Introduction

This first case study is essentially concerned with discussing two separate but interrelated issues: 1) the integration of qualitative methods and a participative co-design approach into a traditional RCT design; and 2) the different approaches to evidencing the effect of a novel prototype visual method, co-developed within the trial design, as an aspect of a complex intervention, for its efficacy in improving the experience and outcomes of rehabilitation following stroke through a set of Phase II RCTs (exploratory) as defined by the MRC and following MRC guidelines for the evaluation of complex interventions (Craig et al., 2008).

The development and evaluation of the visual method has been described previously in some detail (Loudon et al., 2012, 2014). Briefly, the visual method uses motion-capture and motion-sensor technologies to provide data which are visualised onto a prototype virtual mannequin of the patient in ways that allow real-time visual feedback of movements and communication of complex biomechanical data associated with body and limb movements in an accessible manner for both stroke patient and therapist (Figure 17.1).

The problem/issue

The biomechanical concepts of human movement, e.g. forces, moments, angles, velocity and acceleration, although important to assist in improving physical rehabilitation, are ones which the general public and most health professionals, including therapists, understand poorly. The formats used for representing these concepts and biomechanical data have been the sole preserve of biomedical engineers. Consequently, despite almost 40 years of research, biomedical engineers had been unable to represent this data in a format largely usable by anyone outside their own discipline, particularly by rehabilitation therapists or by their patients. These therapists and patients had not been involved in the processes of either the formats of the presentation of data or the design of the interventions. As a consequence, clinicians had to assess patients' movements by eye despite the inaccuracies and missed observations caused by such an approach, with patients having their problems explained to them verbally or using less-than-ideal methods such as mirrors, tables or graphs, or sometimes through video.

Figure 17.1 One of the visual tools developed for the 'lower limb stroke' feasibility trial showing a visually correct target angle indicated by a coloured 'fan' scale which moves as the patient moves.
The patient has to lift their leg sufficiently to enter the coloured zone and this angle can be
customised for each individual and for each stage in the rehabilitation process

Source: © envisage, 2012

Biomechanical preoccupations

Naturally, biomedical engineers have tended to be preoccupied with quantitative biomechanical
metrics, e.g. in a patient's manner of walking (gait), speed, step length, symmetry of steps while
walking, angles of movement of limbs and with the various forces exerted during dynamic
movement. This is illustrated clearly in the primary and secondary outcome measures that
were used to evaluate if the use of the visual interventions improved outcomes in the three
stroke trials in this study. For example, in the lower limb stroke trial the outcomes measured,
in each participant, the differences in the walking velocity, step length, spatial symmetry and
temporal symmetry between baseline and post-intervention assessments.

Utilitarian use of designers?

The biomedical engineer's interests, as project lead, in inviting designers into the core team
was to exploit their novel visual method, prototyped and developed in previous work, to
visually present biomechanical data and information in a user-accessible manner for the
RCTs. This involvement of the designers could perhaps be seen as 'utilitarian', due to the
method's potential for improving outcomes evaluated through quantitative metrics familiar
to the biomedical field as defined above. A further attractor here was the designers' use of a
participative co-design approach to guide the further development of the prototype visual
tools to the versions used as interventions in the RCTs.

Quantitative outcomes

Had the use of traditional biomedical engineering quantitative outcome metrics prevailed as the sole method of data acquisition and analysis in these trials, as might have been the norm in an RCT design of this nature, the in-depth experiences of the stroke survivors and therapists and what was important to *them*, as distinct from what was important to the biomedical engineers, would not have been understood. For example, it was reported in the findings of the lower limb trial that 'All groups demonstrated improvements in most parameters, with changes in spatial and temporal symmetry being relatively small' (Thikey et al., 2014). The statistics in the tables of the findings of the other two stroke trials bear out similar preoccupations with these types of quantitative outcomes (Carse et al., 2014; Jones et al., 2014), whereas discussion and analysis of 'experience', although acknowledged, is limited to short statements such as, 'Importantly, all experimental participants were able to engage with the virtual avatar and expressed that they found it useful to see how they moved' (Thikey et al., 2014).

The requirement for mixed methods

Lewin et al. (2009) highlight the importance of integrating qualitative processes into quantitative trials: 'Complex healthcare interventions involve social processes that can be difficult to explore using quantitative methods alone… Qualitative research can support the design of interventions and improve understanding of the mechanisms and effects of complex healthcare interventions.' This reminds us of the above definition of co-design by Donetto et al. (2014: 45). In joining this study, the designers, as the originators of the visual prototype and the participative co-design process by which it was – and would be further – developed, required to integrate their own qualitative people-centred methods and processes for the development of the prototype visual interventions into the methodological design of the RCTs. In the design of the overall research methodology, the challenge was to integrate the established 'gold-standard' evidence-based approaches fundamental to judgement making in the biomedical sciences with those more concerned with understanding users' experiences.

A qualitative methodology, described in Macdonald (2014), introduced by the designers, involving interviews, observations and focus groups (Figure 17.2), ensured that patients' and therapists' feedback was considered to assist in the co-development of the intervention before the RCTs and also to improve understanding of the effects of these complex interventions during and after the RCTs. Savory's framework was useful here as it sets out a series of four 'ideal strategies' for 'incorporating PPI [public and professional involvement] into the wider process of translative healthcare research involving technological innovation' (Savory, 2010). This framework helped highlight the different attitudes amongst the research team to PPI and to how patients and professionals were involved. Qualitative methods were adopted in each of the four key phases of the trial: intervention design, pre-trial, during-trial and post-trial phases.

Insights from qualitative data

The capture and analysis of extensive qualitative data throughout the four phases of the RCTs provided explicit insights into the experiences of therapists and stroke survivors. Some of these were elicited by conventional means, such as interviews. Other data were elicited through prototypes. For example, in one of the pre-design stage focus groups, where the designers had produced a number of early-stage visual prototypes to explore what features in these

Figure 17.2 Workshop with stroke survivors providing feedback on pre-trial stage prototype visualisation
tools during their development
Source: © Alastair S. Macdonald, 2011

might be appropriate to them for *their* rehabilitation purposes, on seeing these the stroke survivors likened themselves to 'wounded animals' trying to heal, or of 'feeling like a two year old' learning to walk again, having to go through a transitional phase of readapting to the lack of – or relearning – the functioning of their body. From a therapist's perspective, acknowledging survivors' difficulties with speech, it can be very challenging to establish whether patients have understood the aims of the rehabilitation and what they are being asked to achieve. Strategies normally adopted at this time include physical prompts, diagrams and verbal prompts as it is crucial that the patient understands what is being asked of them. These early visual prototypes, as could be evidenced, generated different kinds of responses through patients seeing representations of themselves and their condition in a potentially new 'future' tool for rehabilitation.

The study's findings (Macdonald et al., 2013) suggest that visualisation software can be used in the context of stroke rehabilitation with benefit to both patients and therapists and that through the visualisations: survivors better understand the key aspects of their rehabilitative tasks; an interactive rehabilitation environment is created whereby both patient and therapist are able to communicate and discuss key issues and progress; the visualisation of the patient's own motion provides an aid to their understanding of their movement problems and the purpose of their rehabilitation tasks; the visual representation of the movement and the overlay of specific measures relevant to their rehabilitation provides a medium for improved communication between the patient and the therapist; and the combination of quantitative measurement and clear visual representation of the measures provides an objective tool for therapists to monitor progress and communicate it to patients.

The question of whether these kinds of results could have been achieved without the involvement of designers and their iterative prototyping method is returned to in the Discussion section.

Case study 2: monitoring nutrition in older hospital patients

Introduction

This second study discusses the development, through a participative co-design process, of an innovative technology-based system for addressing issues of malnutrition in older hospital patients. Briefly, the proposed system enables the recording of a person's daily nutritional intake against a series of personalised daily targets set for protein, calories, nutrients and fluids, prompting the system to alert food managers and ward staff to deliver extra foods and fluids as appropriate if these daily targets are in danger of not being met. The system was iteratively developed through a narrative-generating and prototyping process, starting with paper mock-ups derived from earlier evidence-eliciting stages, finally as a demonstration prototype assessed through a heuristic peer-evaluation process from feedback at a series of conference seminars and exhibitions rather than, as in case study 1, through RCTs. The description of the development and evaluation of the system has been described previously in some detail (Macdonald et al., 2012; Comber et al., 2012; Moynihan et al., 2012; Thompson et al., 2014).

The problem and current preoccupations

The alarming scale of malnutrition in hospitals, particularly amongst older patients, provides the context here. The current situation is predominantly one of a totally inadequate 'one-size-fits-all' meal provision service, currently a complex agglomeration of imperfect systems, often with conflicting interests, out of sync with one another, fragmented by a task-driven mentality, a limited awareness of the total system and with no workable way of monitoring the nutrition intake of patients, each of whom has their own individual requirements for calories, protein, nutrients and fluid intake. Isolated interventions, such as 'protected mealtimes' (to prevent the disturbing of patients by clinical staff) and 'red trays' (to identify nutritionally at-risk patients) had been found ineffective in addressing this problem which had traditionally been seen as one involving the expertise of nutritionists, dietitians, food scientists and front-line ward staff (i.e. those largely concerned with identifying patients at risk and their individual nutritional requirements). The urgency of addressing this issue had been recognised to the extent that this research was commissioned through a special competitive ageing nutrition call, part of whose brief suggested the application of innovative technologies might assist in addressing this problem. In this case, design formed one of the core investigating disciplines, attractive due to its co-design, visualisation and prototyping competencies.

A collaborative approach

Because of the very fragmented nature of the current system and the diverse roles and tasks of all those involved in it, it was essential that everyone was brought together through a participative co-design and co-development process. This involved a 'food family' (FF), i.e. those concerned with nutrition, food production, food supply, delivery and catering, as well as ward staff, nurses, physicians, speech and occupational therapists. It also involved key stakeholders (KS) from groups such as the UK's NHS and older people representatives. These were all engaged, in various configurations, in a series of workshops and events over the duration of the project, from the mapping of existing systems to the iterative process of creation and refinement of the new prototype system. As it was a multidimensional project it also included the development of new food and drink products.

Narratives, mock-ups and prototypes

In the course of the development of the proposed prototype system, two principal narrative forms emerged. Both required developing a 'commons', a space where 'individuals bound by a common cause… a dynamic organization of individuals and groups formed by the desire to address an issue' (Le Dantec and DiSalvo, 2013) could tackle this work, as well as the means – the 'infra-structuring' (Björgvinsson et al., 2012), to enable the collective mobilisation of the FF and KS who were essentially co-opted into the design team.

The first narrative form related to the status quo prompted by, e.g., visual mapping of food journeys and the pre-preparation, preservation, storage and reheating of meals, and also understanding the patients' and ward staff's experiences of mealtimes. Various tools were designed for use to engage the KS and FF to help elicit and assemble their fragmented knowledge, insights and experiences to build, from the evidence, the 'big picture' in easily sharable visual formats. These tools took a variety of forms, mostly graphical mapping and visual prompts, to allow for a collective discussion and verification of the current system.

The second narrative form was very much a consequence of stimulating thinking through a number of activities using a range of mock-ups and low-resolution to more refined prototypes about how the experiences, insights and expertise of the FF and KS could be shaped into an improved and workable system taking advantage of new technologies, part of the commissioning brief (Figure 17.3). These narratives were made manifest through an iterative co-prototyping process, 'bringing into being' this innovative (yet still hypothetical) system as a means of opening up, discussing and experiencing the possibility, in a very tangible way, that things could be quite different. These narratives were multidimensional. From the patient's perspective the narrative, supported by the prototypes, helped understand, e.g., how the service presented itself through an easy-to-understand and easy-to-use interface in welcoming him/her and in presenting and assisting in the selection of meal options. From the ward nurse's perspective, this was about, e.g., how the system ensured that food intakes met each individual's daily targets, so here the narratives and prototypes explored what role the various service elements and technologies could play in helping to plan for and respond to a patient's nutritional needs and to enable monitoring of intake. Similarly, this allowed a catering manager to, e.g., keep track of the inventory and particular dietary needs. This set of narratives was iteratively developed, in text form initially, then through story-board scenarios and brought back to the FF and KS for comment. A further stage was the version which appeared in the touring exhibition of the prototype and which appeared on the animation video on the website. Both narrative forms described above were a form of collective sense-making: the first, of an understanding and critique of the present system; the second, of a preferable, hypothetical – yet still tangible – future alternative.

Running concurrently and interconnected with the development of this type of narrative was the iterative prototyping process, which was used to probe and explore possible future

Figure 17.3 The food family and key stakeholders compiling an early narrative for a new food-
        management and nutrition-monitoring system
Source: © Alastair S. Macdonald, 2009

territory. The use of mock-ups and prototypes gave permission to ask the kinds of questions about how to proceed – 'if we used this, could it be like this or that…?' or 'if we had this…?' allowed wrong turns and dead ends to be identified early and to allow progress in a more productive direction. Here, prototyping took a number of forms. An improvised form of service prototyping involved building and enacting a simple system, using low-resolution prototype materials for ideas that were generated during workshop activities (such as mock-ups of interactive screens, food menus and food trays), and testing this through role playing. In contrast, a 'mini-meals' trolley, which formed part of the total system, was developed as a full-scale prototype, from initial computer-aided design concepts, evaluated for its thermodynamic performance in keeping different foods at different temperatures, and for ergonomic performance by the FF in a dedicated workshop.

The core of the proposal was a smart monitoring and management system comprising software and interfaces, including patient- and staff-facing interactive screens used for presenting food menu options, recording individual food intake and monitoring progress – against an individual's needs – towards daily nutritional targets. A 'wipe-away' food-monitoring app using a photo of the meal linked to a smart nutritional database on the patient's bedside touch-screen terminal was also developed. Initially built by team members as a tablet-based mock-up (Figure 17.4), this was then worked up as an Android prototype for testing with

Figure 17.4 Making tangible the interactive system through a working tablet mock-up for one of the
key stakeholders (older person representative)
Source: © Cate Gillon, 2011

the FF and KS. This was further developed, as a large touch-screen version, externally, due to
the sophistication of the data and screens which required to be included for the 'public' version touring to conference meetings of gerontology, design, nutrition, geriatric medicine and
hospital-catering societies. Again, the question of whether these kinds of results could have
been achieved without the involvement of designers and their particular tools and methods
is discussed below.

Discussion

In the Introduction a case was suggested by this author that, due to the reported evidence
and positive outcomes of the EBCD *grand projet*, designers might appear – to some – to be
sceptically regarded as largely redundant in healthcare-related co-design, leaving this author
the challenge of identifying a legitimate case for designers to be involved in the co-design and
co-development of healthcare-related interventions and innovations. As far as this author can
determine there is no other programme of the scale and durability as EBCD being promoted
in the name of 'design' within healthcare and which is able to be replicated in and adapted
to so many different settings by independent groups, while demonstrating economic benefit
alongside service innovation and improved patient and professional experience. This represents
not only a significant achievement for EBCD but also a significant challenge for designers,
more so when various techniques in co-design, regarded by some designers as belonging to

their own design lexicon, are considered by proponents of EBCD as better conducted by non-designers:

> I am less convinced of the unique or added-value of 'designers' in the relational work needed to underpin co-design. We have always managed to find fantastic facilitators of these processes within NHS organizations with a combination of ideal skill sets and professional (typically nursing) knowledge (and not to mention positional authority)... but less so as facilitators of the whole process from start to end (not least because many of [designers'] skills (seems to me at least) are duplicating those of staff in healthcare organizations already but also because I think lots of the benefits of EBCD would be lost if external designers 'hold the ring' – I'm thinking of personal development for NHS staff, staff engagement & ownership and the broader, cultural benefits I think EBCD can engender.
>
> (Robert, 2015)

As a concession, EBCD proponents have identified stages in the co-design process where designers may have a distinct, albeit limited, value and contribution: 'I guess I'm saying yes to seeing a real potential benefit to involving professional designers at the latter stages of an EBCD project (but struggling to see how to make that happen at scale)' (Robert, 2015).

There are points here this author can also concede and which might provide a stark reminder of the need to clearly articulate which deep skills lie truly within design's specialist lexicon and which skills are shared across other disciplines.

To recap, two case studies were presented above, one of the development of a visual tool for stroke rehabilitation, the other of a food-management and nutrition-monitoring system, describing the design team's approaches and contributions within larger multidisciplinary healthcare research groups. They illustrate the designers' intention to use design as 'a set of practices aimed at realising a certain desirable future' (Storni, 2013), to generate narrative forms and prototypes within a 'commons' (Le Dantec and DiSalvo, 2013), through designing situations, activities and materials, i.e. 'infrastructuring' (Björgvinsson et al., 2012) to engage all involved. What the author hopes to illustrate through the two cases cited here is the distinctive design contribution and its value in both simultaneously eliciting and embodying particular forms of evidence (through quantitative and qualitative data) while making progress in providing a tangible and interactive glimpse of the near future. With reference to this chapter's introductory discussion there are instructive lessons emerging from these studies, explored further here.

Case study 1: stroke rehabilitation

In case study 1, pre-trial interviews with both therapists and stroke survivors followed prior glimpses of early visualisation prototypes prompting discussion of how and in what ways to proceed to benefit patients in therapy. Examples of the therapists' narratives of the imagined future benefits can be found in Ballinger et al. (2016). These are borne out in the findings from the trials themselves. Throughout the four stages of the RCT, the role and effect of the visual prototypes is evident, i.e. the process by which these were iteratively co-developed and how these prompted and mediated types of discourse which would not have been possible using more conventional qualitative methods such as interviews, filmed narratives and focus groups. The rehabilitation session may have been regarded previously by the biomedical engineering community in research of this type as a largely 'clinical/technical' challenge to restore function and, from a research perspective, of how to collect, measure and present quantitative biomechanical data to use with the patient to help achieve correct movement: trials and their interventions would be designed on this basis. However, once one starts acquiring the type of qualitative data captured during the development and use of the prototype visualisation tools, it becomes evident that the rehabilitation session is as much an intensely social as a technical challenge. During the design and pre-trial phases of the RCT, the nature – and various iterations of – the prototype visualisation tools came to be understood, by this author, as being *simultaneously* technical and social in nature. The visual interventions proved not only to be a technical mediator in assisting therapists and patients to respectively communicate and understand correct posture, movements and progress but also a social mediator, acknowledging and responding to the patients' and therapists' needs for clearer mutual communication and understanding, as a consequence reducing the social and technical distance between these players. Captured here is a form of evidence different to that of interest to the biomedical engineer, rich not only in the instrumental narrative of therapist-with-patient trying to achieve correct movement, but of how the patient and therapist actually converse and interact during rehabilitation sessions. Clearly evidenced also is the underlying narrative of individuals' disrupted lives, their wells of emotions, hopes and aspirations, the frustrated communications and the expressions of achievement and disappointment – the real challenges, experiences and complexities of their daily lives – all of which may affect the efficacy of any intervention if these factors are not acknowledged within a trials context. This work integrates both a scientifically 'legitimate' evidence-based approach together with a narrative-generated experience-based approach. This is an outcome prompted by the visual prototypes; what these do is allow one to not only imagine, but to tangibly witness and experience the possibility of how different the rehabilitation setting and session could be, and collect evidence on its benefits.

Case study 2: nutrition

Unlike the setting of the stroke rehab therapy session, in which there was an intimate correspondence between the stroke survivor (and perhaps their carer), the therapist and the clinical lead, the series of evolving case study 2 prototypes collated and embodied the collective insights, experiences and expertise of its many stakeholders currently working in a highly fragmented system and proposed a way of making a coherent sense of this through (eventually) a feasible electronic solution which located the care of the patient at its centre. They also provoked, from initial paper mock-ups through to the more advanced elements of the demonstration prototype, conversations between the many different stakeholder communities about what would work or not, eventually about what would make such a system possible and workable. Prototyping offered a tangible and interactive glimpse of a preferable and hypothetically workable solution. The iterative prototyping process provided a means of mobilising collective will and stimulated new kinds of conversations and ideas, many of which are recorded in the end-of-project and impact reports for this work and the many outputs produced by the team (ESRC, 2013).

Beyond research, towards implementation

Both cases describe innovations dependent on existing but not fully exploited technologies. In case study 1, such a system has become feasible, technologically and economically, since the first prototypes were developed over a decade ago. For case study 2, progressing the food-management and nutrition-monitoring prototype into an implementable system was beyond the resources available for this exploratory developmental project. For either to progress, there would still be the very real issues of, e.g., feasibility trials and, if successful, scalability. At a pragmatic level, there would be challenges of the integration of these innovations with current software systems and platforms while negotiating all the attendant issues such as 'platform fatigue' (Jones, 2013: 19), i.e. the learning of new interfaces and new procedures for accessing and logging into multiple systems, together with the problematics of dysfunctional interfaces (Naughton, 2014).

A case for design?

Would it be essential for designers to be included in teams to develop the types of solutions proposed in the two cases above? The author hopes a convincing argument has begun to be made, illustrated by examples of the deep and distinctive expertise required to develop the two solutions presented. The iterative and participative manner of prototype development both elicited and cumulatively embodied 'evidence' into tangible and interactive solutions. Siodmok (2014), while acknowledging that the context of his discussion is with regards to the use of prototyping in policymaking, states: 'to prototype generates imperfect truths but with the right approach it also generates data about the future' and also 'evidence of what works and, more importantly, what does not, can be very powerful'. Siodmok acknowledges that prototyping is not a widely used term (in policymaking) and that this kind of practical tool and the lab in which to explore this is in its infancy. At the time of writing, an examination of the EBCD toolkit on the King's Fund website provides no guidance on prototyping, only providing methods more familiar to qualitative research, e.g. interviews, filming, focus groups, and 'brainstorming' sessions.

Coughlan et al., citing cases of the effectiveness of rapid prototyping in the healthcare setting, discuss the value of prototyping in such terms as: 'building to think', 'giving permission to explore new behaviors, relieving individuals of the responsibility to consciously change what they do', 'in a nonthreatening, low-risk way', as 'learning tools', to 'learn quickly', 'to explore and communicate propositions', 'tangible, created so everyone can grasp the idea', 'as "transitional objects"… objects that support a change from a current behavior to a new behavior' (Coughlan et al., 2007). Similarly, Sanders and Stappers discuss designers' ability to 'make things that describe future objects' stating that 'making is a significant activity for designers' citing how prototyping can play a number of roles and how, e.g., 'in making, people can bring their insights to the surface', 'allow the testing of a hypothesis' and because prototyping 'allows people to experience a situation that did not exist before' (2014: 6).

Integrating evidence-based research and experience-based design

Hagen (2014) calls for the bringing together of 'user experience design and participatory approaches with the evidence-based models which traditionally underpin health promotion, intervention and treatment', identifying differences and challenges in integrating these two approaches. Certainly case study 1 explores this territory and highlights the differences and tensions between the medical-scientific approach evidencing the biomedical outcomes alongside the more psychosocially oriented approach evidencing the engagement, two-way communication and shared understanding from the qualitative data. Both cases used prototype methods, building to think with, to elicit new narratives and to understand effects and, as Hagen acknowledges, 'which perspective [i.e. experience or evidence] has greatest influence can shift depending on the context of the intervention'. Hagen goes on to say (within the context of a discussion of mental health): 'Being able to enrich the application of medical models... through an understanding of people's everyday lived experiences... as well as their behaviours around technology, greatly increases our chances of building products and services that will actually be used and have impact.'

Mutual collaboration?

To be clear, this discussion is not one pitting a preferred social model against a scientific biomedical model as clearly the value, indeed necessity, of integrating the two are acknowledged in discussions of both cases above. Both provide an opportunity, as Parker and Parker (2007, cited in Carr et al., 2011: 13) state, in arguing the case of integrating evidence-based design and experience-based approaches in healthcare, of 'completely redesigning the script and modes of interaction between services and people'. Nor, to be equally clear, is this an argument against EBCD, which has evidenced significant results by exploiting and mobilising latent design capability amongst non-designers and using forms of adapted design methods and tools, along with others, in its online toolkit.

However, despite their separate achievements, and rather than using only those methods and tools largely familiar to – and comfortable for – their respective communities, it is this author's contention that EBCD-based practitioners and non-EBCD-allied designers could mutually benefit by exploring together their respective strengths and limitations. On the one hand EBCD-based practitioners could capitalise more on designers' skills in using prototyping and visual methods both as a means to conduct research and make tangible a greater range and type of possible near-future solutions than appear to be currently generated using EBCD. On the other hand, non-EBCD-allied designers could accommodate less frequently encountered notions of scalability, adaptability, repeatability and rigour in evaluation. Clearly concessions and adjustments are required on both sides but the common ground has already begun to be been explored by Robert and Macdonald (2017) citing, within a larger discussion, a case study of each of their respective approaches to developing complex interventions within RCTs.

Conclusions

What remains? As far as lessons for design, as highlighted earlier, EBCD, through its significant achievements, throws design a set of challenges it should note and address. One is the scale and durability of EBCD's *grand projet* which, with its every new project, offers EBCD the opportunity of demonstrating its ability to be replicated in and adapted to different environments with different problems, a key principle to establishing legitimacy within healthcare: 'Replication, not only collaborative parallel studies but also independent replication, is needed to understand generalizability of findings' (Fanelli, cited in van der Steen and Goodman, 2015). EBCD has demonstrated this kind of viability and legitimacy through a programme of sustained innovation, accumulated evidence and costed improvement. This ability for replication may perhaps be part of what Jones refers to, when he states that 'designers will be expected to understand and adapt to the domain rather than the language of design and user experience' (Jones, 2013: 17). Design in healthcare involving designers has no such programme to match this. Is a programmatic approach covering a series of related studies required, by design, to build legitimacy, to avoid duplication and one-off, standalone studies, many of which are currently poorly reported and lack robust evaluation – in healthcare terms, an issue identified in Chamberlain et al. (2015: 52)?

Marsh (2010), in a discussion referencing Gorb and Dumas' (1987) paper 'Silent Design' where Gorb and Dumas anticipate the 'design without designers' narrative implicit in EBCD, highlights the usefulness of design-led methods, 'within the intangible world of services [which] include techniques to creatively explore ideas through customer or user research' and through 'visualisation methods that designers use to express ideas; and quick low-risk proto-types that help them learn about the best way forward through hands-on experimentation'. But Marsh goes on to say 'design thinking can help silent designers find their voices, as a voice coach might. The singing part, however, is quite a different matter.' Many of these voices have been elicited both through EBCD and more bespoke approaches to design-led healthcare research. The case for making these voices really sing, utilising the added value of the designer's skills and craft in visualising and prototyping, perhaps as one way forward through designers working more closely with the achievements of EBCD, has hopefully begun to be made more convincing here.

Acknowledgements

Case study 1: The envisage project was conducted principally by the University of Strathclyde, the Glasgow School of Art and Glasgow Caledonian University. It was funded by the MRC Lifelong Health and Wellbeing programme, a cross-council initiative in partnership with the UK health departments and led by the MRC. The author acknowledges the contributions of the wider 'envisage' team and all participants: survivors, patients, health professionals and trial leads.

Case study 2: The author acknowledges the contributions of the wider mappmal research team and all participants. The mappmal project was conducted by the Universities of Newcastle and Reading and the Glasgow School of Art in collaboration with Loughborough University. It was funded through the Research Councils' New Dynamics of Ageing Programme led by the ESRC.

References

Ballinger, C., Taylor, A., Loudon, D. and Macdonald, A.S. (2016) Rehabilitation professionals' perceptions of the use of new visualisation software tools with people with stroke. *Disability and Rehab: Assistive Technology*, 11(2): 139–14.

Bate, S.P. and Robert, G. (2007) *Bringing User Experience to Healthcare Improvement: The Concepts, Methods and Practices of Experience-Based Design*. Oxford: Radcliffe Publishing.

Björgvinsson, E., Ehn, P. and Hillgren P.-A. (2012) Design things and design thinking: Contemporary participatory design challenges. *Design Issues*, 28(3): 101–16.

Carr, L., Sangiorgi, D., Büscher, M., Junginger, S. and Cooper, R. (2011) Integrating evidence-based design and experience-based approaches in healthcare service design. *Health Environments Research and Design Journal*, 4(4): 12–33.

Carse, B., Bowers, R.J., Loudon, D., Meadows, B.C. and Rowe, P.J. (2014) Assessing the effect of using biomechanics visualisation software for ankle-foot orthosis tuning in early stroke. *Gait and Posture*, 39(1): S2–S3.

Chamberlain, P., Wolstenholme, D., Dexter, M. and Seals, E. (2015) *The State of the Art of Design in Health: An Expert-Led Review of the Extent of the Art of Design Theory and Practice in Health and Social Care*. Sheffield: Sheffield Hallam University.

Comber, R., Weeden, J., Hoare, J., Lindsey, S., Teal, G., Macdonald, A.S., Methven, L., Olivier, P. and Moynihan, P. (2012) Supporting visual assessment of food and nutrient intake in a clinical care setting. ACM Conference on Human Factors in Computing (CHI'12), 5–12 May. Austin, TX: ACM.

Coughlan, P., Fulton Suri, J. and Canales, K. (2007) Prototypes as (design) tools for behavioral and organizational change: A design-based approach to help organizations change work behaviors. *Journal of Applied Behavioral Science*, 43(1): 122–34.

Craig, P., Dieppe, P., Macintyre, S., Michie, S., Nazareth, I. and Petticrew, M. (2008) Developing and evaluating complex interventions: The new Medical Research Council guidance. *British Medical Journal*, 337: a1655.

Donetto, S., Tsianakas, V. and Robert, G. (2014) *Using Experience-Based Co-design to Improve the Quality of Healthcare: Mapping Where We Are Now and Establishing Future Directions*. London: King's College London.

ESRC (2013) MAPP-MAL: Outputs and impact report details. Available at: www.esrc.ac.uk/my-esrc/grants/RES-354-25-0001/read/outputs/Date/25/1, accessed 13 July 2015.

Gorb, P. and Dumas, A. (1987) Silent design. *Design Studies*, 8(3): 122–84.

Hagen, P. (2014) Integrating user experience and evidence-based approaches to design. Smallfire. Available at: www.smallfire.co.nz/2014/01/25/integrating-user-experience-and-evidence-based-approaches-to-design/, accessed 14 July 2015.

Jones, L., van Wijck, F., Grealy, M. and Rowe, P. (2014) Investigating the feasibility of using visual feedback of biomechanical movement performance in sub-acute upper limb stroke rehabilitation. *Gait and Posture*. 39(1): S48.

Jones, P.J. (2013) *Design for Care*. New York: Rosenfeld.

Kimbell, L. (n.d.) Design practices in design thinking. Available at: www.lucykimbell.com/stuff/DesignPractices_Kimbell.pdf, accessed 13 July 2015.

Kimbell, L. (2009) Beyond design thinking: Design-as-practice and designs-in-practice. Available at: www.lucykimbell.com/stuff/CRESC_Kimbell_v3.pdf, accessed 13 July 2015.

Le Dantec, C.A. and DiSalvo, C. (2013) Infrastructuring and the formation of publics in participatory design. *Social Studies of Science*, 43(2): 241–64.

Lewin, S., Glenton, C. and Oxman, A.D. (2009) Use of qualitative methods alongside randomised controlled trials of complex healthcare interventions: Methodological study. *British Medical Journal*, 339: b3496.

Locock, L., Robert, G., Boaz, A., Vougioukalou, S., Shuldham, C., Fielden J., Ziebland, S., Gager, M., Tollyfield, R. and Pearcey, J. (2014) Testing accelerated experience-based co-design: A qualitative study of using a national archive of patient experience narrative interviews to promote rapid patient-centred service improvement. Southampton: NIHR Journals Library. Available at: www.ncbi.nlm.nih.gov/books/NBK259580/, accessed 13 July 2015.

Loudon, D., Macdonald, A.S., Carse, B., Thikey, H., Jones, L., Rowe, P.J., Uzor, S., Ayoade, M. and Ballie, L. (2012) Developing visualisation software for rehabilitation: Investigating the requirements of patients, therapists and the rehabilitation process. *Health Informatics Journal*, 18(3): 171–80.

Loudon, D., Taylor, A. and Macdonald, A.S. (2014) The use of qualitative design methods in the design, development and evaluation of virtual technologies for healthcare: Stroke case study, in: Ma, M., Jain, L.C. and Anderson, P. (eds), *Virtual and Augmented Reality in Healthcare 1*. Berlin: Springer-Verlag, 371–90.

Macdonald, A.S. (2014) Socio-technical infrastructuring to assist innovation in healthcare technologies, in: Laakso, M. and Ekman, K. (eds), *Proceedings of NordDesign 2014 Conference*. Helsinki: Aalto University, 376–85. Available at: www.designsociety.org/publication/36282/socio-technical_infrastructuring_to_assist_innovation_in_healthcare_technologies.

Macdonald, A.S. and Robert, G. (2014) Reconciling science and art within healthcare service design, in: Sangiorgi, D., Prendiville, A. and Ricketts, A. (eds), *Mapping and Developing Service Design Research in the UK: Final Report 2014*. Lancaster: Imagination, 36–7.

Macdonald, A.S., Teal, G., Bamford, C. and Moynihan, P.J. (2012) Hospitalfoodie: An inter-professional case study of the redesign of the nutritional management and monitoring system for vulnerable older hospital patients. *Quality in Primary Care*, 20(3): 169–77.

Macdonald, A.S., Loudon, D. and Taylor, A. (2013) WP1: Qualitative evaluation of visualisation in stroke rehabilitation. Available at: www.envisagerehab.co.uk/sites/default/files/files/Envisage_WP1_findings.pdf, accessed 13 July 2015.

Marsh, N. (2010) In celebration of 'silent designers'. *Guardian*, 12 March. Available at: www.theguardian. com/service-design/comment-nick-marsh, accessed 27 March 2015.

Moynihan, P., Macdonald, A., Teal, G., Methven, L., Heaven, B. and Bamford, C. (2012) Extending an approach to hospital malnutrition to community care. *British Journal of Community Nursing*, 17(12): 614–21.

Naughton, J. (2014) The NHS's chaotic IT system shows no sign of recovery. *Observer*, 21 December. Available at: www.theguardian.com/technology/2014/dec/21/nhs-it-system-failings-addenbrookes-john-naughton, accessed 27 March 2015.

Parker, S. and Parker, S. (2007) *Unlocking Innovation: Why Citizens Hold the Key to Public Service Reform*. London: Demos.

Robert, G. (2015) Discussion on value of involving designers in EBCD. Personal communication, 23 February.

Robert, G. and Macdonald, A.S. (2017) Design and quality improvement in the healthcare sector: Recognising and reconciling tensions between the 'art' and the 'science', in Sangiorgi, D. and Prendiville, A. (eds), *Designing for Service: Contemporary Issues and Novel Spaces*. London: Bloomsbury.

Sanders, E.B.-N. (2001) Virtuosos of the experience domain. Maketools. Available at: www. maketools.com/articles-papers/VirtuososoftheExperienceDomain_Sanders_01.pdf, accessed 25 January 2015.

Sanders, E.B.-N and Stappers, P.J. (2014) Probes, toolkits and prototypes: Three approaches to making in codesigning. *CoDesign: International Journal of CoCreation in Design and the Arts*, 10(1): 5–14.

Savory, C. (2010) Patient and public involvement in translative healthcare research. *Clinical Governance: An International Journal*, 15(3): 195–7.

Siodmok, A. (2014) Designer policies. *RSA Journal*, 4: 28–9. Available at: www.thersa.org/discover/publications-and-articles/journals/rsa-journal-issue-4-2014/, accessed 25 January 2015.

Storni, C. (2013) Design for future uses: Pluralism, fetishism and ignorance. Proceedings of Nordic Design Research Conference 2013, Copenhagen-Malmö, 9–12 June. Available at: www.nordes.org/opj/index.php/n13/article/view/276, accessed 15 July 2015.

Thikey, H., van Wijck, F., Grealy, M. and Rowe, P.J. (2014) A virtual avatar to facilitate gait rehabilitation post-stroke. *Gait and Posture*, 39(1): S52–S53.

Thompson, J.L., Peace, S., Astell, A., Moynihan, P.J. and Macdonald, A.S. (2014) Food environments: From home to hospital, in A. Walker (ed.), *The New Science of Ageing*. Bristol: Policy Press, 155–79.

van der Steen, J.T. and Goodman, C. (2015) What research we no longer need in neurodegenerative disease at the end of life: The case of research in dementia. *Palliative Medicine*, 29(3): 189–92.

18 Communications

Visual information about medicines for older patients

Karel van der Waarde

Abstract

Situation: People take medicines to cure, to relieve symptoms or to prevent diseases. When people get older, it is likely that more medicines need to be taken to support wellbeing. At the same time, cognitive and physical abilities might diminish, which could make taking medicines an increasingly arduous and challenging task. Most medicines are accompanied by extensive and fairly complex information. Reading, synthesising, understanding and applying written instructions of different medicines will also become increasingly difficult.

Questions: What happens if a patient needs to consider the information that accompanies a simple painkiller? Does the information that is provided with, for example, ibuprofen help to integrate its use into a complex regimen, and does it make allowances for diminishing abilities?

Approach: A collection of European ibuprofen packaging was analysed to evaluate if and how current information relates to both trends. Seventeen patients over 65 years of age were interviewed.

Results: Patients who want to use ibuprofen encounter substantial problems with the information contents and visual design. The main problems relate to difficulties in finding out what ibuprofen is for, deciphering texts, difficulties in applying information to a personal situation, difficulties considering risks and difficulties about establishing the correct dose.

Discussion: There does not seem to be an 'information strategy' that supports people to take medicines. The analysis showed some severe gaps and overlaps in the available information about ibuprofen. This affects the wellbeing of older patients.

Conclusion: There is a need for change in the regulatory framework to accommodate for ageing processes and to make sure that medicines can be taken correctly by older patients. An 'information strategy' that is based on the actions of patients might provide a suitable approach.

Introduction: what is the current situation?

The 'use of medicines by people over a certain age' needs to look at *gerontology* (the study of social, psychological, cognitive and biological aspects of ageing), *healthcare* (all the activities related to patients' wellbeing) and *literacy* (the ability to gain meaning from a critical interpretation of written information (UNESCO, 2005)). Below is a brief and sketchy overview with some of the available data that indicates the scope of the issues.

Gerontology: aspects of ageing

In 2014, in a total population of 506.8 million citizens in Europe, 18.5 per cent is over 65 years of age and 5.1 per cent of that group is over 80 (Eurostat, 2015). These percentages will steadily increase, with a particularly rapid increase in numbers of over 80s. It is likely that there will be about 100 million people over 65 in 2025 of which 30 million people will be over 80 years of age. These figures vary substantially from country to country (Gapminder World, 2015). This variety is caused by a combination of genetic inheritance, individual choices and factors outside the control of individuals (World Health Organization (WHO), 2015: chapter 6).

The practical consequences of the biological reality of ageing are that visual acuity, manual dexterity, and mental abilities might reduce at different rates. Some of the abilities might still be similar to those of a 20-year-old, while others are reduced to an inadequate level. Furthermore, social positions, goals, motivational priorities and preferences change when people get older. The combination of all these factors makes it necessary to take heterogeneity as the main characteristic of ageing: ageing is always dynamic for each individual and it shifts continuously.

The WHO report defines 'healthy ageing' as: 'the process of developing and maintaining the functional ability that enables well-being in older age' (WHO, 2015: 28). The words 'individual' and 'environment' are not mentioned in this definition, but they occur in all the detailed explanations of each of the terms that appear in this definition. The definition makes clear that enabling wellbeing in older age really requires a succinct range of activities that needs to be fully integrated in a society. The WHO report quite rightly suggests that this requires a 'systemic change' (WHO, 2015: 6).

Healthcare: use of medicines

Health – and coping with transforming capacities and changing environments – is an inseparable part of functional ability. Caring for health covers a wide variety of activities ranging from food selection, physical activities and medical care. Medicines – as part of medical care – are an important ingredient of most diagnoses, treatments and preventions of diseases and impairments.

There are accurate figures available about the use of medicines by older people. In Europe, 40 per cent of people aged 65 and over consume between five and nine medicines per week (Eurostat, 2015). There are substantial variations between the different countries. Women take more medicines than men, but this difference disappears for the highest age groups. Education has a clear correlation: people who are higher educated use less medicines. Australian and US data show the same trends. Around two-thirds of Australians over the age of 60 use four or more medicines (Elliott, 2006). And in the United States, 94 per cent of women over 65 took at least one medicine, 23 per cent took at least five prescription drugs and 12 per cent took at least ten medications in the week preceding an interview. The percentages for men over 65 are respectively 91, 44 and 12 per cent (n=2590) (Kaufman et al., 2002). These figures show that it would be rare to find older patients in Europe who don't use several medicines, and even rarer to find people over the age of 60 who use none at all.

People can obtain medicines in Europe in two different ways. Prescription-only medicines can only be acquired through a doctor and pharmacist (in a community or in a hospital). The other category is the 'over-the-counter' medicines, that can be bought without a prescription. There is a third category of 'complementary and alternative products' that can be bought without a prescription. This last category might or might not be included – due to the scientifically unknown status and/or terminology issues – in the statistics mentioned above. Many patients use all three groups at the same time.

Taking different medicines during the day requires the consideration of a personal regimen. Making and understanding these daily schedules can become complex when several medicines need to be taken. Despite this complexity, it is likely that most medicines are taken correctly and are effective as part of a treatment.

However, a substantial number of patients do not take their medicines for a variety of reasons. 'Non-compliance rates' vary from medicine to medicine, but for some medicines the 'not-taking-figure' is as high as 50 per cent (WHO, 2003). The main reasons for non compliance are health illiteracy, forgetfulness, misunderstanding, complex regimes, adverse effects (real or imagined) and reduction or fluctuation of symptoms.

'Not taking medicines' has serious consequences. Medicines cause many more lethal accidents than traffic (non-adherence causes approximately 200,000 premature deaths in Europe per year (Eurostat, 2015)). Between 10 and 45 per cent of medicine costs are ineffective and about 50 per cent of the production of some medicines is wasted (York Health Economics Consortium and School of Pharmacy, University of London, 2010). For individual patients, not taking medicines can be expensive (insurance, additional costs), time-consuming (additional consultations, recovery time) and detrimental for wellbeing.

Literacy: the ability to create meaning from visual information

A substantial number of people have difficulties reading a text in a particular language, either because they have difficulties reading ('low literacy'), have difficulties understanding medical issues ('health literacy') or have difficulties understanding a specific language ('non-native speakers'). The increasing use of screens has added 'digital literacy' to this list.

The Organisation for Economic Co-operation and Development (OECD) defines literacy as 'the ability to understand, evaluate, use and engage with written texts to participate in society, to achieve one's goals, and to develop one's knowledge and potential' (OECD, 2013). The percentages in a society vary substantially according to the definitions and inclusion criteria. As an example, less than 1 per cent of UK citizens are 'illiterate' and around 16 per cent are 'functionally illiterate'.

A comparison of health literacy in eight European countries in 2011 revealed that just under 50 per cent of the 8,000 participants had 'inadequate' or 'problematic' *health literacy*. The report also showed that there are substantial differences between the participating countries (HLS-EU Consortium, 2012). Immigrants and people with a foreign-language background have a significantly lower proficiency. Furthermore, there is a difference in functional literacy between older adults and younger adults.

The data presented in this first section about the increasing elderly population, the increasing use of medicines in combination with a consideration of the changing functional abilities and problematic functional literacy, seem to paint a fairly complex situation. Apart from a common advanced age, there are very few characteristics that older individuals share. The use of medicines is ubiquitous, but the individual needs and abilities vary substantially. The consequences of this variation for individual patients can only be evaluated by considering individual situations in a specific environment.

Visual information about medicines: sources, regulations, developments

In order to take medicines, information is essential. Instructions on how to take them, warnings against potential risks, descriptions of possible positive and negative effects, storage instructions and a description of what a medicine actually does are all required for each medicine.

Sources: more and more information

Since the introduction of European Directive 92/27/EC (1992) most medicines are provided to patients in a standardised combination of 'an outer package', 'an inner package' and a package leaflet. The outer packaging is usually a small cardboard box, the inner package is a blister pack or bottle and the package leaflet is a multiple folded paper sheet or booklet (Figure 18.1). This is applicable to both prescription-only medicines and over-the-counter medicines.

Before a medicine is given to a patient, a pharmacist will add more information. There will be some aural instructions and warnings, and the pharmacist will add printed labels with visual instructions and warnings (Figure 18.2). If a patient receives several medicines at the same time, there will be several printed labels, several aural instructions, several outer packs, several inner packs and several package leaflets (Figure 18.3). Some pharmacists add their own information sheets and brochures, but this depends on the individual pharmacy.

This information changes continuously in both length and visual design. The information on the outer pack frequently changes due to new legal requirements (QR-codes, serialisation numbers, additional warnings). The visual design of medicine packaging is irregularly updated. The amount of information on packaging and in package leaflets has gradually increased into fairly long texts (Wolf et al., 2012). And, depending on the relations with healthcare services and health insurances, cheaper equivalent medicines might be given as a substitute to patients. A consequence is that the information that patients receive about identical medicines might vary substantially both visually and in contents.

A patient has to combine all this information, together with the aural information that is remembered from the consultation with the prescribing doctor, into a usable regimen. Questions like 'which medicine needs to be taken first?', 'which ones do I take with food?' and 'which ones do I only need to take when I notice specific symptoms?' need to be answered. Pharmacists are very helpful, but a lack of time and resources limits their involvement in the design of the daily regimen of individual patients. Fortunately, it is a gradual process that starts with very few medicines and simple regimen schedules. Patients can take time to get used to their medicines. Experienced patients will integrate new medicines into their existing patterns. And if there are questions, there are a range of resources available such as pharmacists, family and the internet.

Legal developments: more and more complex

The information about medicines that appears on the outer package, inner package and package leaflet is strictly regulated. The main aims of the European regulations are to 'safeguard public health' and to 'not hinder the pharmaceutical industry' (Directive 2004/27/EC, 2004, article 4).

The directive prescribes exactly which information must be mentioned on the packaging and the package leaflet. It also stipulates the order (Directive 2004/27/EC, 2004, article 59). In addition, there are product-information templates in 25 languages and guidelines for the writing, design and testing of the information (EMA-QRD, 2015). During the development of information about medicines, this template must be used as a basis. It provides the structure and a number of obligatory sentences and phrases that must be used on every pack and in every leaflet. 'Keep out of the sight and reach of children' and 'Read the package leaflet before use' are examples. A company who wants to market a medicine adds details about a specific medicine to this template. The graphic design of the leaflet is fairly limited. A lot of text must be presented on a fairly small leaflet or booklet. The production requirements – the machines

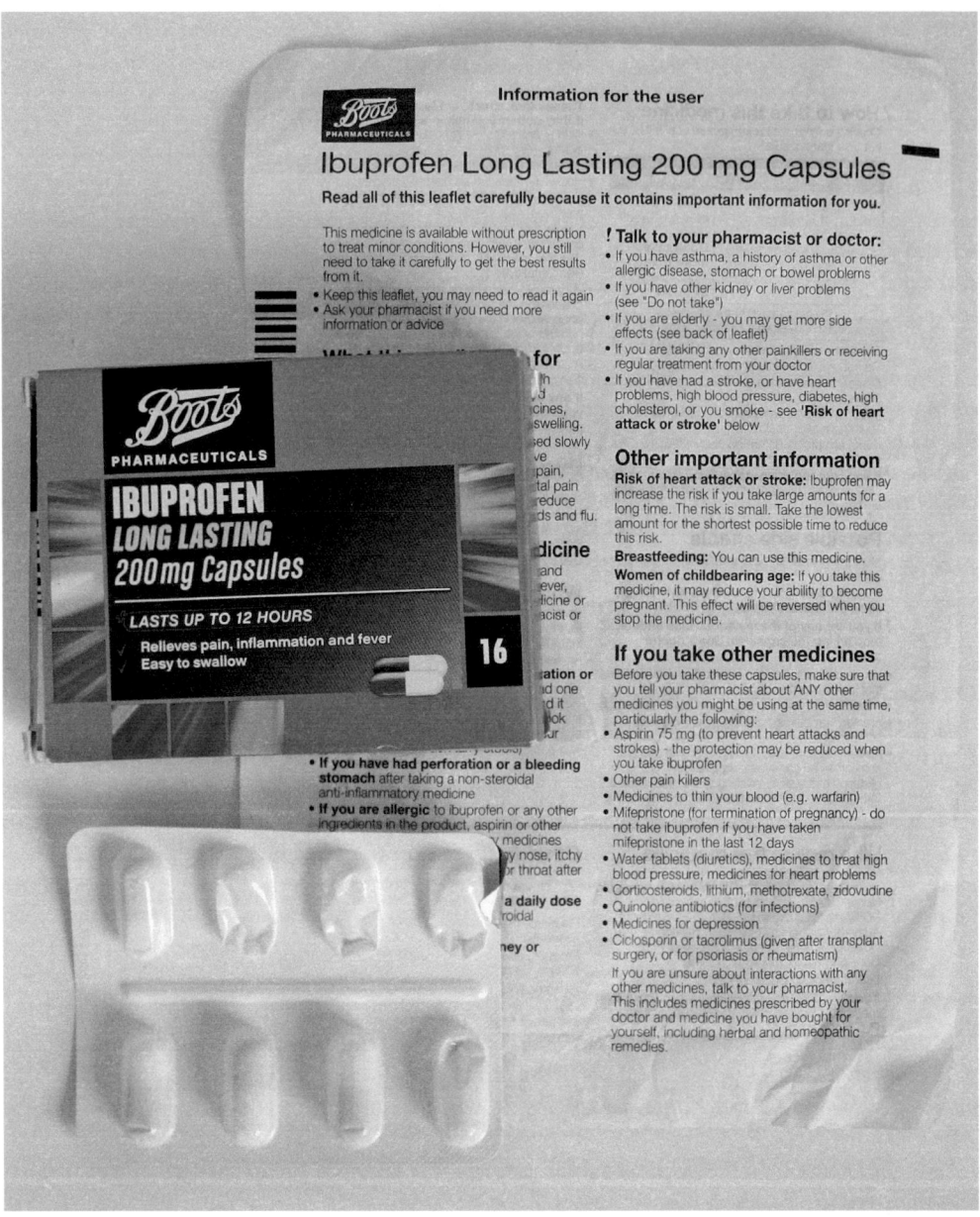

Figure 18.1 Information about ibuprofen in the United Kingdom in 2015: a cardboard box, a leaflet and a blisterpack

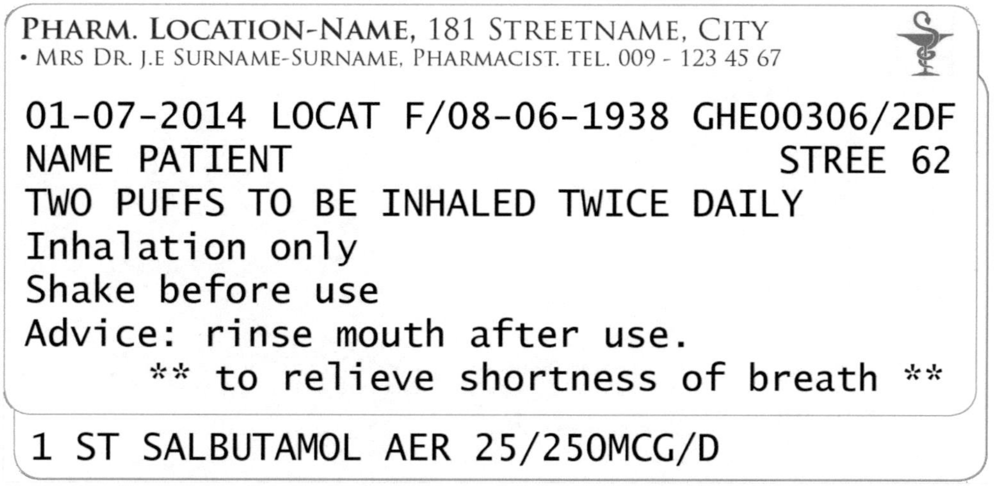

PHARM. LOCATION-NAME, 181 STREETNAME, CITY
• MRS DR. J.E SURNAME-SURNAME, PHARMACIST. TEL. 009 - 123 45 67

01-07-2014 LOCAT F/08-06-1938 GHE00306/2DF
NAME PATIENT   STREE 62
TWO PUFFS TO BE INHALED TWICE DAILY
Inhalation only
Shake before use
Advice: rinse mouth after use.
        ** to relieve shortness of breath **

1 ST SALBUTAMOL AER 25/250MCG/D

Figure 18.2 A pharmacist's label: these are stuck to the outer box of prescription-only medicines to instruct and warn patients. Is the typography and layout suitable for older patients?

that are available – determine the maximum dimensions. And the European legislation also demands that the package leaflet must be tested on a group of patients to make sure that it 'enables the users to act appropriately'. This combination of writing (follow template), design (within production limits) and testing straightjackets the development process into a single standardised mould.

In Europe, the European Medicines Agency and the national regulatory agencies check if the information adheres to the regulations and guidelines. The continuous updates of the legislation, the guidelines and the template demand that both industry and regulatory agencies continuously have to be alert to avoid mistakes. A mistake can be costly and time-consuming. The European Commission is aware that there are 'shortcomings' in the current regulatory framework and that these need to be addressed (Directive 2010/84/EC, 2010, amendment to article 59).

Developments: changing societies and environments

Apart from the increasing amounts of information and the increasing complexity of the regulatory framework, there are other factors that influence the contents and design of information about medicines. The envisaged continuation of the following trends is likely to influence the way that packaging and labelling are produced. These trends are not in any particular order and are likely to occur simultaneously:

• patients are taking a more active role in their treatment;
• the availability of information about medicines on the internet will increase;
• the use of medicines is likely to increase. There will be more medicines, and more people who use more medicines;
• using a combination of different medicines (polypharmacy) will increase;
• internet sales of medicines will increase;

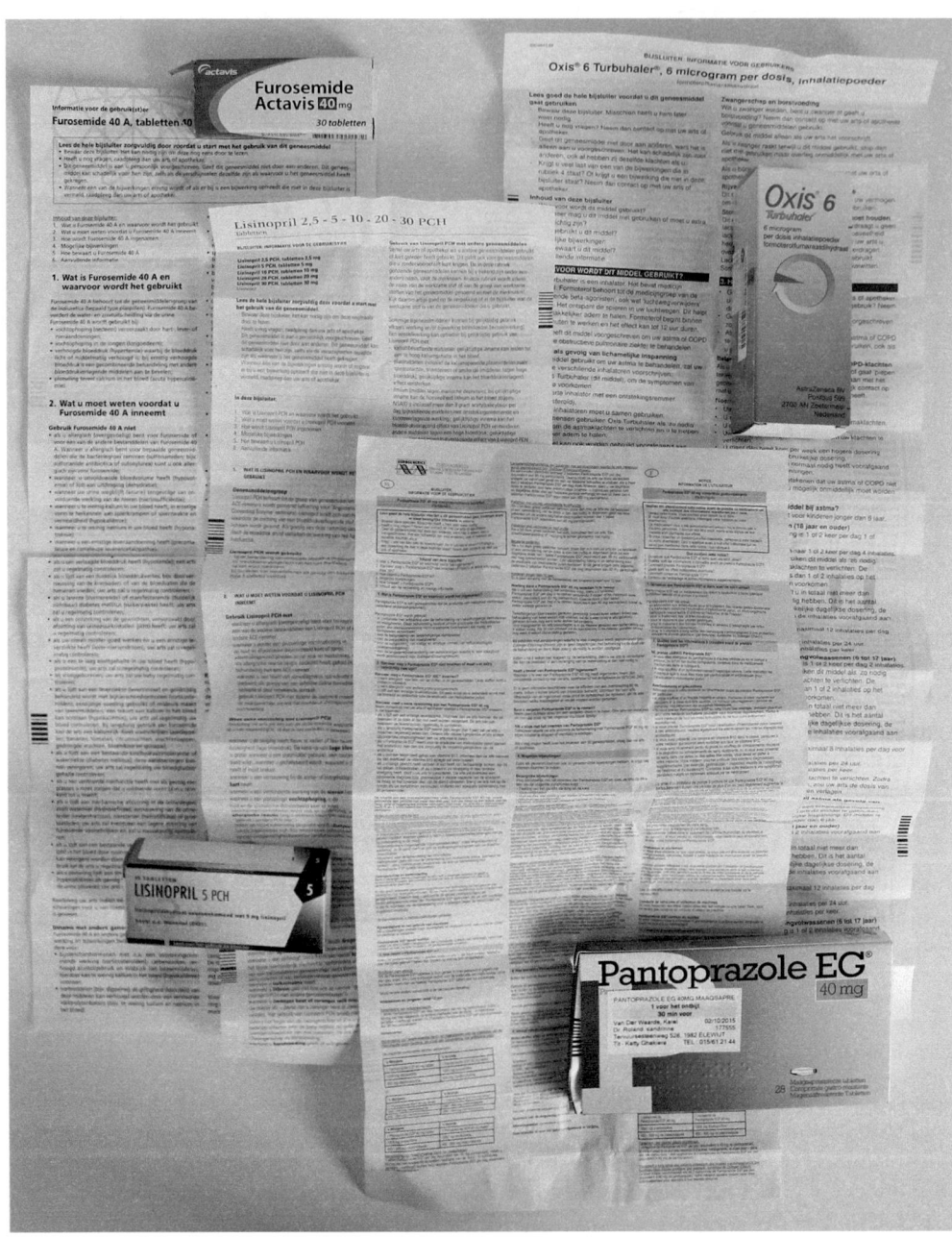

Figure 18.3 The daunting information about four medicines. This patient has asthma, needs to reduce stomach acids, needs to eliminate water and salt and needs to treat high blood pressure. Does the format of these texts help patients to combine these medicines?

- the costs of medicines for patients and for societies (tax and insurance) is likely to increase;
- the internal costs for the pharmaceutical industry to produce packaging and labelling will increase;
- the complexity of the legal framework, including the guidelines, will increase;
- counterfeiting and forgeries of medicines will increase.

None of these are real surprises, and there are already practical actions that anticipate these developments. For example, from 2018 onwards, medicine packaging must be 'tamper evident', which means that it must be possible to see immediately if anyone has tried to open packaging earlier. A second example is the serialisation of all medicine packs by unique identification numbers. Both these developments aim to reduce the risks of counterfeiting and illegal sales of medicines.

The amount of information increases and the visual formats keep changing, the regulatory framework is effective but contains shortcomings and there are many developments outside the pharmaceutical industry and regulations that will influence the ways in which information is provided.

One example: an ibuprofen package

The description in the first two sections provides some background of older patients who need to take medicines. In order to see if factors (diminishing abilities, literacy, personal regimens) are taken into consideration when information about medicines is developed, standard packaging for over-the-counter painkillers was analysed and tested. The research question is:

> Do the contents and design of information about ibuprofen take notice of the functional abilities of older patients, the likelihood that a painkiller needs to be integrated in an existing daily schedule, and a range of functional literacy?

Ibuprofen is one of the most often used medicines (Kaufman et al., 2002) and it is used for the relief of symptoms of pain, inflammation and fever (Rainsford, 2013). However, it is by no means harmless because side effects include kidney damage and ibuprofen can cause gastrointestinal bleeding.

Across the European continent, there are very substantial differences in information provided about ibuprofen. Figure 18.4 shows some of this variation. It is available as an over-the-counter product that can be purchased without a prescription, and as a prescription-only medicine. A complete review of all ibuprofen packaging in all EU countries would be interesting because it is likely to show a substantial variation in the traditions, interpretations of the regulations and a variety in marketing approaches. This article limits itself to a single British example.

The focus of the analysis is only on the contents and the design of the information on the packaging. The quality of the medicine itself, or the way in which it is advertised and sold are not part of this analysis. It has long been known that trust in a specific brand affects the effects of a medicine. People believe that a specific brand provides effective medicines (Branthwaite and Cooper, 1981).

The interaction with the information about ibuprofen were divided in five chronological steps:

1. Finding out what the medicine is for.
2. Reading instructions: is it legible and understandable?

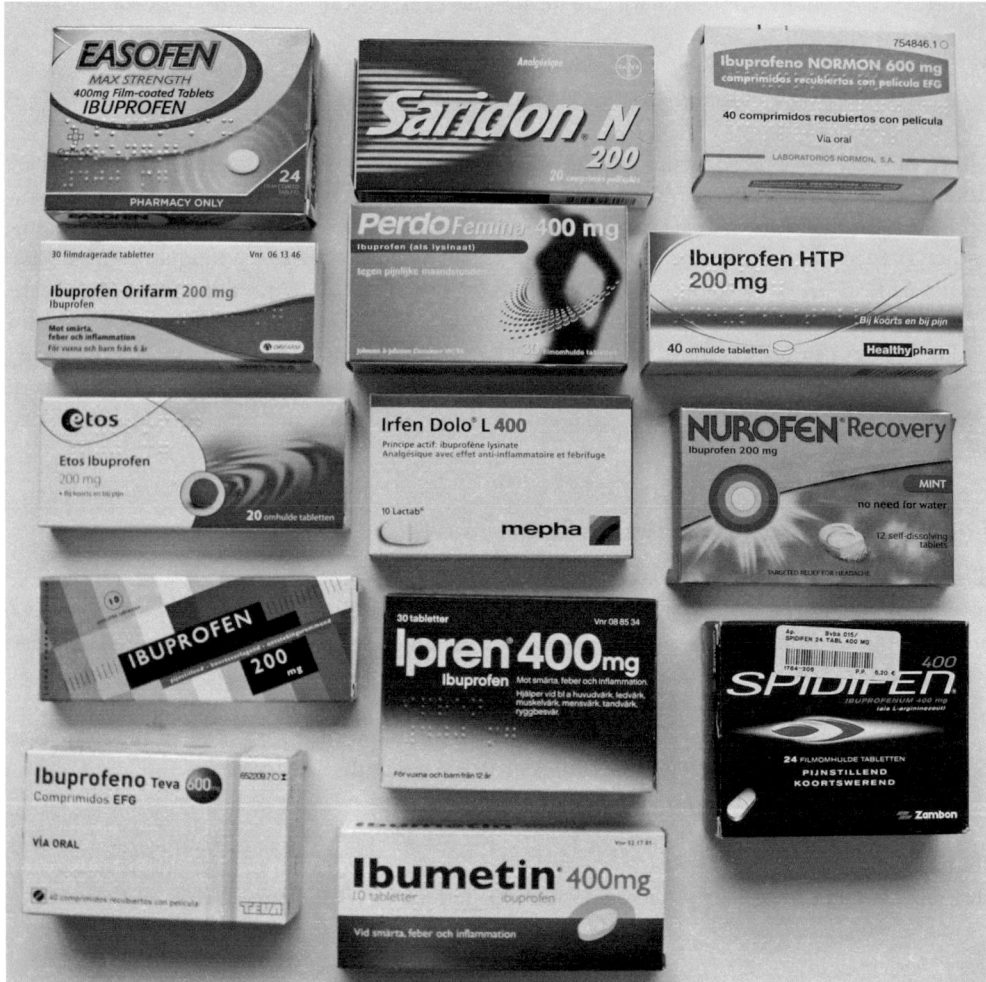

Figure 18.4 A collection of boxes for ibuprofen tablets in Europe. The form (tablets) and active ingredient (ibuprofen) are the same. The strength (200mg or 400mg) and the number of tablets per box (10 to 40) differs

3. Checking: what are the warnings?
4. Considering the risks: side effects.
5. Taking the right dose.

These five steps were used as a basis for interviews with 17 people over the age of 65. Each interview lasted between 30 minutes and an hour. People were asked to have a look at the information as it is shown in Figure 18.1. In the description below, the main remarks of these interviews are integrated. A statistical analysis of these remarks was not performed: each interview provided some new insights about the interpretation of the information about ibuprofen.

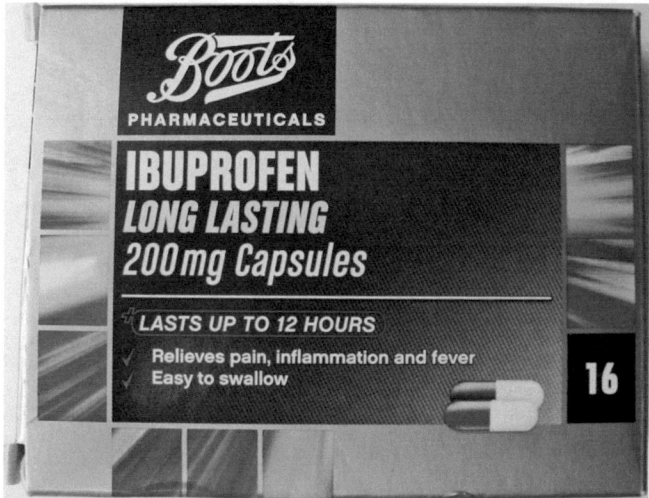

Figure 18.5 The front of a box for ibuprofen as it is sold by pharmacists in the UK

Finding out what the medicine is for

The front of the package does not really indicate a clear visual starting point. At least four items are equally prominent. None of these prominent ones – Boots Pharmaceuticals; IBUPROFEN; LONG LASTING; 200 mg capsules – states what the medicine is for. The text in the smallest type is the most relevant. It states: 'Relieves pain, inflammation and fever' (Figure 18.5). This is part of a list of two items. The visual design implies that both these sentences belong to the same group and have a similar type of meaning. It suggest that, apart from considering the reasons to take a medicine, it is also important to consider the way in which a medicine is taken.

The first sentence on the back of the pack is 'Read all of the enclosed leaflet for full instructions' (Figure 18.6). It is doubtful if a consumer can really do this in a pharmacy. Does this mean that patients have to base decisions on incomplete instructions, and check the full instructions after the package has been bought? The information on the pack continues (Figure 18.6): 'Uses: A slow release capsule for the relief of headaches, rheumatic and muscular pain, backache, migraine, period pain, dental pain and neuralgia. It can also be used to reduce fever and relieve the symptoms of colds and flu.' If this is compared with the information on the front (Figure 18.5) then it seems different. There is a relation between different kinds of pain, but the term 'inflammation' is not in the list on the back. The text 'relieves the symptoms of colds and flu' is not mentioned on the front.

The text in the package leaflet describes the effects of a group of medicines 'which acts to relieve pain and reduce swelling' (Figure 18.7). This suggests that ibuprofen has both these effects as well. If it really has, then it is surprising that 'reduces swelling' is not mentioned on the outer package.

The reasons for taking ibuprofen are mentioned in different ways in different locations on the outer package and the package leaflet. This makes it for the interviewees very difficult to figure out if this medicine is suitable for a particular treatment.

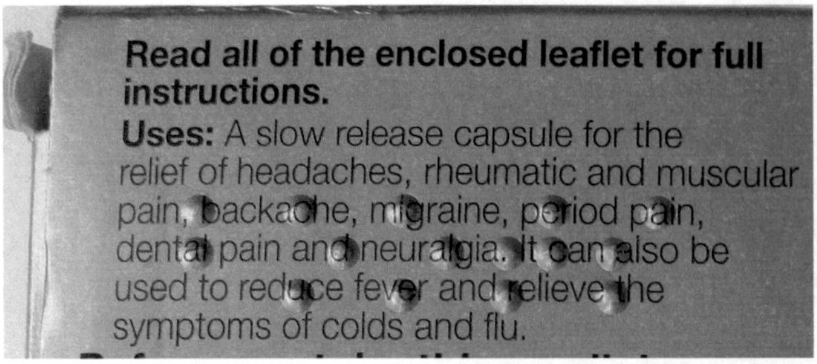

Figure 18.6 A detail of the top-left corner of the back of a box for ibuprofen. Does the combination of typographic variables (type size, type weight, compression, line space, contrast, reflection and Braille dots) really help to make this text readable?

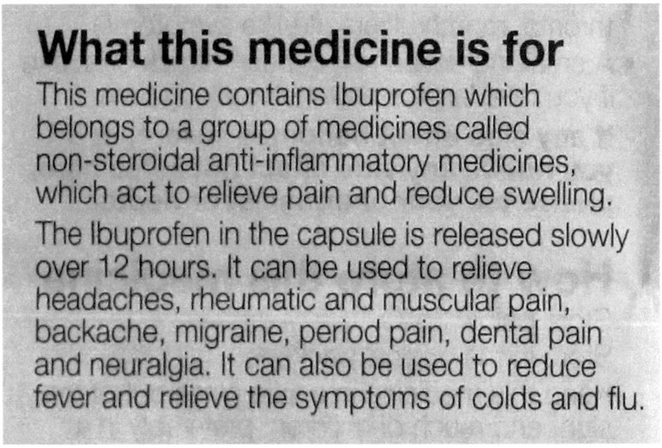

Figure 18.7 A detail of a package leaflet. Does the combination of typography and language help patients to read and understand the indications?

Reading instructions: is it legible and understandable?

The information on the package and in the package leaflet suffer from several linguistic and typographical problems. Two examples, one from the outer pack and one from the package leaflet, give a flavour of these.

The top-left corner of the back of the outer package describes the uses of ibuprofen (Figure 18.6). This text is fairly hard to read for several reasons. The type is small, it is condensed, it is a light version and there is very little space between the lines. The text is printed in black ink on a silver-grey background, the cardboard is shiny and reflective and there are Braille dots pushed right through the text which distort the letter shapes. According to the literature about legible typography, each of these factors influences legibility in a negative way (examples: Spencer, 1968; Baines and Haslam, 2002). The combination of seven (!) of these detrimental factors make the text very hard to decipher.

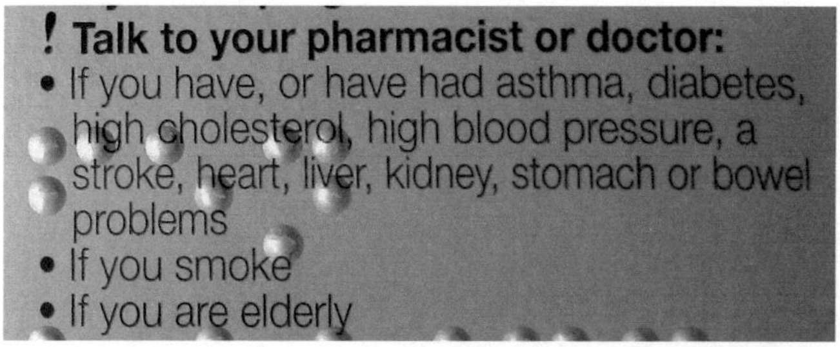

! Talk to your pharmacist or doctor:
- If you have, or have had asthma, diabetes, high cholesterol, high blood pressure, a stroke, heart, liver, kidney, stomach or bowel problems
- If you smoke
- If you are elderly

Figure 18.8 A detail of the back of the box. The information after the first bullet is hard to understand. Does the phrase 'If you have, or have had a heart?' make sense?

The first sentence in the package leaflet is 25 words long. It states: 'This medicine contains ibuprofen which belongs to a group of medicines called non-steroidal anti-inflammatory medicines which act to relieve pain and reduce swelling' (Figure 18.7). The sentence uses an awkward 'which-which' construction (multiple embedded non-restrictive clauses). These are particularly difficult for poorer readers, and for those who are reading quickly.

The interviewees indicated that both the contents (writing style, terminology) and typographical design are not very helpful.

Checking: what are the warnings?

The back of the box shows two lists under the heading 'Before you take this medicine.' The first list is 'Do not take:' and the second list is 'Talk to your pharmacist or doctor' (Figure 18.8). The interviewees had difficulty reading this text because of its poor legibility and raised some questions. For example, the first sentence in the second list can be interpreted in many different ways. It states: 'Talk to your pharmacist or doctor: If you have, or have had asthma, diabetes, high cholesterol, high blood pressure, a stroke, heart, liver, kidney, stomach or bowel problems'. In this 28-word sentence, some of the statements are plainly incorrect ('If you have had diabetes' (some forms are incurable at the moment); 'If you have a heart' or 'If you have had a stomach'). It takes some mental effort to relate 'heart', 'liver', 'kidney' and 'stomach' to 'problems', which does not make this sentence easy to read.

And the last point of this list is 'Talk to your pharmacist or doctor if you are elderly'. This is the only reference to older patients, but 'elderly' seemed fairly vague to the interviewees. Does this mean over 65, over 75 or over 90 years of age? The package leaflet adds to this warning: 'You may get more side effects' and 'if you are elderly, you may be more likely to have some of these side effects'. The difference between these two phrases is not further explained, but they seem to have a different meaning.

Interviewees mentioned that the information on the outer package and in the package leaflet does not really help to consider the warnings. It is very difficult to understand them and apply these to one's personal situation. The information is vague and not very helpful.

Considering the risks: side effects

The potential risks are not mentioned on the outer package and appear only in the section 'Possible side effects' in the package leaflet. Interviewees noticed that the information about possible risks is not available at the time of purchase.

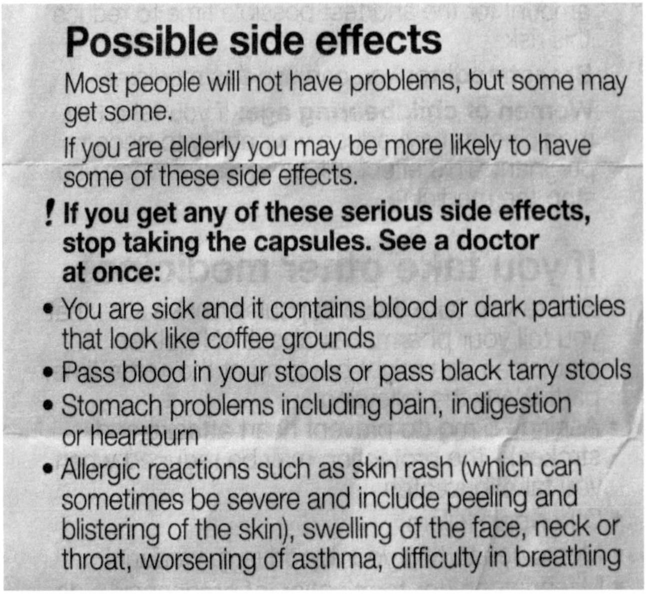

Possible side effects

Most people will not have problems, but some may get some.

If you are elderly you may be more likely to have some of these side effects.

❗ If you get any of these serious side effects, stop taking the capsules. See a doctor at once:

- You are sick and it contains blood or dark particles that look like coffee grounds
- Pass blood in your stools or pass black tarry stools
- Stomach problems including pain, indigestion or heartburn
- Allergic reactions such as skin rash (which can sometimes be severe and include peeling and blistering of the skin), swelling of the face, neck or throat, worsening of asthma, difficulty in breathing

Figure 18.9 The serious side effects of ibuprofen. All of these might occur in less than 1 in 10,000 patients. Are patients really capable of considering these risk levels?

The section starts with a reassuring sentence: 'Most people will not have any problems, but some may get some' (Figure 18.9). This might be the most appropriate way of formulating, but the next sentences are more worrying: 'If you get any of these serious side effects, stop taking the capsules. See a doctor at once'. These are in bold type to visually emphasise their importance.

The information about side effects in the package leaflet separates 'serious side effects' from 'less serious side effects'. Kidney failure, meningitis and heart attacks are now classified as 'less serious' side effects. When these occur, the leaflet advises to 'talk to a pharmacists if they bother you'. In interviews with patients, they indicated that they would classify these side effects as very serious and that they would hope that a doctor would tend to them immediately.

All five possible reasons for taking ibuprofen appear in the list of possible side effects (Figure 18.10). By taking ibuprofen against pain such as a headache, patients might get certain kinds of pain such as a headache. Ibuprofen could be taken to reduce fever, but it might also cause fever. Ibuprofen could relieve flu-like symptoms, but the symptoms of cold and flu are also listed as a side effect of ibuprofen. Ibuprofen can increase the number of infections, if patients take it to relieve an inflammation. And patients can start swelling because they took ibuprofen against swelling.

Interviewees concluded that the lists of side effects are unhelpful. Although they are likely to be correct from a pharmacological point of view, they give the impression that the benefits of ibuprofen are unreliable or to some extent unknown. Ibuprofen might work, but there is a chance that it doesn't work at all, or causes the same symptoms as it intends to relieve. It could even trigger effects that are worse. The numerous irresolute and vague indications do not increase the confidence of the interviewees in the effectiveness of ibuprofen.

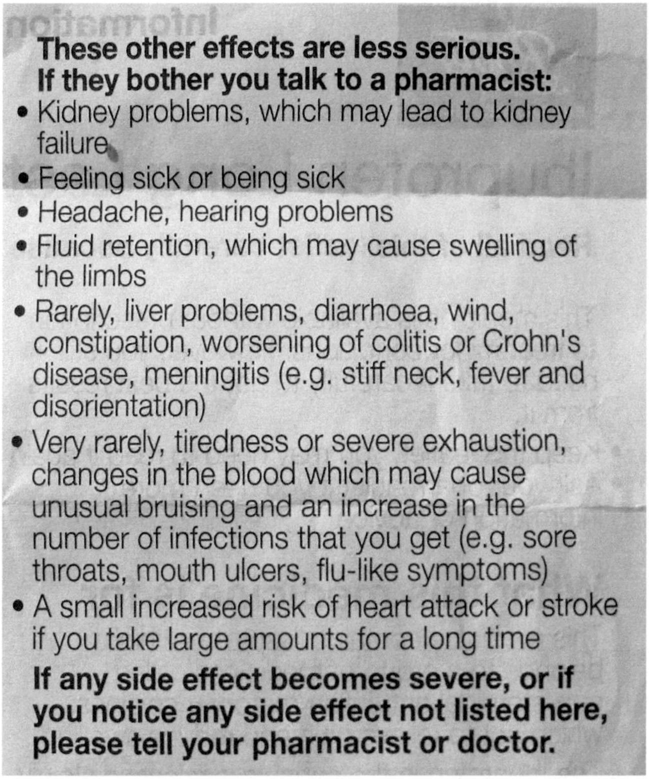

These other effects are less serious.
If they bother you talk to a pharmacist:
- Kidney problems, which may lead to kidney failure
- Feeling sick or being sick
- Headache, hearing problems
- Fluid retention, which may cause swelling of the limbs
- Rarely, liver problems, diarrhoea, wind, constipation, worsening of colitis or Crohn's disease, meningitis (e.g. stiff neck, fever and disorientation)
- Very rarely, tiredness or severe exhaustion, changes in the blood which may cause unusual bruising and an increase in the number of infections that you get (e.g. sore throats, mouth ulcers, flu-like symptoms)
- A small increased risk of heart attack or stroke if you take large amounts for a long time

If any side effect becomes severe, or if you notice any side effect not listed here, please tell your pharmacist or doctor.

Figure 18.10 The less serious side effects of ibuprofen are meningitis, severe exhaustion and heart attacks. Do patients really consider these as 'less serious'?

Handling: selecting the right dose

The instructions on the normal dose are provided on the package and in the package leaflet (Figure 18.11). They are a mixture of instructions and warnings. The instructions under the heading 'How to take this medicine' start with a warning: 'Check the foil is not broken before use. If it is, do not take that capsule'. This confused some of the people during interviews: which foil is meant? It only makes sense from a pharmacological point of view: the granules inside the capsules might attract water (hydrophilic) and could stick together. The third sentence is: 'Swallow each capsule whole with water'. The actual dosage instruction is on the line below: 'Adults and children of 12 years and over: Take two capsules in the morning and evening, if you need to.' This is followed by three warnings: 'Don't take more than 4 capsules in 24 hours', 'Do not give to children under 12 years' and 'Warning: Do not exceed the stated dose'. The last one appears in a box. Interviewees remarked that this might look like a text that needs to be read from top to bottom, but that it is not very well structured and that there are several repetitions. Especially the difference between 'Do not exceed the stated dose' and 'Don't take more than 4 capsules in 24 hours' required some mental gymnastics of the interviewees.

During the interviews, participants asked some questions about the dosage instructions. One of these questions was why is it necessary to always take two capsules? Was it not possible

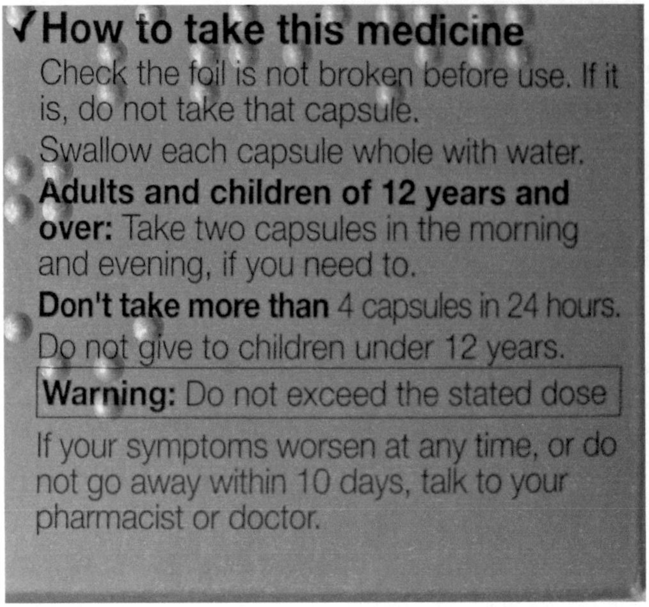

Figure 18.11 The administration instructions for ibuprofen. Should everyone – regardless of age, weight, pain level, liver function or gender – really take the same dose of two capsules?

to put 400 mg into one capsule? Or should patients experiment themselves what an effective dose is? And if that is correct, why is that not stated anywhere? The words 'if you need to' enhance this particular interpretation. Several interviewees also questioned if the instructions were actually correct. Should everyone – regardless of age, weight, pain level, liver function or gender – really take the same dose of two capsules?

The interviewees concluded that it is not very clear how many of these capsules are required for an older person with a simple headache. The practical conclusion most of the interviewees drew was that they would take two capsules and wait for the headache to disappear. If the headache persisted, then they would take another two capsules.

Discussion: learning from a single sample

The conclusions of each of the five sections above show that interviewees found that some of the information about ibuprofen was:

- unclear and inconsistent about the reasons to take it;
- hard to read, both in contents and in typographic design;
- difficult to apply to a personal situation;
- not very helpful if potential risks needed to be considered;
- vague about the number of capsules that needed to be taken.

The interviewees had varying degrees of difficulty reading the texts on the outer packaging and in the package leaflet. Even if a text could be read, it was difficult for several interviewees to understand what it meant, and even more difficult to apply it to a personal situation. There is no information on the package or in the leaflet that provides suggestions on how to integrate ibuprofen in an existing medicine regimen. Some of the difficulties that interviewees mentioned confirm the results of a recent study in the Netherlands (Notenboom et al., 2014: 2342).

These might seem harsh conclusions, but if the results of the interviews are compared with the data about medicine-taking of older patients and functional literacy, it could have been a lot worse. Most interviewees could find most of the information, albeit with some reluctance, a certain amount of effort and spending a sufficient amount of time. It is unlikely that any of the interviewees would have read the information about ibuprofen under normal circumstances.

It is clear that a single series of 17 interviews about one ibuprofen pack needs to be repeated with different ibuprofen packs, in different languages, in different EU countries before firm conclusions can be drawn. Such an extended study would reveal the international variations and might provide significant and generalizable data. However, it should also reveal the individual differences and individual problems that older patients have with information about medicines.

Form teams to cover different frames

The assumption that formed the basis for the interviews was that the information about ibuprofen is intended to be read by people. This assumption is only partly correct. Apart from enabling people to take medicines correctly, there are at least two other perspectives that have a strong influence on the information:

* It must adhere to legal requirements.
* It must consider commercial motivations.

Legal requirements demand that all information about a medicine is submitted to regulatory authorities. The authorities check if the information complies with the legislation and guidelines. The sequence and structure of the information in the package leaflet and on the outer packaging is checked to make sure that the information follows the templates, guidelines and regulations. This singular and standardised approach – 'one-template-fits-all medicines' – has proven to be effective for the registration and trade of medicines in Europe. The application of this approach to the information supply has the unintended consequence that differences between patients, differences between medicines, differences in contexts of use and differences in languages are ignored. An example of such a consequence of this approach is that the 'benefits' of a medicine are mentioned very briefly on the outer pack and on the front of the package leaflet, but the 'harms and risks' are only mentioned on the back of the package leaflet as a fairly extended list. This does not make it easy for people to compare and consider the benefits and risks (or harm) of taking a medicine. Of course, both industry and regulatory authorities are aware of these issues and both try to resolve these on a case-by-case basis.

The commercial requirements for an over-the-counter medicine are clear too. Enhancing the brand and increasing profits are two legitimate aims for any packaging design, and the ibuprofen packaging fits both these aims. It also fits the long-term marketing strategies within a group of related products.

The balance between these three frames – patient information, legal requirements, commercial interests – seems to favour the latter two. If it is really beneficial for patients to know about medicines, then it is necessary to reconsider the balance between these three frames. Reconsidering frames has a long history (Schön and Reid, 1994; Dorst, 2015) and this approach is likely to be beneficial for the provision of information about medicines.

Develop prototypes within a strategy: what do patients actually want to do?

In order to make the information about ibuprofen more suitable for patients, it might be necessary to shift the main focus from 'providing information about ibuprofen for legal and commercial reasons' to 'enabling patients to act appropriately'.

The interviewees clearly indicated what they expected from information about ibuprofen. It should focus on the following five main topics:

- Describe what ibuprofen is for.
- Tell exactly how to take ibuprofen, including its incorporation in an existing daily regimen.
- Help to consider the risks and side effects in relation to the benefits.
- Help to check if ibuprofen can be taken. It should be possible to consider the current personal state of health, as well as to consider combinations with other personal medicines.
- Where to get additional information and personal advice.

This should be presented in a format that does not require a substantial amount of effort and time to read. The information should not contain too much repetition. Related information must be placed together, and it should suggest how to integrate ibuprofen in a daily schedule. Furthermore, although the information frequently suggests that patients should ask a pharmacist or a doctor if there are further questions, this is not made easy. There are no phone numbers, email addresses or websites that people could consult.

In general, patients seem to ask for an 'information strategy' that starts from the perspective of patients. The development of such an information strategy should start with discussions with patients, followed by an iterative process of designing and testing prototypes. Publications like *Writing About Medicines for People* (Sless and Shrensky, 2006) could be used as a guide, in combination with best practice (Sless, 2002) and experimental results (Bix et al., 2009).

The three suggestions in this discussion – more research for specific data, reconsidering frames and the development of an information strategy – might take substantial time to achieve. It requires the reconsideration of legislation, reframing approaches and really starting from the activities of patients. Ignoring these issues is not an option. It is likely that the changes described on page 341 will provoke some fundamental and substantial changes related to the design of information about medicines.

Some improvements can be made within the current legal framework in Europe. In some cases this would require a different emphasis and different interpretations, but it would not require a substantial modification of the legislation. However, for some medicines and some processes, it really is necessary to modify the legislation to make sure that patients receive relevant and reliable information about their medicines.

Conclusion: which way forward?

This investigation showed the context and use of information related to a single ibuprofen package. The results of 17 interviews with older patients indicated that they could read most of the information. However, this required substantial time and effort, and it showed that much of the information is inconsistent, unclear, difficult to apply, not very helpful and vague. The results also show that the information that is provided with ibuprofen does not help to integrate its use in a complex regimen, and it does not make allowances for diminishing abilities.

In order to change the existing situation into a preferred one, it seems essential that the following three activities are undertaken.

Data and statistics: get the facts right

The introduction showed that there is a fair amount of generalizable data about ageing populations, medicine use and functional literacy. However, these generalizable data across large sections of the population do not give an indication of the variation in ability of individual older patients. To get an idea of the scope of this variation and its influence on medicine use, it is necessary to look at the data about individual situations and find out how individuals deal with information about medicines. The data about individuals are vital to focus on the actions that are likely to cause most problems.

Visual information: prototypes within a strategy?

A second way to convince people that change is required is to show prototypes that perform better. The application of established design processes will lead to prototypes that are performance-based. They are based on the actions of people and take the contexts and environments into account. Initially, these prototypes are likely to be in conflict with the legislation and the guidelines. It is also likely that they cause major discussions within companies and externally with the regulatory authorities. Both the discussions and the prototypes are important to make progress.

Form teams and cooperate

The combination of more individual data and performance-based prototypes can be used as a base to involve more stakeholders. A group or team that incorporates all three frames – regulatory, commercial and healthcare – would be the ultimate aim.

The combination of these three activities – data collection, prototype development, forming teams – is a real challenge.

References

Baines, P. and Haslam, A. (2002) *Type and Typography.* London: Lawrence King Publishing.

Bix, L., Bello, N.M., Auras, R., Ranger, J. and Lapinski, M.K. (2009) Examining the conspicuousness and prominence of two required warnings on OTC pain relievers. *Proceedings of the National Academy of Sciences of the United States of America*, 106(16): 6550–5.

Branthwaite, A. and Cooper, P. (1981) Analgesic effects of branding in treatment of headaches. *British Medical Journal*, 282: 1576–8.

Directive 92/27/EEC (1992) Council Directive 92/27/EEC of 31 March 1992 on the labelling of medicinal products for human use and on package leaflets. Official Journal, L 113, 30 April, 107–14.

Directive 2004/27/EC (2004) Directive 2004/27/EC of the European Parliament and of the council of 31 March 2004 amending Directive 2001/83/EC on the Community code relating to medicinal product for human use. Official Journal, L 136, 30 April, 34–57.

Directive 2010/84/EC (2010) Directive 2010/84/EC of the European Parliament and of the council of 15 December 2010 amending, as regards to pharmacovigilance, Directive 2001/83/EC on the Community code relating to medicinal product for human use. Official Journal, L 348, 31 December, 74–99.

Dorst, K. (2015) *Frame Innovation: Create New Thinking by Design*. Cambridge, MA: MIT Press.

Elliott, R. (2006) Problems with medication use in the elderly: An Australian perspective. *Journal of Pharmacy Practice and Research*, 36(1): 58–62.

EMA-QRD (2015) Product-information templates. Available at: www.ema.europa.eu/, accessed 22 October 2015.

Eurostat (2015) Population structure and ageing. Available at: http://ec.europa.eu/eurostat/statistics-explained/index.php/Populationstructureandageing, accessed 14 October 2015.

Gapminder World (2015) Wealth and health of nations. Available at: www.gapminder.org, accessed 22 October 2015.

HLS-EU Consortium (2012) Comparative report of health literacy in eight EU member states. The European Health Literacy Survey HLS-EU. Available at: www.health-literacy.eu, accessed 20 September 2015.

Kaufman, D.W., Kelly, J.P., Rosenberg, L., Anderson, T.E. and Mitchell, A.A. (2002) Recent patterns of medication use in the ambulatory adult population of the United States (The Slone Survey). *Journal of the American Medical Association*, 287(3): 337–44.

Notenboom, K., Beers, E., Riet-Nales, D.A. van, Egberts, T.C.G., Leufkens, H.G.M., Jansen, P.A.F and Bouvy, M.L. (2014) Practical problems with medication use that older people experience: A qualitative study. *Journal of the American Geriatrics Society*, 62(12): 2339–44.

OECD (2013) *OECD Skills Outlook 2013: First Results from the Survey of Adult Skills*. Paris: OECD Publishing. Available at: http://dx.doi.org/10.1787/9789264204256-en.

Rainsford, K.D. (2013) Fifty years of ibuprofen: Advancing pain and fever management. *International Journal of Clinical Practice*, 67 (178): 1–2.

Schön, D. and Rein, M. (1994) *Frame Reflection: Toward the Resolution of Intractable Policy Controversies*. New York: Basic Books.

Sless, D. (2002) Panadol 24 pack: New instructions for consumers. Report prepared for GlaxoSmith-Kline. Melbourne: Communication Research Institute. Available at: www.foodlabellingreview.gov.au/internet/foodlabelling/submissions.nsf/lookupSubmissionAttachments/1SWIN-85JVQG20100518093818ERBI/$FILE/446d.pdf, accessed 22 November 2015.

Sless, D. and Shrensky, R. (2006) *Writing about Medicines for People: Usability Guidelines for Consumer Product Information*. 3rd edition. Sydney: Australian Self-Medication Industry.

Spencer, H. (1968) *The Visible Word: Problems of Legibility*. London: Lund Humphries.

UNESCO (2005) *Education for All: Literacy for Life*. Paris: UNESCO.

Wolf, A., Fuchs, J. and Schweim, H.G. (2012) QRD template texts intended for package inserts. *Pharm. Ind*, 74(9): 1540–9.

World Health Organization (2003) *Adherence to Long-Term Therapies. Evidence for Action*. Geneva: WHO.

World Health Organization (2015) *World Report on Ageing and Health*. Geneva: WHO.

York Health Economics Consortium and School of Pharmacy, University of London (2010) *Evaluation of the Scale, Causes and Costs of Waste Medicines*. York and London: University of York and University of London.

19 Architecture

Workplace health and wellbeing: can greater design participation provide a cure?

Jeremy Myerson and Gail Ramster

Abstract

This chapter looks at current initiatives to improve health and wellbeing in the office workplace, against the background of a loss of productivity and a rise in incidences of stress, depression and burnout. It explores giving employees a greater sense of control over their work environment through participation in the design of their workspace, and describes a UK research study which makes a link between participatory design activities and improved levels of mental wellbeing. A conceptual model is presented which suggests that better health and wellbeing can be achieved in the office workplace by aligning organisational purpose more closely with both the functional and psychological needs of the individual. Co-design is advocated as a way to improve employee belonging and wellbeing despite the relative unfamiliarity of the concept in the workplace.

Introduction

Business leaders and public health experts look at the workplace from very different perspectives. But on the subject of workplace health, they increasingly speak with one voice on the need to find new ways to make the work environment less damaging and more beneficial to the health and wellbeing of employees. The combination of a loss of workplace productivity, which has caused alarm in business circles, and growing concerns among healthcare professionals over the negative effects of a sedentary, long-hours working culture has pushed design for health in the workplace right up the agenda for change.

'We want people to leave the workplace healthier than when they arrive', says Duncan Young, Head of Health and Wellbeing at Lend Lease, one of the world's largest office property developers (Young, 2015). Better diet at work, more exercise, more natural light, improved air quality and frequent breaks are among Young's recommendations to improve workplace health. Dame Carole Black, expert advisor to the UK government on work and health, takes a wider view: 'The workplace, traditionally seen as a source of health problems, in fact represents a huge opportunity to improve the health and wellbeing of the nation' (Black, 2016). Black's focus is on creating a total workplace culture that can deliver better physical and mental health with wider benefits feeding back to families and communities.

The reason why opportunities to improve health at work need to be seized is best understood by looking at the current impact of poor health on productivity. Absence from work costs the UK economy more than £14 billion a year according to the Confederation of British Industry (CBI, 2013). In 2014, around 27.3 million working days were lost in the UK, according to the Health and Safety Executive; 23.3 million of them were due to work-related ill health, and just over 4 million were due to workplace injuries (HSE, 2015). Work-related ill health covers musculoskeletal disorders, which account for most days lost, as well as stress, anxiety and depression, which are generally on the rise. Calculate the knock-on effects in the wider community and the cost becomes even higher.

Not surprisingly, the issue of health and wellbeing is now widely debated within the global industry of professionals who plan, build and manage workplaces, and there is growing consensus that design has a key role to play in a field that becomes more complex the longer you look at it. A Well Building Standard, established by the International Well Building Institute (DELOS Living LLC, 2015), helpfully organises the key elements under seven headings – air, water, nourishment, light, fitness, comfort and mind – in a bid to cover all the angles.

Looking broadly at current practice, the core environmental comfort issues of air quality, light and lighting, acoustics, thermal control, water quality and access to nature affect physical and mental health. These depend very much on design decisions. Other factors include layouts and settings that encourage movement and exercise through activity-based working, and the provision of ergonomic innovations such as sit-stand desks, stand-up meeting rooms and posture-correction devices.

Mindful of the growing threat of obesity, which is becoming the lifestyle epidemic of the 21st century in the way that smoking was in the 20th century, nutrition protocols in the workplace are under scrutiny with a move towards preparing healthier food, growing your own fruit and veg and cutting down on calorific vending machines. Commuting is under scrutiny too with growing emphasis on walking and cycling to work (active transport) as a complement to the formal provision of gyms, exercise spaces and fitness equipment in the workplace.

Indeed, there is a whirlwind of activity around the subject, with many new health and wellbeing technologies coming online – from wearables that count steps and calories to intelligent buildings that use the Internet of Things to monitor health by recalibrating air quality and light levels according to levels of occupancy. But what emerges from a broad look at the field is that, despite the growing physical influence of design and technology, the toughest nut to crack in the workplace relates to mental health. Managing stress, depression and burnout is the red light flashing on the management dashboard. Health in the workplace context is partly in the mind.

At a time when workplace injuries are falling and the workplace is physically safer than a generation ago, incidences of psychological distress have been rising proportionally. One in six people in work are experiencing depression, anxiety or another mental health condition to a diagnosable level at any one time, excluding drug and alcohol dependency (Singleton et al., 2000). The estimated cost to the UK economy of mental health problems is £1,035 per employee (Sainsbury Centre for Mental Health, 2007).

Not all mental health problems affecting work are necessarily caused by the workplace. A 2011 survey by the Chartered Institute of Personnel Development found that 65 per cent of people reporting poor mental health said that this was due to a combination of work and non-work factors, 20 per cent said their poor mental health is just down to non-work issues, while 15 per cent said their poor mental health is the result of work alone. Nevertheless, mental health problems in the workplace bring those knotty issues of identity, belonging, empowerment and work–life balance to the fore – and these tend to be tougher to fix through design interventions than challenges related to the environment or settings.

In this chapter, we want to focus on the importance of mental health and wellbeing in the workplace, explore the concept of 'a sense of control' in supporting psychological comfort and describe and reflect upon a UK research study which we co-directed, looking at the impact of participatory design on team wellbeing.

A sense of control

There are many reasons why people around the world become disenchanted, disassociated or distressed at work – growing stress levels have been recorded from Mexico to China (Regus, 2009). Dame Carol Black (2016) lays some of the blame at the door of managers: 'Poor quality leadership is linked with stress, depression and burnout.' Others point the figure at unreliable IT systems, inadequate training or poorly designed work environments that offer little personal choice and over which employees can exercise no control. Conversely, workplace interventions that improve wellness appear to have financial benefits due to their impact on reduced absence and staff turnover, and they also positively influence employee satisfaction, productivity levels and organisational profile (PwC, 2008). But what exactly constitutes a sense of mental wellbeing in the workplace and how can it be maintained?

One way to understand wellbeing is as the equilibrium between a person's own psychological, physical and social resources on one hand and external circumstances and challenges on the other (Dodge et al., 2012). This approach presents personal wellbeing as subjective and dynamic. The UK Office of National Statistics measure of national wellbeing encompasses happiness, satisfaction, freedom from anxiety and feeling worthwhile (Oguz et al., 2013). Research by the New Economics Foundation (Jeffrey et al., 2014) suggests that factors affecting wellbeing in the workplace include: personal resources ('who you are') – your health, activity, level of relaxation and work–life balance; and organisational systems ('where you work') – environmental factors, social value of work, technology and infrastructure, social interactions and relationships and sense of control.

Indeed a 'sense of control' emerges from the literature as an established driver of wellbeing and happiness at work. It is a factor relevant to successful functioning at work, reducing the negative aspects that can erode wellbeing on an ongoing basis (Marks, 2014; Gensler, 2013). Of course, a sense of control has wide meaning: it can apply to choices regarding work–life balance, the surrounding environment, commuting and travel; it also refers to control in terms of access to tools, resources, spaces, control over territory and privacy and control over relationships and interaction with others in the office community.

However, a sense of control has particular meaning in relation to the level of participation that people have in the design and planning of their own workplace. The levels of control and empowerment associated with participation in office design have been connected to higher levels of wellbeing in a number of research studies. Vischer (2005) suggests that participation in the design process and feeling 'empowered' in environmental decision-making affects the sense of belonging or ownership felt by employees over their workspace. This contributes to what Vischer (2008) terms 'psychological comfort'.

Knight and Haslam (2010) found through workplace-based experiments that environments enriched by workers with plants and artwork had a greater effect on their psychological comfort, autonomy and job satisfaction compared to environments enriched by others. Enrichment by workers also led to improved productivity and reduced errors. When their input was overridden and the workspace reverted to pre-empowerment conditions, the effect on autonomy and psychological comfort fell, reflecting the disempowerment of the worker.

As part of its advice on mental wellbeing at work, NICE guidelines recommend taking action to promote 'a culture of participation, equality and fairness that is based on open communication and inclusion' (NICE, 2009). However participatory design or 'co-design' activities, which give participants a greater sense of control over their environment, are less in evidence in the workplace than in community development, public services and urban environments where they are far more common.

Participatory design

Participatory design or co-design is a growing field. It sees designers working collaboratively with end users as equal partners to create, design and/or produce ideas, spaces, products, technologies or services. By adopting a co-design methodology, people benefit from involvement in the process as well as the end result (Sanders and Stappers, 2008; Ramirez, 2008). According to Bradwell and Marr (2008): 'Co-design broadly refers to the effort to combine the views, input and skills of people with many different perspectives to address a specific problem.'

Co-design methods promote participation, open discussion and collective decision-making, helping people to arrive at decisions even if they do not meet their personal preferences; as a result, solutions are more sustainable due to a sense of collective ownership. Co-design methods have been widely piloted in community development to improve neighbourhood cohesion (Ramirez, 2008; Boyle et al., 2010) and in healthcare where experienced-based co-design has reoriented medical services and systems around patient needs (Macdonald and Teal, 2011). It is not hard to see their value to the creation of office environments, but detailed evidence of practice in the workplace is relatively thin on the ground.

StudioTilt (2014) produced a series of case studies of co-design in workplaces through which it identified a series of methods (role playing, mock-ups, mapping, workshops and so on) as well as a series of advantages in getting dissenting voices out in the open and creating more sustainable results. New Zealand Bank ANZ (Lynch and Roulston, 2015) developed and discussed a new 'Playbox' methodology to enable staff to co-design their own flexible furniture, leading to the design of settings with such names as Scrum, Showcase and Exchange. Clearly, the scope to extend co-design practice within the workplace is considerable. However, a key question is whether greater participation by employees in the design of the workplace environment will increase a sense of control and contribute to higher levels of wellbeing. This is the main question that a one-year study entitled Workplace and Wellbeing (Myerson and Tidd, 2016) set out to explore. This study was jointly led by the Helen Hamlyn Centre for Design at the Royal College and the architectural practice Gensler.

Workplace and Wellbeing research study

The RCA–Gensler research was conducted in two stages over a period of one year. In the first phase of research, the research team conducted a scoping study in four different organisations in London and the south-east of England that have undergone different levels of workplace change over the past three years (relocation to new purpose-built premises, relocation to new premises without refurbishment, introduction of new furniture in existing premises and no workplace change). This phase was conducted through cross-organisation interviews, stakeholder mapping (with managers, building services, department representatives and so on) and observations of teams within the workplace. Thirty interviews were conducted and analysed across the four organisations (22 with employees, eight with other stakeholders).

In the second phase of research, a participatory design project was devised with three teams on one office floor in one organisation in order to test the impact of different levels of design participation (high, low and no participation) on employee wellbeing. Teams worked to create, design and test interventions in their workspace. The intention of this approach was to give employees more sense of control over the environment in two ways: first, by inviting them to participate in the design process using co-design methods; and second, by providing interventions designed for and by them, creating a sense of co-ownership of space. A validated measurement of mental wellbeing, the Short Warwick-Edinburgh Mental Wellbeing Scale, was used to measure the effects on teams of employees.

Based on the findings of the two phases of the study, the research team built a workplace wellbeing conceptual model that illustrates a necessary balance between the functional and psychological needs of the individual that organisations need to provide in the workplace. The model presents two axes of need, from functional need to psychological need, and from the organisation to the individual.

Research findings

Findings from the scoping study presented 'a snapshot of change' characterised by an ever, shifting workplace landscape and a relentless squeeze on space. This constant change was seen by employees as often in the interests of the organisation, while worsening their physical and psychological wellbeing. Huge variations in levels of mobility, choice and flexibility for individuals emerged, with many people feeling excluded from decision-making processes in relation to the work environment.

The scoping study revealed that employee wellbeing and satisfaction was supported by such workplace factors as: a sense of connection with the outside world through natural light, birdsong and plants as well as closeness to leisure amenities and transport links; a positive and purposeful environment which is welcoming and easy to navigate; a variety of spaces to suit different tasks; and control and personal autonomy over space. People felt better about work when invited to participate in the planning and design of the work environment, and unless happily excluded from decision-making processes when not given a voice.

Generally, mental wellbeing was seen to suffer when there were poor connections with the outside world, badly managed communication between teams, difficulties in wayfinding and inadequate provision of a variety of flexible spaces, thus exposing staff to constant noise and distraction. Decision-making that failed to account for the impact on the individual and a general lack of consultation over workplace design was also seen as unhelpful.

Insights into employee views on participatory design provided a bridge to the second phase of the project: the participatory design project. The research team worked with three teams of employees all situated on the same floor. Each team contained between six and nine people who work together and share similar work patterns. Team 1 was offered the highest level of participation by being invited to co-design ideas and interventions and becoming involved in their implementation. Team 2 was offered a lower level of participation through engagement activities to identify those aspects of the workplace that were important to them and where opportunities for improvement lie. However, Team 2 was not involved in how ideas and interventions were developed or chosen for implementation. Team 3 was completely excluded from design participation, but received interventions designed by and for the other teams on the floor.

Team 1 (high participation) and Team 2 (low participation) both focused in their initial engagement workshops on the corporate feel and identity of the space, its dullness and low levels of natural light with poor connections to the outside. Team 1 then went on to co-design a 'Life and Light' intervention with the research team. This comprised the introduction of plants in the space installed in hanging skyplanters (see Figure 19.1), a range of salad crops, herbs and chillies to eat that the team would cultivate. Blinds were fully retracted to increase light. This intervention was delivered to Team 2 (low participation) and Team 3 (no participation). Team 1 and Team 2 also combined to organise a 'Tidy Friday' de-clutter day to clean up their space. Team 3 did not initiate this activity but participated in it.

Figure 19.1 Life and Light design intervention in the workplace, with hanging skyplanters

The participatory design project made use of the Short Warwick-Edinburgh Mental Wellbeing Scale (Warwick Medical School, 2015), a validated tool developed to evaluate the impact of a project on the mental wellbeing of a group of people. It is based on seven positively worded statements about mental wellbeing (such as 'I've been feeling useful' and 'I've been thinking clearly') that can be scored from 1 (none of the time) to 5 (all of the time). This tool was presented to participants as an online survey that they could complete themselves. The survey was distributed before the design participation project began and again after implementation of the design intervention to chart changes in team wellbeing that might be attributed to the project.

The survey was based on a sample of 18 people in total, drawn from the three teams. Results suggested a detectable link between design participation in the workplace and mental wellbeing. The two teams that participated in design recorded bigger increases on the wellbeing scale than the team that was not given the opportunity to participate. However, there was no real difference between the wellbeing scores for Team 1 (high participation) and Team 2 (low participation), indicating that that the level or 'dose' of design participation is less important than the overall invitation to engage in some way. Providing a more intense or prolonged participatory design experience does not automatically boost wellbeing further.

More in-depth feedback from all teams (through a qualitative survey) provided greater context, showing that many people appreciated being invited to participate in an open design process and expressed satisfaction with the staff-designed workspace intervention irrespective of whether or not they had actually participated in the process.

Workplace wellbeing model

A conceptual model to chart and assess wellbeing needs in the workplace was developed by the research team over the duration of the study, based on the thematic analysis from phase 1 (occupancy study in four organisations) and the live findings recorded in phase 2 (participatory design project). The model (see Figure 19.2) illustrates a necessary balance between the functional and psychological needs of the individual that organisations need to provide in the workplace. This approach mirrors to some extent the purpose of the organisation itself, which can also be seen as a combination of functional and psychological needs.

(a)

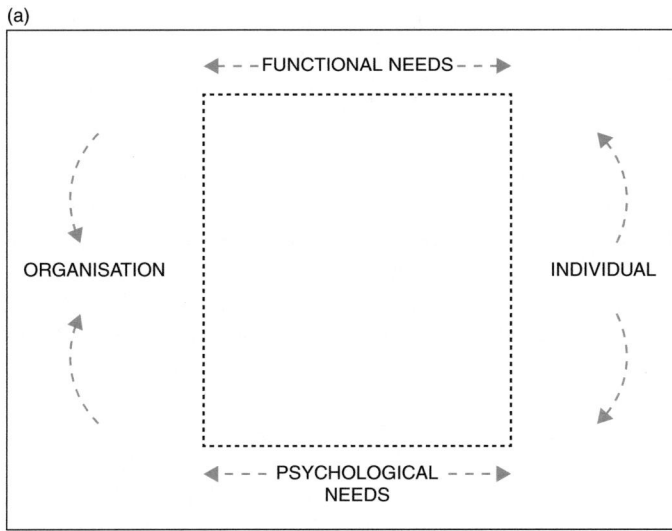

(b)

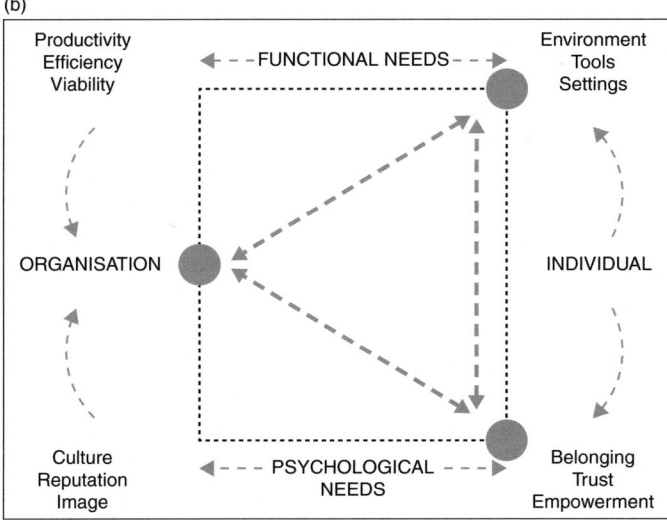

Figure 19.2 Workplace and wellbeing model showing full alignment (above) between organisational purpose and individual needs

The model therefore presents two axes of need, from functional need to psychological need, and from the organisation and the individual. Individual needs are those that appear to benefit the individual more than the organisation; organisational needs are those that benefit the organisation more. At the heart of the model is what has been termed 'the psychological contract' – in return for hard work, commitment and loyalty, the individual worker expects the organisation to be responsible for their workplace wellbeing.

Organisations have a number of functional requirements in order to be productive, efficient and viable. They must capitalise on assets and property, utilising space in an efficient way (for example, by introducing new working practices). They must raise performance and increase commercial competitiveness (for example, through collaboration). Keeping the workforce safe and healthy to work, through provision of ergonomic work settings, is part of this picture. Organisations also have 'softer' psychological needs based around creating and maintaining a positive culture, reputation and brand. These needs are related to motivating the workforce and attracting and retaining talent (for example through training, social amenities and other incentives), as well as exerting influence in the wider world of customers, partners and suppliers.

Individuals have a number of functional requirements to carry out their work. These broadly relate to environment (light, heat, air quality, spatial layout, ambience, décor and so on), tools (technology, furniture, protocols and systems) and settings (spaces for different work and social activities). Individuals have a range of psychological needs in the workplace that are related to belonging, trust and empowerment. They want to feel valued, cared for and acknowledged. They want to feel that their contribution is worthwhile. Factors relating to levels of flexibility, autonomy and choice in the workplace come into play here, as do issues of identity and territory and the process of participating in workplace design.

The model proposes that for wellbeing in the workplace to be optimised, organisational purpose has to be geared towards meeting both the functional and psychological needs of the individual on an equal basis. There are four versions of the model: a Full Alignment model in which the organisational purpose is fully aligned with both the individual's functional and psychological needs; two Partial Alignment versions in which the organisational purpose is aligned with either the functional or psychological needs of the individual, but not both; and a Non-Alignment Model in which organisational purpose is aligned to neither the functional nor psychological needs of the individual.

It is proposed that the ideal state of wellbeing in the workplace is when the organisation's needs and individual needs are aligned, both functionally and psychologically. This state of equilibrium is rare and hard to achieve, although the research team identified examples in the field. In this scenario, the organisation benefits directly from its investment in the workplace and in people's wellbeing because the psychological contract ensures that people will work harder, have more commitment, be more innovative and so on.

More often, the alignment is incomplete or partial in one way or another. Sometimes the psychological contract with employees is strong – staff members feel trusted, empowered and understood. They have a strong sense of belonging based on a commitment and attraction to the organisation's mission and values. Their psychological needs are met. However, their functional needs are unmet. The environmental conditions might not be appropriate given what the organisation is trying to do, or the tools and systems are inadequate, or there is insufficient choice or variety of settings. A vibrant sense of identity with the organisation's mission is therefore undermined by a workplace that is not fit for purpose. This scenario can occur when an organisation has adopted a new workplace culture but not adapted its workspace functionally to reflect new ways of working.

Sometimes the opposite occurs. Functional needs are met in terms of providing the right physical work environment, tools and settings to match the organisation's purpose. However, the psychological contract with employees is weak – staff members do not feel trusted, empowered or understood and they have no real sense of belonging, indicating that their underlying psychological needs have not been considered. This scenario can occur after an organisation has invested in the design of a new workplace without having taken their workforce through a change-management process or without allowing staff to participate in the decision-making for the design of a new space.

In the worst cases, there is a complete non-alignment, resulting in a demotivated workforce adrift in a disorganised workplace. All elements of the model are out of synch with each other. Functional needs of the individual are not met. The organisation is not providing the right environment, tools or settings to get the work done effectively. Psychological needs of the individual are not met either. Employees do not feel they belong. They feel disempowered, mistrusted and misunderstood. This scenario can occur when an organisation is physically stretched – the office is full beyond capacity but there is no budget for improvements and no planned investment. At the same time, there is a failure to compensate for physical workplace shortcomings by meeting psychological needs.

Conclusions

Although a small study as part of an ongoing programme of research, the RCA-Gensler Workplace and Wellbeing study provides evidence that participation in the design of the workplace can have some beneficial effect on wellbeing at work. Those teams that were engaged in the participatory design project at any level (whether high or low participation) registered a higher increase in their mental wellbeing than the team not invited to participate. The study offers insights into how participatory design activities (see Figure 19.3) might be planned and delivered in a busy workplace; it also provides a model to help organisations look at the balance of their provision to meet employee needs and thus address the mental health problems of stress, depression, anxiety, disassociation and burnout that are becoming increasingly prevalent.

Why mental health should be getting worse as offices become more sophisticated and comfortable in terms of design can be attributed to the particular characteristics of knowledge working in the digital age – the always-on, 24/7 nature of the commitment required and the move away from individually assigned desks to more flexible modes of working that can create anxiety as well as offer choice. It is ironic that progressive remote working technologies and activity-based working formats can impact so negatively on an individual's sense of control at work when they were intended to do exactly the opposite.

What is clear is that employees appreciate being given the opportunity to exercise some control over the change process that is now a constant part of working life through participation in workplace design. But the invitation to participate is more important than the level of participation on offer. Both business leaders and public health experts will continue to advocate design changes that influence health and wellbeing in the workplace. These will span the technical considerations of air and water quality, light and lighting, as well as spatial issues such as circulation, movement and provision of varied settings, and cultural factors such as management style, supervision and nutrition. The 21st-century workplace must do everything it can to address the health deficit that is a legacy from the efficiency-at-all-costs mantra of the past 100 years of office design. In the mix, however, we should start paying more attention to how design participation in the workplace can help to improve mental wellbeing. Despite

Figure 19.3 Co-design activities during the Workplace and Wellbeing research study

the relative unfamiliarity of the concept in the workplace, the potential of co-design is there to be adopted.

Acknowledgements

The authors would like to thank Andrew Thomson and Alma Erlich from the RCA worked on the RCA-Gensler Workplace and Wellbeing study described in this chapter. The Gensler team was led by Philip Tidd, Ankita Dwivedi and Namrata Krishna. The research was supported by an industrial consortium comprising Bupa, Kinnarps, Milliken, RBS and Shell.

References

Black, C. (2016) How everyone benefits from company health and wellbeing campaigns. *Guardian Supplement on Workplace Health*, March.
Boyle, D., Slay, J. and Stephens, L. (2010) Public services inside out: Putting co-production into practice. London: NESTA.
Bradwell, P. and Marr, S (2008) Making the most of collaboration: An international survey of public service co-design. DEMOS and PricewaterhouseCoopers Public Sector Research Centre, London.
CBI (2013) Fit for purpose: Absence and workplace health survey 2013. Available at: www.cbi.org.uk/media/2150120/cbi-pfizer_absence___workplace_health_2013.pdf, accessed 31 March 2016.
DELOS Living LLC (2015) Wellbeing standard. International Institute of Wellbeing, February.

Dodge, R., Daly, A., Huyton, J. and Sanders, L. (2012) The challenge of defining wellbeing. *International Journal of Wellbeing*, 2(3): 222–35. Available at: www.ernationaljournalofwellbeing.org/index.php/ijow/article/viewFile/89/238?origin=publication_detail, accessed 4 March 2015.

Gensler (2013) 2013 U.S. workplace survey: Key findings. Gensler. Available at: www.gensler.com/uploads/document/337/file/2013_US_Workplace_Survey_07_15_2013.pdf, accessed 4 March 2015.

HSE (2015) Health and safety statistics annual report for Great Britain 2014/15. Available at: www.hse.gov.uk/statistics/overall/hssh1415.pdf, accessed 31 March 2016.

Jeffrey, K., Mahony, S., Michaelson, J. and Abdallah, S. (2014) Well-being at work: A review of the literature. New Economics Foundation. Available at: http://b.3cdn.net/nefoundation/71c1bb59a2ce151df7_8am6bqr2q.pdf, accessed 4 March 2015.

Knight, C. and Haslam, S. (2010) The relative merits of lean, enriched, and empowered offices: An experimental examination of the impact of workspace management strategies on well-being and productivity. *Journal of Experimental Psychology: Applied*, 16(2): 158–72.

Lynch, K. and Roulston, T. (2015) The playbox: ANZ Bank. Conference presentation at Worktech, London, 17 November.

Macdonald, A. and Teal, G. (2011) Inspiring service innovation through co-design in public sector healthcare. Include conference.

Marks, N. (2014) Guardian readers reveal what makes them happy at work. *Guardian*. Available at: www.theguardian.com/sustainable-business/happy-work-what-makes-you.

Myerson, J. and Tidd, P. (2016) Workplace and wellbeing: What aspects of workplace design are most important to people's wellbeing? Royal College of Art and Gensler research report.

NICE (2009) *Mental Wellbeing at Work*. Manchester: National Institute for Health and Care Excellence.

Oguz, S., Merad, S. and Snape, D. (2013) Measuring national well-being: What matters most to personal well-being? London: Office for National Statistics. Available at: www.ons.gov.uk/ons/dcp171766_312125.pdf, accessed 4 March 2015.

PwC (2008) Building the case for wellness. Available at: www.gov.uk/government/uploads/system/uploads/attachment_data/file/209547/hwwb-dwp-wellness-report-public.pdf, accessed 11 March 2016.

Ramirez, R. (2008) A 'meditation' on meaningful participation. *Journal of Community Informatics*, 4. Available at: http://ci-journal.net/index.php/ciej/article/view/390, accessed 17 March 2016.

Regus (2009) Stress out? A study of trends in workplace stress across the globe. Available at: www.regus.co.uk/images/Stress%20full%20report_FINAL_Designed_tcm294-21560.pdf, accessed 30 March 2016.

Sainsbury Centre for Mental Health (2007) Mental health at work: Developing the business case. Policy paper 8. London: Sainsbury Centre for Mental Health.

Sanders, E B-N. and Stappers, P J. (2008) Co-creation and the new landscapes of design. *Co-Design: International Journal of CoCreation in Design and the Arts*, 4(1): 5–18. Available at: www.tandfonline.com/doi/pdf/10.1080/15710880701875068.

Singleton, N., Bumpstead, R., O'Brien, M., Lee, A. and Meltzer, H. (2000) Psychiatric morbidity among adults living in private households, 2000: Summary report. London: Office for National Statistics.

StudioTilt (2014) *Codesigning Space*. London: Artiface.

Vischer, J.C. (2005) *Space Meets Status: Designing Workplace Performance*. Oxford: Taylor and Francis/Routledge.

Vischer, J.C. (2008) Towards an environmental psychology of workspace: How people are affected by environments for work. *Architectural Science Review*, 51(2): 97–108.

Warwick Medical School (2015) Warwick-Edinburgh Mental Wellbeing Scale. Available at: www2.warwick.ac.uk/fac/med/research/platform/wemwbs/, accessed 30 March 2016.

Young, D. (2015) Walking urbanism and the workplace. Conference presentation at Worktech, London, 17 November.

20 Behaviours

Older adults' behavioural strategies in the adoption of new technology-based products: the effects of ageing and the promising application of smart materials for the design of smart products

Gabriella Spinelli, Massimo Micocci and Marco Ajovalasit

Abstract

In a world that is ageing fast technology can really make a difference to keep people independent, healthy and socially connected. While the physical and sensorial signs of ageing have to some extent been considered in the design of technology for older people, much work is still needed to understand the impact of cognitive and emotional changes in the adoption, deferral or rejection of technology devices. Understanding the behavioural strategies of older people when dealing with technology-based products can help designers as well as marketers to reconsider product attributes and market communication, respectively. A set of smart computational materials suggests novel application opportunities for the design of more immediate and intuitive technology products.

The ageing market

We live in an ageing world. The world's population of those aged 60 years and older has doubled since 1980 and is forecast to reach 2 billion by 2050 (World Health Organization, 2014). People are living longer, remaining more active into older age and desiring to stay in their homes longer before finding the need for 'assisted living' arrangements (Fisk et al., 2009). While this would release the pressure that nursing homes experience and reduce healthcare costs, it generates great pressure on informal carers, such as spouses, children and other family members and friends (Mulvenna et al., 2010). Longevity is also associated with significant deterioration in the human physical and cognitive capabilities, such as hearing and vision loss, osteoarthritis, memory problems, mobility impairments and general frailty (Metz, 2000). As a result of these changes, one of the main challenges for the ageing population involves understanding how to keep older adults independent in their daily activities. Older adults need everyday products that place a relatively low level of demand on their cognitive and physical capabilities in order to ensure they can interact with the product to achieve their desired goal (Elton and Nicolle, 2015).

In addition to the change in demographics, there has been a major change in what current technology can offer for the design of product functionalities, the way they look, act and react to people who use them. With an unprecedented change in the worldwide population structure, increasingly more attention is focused on the design of technology products for older people (Peacock and Künemund, 2007). One of the major caveats for any project that aims to develop assistive devices for older adults is indeed ensuring that the final product will be adopted by intended users and meet real needs. There is a large amount of research (Walters et al., 2000, Blyth et al., 2005, Dröes et al., 2006) which brings evidence that involving target users in the design process, with the goal of developing a device, whose design supports only functional needs seems not to be the best way forward for designing for older adults. Aside from physical problems (such as loss of eyesight and hearing and incontinence), the most frequently identified unmet needs for products or services are in the areas of information (on health condition, treatment, care and support possibilities, etc.), memory problems and communication and psychological distress (anxiety). Research (Hancock et al., 2003) suggests that technology adoption among older people falls short of satisfying very fundamental needs such as the feeling of autonomy. To support autonomy technology could reinforce one's orientation in space and in time, topographic memory and one's ability to maintain contact with their social environment.

Advancements in information and communication technology (ICT), computing and monitoring sensors (Harrison et al., 2009) have led to progress in areas of ubiquitous and pervasive computing and enhanced awareness in their application in the role of assistive technology in the home context for older people. However, research (Blyth et al., 2005) suggests that the adoption of technology in the home of the older person should be approached from a *socioemotional* aspect, whereas most of the current research performed to date concentrates mainly on the usability of the screen device or interface design. Blyth et al. (2005) draw attention to the evidence gathered in the interviews conducted in their studies; they find that personal contact was very important to the older person. They also highlighted that the wearing of a device was perceived as a diminishment of the older user's independence rather than a facilitator of independence as intended.

Ho et al. (2005) found in their studies that older people in the field of monitoring medication intake had less confidence in their own judgement and so were more reliant on the decision made by the technology. Thus they suggested that this trait in the older user should be included into the design process. Experimental research performed by Bickmore et al. (2005) into relational agents–defined as 'computational artifacts designed to build and maintain long term social-emotional relationship with the users'–found that the relationship built up between the person and the agent had a beneficial result in having the technology system accepted by the older person and being also beneficial in reducing loneliness for the older person.

Technological products for the everyday life of older adults

The design of products for the ageing market is encompassing multiple technological innovations that are improving the way older adults experience their everyday life. The growing pervasiveness of these products across all domains of life is facilitating how older people perform independently specific tasks, such as health monitoring and medicine management, but their acceptance is still a challenge. Although older people appear willing to use technological products to support their safety at home and promote their personal wellness and health (Mitzner et al., 2010), still a *digital divide* between those who do and those who do not adopt technology-based products is widely observed (Czaja et al., 2006).

The perceived benefit deriving from the adoption of products is a fundamental aspect that leads older adults to purchase and fully use a new product. Although costs are widely recognised as a barrier to technology adoption (Age UK, 2013a), more likely the inability to clearly comprehend the perceived benefits of a technology-based product prior to purchase is the key hindering factor. The study of Mitzner et al. (2010) with 113 community-dwelling older adults and the data collected by Melenhorst et al. (2006) are consistent in emphasising that perceived benefits are decisive in older adults' choice for the purchase of a new product. It is reasonable to assume that with growing age, and a consequent reduced life-time horizon, personal resources are deemed precious so any investment of energy and time represents a worthless effort unless benefits are unequivocally clear.

The growing difficulty in performing activities of daily living, often caused by decreased mobility, reduced muscle strength and limited stamina, affects the perception, cognition and the control of movements (Fisk et al., 2009; Blaschke et al., 2009) and consequently may impinge on the adoption of complex technological products. As individuals grow older, there is increasing variability in haptic control and increased limit for temperature and vibration perception compared to younger adults. Age-related changes in audition and vision are also considered as basic factors that restrain older people to use products that barely consider these changes in sensorial perception. In addition to changes in perception, reduced cognitive skills, mainly related to an age-related decline, ought to be considered. Working (short-term) memory refers to the capability to temporarily store information while we use it and this affects greatly the information one may retain about a product one wishes to purchase and the necessary instructions that facilitate the learning of products. Long-term memory seems less affected by the ageing process. This type of memory consists of the semantic memory, defined as the store of factual information gathered through a lifetime of learning and the procedural memory, a set of scripts of how to perform activities and tasks (Fisk et al., 2009). This is the reason why automated tasks and activities learned prior to senescence remain intact while older adults encounter difficulties in retaining information and developing automatic processes for new tasks. The use of products that require significant learning instruction not comparable to previous experience may therefore be reduced (Blackler and Hurtienne, 2007). In the attempt to design familiar and intuitive devices, several standalone products exclusively conceived for older people are often designed with commands, features and redundant controls aiming to enhance the appropriate communication of their function. These attempts are not always reported as successful; often these products end up magnifying the physical and cognitive weaknesses of the user that perceive them as demeaning and stigmatising. As reported by Forlizzi (2007) this failure broadens the gap between the elders and their environment, sometimes resulting in frustration and isolation. More successful are products that support elders' values of self-confidence, dignity and that re-establish or maintain one's identity, possibly in defeating the stigmatisation of ageism. Achieving a goal is for older people a fundamental way to still appreciate them as respectful and worthy, and technology could help to facilitate activities, mediate social interactions and evoke experiences that contribute to a positive sense of self (Forlizzi, 2007). Intelligent products and systems for older people could be effectively conceived in a way that they understand the users' behaviour, predict the users' wishes and needs and act accordingly without imposing to the user overwhelming procedures. This would reduce the load of learning that new models and interfaces generally require (Sadri 2011). The advantage in the adoption of these new technologies is to allow old, frail people to remain in their homes longer with increased levels of independence and change the focus of healthcare toward wellness.

The effect of the ageing process on decision-making

Ageing has significant consequences for information processing because it underpins the decision-making we exercise when making choices in any aspects of our life. Decision-making is, in turn, fundamental in the choice we operate to adopt and use products and services around us. Information is processed in two ways during decision-making: affective-experiential and deliberative (Epstein, 1994; Reyna, 2004). These two ways are also referred to as system 1 and system 2, respectively (Kahneman, 2003). Both systems are equally important in decision-making and effective decisions are said to be the results of choices operated by the two systems concertedly (Damasio, 1994). However, the two systems work in fundamentally different ways; while system 1 operates in unconscious, effortless, intuitive and spontaneous ways, system 2 acts consciously, requires effort, it is explicit and analytical (Epstein 1994). Scholars claim that the deliberative system applies some sort of quality control to the instinctive outputted decisions operated by the affective system (Kahneman, 2003). Moreover, research has ascertained that the two systems are interdependent (Epstein, 1994) and that at times they compensate and influence each other. In some cases it has been observed that the affective system may have a greater influence on decisions when the cognitive load is higher or the deliberative skills are lower (Hammond, 1996; Peters and Slovic, 2007). Alhakami and Slovic (1994) have also ascertained that under time pressure, the effective system has a higher influence on the deliberation. These findings have stronger implications on how consumers enact their choice in relation to the point and channel of sale.

The relation between ageing and systems 1 and 2 has been evidenced in several studies. Age seems to be unequivocally linked to a decline of deliberative skills due to a less effective information processing (Salthouse, 1992), learning deficit (Kausler, 1990), inability to filter out irrelevant or false information (Hasher and Zacks, 1988), deterioration of the executive functions (Amieva et al., 2003) and numeracy skills (Kirsh et al., 2002). Less clear are the effects of ageing on the affective system. The most significant theoretical contribution explaining the role of emotions in decision-making among older adults is the socioemotional selectivity theory (Carstensen, 2006). This perspective argues that older adults are more aware of their nearing end of life and consequently they rely more heavily on the affective system in order to achieve positive outcomes. Studies have provided evidence that greater recall of positive advertisements and of emotion-laden information take place among older people (Carstensen and Turk-Charles, 1994; Carstensen, 1993).

The implications determined by the ageing process on decision-making, especially in the realm of technological products, can be summarised in two points:

1. As the older adults have been exposed to technological products for a relatively short period in their life, their decisions are based predominantly on deliberative skills rather than experience and emotions. The former, as discussed above, are cognitively demanding. Consequently, older people may be vulnerable and prone to information overload.
2. Older adults' vulnerability is exacerbated by social-economical circumstances whereby they have: i) less time and, on average, less financial resources to recover from poor-quality decisions (Peters et al., 2007); ii) less access to knowledgeable members of the family due to geographically dispersed family; and iii) less opportunity to benefit from online services and reviews of technological-based products due to their relatively lower lack of experience with internet technologies (Selwyn et al., 2003).

Whilst it has been claimed that decision-making and access to appliances such as microwaves, washing machines and electric gardening tools is a matter of personal choice, hence unproblematic (Peacock and Künemund, 2007), the inaccessibility to digital technologies represents a more challenging issue. Abundant research has taken place to explain why older people are laggards in the adoption of technological products and the reasons offered range considerably: usability issues, product price and the high cost of learning. This composite set of barriers informs the behaviour of people in all three stages of the technology adoption process; the formation of consideration set, the selection of point of purchase and eventually usage. Both affective/experiential and deliberative systems have a fundamental part to play in the three stages listed above, hence ageing will affect the way that older adults will consider, approach and use technology-based products. It would be too vague a generalisation to attribute the behaviours and choices of older adults when it comes to technology-based products only to their chronological age. Studies have found out that higher education attainment and labour-force participation are positively related to the adoption of technology (Korupp et al., 2006). Technology usage is observably different between genders as well with women displaying a lower uptake of technological products. This may possibly be due not to gender differences but simply to a higher level of education more frequently accessible to men in the past (Peacock and Künemund, 2007).

Ageing and ageing-related socioeconomical factors have a profound impact on how information is processed, decisions are made and behaviour is enacted. To some extent the impact of ageing is exacerbated when it comes to technology-based products as they are less known to the ageing population and are also characterised by a fast pace of change due to continuous technological advancement and consequent reduction in costs. In the following section the behavioural strategies adopted by older adults when dealing with technology-based products are discussed.

Behavioural strategies in adoption of technology products

Some attempts have been made in gerontology studies to create a taxonomy of the technologies available (Mollenkopf and Kaspar, 2005). This classification includes *compensation technology*, those used to make up for sensory losses and other physical or cognitive limitations; *daily life technology*, artefacts used to rehabilitate individuals who have suffered temporary conditions/disabilities; and a cluster of *low- and high-tech devices* that are chosen to enhance the wellbeing of individuals who have no condition to cater or compensate for. In contrast with the first two types, this latter set of technology is freely chosen and consists of mainstream technology purchased and accessible to people of all ages. However, in light of the changes determined by the ageing process and discussed above, the behavioural strategies leading to the selection and adoption of technology-based products are worth special attention.

Research has already established that older adults consider selection sets at pre-purchase that contain fewer items (Roedder and Cole, 1986). This can be explained by:

- a lesser ability to retain and process analytical information about a larger number of products;
- a more developed preference for some products/brands achieved through past experience (Lambert-Pandraud and Laurent, 2010); and
- a generally higher cost in searching for product information (Johnson, 1990).

This is particularly important in the selection of technology-based products, as the brands known to the older population are fewer and the familiarity with the product category less developed. Other crucial aspects considered by older adults in purchase decisions are staff availability and knowledge of the products at the point of sale and products' extended warranty (Shekarriz and Spinelli, 2013).

In the consideration of older adults' behaviour towards technology-based products it is important to take into account research regarding decision-making. An attempt to group the behaviour of older adults as consumers of technology leads to the identification of four strategies; these are: i) denial, ii) deferral, iii) delegation and iv) adoption. While extant literature has already considered decision avoidance (Anderson, 2003) across the life span, the account that follows is specific to decision-making regarding observed behaviour of older adults around technologies. It is important to stress that decision avoidance is a class of behaviour usually attributed to a complex set of antecedents and that occurs across life age. This class of behaviour includes inertia, delay, defensive avoidance and omission bias (Tykocinski et al., 1995; Dhar, 1996, 1997).

Denial

This represents the decision of not considering an action, or in other words, the choice to retain the *status quo*. In such events the decision-maker prefers to not consider other alternatives available, therefore settling for the current state of affairs (Schweitzer, 1994). In these cases, the *status quo* is considered less threatening and the avoidance to consider alternative decisions is associated with the prevention of negative emotions that would derive by choosing 'something new'. In choosing to ignore alternatives, the decision-makers deny themselves the opportunity to consider the perceived benefits that a technology may bring to their life, while also preventing feeling frustrated, anxious or regretful if technologies proved to be difficult to use. Older adults may disregard the benefits that smart phones or internet-based technologies may bring to their life by stating that their current set-up (e.g. communicating by letters with remote family and friends) is more personal and that technologies would bring a style of communication that they would consider disrespectful (e.g. texting is considered by some older adults as a nuisance, abrupt and unfriendly). Such denial strategy may be explained by the inability of some older adults to recognise the opportunities that technologies could bring to their life, making them prefer a known state, the present, which presents no negative surprises for them.

Deferral

Still in the attempt to avoid negative emotions, older adults may consider the deferral of decisions as a good way to resolve decision-making situations. Finucane et al. (2002) observed that older adults were more likely to prefer not to feel responsible for choosing their own medical plan. The study of Tversky and Shafir (1992) suggests that it is the compound complexity of choice dimensions that may cause deferral. When overwhelmed by the choice alternatives and by the relevant attributes to consider in the evaluation of the selection set, older adults may postpone their decision and this may lead to irretrievable consequences. When dealing with technologies older adults may link the adoption of new products to events that may never occur so as to attribute the cause of their postponement to external factors outside their control (e.g. save money to purchase a device, prolong search for alternatives or the accessibility to a family member who could teach them to use the device). It is generally accepted that deferred choices are the symptoms of conflicting experience by the decision-makers either because they are overwhelmed by the options or because they are unable to focus on the relevant attributes to operate the choice (Anderson, 2003). Both cases seem highly relevant to older adults and technology adoption given the relative underdeveloped familiarity with this product category.

Delegation

This is another strategy in the avoidance behaviour class and it is observed when the decision is passed in full or in part to another agent. In older consumers who seek to adopt technology, delegation occurs often between spouses, with usually a gender prevalence where males are delegated the responsibility to purchase, set up and indeed use technologies. Differently from the previous two strategies, here the perceived benefits of technology are somehow understood, hence the decision-makers do not wish to prolong the *status quo* but they feel unable to be leading such a decision. The strategy of delegation also occurs between generations where older adults invest their offspring with the responsibility to select the technology they may use. Partial delegation may occur when for lack of confidence in their technology skills, older adults may delegate crucial tasks such as initial technology set-up and privacy management to those whom they believe to be more expert.

Adoption

This is not just the purchase of technology products but also their use. Often technologies are purchased or received as gifts and abandoned for a set of reasons that in part overlap with those analysed in the strategies for decision avoidance, e.g. lack of confidence, unfamiliarity with the product, conflict in the choice, fear of regret, high cost of learning. However, when technology adoption takes place among older adults it is the outcome of a much more complex process that involves other social resources in support of this choice. Adoption is supported often when the older consumer is within a supportive social group and can access peer or structured learning.

Technologies for an ageing population: design considerations

Nowadays, commercially available products for the ageing market use a broad range of modern technology such as necklaces with emergency buttons and fall sensors integrated into mobile phones with wireless notification functionality to caregivers. These are mainly standalone systems, often too difficult for older people to operate (Kleinberger et al., 2007). Ubiquitous input/output devices, such as smartphones or blood pressure machines, are then particularly affected by a low adoption rate, since they involve an interaction with the cognitive and sensorial system of the user, systems that as we discussed earlier undergo significant changes with age (Gamberini et al., 2006). Regardless of such changes, some older people show a vivid curiosity to discover new products but often they rely on their social network or formal training courses to understand the usefulness of a laptop computer (Age UK, 2013b) and overall support technology adoption. Designing for the ageing population should entail specific consideration for changing the behavioural, cognitive and emotional pattern of the users. Fisk et al. (2009) considered usefulness as the sum of *usability* – the possibility to have access to a product – and *utility* – the capability to provide the functionality the product possesses. Usefulness in the design for the ageing population can be embedded through five characteristics:

- *Learnability*: how easy it is to learn to use the device.
- *Efficiency*: how technological applications satisfy users and how the users' needs are met avoiding fatigue and dissatisfaction within a reasonable a amount of time.
- *Memorability*: minimise the effort to remember how a device works after a period of non–use.

- *Errors*: minimise the amount of errors while interacting with the device and allow retrievable errors.
- *Satisfaction*: create pleasurable interactions with the product.

Often a barrier to an enjoyable and effective use of a technology-based product is its interface. Designing for older people challenges standard and traditional input/output modality because of the older adults' changes in sensory and cognitive skills as well as the lack of familiarity with new interaction languages. In this view, the combination of multiple sensory input and output channels for the interaction with technology (multimodality) could have the benefit to let the user choose the interaction modality that is most suitable to his/her own capabilities and to make a redundant message that if communicated in a multisensorial way could be more effective. Blackler et al. (2012) found that the performance of older people when interacting with various interfaces is affected by decline in cognition and familiarity with the product features. Consequently, the emerging factor that contributes to making a product more immediate for the older adults is managing the transfer of the user's existing schema of products to the new device (Moreau et al., 2001; Blackler et al., 2007).

One approach that has been proposed to design more effective technology for older adults is to include them in the design process from the requirement stage, and ideally throughout the development phase. Kurniawan (2008), through a multimethod investigation, identified how older people need to personalise the interface of the mobile phone and how some of the functionalities of the device could be dramatically improved to support the cognitive decline in later life. Using design methodologies that enable the direct observation of the user is also effective to understand the older adults' psychological and socioemotional needs that may conflict with the functional benefit of elderly-related products (Bright and Coventry, 2013). This misunderstanding of the users' needs often causes the users to abandon the technology, resulting in a reduced sense of self-confidence. Bright and Coventry (2013) identify guidelines to avoid embedding negative age stereotypes and the resulting reluctance to engage with them. The researchers propose that assistive technologies should not be considered as medical devices but they should rather stimulate the users' curiosity and interest so as to facilitate early adoption and personalisation of the technologies so that they could enter the lifestyle of older adults without signalling disability.

When considering the behavioural strategies adopted by ageing users and the challenge to bridge the digital divide that still characterises this growing segment of the population worldwide, product-development teams may wish to consider the following practical suggestions:

- Despite being incredibly effective and useful, technologies are perceived differently by the ageing population. Consequently, the pervasiveness of technology-based products may not be seen by older people as the ideal solution to achieve an independent life in older age. Sometimes interventions devoid of technology may be better received.
- In the adoption of technology its perceived benefit must be significantly bigger than the learning resources associated with the use of the same. As a result the marketing communication of the technology products is a key factor.
- In designing for older people technology must consider the evolution of the user, hence be adaptable to a number of co-present conditions and developing consequences.

- The ageing market is far from being homogenous and requires a landscape of products and services that reflects such diversity in conditions, taste, attitude to technologies and aspirations.
- The discovery and application of smart and computational materials in everyday life activities should be considered as a means to simplify current activities performed in interaction with technological devices rather than just providing further functionalities.

Discussion

Research has established that ageing impacts our cognitive skills, emotions and social needs. In turn these changes modify our everyday behaviour making older adults somehow more vulnerable when choosing and adopting technology-based products. However, in a world that is ageing, designers cannot refrain from considering the imperative of designing for the human, regardless of his/her conditions and disabilities. So far the debate on technology for the ageing population has been dominated by the concept of assistive technologies. This in part has skewed the debate and, most of all, has reduced the efforts made by the ICT sector to produce mainstream products that can adapt to the changing needs of people, rather than focusing on the impairments emerging with age. Considering behavioural changes as a consequence of cognitive and physical impairments has damaging consequences on the design rationale and philosophy that is applied to developing products, systems, services and experiences for the older population. If living well with dignity and independently for as long as possible is a societal goal, researchers and practitioners are invested with the role to make transition to older age as acceptable as possible; an evolution rather than a segregation to a group of impaired and frail individuals.

The current advancement in materials and technologies has started to shift the discourse on technology adoption among older people and we observe more applications made to enable people rather than to compensate for their changing skills. For example, products such as Ref, a wearable device[1] that monitors changes in the user's pulse and by communicating them through haptic signal onto the user's wrist, relaxes or enhances the user's behaviour. This demonstrates that supporting the awareness and understanding of correct breathing and emotional patterns has great impact on the overall health and self-confidence of the user while also improving his physical condition.

While the researchers strive to understand more about the ageing mind and body, design efforts in the last two decades have rightly made a case for inclusive design; that is designing for audiences with a wider set of skills and aspirations. This special effort to design inclusively though has often produced products that are 'assistive' making the impairment they try to support more evident, hence more stigmatising. With the introduction of materials that are smart and can adapt and respond to users' needs and desires, technologies are promising us a truly new horizon of products that evolve with the individuals.

An additional challenge is posed by how marketing can communicate the potential of technologies without disenfranchising older adults who invest in products when the perceived benefits are clear and substantial for their lifestyle. Categorisation literature has argued that available mental models developed through past experience can help in transferring knowledge to new products and facilitating the comprehension of how new technology works (Hoeffler, 2003). However, there is still ambiguity on how such insights can become guidance for designers and marketers. The fast pace of technology turnover on the market further confuses older adults by making purchased products obsolete very quickly and demanding a high cost of learning to stay abreast. In the next section the future of technology-based products is discussed considering the application of so-called 'smart material'.

Future directions and conclusions

Evidence-based research (Hancock et al., 2003; Mulvenna et al., 2010; European Commission, 2010) reports that more than 60 per cent of people over 50 years of age feel that their needs are not adequately addressed by current ICT equipment and services. One of the main reasons is due to the lack of *socioemotional engagement* that older adults have with such technology (Bright and Coventry, 2013). Changes in technology can lead to less than desirable interactions with products or services. Despite recent advancements in ICT and growing sales numbers, the industry has been rather reluctant to standardise access technology and to implement them in a 'design for all approach'. Most often, the design and implementation of appliances using modern ICT are driven by the ambition to satisfy users that are already engaged in modern technologies. Thus many people with disabilities, in particular people with cognitive disabilities and older persons, are excluded from their use. Moreover, modern ICT-based products and services for coping with behavioural and psychological changes in people's disabilities and personalised information on the person's condition (Yasuda et al., 2006) are relatively disregarded as yet, while support for social contact seems currently to be effectively realised, for example, through simplified mobile phones or videophones (Lauriks et al., 2007).

Emphasis in the literature points to the need for more flexible, personalised care and support due to the fact that the individual needs of older adults and carers can considerably differ because of a number of personal and contextual factors, such as the symptoms of the person with disabilities, carer characteristics and utilised coping strategies, the relationship between the carer and older people and the perception of the quality of the relief that is offered (Burns, 2000; Clare, 2002).

The field of wellbeing and healthcare highlights the need of products and services that are effective in the way they can track and enhance the wellness of the user, provide information and entertain rather than merely operate when a disease is in progress. Research areas such as Pervasive and Ubiquitous Computing (Weiser, 1991), Internet of Things (Atzori et al., 2010) and Ambient Intelligence (Ducatel et al., 2001) foresee the environments of the future as intelligent in a way that it can unobtrusively understand the users' behaviour, predict the users' wishes and needs and act accordingly.

In this perspective, 'smart objects' are defined as autonomous physical/digital objects augmented by sensing, processing and network capabilities (Kortuem et al., 2010). These objects can sense and interpret what is occurring within them and are aware of the surrounding world, communicate with each other, act on their own and exchange information with people (e.g. Figure 20.1).

For example, Withings[2] has recently commercialised a wireless blood pressure monitor that shows to the doctor the blood pressure of his patients. Data are communicated directly to the doctor so as to unload the user from recording and remembering the information; this results in an easier routine for the patient that is not taxing on his memory. Another example is Vessyl, a smart mug designed at Mark One[3] that automatically knows and tracks everything the user drinks and that displays nutritional information via Bluetooth to a smartphone. AdhereTech[4] also designed another smart object, a smart wireless pill bottle currently used by patients in pharmaceutical and research engagements (Figure 20.2). These bottles automatically analyse

Figure 20.1 Wireless blood pressure monitor, designed by Withings
Source: Withings, 2016

information and if doses are missed, patients can receive customisable alerts and interventions – using automated phone calls, text messages and more. With these products, the user can perform his ordinary activities (run, walk, drink) while objects seamlessly track his wellbeing status as a hidden caregiver. What the user perceives is exclusively the result of his performance, not needing to be concerned about the technology behind the product.

The growing diffusion of computational features in everyday products has blurred the boundaries between materials, interactive technologies and human–computer interaction (Vallgårda and Redström, 2007). Mickael Boulay designed 'Measure less to feel more',[5] a diabetes reader that reduces the stress of the user while measuring blood sugar level by creating an emotional and engaging experience. Current devices focus strictly on quantifying the blood level with numbers with no room for personal feeling and sensation. In the vision of the designer this aloof activity is made personal by the use of a changing LED light to literally express how high/low the blood sugar level is instead of using numbers. Another interesting composite interaction is provided by Future Care Floor (Klack et al., 2011) that shows an instrumental integration of the smart materials into the home environment. This sensor floor seamlessly integrates piezoelectric sensors to support old and frail persons living independently at home. The purpose of this application is to detect abnormal behavioural patterns of the inhabitant and activate rescue procedures in case of falls or other emergency events.

'Smart materials' (SMs) is a relatively new term for materials that have changeable properties and are able to reversibly alter their shape or colour in response to physical and/or chemical influences, e.g. light, temperature or the application of an electric field (Ritter, 2007). The

Figure 20.2 Smart wireless pill bottles, designed by AdhereTech
Source: AdhereTech, 2016

Knowledge Transfer Network defines SMs as materials that display smart behaviours. In their view a smart behaviour occurs when a material can sense a stimulus from its environment and react to it in a useful, reliable, reproducible and usually reversible manner. SMs also incorporate features such as sensors and actuators, which are either embedded within a structural mate-rial or else bonded to the surface of the material (Gandhi and Thompson, 1992). The control capabilities permit the behaviour of the material to respond to an external stimulus according to a prescribed functional relationship or control algorithm. The development of 'smart' or 'intelligent' materials, systems and structures shows how products can actively monitor and optimise themselves and their performance emulating biological systems through their adap-tive and responsive capabilities (Schwartz, 2002).

Designers and engineers are starting to deploy the properties of materials to enhance the experience unleashed by products and unlock design opportunities for creative applications. Such attempts are proceeding by trial and error and despite the promising attempts described above, there seems to be no rationale that can robustly account for the specific matching of SMs to users' experiences/needs. These attempts demonstrate that we still lack a clear under-standing of how the users perceive, respond and maximise their experience with engineered materials embedded in everyday products. The quest to truly embed SMs in new products cannot transcend from the understanding of the users and their contexts of use.

Figure 20.3 Future care floor
Source: Kasugai, 2014

In this perspective it is reasonable to think that materials *per se* are neutral and invested with intelligence only within the framework of the user's experience, hence the need to focus on the latter. Benefits from SMs are not only as add-on interfaces in product development, but as integral constituents of the product. It is instrumental therefore to understand the users' goals and necessities in the continuous agency they perform in everyday tasks. This helps to conceptualise the sensorial and interactive qualities that can become the 'language' of interaction between the users and the immediate products that in this logic don't require interface to achieve smart experiences.

Summary

Designing technologies for the ageing population is a challenging issue. The challenge is represented by an ever-moving goal post in technology advancement that is not an easy match for the relatively inexperienced older user who, generally speaking, is still uncertain and unconvinced that technology can improve their lifestyle in older age. The chapter has reviewed the behavioural strategies displayed by older people when selecting, purchasing and using technology-based products. Such strategies rely not only on the individual's skills and characteristics but also on the social support group that can intervene to make the technology adoption process less demanding. The pressure on social and healthcare systems posed by an ageing society is relentless and smart materials are emerging as a promising opportunity for the design of more intuitive technology-based products. This, combined with a more advanced understanding of the ageing process, may help in the search for solutions to the changes in the demographic structure that are set to stay.

Notes

1 www.dyvikdesign.com/site/portfolio-jens/ref.html#sthash.aoswm1af.dpuf.
2 www.withings.com/eu/blood-pressure-monitor.html.
3 www.myvessyl.com/.
4 www.adheretech.com/.
5 http://mickaelboulay.fr/index.php?/measuring-less/content/.

References

Age UK (2013a) Digital inclusion evidence review. Available at: www.ageuk.org.uk/Documents/EN-GB/For-professionals/Research/Age%20UK%20Digital%20Inclusion%20Evidence%20Review%202013.pdf?dtrk=true.

Age UK (2013b) Pressing the right buttons. Available at: www.ageuk.org.uk/Documents/EN-GB/For-professionals/Research/Report-Computers_and_the_internet.pdf?dtrk=true.

Alhakami, A.S. and Slovic, P. (1994) A psychological study of the inverse relationship between perceived risk and perceived benefit. *Risk Analysis*, 14(6): 1085–96.

Amieva, H., Phillips, L. and Della Sala, S. (2003) Behavioral dysexecutive symptoms in normal aging. *Brain and Cognition*, 53(2): 129–32.

Anderson, C. (2003) The psychology of doing nothing: Forms of decision avoidance result from reason and emotion. *Psychological Bulletin*, 129: 139–67.

Atzori, L., Iera, A. and Morabito, G. (2010) The Internet of Things: A survey. *Computer Networks*, 54: 2787–805.

Bickmore, T.W., Caruso, L., Clough-Gorr, K. and Heeren, T. (2005) It's just like talking to a friend: Relational agents for older users. *Interacting with Computers*, 17: 711–35.

Blackler, A.L. and Hurtienne, J. (2007) Towards a unified view of intuitive interaction: Definitions, models and tools across the world. *MMI-interaktiv*, 13: 36–54.

Blackler, A.L., Popovic, V., Mahar, D.P., Reddy, R. and Lawry, S. (2012) Intuitive interaction and older people. Proceedings of the Design Research Society 2012 Conference, Department of Industrial Design, Faculty of Architecture, Chulalongkorn University, 560–78.

Blaschke, C.M., Freddolino, P.P. and Mullen, E.E. (2009) Ageing and technology: A review of the research literature. *British Journal of Social Work*, 39(4): 641–56.

Blyth, M., Monk, A.F. and Doughty, K. (2005) Socially dependable design: The challenge of ageing population for HCI. *Interacting with Computers*, 17: 672–89.

Bright, A.K. and Coventry, L. (2013) Assistive technology for older adults: Psychological and socio-emotional design requirements. Proceedings of the 6th International Conference on Pervasive Technologies Related to Assistive Environments, ACM, 9.

Burns, A. (2000) The burden of Alzheimer's disease. *International Journal of Neuropsychopharmacology*, 3: 31–8.

Carstensen, L.L. (1993) Motivation for social contact across the life span: A theory of socioemotional selectivity, in Jacobs, J.E. (ed.), *Nebraska Symposium on Motivation: 1992, Developmental Perspectives on Motivation*. Lincoln: University of Nebraska Press, 209–54.

Carstensen, L.L. (2006) The influence of a sense of time on human development. *Science*, 312: 1913–15.

Carstensen, L.L. and Turk-Charles, S. (1994) The salience of emotion across the adult life span. *Psychology and Aging*, 9: 259–64.

Clare, L. (2002) We'll fight it as long as we can: Coping with the onset of Alzheimer's disease. *Ageing and Mental Health*, 6: 139–48.

Czaja, S.J., Charness, N., Fisk, A.D., Hertzog, C., Nair, S.N., Rogers, W.A. and Sharit, J. (2006) Factors predicting the use of technology: Findings from the Center for Research and Education on Ageing and Technology Enhancement. *Psychology and Ageing*, 21(2): 333.

Damasio, A.R. (1994) *Descartes' Error: Emotion, Reason, and the Human Brain*. New York: Avon.

Dhar, R. (1996) The effect of decision strategy on the decision to defer choice. *Journal of Behavioral Decision Making*, 9: 265–81.

Dhar, R. (1997) Consumer preference for a no-choice option. *Journal of Consumer Research*, 24: 215–31.

Dröes, R.M., Boelens, E.J., Meihuizen, L., Ettema, T.P., Gerritsen, D.L., Hoogeveen, F., de Lange, J. and Schölzel-Dorenbos, C. (2006) Quality of life in dementia in perspective: An explorative study of variation in opinions among people with dementia and their professional caregivers, and in literature. *Dementia: International Journal of Social Research and Practice*, 5(4): 533–58.

Ducatel, K., Bogdanowicz, M., Scapolo, F., Leijten, J. and Burgelman, J. (2001) Scenarios for ambient intelligence in 2010. Office for Official Publications of the European Communities.

Elton E. and Nicolle C. (2015) Inclusive design and design for special populations, in Wilson, J. and Sharple, S. (eds), *Evaluation of Human Work*. 4th edition. Boca Raton, FL: Taylor and Francis.

Epstein, S. (1994) Integration of the cognitive and the psychodynamic unconscious. *American Psychologist*, 49: 709–24.

European Commission (2010) *Overview of the European strategy in ICT for Ageing Well*. Brussels.

Finucane, M.L., Slovic, P., Hibbard, J.H., Peters, E., Mertz, C.K. and Macgregor, D.G. (2002) Aging and decision-making competence: An analysis of comprehension and consistency skills in older versus younger adults considering health-plan options. *Journal of Behavioral Decision Making*, 15(2): 141–64.

Fisk, A.D., Rogers, W.A., Charness, N., Czaja, S.J. and Sharit, J. (2009) *Designing for Older Adults: Principles and Creative Human Factors Approaches*. Boca Raton, FL: CRC Press.

Forlizzi, J. (2007) Product ecologies: Understanding the context of use surrounding products. Unpublished dissertation, Carnegie Mellon University, Pittsburgh.

Gamberini, L., Raya, M.A., Barresi, G., Fabregat, M., Ibanez, F. and Prontu, L. (2006) Cognition, technology and games for the elderly: An introduction to ELDERGAMES project. *PsychNology Journal*, 4(3): 285–308.

Gandhi, M.V. and Thompson, B.S. (1992) *Smart Materials and Structures*. New York: Springer.

Hammond, K.R. (1996) *Human Judgment and Social Policy: Irreducible Uncertainty, Inevitable Error, Unavoidable Injustice*. New York: Oxford University Press.

Hancock, G.A., Reynolds, T., Woods, B., Thornicroft, G. and Orrell, M. (2003) The needs of older people with mental health problems according to the user, the carer and the staff. *International Journal of Geriatric Psychiatry*, 18: 803–11.

Harrison, C., Lim, B., Shick, A. and Hudson, S. (2009) Where to locate wearable displays? Reaction time performance of visual alerts from tip to toe. *CHI'09*: 941–4.

Hasher, L. and Zacks, R.T. (1988) Working memory, comprehension, and aging: A review and a new view, in Bower, G.H. (ed.), *The Psychology of Learning and Motivation: Advances in Research and Theory*. San Diego, CA: Academic Press, 193–225.

Ho, G., Wheatley, D. and Scialfa, C.T. (2005) Age differences in trust and reliance of a medication management system. *Interacting with Computers*, 17: 690–710.

Hoeffler, S. (2003) Measuring preferences for really new products. *Journal of Marketing Research*, 40(4): 406–20.

Johnson, M.M.S. (1990) Age differences in decision making: A process methodology for examining strategic information processing. *Journal of Gerontology: Series B Psychological Science and Social Science*, 45: 75–8.

Kahneman, D. (2003) A perspective on judgment and choice: Mapping bounded rationality. *American Psychologist*, 58: 697–720.

Kasugai, K. (2014) *Raumgeist: Prototypen der raumunterstützenden Technik*. Aachen: Apprimus Wissenschaftsver.

Kausler, D.H. (1990) Automaticity of encoding and episodic memory processes, in Lovelace, E.A. (ed.), *Aging and Cognition: Mental Processes, Self-Awareness, and Interventions: Advances in Psychology*. Amsterdam: North-Holland, 29–67.

Kirsch, I.S., Jungeblut, A., Jenkins, L. and Kolstad, A. (2002) *Adult Literacy in America: A First Look at the Findings of the National Adult Literacy Survey*. 3rd edition. Washington, DC: National Center for Education.

Klack, L., Möllering, C., Ziefle, M. and Schmitz-Rode, T. (2011) Future care floor: A sensitive floor for movement monitoring and fall detection in home environments. International Conference on Wireless Mobile Communication and Healthcare. Berlin: Springer, 211–18.

Kleinberger, T., Becker, M., Ras, E., Holzinger, A. and Müller, P. (2007) Ambient intelligence in assisted living: Enable elderly people to handle future interfaces. *Universal Access in Human-Computer Interaction*, 4555: 103–12.

Kortuem, G., Kawsar, F., Fitton, D. and Sundramoorthy, V. (2010) Smart objects as building blocks for the Internet of Things. *Internet Computing*, 14(1): 44–51.

Korupp S.E. (2006) No man is an island: The influence of knowledge, household settings, and social context on private computer use. *International Journal of Internet Science*, 1(1): 45–57.

Kurniawan, S. (2008) Older people and mobile phones: A multi-method investigation. *International Journal of Human-Computer Studies*, 66(12): 889–901.

Lambert-Pandraud, R. and Laurent, G. (2010) Impact of age on brand choice, in Drolet, A., Schwarz, N. and Yoon, C. (eds), *The Aging Consumer: Perspectives from Psychology and Economics*. London: Taylor and Francis, 191–208.

Lauriks, S., Reinersmann, A., van der Roest, H.G., Meiland, F.J., Davies, R.J., Moelaert, F., Mulvenna, M.D., Nugent, C.D. and Dröes, R.M. (2007) Review of ICT-based services for identified unmet needs in people with dementia. *Ageing Research Reviews*, 6(3): 223–46.

Melenhorst, A., Rogers, W.A. and Bouwhuis, D.G. (2006) Older adults' motivated choice for technological innovation: Evidence for benefit-driven selectivity. *Psychology and Ageing*, 21(1): 190.

Metz, D.H. (2000) Mobility of older people and their quality of life. *Transport Policy*, 7(2): 149–52.

Mitzner, T.L., Boron, J.B., Fausset, C.B., Adams, A.E., Charness, N., Czaja, S.J., Dijkstra, K., Fisk, A.D., Rogers, W.A. and Sharit, J. (2010) Older adults talk technology: Technology usage and attitudes. *Computers in Human Behavior*, 26(6): 1710–21.

Mollenkopf, H. and Kaspar, R. (2005) Elderly people's use and acceptance of information and communication technologies, in Jaeger, B. (ed.), *Young Technologies in Old Hands: An International View on Senior Citizens' Utilization of ICT*. Copenhagen: DJOF Publishing, 41–58.

Moreau, C.P., Lehmann, D.R. and Markman, A.B. (2001) Entrenched knowledge structures and consumer response to new products. *Journal of Marketing Research*, 38(1): 14–29.

Mulvenna, M.D., Nugent, C.D., Moelaert, F., Craig, D., Dröes, R.M. and Bengtsson, J.E. (2010) Supporting people with dementia using pervasive healthcare technologies, in Mulvenna, M.D. and Nugent, C.D. (eds), *Supporting People with Dementia Using Pervasive Health Technologies*. New York: Springer, 3–14.

Peacock, S.E. and Künemund, H. (2007) Senior citizens and internet technology: Reasons and correlates of access versus non-access in a European comparative perspective. *European Journal of Ageing*, 4(4): 191–200.

Peters, E. and Slovic, P. (2007) Affective asynchrony and the measurement of the affective attitude component. *Cognition and Emotion*, 21: 300–29.

Peters, E., Hess, T.M., Västfjäll, D. and Auman, C. (2007) Adult age differences in dual information processes: Implications for the role of affective and deliberative processes in older adults' decision making. *Perspectives on Psychological Science*, 2(1): 1–23.

Reyna, V.F. (2004) How people make decisions that involve risk: A dual-processes approach. *Current Directions in Psychological Science*, 13: 60–6.

Ritter, A. (2007) *Smart Materials: In Architecture, Interior Architecture and Design*. New York: Springer.

Roedder, J.D. and Cole, C.A. (1986) Age differences in information processing: Understanding deficits in young and elderly consumers. *Journal of Consumer Research*, 13: 297–315.

Sadri, F. (2011) Ambient intelligence: A survey. *ACM Computing Surveys*, 43(4): 36.

Salthouse, T.A. (1992) Why do adult age differences increase with task complexity? *Developmental Psychology*, 28: 905–18.

Schwartz, M.M. (2002) *Encyclopedia of Smart Materials*. New York: Wiley-Interscience.

Schweitzer, M. (1994) Disentangling status quo and omission effects: An experimental analysis. *Organizational Behavior and Human Decision Processes*, 58: 457–76.

Selwyn, N., Gorard S., Furlong J. and Madden L. (2003) Older adults' use of information technology in everyday life. *Aging Society*, 23: 561–82.

Shekarriz, M. and Spinelli, G. (2013) Ageing consumers: Lifestyles and preferences in the current marketplace. Project Report for Age UK, February.

Tversky, A. and Shafir, E. (1992) Choice under conflict: The dynamics of deferred decision. *Psychological Science*, 3(6): 358–61.

Tykocinski, O.E., Pittman, T.S. and Tuttle, E.S. (1995) Inaction inertia: Foregoing future benefits as a result of an initial failure to act. *Journal of Personality and Social Psychology*, 68: 793–803.

Vallgårda, A. and Redström, J. (2007) Computational composites. *ACM*: 513–22.

Walters, K., Iliffe, S., See Tai, S. and Orrell, M. (2000) Assessing needs from patient, career and professional perspectives: The Camberwell assessment of need for the elderly people in primary care. *Age and Ageing*, 29: 505–10.

Weiser, M. (1991) *The Computer for the 21st Century*. New York: Scientific American.

World Health Organization (2014) 10 facts on ageing and the life course. Available at: www.who.int/features/factfiles/ageing, accessed 20 March 2015.

Yasuda, K., Beckman, B., Yoneda, H., Iwamoto, A. and Nakamura, T. (2006) Successful guidance by automatic output of music and verbal messages for daily behavioral disturbances of three individuals with dementia. *Neuropsychological Rehabilitation*, 16: 66–82.

Part III

Research methods, recommendations and foresight

21 Design insider

The patient perspective

Victor Margolin

The chapters in this book have all been written from the perspective of the expert, based on theory and/or practice in design research and the evidence presented comes from researchers who collect data through observation and/or design practice.

Rarely do we see the environment from the insider. This chapter was written by a design historian/theorist who unfortunately became a patient. It illustrates the plethora of equipment that surrounds the patient throughout diagnosis, treatment and recovery. Victor Margolin describes clearly the strangeness of coming to terms with the processes, the technology and even the names of the technology and procedures.

Looking through this lens illustrates how much more designers and design researchers can do, from process and procedure explanation and understanding, to patient options choice and medical decisions, to the design of the technology, not only from the patient perspective but also from the medical and support team use-ability perspective. Can we even imagine a completely different world where the experience of such patients is holistic, simple and transparent… what will new technologies and new materials do to change this experience? There are so many opportunities to improve our health diagnosis, treatment and healing system. It would be wise to use this chapter to do good design for health and wellbeing.

Design down under

I have been a design historian and design theorist for more than 30 years. In 1982, I was a founder and later first editor of the academic journal *Design Issues*. I published a number of books and anthologies about design history and theory.[1]

On 17 October 2015, I had an accident at a design conference in Gwangju, South Korea. I fainted, fell and dislocated several cervical vertebrae that impinged on my spinal cord. I was left without movement from the neck down. Subsequently, I regained movement in different parts of my body, but there is still a way to go. During my stays at five different hospitals, I lay on my back at different elevations of a bed.

In this period, I became a participant observer of how design for spinal patients works. I came to see that there is an entire system of patient care that involves protocols and objects. These were completely invisible to me as a design historian. I want to outline some of them in this chapter in order to make them visible to other scholars. This chapter is based on my reflective experience as a patient rather than on scholarly research.

Among the protocols used for patients with spinal injuries is the grading of food intake. There are four different levels that depend on the capacity of the patient. When patients are not able to swallow at all, food intake comes from cans of liquid food that are injected through a g-tube placed in the stomach. The next level is pureed food, then soft food and finally regular food. Swallowing capacity is evaluated by a series of tests. The Barium Swallow helps medical staff to see if there is difficulty in the oesophagus while swallowing. The patient ingests a solution of barium sulphate, a metallic compound. A special machine is used that has an x-ray image of the throat. If the barium solution goes down the right channel, the patient can go from stomach feeding to ingesting pureed food by mouth. Another test, the Dynamic Swallowing Study, determines whether a patient can move up to eating soft foods and then to a regular diet. Patients swallow barium-coated foods and x-ray images show the food as it travels through the mouth and down the throat to ensure that it is not going into the breathing tube.

Then there are numerous devices and protocols for determining how patients with shortness of breath will use equipment for breathing support. A first attempt is to find out if the patient can breathe easily with a mask, connected to a ventilator, that is placed over the nose and mouth. If this is not sufficient, a temporary procedure before surgery is to put down the patient's throat a tube that is attached to a ventilator; this requires intravenous feeding and prevents the patient from talking. A final procedure is for the patient to have a tracheostomy; the ventilator is attached to a tube inserted through an incision made in the throat. As patients strengthen their lungs and diaphragm, a weaning process begins that allows them to get off the ventilator in stages. There are different kinds of ventilators such as the Trilogy that can be set to various degrees of breathing support. A passy muir valve can be placed on the hub of the trach tube to enable patients to talk during this weaning process. Eventually, the trach tube can be capped making it possible for the patient to talk and breathe independently. When this occurs all or most of the time, the trach tube can be removed and the hole in the throat closes on its own. I achieved 16 hours off the ventilator and that has remained. Initially, I achieved 16 hours off the ventilator and now I use the ventilator only when I sleep.

There are at least three categories of equipment with which I became familiar: equipment used for maintenance, diagnoses and restoration. Maintenance equipment needed for the protocols already discussed includes the ventilator, the trach collar, suction devices, the passy muir valve, the cough assist, the breathing treatment device and the g-tube for food and medicine intake.

Diagnostic equipment is used for testing various levels of functioning, for example hearing, swallowing and heart rate. I've written elsewhere about an MRI machine that won an industrial design award. Then, there are machines such as the x-ray for taking internal images, the EKG for monitoring heart rate, the ultrasound for looking three dimensionally at internal organs and monitors to evaluate such things as blood pressure and oxygen intake.

Finally, there are restorative devices. This equipment is used in occupational therapy (OT) that involves the upper body, physical therapy for the lower body and speech therapy for helping with talking, swallowing and breathing.

One piece of equipment used in OT is the sling. Two slings, one placed around the hand and the other around the arm, are attached to a rope that is connected to a grid on the ceiling. The arm is able to move in and out as well as back and forth from the elbow without the pull of gravity. This means that different muscles are exercised and the movement of the arm can be increased.

Another piece of OT equipment is a machine that is like an arm bicycle. The patient's hands are attached to handles that rotate a cylinder. When a computer in the machine senses that the patient is slowing down it will send a message to the machine to allow mechanical rotation to kick in. There is also a button that reverses the direction of the rotation so the patient can exercise different muscles.

Another kind of arm sling attached to a standing device lifts the arm above the pull of gravity and lets a patient swing the arm back and forth while in the process of knocking styrofoam cubes off a table and performing related activities. These devices and others have been developed to increase movement of the arms.

There is also equipment used in physical therapy to help the rest of the body move. This is all done with protocols that pass through various exercises to facilitate the patient sitting, standing and walking again. Among the ways a patient learns to sit, an important precedent to walking, is with the support of a foam wedge. Patients are hoisted onto a raised mat. A wedge placed behind them holds them in a sitting position. With the support of a therapist, the patient is lifted from the wedge and is held upright. The goal is to strengthen the spine and increase the time sitting without support. For walking, the most basic device is a flat surface that the patient lies on and gets strapped to; then the device is raised to a vertical position to help acclimate him or her to standing upright. In addition, there are treadmills with slings that help a patient take steps towards eventually being able to walk again. One of the most effective pieces of equipment is a harness attached to a track on a ceiling. The patient is put in a harness and a therapist or trainer can control the amount of body weight that a patient's feet supports. The patient then learns to walk along the track in the harness. Another piece of equipment is an exoskeleton placed about the legs that provides support to help patients, holding onto parallel bars, walk.

One of the most interesting objects of restorative equipment is the electric wheelchair. The function of the chair is to move the patient from place to place, but for those who are not able to propel and direct this process manually, adaptive devices can be attached to the chair. One is a 'sip and puff' device that allows patients who cannot move their hands to drive the chair by breathing through a tube. People who have the use of their hands can manoeuvre a joystick placed on or near one of the chair arms. In addition, the chair can be raised to a sitting position or lowered to a reclining position. For those patients who cannot operate a joystick, sensors can be placed in the wheelchair's headrest. By moving the head against the headrest the patient can control the functions of the chair.

There is equipment used by speech therapists to strengthen the power of the lungs. The Expiratory Muscle Strength Trainer is a device to help patients increase breathing strength. Patients blow into a tube and when the exhalation is strong, the device will make a sound.

To conclude, these are only a few examples of protocols and equipment used to maintain, diagnose and rehabilitate patients with spinal cord injuries. There are, of course, many other types of equipment used for these patients as well as for those with other injuries. As a category of design, medical equipment has been little or not examined. I suggest that it provides a rich field of exploration for design historians and design researchers.

Note

1 This chapter could not have been written without the editorial assistance of my wife, Sylvia Margolin.

22 Foresight

The next big frontier in healthcare

Aaron Sklar and Lenny Naar

The next big frontier in healthcare lies in the hands of an unforeseen bunch. They're not developing the next blockbuster drug or groundbreaking surgery. They're not even publishing their celebrated research in medical journals. Designers are one of the most untapped, underutilised assets in the healthcare industry.

Why? Design has a brand problem in healthcare.

To understand why the healthcare industry at large has been slow to embrace design as a tool for problem solving, let us consider plastic surgery. If a Google image search is any indication, the perception of plastic surgery by the general public is purely cosmetic. Images of face lifts, celebrities and plastic surgery 'gone wrong' fill a seemingly endless scroll of the web browser. Yet unlike other practices of medicine, plastic surgeons do not specialise in a specific anatomic area, organ system or patient group (Panse et al., 2012). Plastic surgery fills a defect – most commonly by moving tissue from one place to another. Plastic surgeons anticipate the behaviour of human tissue – its laxity, mobility and healing capacity. Plastic surgeons problem solve by understanding the *principles* of how tissue behaves and how it will interact with the ecosystem of the human body. Simply put, plastic surgery involves far more complexity than the practice's perception by the general public.

Design in healthcare faces a challenge similar to the practice of plastic surgery. Design is viewed by the general public and healthcare decision-makers as purely aesthetic. Graphic design, device design and architectural design are commonly understood practices of design as their output are tangible, experiential things we can hold in our hands or physically move through. When design is done well, the practice of design is invisible to the end user; a person navigates a hospital with ease, for example. But when design is done poorly, the practice of design is suddenly visible; a person finds themselves lost in hospital. For the healthcare industry to realise the value it can gain from design, designers need to prove their work goes far beyond aesthetics – design in healthcare is about problem solving.

There is an opportunity to challenge the status quo of health and healthcare delivery by leveraging human-centred practices of design. The designer's super powers are empathy and prototyping. Underlying both of these is a commitment to learning – learning about people's needs, learning through experimentation and trial and arriving at a solution through iteration and discovery.

We believe there are 12 distinct areas where design can make a notable difference in healthcare.

Design can help people feel understood and cared for

To achieve this, designers can advocate the patient's point of view and respond through new services, communications and products. Designers can distinguish distinct needs for different clusters of patients and create tailored responses that fit.

Designers can help connect technologies with the people who use (or benefit from) them. Designers spend a great deal of time listening to the stories of end users, extreme users and experts about their everyday experiences. By deeply understanding people's needs, motivations and behaviours, designers are able to engage people in new ways. This first area – design helping people feel understood and cared for – is a foundational principle that we believe should inform all practices of design in healthcare.

Design can empower people to shape the direction of their treatment

To achieve this, designers can make complex healthcare information easily digestible and actionable, facilitating people's imaginations of different scenarios to consider.

HELIX Centre[1] – a hospital-based design studio jointly run by Imperial College London and the Royal College of Art – launched a project to help patients better navigate complex cancer pathways. The project stemmed from an insight that many patients complained of poor experience when receiving cancer treatment at leading London NHS trusts, yet had stellar health outcomes.

Care pathways can be very complex and can often require multiple hospital visits for clinic reviews, investigations and treatments. At a system level, the efficiency and effectiveness of the whole patient journey is dependent on its constituent steps – a process the team discovered to be difficult to understand as the patient was going through them. While many initiatives tackle care pathways at a system level to maximise efficiency, they often leave out understanding the needs, motivations and behaviours of an important stakeholder: the patient. HELIX conducted field research at Imperial College NHS trust (St Mary's Hospital). Designers embedded themselves in the care context, shadowing patients and clinicians through cancer journeys in breast, bowel and brain cancers. During the design research phase, they used tools such as empathy and journey maps to document qualitative discoveries.

The project began as an open-ended exploration, and throughout the design process the team continually engaged clinical stakeholders with artefacts from their design research. One such artefact – a journey map visualising the entire pathway for breast cancer patients – was on a spool that stretched across numerous large tables. The fully outstretched map elicited responses from clinicians that the designers could not ignore: curiosity, surprise and empathy.

As a response to these observations, the HELIX team launched a product to help patients understand their individual cancer care pathway, who their clinical team are, where the key locations of their care are and what third-party services (such as charity support) are available to them. The simplest solution is a printed card brochure that acts as a discussion tool between clinician and patient. This can also be used as a web- or app-based portal, establishing a digital connection between the patient and clinical teams. These tools allow people – both clinicians and patients – to understand and shape the direction of treatment.

Design can enable people to navigate health ecosystems with ease

To achieve this, designers can identify hotspots in the journey where help is needed and create a welcoming environment with clear guideposts.

Healthvana[2] is a patient-engagement platform for sexual health clinics. Focused on delivering real-time lab results and care instructions to patients, their service replaces the traditional 'wait 7–10 days and call us' model of healthcare that keeps patients in limbo for weeks. Healthvana is directly responding to a human insight that the experience of waiting for lab results – especially for sexual health – is loaded with anxiety around the unknown. This new model results in a superior patient experience, more efficient clinical operations and a reduction in patients who 'fall through the cracks' by never receiving lab results or treatment.

Healthvana found that approximately 80 per cent of patients check their lab results and follow-up care instructions through their digital platform. This high level of patient engagement leads to patients experiencing less anxiety while waiting for results, a quicker diagnosis notification and a faster time to treatment.

By responding to a clear human, emotional insight designers can enable people to navigate health ecosystems with ease. Moreover, startups like Healthvana are finding novel methods to incentivise healthcare providers to improve patient experiences, in this case by reducing the administrative burden of the clinic itself. Healthvana recently launched a new digital solution for patients to self-register for visits from a clinic's waiting room. By eliminating paperwork, the new system shortens patient registration time, decreases data entry for staff and reduces data transcription errors. Since launching the electronic registration solution, clinics are indicating a significant increase in the number of patients they can see per day, and patients are experiencing a decrease in time spent at the clinic.

Design can ensure healthy behaviours are encouraged beyond the traditional healthcare walls

To achieve this, designers can create feedback loops to lift engagement outside of healthcare episodes and explore new methods to shift norms.

According to the London Health Commission, London is currently the worst capital city on record for childhood obesity, with 22 per cent of children in London obese (London Health Commission, 2014). The HELIX Centre challenged itself to explore ways to promote physical activity in children that was low-cost, sociable and fun, all outside of the traditional healthcare walls. The team of interaction and industrial designers set out to learn about the daily lives of children aged 9 to 13 – an age range which sees enormous change, including puberty and new schools.

The team arrived at a simple, but profound human insight that brands must talk *with* children rather than *at* them, to successfully connect. Healthcare interventions for kids typically foreground the problem (in this case, childhood obesity) and background the action (physical activity). In response to this insight, the team created a card game called Zilli where participants set physical challenges for each other to be acted out in a light-hearted and amusing manner. The funnier the participants are through their physical activity, the further they progress to winning the game. The card game is competitive, but not in the traditional sense of established sports; it combines physical activity with wit, imagination and humour. HELIX believes the game will appeal to groups of peers and families alike, and will offer an alternative form of ad-hoc exercise with broad appeal.

Design can enable informal caregivers to be acknowledged as credible members of care teams

To achieve this, designers can incorporate family caregivers' needs and contributions into services and tools. Additionally, designers can create tools and toolkits to empower community members to serve medical needs.

With human resources accounting for a large proportion of healthcare costs, it is increasingly important to identify resources to support patients outside of the formal care team. Countless non-profit organisations exist to support people with specific medical conditions.

The British Heart Foundation, for example, runs a service within the NHS to ease the transition from hospital to home. But design has as opportunity to engage a new class of carers: family and friends.

How might we filter and assign care needs to relevant members of the care team – including informal carers? What if designers worked on methods to educate informal carers on how to perform tasks that do not require medical professionals? We believe that design can play an enormous role in expanding the capability of formal carers by engaging informal carers in safe, reliable ways.

Design can enable care coordination across specialties, locations and roles

To achieve this, designers can reshape tools and systems to focus on teams and communication that fit smoothly into workflows.

If we consider the education systems in place to teach future generations of clinicians, it becomes clear why the healthcare context lends itself to siloed working. Our future doctors are categorised into specialties and sub-specialties early on, perpetuating the narrative that coordination across care settings simply cannot be. From an administrative and policy perspective, institutions are not always incentivised to collaborate or share information.

We believe there is an important challenge to designers to collaborate with clinicians and administrators to find novel ways to put the patient at the centre of their care and enable collaboration around them. While many designers have speculatively designed solutions to this problem, few have successfully penetrated the complex economic ecosystems that drive new behaviours.

Design can work to fulfil clinicians by their work and get the support they need

To achieve this, designers can fade technology into the background in order to foster the relationship between the patient and clinician. Additionally, designers can reimagine tools that enable rather than disrupt the clinician's workflow.

We believe it is worthy work to not only put the patient at the centre, but also effectively design the clinician's experience in care settings. How might designers create positive work experiences for clinicians to enable them to deliver better care? What if the tools and systems used by clinicians supported effective working rather than add to the workflow?

There is no question that digital tools and systems are penetrating the healthcare industry just as they did in finance, travel and education. Electronic health records are probably the main touch point clinicians have digitally, but very few clinicians consider these digital experiences 'delightful' or 'fulfilling'. Designers have the opportunity to connect deeply with clinicians through these platforms to unleash greater levels of productivity. The healthcare industry – just as other industries have experienced – is in the early phase of putting technologies in place but not fully embracing their capabilities.

Design can continually challenge healthcare practices in the name of better health outcomes

To achieve this, designers can foster a culture of innovation and experimentation and bring a beginner's mind to practices that haven't altered in years.

Fable Hospital is a fictional 300-bed facility formed by the research findings on healthcare facilities evaluated by the Centre for Health Design in Concord, California. Since 1993, the research group has focused on the impact of healthcare facility design on health outcomes. Fable Hospital was created as a novel way to present evidence in support of the business case for better physical spaces as a key component of better, safer and less wasteful healthcare. By creating a fictional healthcare facility, the team could be unbounded by the status quo of present-day operations and envision a future state without constraint.

Working with a team of architects and designers, the Centre for Health Design created features and hospital layouts that reduced patient falls by 80 per cent – a potential $2 million (USD) in savings – and reduced nosocomial infections by four per month. The team identified methods to reduce patient transfers between rooms by 80 per cent which could allow for increased continuity of care. Overall, the study calculated $11 million (USD) in savings and increased revenue in the first year based on a $12 million investment (Blair et al., 2011).

Design can make data useful and available to patients and clinicians

To achieve this, designers can present data in visually and interactively engaging ways, highlighting the signal from the noise.

Iodine[3] is a digital service that helps people select the best therapies to improve their health. The start-up company's tools help people choose medications, understand what to expect and track their own experience with therapies. In parallel, Iodine aggregates all of the individual patient data to guide the health system and report back on whether treatments are in fact working. Their mission is to amplify the patient's voice in medical care.

Leveraging visual design from the start, Iodine's general framework for comparing drug alternatives turned into a very popular cold and flu medication picker. The tool helped people narrow down hundreds of medications to select the most relevant drug for their symptoms. The simplicity of information visualisation and ease of interacting with a tool that distils complex information down for patients in a vulnerable state led to a positive feedback loop and kept patients coming back. With high involvement from patient users, Iodine's parallel motive of aggregating data about the efficacy of therapies becomes far more valuable. Designers have made it possible for the collection of valuable data to improve long-term outcomes simply by designing a positive user experience on the front end.

Design can make medical costs simple and transparent

To achieve this, designers can rethink the way bills and benefits are communicated and convene diverse stakeholders to disrupt the status quo.

Healthcare costs are notoriously non-transparent in markets like the United States, where patients, employers, insurers and the government cover different treatments and therapies. How might designers make clear the breakdown of medical costs? How might designers enable patients to make the most of insurance deductibles while still receiving high-quality care?

Design can advocate for best in class care to be available and affordable to all

To achieve this, designers can scale great services to reach more people and facilitate remote interaction and collaboration.

Epharmix[4] is an early-stage start-up comprised of clinical researchers, developers and designers working with practising providers to create a portfolio of toll-free, disease-specific, phone-based interventions. These interventions are created to help providers better serve their patients without adding time to their current work flows. Once a practice registers, Epharmix interventions are instantly prescribable. Specifically targeting dialysis patients, Epharmix did a study of patients receiving EpxDialysis (compared to a control group) and phone messages contributed to a reduction of hospital readmissions by 50 per cent. Statistics from DaVita – a leading provider of dialysis services – estimates that dialysis readmissions cost around $8,000 (USD) per readmission (Medicare Payment Advisory Commission, 2015).

Frugal solutions like this telephonic intervention can enable providers to reach more patients and at the same time achieve positive health outcomes, a cornerstone of value-based healthcare models.

Design can allow for health policy to be informed by empathy for all stakeholders

To achieve this, designers can curate the compelling stories that reframe the issues and synthesise complexity down to actionable challenges.

This last principle underscores the need for designers to collaborate with non-designers on a constant basis. While designers have a skillset relevant and necessary to improve health and healthcare delivery, it cannot be without clinical and subject matter support. The best examples of design working effectively in healthcare are when multidisciplinary teams work together to design solutions from different viewpoints.

While we believe design must challenge cultural and operational norms in healthcare, designers must also acknowledge the evidence base upon which most healthcare decisions are made. For design solutions to take root, they must prove their efficacy through appropriate, ethical trials. In doing so, designers can prove the return on investment (ROI) of their solutions. ROI can be one of the most confronting conversations for anyone making the case for innovation in healthcare. For both designers and healthcare natives, the ROI conversation often requires stepping outside of our comfort zones – replacing the languages of design and healthcare with that of business.

The proliferation of design-driven organisations across sectors has shown that there is in fact a business case for design. Countless types of financial return can be attributed to good design, from demanding higher price points to benefiting from increased customer loyalty. As design increasingly becomes a lifeline for business, it will infuse industries like healthcare – industries where design is often relegated as an aesthetic afterthought.

What makes healthcare unique is that ROI is not just financial. It's about the quantifiable improvement of health and wellbeing: 'Return on Impact'. The goal is to cause the greatest impact with the funds we have. In 2013, 17.1 per cent of the US economy was attributed to health expenditure, amounting to about $2.9 trillion (Centers for Medicare and Medicaid Services, 2014). Meanwhile, chronic disease is on the rise and the overall health of the US seems to be getting worse.

As many leaders through the online design in healthcare community Prescribe Design have pointed out, great design can be leveraged to solve a multitude of problems in healthcare – it is more than just aesthetics. Design can engage the unengaged patient, it can improve workflows and make an organisation more effective, and it can increase job satisfaction and engage workers in an organisation's mission. But getting the opportunity to solve these problems is half the battle for designers.

To build momentum around design initiatives designers must be intentional about planning for the measurement of impact from the outset, setting themselves up for success by declaring realistic goals against status quo baselines. This is what we call seeking 'evidence-based design'. Coming to these ROI conversations armed with the intention to measure will go a long way in establishing buy-in with extended teams, especially considering the healthcare industry's deep-seated culture around evidence-based medicine.

Evidence-based design and proving ROI are not easy. The conversation quickly stalls once we consider the challenges of truly quantifying impact. The types of initiatives that design plays a heavy role in are often game changers and so disruptive that simple measurement of ROI may not be straightforward. The true impact may not be knowable for years. Another complexity in measuring health impact is the challenge of measuring the impact of prevention: how do you quantify that which did not occur? Designers must come to the conversation armed with the intention to measure and with recommendations for early indicators that can be monitored as a proxy for long-term impact.

There is a wave of design coming to healthcare. Concurrently, there is a big push for lean and frugal innovation. Partly this comes from the same fear of 'investment' in innovation without knowing the return. Design efforts can either fall victim to these constraints or design processes can become heroes through small, iterative steps that build on each other over time.

We are firm believers in the power of design – people-centred design – to radically transform healthcare. We created an online community called Prescribe Design to bring design natives and healthcare natives together. We call it Prescribe Design for a couple of reasons. First, it's an action. The platform is about sparking conversation that inspires the real, practical collaboration between designers and healthcare natives. Second, it's inclusive. The name suggests a merging of communities and we even designed our logo to hint at this. A mortar and pestle blends two distinct ingredients into one new, combined whole: design plus health.

For clinicians and other type of healthcare natives, our goal is to reveal new ways for them to cause the transformations they care about and help them make connections with like-minded colleagues around the world. For designers, our goal is to bring to light what is unique about working in healthcare and help them discover and share best practices. We aim to be 'match-makers' for designers and healthcare natives to connect and collaborate. Design can be a powerful force for change in the healthcare industry, but designers cannot do it alone.

Notes

1 See www.helixcentre.com/.
2 See https://healthvana.com/.
3 See www.iodine.com/.
4 See www.epharmix.com/.

References

Centers for Medicare and Medicaid Services (2014) National health expenditures 2014 highlights. Available at: www.cms.gov/research-statistics-data-and-systems/statistics-trends-and-reports/national healthexpenddata/downloads/highlights.pdf.
London Health Commission (2014) Better health for London. November. Available at: www.londonhealthcommission.org.uk/wp-content/uploads/London-Health-Commission_Better-Health-for-London.pdf.

Medicare Payment Advisory Commission (US) (2015) Outpatient dialysis services. Chapter 6 in Report to the Congress: Medicare payment policy. Medicare Payment Advisory Commission. Available at: www.medpac.gov/documents/reports/mar2015_entirereport_revised.pdf?sfvrsn=0.

Panse, N., Panse, S., Kulkarni, P., Dhongde, R. and Sahasrabudhe, P. (2012) Awareness and perception of plastic surgery among healthcare professionals in Pune, India: Do they really know what we do? Plastic Surgery International.

Sadler, B.L., Berry, L.L., Guenther, R., Hamilton, D.K., Hessler, F.A., Merritt, C. and Parker, D. (2011) Fable Hospital 2.0: The business case for building better health care facilities. *Hastings Center Report*, 41(1): 13–23.

23 Design for health

Challenges, opportunities, emerging trends, research methods and recommendations

Emmanuel Tsekleves and Rachel Cooper

Introduction

This chapter provides insights and discussion into the challenges, opportunities and trends in design for healthcare that emerge from analysis of the chapters presented in Theme 2 of the book (Design in acute health) as well as drawing from the literature. This is done by examining the current as well as emerging challenges, opportunities and trends across the four healthcare settings (public, acute, chronic, ageing well) and five design disciplines (architecture, communication, product, service, behaviour design) presented in the book. Thematic analysis was employed for data analysis (Gibbs, 2007), where all data collected are involved in a process of identifying themes throughout coding, indexing and categorising towards drawing themes. Based on the 26 case studies presented in the book the authors draw on the research methodologies and methods in design in healthcare and present these in relation to the healthcare settings and design disciplines they have been employed in. Finally the authors present the way forward for design in healthcare.

Challenges, benefits and emerging trends

A number of themes have emerged, following the thematic analysis of the contributed chapters. A total of 18 themes have appeared across the four different healthcare settings and five design disciplines. The word cloud in Figure 23.1 illustrates the main themes and their importance, as measured in terms of their frequency rate within the chapters.

For instance, it is clear that long-term healthcare, health communication and prototyping are discussed the most within the book. Closer analysis and further categorisation of the themes revealed three main categories under which each one of the themes can be grouped. These are challenges, opportunities and emerging trends for design in healthcare (see Figure 23.2).

More precisely the thematic grouping of 'challenges' refers to current and emerging demands and issues that healthcare is facing and design is called upon to respond to. Under this group seven main themes have been identified, namely *long-term healthcare, ageing, social interaction and support, environment and lifestyle, non-communicable diseases, wellbeing and mental health, active life/living*. These themes have either been highlighted explicitly by authors in this book as key challenges or have implicitly been discussed across several of the book chapters.

Moving on, under the thematic group of 'opportunities' seven themes have emerged, namely *health communication, prototyping, co-design, evidence-based design, digital design, salutogenic design* and *holistic design*. Within the context of the book the thematic group of opportunities refers to methodologies and approaches where design offers value and benefits within health, as identified and discussed by authors across several chapters of this book. The value and

Figure 23.1 Word cloud of the main book chapter themes. The word length and size represents the theme's significance and frequency within the book

importance of several of these, in terms of their contribution to problem finding and problem solving across different sectors of healthcare (public, acute, chronic) can be more explicitly found in the case studies presented in this book.

As its name suggests, the third thematic group of 'emerging trends' refers to emerging and future directions of healthcare practices, services and provision as dictated by several of the challenges identified and discussed in this book (see Figure 23.2) as well as opportunities created by digital technology. Under this thematic group five themes have been identified, namely *self-care/health management, person-centric healthcare, holistic healthcare, community healthcare and preventative healthcare.*

Figure 23.3 illustrates how the three thematic groups are interconnected. More precisely, the challenges in health are influencing the emerging trends, whilst the opportunities created by design can contribute in addressing the health challenges and emerging trends. Each one of the aforementioned thematic groups and their corresponding themes are explored and discussed in more detail within the following sections.

Challenges in design for health

Further analysis of the themes under the thematic group of challenges indicated a causal (although often not proven) relationship and a sphere of influences between these, as depicted in Figure 23.4. Starting from the inner circle of the nested circle diagram, we can see that the environment and lifestyle affect our personal health at a holistic level, influencing our wellbeing and mental health, our opportunities for social interaction and the extent of how

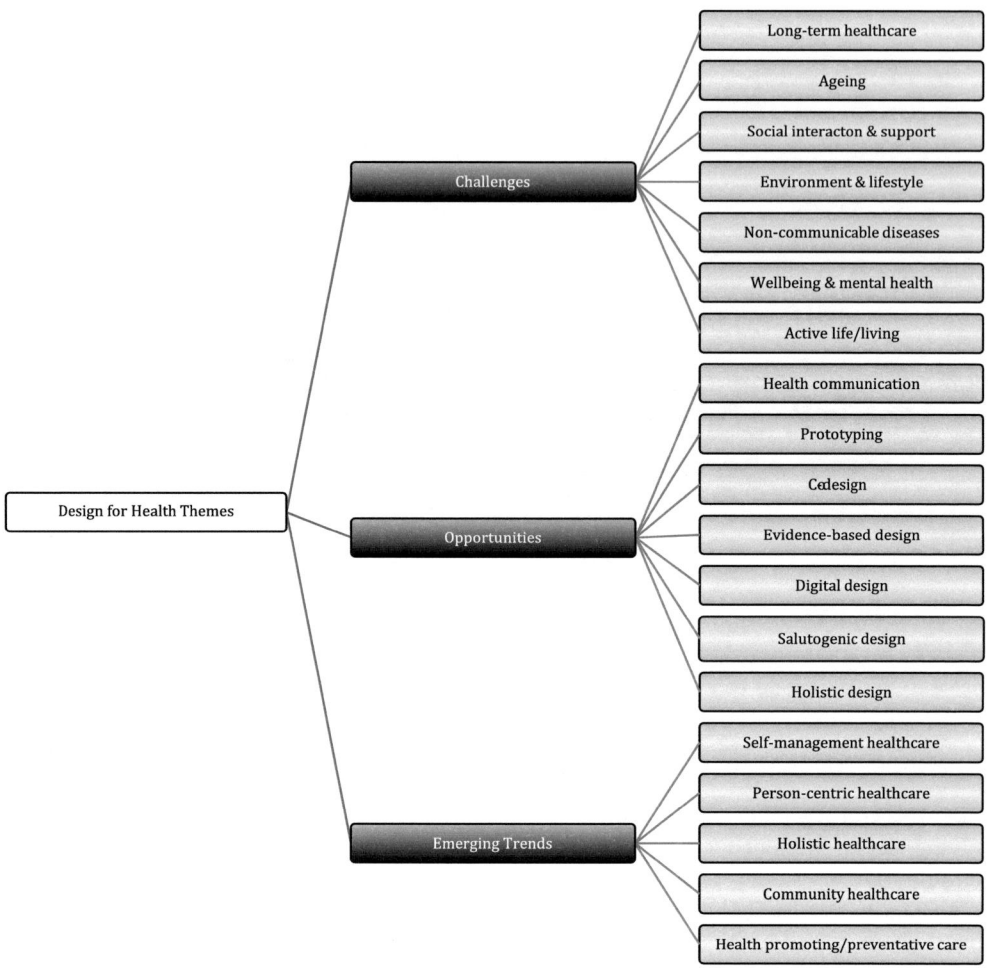

Figure 23.2 Main themes and their grouping following thematic analysis of the book chapters

active our lives are. These in turn have an impact on our ageing process and the prevalence of non-communicable diseases. The rise of those along with an ageing population pose a massive challenge and strain to long-term healthcare access, provision and management affecting each individual.

Looking at the frequency of appearance of the challenges themes across the book chapters reveals that the theme of long-term healthcare has been discussed the most, whilst the majority of the other themes (ageing population, environment and lifestyle, social interaction and support, wellbeing and mental health) have been discussed across most of the chapters, as Figure 23.5 illustrates. In addition to this, it is interesting to note that although the challenges appear across the four healthcare settings, most challenges appear in the public and chronic healthcare setting, followed by that of ageing well (see Figure 23.6).

Looking at how the challenges are distributed across the five different design disciplines shows that a third of the challenges appear under the discipline of architecture design;

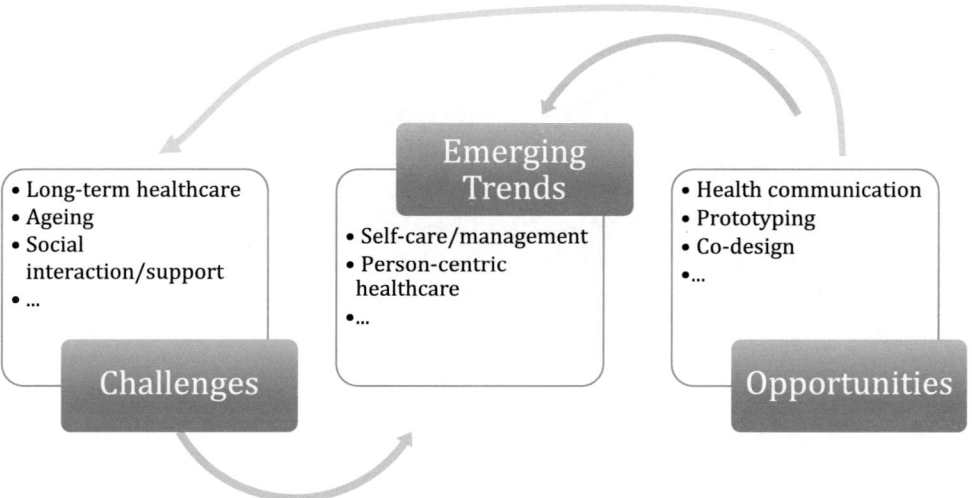

Figure 23.3 Main themes and their grouping following thematic analysis of the book chapters

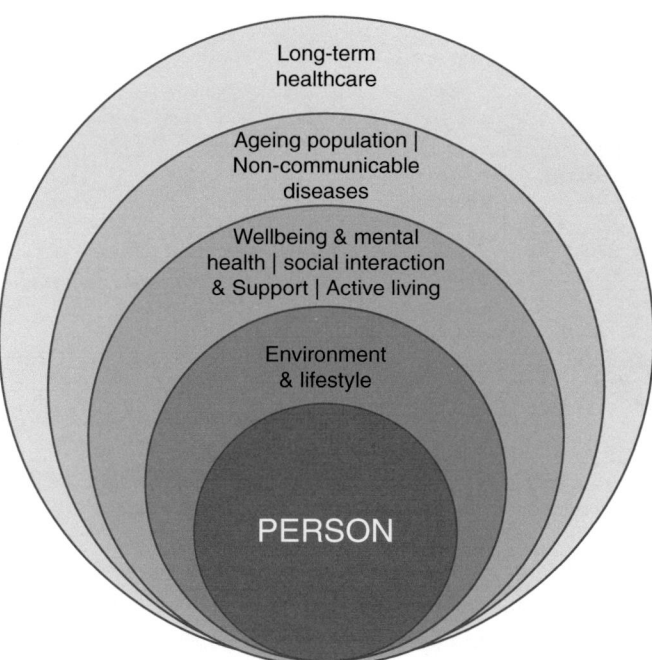

Figure 23.4 Causal relationships between the challenges in design for health

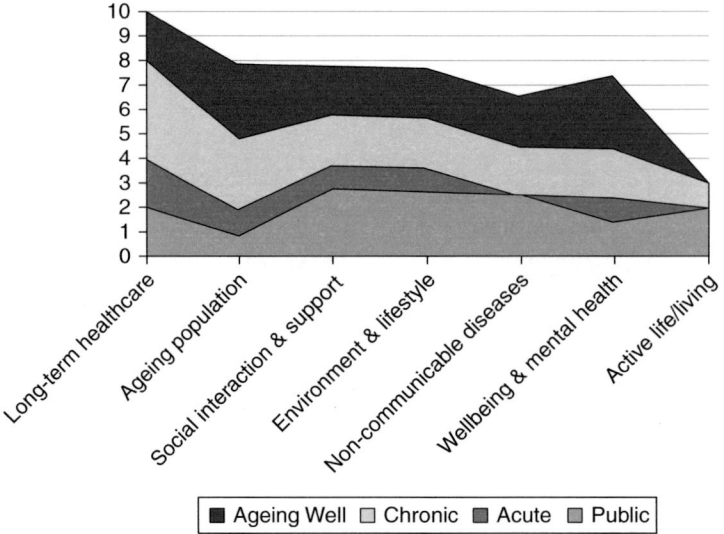

Figure 23.5 Challenges theme appearance across the four healthcare settings. Axis Y refers to the number of chapters in which each theme appears

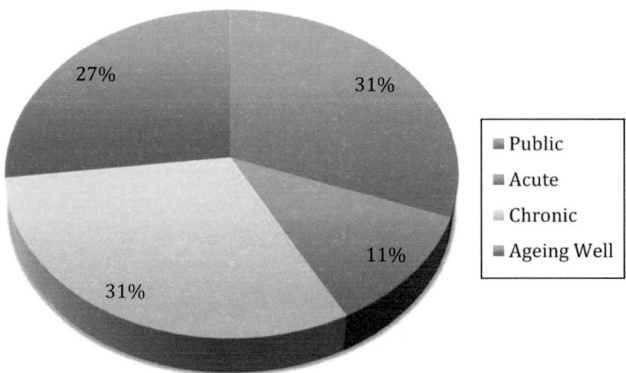

Figure 23.6 How the challenges themes are distributed across the four healthcare settings based on their appearance frequency (%) in the book

whereas nearly a quarter of challenges can be found under service and behaviours design (see Figure 23.7).

Let us examine in more detail each one of the aforementioned challenges identified by the thematic analysis. Within the context of the book the *environment and lifestyle* theme refers to the built and natural environment as well as the lifestyle affordances they encourage or discourage. The built environment encompasses all public, social, institutional and domestic infrastructure. This incudes the physical context in which people live, work, educate, socialise,

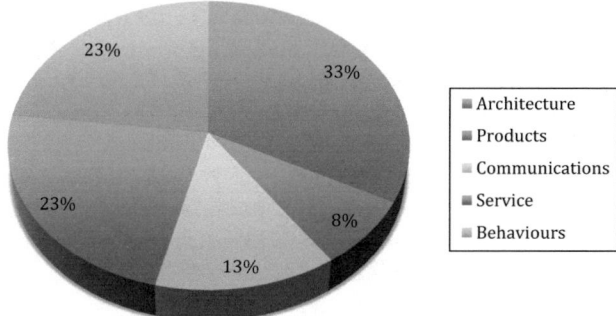

Figure 23.7 How the challenges themes are distributed across the five design disciplines based on their appearance frequency (%) in the book

travel and entertain. It includes buildings but also cities and urban environment as well as transportation infrastructures and systems as a whole.

The link between the design of the built and natural environment and its role in our health and wellbeing, which has been well presented by several of the authors in this book and discussed across several of the book chapters, is well echoed in the literature too (Rao et al., 2007; Codinhoto et al., 2009; Renalds et al., 2010). For instance Codinhoto in Chapter 7 presents several established research theories that explain how the design of the built environment affects human life and behaviour and Dilani in Chapter 5 and Boyko in Chapter 14 point to and present a bulk of research, which has shown that well-designed and people-friendly spaces stimulate walking, cycling and the reduction of the risk of non-communicable diseases.

A key challenge that emerges under this theme is how should we shape our *built environments* and infrastructure to support *healthier behaviours*? How can this be designed and realised at a building, neighbourhood and urban level? Another interesting challenge to emerge as a high priority in research relates to the *environmental consequences of the workplace*. There are several challenges there in terms of not only the built but also the workplace infrastructure environment as a whole that require rethinking. What is abundantly clear here is that as we shape our environment it is shaping us, our psychological, physiological and physical status as well as our interactions with other people and with the natural environment too.

The environment is closely linked to the lifestyles we adopt and again it is clear from the wealth of research material provided in this book that the current state of our environment plays a significant role in the predominantly sedentary lifestyles adopted today. The physical, social and socioeconomic environments in which people live shape their behaviour and directly affect population health. In fact the Marmot report drew a link between better health and higher socioeconomic position in society providing six policy recommendations for reducing health inequalities. According to the report there is a social gradient in health – the lower a person's social position, the worse his or her health (Marmot et al., 2010).

Apart from population health, sedentary lifestyles have a negative impact on *social interaction and mental wellbeing*. Within this context lifestyle refers to the habits, behaviours, attitudes interests and socioeconomic environment that together constitute the mode of living of an individual or a group. The lack of health-promoting lifestyles along with the wide adoption of sedentary lifestyles are key challenges design for health should address. Critical in addressing these is tackling the challenge in changing behaviour patterns in extending life and improving quality of life. This should be addressed both in terms of our existing environment but also in the design of new environments by ensuring that lifestyle design receives a central focus in the design of new environments at a micro and macro level (building, neighbourhood, city).

Related to the aforementioned discussion is the theme of *wellbeing and mental health* (another emerging theme under challenges), which is affected by environmental factors and social determinants of illness and wellness, such as housing, social lifestyle, healthy food access, socio-economic level, etc. Independent research reviews, such as the National Prevention Research Initiative (NPRI) report, have also indicated that there needs to be better understanding of the complex interaction between individual behaviour and risk factors, and social, cultural, health-care and other determinants of health (NPRI Scientific Review Group, 2015). Our current environment and adopted ill-health lifestyles have contributed to an increasingly high negative impact on our mental health and wellbeing. Wellbeing can be thought of in the context of an individual, community but also national wellbeing. In 2010 a Measuring National Wellbeing Programme was launched in the UK aimed at providing a better understanding of national wellbeing. Amongst other findings the report concluded that the biggest challenge is to turn the evidence on wellbeing into action, so that policies truly reflect our quality of life (Self, 2014). In addition to this the Foresight Project on Mental Capital and Wellbeing has used the available scientific and other evidence to develop a vision for the opportunities and challenges facing the UK over the next 20 years and beyond, and the implications for everyone's 'mental capital' and 'mental wellbeing' (Foresight Mental Capital and Wellbeing Project, 2008).

Several chapters comment on the rise of *mental health issues* and the increasing need for mental health support and wellbeing integrated across all aspects of our lives (home, school place, workplace). In Chapter 3, Jones draws on research that shows a large and increasing proportion of emergency department visits being made from persons suffering from chronic mental health disorders. This highlights the strain mental health places on the already stretched healthcare system both in terms of chronic but also in terms of acute healthcare.

Social interaction and support was another theme identified by our analysis. Socialising forms an essential human function and social interaction is often a part of healing and wellbeing (Lloyd and Auld, 2002; Sandstrom and Dunn, 2014). More precisely lack of social interaction was recognised across several chapters as an emerging issue and a challenge that needs to be addressed. The roots for this can be partly found on the built environment our communities form and public service design, as their design can support or hinder social interaction. This was found to be more prominent in older people with loneliness and social isolation being identified as priority risks to emotional wellbeing (Tomaka et al., 2006; Steptoe et al., 2013). Therefore the *supporting social interaction through the built environment but also our communities and social services* emerges as another challenge.

Active life and living, or more precisely the lack of, forms another challenge. The literature provides a clear link between lack of physical exercise and the rise of non-communicable diseases (Daar et al., 2007; Bauman et al., 2012; Kohl et al., 2012). Within this context active living refers to a lifestyle that integrates predominantly physical activity into daily routines. This is closely linked to urban and natural environment, transport and lifestyle. Another important challenge for design in health within this context is the introduction but more significantly adherence to physical activities into our daily habits and routines.

Another theme that has emerged as a *challenge for health is that of non-communicable diseases* (NCDs). NCDs refer to non-infectious chronic diseases, lasting for long periods of time and progressing slowly. According to the WHO NCDs kill 38 million people each year, with eight out of ten deaths being preventable (Alwan, 2011). Tobacco use, physical inactivity, excessive alcohol use and unhealthy diets all increase the risk of dying from an NCD. Challenges under this theme include raising awareness and engaging the public in understanding the risk factors of developing NCDs; shaping health-promoting behaviours through design that minimise the risk factors; and designing interventions for managing NCDs whilst improving quality of life and reducing death rates.

The theme of an *ageing population* is one of the most widely discussed challenges within this book. We live in an ageing world. The United Nations estimate that 1.4 billion people will be over 60 years old by 2030 (United Nations, 2015). In the UK there are currently 11.4 million people over 65 and by 2040, 24.2 per cent will be aged over 65 (Age UK, 2016). The challenges that an increasingly ageing population brings into healthcare are several and multifaceted. The changing age demographics mean that the likelihood of acquiring a chronic disease is on the increase. On top of that an increased number of older people are suffering from multiple and complex health conditions (Marengoni et al., 2011; Salive, 2013), placing an additional demand on the existing healthcare and in particular chronic healthcare services. This changing age structure means a diminishing workforce to sustain public healthcare raising challenges on the funding and existence of public healthcare provision. Within the context of living longer comes the *challenge of strategically placing research focus on preventative services, interventions and support mechanisms that favour and place emphasis on living healthier into older years* (disease-free life expectancy) rather than solely focusing on life expectancy. Currently though one of the key challenges designers and healthcare professionals need to address within this context is the increasing demand for supporting independence and independent living at home and in community settings.

In addition the theme of *long-term healthcare* emerged in this book as one of the main challenges faced in design in healthcare today. The theme was discussed in several chapters across all four healthcare settings presented in the book. Long-term conditions fit well to the 'wicked problem' definition of Rittel and Webber's (1973) as already indicated by Prendiville in Chapter 11. As the number of people with long-term (or chronic) health conditions increases through living longer and with changing lifestyles a massive challenge in maintaining present levels of high-quality patient care at an affordable cost emerges. This is further exacerbated by the rise of the number of people with two or more long-term conditions (comorbidity and multiple morbidity[1]) (Barnett et al., 2012; Uijen and van de Lisdonk, 2008). The challenges created by comorbidity and multimorbidity require a personalised approach to the design of interventions and to the service design of patient pathways within the existing chronic healthcare system. Other current challenges with long-term healthcare include the design of preventative interventions that enable service users to adhere to therapy and manage their condition to prevent further deterioration and development of multimorbidities.

Furthermore, design challenges can be found in extending preventative interventions at a public healthcare level to decreasing the demands currently placed on long-term healthcare. *This is a strategic point at which design for health research and practice should be focused in tackling chronic healthcare issues in the long-term and for prevention.* Lastly, the difficulties of living with a chronic condition place challenges not only on the healthcare system but also the families and friends of service users, communities and society as a whole, and thus solutions can have a far wider impact on society and the economy than just the individuals.

Opportunities in design for health

A number of opportunities for design for health have emerged from our thematic analysis of the book chapters. The themes of health communication and prototyping have been discussed across the majority of the chapters followed by that of co-design, as Figure 23.8 illustrates. The

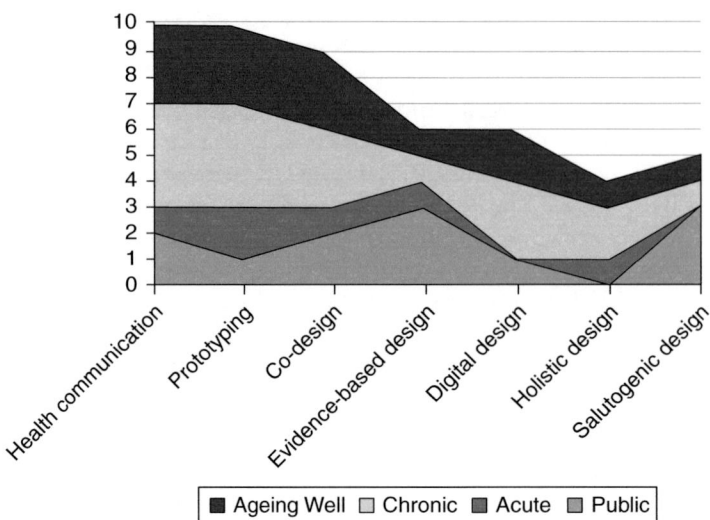

Figure 23.8 Opportunities theme appearance across the four healthcare settings. Axis Y refers to the number of chapters in which each theme appears

themes of evidence-based design and digital design are featured in nearly half of the chapters whereas the themes of holistic and salutogenic design are discussed in over a third of the book.

There are several opportunities for health communication in design for health, as health communication takes many different forms and all can contribute to a better healthcare provision. As depicted in Figure 23.8 the theme of health communication is relevant to all four healthcare settings presented in this book (public, acute, chronic, ageing well) and, as depicted in Figure 23.9, it spans all traditional design disciplines featured in the book, namely architecture, communication, product, service and behaviour design.

In terms of public health, *health communication* adds value in health promotion and disease prevention through enhancing people's understanding and raising awareness about lifestyle choices (Hornik, 2002). Beyond its contribution to preventative healthcare, health communication can provide information in a service user-friendly way to support treatment choices and, by making visible what is often taken for granted, actions it can take to help improve the effectiveness of clinical care. Another key benefit where issues often arise lies in poor communication between healthcare professionals (i.e. doctors, nurses, administrators and other clinical staff) and between service providers and service users. Within this context health communication provides opportunities for enhancing communication and improving interactions amongst different healthcare stakeholders with regards to treatments and patient care pathways, medical products and medicine labelling and information, consultation appointment letters and information. As evident from the work presented in Chapters 6 and 9, despite the move to electronic communication, paper documentation remains a powerful support tool for public and acute healthcare. Lastly, another opportunity for health communication can be found in the effective dissemination of information regarding care pathways and the clinical built environment, such as physical signposting in hospitals and patient-friendly environment design.

The theme of *prototyping* dominated discussions across several chapters in all four healthcare settings and all five design disciplines in the book (see Figures 23.8 and 23.9). Prototyping is

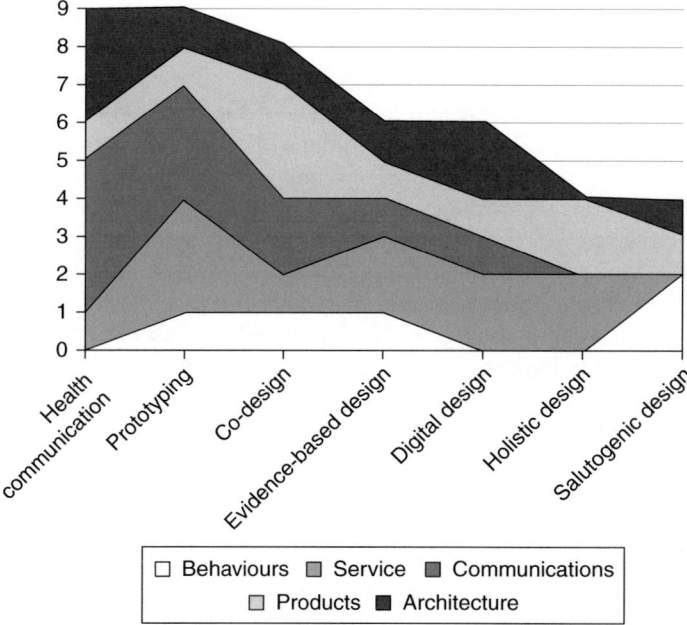

Figure 23.9 Opportunities theme appearance across the five design disciplines. Axis Y refers to the number of chapters in which each theme appears

an immensely useful tool for design for health providing opportunities that extend beyond the traditional employment of prototypes as an early proof-of-concept evaluation vehicle. The values of prototyping can be found both in its making, its use as a discussion prompt and its output as a communication medium (Coughlan et al., 2007; Verlinden and Horváth, 2009). The availability of early prototypes can provide an immediate basis for focused discussion between service users, healthcare professionals and designers. It can become a catalyst for storytelling and rich narratives that on one hand help service users in sharing their experiences (Buchenau and Suri, 2000) and journeys in healthcare; and on the other hand support clinical staff to make sense of the current challenges across different healthcare settings and together to negotiate a way forward. Lastly there are opportunities for prototypes to be used as an innovation tool, as they can assist in convincing people that change is needed and required by showing prototypes that perform better when compared to current solutions.

Similarly to health communication and prototyping, the theme of *co-design* has ben widely addressed in the book chapters. Co-design (Sanders and Stappers, 2008) has shown value as a means of developing health-related services, products and interventions (Tsianakas et al., 2010; De Couvreur and Goossens, 2011; Robert, 2013) where the intended recipient of these becomes an active and equal member in the design process. This has shown to increase the rate of innovation and the adoption and use of the designed outputs. There are several opportunities for co-design in health. In public healthcare, co-designing with service users creates a sense of inclusion, personal value and self-control, all essential in the successful design and roll-out of enhanced public health services, communication material and public-engagement campaigns as well as interventions for behaviour change. The case studies included in the book have also demonstrated the opportunities and benefits created by co-design in care-related documentation and products. In chronic healthcare positioning service users as experts since they are experts in living with their health condition can lead to innovation in products, services, increased quality of service and higher levels of acceptance and adherence to health interventions. Opportunities for co-design have also been presented in managing innovation and change (Chapter 15) as well as increasing wellbeing in the workplace (Chapter 19).

Several chapters in this book have showcased through a number of use cases the benefits of *evidence-based design* (EBD) as a means of combining clinical expertise with the best available external clinical evidence from systematic research to guide design briefs and healthcare interventions (Ulrich et al., 2008; McCullough, 2009). Opportunities for augmenting evidence-based design with qualitative design research have also been provided in the book showing that EBD is applicable across all healthcare settings and design disciplines. EBD is therefore an opportunity that designers working in healthcare should embrace and use in conjunction with other design research methods.

Digital design has appeared as a theme across several chapters in different forms, indicating opportunities for design in the digital domain. Especially as digital technologies have been embedded across different healthcare environments, products and services design has a potent role to play. Firstly in ensuring that any digital technology embedded in healthcare practice is led by service user needs and not driven solely by technology innovation. Secondly in employing digital design as a tool for enhancing design practices, such as prototyping (digital/virtual prototyping and simulation) but also for enhancing communication by making sense of medical data through meaningful visualisation (Chapter 17) and designed outputs aimed at healthcare (Chapter 8). Several chapters have presented how digital technologies, such as additive manufacturing, computer-aided modelling and simulation (Chapter 13) and smart materials (Chapter 20) are shaping the pace of service innovation and medical products in healthcare.

The theme of holistic design was not explicitly described in this book but it was implicitly described in many chapters. Within this context (holistic) design is considered here not simply as a problem-solving activity but also as an issues-led, question-asking problem-finding activity with the ability to create visions and scenarios that expand the space of possibility. It is design that encompasses both the physical elements of design, exploring objects and physical spaces, alongside digital communication and relations with people. Necessitated by the 'wicked' problem of the healthcare challenges discussed above there is a need and an opportunity for design in health that starts with people fitting the services and environment (physical, organisational and social systems) around the person. There are opportunities therefore for design innovations in health that move beyond the product and especially away from medical products and interventions developed in isolation of the service. Chapters 8 and 13 in particular highlight the challenges created by product design outside of the context of service deign and Chapters 11 and 19 present some of the benefits of the application of holistic design in problem finding and product/service innovation.

The theme of salutogenic design (Dilani and Armstrong, 2007; Golembiewski, 2012) also emerged, especially in the public healthcare setting and architecture design discipline. Salutogenic design (as presented in detail in Chapter 5) forms a unique opportunity for design in health. Following the embedding of its preventative care strategies in our built environment it has the potential to change our lifestyle for the better. The change of mindset from the current focus on risk factors and disease treatment to a more holistic understanding and evolution towards a healthier society offers a new way of looking at the role of the built environment within the context of health and wellbeing. Although predominately

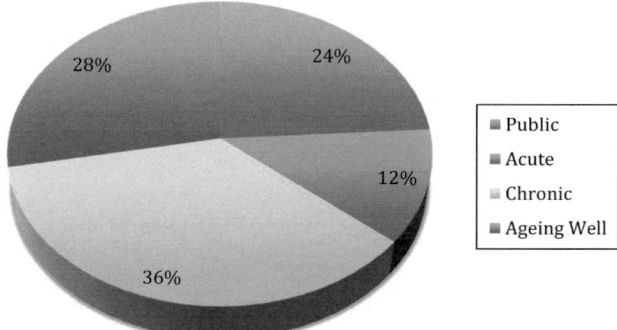

Figure 23.10 How the opportunities themes are distributed across the four healthcare settings and their appearance frequency (%) in the book

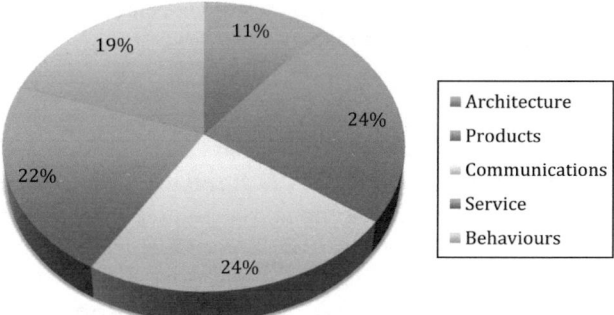

Figure 23.11 How the opportunities themes are distributed across the five design disciplines and their appearance frequency (%) in the book

architecture-focused, salutogenic design also has applications in other design disciplines within public health and ageing well, such as in behaviour and service design.

Lastly, looking at how the opportunities are distributed across the four healthcare settings, as they appear in this book (see Figure 23.10), reveals that most opportunities for design in healthcare can be found in chronic healthcare, followed by ageing well and public health. If we look at where the opportunities lie in terms of the five design disciplines explored by authors in this book (see Figure 23.11), products, communication and service design offer the most opportunities for new areas of work, followed by behaviours and architecture where work is already underway.

Emerging trends in design for health

The thematic analysis revealed a number of emerging trends in the field of design for health, which have been depicted in Figure 23.12. With a focus on the person (starting from the centre of the diagram), person-centric healthcare appears first, followed by the emerging trend of self-healthcare management, community and holistic healthcare. Preventative/

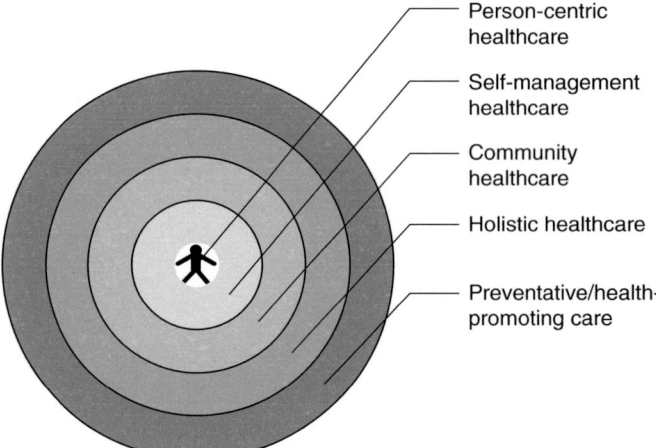

Figure 23.12   Circle of emerging trends in design for health: hierarchical depiction of emerging trends revealed by the thematic analysis with a focus placed on the individual person

health-promoting care is situated at the outer edge of the circle of the healthcare diagram. We shall examine these in more detail below.

Person-centric healthcare forms one of the key emerging themes in this book, having been encountered across several chapters. The move from patient-centred to person–centric healthcare is starting to emerge in the literature and relevant reports (Royen et al., 2010; Peek et al., 2007; Price, 2006; Eaton et al., 2015; Raleigh et al., 2015; Health Foundation, 2014). Within this context the challenge and opportunity for design for health is to place the person as an active agent in all aspects of healthcare, from the promotion to the delivery and treatment. The focus here is on designing for a person rather than for a patient, aiming at improving a person's quality of life along with health.

Service design has an essential role to play here by placing the person at the epicentre of the design and development process, leading to a service responsive to the needs of the individual. Co-design will contribute actively in this process by empowering the individual in the process of redesigning healthcare services towards their needs but also recognising the value of healthcare on the person. In terms of behaviour design, person-centric healthcare will place focus on a person's internal and external behaviour, where the interests, needs and motivations will be at the centre of the design process. Instead of explicitly changing a person's behaviour, person-centric healthcare design will seek to minimise or eliminate (design out) the problems and barriers that prevent health-promoting behaviours. For architecture design, person-centric healthcare design will create a more direct link between the place, person and health, placing the person's health at the forefront of the environment design. Salutogenic design, identified as an opportunity in the previous section, can actively contribute towards this. Within product design the core value of person-centricity in healthcare will be reclaimed and reflected not only on the product outcomes, but also the process. Person-centric healthcare design teams will place empathetic design and deep ethnographic insights at the heart of the process, combining their qualitative findings with evidence-based design.

The implications and impact of person-centric healthcare are twofold. On one hand it will provide more person-agnostic services and on the other hand it will partly shift the responsibility of care from the service provider to the service user. This leads into the next emerging theme of self-management healthcare.

Self-management healthcare programmes are being increasingly introduced across the world (Ouwens et al., 2005; Beaglehole et al., 2008; Brady, 2013) as a response to several of the challenges discussed above, as well as the high economic burdens placed by an ageing population and the increased prevalence of chronic disease. In light of the increase and penetration of digital technologies across both the home and the healthcare setting, there is the expectation that patients with the support of technology and in particular personal medical devices may be motivated and empowered to monitor and manage their own health status. Several chapters in this book have presented the design of personal medical devices for the self-management of different health conditions for public as well as chronic health, such as weight management in Chapter 4, diabetes management in Chapter 11 and stroke-rehabilitation management in Chapter 12. Although each project and personal health device presented is different, they all agree in that to enable self-management, the person with the chronic illness and the health professional need to work together within a participatory network of relatives, friends and service organisations. This presents opportunities for the application of co-design in the shaping of self-management products as well as services, since within co-design lie key characteristics, such as empowerment, control and motivation that allow this goal to be realised.

Particularly for service design, self-management of healthcare poses a challenge and opportunity at the same time. In order to facilitate effective self-management of chronic health conditions at a national healthcare scale, radical rethinking is required about how public health services are organised and delivered, including how technologies can be integrated into healthcare systems to promote and support self-management. On top of and within the redesign of self-management healthcare there are opportunities for design research and practice to create the necessary conditions required to provide people with chronic health conditions not only with personal health products but also the required skills and knowledge to manage their own condition more easily and efficiently in order to maintain or enhance their health, emotional and social wellbeing.

Embracing and implementing a self-care management model will undoubtedly have implications on service delivery, shifting more services into the community and patients' homes. *Community healthcare* is, hence, another of the emerging trends our thematic analysis revealed. Community-based healthcare services are expected to increase on one hand placing personal health within a social context and, on the other hand, facilitating healthcare outside the envelope of primary and secondary healthcare provision. Within this context of service migration into the community there are design opportunities in terms of community-located service design, products and behaviour design within community healthcare services, as well as design of built environments that promote a more social and community-based healthcare delivery system.

Within the topic of design for health, the theme of *holistic healthcare* emerges as a key trend. More precisely several chapters in the book highlighted the need for a holistic approach and mindset in the design of products, services, built environments and behaviours with healthcare. In this context holistic refers to every aspect of a person's life including physical functioning, mental wellbeing, social and professional aspects of their lives. It is within the envelope of holistic healthcare where the challenges of wellbeing and mental health as well as social interaction, which were discussed in the challenges section above, should be addressed by design. In addition to this the values and benefits offered by the design opportunities of holistic and salutogenic design (as discussed in the previous section) should be sought and employed here.

Salutogenic design can also play a key role in the emerging trend of *preventative and health-promoting care*. Similarly to the trend of self-management healthcare, this trend is also necessitated by the economic challenges and the prevalence of chronic diseases. The environment and lifestyle are catalysts for the increase of ill-health-promoting risk factors, such physical inactivity, unhealthy diet, anxiety and stress. Shifting the focus of healthcare delivery and provision from chronic healthcare into public healthcare will require the redesign of our current services as well as built environment and it will be a long-term strategy. However, the benefits from such change will be invaluable for people's health and wellbeing. Communication and behaviour design can significantly contribute towards the realisation of health-promoting and preventative care too.

Preventative and holistic healthcare should be viewed in combination. The importance of this has been highlighted by the National Prevention Research Initiative (NPRI) report. The NPRI report was created based on a scientific group established to review the outputs from 70+ projects (receiving £34 million of funding by 16 research funders in the UK between 2005 and 2014), aimed at reducing the burden of chronic non-communicable disease by investigating the role of health-related behaviour, particularly alcohol consumption, smoking, diet and physical activity. Based on the report to achieve greater reductions in the population illness or health risk could result from applying these interventions at multiple levels (individual, group, community and/or population-level) (NPRI Scientific Review Group, 2015).

Research methodologies and methods in design for health

A total of 26 case studies in design for health have been presented in the book, of which three cover public healthcare, four acute healthcare, 12 chronic healthcare, seven ageing well, and four architecture, three communication design, eight product design, seven service design and four behaviour design. Following the number and diversity of case studies of design in healthcare presented in this book we have conducted an analysis of the design research methodologies and research methods employed. Although this is not an exhaustive list of the research methodologies and methods applied in design in healthcare nor a systematic review of these (see for a systematic review Chamberlain et al., 2015), it still provides the reader with some insights regarding the most popular research methodologies and research methods designers are employing across different healthcare areas (public, acute, chronic and ageing well) as well as design disciplines (architecture, communication, product, service and behaviour design).

Our analysis revealed a total of nine research methodologies and 19 research methods employed across the different case studies in this book. More precisely, as Figure 23.13 illustrates, co-design along with participatory design and design ethnography are the most popular design research methodologies encountered across all four different healthcare settings. Participatory design and co-design have also been employed across all design disciplines, as depicted in Figure 23.14, whereas design ethnography has been employed mainly in service, communication and product design. One observation is that five or more different research methodologies have been employed across all the case studies reported in the different healthcare settings and three to five research methodologies have been employed in each of the design disciplines (see Figures 23.13 and 23.14). The adoption of several research methodologies shows on one hand the mixed and multimethodological approach often required for projects in design in healthcare; and on the other hand it shows the diversity of methodologies design can draw from its research 'quiver'.

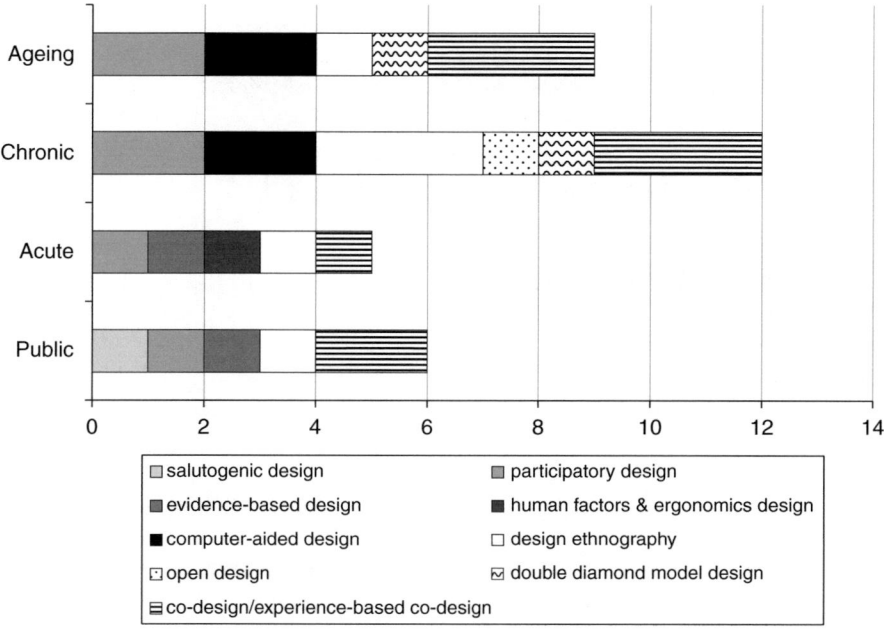

Figure 23.13 The design research methodologies employed in the case studies according to the health–care settings in which they appeared

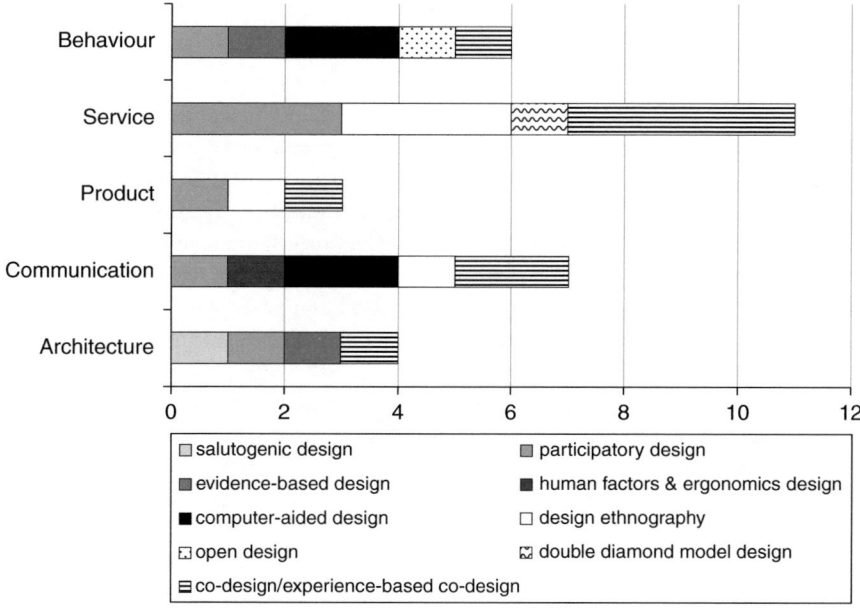

Figure 23.14 The design research methodologies employed in the case studies according to the design disciplines in which they appeared

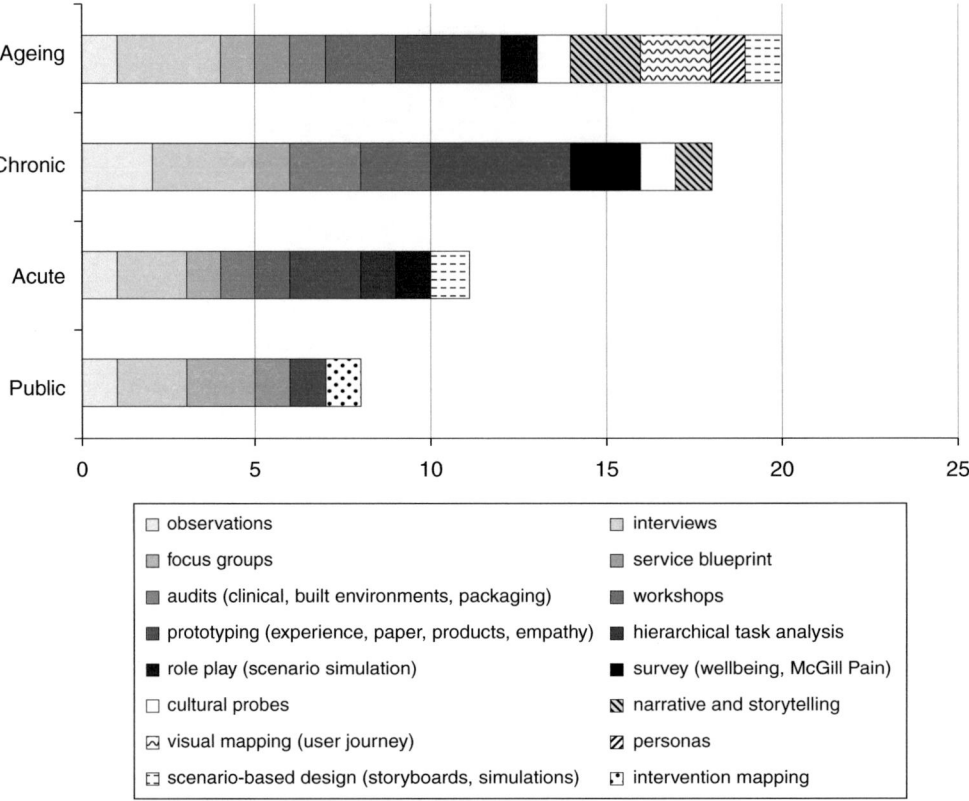

Figure 23.15 The design research methods employed in the book case studies according to the health-care settings in which they appeared

Moving onto the research methods, a similar case to that presented above is revealed. A mixed methods approach has been employed in the vast majority of case studies. A minimum of six and maximum of 13 different research methodologies have been used across the different healthcare settings, as Figure 23.15 illustrates. Observations, interviews, focus groups and prototyping have been popular research methods in all four healthcare settings. Workshops and audits (clinical, built environments, packaging) have also been fairly widely used research methods being employed across the acute, chronic and ageing-well healthcare settings.

Looking at the research methods employed according to the different design disciplines explored in this book (see Figure 23.16), it is clear that some disciplines, such as service blueprint, intervention mapping and hierarchical task analysis, are more discipline-specific whereas others, such as interviews, focus groups, prototyping and audits are more widely employed across most design disciplines. Again it is evident that a mixed methods approach is employed within design in healthcare.

The way forward for design for health

In this book we brought together a disparate knowledge base and illustrated how designers contributed to the different dimensions of health (public, acute, chronic and ageing well). The

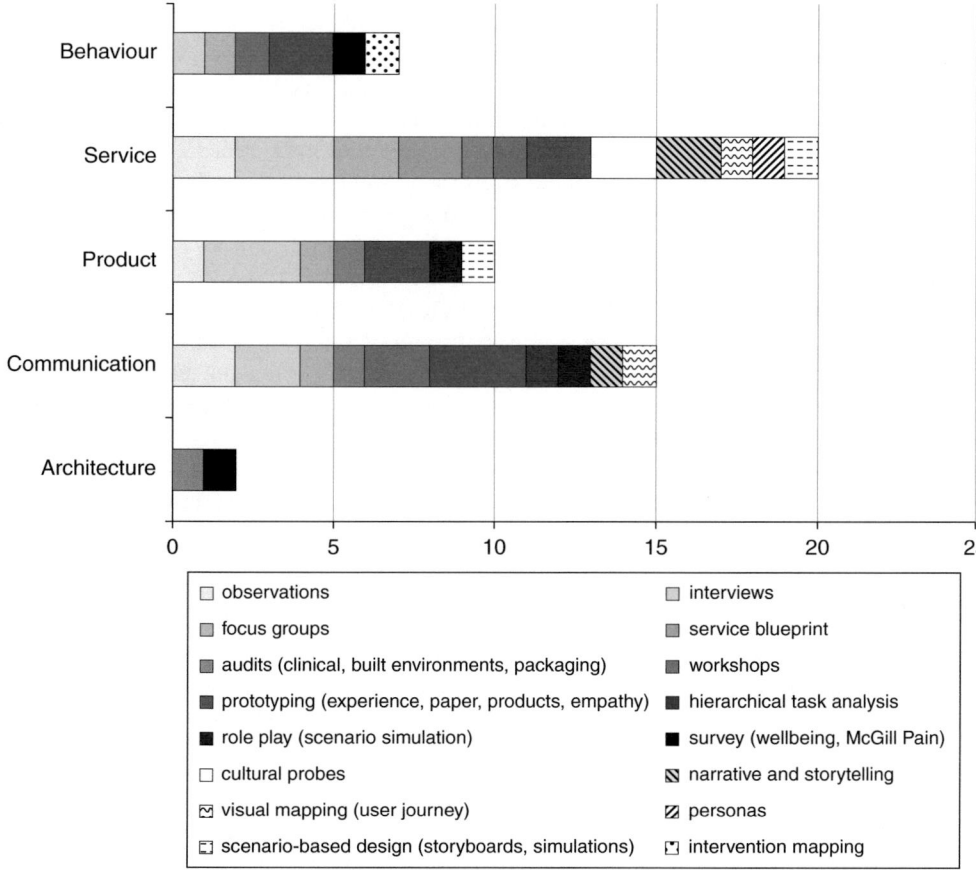

Figure 23.16 The design research methods employed in the book case studies according to the design disciplines in which they appeared

26 case studies presented in this book have revealed a plethora of design research methodologies and research methods employed in design for health. Their application across the four different healthcare settings and five design disciplines has shown the mixed and multimethodological approach often required for projects in design in healthcare and the diversity of methodologies designers can employ from their research 'toolbox'.

We have also presented, following a thematic analysis of the book chapters, and discussed seven challenges (*long-term healthcare, ageing, social interaction and support, environment and lifestyle, non-communicable diseases, wellbeing and mental health, active life/living*) and seven areas of opportunity (*health communication, prototyping, co-design, evidence-based design, digital design, salutogenic design* and *holistic design*) designers are called upon to address within the context of healthcare. Furthermore, five emergent trends in design in healthcare (*self-care/health management, person-centric healthcare, holistic healthcare, community healthcare* and *preventative healthcare*) have been presented.

What the analysis of the book chapters has illuminated is the propensity of design to contribute significantly. Also it has revealed that the key agenda going forward and requiring immediate attention is that of preventative healthcare. We know that the cost of healthcare delivery is increasing (Appleby, 2013; Thomas and Wise, 2015). We know that we have an increasing and ageing population (Ortiz-Ospina and Roser, 2016; Deloitte, 2016). The issue is how to reduce the cost and burden of disease, particularly of non-communicable disease, by focusing more research work around prevention and looking at how design can work in prevention.

If designers are to play the leading role that we have seen they can do, there are some imperatives to address; first how we train designers for a future role where they not only apply design to health challenges, but are able to lead multidisciplinary groups and make major decisions that will influence behaviour contributing to long-term prevention and better overall population health. This raises a second imperative as to how designers work with different sectors, how they provide evidence of the impact of design, how they influence these sectors and indeed who they should be; for instance how can town planners or healthcare professionals or policy-makers understand the value of bringing a design perspective in? We need designers trained to understand these diverse perspectives and be able to converse in a manner that the specialists in other areas can understand.

Designers will still continue to design products and services for health but if we are to reduce the cost of healthcare and improve the quality of life in and beyond Western societies, we need to look at how to ensure designers are a key part of teams identifying the problems and designing the solutions.

Note

1 Comorbidity refers to index chronic diseases coexisting with other diseases, whereas multimorbidity refers to any co-occurrence of medical conditions within a person. Based on definitions by van den Akker et al. (1996).

References

Age UK (2016) Later life in the United Kingdom. Report, February. Available at: www.ageuk.org.uk/Documents/EN-GB/Factsheets/Later_Life_UK_factsheet.pdf?dtrk=true.

Alwan, A. (2011) Global status report on noncommunicable diseases 2010. Geneva: World Health Organization.

Appleby, J. (2013) *Spending on Health and Social Care over the Next 50 Years: Why Think Long Term?* London: King's Fund.

Barnett, K., Mercer, S.W., Norbury, M., Watt, G., Wyke, S. and Guthrie, B. (2012) Epidemiology of multimorbidity and implications for health care, research, and medical education: A cross-sectional study. *Lancet*, 380(9836): 37–43.

Bauman, A.E., Reis, R.S., Sallis, J.F., Wells, J.C., Loos, R.J. and Martin, B.W. and Lancet Physical Activity Series Working Group (2012) Correlates of physical activity: Why are some people physically active and others not? *Lancet*, 380(9838): 258–71.

Beaglehole, R., Epping-Jordan, J., Patel, V., Chopra, M., Ebrahim, S., Kidd, M. and Haines, A. (2008) Improving the prevention and management of chronic disease in low-income and middle-income countries: A priority for primary health care. *Lancet*, 372(9642): 940–9.

Brady, T.J. (2013) A meta-analysis of health status, health behaviors, and health care utilization outcomes of the chronic disease self-management program. *Preventing Chronic Disease*, 10.

Buchenau, M. and Suri, J.F. (2000) Experience prototyping. Proceedings of the 3rd Conference on Designing Interactive Systems: Processes, Practices, Methods, and Techniques, ACM, 424–33.

Chamberlain, P., Wolstenholme, D., Dexter, M. and Seals, E. (2015) *The State of the Art of Design in Health: An Expert-Led Review of the Extant of the Art of Design Theory and Practice in Health and Social Care.* Sheffield: Sheffield Hallam University.

Codinhoto, R., Tzortzopoulos, P., Kagioglou, M., Aouad, G. and Cooper, R. (2009) The impacts of the built environment on health outcomes. *Facilities*, 27(3/4): 138–51.

Coughlan, P., Suri, J.F. and Canales, K. (2007) Prototypes as (design) tools for behavioral and organizational change: A design-based approach to help organizations change work behaviors. *Journal of Applied Behavioral Science*, 43(1): 122–34.

Daar, A.S., Singer, P.A., Persad, D.L., Pramming, S.K., Matthews, D.R., Beaglehole, R., Bernstein, A., Borysiewicz, L.K., Colagiuri, S., Ganguly, N. and Glass, R.I. (2007) Grand challenges in chronic non-communicable diseases. *Nature*, 450(7169): 494–6.

De Couvreur, L. and Goossens, R. (2011) Design for (every)one: Co-creation as a bridge between universal design and rehabilitation engineering. *CoDesign*, 7(2): 107–21.

Deloitte (2016) 2016 global health care sector outlook: Battling costs while improving care. Available at: www2.deloitte.com/content/dam/Deloitte/global/Documents/Life-Sciences-Health-Care/gx-lshc-2016-health-care-outlook.pdf.

Dilani, A. and Armstrong, K. (2007) The 'salutogenic' approach: Designing a health-promoting hospital environment. *World Hospitals and Health Services: The Official Journal of the International Hospital Federation*, 44(3): 32–5.

Eaton, S., Roberts, S. and Turner, B. (2015) Delivering person-centred care in long-term conditions. *British Medical Journal*, 350: h181.

Foresight Mental Capital and Wellbeing Project (2008) Final project report: Executive summary. London: Government Office for Science.

Gibbs, G. (2007) *Analyzing Qualitative Data*. 1st edition. London: Sage.

Golembiewski, J.A. (2012) Salutogenic design: The neurological basis of health-promoting environments. *World Health Design: Architecture, Culture, Technology*, 5(3): 62–9.

Health Foundation (2014) Person-centred care made simple: What everyone should know about person-centred care. London: Health Foundation. Available at: www.health.org.uk/sites/default/files/PersonCentredCareMadeSimple.pdf.

Hornik, R. (ed.) (2002) *Public Health Communication: Evidence for Behavior Change*. London: Routledge.

Kohl, H.W., Craig, C.L., Lambert, E.V., Inoue, S., Alkandari, J.R., Leetongin, G., Kahlmeier, S. and Lancet Physical Activity Series Working Group (2012) The pandemic of physical inactivity: Global action for public health. *Lancet*, 380(9838): 294–305.

Lloyd, K.M. and Auld, C.J. (2002) The role of leisure in determining quality of life: Issues of content and measurement. *Social Indicators Research*, 57(1): 43–71.

Marengoni, A., Angleman, S., Melis, R., Mangialasche, F., Karp, A., Garmen, A., Meinow, B. and Fratiglioni, L. (2011) Aging with multimorbidity: A systematic review of the literature. *Ageing Research Reviews*, 10(4): 430–9.

Marmot, M.G., Allen, J., Goldblatt, P., Boyce, T., McNeish, D., Grady, M. and Geddes, I. (2010) Fair society, healthy lives: Strategic review of health inequalities in England post-2010. London: Institute of Health Equality.

McCullough, C.S. (2009) *Evidence-Based Design for Health Facilities*. Indianapolis, IN: Sigma Theta Tau.

NPRI Scientific Review Group (2015) National prevention research initiative report. September. Available at: www.mrc.ac.uk/research/initiatives/national-prevention-research-initiative-npri/.

Ortiz-Ospina, E. and Roser, M. (2016) World population growth. Available at: https://ourworldindata.org/world-population-growth/.

Ouwens, M., Wollersheim, H., Hermens, R., Hulscher, M. and Grol, R. (2005) Integrated care programmes for chronically ill patients: A review of systematic reviews. *International Journal for Quality in Health Care*, 17(2): 141–6.

Peek, C., Higgins, I., Milson-Hawke, S., McMillan, M. and Harper, D. (2007) Towards innovation: The development of a person-centred model of care for older people in acute care. *Contemporary Nurse*, 26(2): 164–76.

Price, B. (2006) Exploring person-centred care. *Nursing Standard*, 20(50): 49–56.

Raleigh, V., Thompson, J., Jabbal, J., Graham, C., Sizmur, S. and Coulter, A. (2015) Patients' experience of using hospital services: An analysis of trends in inpatient surveys in NHS acute trusts in England

2005–13. London: King's Fund and Picker Institute Europe. Available at: www.kingsfund.org.uk/publications/patients-experience-using-hospital-services.

Rao, M., Prasad, S., Adshead, F. and Tissera, H. (2007) The built environment and health. *Lancet*, 370(9593): 1111–13.

Renalds, A., Smith, T.H. and Hale, P.J. (2010) A systematic review of built environment and health. *Family and Community Health*, 33(1): 68–78.

Rittel, H. and Webber, M. (1973) Dilemmas in a general theory of planning. *Policy Sciences*, 4: 155–69.

Robert, G. (2013) Participatory action research: Using experience-based co-design to improve the quality of healthcare services. London: King's College London.

Royen, P.V., Beyer, M., Chevallier, P., Eilat-Tsanani, S., Lionis, C., Peremans, L., Petek, D., Rurik, I., Soler, J.K., Stoffers, H.E. and Topsever, P. (2010) The research agenda for general practice/family medicine and primary health care in Europe. Part 3. Results: Person-centred care, comprehensive and holistic approach. *European Journal of General Practice*, 16(2): 113–19.

Salive, M.E. (2013) Multimorbidity in older adults. *Epidemiologic Reviews*, 35(1): 75–83.

Sanders, E.B.N. and Stappers, P.J. (2008) Co-creation and the new landscapes of design. *Co-design*, 4(1): 5–18.

Sandstrom, G.M. and Dunn, E.W. (2014) Social interactions and well-being: The surprising power of weak ties. *Personality and Social Psychology Bulletin*, 40(7). doi: 0146167214529799.

Self, A. (2014) Measuring national well-being: Insights across society, the economy and the environment. Available at: http://webarchive.nationalarchives.gov.uk/20160105160709/ and www.ons.gov.uk/ons/dcp171766_371427.pdf.

Steptoe, A., Shankar, A., Demakakos, P. and Wardle, J. (2013) Social isolation, loneliness, and all-cause mortality in older men and women. *Proceedings of the National Academy of Sciences*, 110(15): 5797–801.

Thomas, J. and Wise, S. (2015) 2016 global health care outlook: Reconciling rapid growth and cost consciousness. New York: Carlyle Group. Available at: www.carlyle.com/sites/default/files/market-commentary/october_2015_-_global_health_care_investment_outlook.pdf.

Tomaka, J., Thompson, S. and Palacios, R. (2006) The relation of social isolation, loneliness, and social support to disease outcomes among the elderly. *Journal of Aging and Health*, 18(3): 359–84.

Tsianakas, V., Maben, J., Wiseman, T., Robert, G. and Richardson, A. (2010) Using experience-based co-design to improve breast and lung cancer services. *European Journal of Public Health*, 20: 63.

Uijen, A.A. and van de Lisdonk, E.H. (2008) Multimorbidity in primary care: Prevalence and trend over the last 20 years. *European Journal of General Practice*, 14(sup1): 28–32.

Ulrich, R.S., Zimring, C., Zhu, X., DuBose, J., Seo, H.B., Choi, Y.S., Quan, X. and Joseph, A. (2008) A review of the research literature on evidence-based healthcare design. *Health Environments Research and Design Journal*, 1(3): 61–125.

United Nations (2015) World population ageing: Highlights. Available at: www.un.org/en/development/desa/population/publications/pdf/ageing/WPA2015_Highlights.pdf.

van den Akker, M., Buntinx, F. and Knottnerus, J.A. (1996) Comorbidity or multimorbidity: What's in a name? A review of literature. *European Journal of General Practice*, 2(2): 65–70.

Verlinden, J. and Horváth, I. (2009) Analyzing opportunities for using interactive augmented prototyping in design practice. *Artificial Intelligence for Engineering Design, Analysis and Manufacturing*, 23(3): 289–303.

Index